Victoria Crosses on the Western Front
1 July 1916–13 November 1916

Victoria Crosses on the Western Front 1 July 1916–13 November 1916

Somme 1916

Paul Oldfield

Pen & Sword
MILITARY

First published in Great Britain in 2016 by
Pen & Sword Military
an imprint of
Pen & Sword Books Ltd
47 Church Street
Barnsley
South Yorkshire
S70 2AS

ISBN 978 1 47382 712 7

A CIP catalogue record for this book is available from the British Library

Typeset in Ehrhardt by
Mac Style Ltd, Bridlington, East Yorkshire
Printed and bound in the UK by CPI Group (UK) Ltd, Croydon, CRO 4YY

Pen & Sword Books Ltd incorporates the imprints of Pen & Sword Archaeology, Atlas, Aviation, Battleground, Discovery, Family History, History, Maritime, Military, Naval, Politics, Railways, Select, Social History, Transport, True Crime, and Claymore Press, Frontline Books, Leo Cooper, Praetorian Press, Remember When, Seaforth Publishing and Wharncliffe.

For a complete list of Pen & Sword titles please contact
PEN & SWORD BOOKS LIMITED
47 Church Street, Barnsley, South Yorkshire, S70 2AS, England
E-mail: enquiries@pen-and-sword.co.uk
Website: www.pen-and-sword.co.uk

Contents

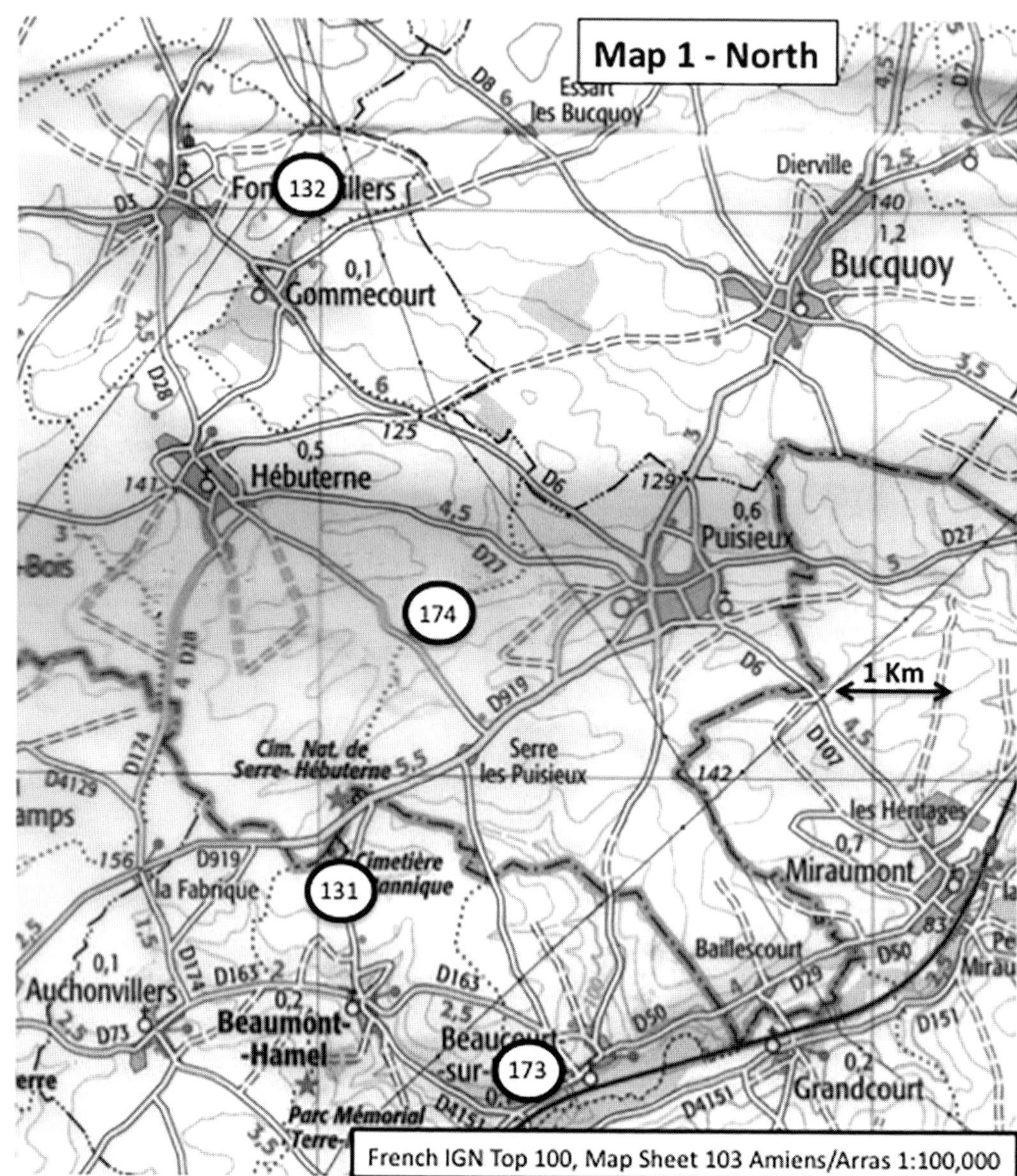

Map 1 - North
Essart les Bucquoy
Dierville
Bucquoy
Gommecourt
Hébuterne
Puisieux
1 Km
Cim. Nat. de Serre-Hébuterne
Serre les Puisieux
les Hentages
Miraumont
la Fabrique
Baillescourt
Auchonvillers
Beaumont-Hamel
Grandcourt
Parc Mémorial
132
174
131
173
French IGN Top 100, Map Sheet 103 Amiens/Arras 1:100,000

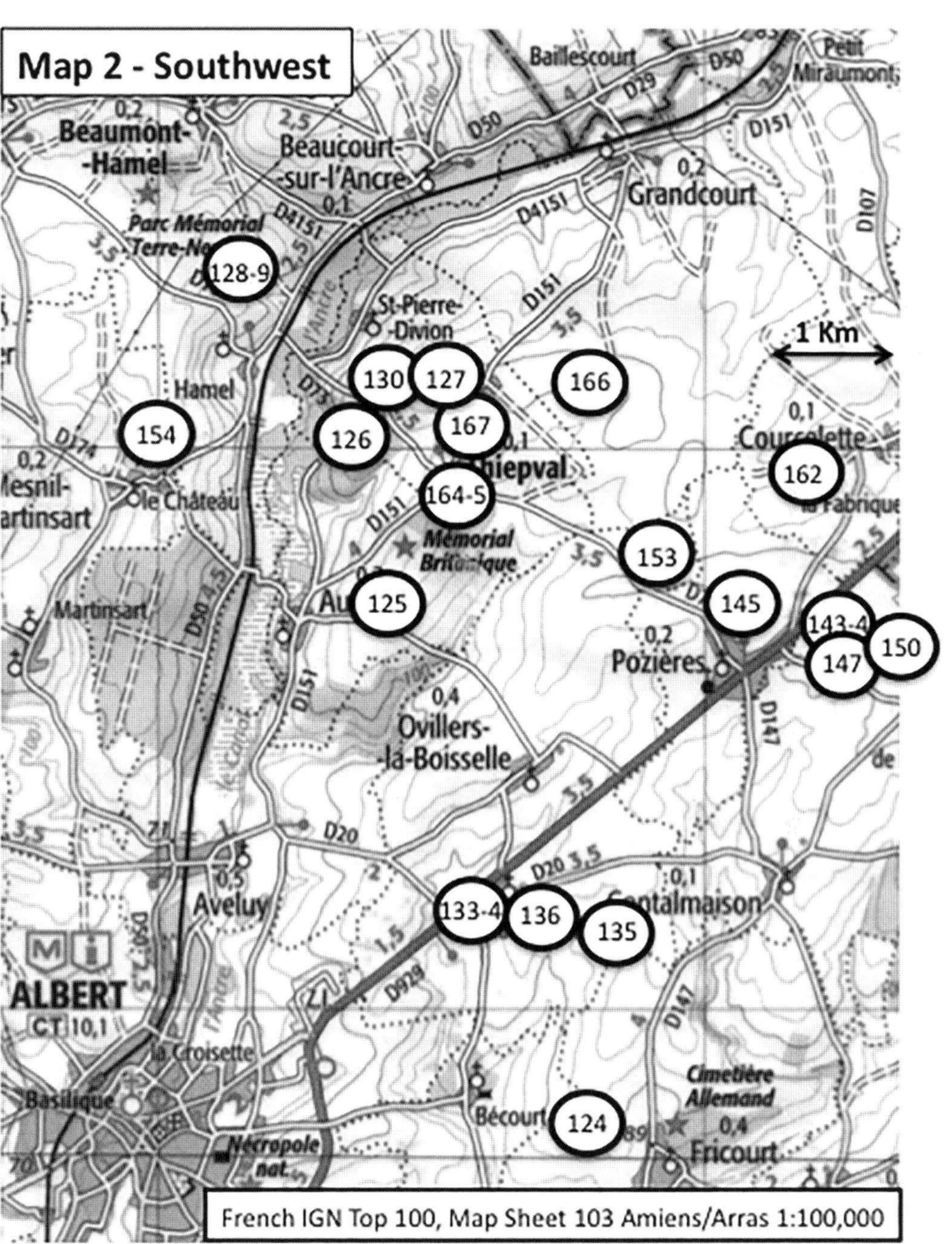

Map 2 - Southwest
Baillescourt
Petit Miraumont
Beaumont-Hamel
Beaucourt-sur-l'Ancre
Grandcourt
Parc Mémorial Terre-Neuve
St-Pierre-Divion
Hamel
1 Km
Courcelette
Mesnil-Martinsart
le Château
Thiepval
Mémorial Britannique
la Fabrique
Martinsart
Pozières
Ovillers-la-Boisselle
Aveluy
Contalmaison
ALBERT
la Croisette
Basilique
Bécourt
Cimetière Allemand
Fricourt
Nécropole nat.
128-9
130
127
166
154
126
167
162
164-5
153
125
145
143-4
150
147
133-4
136
135
124
French IGN Top 100, Map Sheet 103 Amiens/Arras 1:100,000

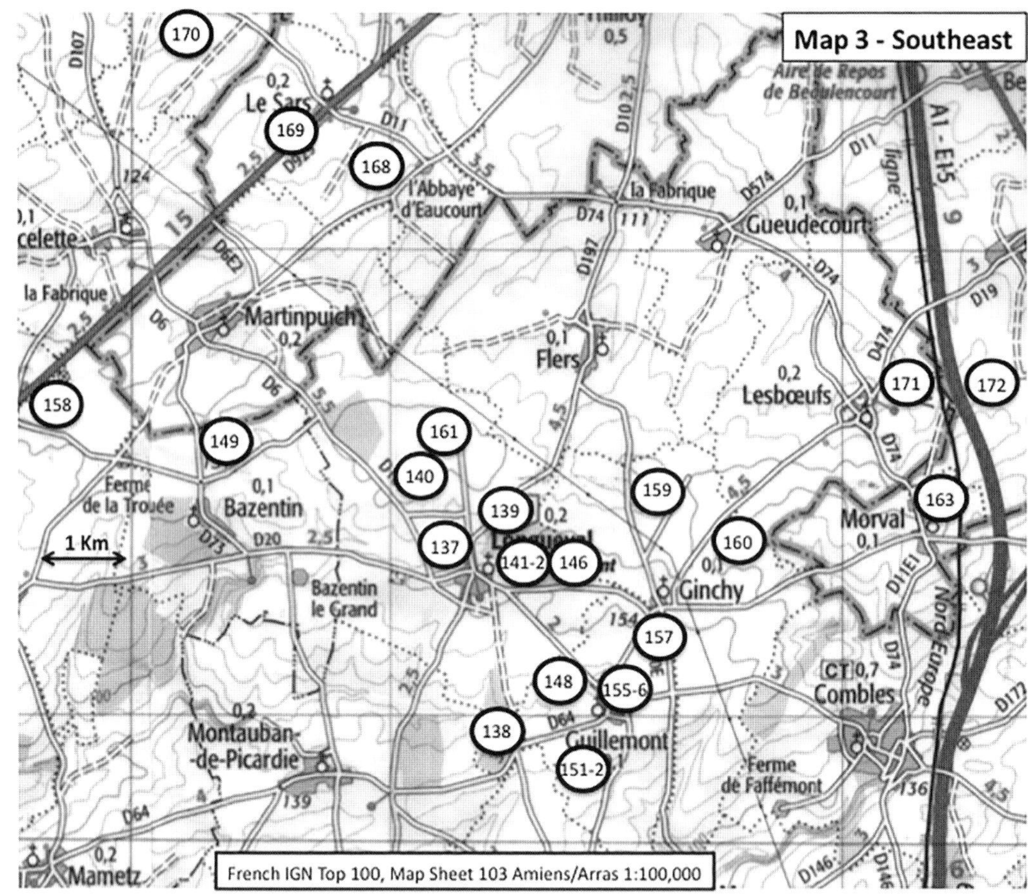

Map 3 - Southeast
170
Le Sars
169
168
l'Abbaye d'Eaucourt
la Fabrique
Gueudecourt
Martinpuich
la Fabrique
Flers
Lesbœufs
171
172
158
149
161
140
139
159
163
Morval
Ferme de la Trouée
Bazentin
1 Km
137
141-2
146
160
Ginchy
Bazentin le Grand
157
148
155-6
Combles
138
Guillemont
151-2
Montauban-de-Picardie
Ferme de Faffémont
Mametz
Aire de Repos de Beaulencourt
A1 - E15
Nord-Europe
French IGN Top 100, Map Sheet 103 Amiens/Arras 1:100,000

Abbreviations

AA	Anti-Aircraft
ADC	Aide-de-Camp
ADS	Advanced Dressing Station
AIF	Australian Imperial Force
ASC	Army Service Corps
ATS	Auxiliary Territorial Service
Att'd	Attached
BA	Bachelor of Arts
BCh or ChB	Bachelor of Surgery
BEF	British Expeditionary Force
BSc	Bachelor of Science
Capt	Captain
CB	Companion of the Order of the Bath
CBE	Commander of the Order of the British Empire
CCF	Combined Cadet Force
CCS	Casualty Clearing Station
CEF	Canadian Expeditionary Force
Ch.M	Master of Surgery
C-in-C	Commander-in-Chief
CMG	Companion of the Order of St Michael & St George
CO	Commanding Officer
Col	Colonel
Cpl	Corporal
CQMS	Company Quartermaster Sergeant
CSgt	Colour Sergeant
CSM	Company Sergeant Major
CStJ	Commander of the Most Venerable Order of the Hospital of Saint John of Jerusalem
Cty	Cemetery
CWGC	Commonwealth War Graves Commission
DCLI	Duke of Cornwall's Light Infantry
DCM	Distinguished Conduct Medal
DJStJ	Dame of Justice of the Most Venerable Order of the Hospital of Saint John of Jerusalem

DL	Deputy Lieutenant
DSC	Distinguished Service Cross
DSO	Distinguished Service Order
Dvr	Driver
FM	Field Marshal
FRCS	Fellow of the Royal College of Surgeons
GCMG	Knight Grand Cross of the Order of St Michael and St George
Gen	General
GOC	General Officer Commanding
GOC-in-C	General Officer Commanding-in-Chief
GSO1, 2 or 3	General Staff Officer Grade 1 (Lt Col), 2 (Maj) or 3 (Capt)
HE	High Explosive
HMAT	Her/His Majesty's Australian Transport/Troopship
HMCS	Her/His Majesty's Canadian Ship
HMHS	Her/His Majesty's Hospital Ship
HMNZT	Her/His Majesty's New Zealand Transport/Troopship
HMS	Her/His Majesty's Ship
HMT	Her/His Majesty's Transport/Troopship/Hired Military Transport
HRH	His/Her Royal Highness
JP	Justice of the Peace
KBE	Knight Commander of the Most Excellent Order of the British Empire
KCB	Knight Commander of the Order of the Bath
KCMG	Knight Commander of St Michael and St George
KCVO	Knight Commander of the Royal Victorian Order
KGStJ	Knight of Grace of the Most Venerable Order of the Hospital of Saint John of Jerusalem
KJStJ	Knight of Justice of the Most Venerable Order of the Hospital of Saint John of Jerusalem
Kms	Kilometres
LCpl	Lance Corporal
LG	London Gazette
LL.B	Bachelor of Laws (Legum Baccalaureus)
LRCP	Licentiate of the Royal College of Physicians
Lt	Lieutenant
Lt Col	Lieutenant Colonel
Lt Gen	Lieutenant General
Maj	Major
Maj Gen	Major General
MA	Master of Arts
MB	Bachelor of Medicine
MBE	Member of the Order of the British Empire

MC	Military Cross
MD	Medical Doctor
MID	Mentioned in Despatches
MM	Military Medal
MO	Medical Officer
MP	Member of Parliament
MRCS	Member of the Royal College of Surgeons
MRCVS	Member of the Royal College of Veterinary Surgeons
MSM	Meritorious Service Medal
NATO	North Atlantic Treaty Organisation
NSPCC	National Society for the Prevention of Cruelty to Children
NZHS	New Zealand Hospital Ship
OBE	Officer of the Order of the British Empire
OP	Observation Post
OTC	Officers' Training Corps
PC	Police Constable
Pte	Private
QC	Queen's Counsel
RA	Royal Artillery
RAAF	Royal Auxiliary Air Force/ Royal Australian Air Force
RAF	Royal Air Force
RAFVR	Royal Air Force Volunteer Reserve
RAMC	Royal Army Medical Corps
RASC	Royal Army Service Corps
RCN	Royal Canadian Navy
RE	Royal Engineers
REME	Royal Electrical and Mechanical Engineers
RFA	Royal Field Artillery
RFC	Royal Flying Corps
RGA	Royal Garrison Artillery
RMS	Royal Mail Ship/Steamer
RN	Royal Navy
RNR	Royal Naval Reserve
RNZAF	Royal New Zealand Air Force
RSL	Returned and Services League
RSM	Regimental Sergeant Major
SAI	South African Infantry
Sgt	Sergeant
Spr	Sapper
SS	Steam Ship
TD	Territorial Decoration
TF	Territorial Force

TMB	Trench Mortar Battery
TSS	Twin-Screw Steamer
UN	United Nations
VAD	Voluntary Aid Detachment
VC	Victoria Cross
VIP	Very Important Person
WAAC	Women's Auxiliary Army Corps
WAAF	Women's Auxiliary Air Force
WO1 or 2	Warrant Officer Class 1 or 2

Introduction

This third book in the series is devoted exclusively to the 1916 Battle of the Somme. Fifty-one VC recipients are included. As with previous books, it is written for the battlefield visitor as well as the armchair reader. Each account provides background information to explain the broad strategic and tactical situation, before examining the VC action in detail. Each is supported by a map to allow a visitor to stand on, or close to, the spot and at least one photograph of the site. Detailed biographies help to understand the man behind the Cross.

As far as possible chapters and sections within them follow the titles of battles, actions and affairs as decided by the post-war Battle Nomenclature Committee. VCs are numbered chronologically 124, 125, 126 … 174 from 1st July–13th November 1916. As far as possible they are described in the same order, but when a number of actions were fought simultaneously the VCs are covered out of sequence on a geographical basis in accordance with the official battle nomenclature.

Refer to the master maps to find the general area for each VC. If visiting the battlefields it is advisable to purchase maps from the Institut Géographique National. The Top 100 series at 1:100,000 scale are ideal for motoring, but the Serie Bleue 1:25,000 scale maps are necessary for more detailed work. They are obtainable from the IGN or through reputable map suppliers on-line.

Ranks are as used on the day. Grave references have been shortened, e.g. 'Plot II, Row A, Grave 10' will appear as 'II A 10'. There are some abbreviations, many in common usage, but if unsure refer to the list provided.

Thanks are due to too many people and organizations to mention here. They are acknowledged in 'Sources' and any omissions are my fault and not intentional. However, I must again single out my fellow researchers in the Victoria Cross Database Users Group, who have provided information and other assistance selflessly over many years – indeed some arrived on the last day of writing: Doug and Richard Arman, Vic Tambling and Alan Jordan, assisted by Alasdair Macintyre.

Paul Oldfield
Wiltshire
March 2015

Chapter One

Battle of Albert

1st July 1916

124 Maj Stewart Loudoun-Shand, 10th Yorkshire (62nd Brigade, 21st Division), Fricourt, France
125 Sgt James Turnbull, 17th Highland Light Infantry (97th Brigade, 32nd Division), Authuille, France
126 Pte William McFadzean, 14th Royal Irish Rifles (109th Brigade, 36th (Ulster) Division), Thiepval Wood, France
127 Capt Eric Bell, 9th Royal Inniskilling Fusiliers att'd 109th Trench Mortar Battery (109th Brigade, 36th (Ulster) Division), Thiepval, France
128 Lt Geoffrey Cather, 9th Royal Irish Fusiliers (108th Brigade, 36th (Ulster) Division), Hamel, France
129 Pte Robert Quigg, 12th Royal Irish Rifles (108th Brigade, 36th (Ulster) Division), Hamel, France
130 Cpl George Sanders, 1/7th West Yorkshire (146th Brigade, 49th (West Riding) Division), Thiepval, France
131 Dmr Walter Ritchie, 2nd Seaforth Highlanders (10th Brigade, 4th Division), Beaumont Hamel, France
132 Capt John Green, RAMC att'd 1/5th Sherwood Foresters (139th Brigade, 46th (North Midland) Division), Foncquevillers, France

At the end of 1915 the British and French started making plans for a major joint offensive in 1916; whilst their allies in Russia and Italy would simultaneously launch their own offensives. However, the German onslaught at Verdun, beginning in February, forced the French to reduce their contribution to the joint venture. The final plan was for the French Sixth Army and the newly formed British Fourth Army to attack astride the River Somme, while the British Third Army made a diversionary attack at Gommecourt. The opening day of the Somme offensive was a watershed in the conflict, being just several weeks before the mid point of the war. It was also the last major battle opened solely by volunteers – Regulars, Territorials and Kitchener men – and, with a few small exceptions, exclusively by the county regiments of the British Army. Expectations were high that the 'Big Push' would lead to a major success.

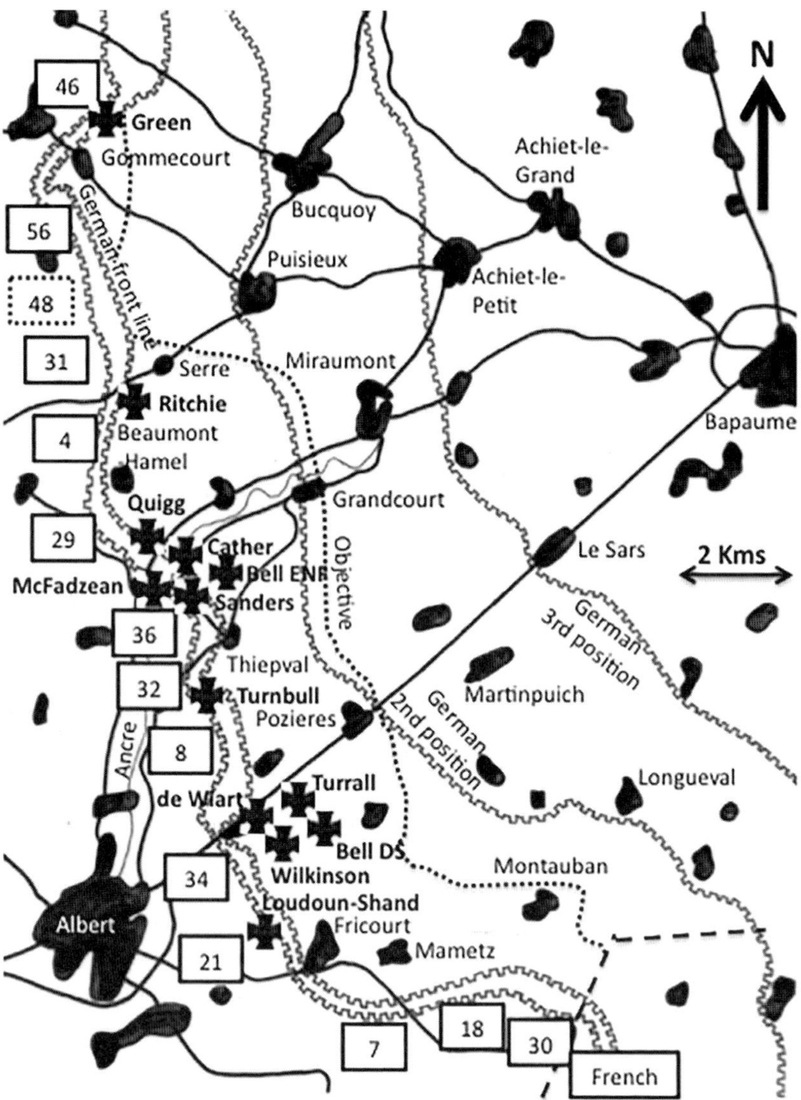

The attack frontage on 1st July 1916; the first day of the Somme. The general location of each of the nine VCs is shown, the main concentration being around Thiepval. Only the British divisions are annotated. Note there was no attack in 48th Division's area. The three German positions illustrate their strength in this area. The objective for the first day, the dotted line, takes in the second position in the centre of the attack area. The simultaneous French attack to the south initially covered about half the British frontage.

On the first day, Fourth Army was to launch a general assault on a frontage of twenty-three kilometres. The objective was the first enemy defensive system along the line Montauban – Pozières – Serre and the second system from Pozières to Serre. This necessitated an advance of at least two and half kilometres along the whole front; a daunting prospect. Attempts to maintain secrecy were futile; it was impossible to hide 400,000 men, 100,000 horses and huge quantities of stores. Efforts to divert enemy attention to other areas by raids and mock preparations failed because there was insufficient artillery ammunition to make the deception convincing.

The preparatory bombardment commenced on 24th June and continued until the attack on 1st July, two days later than originally planned, due to bad weather. Over 1,700,000 shells were fired, but they were generally of light calibre and insufficient to destroy the enemy's deep dugouts; and in many places the wire remained intact or was rapidly repaired. Each morning the bombardment was intensified for eighty minutes, except on the morning of the attack. On that day it was shortened by fifteen minutes in the hope that the Germans would remain in their dugouts long enough for the British to cross no man's land.

During the evening of 30th June, the assault troops made their way into the trenches, each man carrying at least thirty kilogrammes. Ominously a number of raids that night failed, as the fully alert Germans steadfastly defended their trenches. At 6.25 a.m. the final bombardment began, with the trench mortars joining in at 7.20 a.m. Ten minutes later the fire lifted off the enemy front line and tens of thousands of infantrymen advanced across no man's land. It was a cloudless summer day, with a little mist lingering in the hollows. In the words of the Official Historian, '*If ever a decisive victory was to be won it was to be expected now*', but this was not to be. Nine men were awarded the VC for their actions on 1st July 1916.

On the right flank, the attack by XIII Corps alongside the French was successful. Next in line to the north was XV Corps, tasked with capturing the Fricourt salient. In deference to the strength of the enemy defences, the village was to be left until the ground either side had fallen. Accordingly, 7th Division attacked south of Fricourt and 21st Division to the north; their objective was the German second intermediate position. Each division was to push its outside brigade forward to meet at Bottom Wood, while the inside brigades formed defensive flanks to seal off Fricourt and awaited orders to take the village. The final bombardment included gas and smoke and at 7.28 a.m. three mines were blown at the Tambour to divert the enemy's attention and mask enfilade fire against 21st Division's right flank.

21st Division attacked with three brigades in line; from the left these were 64th, 63rd and 50th (attached from 17th Division). 62nd Brigade was in reserve, providing 800 men for carrying parties to the forward brigades and Royal Engineers. As soon as the assault brigades went forward, 62nd Brigade was to move into the vacated front line. 10th West Yorkshire (50th Brigade) was to form the defensive flank against the north face of Fricourt, while the rest of this Brigade awaited the order to attack the village.

At zero hour the assault lines swept forward, meeting little initial resistance, but the Germans recovered quickly. Machine-guns north of the village around the Tambour and on the high ground south of La Boisselle caused horrific casualties. Despite the losses, some of the attackers penetrated a mile into the enemy positions, but they were weak and both flanks were left in the air due to the failure or delay of the troops on either side.

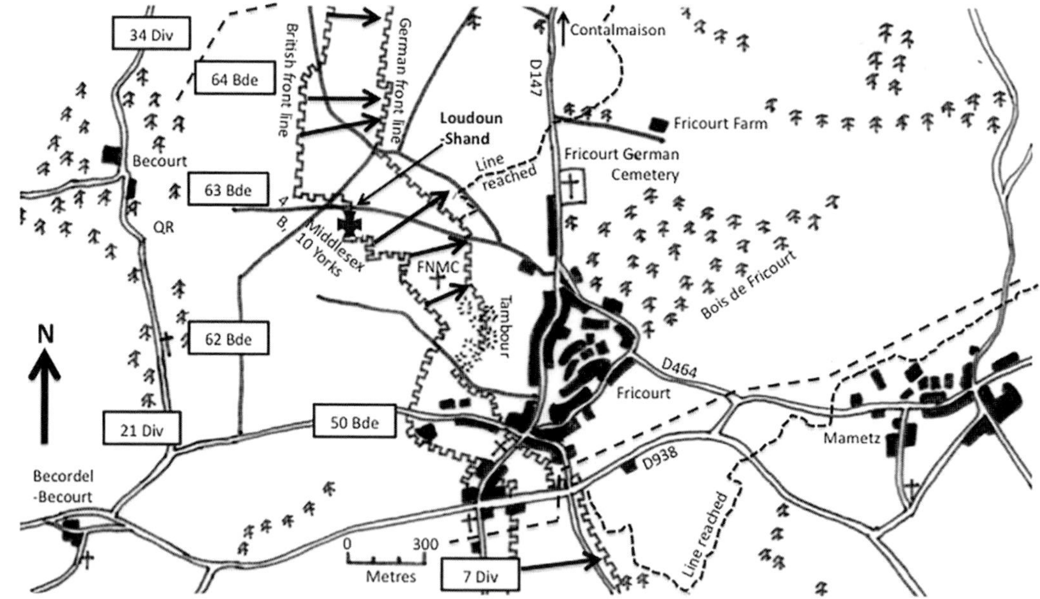

The attack north of Fricourt by 21st Division on 1st July 1916. The village was to be isolated by attacks to the north and south (7th Division), and taken later once it had been cut off. Two abbreviations are used; QR = Queen's Redoubt and FNMC = Fricourt New Military Cemetery. To reach the site of Stewart Loudoun-Shand's VC action, drive south on the D147 from Contalmaison. Pass Fricourt German Cemetery on the left and 250m further on turn right onto a single track road. After 200m, where the track forks, park on the area of hard standing. Walk along the track on the left, passing the path leading south to Fricourt New Military Cemetery after 150m. Continue westwards for another 400m, until about 100m short of a lone tree. This is where the British front line crossed the track and about 100m south of it is where Stewart Loudoun-Shand urged on his men until his death.

During the initial assault, B Company, 10th Yorkshire (62nd Brigade), was tasked to follow 4th Middlesex (63rd Brigade) to mop up enemy resistance. The Company, led by **Major Stewart Loudoun-Shand**, left Queen's Redoubt and made its way through the trenches. It was to arrive in the front line five minutes before zero, just as 4th Middlesex went forward to close the distance to the enemy lines before the artillery lifted. The machine-gun fire was so severe that 4th Middlesex was driven back. Despite being severely depleted and shaken, the survivors left the trench

From the track northeast of Fricourt at the point where the British front line crossed. Stewart Loudoun-Shand was 100m south of the track, in line with Fricourt New Military Cemetery on the extreme right of picture.

again one minute before zero, but only 140 men succeeded in reaching the enemy support line.

Just before zero, Loudoun-Shand led his men into the front line in readiness to follow 4th Middlesex. When the time came to advance at 7.30 a.m., the men hesitated to go over the top as the Germans were spraying the parapet with machine-gun fire. Loudoun-Shand climbed out and ran along the parapet, shouting encouragement to his men and assisting them out of the trench. He was hit by three machine-gun bullets and fell back into the trench, but insisted on being propped up so he could continue to encourage his men as they advanced into the hail of fire. He died just as the enemy trench fell and the machine-gun was destroyed. At the end of the day, B Company mustered only one officer and twenty-seven men. The rest of 10th Yorkshire reached Crucifix Trench. During the night 62nd Brigade took over the line from 64th Brigade until relieved early on 4th July, having suffered 973 casualties.

Optimistic reports led HQ XV Corps to order the attack on Fricourt, which failed, and 21st Division only managed to maintain the positions reached during the morning. Conversely, during the afternoon, 7th Division to the south took Mametz. At the end of the day the right of XV Corps had advanced 2,250 metres while the left had managed only 1,800 metres. During the night the Germans abandoned Fricourt as it was untenable.

III Corps at La Boisselle had very few gains to show for its heavy losses. To the north, X Corps' task was also a difficult one; the capture of the Thiepval Spur and village, the Schwaben Redoubt and the north bank of the Ancre. The German positions were well protected, covered by flanking fire from other units and almost everywhere overlooked the British lines. On the right, 32nd Division was to capture Thiepval Spur, including the Leipzig Salient. On the left, 36th Division was to capture the plateau north of Thiepval and north of St Pierre Divion, beyond the Ancre. Both divisions were then to take the German second position. 49th Division was held in reserve in Aveluy Wood.

32nd Division was already tired, having spent the days preceding the attack digging assembly trenches and carrying stores. The assault was led by 96th Brigade on the left, 97th Brigade on the right and 14th Brigade in reserve. The junction with III Corps on the right was in Nab Valley, which neither Corps attacked, leaving the defenders free to pour enfilade fire into the flanks of both formations.

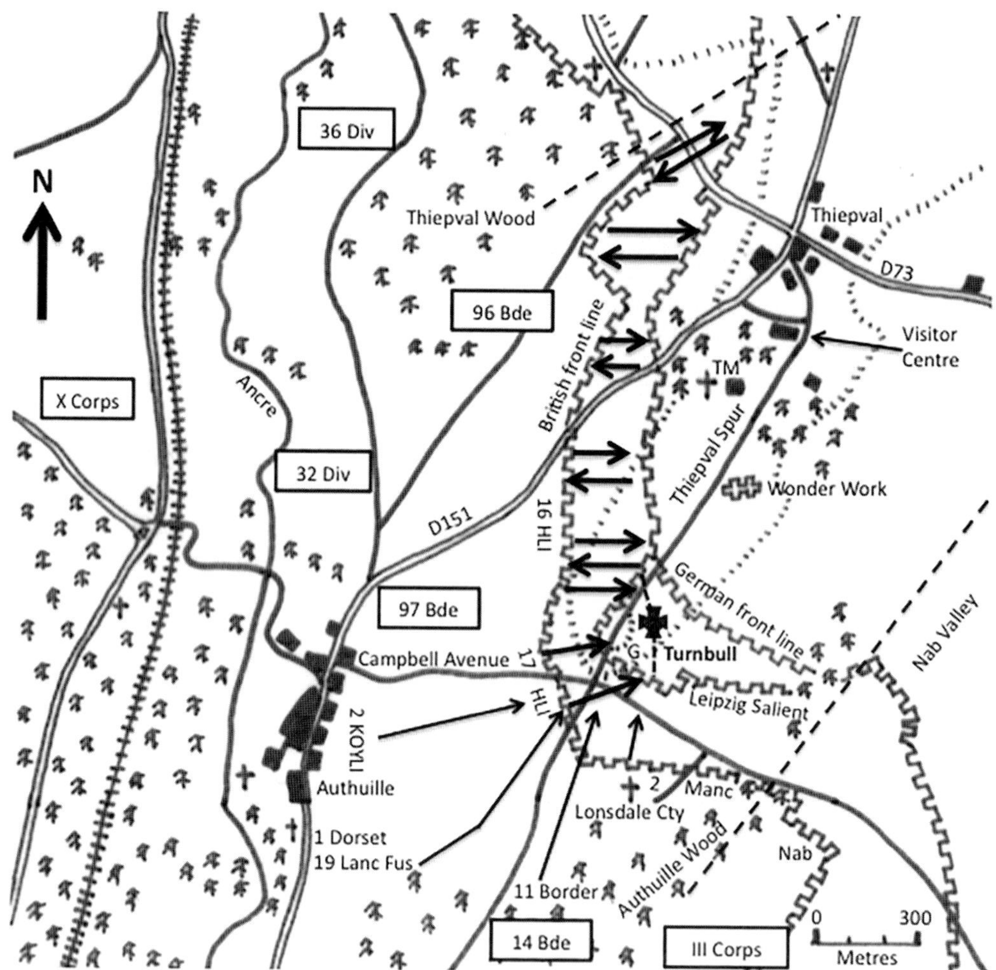

32nd Division on 1st July had only one success; seizure of part of the Leipzig Salient south of Thiepval. Two abbreviations are used: TM = Thiepval Memorial and G = Granatloch. A short dotted line east of the Granatloch marks the limit of the gains by 97th Brigade. To reach the Granatloch, park at the Thiepval Visitor Centre, where it is worth spending some time, but it can become very busy at times. Walk southwest for 900m along the track on top of Thiepval Spur, passing the Memorial on the right. The Granatloch is the small overgrown quarry through which the track passes. Lonsdale Cemetery, where James Turnbull is buried (IV G 9), is a few hundred metres to the south and can be seen from the track. The quarry can be quite oppressive and finds of live ammunition and human bones are not uncommon. Some years ago, the author visited on a hot day to find the contents of a huge shell lying by the side of the track. A very bold/suicidal collector had cut off the base with a power tool and shaken out the explosives in a solid shell-shaped lump. Beads of nitro-glycerin were weeping from it; the visit was short. An alternative parking place is on the track south of the Grantloch. This is reached from Authuille on the unclassified Ovillers road (Campbell Avenue) and also makes it easier to visit Lonsdale Cemetery, with a field path accessible off the same road.

The 97th Brigade plan was for 16th and 17th Highland Light Infantry, left and right respectively, supported by 2nd King's Own Yorkshire Light Infantry, to capture the enemy forward defences on a frontage of 700 metres. One company of 17th Highland Light Infantry was to advance on the right, just beyond the divisional boundary. The southern face of the Leipzig Salient, a small quarry known as the

From the German front line south of Nab Valley, illustrating how exposed the attackers were from flanking fire as they tried to advance towards Thiepval.

Granatloch, was not to be attacked; but once the defences had been overcome, 11th Border (14th Brigade), on the far right, was to cross no man's land and clear up the trenches prior to continuing the advance with 2nd King's Own Yorkshire Light Infantry to the Brigade's final objective.

At 7.23 a.m., the leading companies of 17th Highland Light Infantry (either side of Campbell Avenue) left their trenches and crawled across no man's land to within forty metres of the exploding shells. This was a tactic Brigadier General Jardine had observed the Japanese using successfully during her war with Russia over ten years earlier. When the barrage lifted at 7.30 a.m., the Highlanders were in the German trenches within seconds. They caught the garrison in its dugouts and the Leipzig Redoubt at the tip of the Salient was taken with few losses. Would the results of the day have been different if this tactic had been adopted universally? However,

17th Highland Light Infantry started their crawl towards the Granatloch, on the right, from here.

on the left, 16th Highland Light Infantry was stopped by machine-guns at the German wire, except on the right, where a small party joined up with 17th Highland Light Infantry. About 150 men of 2nd King's Own Yorkshire Light Infantry followed on behind and also joined 17th Highland Light Infantry.

Inside the Granatloch.

As the leading waves pressed on towards the second line they came under very heavy machine-gun fire from the Wonder Work on the left and were forced to withdraw into the Redoubt. The Wonder Work should have been taken by 16th Highland Light Infantry, but uncut wire and undamaged trenches foiled the attack. However, a few men from 16th Highland Light Infantry managed to get through on the right and joined up with 17th Highland Light Infantry in the salient into the German line.

On the right, 11th Border advanced as planned at 8.30 a.m., unaware that the defences had not been subdued. Apart from a few men on the left, who managed to reach the Leipzig Redoubt, the rest were either killed in no man's land or forced back into Authuille Wood. 1st Dorset and 19th Lancashire Fusiliers also tried, but only a few survivors made it into the salient. By 11 a.m. the survivors of 17th Highland Light Infantry and elements of 2nd King's Own Yorkshire Light Infantry and three other battalions were holding the Redoubt. They were cut off and unsupported due to the failure of the attacks on either side.

Captain Hibbert (19th Lancashire Fusiliers), the only officer in the Redoubt, realised it was overcrowded and sent a runner back through one of the recently opened Russian saps to stop further reinforcements. Attempts in the afternoon to take Thiepval failed, largely because of ineffective artillery support. Two companies of 2nd Manchester moved through the Redoubt to bomb towards the Wonder Work but were driven off. During the night the assault troops were relieved by 2nd Manchester and 2nd King's Own Yorkshire Light Infantry. The capture of the Leipzig Salient was the only success of the day for 32nd Division, which suffered almost 4,000 casualties.

Sergeant James Turnbull took part in the initial assault on the Leipzig Redoubt and then helped defend it against heavy German counterattacks. The Germans kept up constant pressure, particularly from the strongpoints to the east, which Turnbull countered with a hail of bombs. When supplies ran short, he took over a machine-gun while his men collected bombs from a German store he had discovered during the attack. Although his small party was almost wiped out on a number of occasions,

Looking south over the Granatloch, with Lonsdale Cemetery, where James Turnbull is buried, in the low ground beyond. The importance of this position at the southern end of Thiepval Spur is evident. Authuille Wood is in the background and the track to Thiepval is on the left. Turnbull's post was to the left of the Granatloch.

Turnbull survived and was reinforced to fight on. Had his post fallen the whole position would have been untenable. Later in the day he climbed onto the parados to throw bombs during a counterattack and was killed by a sniper. He had held his position for fourteen hours.

After dark, elements of 2nd Manchester and 2nd King's Own Yorkshire Light Infantry took over the defence of the Leipzig Salient and 16th and 17th Highland Light Infantry moved back to the British front line.

36th Division's objective on the plateau north of Thiepval was overlooked on the right from the village and on the left from across the Ancre valley. Behind the German front line lay the formidable Schwaben Redoubt, which had to be secured before the second position in front of Grandcourt could be attacked. 109th Brigade was to attack on the right, in contact with 32nd Division, and 108th Brigade on the left, astride the Ancre. 107th Brigade in reserve was to pass through the leading brigades later to reach the Division's final objective. Each battalion had a frontage of about 230 metres and was to advance with two companies leading in columns of platoons. This resulted in each company advancing in four lines fifty metres apart. There was a gap of three metres between each man. A smoke barrage was to be fired into the Ancre valley on the left flank to mask off the high ground either side and avoid flanking fire.

Preparations were meticulous. For weeks prior to the attack large stores of grenades, ammunition and other munitions had been brought into the front line. Gaps were cut diagonally in the British wire. Ramps and ladders were constructed

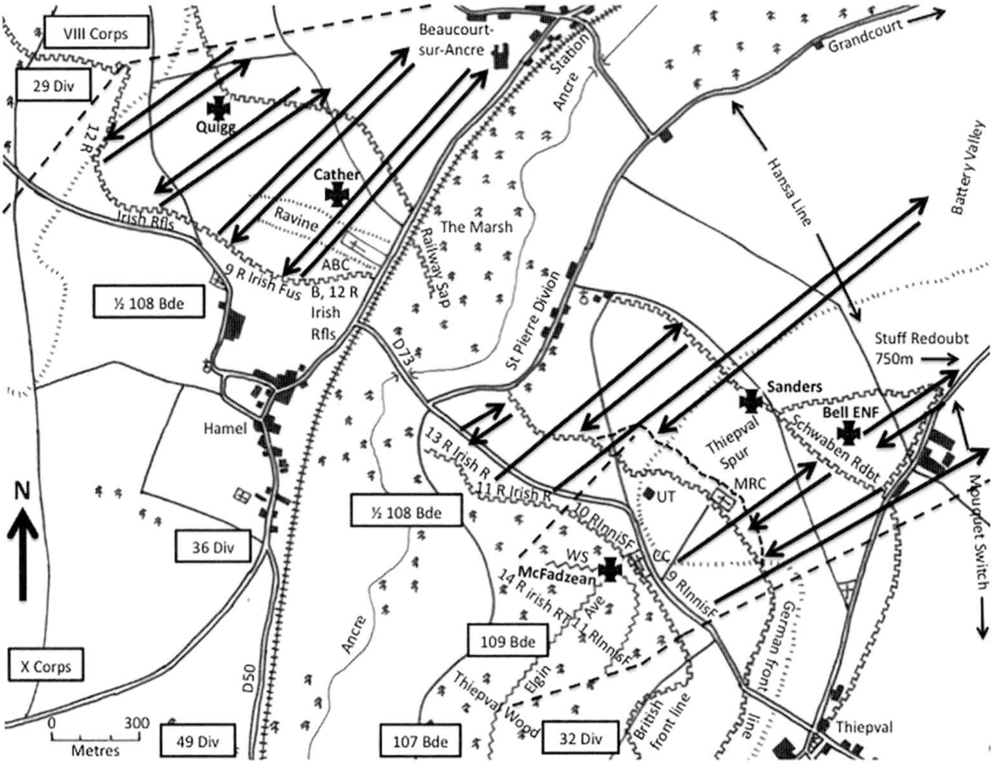

Despite heroic efforts and huge losses, the gains made by 36th Division could not be held once the attacks on the flanks had failed. The dashed line east of the German front line on Thiepval Spur denotes the gains held at nightfall on 1st July. Five abbreviations are used: ABC = Ancre British Cemetery; CC = Connaught Cemetery; MRC = Mill Road Cemetery; UT = Ulster Tower; and WS = Whitchurch Street. A good starting point for a tour of the area is the Thiepval Visitors' Centre, which has toilets and drinks machines. Parking is also available at Ulster Tower, where there is a café and toilets (seasonal opening). A visit to the reconstructed trenches in Thiepval Wood is recommended. There is also parking at Ancre British Cemetery, which is a good starting point to visit the actions of the left half of 108th Brigade.

to allow the assault troops to leave the front line more easily and rides were cleared through Thiepval Wood to aid the rapid deployment of troops and stores. Bridges were constructed for following troops to cross the reserve, support and front lines above ground.

From the crossroads in Thiepval. 109th Brigade attacked from the edge of Thiepval Wood on the left up the slope to the right, between the camera position and Mill Road Cemetery towards the top of the hill, where the Schwaben Redoubt was situated.

The junction of Whitchurch Street running away from the camera, with Elgin Avenue entering it from the right. This is where William McFadzean threw himself on two grenades to save his comrades. This trench junction is just behind Connaught Cemetery on the D73 Thiepval – Hamel road and is not accessible to the public. However, access to the restored trenches inside the Wood can be arranged through the café at the Ulster Tower, although entry is seasonal and timings are limited.

As 14th Royal Irish Rifles (109th Brigade) made its way through Thiepval Wood into the assembly trenches, **Private William McFadzean** provided the banter to keep up spirits in his platoon, even singing his favourite song, *My Little Grey Home in the West*. At about 1 a.m. they arrived at their positions in a narrow trench (Whitchurch Street, astride Elgin Avenue) and began to distribute grenades. As McFadzean lifted a grenade box the rope handle broke, spilling the bombs onto the floor of the trench. The pins fell out of two grenades and the fuses had only four seconds to burn. Everyone froze except for McFadzean, who threw himself on top of the grenades and was blown to pieces. Private George Gillespie's injuries resulted in his left leg being amputated above the knee, but had it not been for McFadzean's unselfish action the explosions in the close confines of the trench would have caused many more casualties.

By 6 a.m. the assault battalions were in position and from 7 a.m. onwards field artillery and trench mortars in the Wood joined in the bombardment. At 7.15 a.m. the leading battalions of both brigades left their trenches under cover of the barrage. They crept forward through gaps in the wire to within a hundred metres of the enemy front line. At 7.30 a.m. the whistles blew, bugles sounded 'Advance' and the Ulstermen moved forward at a steady pace.

In 109th Brigade, 9th (right) and 10th (left) Royal Inniskilling Fusiliers passed through gaps in the wire. Some troops advanced a little before zero. They fell amongst the Germans as they emerged from their dugouts. Following in support were 11th Royal Inniskilling Fusiliers (right) and 14th Royal Irish Rifles (left). The front and support trenches were carried quickly and the advance continued to the

reserve trench 450 metres further on. However, by this time the machine-gunners in Thiepval village had repulsed 32nd Division's attack and turned their attention to the advancing Ulstermen. Supplies of ammunition were moved forward on hand carts but fallen trees on the edge of Thiepval Wood meant boxes had to be manhandled from there forward. Some got through on the left, but any route overlooked from Thiepval village was impassable.

Despite heavy losses, the Schwaben Redoubt was entered at 8 a.m. Flanking fire from Thiepval on the right and around St Pierre Divion on the left increased in intensity, but there was little resistance to the front and the advance continued. By 8.30 a.m. the Redoubt had fallen after a short but bloody fight and Mouquet Switch and the Hansa Line had been reached. Over 500 prisoners were taken.

Captain Eric Bell (9th Royal Inniskilling Fusiliers) was attached to the Brigade Trench Mortar Battery. Six of the twelve Stokes trench mortars had been dug into prepared positions at the head of No.6 tunnelled sap, from where they joined in the final hurricane bombardment. The mortarmen then acted as carriers for the other six mortars, which were to follow the rear waves of infantry.

Bell advanced with the infantry into the Schwaben Redoubt, where the advance was held up by a machine-gun. Bell crept close to it and shot the gunner. On three other occasions the bombers were held up. Each time Bell went forward and threw trench mortar bombs at the enemy, which proved most effective in overcoming resistance. Later, when his bombs ran out, Bell took command of a party of infantrymen who had lost their officer. He was last seen during a counterattack, standing on the parapet and firing his rifle until he was hit and killed.

108th Brigade on the left of 36th Division was spread more thinly. 11th (right) and 13th (left) Royal Irish Rifles attacked on the left of 109th Brigade, with 15th

Leave the crossroads in Thiepval northeast on the D151 towards Grandcourt. After 400m park on the left at the village cemetery. There is space to tuck a car against the hedge without blocking the track or the cemetery gate. Follow the track north-northwest for 600m to just beyond the top of the hill. This is the western tip of the Schwaben Redoubt. Look right. About halfway to La Grande Ferme is the centre of the Redoubt, where Capt Eric Bell was in action. Now look northwest. About 100m along the track and fifty metres to the left is where George Sanders won his VC. The picture looks east from the western tip of the Schwaben Redoubt towards La Grande Ferme, alongside the D151. The southwest face of the Redoubt ran from the camera position to the two prominent trees on the extreme right.

Royal Irish Rifles (107th Brigade) attached in support. On the left there was a gap of 600 metres in the Ancre valley, before the line was continued by 9th Royal Irish Fusiliers (right) and 12th Royal Irish Rifles (left).

On the right of 108th Brigade, 11th Royal Irish Rifles enjoyed the same initial success as 109th Brigade, but 13th Royal Irish Rifles struggled against the machine-guns in St Pierre Divion and only two platoons reached the German support line. North of the Ancre, 9th Royal Irish Fusiliers and 12th Royal Irish Rifles advanced in conjunction with 29th Division (VIII Corps) to the north. Two platoons of B Company, 12th Royal Irish Rifles, on the right of 9th Royal Irish Fusiliers, had the task of capturing the marsh and Railway Sap. The other two platoons were in support behind 9th Royal Irish Fusiliers.

The first wave of 9th Royal Irish Fusiliers moved into no man's land at 7.10 a.m. and suffered little loss when passing through gaps in the British wire. As the advance started casualties mounted from enfilade machine-gun fire from the left. It was particularly heavy in the approach to the ravine halfway over no man's land. The remaining three waves were badly mauled before reaching their own wire, but kept going. The survivors charged and some of the enemy surrendered, until they realised how weak the attackers were. The centre right company suffered less than the other three and reached Beaucourt Station, but as no supporting troops could get over no man's land, there were no lasting gains.

12th Royal Irish Rifles' experience was similar. The remaining three companies advanced in line with C Company on the right, D Company in the centre and A Company on the left. 16 Platoon led D Company's advance, commanded by Lieutenant Sir Harry MacNaghten, attached from 1st Black Watch. At zero they rushed forward and took the enemy front line but, fire from the second line was very heavy. MacNaghten twice reformed the remnants of his Company, but was unable to get through the heavy fire and uncut wire. As he left the front line trench to halt a retirement, he was shot in both legs and fell back into the trench. The machine-gunner responsible was bayoneted, but it made no difference to the outcome and D Company fell back. A few men from the other companies reached the German support line, but were too weak to make a difference and were quickly overcome there.

At 9.15 a.m., 107th Brigade passed through 108th and 109th Brigades in Mouquet Switch and the Hansa Line and, with survivors of these brigades in tow, set off towards the second position in front of Grandcourt, 550 metres away. At 10 a.m. the attacking troops ran into their own barrage and had to wait for it to lift. Lying in the open they suffered many casualties from flanking fire, but at 10.10 a.m. the advance recommenced and the second position was entered at Stuff Redoubt. 36th Division's flanks were now wide open, the attacks on either side having failed completely. The Germans concentrated all their efforts on the handful of Ulstermen holding out inside their lines. Reinforcements and ammunition were desperately needed, but only arrived in a trickle due to the complete domination of the plateau by German machine-gunners.

A patrol found Mouquet Switch deserted and a golden opportunity presented itself to envelop the entire German position on the Thiepval Spur. However, battalion commanders had been forbidden to go into action and there was no one with sufficient authority at this critical moment to take the initiative.

At 2 p.m. the Germans launched two attacks. On the left they came out of the Ancre valley and forced the troops sheltering in Battery Valley back to the lower part of the Hansa Line by 3 p.m. On the right the troops in the second position were pushed back to within 200 metres of the Redoubt. Attacks continued throughout the afternoon. With few officers remaining and ammunition almost exhausted, each attack weakened the defenders further.

At 8.58 a.m., 146th Brigade (49th Division) in reserve, was ordered to cross the Ancre and assemble in Thiepval Wood. The move was completed at 11.35 a.m. A little later, 147th Brigade also crossed and took up positions between the Ancre and Authuille Wood on X Corps' right flank. Officer patrols were sent forward prior to orders being given at 2.45 p.m. for 146th Brigade to attack Thiepval village at 4 p.m. There was little time to prepare and carry out effective reconnaissance. 1/5th West Yorkshire (right) and 1/6th West Yorkshire (left) were to attack, with 1/8th West Yorkshire in support and 1/7th West Yorkshire in reserve to man the edge of the Wood in case of a German counterattack. The attack was launched at 4 p.m. after an ineffective thirty minutes bombardment. Only 1/6th West Yorkshire and a company of 1/8th West Yorkshire were in position. Emerging from the Wood they were met with a hail of machine-gun fire. The survivors made their way back or sought cover in No Mans Land. The attack by 1/5th West Yorkshire was halted with some difficulty to avoid further unnecessary casualties.

Almost simultaneously with the attack, 146th Brigade was ordered to place two battalions at the disposal of 36th Division. The intention had been to use the two battalions not directly committed to the assault, but with the attack on Thiepval underway and the units in some confusion, this was not possible. Due to confusion, a renewed attack by 1/5th West Yorkshire and half of 1/7th West Yorkshire did not get underway until 9 p.m. Instead C and D Companies, 1/7th West Yorkshire, were

Looking west from the western tip of the Schwaben Redoubt towards the Ancre valley and beyond. George Sanders approached roughly from the direction of the Ulster Tower on the left.

sent forward from Thiepval Wood, but went too far to the left and failed to link up with the Ulstermen in the Schwaben Redoubt. Finding the reserve line unoccupied northwest of the Redoubt, they set up a position there to await developments.

At 10 p.m. the survivors of 36th Division in the Redoubt, retired in good order to the German front line. Ironically, as they fell back they met the reinforcements arriving from 1/5th and 1/7th West Yorkshire, but it was too late to reverse the retirement. During the night most of the survivors were withdrawn to Thiepval Wood, leaving isolated parties in the German front and support lines. About thirty men from 1/7th West Yorkshire, commanded by **Corporal George Sanders**, did not receive the order to withdraw. Sanders impressed on everyone the need to hold on at all costs. Next morning he drove off an enemy attack and rescued some British prisoners. All the available water and food was given to the wounded. Two strong bombing attacks were driven off later in the day. On 3rd July the position was finally relieved after a magnificent stand; only nineteen men returned. In addition to Sanders' VC, the party was awarded five MMs, one of whom was 3000 Lance Corporal L Kirk, who died on 21st July 1916 and is buried at St Sever Cemetery, Rouen (A 32 13).

36th Division suffered over 5,100 casualties and it took three days to recover the wounded from no man's land, even with the occasional German cooperation. It was while the wounded were being rescued that two more VCs were won. **Private Robert Quigg** was Lieutenant Sir (Edward) Harry MacNaghten's servant in 12th Royal Irish Rifles. Quigg advanced three times during the day, but that night he heard a rumour that his officer had only been wounded and went out into no man's land again to search for him. Despite the heavy fire, he went out seven times, on each occasion returning with a wounded man. He dragged the last man back on a waterproof sheet from just in front of the enemy wire. After seven hours, Quigg had to give up due to sheer exhaustion. Sir Harry's body was never recovered and he is commemorated on the Thiepval Memorial. He was the great nephew of Captain Dighton MacNaghton Probyn, who was awarded the VC in the Indian Mutiny.

Nearby **Lieutenant Geoffrey Cather**, Adjutant 9th Royal Irish Fusiliers, was engaged in the same work. When the extent of the disaster became apparent

Drive northwest from Hamel on the D73 towards Newfoundland Park and Auchonvillers. Pass the village cemetery on the left and after 150m turn right onto a narrow metalled track with a reservoir on the corner. Park on the hard standing on the right and walk to the end of the reservoir fence, which is on 12th Royal Irish Rifles' front line. Robert Quigg rescued seven men from the area north of this point, but had to give up searching for Sir Harry MacNaghten.

(532 casualties out of the 615 who went into action), all able bodied survivors were gathered to hold the original front line, reinforced by two companies of York and Lancasters. From 7 p.m. until midnight, Cather searched no man's land and brought in three wounded men. At 8 a.m. on the 2nd, despite constant artillery and machine-gun fire, he went out to a fourth man and rescued him successfully. On each trip he also gave water to other wounded men and made arrangements for them to be picked up later. At 10.30 a.m., he set out again and while giving a man a drink he was killed by a machine-gun. Search parties from the Battalion returned to no man's land for the next three nights to finish the task of clearing the wounded. Cather's body was recovered by other officers and buried near where he fell, but the grave was subsequently lost.

Sir Harry MacNaghten's name on Pier Face 10A of the Thiepval Memorial.

VIII Corps' plan was for 29th (right) and 4th Divisions (centre) to advance 3,600m to the second position, while 31st Division (left) wheeled left to protect the northern flank of the whole offensive. In 29th and 31st Divisions, few men reached the German lines and there were no gains. Although the German wire and forward trenches in 4th Division's area had been badly damaged, the deep dugouts were unaffected. The initial assault was made by 11th Brigade along the whole divisional front of 1,350m. Six battalions attacked (including two attached from 48th Division) in two lines of three. Once 11th Brigade had secured Munich

Trench, 10th and 12th Brigades were to pass through and take the second position at Puisieux Trench.

The few men of the leading battalions of 11th Brigade (1/8th Royal Warwickshire attached from 143rd Brigade, 48th Division (left), 1st Rifle Brigade (centre) and 1st East Lancashire (right)) who reached the enemy trenches were either killed or captured there, and the survivors were trapped in no man's land. The exception was on the left, where a small party got into a pronounced salient into the British lines, known as the Quadrilateral (Heidenkopf). The Germans recognised the vulnerability of the position and defended it with only one machine-gun and a few engineers, who were to blow a mine under the Redoubt if the enemy overran it. By a stroke of good fortune, the machine-gun jammed and the mine exploded prematurely, wiping out the garrison instead of the attackers.

At 7.40 a.m., the three support battalions of 11th Brigade (1/6th Royal Warwickshire [attached from 143rd Brigade, 48th Division], 1st Somerset Light Infantry and 1st Hampshire), moved forward and met the same fate as the leading wave. However, some troops got into the Quadrilateral and pressed on for another 400 metres to the rear of the first German position, but by this time fire was coming

From Hamel drive northeast on the D50 towards Beaucourt-sur-l'Ancre and park on the left at Ancre British Cemetery. Walk up the track to the north for 225m, which is in front of the German front line. Look left over the ravine towards the trenches from which 9th Royal Irish Fusiliers attacked towards the camera. Geoffrey Cather made his daring rescues in this exposed field and may still lie there.

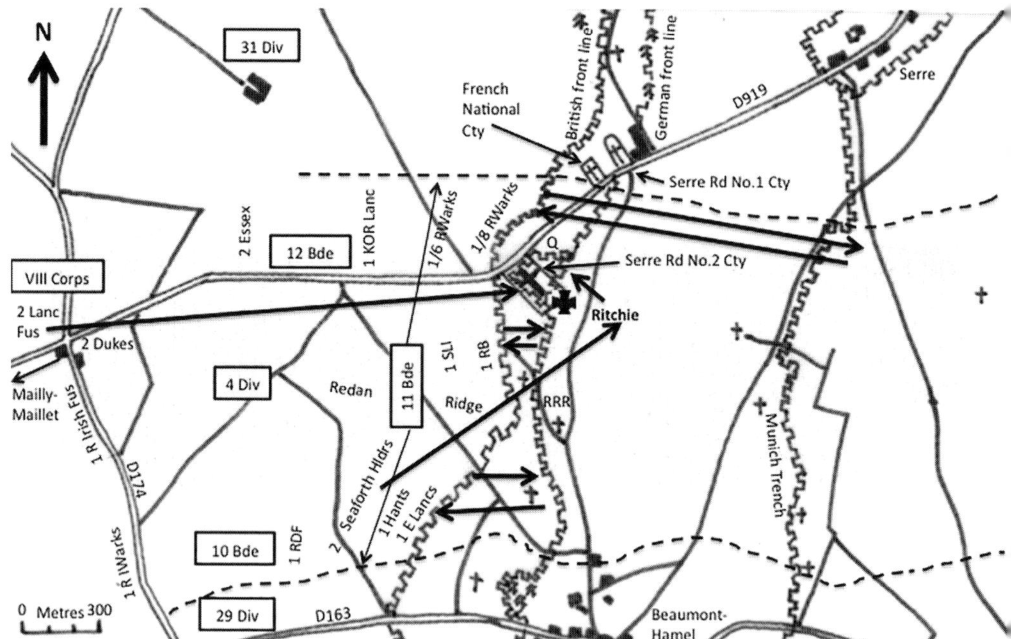

To visit the site of Walter Ritchie's VC action on 1st July 1916, approach Beaumont-Hamel eastwards on the D163 from Auchonvillers. In the centre of the village is a sharp left turn on to Rue de la Montagne. Follow the steep hill upwards and at the water tower keep left. Pass a series of small CWGC cemeteries on the left until reaching the rear of Serre Road Cemetery No.2. This is not a busy road, but try not to block it as local residents often use it as a short cut. Walter Ritchie's action was in the field at the rear of the cemetery. The site can also be approached from the opposite direction by driving northeast along the D919 from Mailly-Maillet. Pass the entrance to Serre Road Cemetery No.2 on the right and 450m beyond turn right opposite Serre Road Cemetery No.1. Follow the minor road 600m to the rear of Serre Road Cemetery No.2. Two abbreviations are used; Q = Quadrilateral (Heidenkopf) and RRR = Redan Ridge Redoubt. While in this area there is an opportunity for refreshments at Ocean Villas (Avril's), 100m southeast of the crossroads in the centre of Auchonvillers.

in from both flanks due to the failure of the flanking divisions. The position was untenable.

Nothing could be gained by committing 10th and 12th Brigades in reserve, but orders to halt the advance did not reach the leading waves. On Redan Ridge, 2nd Seaforth Highlanders (10th Brigade) sent a patrol to investigate the situation, but it was hit by machine-gun fire from Beaumont-Hamel. With no instructions to the contrary, the Battalion set off at 9 a.m. as planned and was hit by flanking fire from Ridge Redoubt and Beaumont-Hamel. By 9.30 a.m. another four and a half battalions were moving across no man's land under fire from Ridge Redoubt. 2nd Seaforth Highlanders avoided the worst of it by veering to the left and, together with two companies of 2nd Lancashire Fusiliers, pressed on to reinforce 11th Brigade in and around the Quadrilateral. Some men even reached Munich Trench, 450 metres further on. However, these gains were soon lost due to the failure of the flanking divisions.

The Seaforth's CO organised the defence of the Quadrilateral, allocating a sector of the perimeter to the survivors of five battalions. At 1 p.m. the Germans evicted

From the minor road behind/east of Serre Road Cemetery No.2, which is on the right. 2nd Seaforth Highlanders advanced towards this position from the left side of the picture.

the defenders of the third line trench and they fell back. Seeing this, **Drummer Walter Ritchie** climbed onto the parapet and, ignoring the heavy machine-gun fire and bombing attacks, repeatedly played the 'Charge' to encourage them to go back. During the rest of the day, Ritchie carried numerous messages over fire swept ground.

During the afternoon the Germans closed in on the Quadrilateral, which was VIII Corps' only gain. Although four more companies were sent to reinforce, they made little difference. Communication across no man's land was all but impossible. By 5 p.m. 2nd Seaforth Highlanders numbered only forty men and was back in the German front line. 11th Brigade was relieved by 12th Brigade after dark and the garrison was reduced during the night. 2nd Seaforth Highlanders finished handing over to 1st Royal Irish Fusiliers (10th Brigade) at 1 a.m. on 2nd July, having suffered 394 casualties. At 11.30 a.m. the last defenders of the Quadrilateral withdrew in good order. By then, 4th Division had suffered 5,752 casualties.

To cover the Fourth Army's exposed left flank, VII Corps (Third Army) was ordered to make a simultaneous diversionary attack against the Gommecourt salient. The plan was simple; 46th and 56th Divisions were to attack the base of the salient from north and south respectively, meeting east of Gommecourt village. No attempt was made to hide the preparations; it was, after all, a diversionary attack. This succeeded in attracting an extra German division into the area and away from the main offensive. As if to confirm they knew what was coming, the German artillery opened fire on the British assembly trenches at 4 a.m.

In 56th Division's area the opposing trenches were 700 metres apart. Over the three nights prior to the attack, a forward assault trench was dug 350–450 metres from the enemy lines to reduce the distance over which the assault troops would be exposed. As a result the attack got off to a good start and the objective was almost reached; but when the enemy artillery sealed off no man's land behind the attackers,

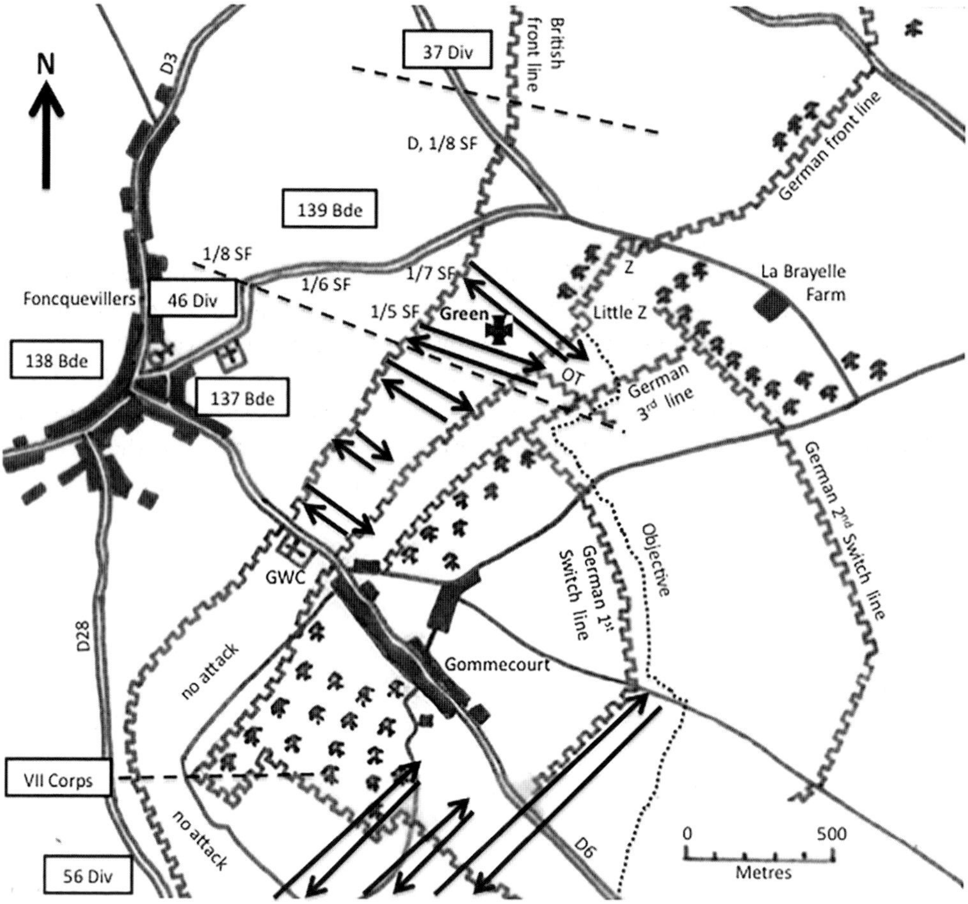

Leave Foncquevillers southeast on the D8 towards Gommecourt. Just after passing under the power lines, park at Gommecourt Wood New Cemetery on the right. From the cemetery walls look northeast. The opposing trench lines were either side of the long re-entrant running away from you. If time permits turn back on yourself towards Foncquevillers. After 300m turn right and follow this narrow lane to a T-junction after 400m. Park here without blocking any of the routes. Turn right and walk 750m east, passing under the power lines halfway. The Little Z is in front. This point marks the midpoint in no man's land through which John Green carried Captain Frank Robinson in an attempt to get him to safety. Two abbreviations are used on the map; GWC = Gommecourt Wood Cemetery and OT = Orinoco Trench. There is a café in Hébuterne.

From the Little Z looking southwest. Gommecourt village is on the left and Fonquevillers church in the right distance. Gommecourt Wood New Cemetery is at the head of the shallow valley, under a pylon. The British front line ran along the opposite hillside. John Green's brave rescue attempt was in the centre right low ground.

it was only a matter of time before the Germans regained control. At about 9 p.m., the last British survivors were pushed back into no man's land.

In 46th Division's area the ground dipped between the opposing lines and was very wet. Attempts to dig advanced trenches failed, as the rain turned these shallow ditches into impassable mud baths and the work merely exhausted the men. The assault troops were in position on time and the trenches were beginning to dry out, although there was still a great deal of heavy mud, making movement difficult. The attack was carried out by 137th Brigade (right) and 139th Brigade (left). 139th Brigade's attack was led by 1/5th Sherwood Foresters (right) and 1/7th Sherwood Foresters (left), supported by 1/6th Sherwood Foresters with 1/8th Sherwood Foresters in reserve. The objective of 1/5th Sherwood Foresters was the German third line, from the northern end of Gommecourt Wood 220 metres northwards to where the third line was crossed by Orinoco communications trench.

The first three waves got away on time, but the fourth wave and the carrying parties behind it were delayed by the poor state of the trenches. The attack got off to a bad start, with the smoke screen dispersing too quickly and the wire being poorly cut. Very few made it to the enemy lines. 139th Brigade fared slightly better than its neighbour, with the first three waves making it over no man's land and fighting their way into the German second line. However, the support waves were cut off by enemy artillery fire in no man's land. Those who did get into the enemy lines were trapped there as the Germans emerged from their front line dugouts and turned on them from behind. Attempts to coordinate further attacks came to nothing in the confusion. The lodgements in the German lines were soon lost.

Captain John Green followed the assault waves of 1/5th Sherwood Foresters across no man's land to deal with the injured. He was wounded early in the action, but refused to give up his work. When the initial assault had been defeated, the enemy turned their attention to the survivors in no man's land. Green went to assist Captain Frank Bradbury Robinson (1/6th Sherwood Foresters), 139th Brigade's Machine Gun Officer, who was badly wounded and entangled in the enemy wire. Green managed to get him into the shelter of a shell hole while under constant bombardment from bombs and rifle grenades. Having bandaged Robinson's wounds, Green dragged him back to safety and had almost succeeded when he was hit again and killed. Robinson died of his wounds on 3rd July and is buried in Warlincourt Halte British Cemetery (I F 6).

From Gommecourt Wood New Cemetery looking northeast, with the respective front lines running away along the hillsides on either side of the shallow valley in the centre. The Little Z is under the second pylon from the right. John Green's rescue of Frank Robinson was in the low ground left of the Little Z.

After dark the survivors came in, but it took days, even with German help, to clear no man's land of the wounded. The attack cost VII Corps over 6,700 casualties, a very heavy price to pay for a diversion.

In summary, the British right (XIII and XV Corps), on the boundary with the French, enjoyed almost complete success, but elsewhere there was almost universal failure. In total, the British Army suffered 57,470 casualties and 19,240 were killed. To put these figures into perspective, the present day Regular Army is about 80,000 strong.

2nd July 1916

133 Lt Col Adrian Carton de Wiart, 4th Dragoon Guards att'd 8th Gloucestershire (57th Brigade, 19th Division) La Boisselle, France

134 Pte Thomas Turrall, 10th Worcestershire (57th Brigade, 19th Division) La Boisselle, France

135 2nd Lt Donald Bell, 9th Yorkshire (Green Howards) (69th Brigade, 23rd Division) La Boisselle, France

136 Lt Thomas Wilkinson, 7th Loyal North Lancashire (56th Brigade, 19th Division) La Boisselle, France

La Boisselle stands on the spur separating Sausage Valley to the south from Mash Valley to the north. On 1st July, 34th Division had attacked the village with the intention of driving on to Contalmaison. Lodgements were made in the German lines southeast of Sausage Valley and around the Lochnagar Crater. However, elsewhere the Division failed to break into the enemy positions. Late that evening,

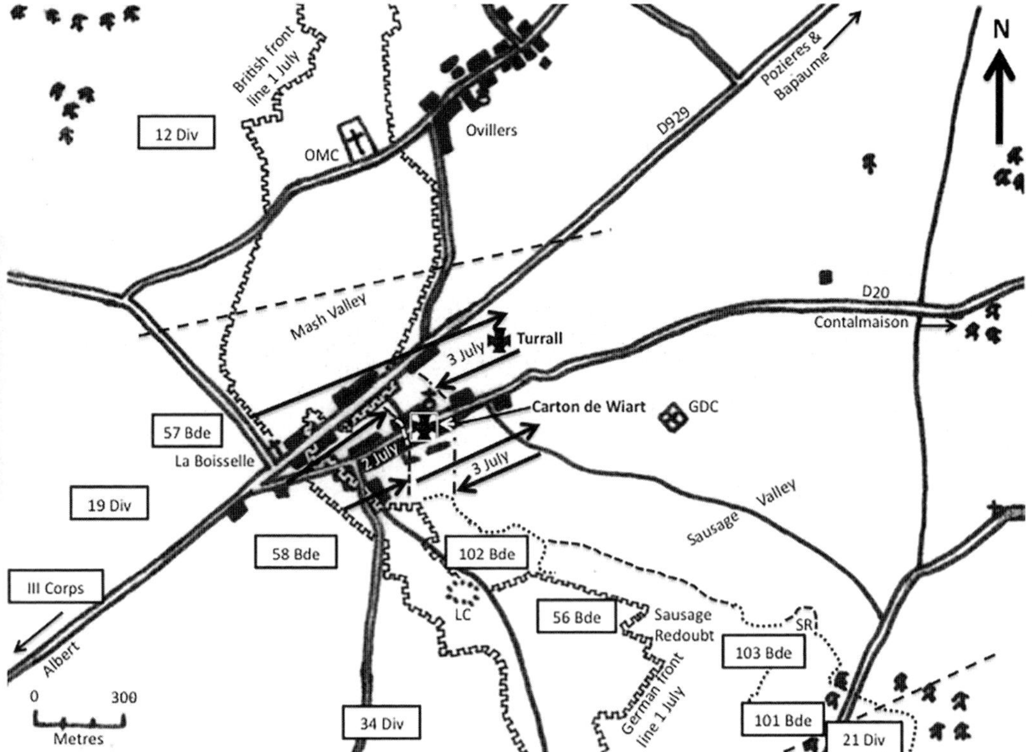

From Albert drive northeast on the D929 towards Bapaume. At La Boisselle take the right fork on the D20 towards Contalmaison. After a few hundred metres on the left is the Old Blighty Tea Rooms, a convenient watering hole for a break. After 700m park near the church on the left. The 19th Division memorial stands in front of it and there are clear views back along the main street towards Albert, where the Golden Virgin on the Basilica can be seen in the far distance. After the debacle on 1st July 1916, the main action for a few days centred around La Boisselle; gains were made gradually, with much opposition from the German defenders. The front lines before the offensive opened on 1st July are shown as trenches. The gains made by the end of that day are shown as a dotted line. Gains made on 2nd July by a dashed line and on 3rd July by a dot-dash line. Four abbreviations are used: GDC = Gordon Dump Cemetery; LC = Lochnagar Crater; OMC = Ovillers Military Cemetery and SR = Scots Redoubt.

57th and 58th Brigades (19th Division) were ordered to continue the attack at La Boisselle, but they were unable to get forward in time through the congested trenches or indeed over the torn, body-littered ground.

On 2nd July, 19th Division was ordered to continue supporting 34th Division. 57th and 58th Brigades deployed left and right of the Albert-Bapaume road respectively, while 56th Brigade worked in direct support of 34th Division, south of the village. 9th Cheshire (58th Brigade) relieved the defenders of the Lochnagar Crater. Later, two companies of 7th East Lancashire (56th Brigade) took Sausage Redoubt and consolidated 900 metres of the front. At the same time, 69th Brigade (23rd Division) relieved 34th Division units opposite Horseshoe Trench.

At 4 p.m., 58th Brigade (6th Wiltshire and 9th Royal Welsh Fusiliers) attacked the western end of La Boisselle, preceded by a deceptive bombardment and smoke screen against Ovillers, which diverted German attention from the real objective.

The forward trenches were taken very quickly and the enemy was cleared from the cellars and other shelters; by 9 p.m. the village was cleared to just short of the church, with 9th Cheshire joining in on the right.

The D20 road through La Boisselle was the axis of the attack led by Adrian Carton de Wiart, advancing towards the church. This is where he also consolidated a line, having held the German counterattacks.

Before dawn on 3rd July, 57th Brigade attacked La Boisselle from north of the Albert-Bapaume road. During the move forward to the attack positions, 8th North Staffordshire began to retire in confusion, believing it had been ordered to pull back. According to 57th Brigade's war diary this was caused by a man shouting, *About turn and double.* The retirement was stopped by **Lieutenant Colonel Adrian Carton de Wiart**, commanding 8th Gloucestershire. At 2.15 a.m., 8th North Staffordshire and bombers from 5th South Wales Borderers (Pioneers) advanced between the village and the Albert-Bapaume road, while 10th Worcestershire covered the open flank on the left. Then at 3.15 a.m., simultaneously with 12th Division's attack against Ovillers on the left, 57th and 58th Brigades attacked. The whole village was cleared and the trenches 350 metres beyond it in fierce hand-to-hand fighting in which 373 prisoners were taken.

The Germans were far from finished. At 8.30 a.m., a counterattack fell on 58th Brigade from the direction of Pozières, forcing it back to its start point. Reserves were rushed up to stabilise the situation and most of the lost ground was recovered by 12.30 p.m.

Meanwhile, at 11 a.m., the Germans attacked 57th Brigade, forcing it back halfway down the village. The situation was desperate; all battalion commanders had been killed or wounded, except for Adrian Carton de Wiart. Reinforcements from 8th Gloucestershire and two companies of 10th Royal Warwickshire came forward and consolidated a line behind the church, while the survivors of 10th Worcestershire established another line thirty metres behind. The divisional commander (Major General GTM Bridges CMG DSO) gave Carton de Wiart command of all the battalions when he came forward on a reconnaissance. From the time Carton de Wiart took over no more ground was lost. He was an inspiration to all, fearlessly walking about, encouraging everyone, organising the defence, attending to supplies of bombs and also getting stuck into the fight. He solved the problem of extracting pins from Mills bombs with only one hand by using his teeth; he was a very tough man indeed. Through his leadership the Germans were held at the church at nightfall. However, the cost was high and at 4 p.m. 10th Worcestershire had to bring forward its reserve officers as there were no others left.

From the church in La Boisselle looking along the main street towards Albert. The 19th Division memorial is on the left.

During the dawn attack, small parties of 10th Worcestershire had pressed ahead of the main body. After a hard fight they broke out of the village into open ground to the northeast, having taken three lines of trenches. However, as their bombs ran out they were forced back into the village. One party, led by Lieutenant Richard W Jennings, the Bombing Officer, included **Private Thomas Turrall**, who was well known in the Battalion and had just been released from arrest. As the light increased, a hidden machine-gun opened fire and Jennings was hit in the arm and leg. Turrall risked a quick look from where he had dived for cover and saw the officer lying nearby with a shattered leg; the rest of the party had been killed.

Crawling over open ground, Turrall reached Jennings and dragged him into a shell-hole. He bandaged the wounded leg using an entrenching tool handle as a splint and one of his own puttees as a bandage. A party of Germans saw him moving

From the church in La Boisselle continue just under 400m towards Contalmaison on the D20 and park on the left at the track junction. From the roadside bank there are excellent views northwards to Ovillers round to the southwest to La Boisselle. On the left is La Boisselle with its distinctive church and just before the first tree in the foreground is the white base of the 34th Division memorial. Behind the last tree on the right is Ovillers Military Cemetery, with the village on the extreme right. Thomas Turrell's VC action was in the fields through the trees in the foreground.

about and soon bombs were exploding all around. Turrall picked up his rifle and set about defending the shell hole. The Germans tried to work their way closer, using a hedge to cover their approach; but they had to cross a gap at one point and when they did Turrall shot two of them and the rest withdrew. Later the German counterattack swept over the area. It was useless to resist in the circumstances, so Turrall feigned death alongside the unconscious officer. Although prodded by several bayonets, he got away with it.

Turrall looked after Jennings until nightfall and then carried him on his back cautiously towards the village. Jennings was much taller than Turrall, and his feet dragged on the ground while his head towered above Turrall's. When Turrall approached the British positions he was ordered to put up his hands by a sentry who added, *and that man behind you – quick*. Jennings died a few hours later at Dernancourt, but not before he had dictated a full account of Turrall's actions. He is buried in Méaulte Military Cemetery (D 34). Turrall returned to the front and continued to fight with great gallantry until the battalion was withdrawn.

At 8.30 a.m. on 4th July, 57th and 58th Brigades attacked again; first to consolidate a line running northeast to southwest across Mash Valley, then to turn east across the north of La Boisselle and finally to follow Alte Jager Strasse to a point close to Gordon Post. During this attack, 7th Royal Lancaster (56th Brigade) bombed forward across the entire width of the village, supported by the bombers and Lewis gunners of 7th Loyal North Lancashire. Eventually three companies from the latter battalion were committed to the battle for La Boisselle. The Germans fought very determinedly, but by 2.30 p.m. the whole village had been taken, less a few ruins at the eastern end. That afternoon a terrific thunderstorm hit the area, completely flooding the trenches.

5th July 1916

XV Corps attacked to the south at 12.45 a.m. on 5th July, to secure the southern end of Mametz Wood and Wood and Quadrangle Trenches. 69th Brigade (23rd

Leave Contalmaison southwestwards on the D147 towards Fricourt and 150m after passing the church on the right, turn left, signed for Bell's Redoubt. The memorial is 100m on the left and there is space to park off the road and turn round. Return to the D147 and turn left towards Fricourt. Pass Peake Wood Cemetery on the right and 500m further on stop on the right at the start of a track, where there is a large area of relatively hard standing. Walk northwest along the track for just over 600m. Donald Bell's VC action was 50m into the field on the right. At the end of the track is La Boisselle and 100m left of the sunken section close to the village is the site of Thomas Wilkinson's VC action.

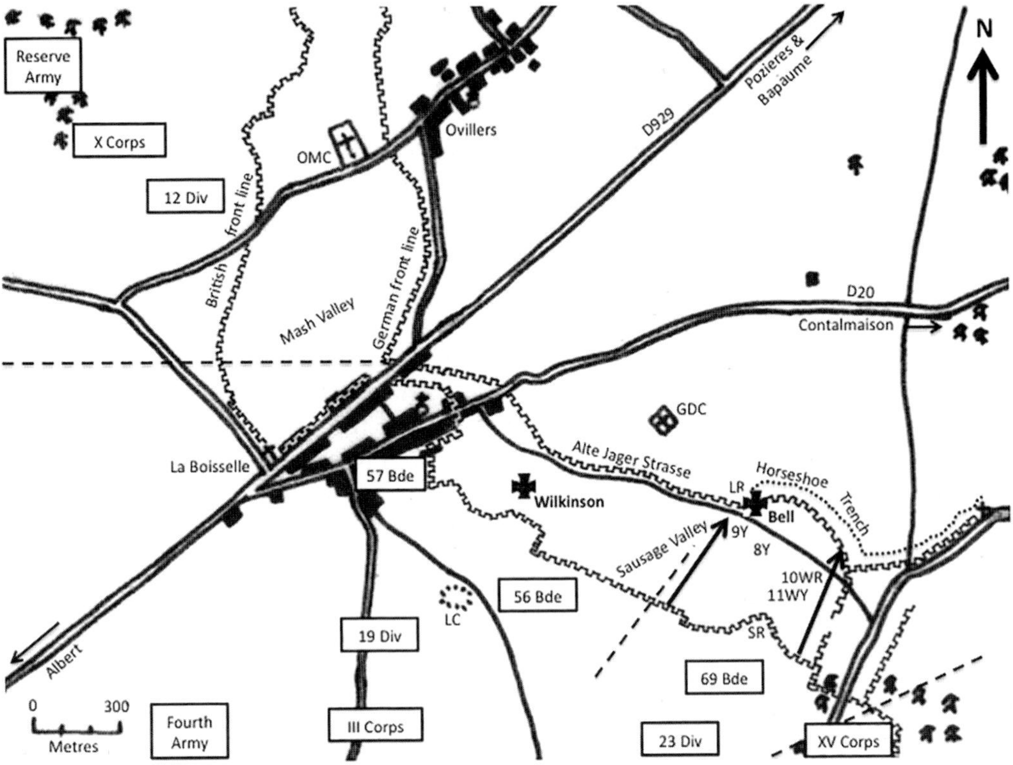

The gains made at La Boisselle on 5th July are shown as a dotted line around Horseshoe Trench. Abbreviations are as for the previous map, plus LR = Lincoln Redoubt.

Division) was ordered to support XV Corps' left flank and to improve its own positions in front of Contalmaison; an attack on Horseshoe Trench was therefore ordered. 69th Brigade launched its attack at 4 a.m. Bombing parties of 9th Yorkshire went forward on the left flank, while 10th West Riding and 11th West Yorkshire advanced on the right. Fighting continued in Horseshoe Trench until 10 a.m., when the Germans counterattacked and retook most of the ground gained.

In the afternoon the British gradually gained the upper hand and a frontal assault by 10th West Riding and 8th and 9th Yorkshire (right to left respectively) was planned to retake Horseshoe Trench at 6 p.m., although much ground had been seized before then by 11th West Yorkshire and 10th West Riding. As a preliminary to the main attack, a machine-gun on the left flank was to be dealt with by a party

The memorial at Bell's Redoubt, where he was killed on 10th July 1916.

of bombers, led by Lieutenant John Gibson. They were detected, Gibson was killed (Thiepval Memorial) and the rest of the party withdrew to safety.

When the main attack began it was subjected to accurate enfilade fire and heavy casualties were sustained. On his own initiative, **Second Lieutenant Donald Bell** crept along a communications trench towards the machine-gun position, followed by 15958 Corporal H Colwill and 16748 Private J Batey. When close to the gun, Bell charged over the open, shot the gunner with his revolver and knocked out the rest of the crew with grenades. His prompt action undoubtedly saved many lives and

Leave La Boisselle eastwards on the D20 towards Contalmaison. After 650m park at the end of the path leading to Gordon Dump Cemetery (Donald Bell VC is buried there) on the right and look back towards La Boisselle. Thomas Wilkinson's VC action was on the spur to the left of the trees around La Boisselle. To get closer to the site, walk southeast along the track starting from the eastern limits of La Boisselle village. After 300m there is a sunken section and Wilkinson's action was 100m southwest of it. Continuing along the track for another 750m brings you to the site of Horseshoe Trench and Donald Bell's VC site.

From Bell's Redoubt looking southwest. Donald Bell's VC action was just over the crest of the hillside in the centre. Peake Wood Cemetery is alongside the road to Fricourt, on the left.

ensured the success of the attack. Colwill and Batey were awarded the DCM for their part in this action. Bell was killed at Contalmaison five days later.

The enemy began to crack and at 6 p.m. a determined attack by 9th Yorkshire on the left completed the demoralisation of the Germans. Horseshoe Trench and another beyond it were cleared by 7 p.m. and consolidated during the evening, as was part of Lincoln Redoubt. More than 200 prisoners and two machine-guns were taken at a cost of 195 casualties.

In 56th Brigade, 7th East Lancashire made a bombing attack at 2.30 p.m., supported by D Company and the bombers of 7th Loyal North Lancashire. 1st Sherwood Foresters (24th Brigade, 23rd Division, attached to 57th Brigade) cooperated on the left. Fire support was provided by the Trench Mortar Battery, but the attack was not well organised. Many messages came back to Brigade HQ for resupply of grenades, but there were large stocks in the front line. This seems either to have been ignored or they were not known about. Due to a misunderstanding, at about 3 p.m. 7th East Lancashire began to withdraw on the left to the old German front line, giving up much of the ground gained. By 6.23 p.m., 7th East Lancashire reported it was back in its start positions and was assisted by 7th Loyal North Lancashire to reorganise there. The right flank was wide open, but this was not apparent until next morning, when the brigade commander visited.

During the retirement, **Lieutenant Thomas Wilkinson,** on the left, noticed a Lewis gun abandoned by the retiring troops. With two men he rushed forward and

brought the gun into action, just in time to drive back a determined German attack down a trench. C Company, 7th Loyal North Lancashire, then charged over no man's land to retake most of the lost ground. Forcing his way to the front, Wilkinson found an earthwork block over which the Germans were throwing grenades. Quickly mounting the Lewis gun on top of the parapet, he dispersed the enemy. Later in the day he made two attempts to rescue a wounded man lying fifty metres out in no man's land; on the second attempt he was shot through the heart and died instantly. He was recommended for the VC by Lieutenant Colonel RL Sherbrooke, CO 1st Sherwood Foresters (24th Brigade, 23rd Division).

Chapter Two

Bazentin Ridge and Delville Wood

Battle of Bazentin Ridge 14th–17th July 1916

138 Sgt William Ewart Boulter, 6th Northamptonshire (54th Brigade, 18th Division) Trônes Wood

The Battle of Bazentin Ridge marked the opening of the second phase in the 1916 Somme campaign. The days preceding the dawn attack on 14th July saw a series of sharp preliminary operations for Mametz Wood and Contalmaison to establish the start line for the assault on the ridge. Attempts to take Trônes Wood failed. Four divisions (3rd and 9th in XIII Corps and 7th and 21st in XV Corps), made the initial assault at 3.25 a.m. on a frontage of 3,600m. The attack

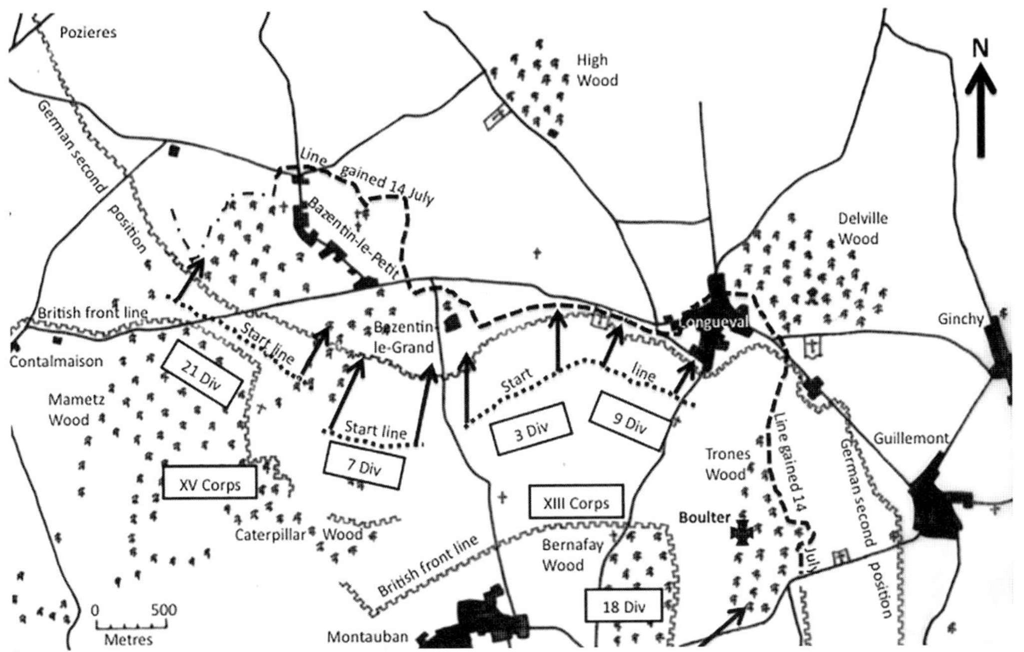

The dawn attack on the Germans Second Position on 14th July 1916 was made from an advanced start line to cut down the assault distance. The operation included an attack by the 18th Division to secure the right flank at Trônes Wood.

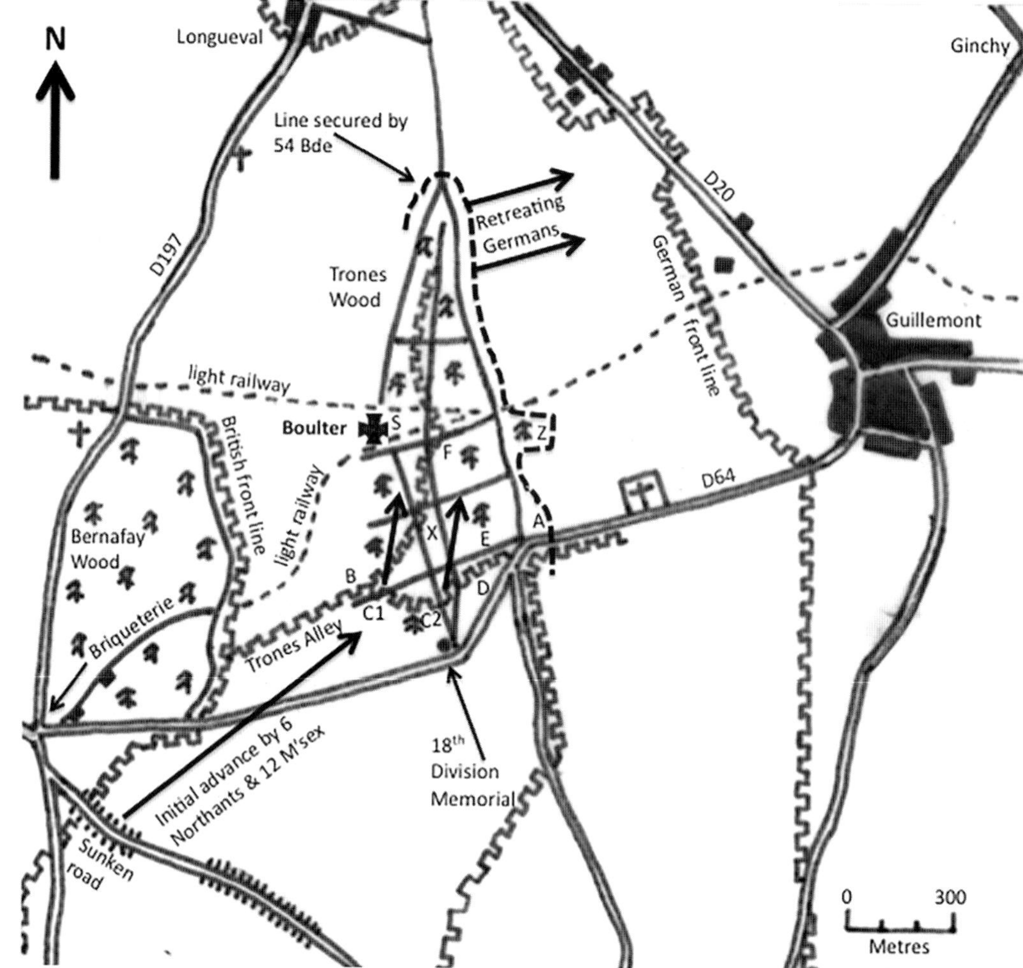

Leave Montauban-de-Picardie eastwards on the D64 towards Guillemont. After a crossroads, pass Bernafay Wood on the left and continue to the next wood, which is Trônes. There is space to park a car either side of the 18th Division memorial at the southern tip, but care is required when emerging back onto the road. Walk northwards through the wood. There are numerous shell holes and occasional collapsed dugouts, but the going is relatively easy if you avoid the patches of thicker undergrowth. Head slightly west of north until reaching the obvious former railway embankment. Just beyond it, on the western edge of the wood, is where Strongpoint S, taken by William Boulter, was located.

was preceded by a hurricane bombardment of only fives minutes, following which the advance was supported by the first true creeping barrage. The objective was to break into the German Second Position.

Although progress on the right was slow and fighting for Longueval continued, XV Corps had seized the Bazentins by 9 a.m. 2nd Indian Cavalry Division was ordered forward, but it was too far back and made slow progress over the broken battlefield. It did not arrive until evening, by when the opportunity had passed and the Germans had begun to reoccupy High Wood. The cavalry charged and held the Wood overnight but, without support, withdrew in the morning. It would be two months before High Wood was captured.

The 18th Division memorial at the southern tip of Trônes Wood.

On the right flank, 55th Brigade (18th Division) carried out a preliminary operation to capture Trônes Wood the evening before the main attack. 12th Middlesex and 6th Northamptonshire (both 54th Brigade) were placed at the disposal of 55th Brigade. Only the southernmost part of the wood was captured, which left this flank of the main attack dangerously exposed.

Just after midnight on 14th July, 54th Brigade was ordered to complete the operation, attacking at 3.20 a.m. By then 6th Northamptonshire was deployed, with two companies each in Dublin Trench and Maricourt. There was little time for preparation and none for reconnaissance, so the brigade commander adopted a simple plan; 12th Middlesex was to sweep the Wood from south to north, with 6th Northamptonshire following to clear pockets of resistance and to establish a secure flank along the eastern face. Both battalions were under the command of Lieutenant Colonel FA Maxwell (a South African War VC), commanding 12th Middlesex. The position of other troops south of the Briqueterie – Guillemont railway was uncertain, so it was decided that there would be no barrage to the south of it. The attacking troops were estimated to arrive at the railway at 4.30 a.m., at which time a barrage was to commence from it, stepping northwards ahead of the assault troops.

From the southern tip of Trônes Wood looking southwest, with Bernafay Wood in the right background. 6th Northamptonshire advanced towards the camera from the direction of the trees on the far left horizon.

Maxwell arrived at the sunken road selected as the start line and realised that only one company of 12th Middlesex was in position, with another on the way from Dublin Trench. The battalion would not be complete before zero hour, but 6th Northamptonshire was in position and ready to move. Maxwell switched the battalions' roles.

6th Northamptonshire began the attack at 4 a.m., with A and B Companies advancing from the sunken road about 900 metres from the wood. C Company followed in support, while D Company remained in reserve. A number of casualties were suffered from heavy shellfire as they crossed the open ground. At 4.30 a.m. the southwest edge was reached and the troops plunged into the trees. They paused while the temporary CO, Major Clark, tried to ascertain from CO 7th Royal West Kent where his troops were disposed.

The situation was very confused as the advance up the wood commenced. After less than 200 metres from the southwest edge, the leading companies came under heavy rifle and machine-gun fire. By 4.50 a.m. the leading company was bombing along Trench C1 towards Strongpoint X at the southern end of Central Trench. Twenty minutes later it was in touch with two others from the battalion on the right, but reported it was held up by Strongpoint X and that Major Clark had been killed. Major Charrington went forward to find two companies advancing on Strongpoint X against heavy small arms fire. A resupply of bombs arrived and soon after 6 a.m. the strongpoint was overrun; fifty dead Germans were discovered there.

6th Northamptonshire pressed on in small groups, but lost direction whilst struggling through the tangle of fallen trees, thick undergrowth and shell holes. The battalion was also fired upon by survivors of 55th Brigade, who believed the Germans had infiltrated behind them. A party under Second Lieutenant Redhead cleared the west side of the wood to the northern tip and then swept down the east side, joining other elements of 6th Northamptonshire near Strongpoint A. Second Lieutenant Price reported his men were occupying Central Trench and that the wood was clear in the south and east but that snipers were still active to the north. A projection on the eastern face of the wood, Copse Z, was mistaken for the northern apex and, believing they had reached their objective, the troops began to consolidate at 9 a.m. The exception was Strongpoint A, which was attacked by a party of 7th Royal West Kent supported by a Stokes trench mortar and finally fell to a combined force of 12th Middlesex and 7th Royal West

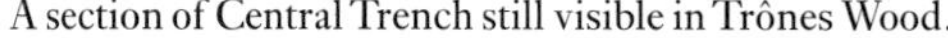
A section of Central Trench still visible in Trônes Wood.

Kent. Retreating Germans were fired on from Strongpoint A and by Lewis guns at Copse Z on the eastern edge of the Wood. There was no further communication from 6th Northamptonshire until 11.30 a.m., when B Company reported it was lining the eastern edge of the Wood.

Meanwhile, at about 8 a.m., Maxwell left his HQ between C1 and C2 and went to the south-eastern edge of the wood at Point D. He found a mixture of units and met Captain Dennis of 12th Middlesex, who reported Strongpoint A had not been taken. At Point E, Maxwell found a group of 6th Northamptonshire, but no other formed units and could hear no activity in front. He reorganised his force to try again. A company of 12th Middlesex and elements of 6th Northamptonshire formed a new line and swept up the wood, with frequent halts to check direction.

The railway embankment running through Trônes Wood. This view looks east from the western edge. Strongpoint S was off to the left of picture.

Little resistance was encountered until the southern railway line was reached, when the sweep came under very heavy fire from Strongpoint S. Maxwell took seventy men and captured the Strongpoint. The advance continued, sweeping up the wood and encountering little resistance. The men were ordered to fire as they advanced, which improved their morale. Many Germans broke out of the northeast side of the wood to escape towards Guillemont and were shot down by the Lewis guns of 6th Northamptonshire and 12th Middlesex already in position. Maxwell believed his force was the first to reach the northern apex, but this is at variance with reports from a number of officers of 6th Northamptonshire, which suffered heavy casualties in clearing the wood, and this may account for the lack of opposition Maxwell encountered except for Strongpoint S.

Looking north from the railway embankment over the site of Strongpoint S, the most likely location for William Boulter's VC action.

It is not entirely clear precisely where or when **Sergeant William Boulter's** VC action took place. The description in various accounts indicates that just before 9 a.m. the remnants of two companies

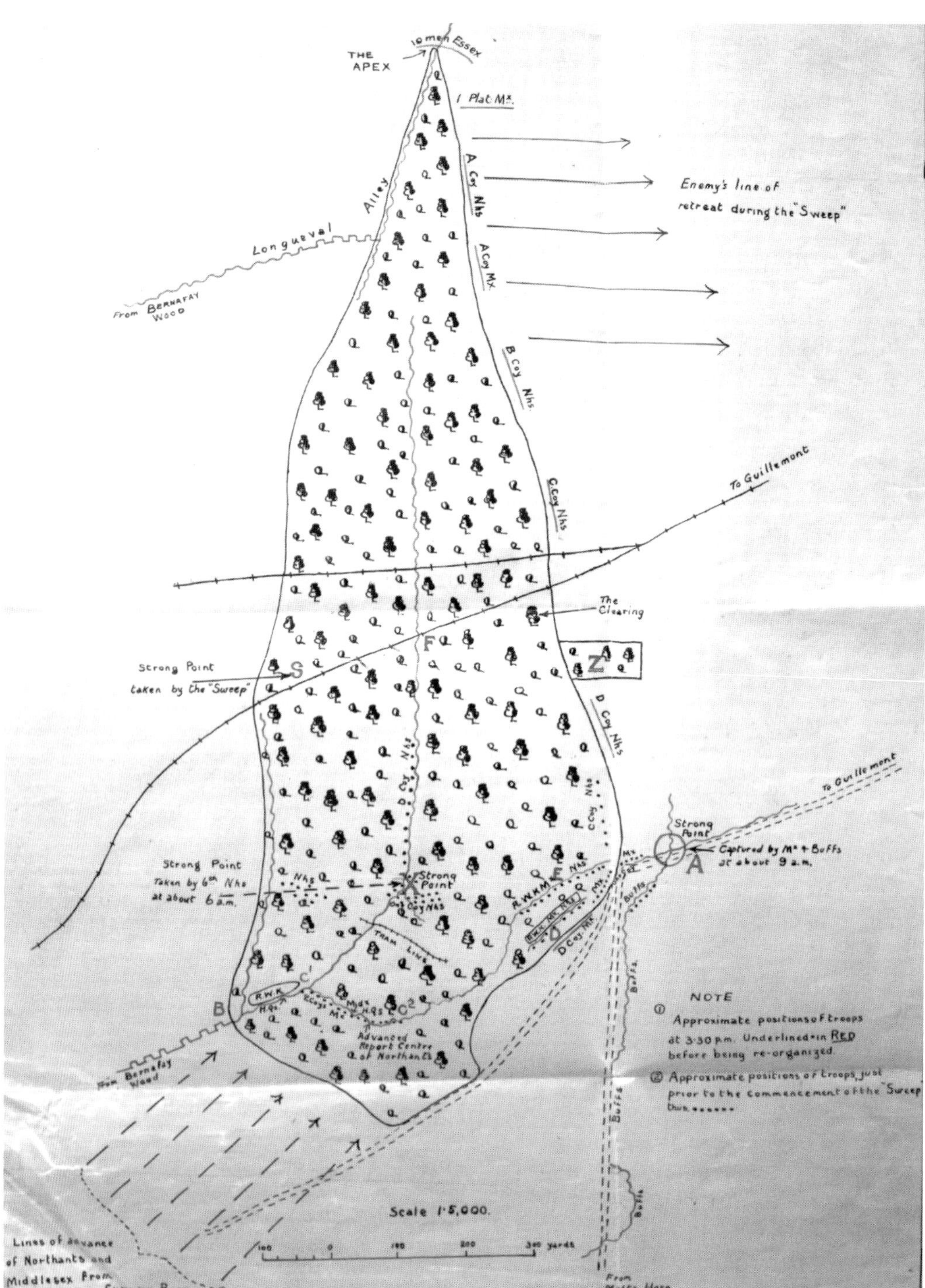

Contemporary sketch map of the action in Trônes Wood on 14th–15th July 1916.

were pinned down by a machine-gun as they approached the northern apex of the Wood. This fits the action at Strongpoint S, except it was not at the northern apex. However, after seizing Strongpoint S no major opposition was encountered by the sweep. The weight of evidence points to Boulter's VC action being during the storming of Strongpoint S.

Boulter was commanding his platoon after his officer had become a casualty. A shell landed close to him, wounding Lance Corporal Frederick Cordaroy in nineteen places. With complete disregard for his own safety, Boulter grabbed a bag of bombs and dashed forward alone. He was badly wounded in the left shoulder by a sniper, but continued. When he was close enough, he bombed the Germans out of their positions and the final objective was secured. Boulter then walked back 1,800 metres to the aid station for treatment.

The fight for Trônes Wood cost 6th Northamptonshire 317 casualties, including fourteen of the seventeen officers who went into action. 12th Middlesex had about 150 casualties. With Trônes Wood in British hands, the Germans bombarded it heavily, but made no attempt to counterattack.

Attacks on High Wood 20th–25th July 1916

140 Pte Theodore Veale, 8th Devonshire (20th Brigade, 7th Division)

A major struggle for Longueval and Delville Wood developed on Fourth Army's right flank (XIII Corps) and III Corps pressed ahead on the left towards Martinpuich. In between, XV Corps made another attempt to secure High Wood after the missed opportunity on 14th July. 19th Brigade (33rd Division) on the left was tasked to capture the Wood, while 20th Brigade (7th Division) in the centre and 13th Brigade (5th Division) on the right were to secure Wood Lane Trench, between the wood and Longueval.

20th Brigade was led by 8th Devonshire on the right and 2nd Gordon Highlanders on the left. They began to move into position at 10 p.m. on the 19th; it was a fine night with a clear moon. Each battalion was to attack with two companies, each with a frontage of two platoons. A third company was held in trenches in support and the fourth was further back in reserve. Behind the leading battalions were 9th Devonshire, 2nd Border and 1st Royal Welsh Fusiliers, the latter attached from 22nd Brigade for the operation.

At 2.55 a.m. on 20th July the bombardment intensified and at 3.15 a.m. the leading companies of 8th Devonshire (A and C Companies) and 2nd Gordon Highlanders moved forward uphill in a north-easterly direction under cover of the barrage. There were some casualties as they crawled forward because the barrage was not as accurate as expected. The first objective was Black Lane, on the reverse

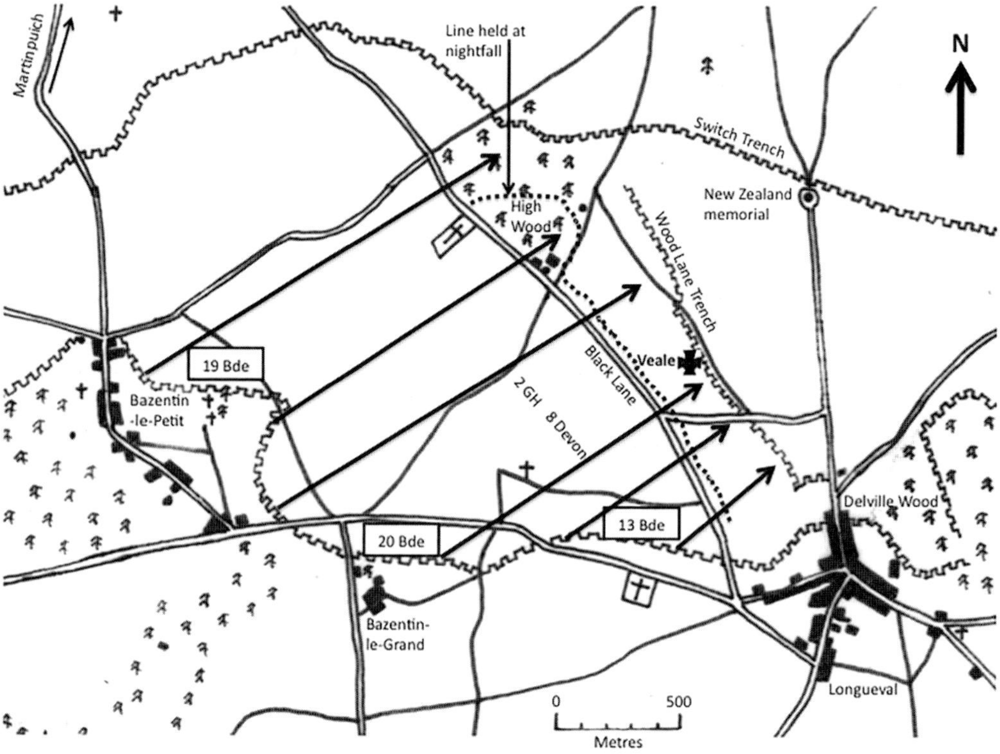

Drive north out of Longueval on the D197 towards Flers. Just as you leave the village turn left, signed for the New Zealand Forces Memorial. After 350m turn left and continue for another 300m, where there is a track on the right. Park here and walk northwest along the track towards High Wood for 280m. Climb on the bank on the left side of the sunken section. In front of this point is where Theodore Veale won his VC.

slope from the German positions and about forty metres back from the crest; as a result it was secured quickly at zero (3.25 a.m.).

The assault pressed on over the crest of the ridge towards Wood Lane, the second objective, roughly 450 metres away. Only ten minutes were allowed before the barrage lifted again. This was not enough time for 19th Brigade on the left in High Wood. As 20th Brigade continued, it came under fire from the east side of High

From Wood Lane looking northeast, with High Wood in the background. 8th Devonshire attacked from the left. Lieutenant Eric Savill was rescued by Theodore Veale about fifty metres into this field and taken to the left towards Black Lane.

Wood, Switch Trench, strongpoints along Wood Lane, troops dispersed in crops (which in places were breast high) east of the Lane and machine-guns concealed in the northern corner of Delville Wood. The British shelling was falling short and added to the impact of the German barrage.

In the face of such strong opposition, the attack was stopped twenty-five metres from Wood Lane, with both flanks open. The two leading platoons of the left company of 2nd Gordon Highlanders were reduced to a wounded officer and five men. All the officers in A and C Companies, 8th Devonshire, were casualties. For an hour the men attempted to dig in where they were, but every time a man rose to dig he was invariably shot, often from the left rear. The British artillery was still falling short, despite numerous green flares being put up to indicate the position of the forward troops. The survivors were forced to crawl back in small groups to Black Lane, covered by the Lewis guns. The support companies and part of the reserve companies were required to consolidate this line, and contact was made with the formations on either flank.

Plans were made for another attack on the second objective, but it soon became clear that even if it was taken it would be untenable in daylight unless Switch Trench was also taken and that was very strongly held. HQ 20th Brigade then investigated the possibility of approaching the second objective from the left flank, through High Wood. An officer of 2nd Gordon Highlanders was sent to reconnoitre and found the southeast edge occupied by 2nd Royal Welsh Fusiliers (19th Brigade, 33rd Division), but the situation in High Wood was in some confusion. Although 19th Brigade had captured the Wood, it was so weak that by evening the Germans had forced the survivors back to the southern corner.

The officer was unable to reach the eastern corner, but could see Switch Trench, which appeared to have no wire in front of it, although trench maps show it was wired. A patrol was sent out, but only one man returned and without any useful information. The situation remained largely unchanged and during the rest of the day and night Switch Trench and the crop fields were kept under indirect machine-gun fire. Overhead in the early evening an aerial combat resulted in one aircraft on each side being shot down.

While 8th Devonshire was preparing positions in Black Lane a hand was seen waving from no man's land. Thinking it was a German wanting to surrender, a

The opposite view from the previous picture. Black Lane runs towards High Wood on the left. Eric Savill was rescued by Theodore Veale in front of the bushes on the right, which are along the sunken section of Wood Lane.

close watch was kept on the area. After twenty minutes the man had made no move, but cries for help were heard from the same area. Grabbing his rifle and a grenade, **Private Theodore Veale** set off into no man's land. Bullets whistled past him and he dived for cover, but he pressed on and eventually reached the wounded man lying close to Wood Lane; it was Lieutenant Eric Savill, OC C Company.

Because the Germans were only fifty metres away, Veale decided to pull Savill some way back, but at first he mistakenly moved closer to the enemy. Under intense close range fire, he managed to get Savill into a shell hole, and then crawled back for water. He was unable to move Savill any further and returned to the trenches again to organise a rescue party consisting of 6636 Corporal Albert Edgar Allen, Private Lord and another man. After carrying Savill on a waterproof sheet for about seventy metres they stopped for a rest. One hundred metres away, five Germans appeared out of the long grass and the rescuers immediately set off again. However, as they crossed a little bridge (presumably over a trench) Allen was shot through the head and killed (Thiepval Memorial). Veale's other helpers became worried for their own survival. Sending them away, Veale pulled Savill a little further, hid him in a shell hole and went back for more water to keep him alive.

Two British Mills bombs alongside Black Lane in March 2015. Of all the unexploded ordnance hazards encountered on the Western Front, these are the most unstable and dangerous. Leave well alone.

That evening Veale led out another rescue party. This time he was accompanied by the Reverend EC Crosse DSO, Lieutenant Duff MC and Sergeant Smith DCM; a distinguished, gallant and appropriate supporting act for a VC. They reached Savill just before dark and were about to carry him back when some Germans were seen approaching. Duff kept them occupied with his revolver while Veale dashed back 135 metres to the trench, fetched a Lewis gun and brought it into action. He and Duff covered the others, while they carried the wounded officer to safety.

During the night, 19th and 20th Brigades were relieved during a German counterattack; in spite of the heavy fire the relief was achieved smoothly and with few additional casualties. Losses overall had been heavy. 8th Devonshire's post action report showed eight officers and 193 other ranks were lost out of twenty officers and 564 other ranks deployed. Another attempt was made on High Wood on the night of 22nd/23rd July. No significant gains were made and losses were again heavy.

Battle of Delville Wood 15th July–3rd September 1916

137 Maj William Congreve, Rifle Brigade att'd HQ 76th Brigade (3rd Division) Longueval, France
139 Pte William Faulds, 1st South African Infantry (South African Brigade, 9th Division) Delville Wood, France
141 Cpl Joseph Davies, 10th Royal Welsh Fusiliers (76th Brigade, 3rd Division) Delville Wood, France
142 Pte Albert Hill, 10th Royal Welsh Fusiliers (76th Brigade, 3rd Division) Delville Wood, France
146 Sgt Albert Gill, 1st King's Royal Rifle Corps (99th Brigade, 2nd Division) Delville Wood, France
148 CSM George Evans, 18th Manchester (90th Brigade, 30th Division) Guillemont, France
151 2Lt Gabriel Coury, 1/4th South Lancashire (Pioneers) (55th Division) near Arrow Head Copse, Guillemont, France
152 Capt Noel Chavasse, RAMC att'd 1/10th King's (Liverpool) (166th Brigade, 55th Division) Guillemont, France

15th July 1916

While the preliminary operation to secure Trônes Wood was taking place on 14th July, the main attack on the German second position got underway. In 3rd Division, 8th and 9th Brigades made the assault, leaving 76th Brigade in reserve south of Montauban. 3rd Division had prepared for this attack since 6th July, during which time **Major William Congreve**, Brigade Major of 76th Brigade, displayed the utmost dedication to duty. He led a number of dangerous reconnaissance missions under heavy fire, often penetrating 900 metres forward of the British lines. On each occasion he took parties of officers and senior NCOs to acquaint them with the ground that they were about to fight over. This type of work was not the business of a brigade major, but Congreve gladly accepted the risks to ensure success and avoid casualties. His father, the Corps Commander, wrote in his diary, *Very wrong of him to be out on such work .... bless him.*

The main attack caught the Germans by surprise and the Second Position was captured on a frontage of 5,400 metres from Contalmaison Villa to Longueval. At 10 a.m., the centre was wide open, but the infantry were forbidden to continue. The continuing hard fighting for Longueval and Delville Wood, the key to the right flank, made the commanders cautious. With the benefit of hindsight this was a mistake. Eventually a combined force of cavalry and infantry did advance at 7 p.m. Part of High Wood and ground either side of it was secured, but on the right, around Longueval, the situation had not improved by the end of the day.

A German counterattack on the morning of 15th July failed to develop due to confusion and the strength of the British artillery. However, sufficient German

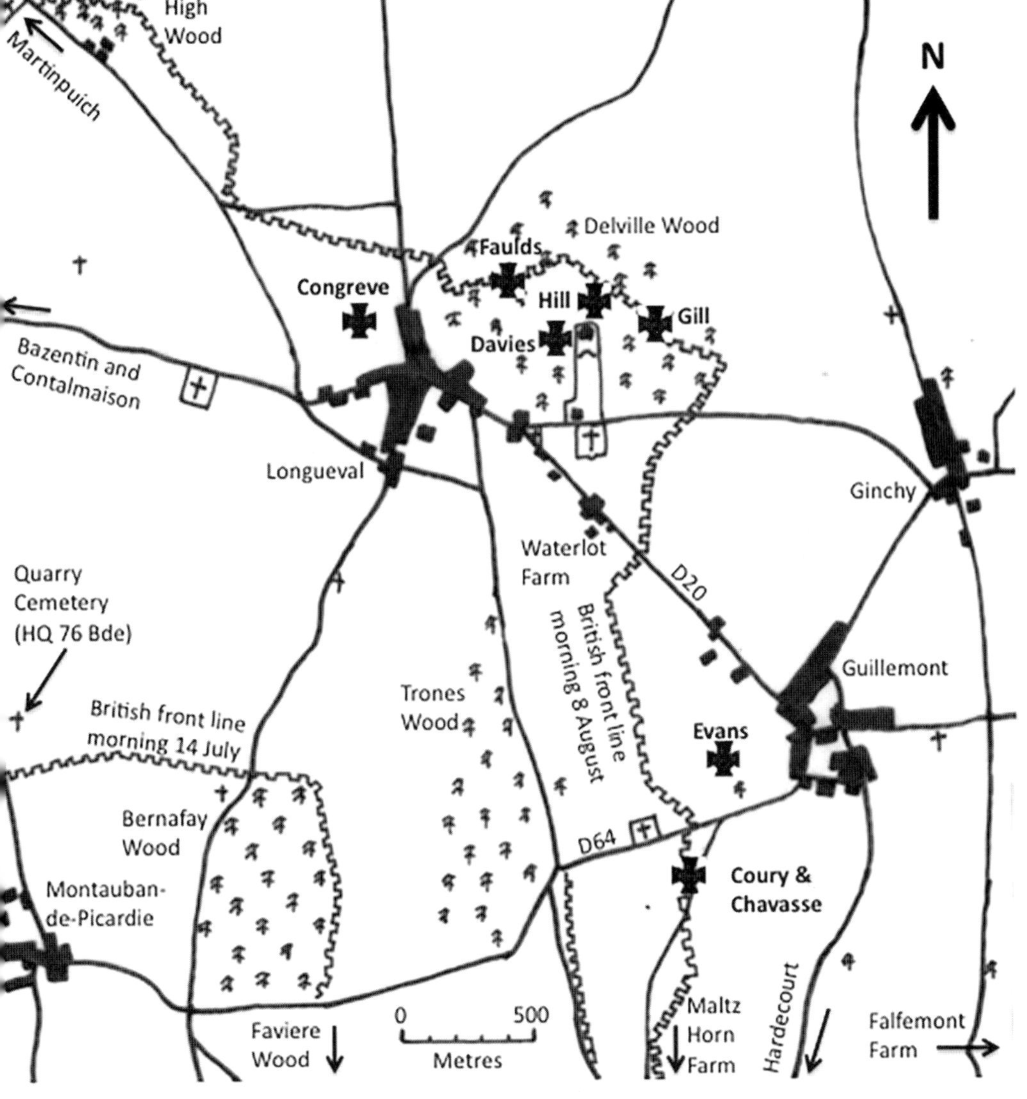

The relative location of the VC's in the Battle of Delville Wood, 15th July – 3rd September 1916.

reserves came forward to resist any further move forward. Waterlot Farm was finally captured on the extreme right, but German shelling made it untenable for a few days.

9th Division's main task was to complete the capture of Longueval and Delville Wood. The Wood was a thick tangle of trees and bushes intersected by grassy rides. The northern part was in dead ground, which provided the Germans with a covered approach into Longueval from the northeast. 27th Brigade was ordered to make a fresh attack through Longueval with 1st South African Infantry (South African Brigade) attached for the operation. 12th Royal Scots led the way, bombing up North Street and also through the orchards to the west. However, all the gains were retaken by the Germans. Another attempt at 7.30 p.m. was to no avail.

Meanwhile the rest of the South African Brigade (which had arrived in France in April 1916 and replaced 28th Brigade in 9th Division when the latter was broken up) had come forward. Its mission was to clear the Wood at all cost, regardless of success or otherwise by 27th Brigade on its left flank. The attack was to be launched eastwards from Longueval, but if the north of the village was still in German hands the attack was instead to be made from the southwest corner of the Wood.

Lieutenant Colonel WEC Tanner, CO 2nd South African Infantry, was in command of the attack. He decided to clear the south of the Wood first, before turning attention to the north. 3rd South African Infantry led the attack, followed by 2nd South African Infantry with 4th South African Infantry in reserve; 1st South African Infantry was already detached to 27th Brigade. At 6.15 a.m., the South Africans advanced through 26th Brigade's line on the southwest edge of the Wood. Battling through the downed trees and confusion of shattered undergrowth and shell holes, the southern half of the Wood was cleared by 3rd South African Infantry and a company of 2nd South African Infantry by 7 a.m. The advance was continued by three companies of 2nd South African Infantry and the remainder of the Wood was cleared by noon, except for the northwest sector. About 140 prisoners were taken and a machine-gun.

The South Africans settled down to consolidate their gains, although digging through the numerous tree roots was extremely arduous and slow. The Germans shelled the positions throughout. Machine-gun fire into the north and east sides of the Wood was also incessant and just about every man was required to hold the gains against successive counterattacks in an arc from the southeast to the northeast. However, the British artillery support was effective. A company each of 1st and 4th South African Infantry came up in support and 9th Seaforth Highlanders (Pioneers) sent a company to wire the north-eastern edge of the Wood. 1st South African Infantry returned to the South African Brigade at 11.15 a.m. and it sent a second company to reinforce 2nd South African Infantry.

As it grew dark the German artillery opened a furious bombardment, which preceded a strong counterattack. It was stopped fifty metres short of the Wood by the weight of small arms and artillery fire, but the German artillery continued firing all night. Up to 400 shells per minute were arriving. Despite their exhaustion the men were urged to dig in and hold on. A Lewis gun and Vickers machine-gun were set up at the southwest corner to cover along the southern edge of the Wood and ten other machine-guns were set up in the perimeter. The Brigade was not well placed; it had a long perimeter to hold against a determined enemy who had the advantage of a covered approach to bring up reserves.

16th July 1916

On the morning of 16th July, Major General Furse, GOC 9th Division, ordered another attack. 11th Royal Scots (27th Brigade) advanced to the west of North Street at 10 a.m., while A and B Companies, 1st South African Infantry, advanced northwards from the western end of Princes Street. C and D Companies were under command of 2nd South African Infantry for the defence of the Wood. A bombing section was to rush a trench at 10 a.m., while the rest of the assault troops followed. Two companies of 4th South African Infantry were in support and another 1st South African Infantry company with 2nd South African Infantry was to advance west from the Strand.

Both attacks were forced back by intense machine-gun fire and also uncut wire in 27th Brigade's area. The trench mortars continued to bombard the German positions and fighting continued without gaining ground. B Company, 1st South African Infantry, was delayed starting due to a platoon of D Company being in the start line trench by mistake. Survivors of the 1st South African Infantry attack fell back to Princes Street.

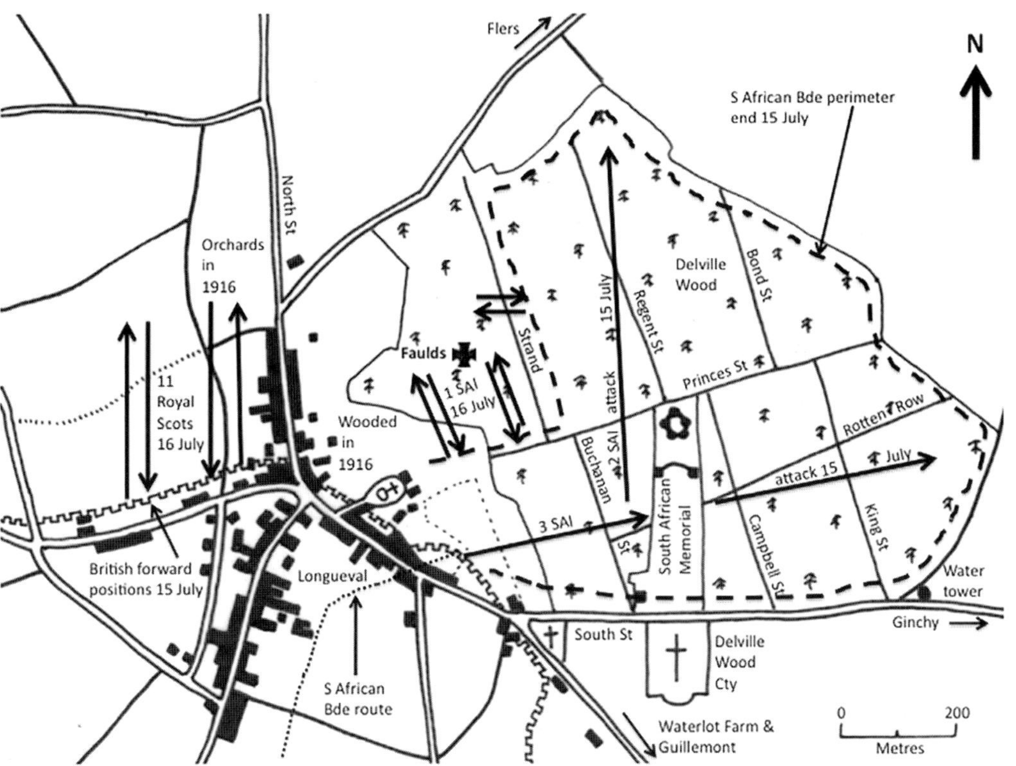

To visit the sites of all the Delville Wood VCs, park at the visitors' centre. It opens in winter 1000–1600 and in summer 1000–1730. The information centre and museum are closed on Mondays and do not open on Tuesdays until 1100. Walk along the road to the east, keeping the Wood on your left, to the entrance opposite Delville Wood Cemetery, where one of the Delville Wood VCs, Albert Gill is buried. Once inside the Wood the rides are clearly marked and navigating around is simple. Beware the rides in wet weather, as they can be extremely slippery. From the rear of the South African Memorial, join Princes Street and walk along it to the western edge of the Wood. Look north. This is the centre of the start line for the attack by 1st South African infantry on 16th July. Turn right (north) along the edge of the Wood for fifty metres until the path swings left. To the north a narrow grassy path can be seen. Faulds VC action was about a hundred metres north of this path.

From the centre of 1st South African infantry's start line looking north. On the left is Longueval, with its church spire just visible through the trees. On the right is Princes Street.

The grassy track and beyond it the northwest corner of the Wood where Mannie Faulds won his VC on 16th July.

Private Mannie Faulds, 1st South African Infantry, with Privates Alexander Estment and George F Baker spotted their platoon commander, Lieutenant Arthur William Craig, lying severely wounded in the open between the lines. He had been wounded in the charge over open ground and managed to roll into a shallow trench running at right angles towards the German lines. He was only fifteen metres from the Germans, but the main threat was a machine-gun about seventy metres away on the left. About 10.30 a.m., Faulds scaled the parapet, doubled to Craig and attended to his wounds as best he could under heavy fire. He was joined by Estment and Baker. It took them twenty-five minutes to drag Craig back by his left leg along the shallow trench and over a barricade. His uniform and equipment were shredded by machine-gun bullets, but he survived. Baker was also wounded in the withdrawal and received the MM for his part in the rescue; he was killed on 12th April 1917 (Level Crossing Cemetery, Fampoux I B 79). Estment received the DCM.

A fresh attack was planned for next morning, but during the preparations HQ XIII Corps ordered that the objectives must be secured by dawn on 17th July. The most forward infantry had to be withdrawn before the Corps' heavy artillery opened fire against the northwest corner of the Wood and the north of the village at 12.30 a.m. Before this the South Africans endured another German attack at 11 p.m.

The attack was launched at 2 a.m. on 17th July. 27th Brigade was astride North Street and 1st South African Infantry started from south of Princes Street and east of the Strand. It was almost a repetition of the previous day's attack. German machine-guns survived the bombardment and, although trench mortars were used again, by midday the operation had failed with heavy losses. Heavy German gas and high explosive shelling concentrated on the village and Wood that night. That evening Tanner was wounded and Lieutenant Colonel EF Thackeray, CO 3rd South African Infantry, took command of all South African troops in the Wood.

18th July 1916

By the evening of 17th July, 9th Division had exhausted itself in gaining the southern end of the Wood and village. HQ XIII Corps changed tactics and ordered 3rd Division to seize the objectives before dawn on 18th July by attacking from the west. In the meantime the Germans made plans to regain control of their lost ground. That evening the forward German troops were withdrawn to allow for a massive bombardment, which commenced at 11.45 p.m. There were 116 field guns and at least seventy medium and heavy guns involved. The South Africans were pushed back and forced to make a stand in their support trenches on Buchanan Street and Princes Street.

76th Brigade was tasked to make the 3rd Division attack and Congreve personally led the units to their assault positions. At 3.45 a.m., after a one-hour bombardment, 1st Gordon Highlanders, supported by two companies of 8th King's Own Royal Lancaster, left its north facing trenches, formed 90° to the right and advanced eastwards. Longueval was taken as far north as Duke Street and a line was occupied on the north-western edge of Delville Wood, in contact with the South African Brigade. Much of the credit for this success was due to Congreve, who established himself in an exposed position and gave the necessary orders to drive the enemy from the village.

While 76th Brigade was securing Longueval, the South African Brigade was recovering the remainder of Delville Wood. The situation looked promising until the Germans opened a furious counter-bombardment, setting Longueval and

Delville Wood ablaze. At 3.30 p.m., the Germans counterattacked. The attack from the east was halted by the British artillery and small arms fire from the South African Brigade in the south-eastern edge of the Wood. Another attack from the north pushed the surviving South Africans back to Princes Street, except for some men who hung on in the southeast corner until next morning. This German attack reached the south of the Wood where it was hit by artillery and machine-gun fire. Another attack from the north and northeast against Longueval forced 27th Brigade back to the southern edge of the village. 26th Brigade assisted and the line of Clarges Street was regained. 76th Brigade was forced back to its starting positions, where 1st Gordon Highlanders and 8th King's Own Royal Lancaster were relieved by 1st Duke of Cornwall's Light Infantry.

During the 18th Mannie Faulds made a second daring rescue under very heavy fire. Stretcher-bearers were aware of a severely wounded Highland soldier. He had been hit by a shell fragment in the back and was lying in the open. Despite the scale of the challenge and the heavy fire, Faulds went out alone and carried the man 700 metres to a dressing station.

Early on the 19th, 53rd Brigade (18th Division, attached to 9th Division) tried again. 8th Norfolk had no time for food or reconnaissance before it set off from the southwest of Longueval at 7.15 a.m., having missed the barrage. Despite the disadvantages, it retook the southern part of the Wood. Further attempts by 53rd Brigade failed to achieve much more.

Congreve again distinguished himself when HQ 76th Brigade was shelled in the Quarry north of Montauban (now Quarry Cemetery), on 19th July. Although badly shaken and suffering from gas, he helped the MO to look after the wounded and move them to safety. The Brigade Signals Officer, Lieutenant M Hill DCM RE, was killed by a shell there (Carnoy Military Cemetery – K31). Brigade HQ was forced to move to the sunken road between Montauban and Caterpillar Valley. Meanwhile

The Quarry north of Montauban now houses Quarry Cemetery. Billy Congreve distinguished himself here when HQ 76th Brigade was shelled on 19th July.

the Brigade also practised its part in the forthcoming attack repeatedly over taped ground behind the lines. During the night, 3rd Division began relieving 9th Division, but not 53rd Brigade or the remaining South Africans under Thackeray still in the Wood.

20th July 1916

Plans were further revised with a view to a combined advance with the French; but the latter would not move until the British right had advanced further. Haig allocated more frontage to the Reserve Army, allowing Fourth Army to shorten its frontage and concentrate for another effort. However, the reorganisation was slowed considerably by poor roads, wet weather and the need to relieve exhausted divisions. The renewal of the general offensive therefore had to be delayed until 22nd July.

In the meantime Haig remained concerned at the situation around Longueval and Delville Wood, where a short German advance would endanger the gun positions in Caterpillar Valley. He therefore gave instructions that the line was to be pushed forward to Longueval – High Wood – Bazentin-le-Petit. Then, in cooperation with the French, the advance was to continue to Guillemont and Falfemont (Faffemont) Farm. As a result, on 20th July XIII Corps tried to seize Longueval and Delville Wood, while XV Corps was to make another attempt to secure High Wood.

76th Brigade made another attack using the two battalions not yet committed. At 3.35 a.m., 2nd Suffolk advanced eastwards from Pont Street, northeast of the windmill. 10th Royal Welsh Fusiliers was due to attack northwards at the same time from Princes Street between the Strand and the eastern edge of the Wood. Guides were met at the southwest corner of the Wood and they led the Battalion east along South Street and then north along Buchanan Street. Here they came under heavy fire under Very lights. The guides insisted they had reached the start position behind Princes Street, but this was clearly untrue. The battalion turned 90° right and deployed eastwards along the start line.

The intention was for each of the three forward companies to have a frontage of a little under 200 metres. B Company on the right was to continue until its head reached the eastern edge of the Wood. The right of D Company in the centre was to march about 350 metres before halting and C Company on the left about 180 metres. However, having progressed only a hundred metres along the start line, B Company was attacked, but repulsed the enemy. After lying down for a while to avoid the heavy machine-gun fire, it set off again and covered 200 metres before coming under fire from front and rear. The Germans attacked again and were once more repulsed. It was then decided that the battalion would attack from where it was on a restricted frontage.

A party of nine men from D Company was cut off after the first German attack and during the second attack was surrounded and forced to take cover in a shell hole. **Corporal Joseph Davies** took charge and conducted a most aggressive defence. When the attack petered out, Davies rushed after the fleeing Germans and

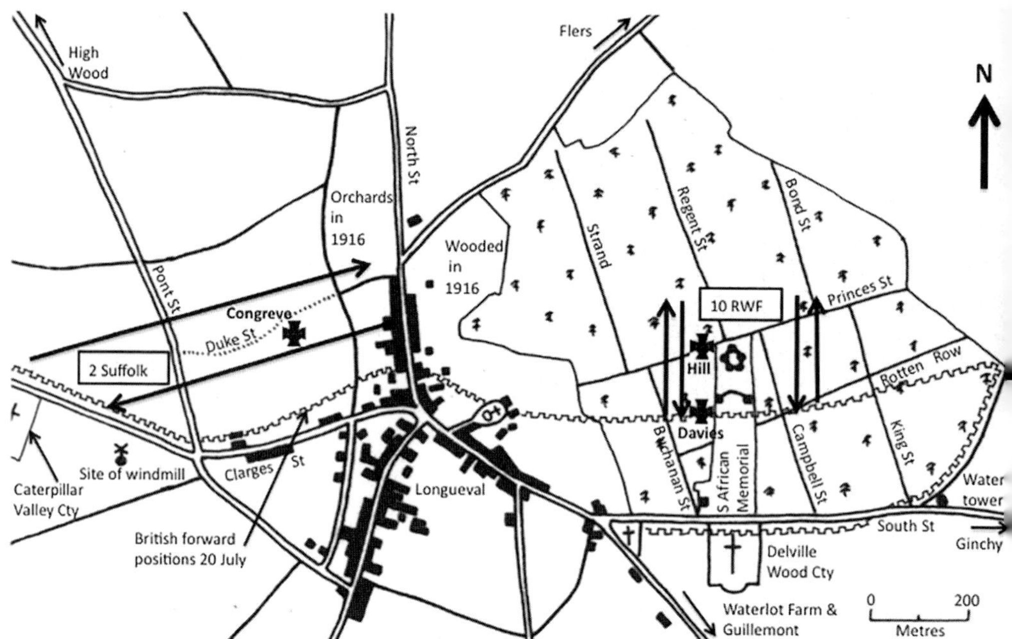

Walk north along the left side of the memorial avenue in Delville Wood until just before the memorial itself. 10th Royal Welsh Fusiliers emerged from the trees on the left to reach this point before attacking northwards. Joseph Davies' VC action was in this area. Continue north, with the memorial on the right. On reaching Princes Street turn left along it for thirty metres. This is about where Albert Hill won his VC. There is a memorial to both men nearby, close to the only surviving tree from 1916.

bayoneted a number of them. This was a remarkable performance in a thick wood on a dark night.

To add to the difficulties, 11th Essex, holding the line in this area, had not been told about the attack and opened fire on 10th Royal Welsh Fusiliers. Having driven off the enemy and identified themselves to 11th Essex, 10th Royal Welsh Fusiliers commenced the attack at 3.45 a.m. It was ten minutes late, but this delay

10th Royal Welsh Fusiliers emerged from the trees on the left, turned left and attacked northwards past the memorial. This is where Joseph Davies' VC action took place.

Looking north along Buchanan Street, the route 10th Royal Welsh Fusiliers took to get into the Wood. The memorial on the left marks the location of the South African Brigade HQ.

A well defined trench in the area where Albert Hill won his VC.

was discretionary for the CO to allow the 2nd Suffolk's attack to develop first. The advance was met with heavy machine-gun fire and numerous bombs. The line was broken up and, with severe casualties, it was impossible to continue. The line gradually withdrew, leaving many isolated parties in front to engage the enemy for the rest of the day.

In C Company on the left, **Private Albert Hill** charged forward and immediately bayoneted two Germans. Later, when he was sent by his platoon sergeant to make contact with the company, he was surrounded. Instead of lying low, he immediately attacked a party of about twenty Germans with bombs. Many were killed and wounded and the remainder ran off. He then joined forces with a sergeant and they fought their way back to the company. On returning, he learned that the company commander, Captain George B Devereux Scale, and his scout had been wounded and immediately went out with two other men to recover them. Hill personally brought in the officer; the scout was recovered by the others. Finally, he went out on his own and captured two prisoners. Before Captain

The memorial to Joseph Davies and Albert Hill on Princes Street, with Longueval church in the background. This was the area of Albert Hill's VC action. A close up of the memorial is inset.

Scale died of wounds (Thiepval Memorial) he submitted a recommendation for the VC for Hill.

Both battalions attempted to press on, but the attack degenerated into a series of isolated actions and broke down. The last of the South Africans were relieved after five days of incessant fighting under heavy enemy artillery fire, including gas

From the crossroads in the centre of Longueval, drive west on the D20 towards Bazentin. After 450m turn left and park without blocking any of the roads. Climb onto the bank to the west and look northwards to see the line of bushes and trees along Duke Street leading towards Delville Wood, where Billy Congreve was killed. There is a café in the centre of Longueval (Le Calypso II).

shells. At 6 p.m., Thackeray marched out with only three other officers (two were wounded) and 140 other ranks. Of the 121 officers and 3,032 other ranks that went into the Wood on 15th July, only 29 officers and 751 other ranks were present for the roll call on 21st July. The South African Brigade had ceased to be an effective fighting force. However, its defence of the Wood for six days and five nights is one of the most remarkable feats of determination and endurance of the First World War.

Congreve went forward to sort out the mess, although he was already exhausted by days of exertion and lack of sleep. Accompanied by Major Stubbs, commanding 2nd Suffolk, and Congreve's orderly, Private Edward Roberts of 10th Royal Welsh Fusiliers, they passed along a communication trench running alongside Duke Street. At the end they found some soldiers digging an extension to the trench. Congreve climbed out and took cover in a disused German gunpit from where he could observe the enemy and take notes. Having finished his work, Congreve returned to the trench. At about 10.55 a.m. he stopped to talk to Sergeant Sheen about the fine job his work party was doing. As he spoke, a sniper shot him in the throat and he died within minutes.

Both 76th Brigade battalions were relieved that night and during the 21st, having suffered heavy casualties. It was clear that isolated attacks on the Wood were unlikely to succeed in the face of heavy artillery fire.

On the night of 22nd/23rd July, there was a general attack by the British. III Corps was to continue towards Martinpuich, XV Corps towards the Switch Line either side of High Wood and XIII Corps was to complete the clearance of Delville Wood. XIII Corps attacked at 3.40 a.m. 30th Division headed for Guillemont, while 3rd Division's objective was from Guillemont Station to Longueval inclusive, including Delville Wood. 30th Division's attack became confused in the darkness and smoke and, although there was some initial success in places, no progress was made. 3rd Division's attack was made by 9th Brigade from Pont Street, supported by 95th Brigade (5th Division) on the left. It met with some success, but heavy flanking fire from the left and counterattacks forced the attackers back to their start positions.

A closer view of Duke Street. Longueval church is on the right, with Delville Wood behind. The line of bushes and trees from the centre leading to the left are along the line of Duke Street. In the distance on the left is the New Zealand Memorial.

27th July 1916

The next major attack was at 7.10 a.m. on 27th July. The aim remained the same, to secure the right flank, and plans were made for XIII and XV Corps to combine in securing Longueval and Delville Wood. 5th Division was to clear Longueval, while 2nd Division was to capture Delville Wood. The combined artillery of both Corps (200 field guns and 200 medium/heavy guns) would saturate the objectives for an hour before the attack commenced. About eighty Germans surrendered during the bombardment, but some shells dropped short, causing casualties to the assault troops.

2nd Division's attack was led by 99th Brigade, with 1st King's Royal Rifle Corps on the right, 23rd Royal Fusiliers on the left and 1st Royal Berkshire in support. Two of the Royal Berkshire companies were directly under command of the assault battalions, which each had four machine-guns and two Lewis guns attached. The company on the left also had a section of the Brigade Trench Mortar Battery with it to assist 15th Brigade's (5th Division) attack on Longueval. The right company's task was to guard that flank, while the two inner companies consolidated on Princes Street as the advance of the assault battalions continued. 22nd Royal Fusiliers had two companies as Brigade reserve and the other two companies were under the Staff Captain as carrying parties.

The boundary between the assault battalions was a north-south line through Campbell Street and Regent Street. At 7.08 a.m., B and D Companies, 1st King's Royal Rifle Corps, advanced. The barrage lifted at 7.10 a.m. and by 7.13 a.m. Princes Street had been taken with little loss. Many dead Germans were found there and three knocked out machine-guns. At 8.08 a.m. the second wave passed through to take the next objective. At 8.38 a.m. A and C Companies reached the final objective, 135 metres inside the northern edge of the Wood, which was secured by 8.50 a.m. A Company threw back its right to connect with B Company, which was holding three strong points in the southeast corner of the Wood. Battalion

headquarters was established in South Trench, opposite Angle Trench. As the gains were being consolidated, casualties were caused by the British artillery falling short, particularly in B Company.

Although hampered by enfilade fire from Longueval and a stubborn redoubt in a small quarry, 23rd Royal Fusiliers was also successful on the left of 99th Brigade, reaching the final objective at 9.40 a.m. On the far left, 15th Brigade had a difficult

Enter Delville Wood and go north beyond the impressive South African Memorial to reach Princes Street. Turn right and continue for 330m. This is where Albert Gill was in action on 27th July.

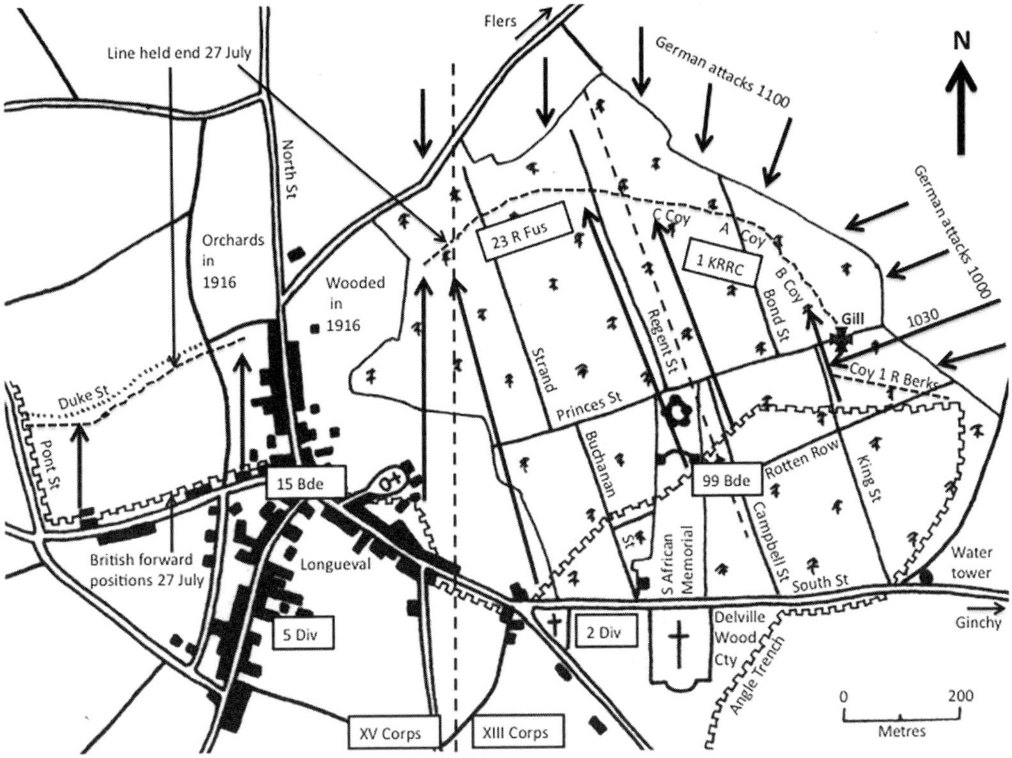

time clearing the western edge of the Wood and Longueval up to Duke Street, but it was achieved and contact was made with 99th Brigade on the right. However, the orchards at the northern end of Longueval remained in Germans hands.

The 1st Royal Berkshire company on the right, which was to help consolidate the eastern side of the Wood, was not in contact with B Company, 1st King's Royal Rifle Corps. At 9 a.m. the Germans commenced to sweep the Wood with heavy artillery fire and at 10 a.m. B Company came under heavy enfilade shrapnel fire from the east and northeast. The Germans launched strong bombing attacks against the eastern side of the Wood, despite being under very heavy British artillery fire. 1st King's Royal Rifle Corps held on, supported by the Brigade machine-guns, but at about 10.30 a.m. a German bombing party penetrated behind the defenders due to the gap left by the 1st Royal Berkshire company. This allowed the Germans to make a lodgement sixty metres south of Princes Street and the right of the line bent back and withdrew slightly to face northeast. Bombing fights took place at ranges of less than fifteen metres.

At 11 a.m. A and C Companies, 1st King's Royal Rifle Corps, were also attacked from the north and northeast. Close quarter fighting followed, with the Germans sniping constantly from shell holes. To add to the difficulties, British SOS rockets failed due to dampness and there was no artillery support. Extra bombers were sent by 23rd Royal Fusiliers and 1st Royal Berkshire and the Germans were eventually halted, but the pressure was relentless for the rest of the day. Further attacks against B and D Companies took place for one and a half hours from 1 p.m. along the east face of the Wood. During the course of the afternoon reinforcements were received from 17th and 22nd Royal Fusiliers, 17th Middlesex and 2nd South Staffordshire (the latter two battalions from 6th Brigade). 17th Middlesex gradually relieved 1st King's Royal Rifle Corps in the forward positions during

Looking east along Princes Street, with King Street on the right. A few metres beyond the junction is where Albert Gill stopped the German counterattack.

the night, but the battalion was not relieved completely until the 29th, having sustained 322 casualties.

At the critical moment in the German attack on the right flank, **Sergeant Albert Gill** of 1st King's Royal Rifle Corps saw one of the Battalion's bombing posts wiped out. He called on the remnants of his platoon to follow him and defend the post. None were trained bombers and the trench was very shallow and battered. Shortly afterwards the enemy surrounded the post and sniped from the thick undergrowth only twenty metres away. Gill stood up to be able to direct fire and had just passed on information about the location of the Germans when he was shot through the head and killed instantly. However, his action prevented the Germans breaking into the battalion's position. It is not known for certain precisely when this happened, but was probably during the initial German penetration behind B Company.

30th July 1916

Although Longueval was cleared over the next two days by 95th Brigade (5th Division) and the right flank made relatively secure, High Wood continued to hold out. 51st Division's attempt to seize it on 29 July failed. The next major action in this area was a combined British – French attack against the German Second Position north of the Somme on 30th July 1916. XIII Corps on the right was allocated the front from Waterlot Farm to the junction with the French at Maltz Horn Farm. III and XV Corps on the left launched subsidiary attacks at 6.10 a.m. to keep the Germans under pressure.

30th Division led the XIII Corps assault, passing through 35th Division. 89th Brigade on the right, flanking the French, attacked south of Guillemont towards Falfemont Farm and the German Second Position northwest of it. 90th Brigade on the left attacked Guillemont itself. 5th Brigade (2nd Division) was ordered to take Guillemont Station. The move into the assembly trenches on the eastern edge of Trônes Wood was made very difficult by thick fog, heavy German artillery fire and gas.

The main attack began at 4.45 a.m. in fog, which did not clear until 8 a.m. On the right of 89th Brigade's area, Maltz Horn Farm and trenches to the north were taken by a combined assault by a company of 2nd Bedfordshire from the west and a company of the French 153rd Regiment from the south. The advance continued eastwards to the Hardecourt – Guillemont road, but there were many casualties.

90th Brigade was led by 2nd Royal Scots Fusiliers (right) and 18th Manchester (left). The former, astride the Trônes Wood – Guillemont road, reached the northeast corner of Guillemont at about 5.45 a.m. with little loss, consolidated its position and drove off a counterattack from the direction of the cemetery.

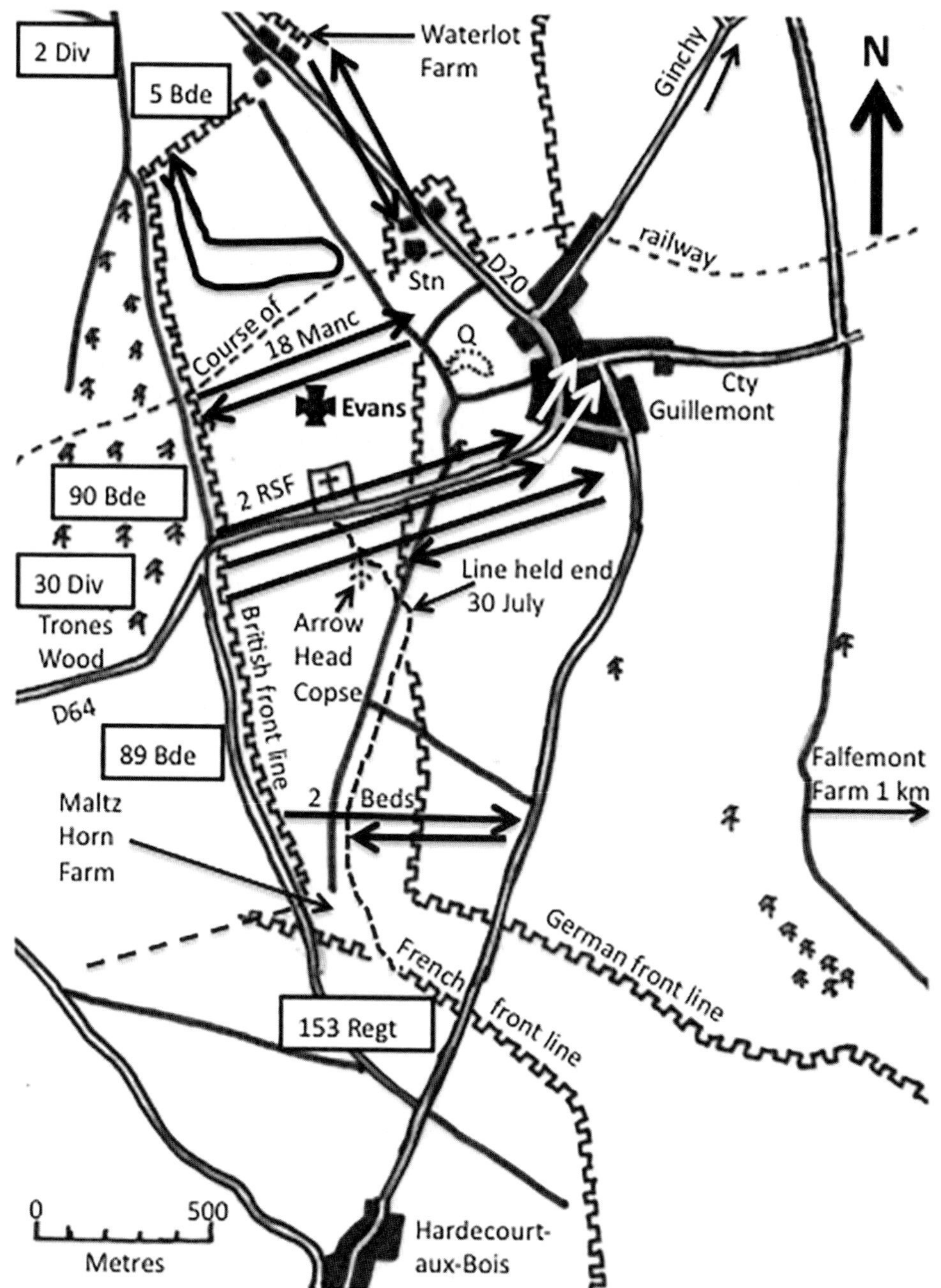

Park at Guillemont Road Cemetery 800m west of Guillemont on the D64. Look north over the low ground. This is where George Evans earned his VC.

18th Manchester's move through Trônes Wood in single file was particularly difficult, being carried out in gas helmets. The assembly trenches were not reached until just before zero hour. These were old trenches that had been improved by 17th Manchester and 11th South Lancashire on the preceding nights. Keeping the Trônes Wood – Guillemont railway on its left, the Battalion's advance started well at 4.45 a.m., although it was unsupported on that flank. A (right) and C (left) Companies led, with B and D Companies following. C Company, under Captain Blythe, cleared the trench west of the village and took a hundred prisoners before pressing on. It then ran into heavy machine-gun fire from the Quarry and the Station. A Company, under Captain Routley, moved to assist C Company, but a German barrage behind the leading troops cut them off from the rear. The line of the church had been reached before an erroneous order to retire was given; it is not known who gave it. About fifty men fell back while the remainder clung to the trench on the outskirts of the village. Meanwhile D Company swung to the left in an attempt to reach the station, where 5th Brigade's (2nd Division) attack had foundered. Elements of the brigade got into the enemy front line but were cut off and destroyed there. Two companies of 16th Manchester on the extreme left flank of 90th Brigade were checked by uncut wire south of Guillemont Station and forced to retire.

At 7.45 a.m., a second attack was launched, which included those who had previously fallen back. Despite the support of two companies each from 16th and 17th Manchester, this attack also failed. An attempt to reach the Quarry failed due to direction being lost in the fog. Enemy shelling continued and the support waves were heavily engaged from the left flank, which was in the air throughout the day. Communications also broke down; telephone lines were cut, only a few pigeons got through, runners were vulnerable to machine-gun fire and, until the fog lifted, visual signalling was impossible.

In the outskirts of Guillemont, **CSM George Evans** of B Company, 18th Manchester, saw five runners killed attempting to take an important message back. Evans had already distinguished himself at Montauban and Trônes Wood, setting an excellent example to his men. He volunteered to make the next attempt, which entailed crossing 650 metres of bullet swept ground, much of it devoid of cover and in full view of the enemy. However, by dodging and weaving and occasionally taking cover in shell holes, he got through and delivered the message. Although wounded in the arm, he insisted on returning to his Company. Evans was taken prisoner in the southwest of the village at about 2.30 p.m. and his bravery was not recognized formally until after the war.

Due to the position of the forward troops, it was difficult for the British artillery to support them. A German counterattack struck 2nd Royal Scots Fusiliers in Guillemont. Cut off by the German barrage and with all local reserves already used, the survivors of the battalion were overwhelmed.

89th Brigade gained some ground around Arrow Head Copse, but at an appalling cost. At one time this copse had to be defended by runners and battalion headquarters signallers. The rest of the day was spent consolidating the line from Arrow Head Copse along the Hardecourt – Guillemont road to Maltz Horn Farm, these in touch

From Guillemont Road Cemetery looking north. 18th Manchester advanced from the edge of Trônes Wood on the left, across the low ground beyond the cemetery towards the quarry and station on the right. It was along that route that George Evans carried the important message and returned to Guillemont, where he was later taken prisoner.

with the French. That night the exhausted 30th and 35th Divisions were relieved by the newly arrived 55th Division.

A number of subsidiary attacks were made in the evening either side of High Wood. Overall the results of the day were disappointing. Some limited gains were made at great cost in casualties and required massive expenditure of ammunition against an enemy holding his front lightly but in considerable depth. Although the Germans were under extreme pressure, they were holding on. Before another effort could be made, considerable reorganisation and resupply was needed. This respite was also of benefit to the hard-pressed Germans, who were also under pressure on the Eastern Front and at Verdun.

8th–9th August 1916

Haig realised that progress would only be made with meticulous preparations. In the meantime existing gains had to be protected against counterattacks. The intention was to continue on the right flank in contact with the French, but only when local commanders were satisfied that everything possible had been done to ensure success.

On the night of 4th/5th August, XV Corps took over the Delville Wood area in order to allow XIII Corps to concentrate on Guillemont. 55th Division was tasked to capture the village on 8th August. On the right, from the Hardecourt – Guillemont road to the junction with the French 77th Infantry Brigade, was 165th Brigade and, on the left, 164th Brigade. Each brigade had a company of 1/4th South Lancashire (Pioneers) attached. To the north, 2nd Division was to capture the northern edge of the village, the station and Waterlot Farm. To cut down the assault distance, both divisions advanced their trenches in the preceding days. On 7th August, the bombardment was interspersed with six feint 'Chinese'

attacks, in which the artillery lifted as it would just before an infantry assault. Much was done to improve communications once battle was joined, using flares, tin disks on the troops' backs, mirrors, lamps, panels, visual signalling posts, relay posts for runners and a wireless station in the trenches northeast of Favière Wood.

At 4.20 a.m. on 8th August the infantry advanced, supported by the artillery lifting in five steps every ten minutes. The wind was from the east, adding the smoke of the barrage to the early morning mist. Visual signalling was impossible and aircraft could not distinguish what was happening below accurately. As a result, it was not until 6 a.m. that HQ 55th Division received the first news from its forward units. 165th Brigade made a little progress against the spur south of Guillemont, with 1/5th King's bombers pushing along Cochrane Alley to reach the bottom of Maurepas Ravine. However, it was out of touch on both flanks and this was the only gain of the day.

164th Brigade attacked with 1/4th King's Own Royal Lancaster on the right, opposite the southwest corner of Guillemont, and 1/8th King's on the left. Two companies of 1/4th North Loyal Lancashire were to follow the assault battalions to consolidate the German front line. 1/4th King's Own Royal Lancaster was also followed by two platoons of D Company, 1/4th South Lancashire (Pioneers), led by **Second Lieutenant Gabriel Coury**. Two minutes after the assault troops set off, the Pioneers began digging a communication trench across no man's land, covered by their Lewis guns. They dug a hundred metres of trench to a depth of one and a half metres within an hour. When small parties began to drift back, Coury halted those near him and rallied them. He constantly patrolled the line of the trench, inspiring his men with confidence through his coolness under fire.

1/4th King's Own Royal Lancaster was halted in front of the enemy wire opposite the southwest corner of Guillemont. The survivors were ordered to dig a new front line and link up with the trench being dug by the Pioneers. There was some confusion over an order to retire. Lieutenant Colonel JL Swainson DSO DCLI, CO 1/4th King's Own Royal Lancaster, told Coury that he had given no

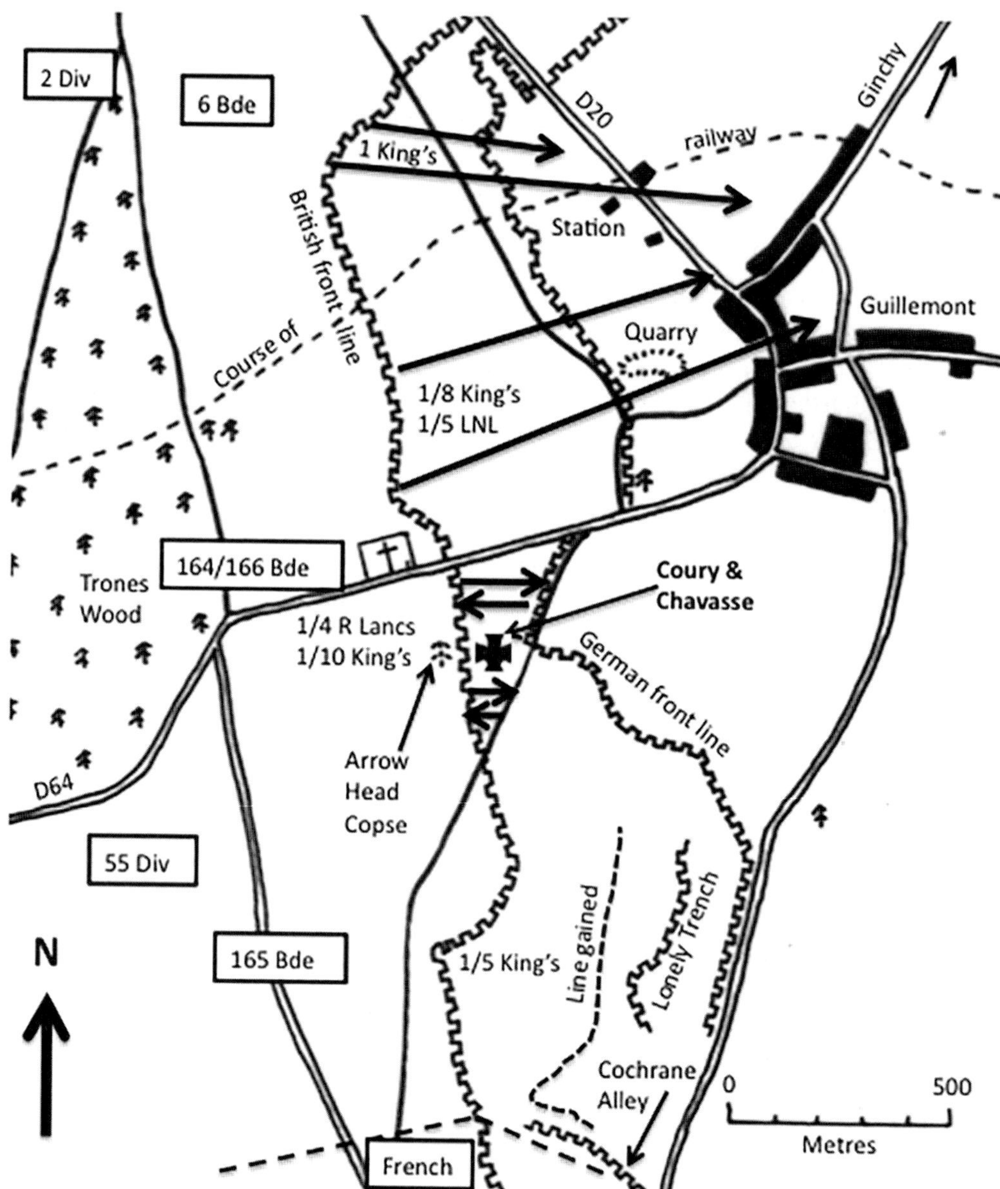

From Guillemont Road Cemetery continue eastwards towards Guillemont on the D64. After 275m turn sharp right onto a track and park on the relatively hard standing on the right. Walk southwest along the track for 275m, where it emerges from the sunken section onto the plateau. This is the tip of the German front line. Arrow Head Copse was 200m east-southeast of this point. The area between the track and the site of the former copse is where both Gabriel Coury and Noel Chavasse earned their VCs.

such order and work resumed on the trenches. The new line was roughly wired by 1.30 p.m., but the situation was hopeless and eventually the attackers withdrew to the assembly trenches. While pulling back, Swainson fell wounded in front of the new line near Arrow Head Copse. A sergeant from 2/2nd West Lancashire Field

Company who went to assist him was killed. Hearing about this, Coury immediately dashed forward in full view of the enemy and single-handedly brought Swainson to safety, but he died shortly afterwards (Corbie Communal Cemetery Extension – 2 A 72 – close to Major WLT Congreve VC). Coury pulled his men back and took up supporting positions behind the original front line, where he remained until relieved at 3.55 a.m. the next morning.

Further north, 1/8th King's broke into the village, but was cut off by enemy machine-guns covering no man's land. 6th Brigade (2nd Division) penetrated as far as the northern edge of the village, but was also cut off as the enemy reoccupied their front line behind the attackers. At the end of the day the left had been partially successful, the centre had failed completely and although the right had succeeded, it was perilously isolated.

166th Brigade relieved 164th Brigade during the night in very difficult circumstances. A repeat attack was ordered for the same time on the 9th. The defenders still had numerous machine-guns and the bombardment was hurried and ineffective. 1/5th Loyal North Lancashire on the left was late starting through no fault of its own, but the barrage had already lifted and it stood no chance of success. 1/10th King's on the right reached its assault positions only twenty minutes before zero. 5th South Lancashire had two companies behind each leading battalion to consolidate the German front line, but this was later changed to the whole battalion being behind 1/10th King's. The battalion advanced against the village, keeping close behind the barrage, but was halted in front of the uncut enemy wire. The CO was wounded and the battalion suffered heavily in four unsuccessful attempts to break into the German defences. The Germans fired a standing barrage across no man's land halfway between the opposing lines. Most of the officers were wounded or killed. At 10.45 p.m. the survivors were relieved by 1/5th King's Own Royal Lancaster and moved back into Liverpool and Lancaster Trenches under the command of a second lieutenant. Casualties totalled 280 out of the 620 who went into action.

Attacks by 165th Brigade and 6th Brigade (2nd Division) also came to nothing. Troops of both Divisions cut off in Guillemont were hit by counterattacks as the Germans recovered from the confusion more quickly. Detachments of 1/8th Kings (55th Division) and 1st King's (2nd Division) held out at the station until the evening of 9th August, when they ran out of water, ammunition and bombs. These soldiers were seen from the British front line as they were marched into captivity.

1/10th King's MO, **Captain Noel Chavasse**, was exposed to enemy fire in no man's land throughout the day as he attended to the wounded and organised rescue parties. That night he scoured the ground in front of the enemy line for four hours. The following day he and another man rushed to the advanced line and carried a badly wounded soldier over 450 metres to safety, under heavy shellfire throughout. Chavasse was wounded in the side by a shell splinter, but carried on with his duties.

From the tip of the German front line looking west. Gabriel Coury's and Noel Chavasse's VC actions were in this field near Arrow Head Copse.

That night he led a party of twenty volunteers into no man's land and recovered three men from a shell hole only twenty-five metres from the enemy front line. They had been cared for by Corporal Aldritt (awarded DCM), who had kept them supplied with water at great personal risk. He had crawled back to the British lines with one of the wounded men and then guided Chavasse to the shell hole to rescue the remaining three, although two died later. During the night Chavasse buried two officers and recovered a number of identity disks. He made a point of doing this so that the men would not be posted missing and thus raise false hopes amongst their families.

A second attempt that night to rescue more wounded was halted by enemy bombers. Chavasse was slightly wounded again by a few grenade splinters in his back. Private Jackson remembers seeing him wandering around no man's land with a torch, calling out to the wounded, apparently oblivious to the danger. By the time the battalion left the line, Chavasse had personally seen to the rescue of twenty seriously wounded men who would otherwise have died. At one stage he also rallied the fighting troops when all other officers had become casualties. Five soldiers who helped in these rescues were awarded the DCM, including Chavasse's orderly, Corporal A Baybut, who by the end of the war had been awarded a Bar to the DCM and the MM.

General Rawlinson halted further attempts to take the village until the most thorough preparations had been made. It was clear that small scale operations were not succeeding. Joffre and Haig met on 12th August and agreed that they needed to return to the previous plan for large combined attacks on a broad front. The target date for renewal of the offensive was 18th August. A preliminary operation on the British right in cooperation with the French 153rd Regiment gained little, as did

another attack on the 17th. The main attack on 18th August achieved some success, although not as much as desired.

As plans developed for a major offensive in the middle of September, the requirement to secure a suitable starting position on the main ridge remained. Time was running out and resources were limited, as six fresh divisions were to be kept back to exploit the expected success of the first use of tanks. Small scale operations were again the order of the day, to take advantage of any opportunity to push the line forward, particularly in surprise night operations.

Chapter Three

Battle of Pozières Ridge

143 2Lt Arthur Blackburn, 10th Australian Infantry Battalion AIF (3rd Australian Brigade, 1st Australian Division) Pozières, France
144 Pte John Leak, 9th Australian Infantry Battalion AIF (3rd Australian Brigade, 1st Australian Division) Pozières, France
145 Pte Thomas Cooke, 8th Australian Infantry Battalion AIF (2nd Australian Brigade, 1st Australian Division) Pozières, France
147 Sgt Claude Castleton, 5th Machine Gun Company AIF (5th Australian Brigade, 1st Australian Division) Pozières, France
149 Pte James Miller, 7th King's Own (Royal Lancaster) (57th Brigade, 19th Division) Bazentin-le-Petit, France
150 Pte William Short, 8th Green Howards (69th Brigade, 23rd Division) Munster Alley, France
153 Pte Martin O'Meara, 16th Australian Infantry Battalion AIF (4th Australian Brigade, 4th Australian Division) Pozières, France
154 Capt William Allen, 1/3rd Field Ambulance RAMC att'd 246th Brigade RFA (49th Division) Mesnil, France
158 Cpl Leo Clarke, 2nd Battalion CEF (1st Canadian Brigade, 1st Canadian Division) Pozières, France

23rd July 1916

While Fourth Army made the main effort on the right flank against High Wood, Longueval and Delville Wood, the Reserve Army began to take an increasing role in the offensive. On 23rd July, in conjunction with Fourth Army, the Reserve Army attacked at Pozières with 1st Australian Division on the right and 48th Division on the left; the first of many attacks in this area over the following weeks. The preparatory bombardment started on 19th July and went on steadily until the 22nd, when the rate of fire was increased. In addition to the guns of the divisions involved and corps artillery, the field artillery of 25th and 34th Divisions and some French batteries were also used.

Zero hour was at 12.30 a.m. on 23rd July and for five minutes before then the heavy artillery bombarded the western side of Pozières in addition to the Old German (OG) Lines and Pozières Trench. It was a dark night and the gun flashes

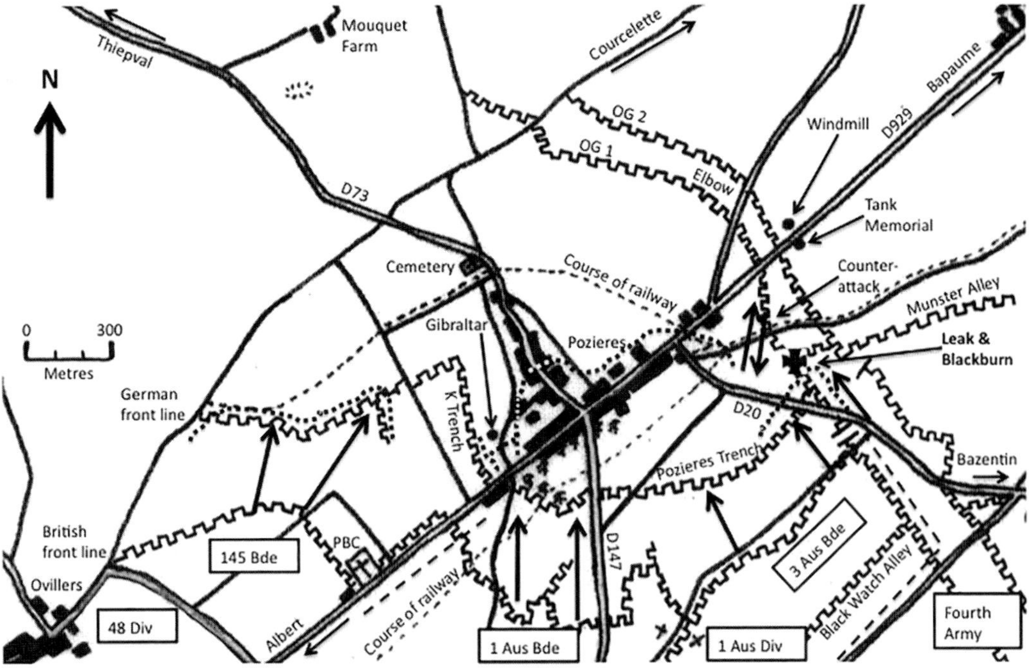

Turn off the D929 Albert-Bapuame road in Pozières southeast towards Bazentin on the D20/D73. After 600m pull over on the right, where there is a strip of hard standing. The windmill at Pozières is the highest point on the Somme battlefield, hence the importance of the position. The initial attack on the village by 1st Australian Division was a success, albeit with exceptions, particularly on the right flank, where a gap remained and the OG Lines proved difficult to penetrate.

The trench on the west side of the village is shown on British maps as Western Trench, but was known to the Australians as K Trench. The only abbreviation is PBC = Pozières British Cemetery and Memorial. The site of the OG Lines VCs (Leak, Blackburn, Castleton and Short) was on the left (northern) side of the road. The dotted line around Pozières is the limit of the advance on 23rd July. When finished considering the various actions in this area, there is 'Le Tommy' in Pozières in the direction of Albert on the left of the D929, serving drinks and meals. There is also a museum of battlefield artefacts.

and shell explosions could be seen thirty kilometers away. Other batteries simulated an attack from the southwest.

On the right of 1st Australian Division, 3rd Australian Brigade was to attack with 9th (right) and 11th (left) Battalions. The right company of 9th Battalion was to deal with OG1 and OG2, supported by a section (four guns) of 3rd Machine Gun Company and a company of the 10th Battalion. Attempts by British and Australian units in the nights before the attack to secure the junctions of OG1 with Pozières Trench and OG2 with Switch Trench (renamed Munster Alley) failed. 10th Battalion and 12th Battalion, in reserve in Black Watch Alley, were to pass through the leading battalions to take the 3rd and 4th objectives.

On the left, 1st Australian Brigade was to attack with 1st and 2nd Battalions. Most of the German retaliatory fire fell on the supports. The assault troops moved out into no man's land early in order to gain as much distance before the barrage lifted. Any noise they made was covered by the barrage and in places they got to within fifty metres of the enemy lines.

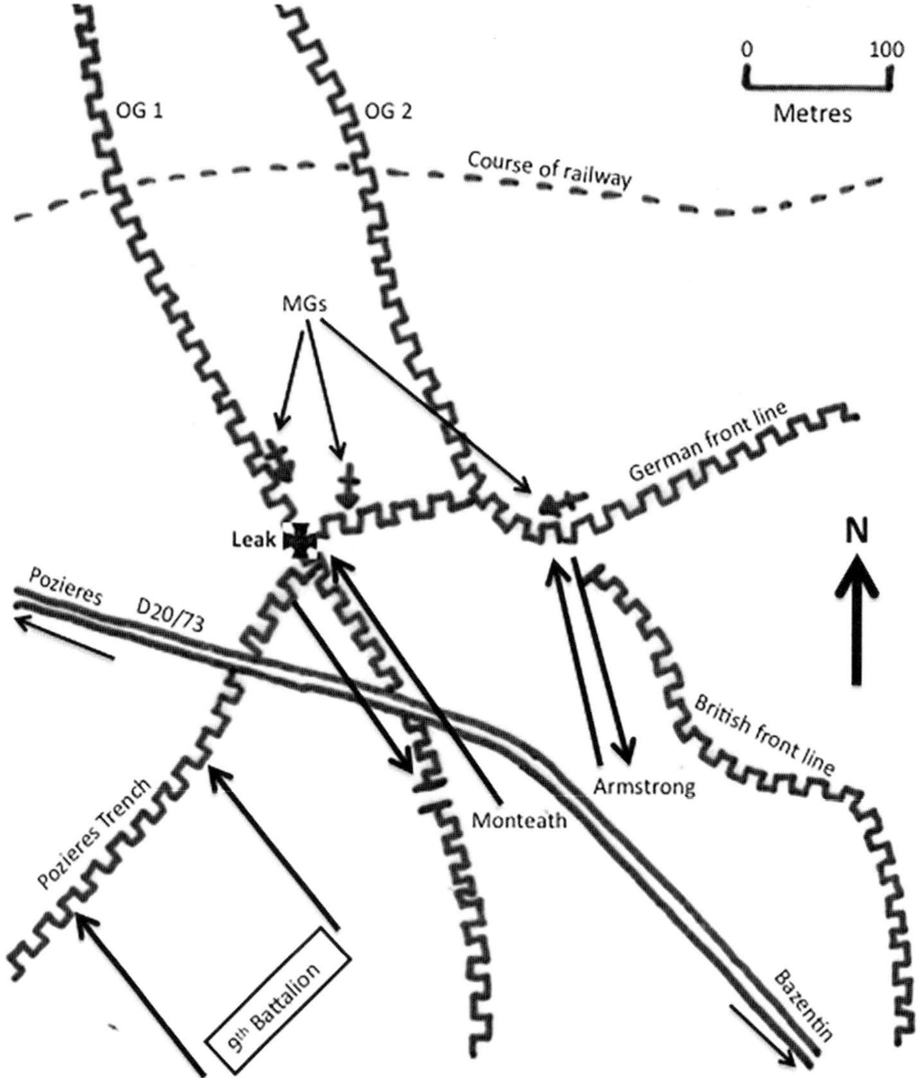

The situation during the initial attack by the platoons under Lieutenants Armstrong and Monteath, during which John Leak attacked and seized a German position.

At zero hour the assault troops surged forward and seized Pozières Trench with little loss. There was some resistance on the right; but otherwise the defenders pulled back quickly. On the extreme right, the company of 9th Battalion advanced above ground level, with two platoons leading, between OG1 and OG2. It came under heavy machine-gun fire and had to get into the trench and bomb along it instead, which was slower. The platoon on the left managed to push along OG1 to the junction with Pozières Trench, where it was stopped by two machine-guns, one further north along OG1 and another just off to the right in a short section of trench linking OG1 to OG2.

The Germans were able to outdistance the Australian bombers using their egg-bombs. While a means of breaking this deadlock was being devised, **Private John Leak**, entirely on his own initiative, leapt out of the trench, dashed forward and threw three bombs into the German position. He then jumped down into it and bayoneted three unwounded German bombers. Lieutenant Monteath caught up, to find Leak calmly wiping the blood off his bayonet with his felt hat; it was 12.50 a.m.

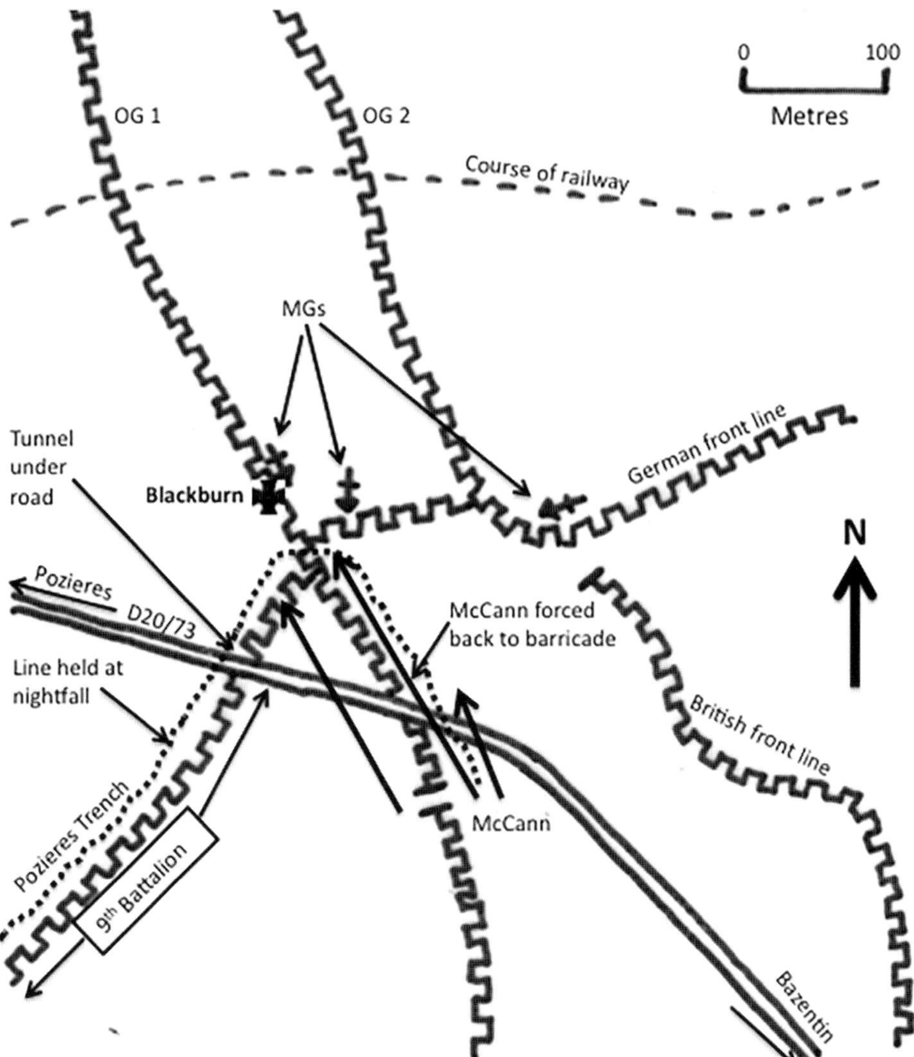

Captain McCann's attack with two platoons astride OG1 reached the junction with Pozières Trench before it was stopped and driven back down OG1 for 100m, where a barricade was erected. It was from that point that Arthur Blackburn took up the fight, reaching thirty metres beyond the junction with Pozières Trench. Despite his efforts the most advanced gains could not be held and the junction became the new forward position.

Monteath had only six or seven men and the enemy appeared to be all around them. They were short of grenades and as Monteath went back to get more he ran into two Germans and shot them. To hold the gains they needed reinforcements. Meanwhile, the platoon attacking along OG2 under Lieutenant Armstrong could not find the trench due to the ground all around being leveled by the artillery. Attempts to press on were halted and no progress was made in OG2.

The advance to the second objective was to commence at 1 a.m., but there was so much other artillery fire that the lift was indistinguishable to the men. Officers just had to rely on their watches. On the left, 11th Battalion and a platoon of 9th Battalion swept on, but the right flank remained stuck and no progress was made in OG2 at all. The second objective on the left was taken at 1.15 a.m. and consolidation commenced. Seeing the Germans fleeing, some soldiers surged after them and it took a great deal of effort by officers and NCOs to bring them under control.

At 1.30 a.m. the leading company of 10th Battalion arrived at 9th Battalion's HQ and was sent to relieve Lieutenant Monteath's party. As it reached the point from where the original 9th Battalion attack had started, it was met by a rush of 9th Battalion men coming back, having been forced out by a counterattack on the OG Lines. The company commander, Captain McCann, ordered two of his platoons into shell holes left and right of OG1 and positioned himself with a central party in OG1 between them. They advanced again but near the junction with Pozières Trench were stopped by wire and heavy machine-gun fire from the right front. The platoon on the right was some distance behind. McCann formed a line with ten to twelve others and bombed the machine-gun crews. Just before ordering them to change in with the bayonet, McCann was hit in the head, but survived. Lieutenant Ruddle, Adjutant of 9th Battalion, who had gone forward to assist in the supply of bombs, was shot dead when peering over the parapet. With bombs running out, the survivors were driven back down OG1 again and formed a barricade about a hundred metres short of the junction with Pozières Trench.

McCann reported to CO 9th Battalion on the situation just as D Company, 10th Battalion, arrived under Major Giles by way of Black Watch Alley. Giles sent **Lieutenant Arthur Blackburn**, one of his platoon commanders, with fifty men and two teams of battalion bombers to drive the enemy back from a strongpoint.

At the barricade Blackburn found the exhausted remnants of McCann's company with the Germans just ahead. He and some bombers, supported by some of his own men, leapt over the barricade and rushed the next traverse. They then tore down the barricade to allow others to reach them and pressed on through bay after bay. They expended large quantities of grenades, but pushed the enemy back inexorably. They had to remain in the trench due to machine-guns in OG2 and snipers in Munster Alley dominating the area above ground.

After about ninety metres, they found that the trench had been flattened by the artillery and they had to crawl forward to avoid the machine-guns. The next party of Germans was in a crater thirty metres ahead and they had the advantage when it came to a bombing duel. Blackburn called a halt and crept forward with four men, all of whom were killed. Blackburn detected a German post in a cross trench a little to the right, probably the one that had held up previous attempts. Blackburn returned to the CO of the 9th Battalion to arrange a trench mortar bombardment. He then tried to rush the position again, but the machine-gun had not been subdued and four more men were hit. The CO arranged for artillery and trench mortars to support the next attempt, with Blackburn reinforced by a fresh bombing team. He managed to gain thirty metres before Germans resistance again stiffened.

Blackburn then crawled forward with 1533 Sergeant Robert Minney Inwood (brother of Roy Inwood VC) to reconnoitre the ground. He discovered that the resistance was coming from the cross trench that cut across OG1 at right angles. His fourth attack captured the part of the cross trench west of OG1 but, as he was consolidating this gain, he found that the junction with OG1 was impassable due to the machine-guns in Munster Alley and the German post. Inwood was killed during the action (Serre Road Cemetery No.2 – XXIV M 6) and Blackburn's party was cut off. He crawled west along the trench and found a company of 9th Battalion after crawling through a tunnel. He had reached Pozières Trench and the tunnel was under the Pozières – Bazentin road. Capt Chambers, the 9th Battalion company commander in this area, opened up the tunnel and tools were passed along to consolidate Blackburn's gains.

The 9th Battalion's CO ordered another advance. Blackburn made three more attempts, but his party was stopped on each occasion by heavy fire over the exposed ground. Howitzers were arranged to support the eighth attempt, but they were old and unreliable for such close shooting and the infantry was hit by heavy fire again when it tried to rush the post. Blackburn was then ordered to hold where he was. His efforts had saved the situation in OG1, but of the seventy men with him, including the bombing teams, forty were casualties. The survivors were relieved, while fresh troops and pioneers set to work to consolidate the gains. About 300 metres of OG1 had been taken by daylight, up to the junction with Pozières Trench.

Meanwhile the advance to the second objective had been successful, fighting through the gardens of the houses along the Bapaume road. By 3 a.m., 3rd and 4th Battalions on the left and 10th and 12th Battalions on the right had reached the road and were digging in amongst the rubble. 10th and 12th Battalions were late starting due to being hit by gas shells in the approach to the assembly trench and consequently became mixed up. In addition, troops in earlier waves, finding almost no resistance, had pushed on and almost all the third objective had been taken by the time the support battalions arrived. However, due to the hold up in the OG Lines and the failure of the 1st Division attack on Munster Alley on the right flank, 3rd Australian Brigade had to throw back its right flank to face OG1.

As the position was being consolidated, patrols went forward to clear small pockets of Germans from the cellars. Resistance in the village ceased, although it

From the point where OG1 crossed the D20/D73 Pozières - Bazentin road looking north. The relative position of the four VCs in this area are shown.

was under fire from snipers. At 5.30 a.m. the Germans counterattacked into the gap on the right flank, but were easily repulsed.

On the left, 48th Division had a much worse experience. 144th Brigade on the left came under intense machine-gun fire and suffered huge casualties for no gains. Only a few bombers reached the German lines, where they were soon overwhelmed. 145th Brigade on the right led with 1/5th Gloucestershire (left) and 1/4th Oxfordshire & Buckinghamshire Light infantry (right). The former suffered the same fate as 144th Brigade, but on the right about 600 metres of trench were taken and a counterattack from the area of the cemetery was pushed back. 145th Brigade attacked again with fresh troops and caught the Germans by surprise. The left was successful, but the right remained much as it was.

On the Australian left, a small party of 2nd Battalion crossed the Bapaume road and seized the strongpoint known as Gibraltar. It was found to be a major observation position and was defended by four machine-guns. However, the party was too weak to hold it alone and took its prisoners back, keeping the area under fire to prevent it being reused.

In the afternoon the intention was to launch another major attack to complete the seizure of Pozières, but reports from air and artillery observers indicated that the Germans had abandoned the village. The Army Commander, Gough, decided to press ahead, but it took time for orders to be issued and for the British artillery to be lifted onto other targets. It was 5 p.m. before patrols began moving forward again. Gibraltar was reoccupied and the southern end of K Trench, running along the western side of the village, was captured.

Two companies of 8th Battalion (2nd Australian Brigade) in reserve and attached to 1st Australian Brigade, moved ahead. One company reached the cemetery, but realised that it was dangerously exposed. It pulled back in line with the other company and dug in halfway between the Bapaume road and the cemetery. This took until midnight. On the right, in 3rd Australian Brigade's sector, 12th Battalion

crossed the road and dug in beyond the railway on the right flank. An attempt to get ahead along the OG Lines, in cooperation with 1st Division on the right, came to nothing in the face of heavy machine-gun fire.

On the left, in 48th Division's area, there was considerable bombing activity during the day and 143rd Brigade relieved 145th Brigade. However, despite all the efforts, there was still no link up with the Australians on the right.

24th/25th July 1916

Gough was determined to get on. Having gained the Second Position, he wanted to drive north through Mouquet Farm to the Ancre, thereby cutting off Thiepval and gaining observation over Courcelette and Grandcourt. At 7 p.m. on 23rd July he ordered the capture of the OG Lines southeast of the Bapaume road. To achieve this, I ANZAC Corps was to cooperate with III Corps to the east. At the same time, 48th Division (X Corps) on the left was to join up with the Australians and continue the advance alongside them. The intention was to attack before dawn on 24th July, but preparations could not be made in the time available. Instead the Australians were to attack as soon as they were ready on the night of 24th/25th July. During the 24th, while preparations were being made, 48th Division made a few bombing attacks in an attempt to join up with 1st Australian Division, but no progress was made.

Two separate operations were to be undertaken. 3rd Australian Brigade was to take about 550 metres of the OG Lines at 2 a.m. on 25th July by frontal assault, whilst at 3.30 a.m. Pozières was to be taken by 1st Australian Brigade. The attacks could not be made simultaneously as the assault troops for both attacks needed the same approaches. III Corps was to attack on the right at about the same time. Heavy artillery preparation was fired against both OG Lines. The German artillery also intensified its fire during the evening and many men were buried in collapsed trenches and had to be dug out by their comrades. One man quipped to another who had just been dug out stunned and dazed, *Well, at least you weren't hit*. 3rd Australian

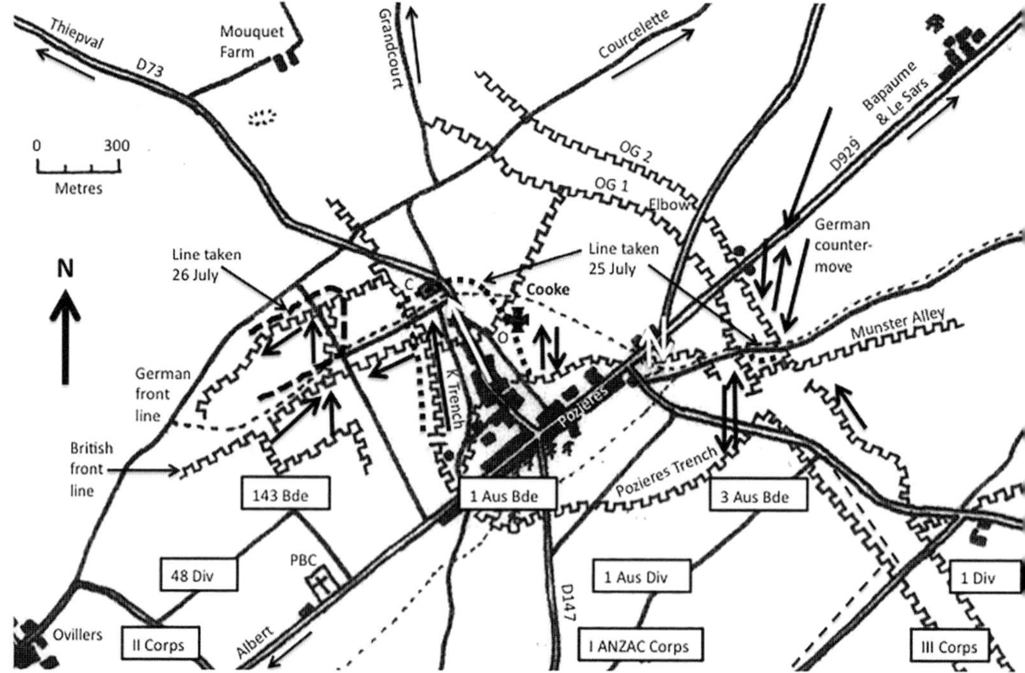

The attacks on 25th and 26th July resulted in the rest of Pozières northwards to the cemetery being secured and the 1st Australian Division was able to join with the 48th Division on the left flank. However, little progress was made on the right flank against the OG Lines, except for a small gain in the cross trench between OG1 and OG2 and a small section of OG1 south of the railway. There are a few abbreviations used – C = cemetery, O = orchard and PBC = Pozières British Cemetery and Memorial. The right company of 8th Battalion reached the orchard and this is where Thomas Cooke was sent forward with his Lewis gun team.

Brigade was reinforced by 5th and 7th Battalions and 1st Australian Brigade by 8th Battalion, all from 2nd Australian Brigade.

The divisional artillery was to fire an intense two minutes barrage against OG1 just before zero, at which time III Corps' artillery was to hit OG2 for fifteen minutes before moving east for an hour. II Corps' (HQ II Corps relieved HQ X Corps on the left of I ANZAC Corps during the day) artillery was to hit the area about the windmill for an hour, commencing at zero.

The assault troops on the right (5th Battalion (right) and two companies of 7th Battalion (left), all under CO 5th Battalion), had to file out of Pozières Trench and then turn right to form up for the attack. Tapes had been laid, but most of the 7th Battalion companies, which were to flank the Bapaume road, lost their way and did not take part. Half the bombers and two platoons of 10th Battalion were also to attack to secure the strongpoint that thus far had resisted all progress along the OG Lines.

At 2 a.m., 5th Battalion seized OG1 and followed the barrage to OG2, which was almost unrecognisable as a trench. However, in OG2 they came under attack from left and right and from Germans in OG1 behind them on the flanks and had to fall back to OG1. The Germans attacked along OG1 from the north, where most of 7th Battalion had failed to start the attack, and reached the junction with the communications trench leading to Munster Alley. 5th Battalion was reinforced with all available men of 9th and 10th Battalions and the two uncommitted companies of 7th Battalion. The battle swayed back and forth about thirty metres either side of the cross trench junction. At one time the Germans were almost driven north to the railway, but they rallied and forced the Australians back almost to the trench junction again. A barrier was finally established halfway between the railway and the cross trench.

On the extreme right, 10th Battalion captured the strongpoint after it had been subjected to an intense trench mortar barrage, but the Germans managed to hang on to the junction of OG2 with Munster Alley. An attack by 1st Division on the right of the Australians also failed to reach OG2.

At 3.30 a.m. the main attack against Pozières commenced. When preliminary orders reached HQ 1st Australian Brigade it was noted that the attack was scheduled for 26th July. The brigade commander sent the battalion commanders back to their units, but soon after the mistake was corrected and runners were sent to recall the COs; those of 2nd and 3rd Battalions could not be found, but those of 4th, 8th and 1st were and orders were hurriedly passed on.

On the left, the aim was to get behind the enemy holding up 48th Division. This was to be achieved by 4th Battalion advancing north along K Trench, but due to the mix up with dates, the Battalion started ten minutes after the bombardment ended. Progress was slow and costly.

4th Battalion's action had the effect of diverting German attention from 8th Battalion, which advanced steadily through the village and reached the cemetery on the left and an orchard on the right. The left company of the 8th Battalion got well ahead of the 4th Battalion and was able to cut off retreat by the Germans

Leave Pozières northwestwards on the D73 towards Thiepval. After 650m park on the right, opposite the cemetery. Walk back 100m towards Pozières and turn left along a track. Follow it for 120m and look east towards the mast and Pozières Windmill in the centre of the picture. Thomas Cooke's VC action was about 100m into the field in the foreground, which was then an orchard.

defending K Trench and many were killed trying to escape. The right company was met with heavy fire and lost three officers, but reached its objective. However, further right the intended positions between the village and the OG Lines had not been occupied. **Private Thomas Cooke**, in the right company of 8th Battalion, was ordered to take his Lewis gun team forward to cover the open flank. They came under very heavy fire until he was the only man left alive. He continued firing his gun but when support arrived later he was found dead beside it.

The 4th Battalion drive along K Trench eventually met up with 8th Battalion. The trench ahead was unoccupied and CSM FW Goodwin pressed forward until he could see Mouquet Farm.

On the right of the main attack, 12th Battalion was hit by fire from the portion of OG1 that was not attacked south of the Bapaume road. It could make no progress and the hope of linking up both parts of the assault failed. Next on the left, 11th Battalion reached the railway, but came under fire from 8th Battalion in the confusion. By daylight shelling was so intense that 12th Battalion pulled back to its start line.

3rd Battalion was still south of the Bapaume road. It advanced to link up the right of 2nd Australian Brigade with the left of 3rd Australian Brigade. 6th Battalion also came forward to consolidate, managing to do so during a lull in the intense shelling and dug in from the cemetery to the orchard, then southwards.

At 7.15 a.m. the Germans guns opened fire and at 8.30 a.m. what appeared to be a German counterattack was launched southwards over the crest near the windmill. It was actually supports coming forward to resist further attacks, but this was not known to the Australians. The German advance was hit by the artillery of 23rd and 1st Australian Divisions with devastating effect. The machine-guns of 3rd Australian Brigade did the rest and the attack was swept away.

During the day the Australian positions were shelled heavily. The smoke and dust were visible from ten miles away. It was claimed that the shelling of Pozières was the worst the Australians experienced throughout the war. Counter-battery fire was hampered by poor observation and the gunners having other tasks. Many German guns were disabled, but there was no noticeable effect in Pozières.

The relief of the troops who made the assault the previous day was imperative. Having been under the most intense artillery fire all day, the men were at the limit of their endurance. That night, 2nd Australian Division moved into the line to relieve 1st Australian Division. 5th Australian Brigade relieved 3rd Australian Brigade on the right and 2nd Australian Brigade took over on the left until relieved by 6th Australian Brigade that night; but 4th Battalion remained until a link up could be made with 48th Division. 1st Australian Division's fight for Pozières has become legendary, but the somewhat reckless attitude of the troops, effective at times, but costly at others, resulted in 5,285 casualties; slightly less than those suffered by 5th Australian Division in the disastrous attack at Fromelles on 19th July.

As survivors of 1st Australian Division marched to rest camps in the rear areas, they passed elements of 4th Australian Division moving towards the front. A sergeant of the latter wrote:

> *Although we knew it was stiff fighting, we had our eyes opened when we saw these men march by. Those who saw them will never forget it as long as they live. They looked like men who had been in Hell. Almost without exception each man looked drawn and haggard, and so dazed that they appeared to be walking in a dream, and their eyes looked glassy and starey. Quite a few were silly, and these were the only noisy ones in the crowd... We could see that they had lost a lot of men.... In all my experience I have never seen men quite so shaken up as these.... When our battalion came out of the same ordeal nine days after this, we were in no position to compare our boys with the 1st Division, but we were in a position to know what they suffered; and it was easily the worst battering we ever had to stand.*

Early on the morning of 26th July, 1/7th Royal Warwickshire (143rd Brigade, 48th Division) made contact with the Australians northwest of the village. German artillery fire into the village intensified again, with up to twenty heavy shells a minute landing in the southwest corner alone. However, no attack followed. A series of minor actions were fought over the next few days. 143rd Brigade improved its positions on the left and on the right the Australians were involved with 23rd Division in the fight for Munster Alley, where some minor gains were made. In preparation for the next move forward, 2nd Australian Division advanced its trenches and made adjustments to its line while the artillery suppressed German gun positions around Le Sars and Courcelette to reduce the volume of hostile fire received.

28th/29th July 1916

Gough did not want the Germans to have time to recover and wanted the next attack to take place as quickly as possible. HQ I ANZAC Corps left the timing to the commander of 2nd Australian Division (Major General Legge), who selected 12.15 a.m. on 29th July. This was to be the division's first major offensive operation.

The overall intent was to work northwards, rolling up the German Second Position from Pozières to Grandcourt, thereby securing the high ground and cutting off Thiepval. I ANZAC Corps was to make the main effort, supported by II Corps on the left. However, before any of this, the high ground northeast of Pozières, which included the OG Lines and the windmill, had to be secured first.

On the right the plan was to take OG1 south of the Bapaume road by frontal assault, then bomb northwards along OG2. North of the Bapaume road the main attack was to seize the whole of the OG Lines as far west as the track from Courcelette to Ovillers. Extra artillery from divisions not in the line assisted. Heavy artillery also engaged targets as far back as Mouquet Farm and Courcelette.

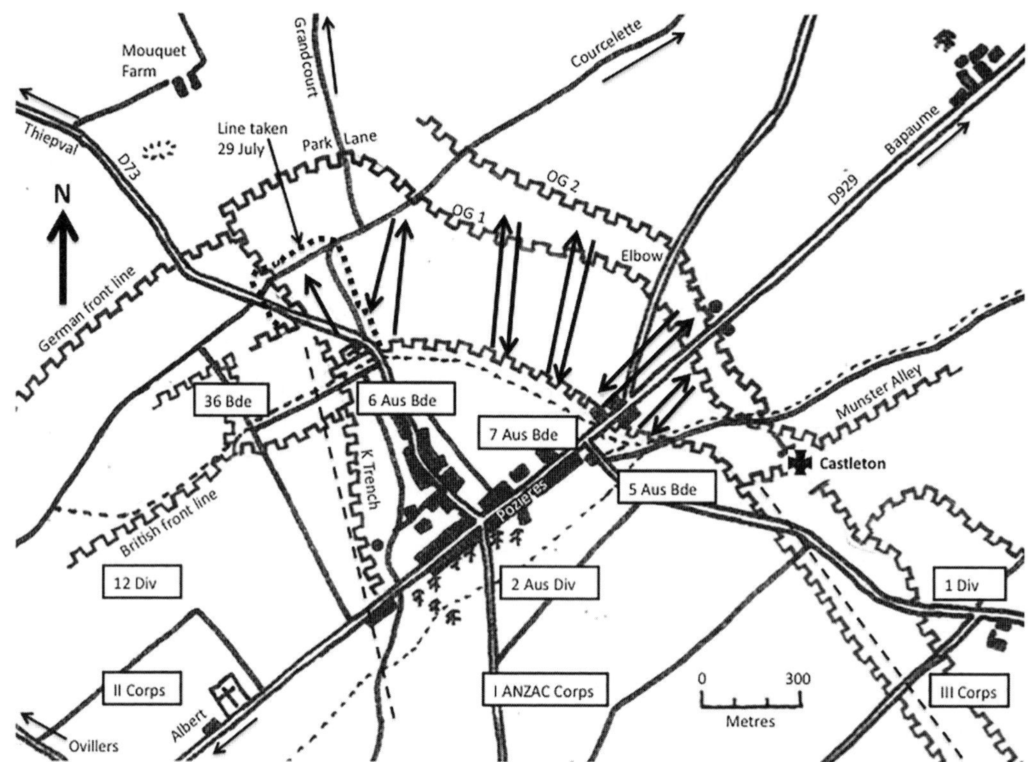

The action on 28th/29th July at Pozières.

A number of unsuccessful attempts were made by III Corps on the right to get into Munster Alley. On 26th July, troops of 1 Division (two companies of 2nd Welch) had come into 17th Battalion's (5th Australian Brigade) area and advanced from the post it held in the trench connecting OG1 and OG2. A furious bombing fight followed, supported by 17th Battalion. When the 2nd Welch bombers were exhausted, those of 17th Battalion took over. When the supply of bombs ran out a chain of men over 400 metres long was formed to pass fresh supplies forward. A post was established and men went forward to hold the Germans while barricades were constructed. When the 17th Battalion bombers were exhausted, they were replaced in turn by those of the 18th Battalion and 20th Battalion. When they too were exhausted, it fell to volunteers and some bombers of the 19th Battalion to continue. Part of 10th Northumberland Fusiliers (68th Brigade, 23rd Division) eventually persuaded the Australians to pull back to OG1. In the ensuing battle, 10th Northumberland Fusiliers was driven back past the junction of OG2 and Munster Alley. The Germans counterattacked strongly and got into the section of communication trench between the two OG lines. Platoons of 18th and 17th Battalions were drawn in and the Germans were pushed back to the original starting point. At dawn, 13th Durham Light Infantry pushed the Germans back again and regained fifty metres of Munster Alley. When the fighting died down the barricade was a few metres short of where it had all started the previous day; 15,000 grenades had been used by the Australians and British alone.

During the 27th, the trenches of 5th Australian Brigade just north of the Bapaume road were flattened in places. Preparations for the next attack were being rushed and would result in it being the only action at the time; the British were not going to attack again until 30th July at Guillemont. Dust and smoke hampered the artillery observers and it was not known if the enemy wire had been cut. In places the wire in front of OG2 was in dead ground. On the night of 27th July, patrols of 6th Australian Brigade north of the Bapaume road found the wire well cut, but in 5th Australian Brigade's area patrols found the damage intermittent and in places it was still an obstacle. The rush also meant there was no time to dig advanced trenches for assembly and the final assault to reduce the distance to be covered. The best that could be achieved was strengthening some strongpoints in advance of the front line.

The main attack was to be made by 6th Australian Brigade on the left and 7th Australian Brigade on the right, while 5th Australian Brigade, south of the Bapaume road, was to attack the OG Lines. The latter brigade would be covered by trench mortar fire only. 6th Australian Brigade's objective on the Ovillers – Courcelette road was quite narrow and the task was allotted to 23rd Battalion alone. 7th Australian Brigade's objective was the OG Lines between the Ovillers – Courcelette road and the Bapaume road. This required three battalions – 26th (left), 25th (centre) and 28th (right), with 27th in reserve. 5th Australian Brigade would attack with half of 20th Battalion, while 17th Battalion formed up between OG1 and OG2 and bombed along OG2. The British to the right of the Australians would make another attempt on Munster Alley. The artillery preparation went on by stages throughout the 28th. 7th Australian Brigade was not yet in the line and a hurried reconnaissance was made.

Just before midnight on 28th July, 28th, 25th and 26th Battalions of 7th Australian Brigade were assembled along the line of the railway. On the left, 23rd Battalion of 6th Australian Brigade was also in position. At midnight they advanced to cut down the assault distance as the German lines were about 550 metres away. German shelling destroyed all signal cables and flashes of signal lamps could not be distinguished in the smoke and dust. The assault was launched at 12.15 a.m. as planned. After three minutes, intense barrage on the enemy lines, the artillery lengthened at a slower rate on OG2 while the infantry assaulted OG1. The following waves were planned to pass though to take OG2.

South of the Bapaume road, 5th Australian Brigade's 20th Battalion had been seen assembling by the Germans as the troops filed out of their trenches. They had to cross the railway near its fork. Most of the first wave had settled into their assault positions and the second was crossing the embankment at 11.40 p.m. when it was hit by heavy machine-gun fire that had not been subdued by the trench mortar barrage. Flares rose and other machine-guns joined in from the north. Then a barrage of high explosive, phosgene and tear gas shells descended. Platoon commanders tried

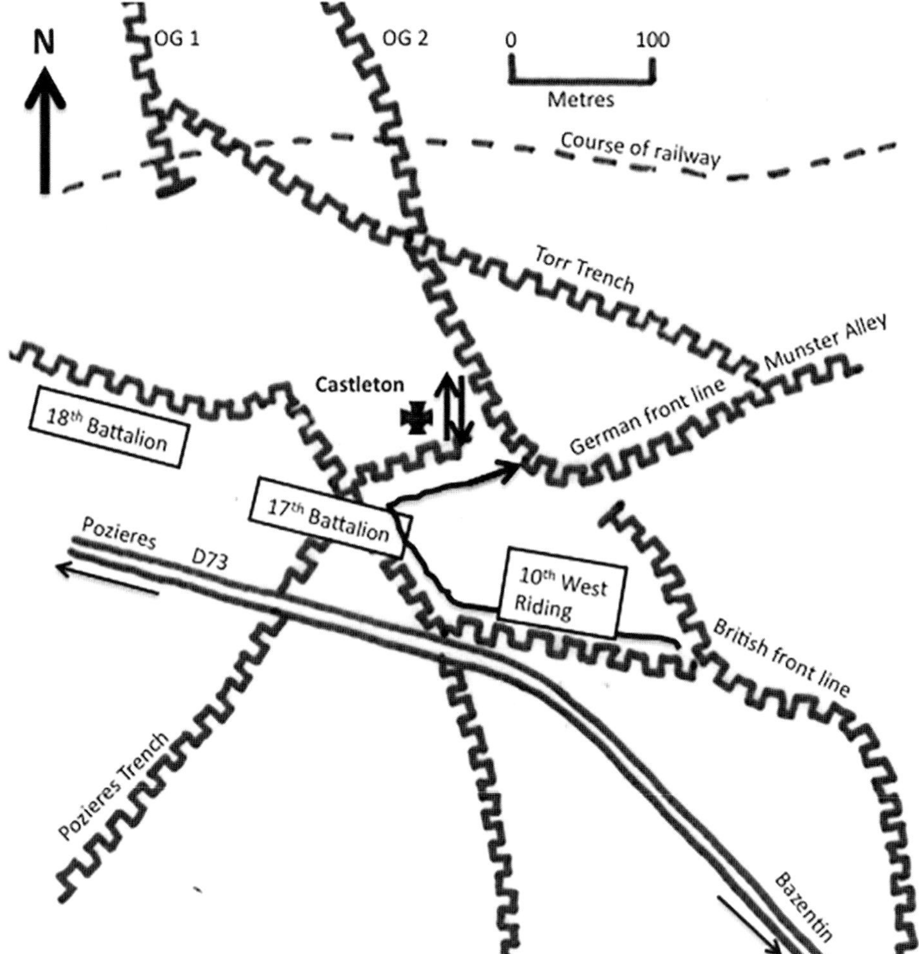

The site of Claud Castleton's gallantry on 29th July 1916 is very close to the VC sites of John Leak and Arthur Blackburn on 23rd July, just north of the Pozières - Bazentin road.

to move forward from crater to crater, but the flares turned night into day. When zero hour came, the overwhelming fire stopped the attack dead.

20th Battalion had no chance of reaching OG1 and on the right this meant the attack by 17th Battalion on OG2 could not succeed. Five waves formed up and the first two moved off before the third was caught by heavy machine-gun fire. The survivors took whatever cover they could find until 3 a.m., when the German fire subsided and most withdrew in the remaining hour before dawn. The attack was eventually called off with 146 casualties, mainly in 20th Battalion. On the extreme right, in III Corps, 10th West Riding (69th Brigade, 23rd Division) made another attempt on Munster Alley. 17th Battalion assisted with supplying bombs and some progress was made initially, but the gains were lost in counterattacks.

Meanwhile, in front of 17th Battalion many wounded remained in no man's land. **Sergeant Claude Castleton** of 5th Machine Gun Company was at the junction of

Munster Alley ready to move forward to assist with the consolidation of the captured position, which never happened. Instead he made two journeys on his own initiative under heavy machine-gun, rifle and shrapnel fire to bring in two wounded men on his back. He went out a third time and was in the act of bringing in another man when he was hit twice and killed. Private Thompson, who had been wounded earlier, and Corporal Field went out and brought in Castleton's body. Next morning he was buried near Contalmaison and his comrades put a small cross on the grave.

On the right of the main attack, 28th Battalion fought through some advanced enemy posts and seized OG1, but the wire in front of OG2 was impenetrable and the survivors had to fall back to OG1 and eventually to the start line. 25th and 26th Battalions had similar experiences and 7th Australian Brigade had gained nothing by the end of the day.

However, on the left, 23rd Battalion in 6th Australian Brigade swept forward and reached the Ovillers – Courcelette road. The objective was unrecognisable and the advance continued until it became involved in its own barrage and fell back to the real objective. Thick fog then formed and covered consolidation. Although successful, the cost to 23rd Battalion was 333 casualties. When the survivors of 7 Australian Brigade on the right fell back, 23rd Battalion held on and a reserve company of 22nd Battalion was sent forward to secure the open flank.

On the left in II Corps' area, 11th Middlesex in 36th Brigade (12th Division had relieved 48th Division on 28th July) captured the extension of K Trench and joined up with 23rd Battalion, resulting in a narrow salient jutting out from the north of Pozières along the ridge towards Mouquet Farm. However, attempts to seize the strongpoint at the junction of Park Lane and K Trench failed.

2nd Australian Division had suffered 3,502 casualties. 7th Australian Brigade was shattered and had to be withdrawn into reserve. The failure was due to a number of circumstances – hurried preparations, uncut wire, no time to dig advanced assault positions and the Germans were pre-warned. The Australians resolved to try again on 30th July, but this time taped routes, jumping off trenches and more effective artillery preparation would be employed.

30th July 1916

On 30th July a number of subsidiary attacks were made in the evening in support of Fourth Army's continuing drive on the right flank towards Guillemont and also to support the Reserve Army against Pozières. At Longueval, 13th Brigade (5th Division) was mainly repulsed but made a small gain to the northwest of Delville Wood. 153rd Brigade (51st Division) advanced against Wood Lane and, although repulsed, did manage to move the line forward about 150 metres.

In III Corps' area in contact with the Australians, 57th Brigade (19th Division) launched an attack to seize Intermediate Trench, north of Bazentin-le-Petit. The Switch Line further north and the northwest of High Wood were masked by the

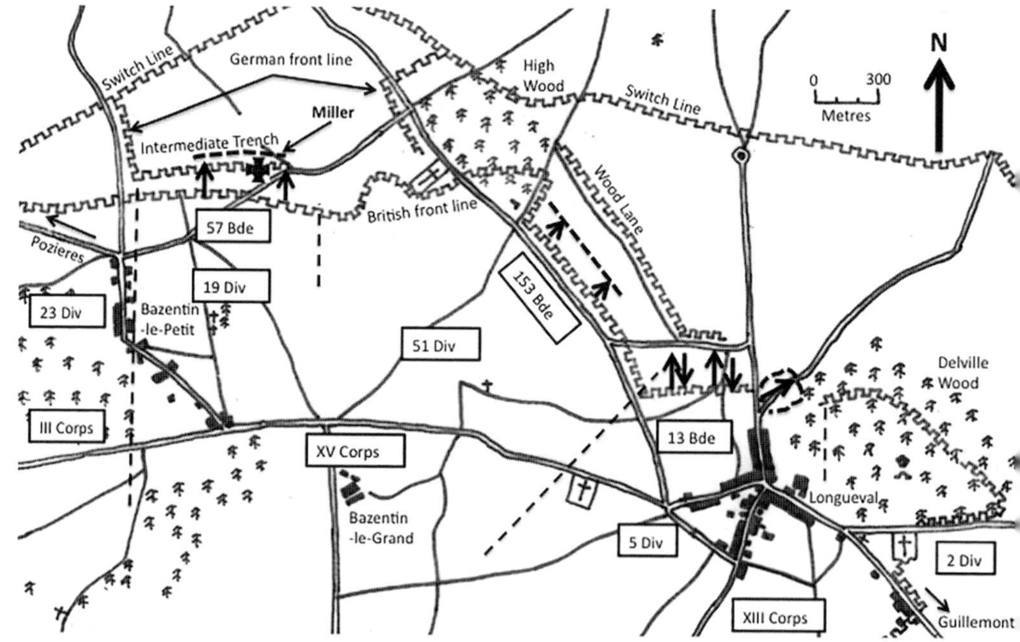

The subsidiary operations on 30th July between Bazentin and Longueval.

Corps artillery. The Special Brigade RE fired seventy-nine smoke shells to screen the right of the advance from machine-guns on the west side of High Wood and this seems to have been effective as no fire was received from this direction. The assault battalions from right to left were: 7th Royal Lancaster (attached from 56th Brigade), 10th Royal Warwickshire, 10th Worcestershire and 8th Gloucestershire.

7th Royal Lancaster, northeast of Bazentin-le-Petit, and 10th Royal Warwickshire followed closely behind the barrage and, immediately the guns lifted at 6.10 a.m., captured the right half of the trench and the strongpoint at the eastern end. However, on the left the other battalions were slower in following the barrage and were caught by the enemy machine-guns; this part of the attack failed. The gains on the right were consolidated with the assistance of 5th South Wales Borderers and 81st Field Company RE. A counterattack was driven off, but rearward communication remained very dangerous due to incessant enemy artillery fire.

The CO of 7th Royal Lancaster ordered **Private James Miller** to take an important message to D Company in another part of the line and return with a reply at all costs. He mentioned that getting the message through would undoubtedly save many lives. As soon as he set off, Miller was shot in the back; the bullet exiting through a gaping wound in his abdomen, leaving a portion of his bowel protruding. Despite being in agony, he compressed the wound with his hand and delivered the message before collapsing. Shortly afterwards he recovered a little. The officer to whom he had delivered the message offered a replacement runner to take the reply, but Miller insisted on taking it himself, as there was no point risking another life. Having delivered the reply, he collapsed and died soon afterwards.

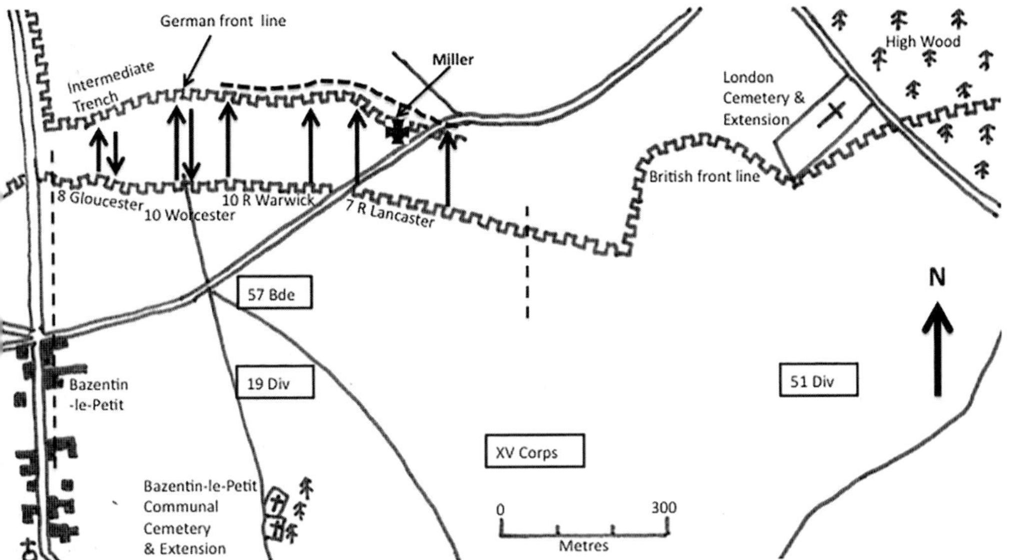

Leave Longueval northwestwards on the D107 towards Martinpuich. Pass High Wood on the right and London Cemetery on the left. As the Wood runs out, turn left on an unclassified road towards Bazentin. After 700m there is a left hand bend with a rough track running off to the right. Park here and look southwest. 7th Royal Lancaster attacked across the road from left to right. James Miller's VC action was 120m from the road/track junction where you parked, to the right of the road and in a roughly west-southwesterly direction.

As July passed into August, Haig began thinking of an attack north of the Ancre to assist in the capture of the Pozières – Grandcourt ridge. While the Reserve Army began preparing plans for this attack, its immediate task was the capture of the old German Second Position between Munster Alley and Mouquet Farm, the latter forming a strong outpost of the main position. However, in order to launch the new attack north of the Ancre, forces had to be conserved and therefore only one division per corps was available for immediate tasks. To the left of I ANZAC Corps was II

From the road/track junction looking southwest towards Bazentin, beyond the sunken section of the road. James Miller's VC action was in the field to the right of the road, on the crest line.

The reverse view to the previous picture. Delville Wood is on the extreme right, with High Wood and London Cemetery right of centre. The spire of Martinpuich church is on the extreme left. James Miller's VC action was in the field just beyond the sunken section of road in the foreground.

Corps, facing converted communications trenches running back from Thiepval. On 3rd August, 36th Brigade (12th Division) charged and captured a section of Fourth Avenue, supported on the left by a battalion of 37th Brigade. Next day 36th Brigade also gained a footing in Ration Trench, but further advance was stopped by machine-guns and the appearance of about 300 Germans from the direction of Mouquet Farm.

2nd Australian Division prepared for the next attack at Pozières by digging assembly trenches closer to the German lines. The artillery of I ANZAC and II Corps carried out four one-hour long bombardments each day, while the field artillery cut the enemy wire and simulated the final preparations for an attack with hurricane barrages. German retaliation was effective, despite counter-battery fire, and many casualties were suffered digging the new trenches.

At 9.15 p.m. on 4th August 2nd Australian Division's attack was made at Pozières. Both flanks were masked with smoke and 49th Division on the left (II Corps) made certain moves to simulate an attack as a diversion. Assembling the assault troops was confusing and was disrupted by the German artillery, but most troops moved off on time. South of the Bapaume road, 5th Australian Brigade captured OG1 easily, but OG2 did not fall until the supporting waves became involved. 7th Australian Brigade reached OG1 just behind the barrage and took it easily. Pressing on to OG2, it was hit by the German barrage and lost direction, but OG2 was eventually taken. On the left, 6th Australian Brigade was held up by a machine-gun to the north and did not reach the Courcelette track until late on the 5th. This joined up the salient to the northwest of Pozières to the new gains in OG2 on the right. 12th Division seized the remainder of Ration Trench and connected it with K/Western Trench. A number of heavy counterattacks were repulsed over the next few days and, on 5th August, 7th Australian Brigade pushed forward to seize the Windmill position, the highest point on the Somme battlefield. Gough intended launching the next attack from the Courcelette track to capture Mouquet Farm.

6th August 1916

2nd Australian Division was exhausted and it was vital to relieve it before heavy German counterattacks were encountered. 12th Australian Brigade (4th Australian Division) relieved 5th Australian Brigade on the right. Part of 7th Australian Brigade was relieved up to the Elbow before proceedings had to be halted to throw back a strong counterattack. Heavy German artillery fire throughout 6th August caused many casualties.

Meanwhile, on the extreme left of III Corps, 23rd Division made fresh attempts to gain Munster Alley. The first attack was on the night of 4th/5th August, when 68th Brigade bombed along fifty metres of the Alley, but an attack on Torr Trench failed. On 5th August, 69th Brigade relieved 68th Brigade and 8th Yorkshire went into the

Although trench lines are shown, in some cases they were flattened beyond recognition by heavy artillery barrages. The capture of Torr Trench and Munster Alley by 69th Brigade on 8th August marked the end of a long chapter of fighting in this small area east of Pozières, which had already resulted in the award of three VCs.

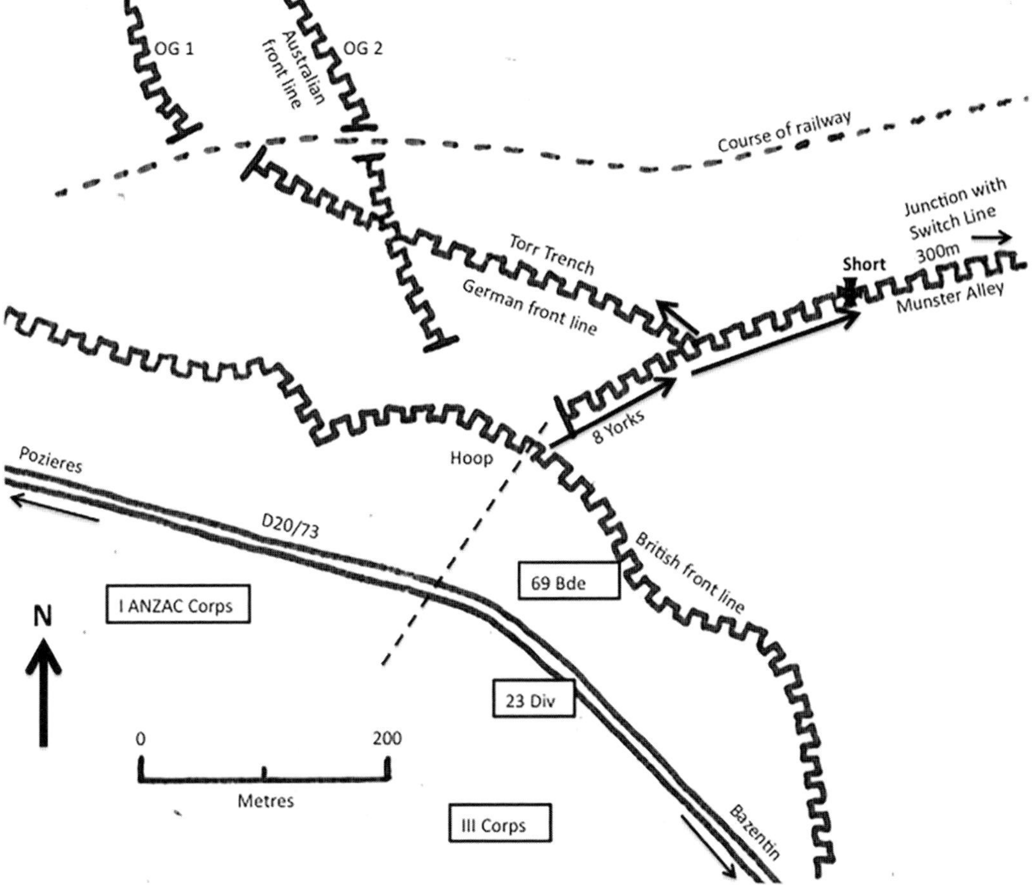

line with orders to secure Munster Alley fifty metres either side of the junction with Torr Trench. Having constructed double blocks, the advance was to be continued along Munster Alley to the Switch Line. One company was detailed for the attack, led by a party of twenty volunteer bombers under Second Lieutenant Lister. Two platoons were to follow close behind, the second under Second Lieutenant Watson and the third, under Second Lieutenant Cole, carrying tools to clear and consolidate the gains.

After a heavy bombardment, the bombers moved forward at 4.10 a.m. on 6th August, only a few minutes after a German attack had been driven off. They pushed the enemy 150 metres along Munster Alley before resistance stiffened and they were forced to give up twenty metres of their gains; they set up a block. Second Lieutenant Lister was wounded and Second Lieutenant Watson took over. One of the bombers, **Private William Short** of C Company, was badly wounded in the foot by enemy shellfire, but refused to go for assistance and continued to throw bombs. Later his leg was shattered by a shell, but he still refused to leave his post. When he could no longer fight, he adjusted the detonators and straightened grenade pins before passing the bombs to his comrades to throw. He died just before his wounds could be attended to.

With the assistance of the Australians to the north, the east end of Torr Trench was secured and during the night a post was established about fifty metres from the junction with Munster Alley. The Battalion was reinforced by two and a half companies of 11th West Yorkshire. Next night Torr Trench was joined to the Hoop, in the old British lines, thus completing the capture of this important position.

On 7th August a German counterattack broke in at the Elbow in the OG Lines north of the Bapaume road, but the British artillery held the supports and those who had infiltrated were destroyed. In this fighting Lieutenant Albert Jacka of 14th Battalion was awarded the MC for attacking the enemy in the rear and releasing a number of Australian prisoners to rejoin the fight. Jacka had been awarded the first Australian VC of the war at Gallipoli as a private. By 10.30 a.m., 4th Australian Division completed taking over the whole of I ANZAC Corps' front.

9th–12th August 1916

The next objective set by Gough for the Australians was a line cutting across the OG Lines through a small quarry to the Pozières – Thiepval road, essentially the line of Quarry Trench. West from that point was the responsibility of 12th Division, which was to seize Skyline Trench and westwards to the original German front line of 1st July. From there, 49th Division would make holding attacks to tie the Germans down. Zero was set for 10.30 p.m. on 12th August and the barrage opened immediately. In the meantime, 4th Australian Division resolved to make as much progress as possible.

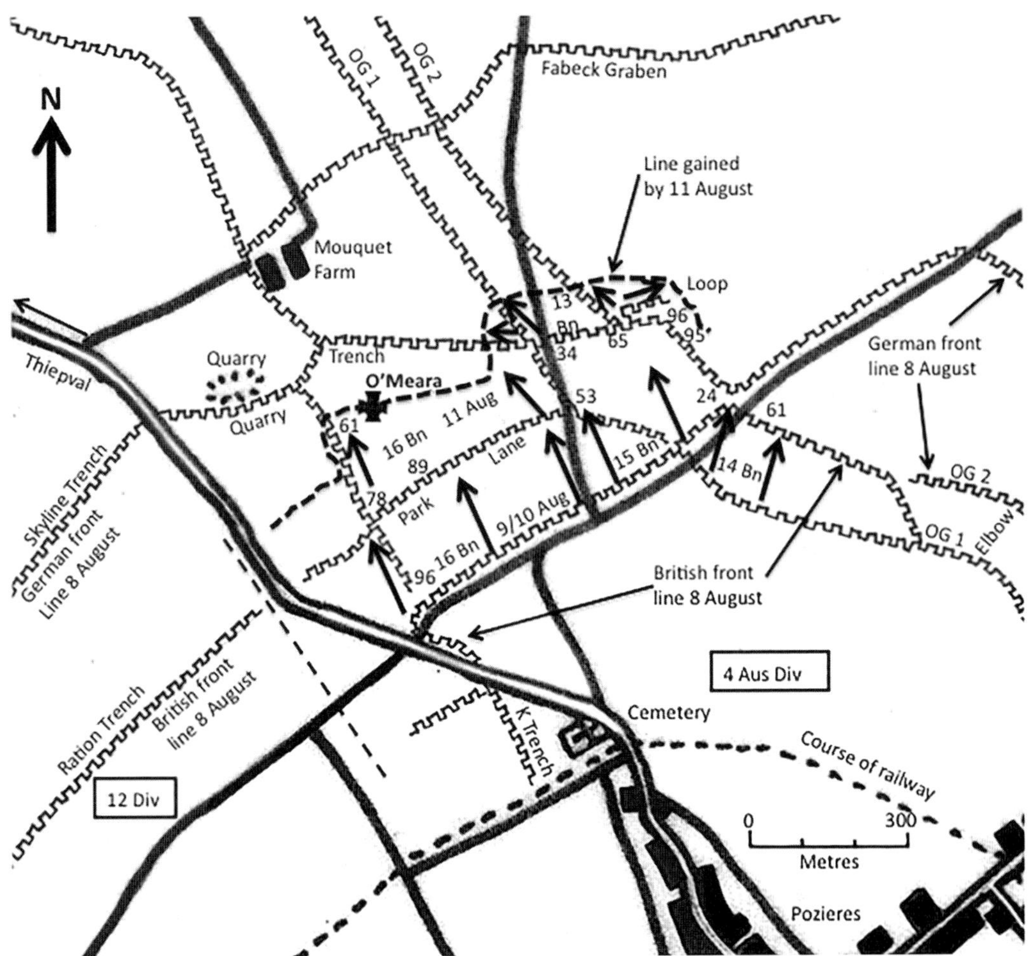

Park at the cemetery north of Pozières on the D73 Thiepval road. Walk north-northwest along a gradually rising track. After 300m the track swings to the right, parallel with and just behind the front line from which 16th Battalion attacked on 11th August. Look northwest towards Thiepval and Mouquet Farm, which is 650m away. Martin O'Meara's VC action was on this line, about 250m short of the Farm, in the low ground. To gain a clearer view, follow the track for another 125m northeast, where there is a large pile of chalk. Climb to the top to look down into the low ground near the Quarry.

Return to your vehicle, drive towards Thiepval on the D73 for 1,100m and pull in on the right where there is a Ross Bastiaan memorial, just before the right turn to Mouquet Farm. Walk back along the road towards Pozières for 175m, remaining alert to the traffic. Turn right uphill along a track and follow it for about 150m and then turn around to look eastwards. Beyond the tree covered Quarry and slightly to the right of it is where Martin O'Meara rescued the wounded. To the north of the Quarry is a patch of ground still bearing the scars of the shelling.

At 9.20 p.m. on 8th August, 15th Battalion and 7th Suffolk (35th Brigade, 12th Division) advanced against Park Lane on the way to Mouquet Farm. 15th Battalion was successful on the right, where the wire had been cut sufficiently, and also got into the OG Lines. The state of the trenches was such that 15th Battalion believed it had reached the line Point 53 – Point 95. In reality it appears more likely it had crossed this levelled trench and reached the line Point 34 – Point 65 and the Loop.

On the left, 7th Suffolk was checked by uncut wire covered by three or four machine-guns, except for a few men on its right. 7th Suffolk tried again by bombing along Ration Trench towards Point 78 and came close, but did not reach it. Patrols discovered that Point 96 was also held by the enemy. The Australian left was thus in the air and twenty bombers of 16th Battalion were sent to reinforce it; only six got through.

Without support, the Australians were forced to withdraw from the western part of their gains in Park Lane just after daybreak. The survivors came out with all their weapons and their wounded were carried by prisoners. As a result of overshooting the objective, 15th Battalion found itself under the preparatory barrage for a new attack late on 9th August. It was forced to withdraw, intending to return once the barrage lifted.

It was realised that making all the objectives the responsibility of one formation would enhance coordination and increase the chances of success. The boundary between I ANZAC and II Corps was shifted to bring K Trench into 4th Australian Division's area and 4th Australian Brigade took over from 12th Division up to the Pozières – Thiepval road. 16th Battalion was tasked to seize Point 78. Learning from 7th Suffolk's experience the previous day, 16th Battalion's CO, Lieutenant Colonel Drake Brockman, decided to attack obliquely instead of frontally. One company had been in reserve to 15th Battalion, but the other three did not start moving forward until 7 p.m. on 9th August. However, all the officers and senior NCOs of the Battalion had the opportunity to study the ground over which they would attack from the front line trench.

From the British front line on 11th August looking in the direction of 16th Battalion's attack. Martin O'Meara made his daring rescues on the forward slope of this hillside, between the camera position and Mouquet Farm. This picture illustrates the strength of the German positions in this area in terms of depth and mutual support.

Point 96 and K Trench were allocated to two platoons and the bombers of 16th Battalion under Lieutenant Wilton. The bombardment was a repetition of the previous attack, but more attention was paid to the machine-guns that had halted 7th Suffolk.

At midnight on 9th August, after five minutes' intense bombardment, the troops rushed the vital trench junction on the left and the whole of Park Lane was occupied with few casualties. They were guided by shielded torches in no man's land put out by the scouts and invisible to the enemy. 15th Battalion managed to reoccupy the positions evacuated earlier. On the extreme right, 14th Battalion also managed to reoccupy Points 61 and 24. By dawn on 10th August the Australian front line was just over the skyline north of Pozières.

During the day a little rain fell and the German artillery was active intermittently until 4 p.m., when the shelling came down heavily. 15th Battalion was relieved by 13th Battalion. Rather than wait for the Germans to recover and counterattack, Commander 4th Australian Division ordered 13th and 16th Battalions to press on while the enemy was still unsettled. 13th Battalion was to seize the line Point 34 – Point 96, but this appeared to be the line reached in the previous night's attack. 16th Battalion was to push forward, establish a series of posts and dig a communication trench from Ration Trench to the left of the new line. To be prudent, the artillery asked the infantry to pull back at least 180 metres before the barrage fell, just in case.

At 1 a.m. on 11th August, 13th and 16th Battalions moved forward. 13th Battalion pushed along OG 1 and OG 2, suffering only thirty casualties, including a few from the British shelling by getting too far ahead. 16th Battalion advanced along K Trench to Point 61 and established its posts just about as planned, overlooking the Quarry. During the day the Germans shelled the new positions and launched a counterattack, which was repulsed. Both battalions were ordered to improve their positions on the night of the 11th. Little was gained, but a strong German attack on 13th Battalion was devastated by close range fire.

Looking across the D73 Pozières-Thiepval road to the east.

The resulting gains from the 8th onwards were held during counterattacks that day and the following night. **Private Martin O'Meara** was involved throughout, including during 16th Battalion's assault on Point 78 (junction of K Trench with Park Lane) on 9th August. During the next four days of heavy fighting, O'Meara, a stretcher-bearer, went out repeatedly to bring in the wounded from no man's land despite intense artillery and machine-gun fire. He was particularly busy during critical barrages and counterattacks. Four times he carried water and supplies forward under bursting shells and returned carrying wounded. It is likely that he brought in over twenty-five wounded men. On one occasion he also volunteered to carry ammunition and bombs to a portion of trench that was being heavily shelled.

On 12th August, the main attack was launched at 10.30 p.m. from the OG Lines westwards to the Nab, in conjunction with III Corps on the right, which was attacking Intermediate Trench and Switch Trench near Munster Alley. On the right, 13th Battalion was already in the final position and had little to do, but had to fight hard to maintain contact with 50th Battalion on the left, which had relieved 16th Battalion. Some platoons of 50th Battalion did not receive their orders until late. The advance from Ration Trench and Park Lane did not go well. The left advanced well in contact with 12th Division, but the centre swung to the right. One party actually reached Mouquet Farm, but was too weak to hold it.

In 12th Division, 35th Brigade advanced against Skyline Trench behind an excellent barrage. There was little opposition and the objective was taken but, as

patrols attempted to press on into Nab Valley, they met considerable resistance and consolidated on Skyline Trench, thinning out men not required to hold it.

At midnight on 13th August the weak garrison of Skyline Trench was pushed back. The attack was to be resumed by 1 ANZAC Corps on the 14th to beyond Mouquet Farm, in conjunction with II Corps on the left. However, an attempt to regain Skyline Trench by a battalion of 145th Brigade failed. Loss of Skyline Trench exposed the left of I ANZAC Corps' line and shelling that evening stopped a coordinated attack before it could commence. It eventually started at 10 p.m. under a full moon. Some gains were made, including sections of Skyline Trench.

The exhausted 4th Australian Division was relieved by 1st Australian Division on 16th August. The next attack was to be coordinated with Fourth Army, but the planned operations north of the Ancre were postponed for the time being. Plans were also being made for a major new offensive in mid-September, so troops available for other operations in the meantime were limited to husband resources.

As it turned out, the attack of 1st Australian Division on 18th August was not coordinated with Fourth Army. The left brigade of 48th Division attacked at 5 p.m. and was successful, having isolated its objective with artillery fire. At 9 p.m. the Australians advanced. Southeast of the Bapuame road, 2nd Australian Brigade had halved its assault distance but did not have the artillery timetable and ran into heavy machine-gun fire. Despite a number of attempts, no progress was made and the survivors withdrew to the start line. Northwest of the Bapaume road, 1st Australian Brigade was hit by the artillery falling short. The right battalion was stopped but, on the left, 4th Battalion established a post in Quarry Trench and repulsed several counterattacks.

At 6 p.m. on 21st August I ANZAC and II Corps attacked again. Although heavily shelled as a result of preparations being observed during the day by German aircraft, some progress was made. The former aimed to push northwest along Pozières Ridge, while the latter continued towards Thiepval. Most of the successes over the next few days were in II Corps' area. On the right, I ANZAC Corps was held up, particularly by the strongly held position at Mouquet Farm. The weather did not help as heavy rain turned the ground into a quagmire.

Plans were now laid to take Thiepval by I ANZAC and II Corps. The latter was to attack astride the Ancre, while the former secured Fabeck Graben and Mouquet Farm, acting in coordination with a Fourth Army/French attack to the south. Because of the weather this next phase could not commence until 3rd September.

Overview of the Ancre operations on 3rd September 1916. C/246 Battery was about 2,500 metres behind the front line, at Mesnil.

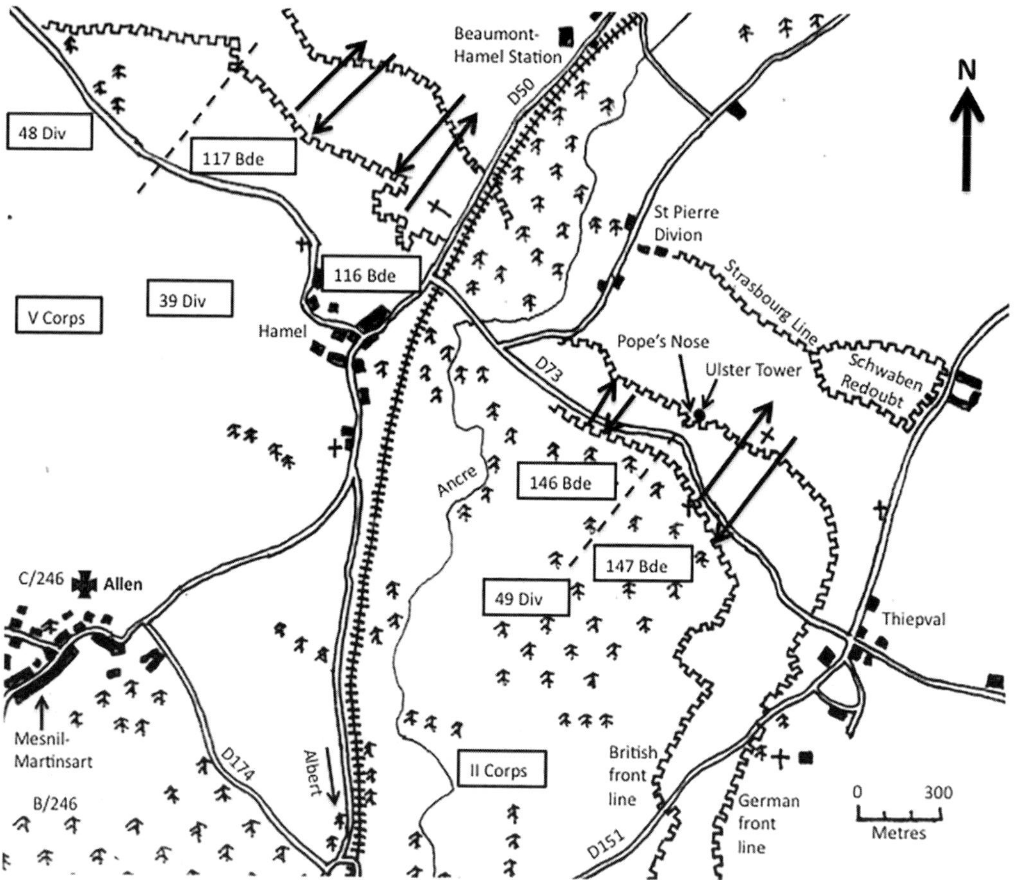

3rd September 1916

Gough's plans to envelop Thiepval were pressed ahead energetically. Officially the attack north of the Ancre was not part of the Battle of Pozières Ridge, which ended on 3rd September, but it seems more appropriate to deal with it in this chapter.

On the right, I ANZAC and II Corps were allocated limited objectives, but on the left the attacks astride the Ancre were more ambitious. South of the river, 49th Division (II Corps) was expected to capture two lines of trenches on a frontage of 900 metres and press on the following day to secure St Pierre Divion and the Strasbourg Line, which linked it to the Schwaben Redoubt. 39th Division (V Corps), north of the Ancre, was expected to take three lines of trenches on the spur south of Beaumont-Hamel and advance along the river to cover 49th Division's left flank. If successful, II Corps was to push north into Thiepval over the following days.

49th Division attacked at 5.13 a.m. from the Hamel – Thiepval road. The barrage was excellent and Thiepval was covered in gas shells and ammonal bombs by the Special Brigade RE. On the right, 147th Brigade occupied the enemy front line and penetrated to the support trench, but pockets of enemy remained in the front line. Due to losing direction, the Pope's Nose salient was not captured. Heavy machine-gun fire was encountered from the Schwaben Redoubt and Strasbourg Line and there was a counterattack by bombing parties from the latter. On the left, 146th Brigade was enfiladed from the Pope's Nose and failed to get into the German lines, although a few men on the river did get to the support line.

Mist and the German barrage prevented messages getting back. By 7.30 a.m., 146th Brigade was back in its trenches and by 10 a.m. the remnants of 147th Brigade, having expended their ammunition and lost most of their officers, were forced out of their gains. Plans to renew the attack in the evening came to nothing, as it was clear that the troops were in no condition to participate. Failure could not be blamed on the artillery, whose support was excellent. However, a frontal assault on the same positions as on 1st July, still commanded by the Schwaben Redoubt, stood little chance of success. Many of the soldiers were replacements and lacked experience, despite herculean efforts by their leaders and older soldiers supporting them.

From north of Mesnil-Martinsart, on the right, looking south. C/246 Battery was on the slope in line with the water tower.

Captain William Allen was the MO with C Battery, 246th Brigade RFA, situated southwest of Hamel, near Mesnil. The Battery was involved in the supporting bombardment from 5.10 a.m. and was subjected to sporadic shelling. At 12.30 p.m., while ammunition was being unloaded, the

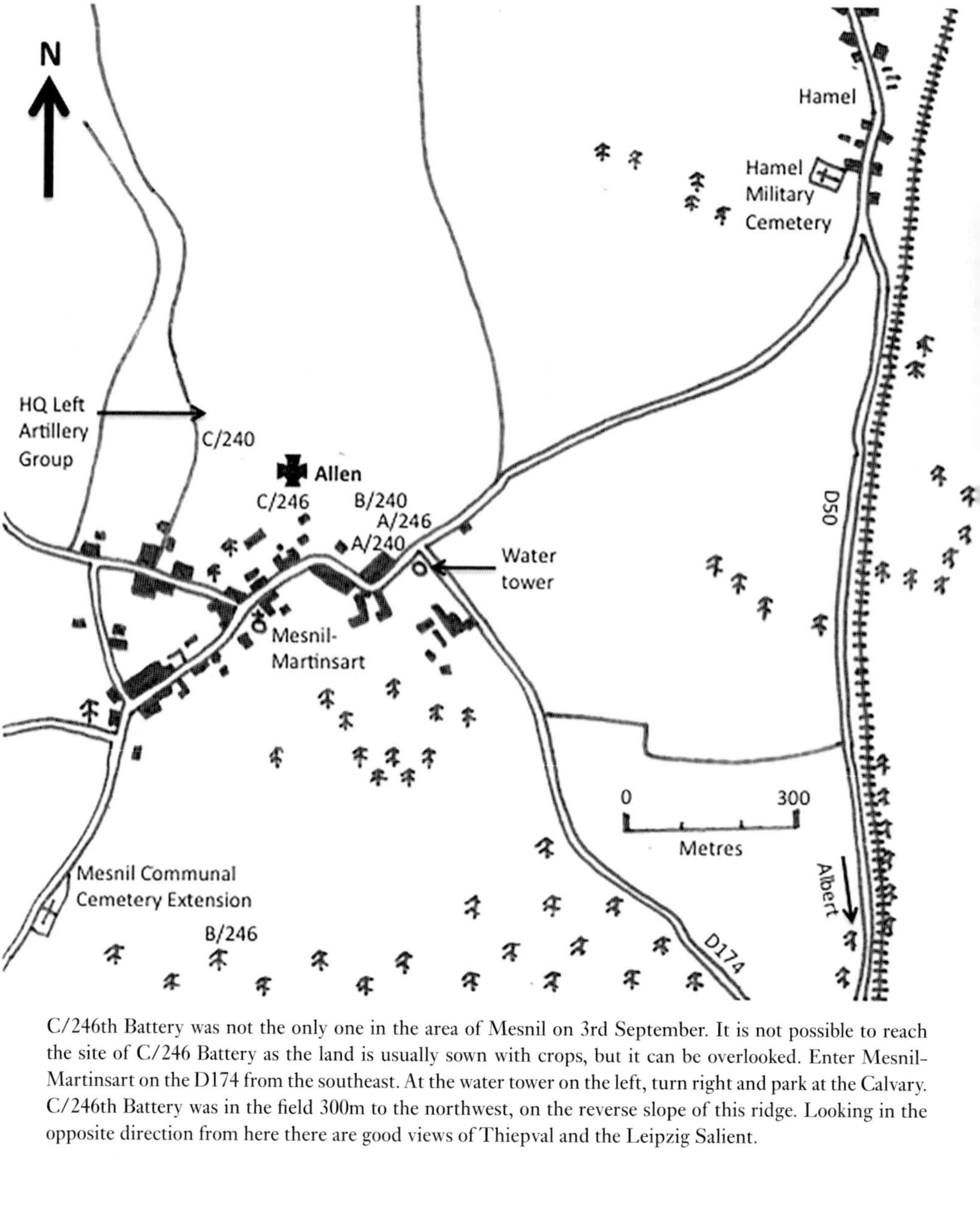
N
Hamel
Hamel Military Cemetery
HQ Left Artillery Group
C/240
Allen
C/246
B/240
A/246
A/240
Water tower
Mesnil-Martinsart
D50
0
300
Metres
Mesnil Communal Cemetery Extension
B/246
Albert
D174

C/246th Battery was not the only one in the area of Mesnil on 3rd September. It is not possible to reach the site of C/246 Battery as the land is usually sown with crops, but it can be overlooked. Enter Mesnil-Martinsart on the D174 from the southeast. At the water tower on the left, turn right and park at the Calvary. C/246th Battery was in the field 300m to the northwest, on the reverse slope of this ridge. Looking in the opposite direction from here there are good views of Thiepval and the Leipzig Salient.

From near the Tank Memorial looking east, with the D929 Bapaume road on the left, Martinpuich right of centre and High Wood in the background on the far right. The site of Leo Clarke's VC action was 360m into the fields in line with the buildings in Martinpuich, which are 1,400m from the camera position.

Ligne de Front
1er septembre 1916

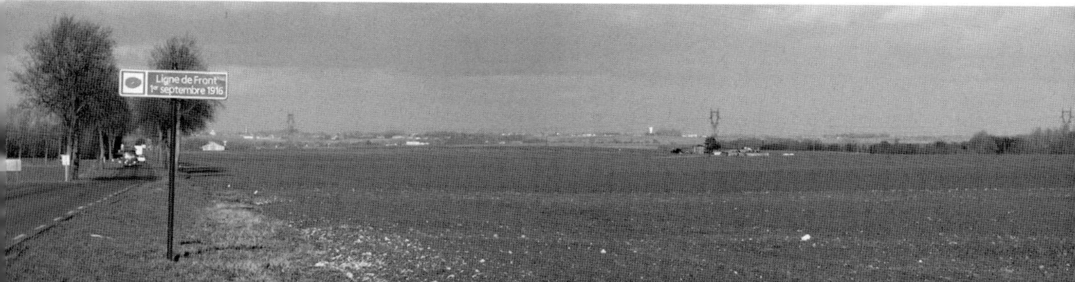

From the Calvary near the water tower looking northwest, with Mesnil-Martinsart on the left. C/246th Battery was 300m into the field in the foreground.

Battery came under heavy artillery fire. An ammunition limber was hit by the first salvo and much of the ammunition exploded. Six men were killed outright and another fourteen were severely wounded, of whom three eventually died. Only four men were left to serve the guns and they naturally took cover to avoid the lethal splinters. Allen dashed to the scene, ignoring the shellfire. He dressed all the wounded, thereby preventing many of them from bleeding to death. He was hit four times in the space of an hour and his injuries included two broken ribs. However, he carried on until the last man had been evacuated. He then went to another battery to attend to a wounded officer before returning to his dugout to report his own injuries.

39th Division's attack was also on a frontage of 900 metres. It started well, behind a good barrage and the wire was well cut, but all of the battalions were well under establishment. Some gains were made and in places the final objective was reached, but it was not consistent. Once 49th Division had been forced back, flanking fire was also received from across the Ancre. Parties began to drift back as their bombs and ammunition ran out. The Corps Commander knew how weak the division was and decided not to renew the attack.

The right of II Corps made some significant advances but was unable to hold them in isolation and had to withdraw. I ANZAC Corps had a little more success and managed to take Fabeck Graben and reach Mouquet Farm, but the three battalions involved were not in touch with each other. A heavy counter-barrage was followed

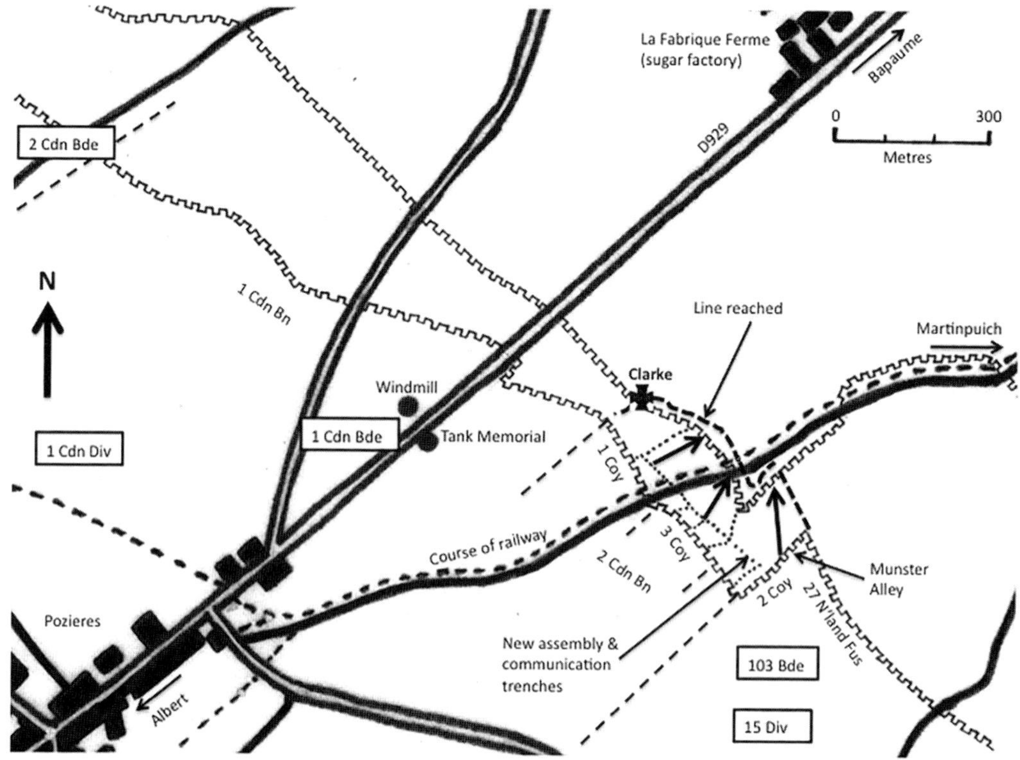

Leave Pozières on the D929 northeastwards towards Bapaume. After a few hundred metres park on the right at the Tank Memorial, opposite Pozières Windmill. Walk to the northern end of the fence surrounding the telecommunications mast and look east-northeast towards Martinpuich. Leo Clarke's VC action was 360m along that line. The area is utterly featureless and there are no tracks to get any closer.

by a strong counterattack and the Farm was lost, but the gains in Fabeck Graben were linked to the Australian positions astride the OG Lines and held.

9th September 1916

The Canadian Corps began replacing I ANZAC Corps on 30th August. 4th Australian Division handed over to 1st Canadian Division, the handover being completed on the morning of 5th September. There was a hope that the Canadians would have a little time to find their feet before any offensive operations. However, during a routine battalion rotation at Mouquet Farm on 8th September, the Germans made several attempts and finally succeeded in regaining the portions of Fabeck Graben that they had lost previously. That evening two more attacks were made near the Farm and repulsed. Other attempts by the Germans followed over the next four days.

Early on 9th September, 2nd Canadian Battalion (1st Canadian Brigade) relieved 4th Canadian Battalion in the front line in preparation for an attack on the German front line later that day astride the railway leading to Martinpuich, south of the Bapaume road. Prior to the attack a series of advanced saps were dug fifty metres out into no man's land, the heads being connected together to form an advanced trench. In addition an assembly trench was dug for the assault troops fifty metres behind the front line from the end of Munster Alley to the left of the attack frontage. The attack was made by three companies in line (from the left, Nos. 1, 3 and 2), each of two waves and separated by forty-five metres. No.2 Company started from the line held by 27th Northumberland Fusiliers (103rd Brigade, 15th Division). The battalions on each flank were to support the attack with machine-gun fire. The assault troops were in the assembly trenches by 4.25 p.m.

At 4.45 p.m. an intense bombardment by the field artillery of 18th and 50th Divisions fell on the German trenches as the assault troops moved forward. The bombardment lifted after three minutes and 2nd Canadian Battalion attacked against considerable resistance, particularly on the left, where the barrage had not been as effective. Hand to hand fighting followed and by 5.08 p.m., 450 metres of trench were secured and more than sixty prisoners were taken. Touch was maintained with 27th Northumberland Fusiliers (15th Division, III Corps, Fourth Army) on the right. During the action, one of the company commanders was shot dead. Lieutenant JP Pringle MM charged a machine-gun that was being set up to sweep the stalled attack. Inspired by this example, the company made a headlong charge for the enemy trenches. Fighting was fierce, mostly with bomb and bayonet.

The second wave arrived to begin consolidation, reversing the captured trench, constructing blocks and digging new communication trenches. The new line was shelled incessantly by the Germans and several counterattacks were beaten back during the night. In total 138 prisoners were taken, but the battalion suffered 270 casualties, including seventy-one killed.

The Battalion Bombing Platoon was divided in half, with one and a half sections being allocated to each flank to set up bombing blocks. Sergeant W Hugh Nicholls and a section of bombers on the left flank moved into the German trenches successfully and set up its block. Once it was established, the party moved along the trench to clear it. **Corporal Leo Clarke** and his section of bombers was ordered by Lieutenant Hoey to clear the continuation of a newly captured trench (Walker Avenue) before meeting up with Sergeant Nicholls and were then to cover the construction of another block.

Most of Clarke's party became casualties and their supply of grenades was exhausted. He was building a block with Private Soppitt when about twenty Germans with two officers counterattacked down the trench. Clarke coolly emptied his revolver twice into the enemy and then grabbed two enemy rifles, which he also emptied. One of the German officers attacked him with a bayonet, wounding him in the leg, but he shot him dead. It is possible that Clarke killed or wounded sixteen of the enemy party. The remainder ran away, pursued by Clarke, who shot four more and captured a fifth, whom he handed over to Sergeant Nicholls. Clarke was later ordered to the dressing station by Lieutenant Hoey to have his wounds tended to, but returned to duty next day. He was killed five weeks later and never knew he had been awarded the VC.

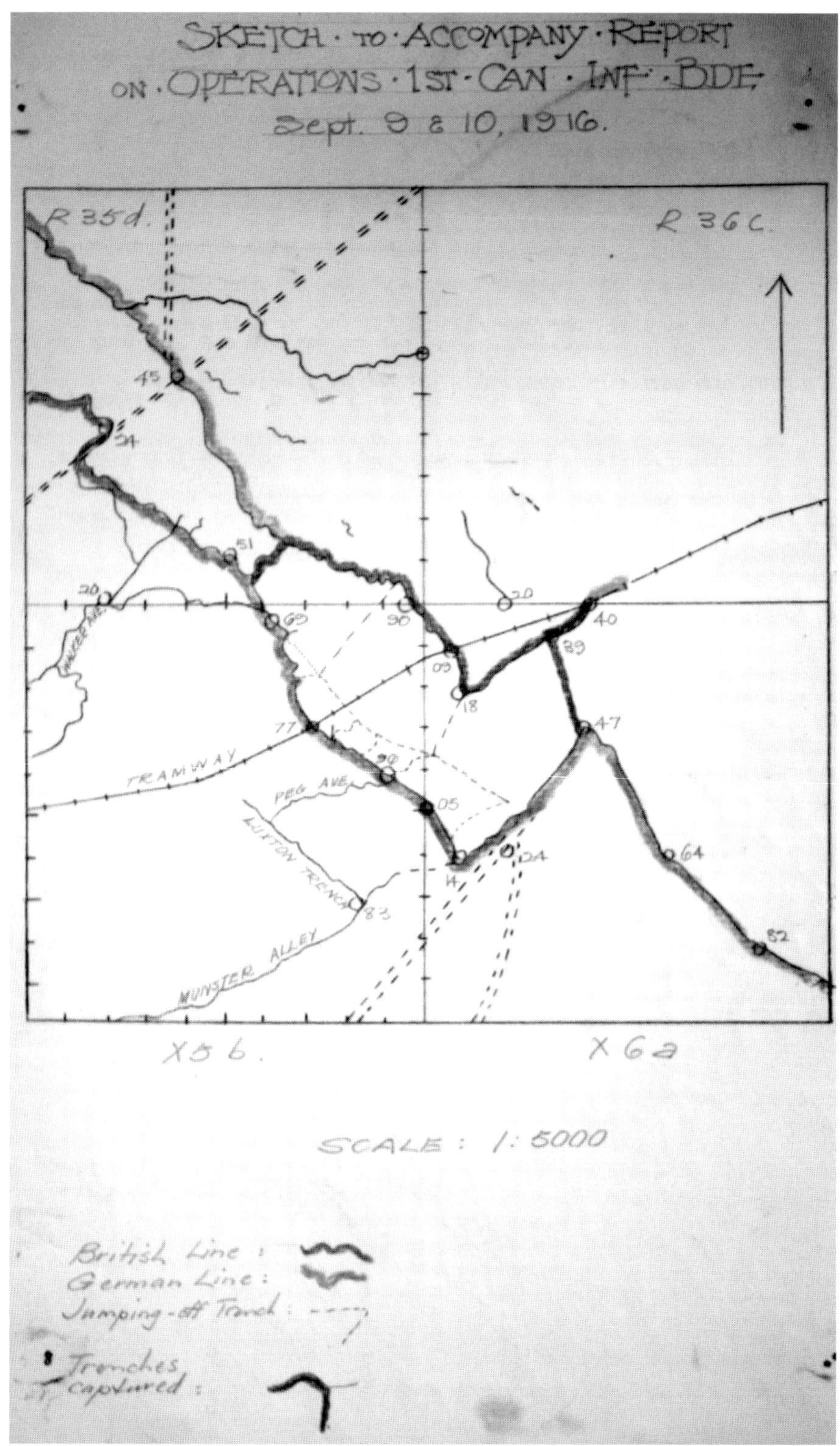

Contemporary sketch of the 2nd Canadian Battalion attack on 9th September.

Chapter Four

Guillemont and Flers-Courcelette

Battle of Guillemont – 3rd – 6th September 1916

155 Lt John Holland, 7th Leinster (47tf Brigade, 16th (Irish) Division)
156 Pte Thomas Hughes, 6th Connaught Rangers (47th Brigade, 16th (Irish) Division)
157 Sgt David Jones, 12th King's (Liverpool) (61st Brigade, 20th (Light) Division)

A combined Fourth Army and French attack took place on 3rd September, involving the British XIV and XV Corps and a division of III Corps. The main objective was to seize Ginchy and Guillemont, while the French captured Falfemont Farm in a preliminary operation some three hours earlier. The artillery bombardment commenced at 8 a.m. on 2nd September. On the right of XIV Corps, the left of 5th Division secured the German second position and by mid afternoon was in touch with 20th Division on the Wedge Wood – Ginchy road. However, on the right the attack failed, as did a second attempt, and at 7.35 p.m. operations were halted for the day.

On the left of XIV Corps, 20th Division was ordered to capture Guillemont, but 59th Brigade could muster only 1,650 riflemen and had to be reinforced by a battalion each from 60th and 61st Brigades. 60th Brigade was so weak that it had to be replaced by 47th Brigade (16th Division). 59th and 47th Brigades attacked the south and north of the village respectively. The advance was to be in three stages to the Wedge Wood – Ginchy road. The barrage crept forward ninety metres every four minutes and by zero hour the village had been obliterated, although many dugouts survived.

59th Brigade's attack was launched from left to right by 10th King's Royal Rifle Corps, 10th Rifle Brigade and 11th Rifle Brigade. 47th Brigade attacked with two battalions initially, 6th Connaught Rangers on the right and 7th Leinster on the left.

10th King's Royal Rifle Corps in 59th Brigade and 6th Connaught Rangers in 47th Brigade, either side of Mount Street, attacked from assembly trenches dug near to the German positions. By keeping close to the bombardment, they pressed forward ahead of zero hour (12.00 p.m.) and, although they suffered some casualties from their own artillery, caught the enemy by surprise. At noon the other battalions set off and within twenty minutes the second objective on the Hardecourt road had been taken.

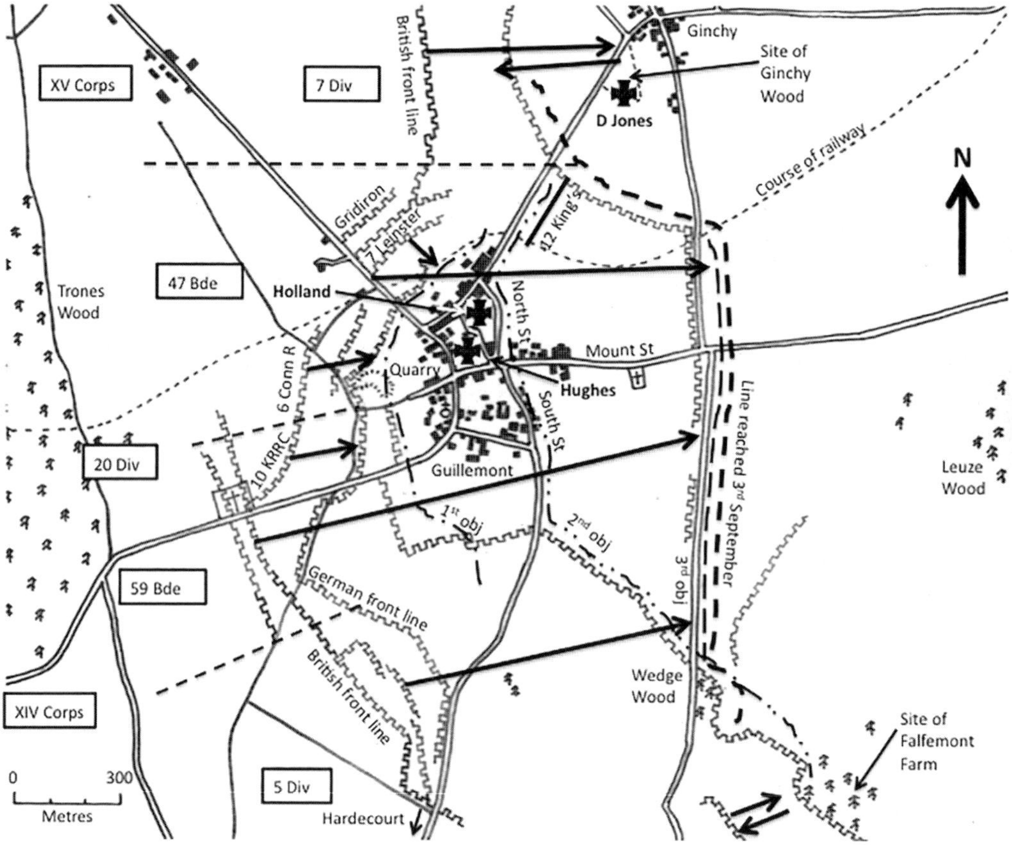

The attack on Guillemont on 3rd September 1916.

C Company (left) and D Company (right), 6th Connaught Rangers, subdued the opposition quickly and by 12.09 p.m. had taken the first objective. The Battalion swept on to the second objective, but in its impatience overlooked many small pockets of enemy, particularly around the Quarry, and a company of 10th King's Royal Rifle Corps had to deal with them. The only Connaught Rangers VC of the

From Guillemont Road Cemetery continue eastwards towards Guillemont on the D64. After 300m turn left onto a track and park at the next junction after 200m. Walk along the track to the northwest for 300m. This is the northern boundary of 6th Connaught Rangers. The start line ran from here a little west of south and the attack was in a generally easterly direction into Guillemont. The picture is from just north of the D64, looking northeast.

Looking west along Mount Street, the right boundary of 6th Connaught Rangers' attack. In the far distance is Trônes Wood. Thomas Hughes' VC action was amongst the buildings on the right.

Great War was won during this attack. **Private Thomas Hughes** was wounded in the initial assault and went for medical assistance, but when his wound had been dressed he insisted on returning. As the advance resumed he charged a machine-gun post alone, shot the gunners and captured the gun. He was wounded again in this action, but managed to bring in four prisoners and the machine-gun.

On the extreme left of 20th Division, 7th Leinster attacked southeast from the Gridiron with great dash. The previous night the Battalion had waded through a sea of water filled shell holes to reach its assembly positions and had endured a number of gas attacks. The men had then waited for eight hours whilst crammed into very shallow trenches. However, when the barrage lifted, the Leinsters rushed forward and secured the first objective quickly. **Lieutenant John Holland** led the bombers in clearing some dugouts and then pressed on through the barrage to clear the majority of the centre of the village. This action broke the enemy's spirit and fifty prisoners were taken. Of the twenty-six bombers who attacked with Holland, five were killed and fifteen wounded; two were awarded the DCM and six the MM.

The headquarters of 20th Division knew by 12.30 p.m. of the success, mainly due to accurate reporting from aircraft patrols. At 12.50 p.m. fresh battalions came forward to continue the advance towards the third objective, which was to be made

Leave Guillemont northwest on the D20 towards Longueval. After 300m park in the entrance to the silos on the left. Across the road is a large barn, on the start line for 7th Leinster. The trench ran away in the direction of Ginchy church. The attack was in a southeasterly direction through Guillemont. From the barn/start line, looking southeast into Guillemont in the direction of 7th Leinster's attack. The road on the right leads to Longueval. Guillemont church is through the trees on the far right.

in two bounds. Enemy fire increased, but there was no check. In 59th Brigade the leading battalions were reinforced by 6th Oxfordshire & Buckinghamshire Light Infantry and 7th Somerset Light Infantry. In 47th Brigade, 8th Royal Munster Fusiliers and 6th Royal Irish passed through 6th Connaught Rangers and 7th Leinster.

At 2.50 p.m. the advance commenced to the third objective, the Wedge Wood – Ginchy road. Opposition was light. The commander of 59th Brigade sent back reports that the front was clear of enemy and fresh troops should take advantage of the situation. In 47th Brigade, 6th Royal Irish Regiment pushed ahead with 140 Connaught soldiers following. The rest of the battalion dug in parallel with Brompton Road (south of and parallel with the railway north of Guillemont), with its left in contact with 7th Leinster. By 3.30 p.m. reinforcements were arriving and the positions were being consolidated.

Reverse of the previous view. Trônes Wood is in the left distance behind the silos on the site of Guillemont Station. The barn in the centre is on the start line trench from which 7th Leinster attacked towards the left of view. On the far right is Delville Wood.

Apart from the success at Guillemont and the penetration of the German second position by 5th Division to the south, the rest of the attack had failed and it was considered foolhardy to press on that day. Instead Rawlinson ordered a resumption of the attack for 3.10 p.m. on the 4th. 47th Brigade's success came at considerable cost; 1,147 casualties, including the CO of 6th Connaught Rangers, out of approximately 2,400 men committed. About 300 prisoners, six machine-guns and a minenwerfer were taken, in addition to numerous enemy dead.

At 5.15 p.m. 47th Brigade reported that 7th Division on the left flank had been forced out of Ginchy. The situation was critical, with 20th Division's left flank unprotected. A protective barrage was fired and GOC 20th Division halted any further advance except for patrols. Earlier, 12th King's (61st Brigade) had been sent forward to reinforce 47th Brigade, having spent the day moving forward through Trônes Wood. At about 4 p.m. C and D Companies went to help 6th Connaught Rangers and 7th Leinster consolidate their gains. They established themselves in a trench on the east side of the Guillemont – Ginchy road, about 540 metres northeast of Guillemont church, in contact with the Manchesters on the left. When 7th Division pulled back, Captain Cleminson, commanding the King's companies, took the initiative and advanced towards Ginchy to establish a defensive line short of the village.

German counterattacks on this flank at 5.30 and 6.30 p.m. were stopped by small arms fire from 12th King's. A platoon sent forward to Ginchy Wood, southwest of

Leave Guillemont on the unclassified road northeast towards Ginchy. Immediately on entering the village of Ginchy, turn left and park. Walk back fifty metres towards Guillemont. The axis of 12th King's advance was towards you from the direction of Guillemont. David Jones' VC action was in the field left of the road, where there used to be a copse (Ginchy Wood).

the village, came under heavy fire and the commander and a number of men were killed. The platoon sergeant, **Sergeant David Jones**, took command and got his men into position and the Lewis gun into action. He reported to Cleminson that there was no sign of 7th Division and then rejoined his platoon.

47th Brigade repulsed three counterattacks on the night of 3rd/4th September. During the couese of 4th September Jones drove back three heavy attacks. 47th Brigade was relieved by 16th Division by 9.25 a.m. on 5th September. When 12th King's was relieved at 5.20 a.m. on 5th September, Jones remained in position with two Lewis gun teams. For an unknown reason the relieving unit (9th Border) had not brought their own Lewis guns. Jones brought his party out at 9.30 a.m. next morning and rejoined the Battalion at the sand pit east of Méaulte. He was without food or water throughout.

Battle of Flers – Courcelette 15th–22nd September 1916

159 Lt Col John Campbell, 3rd Coldstream Guards (1st Guards Brigade, Guards Division) Ginchy, France

160 LSgt Fred McNess, 1st Scots Guards (2nd Guards Brigade, Guards Division) Ginchy, France

161 Sgt Donald Brown, 2nd Otago (2nd New Zealand Brigade, New Zealand Division) High Wood, France

162 Pte John Kerr, 49th Battalion (Edmonton) CEF (7th Canadian Brigade, 3rd Canadian Division) Courcelette, France

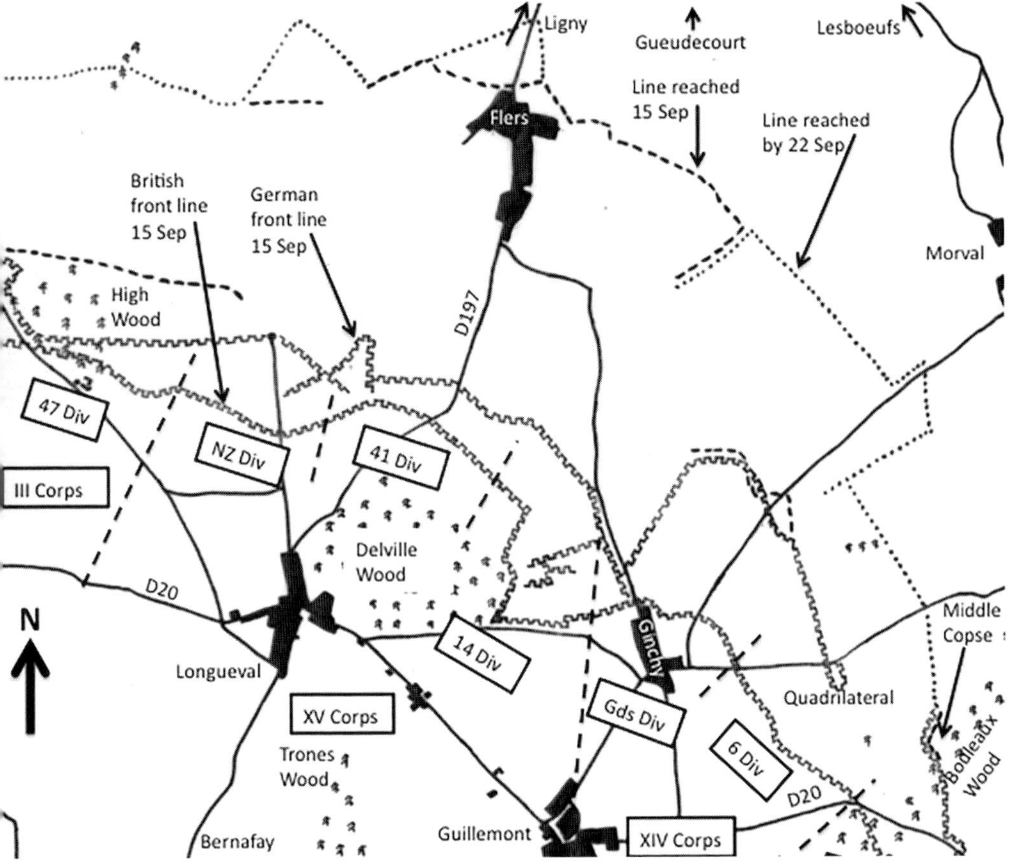

The Fourth Army area during the Battle of Flers - Courcelette, 15th-22nd September 1916.

In early September 1916 plans were made to reinvigorate the Somme offensive, including the first use of tanks. The Battle of Flers – Courcelette opened on 15th September on a frontage of fourteen kilometres, from Thiepval to Combles. Fourth Army delivered the main attack against the principal objectives of Flers, Morval, Lesboeufs and Gueudecourt in the German 3rd Position. Zero hour was at 6.20 a.m. and the fourth objective was expected to be reached by noon, leaving eight hours of daylight for exploitation. A series of colour-coded intermediate objectives were set:

First objective/Green Line – the Switch Line, covering Martinpuich and the forward slopes of the high ground northwest of Combles. This involved an advance of up to 900 metres. The infantry were scheduled to reach it at 6.26 a.m. behind the creeping barrage, which was moving at fifty metres per minute. At 6.40 a.m. the creeping barrage was to move ahead again.

Second objective/Brown Line – included the German 3rd Position in front of Flers and involved an advance of another 450–700 metres. The infantry and tanks were to assault at 7.20 a.m., following the creeping barrage, which would

> be moving at ninety metres every three minutes. At 7.45 a.m. the barrage was to lift again.
>
> Third objective/Blue Line – up to 1,100 metres beyond the second objective, consisted of the German 3rd Position covering Morval, Lesboeufs and Flers. The barrage was to lift at 8.05 a.m. to allow the tanks to destroy the wire, which could not be hit accurately by the artillery beforehand. The infantry were to assault at 8.20 a.m. A covering barrage, just beyond the Blue Line, was to lift at 10.35 a.m.
>
> Fourth objective/Red Line – up to 1,700 metres beyond the third objective, included Morval, Lesboeufs and Gueudecourt. The infantry were to assault it from 10.50 a.m. to 11.20 a.m. The operation was timed to be completed at 11.50 a.m.

The French were to cooperate on the right and the Reserve Army on the left. Subsequent operations would aim to bring the full force of the Reserve Army into action once Courcelette and Martinpuich had been secured.

Four Corps were involved, mainly in Fourth Army; from right to left these were – XIV, XV, III and Canadian (Reserve Army). Two cavalry divisions were poised to pass through the Morval – Gueudecourt gap and the intention was for the rest of Fourth Army to follow and roll up the German line northwards. The preliminary bombardment commenced at 6 a.m. on the 12th and went on continuously, including gas on battery positions and indirect machine-gun fire.

Since 1st July a number of changes had been made to tactics. These included the infantry thoroughly mopping-up, proper consolidation, use of machine-guns in direct and indirect support, Lewis guns covering the flanks and Stokes trench mortars as a close support weapon. Procedures were also changed. It was recognised that the passage of orders from Corps HQs down to company level took six hours in good conditions and time was required in addition to that for commanders at all levels to make their plans and carry out vital reconnaissance. Accordingly, the practice of issuing preliminary instructions ahead of detailed orders was adopted. More contact aircraft were provided to keep senior HQs informed of progress. Signal troops were to concentrate on establishing a single telegraph line from brigade back through division to corps HQs, supplemented by runners, cyclists, riders and motorcyclists in addition to pigeons and some wireless stations.

Fourth Army's artillery was reinforced with five 60 Pounder, one 6″ and two 9.2″ Howitzer batteries. This resulted in there being a field gun for every ten metres of front and a heavy gun for every twenty-five metres; double the concentration achieved on 1st July. The Canadian Corps in the Reserve Army allocated three heavy artillery groups (sixty-four guns and howitzers) and nine field artillery brigades to 2nd Canadian Division.

The first use of tanks demanded changes to the artillery programme, including leaving lanes ninety metres wide along which the tanks could progress in advance of the infantry to deal with strong points. They were intended to arrive at the Green Line five minutes ahead of the infantry. The tanks began leaving Thetford on 13th August and were established at Yvrench, fourteen kilometres northeast of Abbeville. Staff officers came to see them and some limited training was carried out, but not with the assaulting infantry, except for detachments from 56th Division (XIV Corps). Forty-nine tanks of C and D Companies were expected to be available and were distributed amongst the assaulting corps: sixteen to XIV Corps, eighteen to XV Corps, eight to III Corps and six to the Canadian Corps. Two nights before the attack the tanks moved up to positions a few kilometres behind the front.

The night before the attack the tanks moved forward again, the noise being covered by low flying aircraft. On arrival behind the lines the crews found stockpiles of fuel, water, rations and ammunition. They began moving forward again to be at their points of departure on the front line before dawn. Despite taped routes and bright moonlight, progress was slow in the mud and mist. A number were lost for mechanical reasons and others ditched, but all six allocated to the Canadian Corps made it. Despite rumours of armoured vehicles reaching the Germans and some kite balloon observers spotting 'armoured cars' behind the British front, the Germans in the front lines facing Fourth Army had no inkling of what they were facing. The assault battalions made their way to their start positions with little interference or fuss. On arrival they were fed and most men managed a few hours' sleep.

XIV Corps formed the right flank, with three divisions deployed in line. 56th Division was to secure the right flank in contact with the French and the more it advanced the more it would ease pressure on the other divisions. 6th Division in the centre faced the Quadrilateral, 800 metres north of Leuze Wood, before reaching its first objective. On the left was the Guards Division.

In 56th Division, 169th Brigade on the right advanced against Loop Trench. Initially it was successful, but increasing resistance from machine-guns slowed progress. Bombing attacks continued all day and by nightfall the brigade was still seventy metres short of the objective. 167th Brigade on the left was to clear Bouleaux Wood and establish a link with 6th Division on the left. 168th Brigade was due to pass through to secure the British right while Morval was taken by 6th Division. The advance was held up by uncut wire and accurate machine-gun fire, but on the left progress was made to Middle Copse.

6th Division faced the Quadrilateral which, despite close attention from the artillery, was still a considerable strongpoint. Only one of three tanks for the attack on the Quadrilateral reached the rendezvous east of Guillemont, where it opened fire by mistake on the waiting infantry. 16th Brigade's attack on the Quadrilateral failed in the face of withering machine-gun fire, as did 71st Brigade's on the left. At 8.20 a.m. another attempt was made, but the machine-guns in the Quadrilateral added to the casualty list for no gain.

The Guards Division attacked with 2nd Guards Brigade on the right and 1st Guards Brigade on the left, each with two battalions leading. Ten tanks were

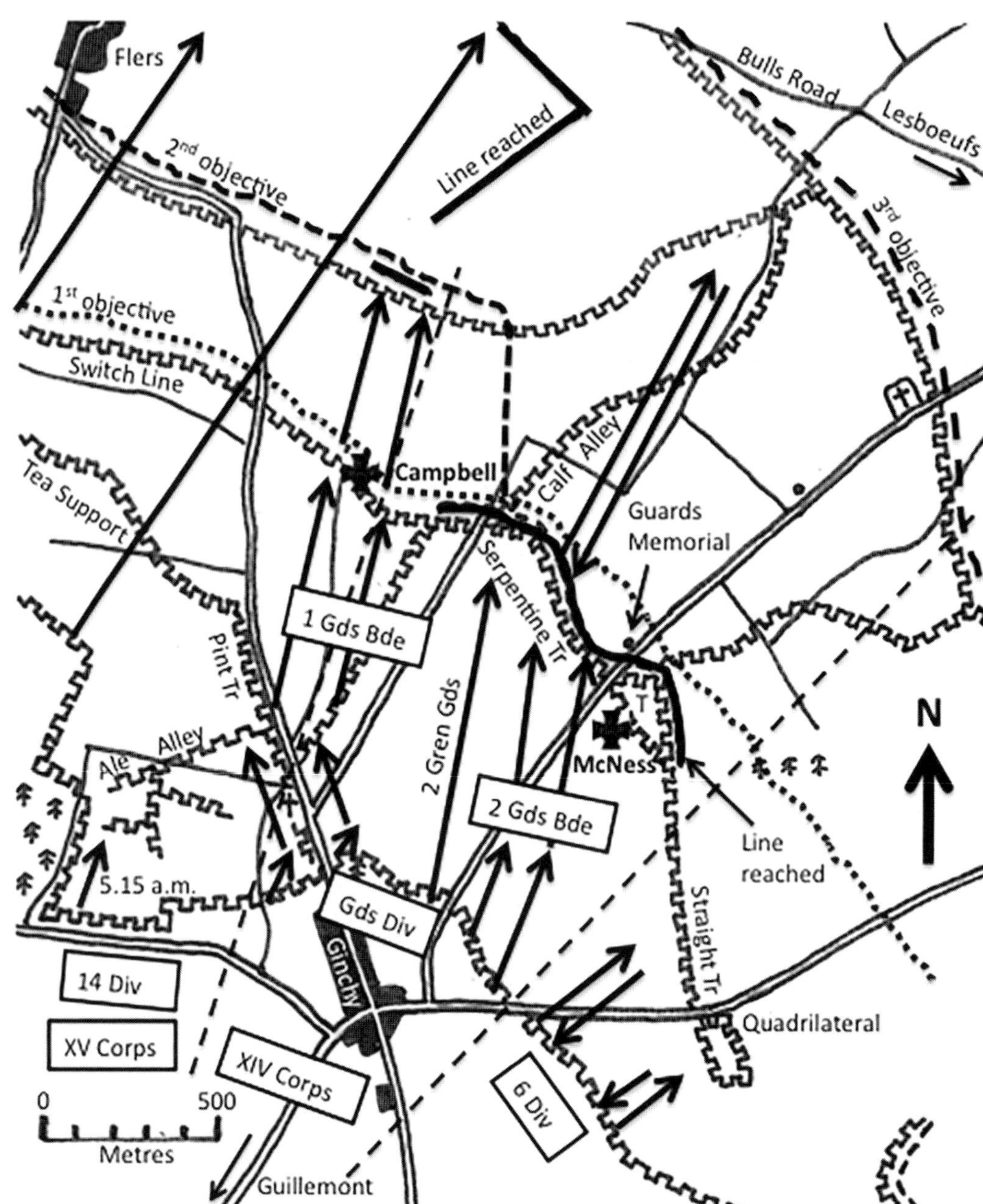

To visit the site of Fred McNess' VC action, leave Ginchy on the unclassified road eastwards towards Morval. After 150m turn left. The road bends round to the right and after 1,150m park at the Guards Memorial on the left. This was the limit of the advance on 15th September 1916. Look back towards Ginchy church. On the map T = Triangle. To visit the site of John Campbell's VC action, leave Ginchy northwards on the unclassified road towards Flers. As you leave the village, stop and look north towards the cemetery. This is where the attack diverted to deal with the machine-guns firing into the left flank. Continue to just before the cemetery and turn right. Continue for almost one kilometre northeastwards and stop when the hill flattens out. There is hard standing on the left on which to park. Look back towards Ginchy. 1st Guards Brigade advanced roughly parallel with and to the right of the track you just drove up. John Campbell led his men in securing the 1st objective about 300m east-northeast of this point, in line with the New Zealand Memorial, which is 2,500m away, with High Wood beyond.

allocated and artillery free lanes were designated to assist their passage towards the enemy lines. In the event all the tanks ditched, lost direction or broke down before reaching the German trenches and as a result enemy resistance was fiercest in these lanes.

2nd Guards Brigade was led by 3rd Grenadier Guards on the right and 1st Coldstream Guards on the left, supported by 1st Scots Guards and 2nd Irish Guards respectively. The brigade was scheduled to go all the way to the final objective. The first wave kept thirty metres behind the barrage but, as it crossed the ridge, came under very heavy fire from the Quadrilateral and Straight Trench in 6th Division's area on the right. The battalions pressed on despite drifting to the left, with the supporting battalions close behind.

The German position beyond the crest consisted of a line of shell holes, where most of the defenders were bayoneted or shot. Then, without waiting, the advance swept on into the north of the Triangle and part of Serpentine Trench, the three belts of wire in front having been well cut by the artillery. By 7.15 a.m., the first objective had been reached, although the battalions had been severely weakened. Bombers from all battalions engaged in fierce fighting to clear the Triangle, which was completed by noon to form a defensive right flank where 6th Division was unable to keep up. Soon after noon a mixed party of one hundred Scots, Irish and Grenadiers Guards pressed on for 800 metres to a point in front of the third objective. They were later forced back by a counterattack to the Green Line.

Soon afterwards the Germans counterattacked and bombed into the right flank of 2nd Guards Brigade. In 1st Scots Guards, **Lance Sergeant Frederick McNess** had led his men forward with great courage in the initial attack. He then personally led an attack against the enemy bombers. The fight went on for about one and a half hours and the Germans were gradually driven back. Despite being wounded, McNess continued to throw bombs and organised the establishment of a block. One of his men was shot through the lungs and fell behind McNess, who comforted him by supporting his head with his left hand while continuing to throw bombs with his right. The soldier died just as McNess was preparing to throw another bomb. A German grenade exploded on the parapet, seriously injuring McNess. His carotid artery, jugular vein and windpipe were exposed. Part of his lower and upper left jaws were blown away and the teeth exposed. His shoulder blade was badly out of place and his left arm was blown behind his neck, the force of the explosion peeling back the biceps muscle to the top of his shoulder. He could not lift his head off his shoulder and occasionally it slipped onto his back.

When he recovered from the initial shock, McNess staggered to the rear, but had not gone far when he met a bomb carrying party heading for his position. Knowing the bombs were needed urgently, he guided the party forward through a barrage of enemy grenades and repeated this journey four times. On the fifth occasion the carrying party was wiped out by a shell and McNess' jaw was broken in two places.

From the Guards Memorial looking southwest towards Ginchy and the area of the Triangle is to the left of the road, where Fred McNess was in action on 15th September.

Blinded by blood, he crawled and staggered back, falling over every four or five paces, but eventually reached an aid station. At one time he is reputed to have been treated by Captain Noel Chavasse VC.

On the left, 1st Guards Brigade was led by 2nd and 3rd Coldstream Guards (left and right respectively), with 1st Irish Guards in support and 2nd Grenadier Guards following. The troops formed up in a tangle of overlapping shell craters to get clear of the ruins of Ginchy. Space was limited and the waves were crammed in with little room to spare. The shape of the ground meant that none of the objectives could be seen from the British front line and the whole area was badly cut up with shell holes. On the left of the brigade, troops from 14th Division and a tank (referred to in one war diary as an armoured creeper) advanced at 5.15 a.m. to clear the German pocket on this flank. There was some opposition, but to the waiting Guardsmen it appeared to be successful.

When the main advance began at 6.20 a.m., 1st Guards Brigade came under heavy fire from the junction of Pint Trench with the sunken Flers – Ginchy road on the left. This was a known machine-gun position and had received extra attention from the heavy guns in the days before the attack. In addition a tank had been detailed to deal with it, but did not reach the objective. The leading battalions were checked with heavy casualties. **Lieutenant Colonel John Campbell**, CO 3rd Coldstream Guards, realised the enemy in the sunken road must be cleared before

Looking north from the outskirts of Ginchy towards the cemetery on the left of the road. Beyond the copse in the centre was Pint Trench, parallel with the road. This is the direction in which John Campbell diverted 1st Guards Brigade's advance to deal with the devastating fire received from its left flank.

progress could be made on the left flank. Blowing his hunting horn, Campbell led the third wave forward. The German position was rushed and four machine-guns and a few trench mortars were taken. Keen to get into the fight, 1st Irish Guards became mixed up with the leading battalions, as did 1st Coldstream Guards on the left of 2nd Guards Brigade.

Direction was lost, partly due to the featureless terrain and also because 2nd Guards Brigade on the right was pushed left into 1st Guards Brigade. As a result, the two leading battalions of 1 Guards Brigade strayed to the north into 14th Division's (XV Corps) area and stormed into the first objective about the same time as 2 Guards Brigade, having taken three lines of trenches, two of which were unexpected. As a result of the change in direction, the Germans holding Serpentine Trench around the junction with Calf Alley were not engaged by either Guards brigade. However, about 7.30 a.m. 2nd Grenadier Guards emerged from Ginchy astride the Lesboeufs road under heavy fire from Serpentine Trench. The Battalion charged, gained a foothold in the trench and after a hard fight by bombing parties, captured it, thus filling the gap between the two brigades. This completed the taking of the Guards Division's first objective.

At about 7.15 a.m. three of the battalion COs of 1st Guards Brigade (CO 1st Coldstream Guards had been killed) held a hurried conference. They assumed they had reached the third objective (Blue Line), but were in fact only on the first objective (Green Line). The troops were being reorganised when Campbell realised the mistake and got the advance started again. Spurred on by Campbell's hunting horn, 2nd and 3rd Coldstream Guards and some men from 1st Irish Guards set off through a very heavy enemy bombardment. Campbell led his men through a small opening in the wire and was one of the first to enter the enemy trench. Fighting their way forward in a mad but irresistible rush, they captured part of the second objective (Brown Line) by 11.15 a.m., although it was outside the divisional boundary. This position was again mistaken for the third objective and reports were sent back accordingly. Sergeant Oliver Brooks, who had been awarded the VC for his gallantry on 8th October 1915, was serving with 3rd Coldstream Guards and was wounded in this action.

From the junction of Calf Alley with Serpentine Trench, the limit of the Guards advance on 15th September 1916, looking west. 1st Guards Brigade's direction of assault is shown.

Contact aircraft patrols confirmed to HQ XIV Corps that no troops had got that far. The ground gained was consolidated, but the assault brigades were severely under-strength and reinforcements were required. Two battalions of 3rd Guards Brigade were allocated, one each to 1st and 2nd Guards Brigades and a brigade of 20th Division was behind at the division's disposal. By then both flanks of the Guards Division were unsupported, as 6th Division on the right and 14th Division on the left had been held up. A company of 4th Grenadier Guards assisted in securing the right flank and 2nd Scots Guards joined Campbell's depleted force on the Brown Line.

XV Corps attacked with three divisions, from right to left: 14th, 41st and New Zealand. Most of the tanks allocated were to deal with Flers and strongpoints around it. In 14th Division, 41st Brigade was to lead to the second objective from where 42nd Brigade would pass through to the fourth objective. Heavy casualties were sustained from machine-guns in Pint Trench, but the troops pressed on to take it and Tea Support. The first objective (Switch Line) was taken by 7 a.m., but there was no contact with 41st Division on the left, so a defensive flank was formed. At 9 a.m., half an hour behind schedule, 42nd Brigade passed through on the way to the third and fourth objectives. It was ahead of both flanking formations and exposed to enfilade fire, particularly from the right as the Brigade approached Bulls Road.

41st Division, in the centre of XV Corps, was to capture Flers and the majority of the tanks were allocated to it. 124th Brigade on the right and 122nd Brigade on the left were to go through to the fourth objective. There was a preliminary operation at 5.15 a.m. to clear a German pocket east of Delville Wood centred on Hop Alley and Ale Alley. These troops came under machine-gun fire from their right rear, which had to be dealt with before the main advance could begin. One tank assisted, until its steering was knocked out.

There was little initial resistance to 124th Brigade though in places casualties were suffered by catching up with the creeping barrage. The first objective (Switch Line) was taken at 7 a.m. and twenty minutes later the attack continued towards the second objective (Flers Trench), which fell at 7.50 a.m. 122nd Brigade had

seized the first objective in twenty minutes and Flers Trench was reached with little opposition. There were only four tanks left as the advance continued to Flers and the third objective beyond the village. Just before 8.20 a.m. tank D16 led the infantry up the main street, firing as it went. Three other tanks (D6, D9 and D17) moved around the east of the village, smashing strongpoints and houses to break resistance. The village was secured by 10 a.m., but there were few officers left and the troops were inclined to seek cover from the shelling. However, some small groups did press on and reached the third objective on the northern edge of the village.

The New Zealand Division, on the right of XV Corps, had to advance over the crest east of High Wood. The final objective was a continuation of the defensive left flank formed by 41st Division. As a result, the latter part of the advance involved wheeling northwest and pivoting on the left. 2nd New Zealand Brigade led up to the Switch Line with 2nd Auckland Battalion (right) and 2nd Otago Battalion (left), supported by 2nd Canterbury Battalion and 2nd Wellington Battalion in reserve. 3rd New Zealand (Rifle) Brigade was to pass through, with 4th Rifles taking the second objective and 2nd and 3rd Rifles the third. Finally, 1st Rifles would establish the defensive flank. None of the four tanks managed to get forward before the infantry advanced. 1st New Zealand Brigade was in reserve.

2nd Otago Battalion set off thirty seconds early in their keenness and also because 1/7th London in 47th Division on the left had also set off early. Some men fell to the British barrage and then to machine-guns in High Wood, but there was no wavering. Occasionally they sheltered in shell holes to allow the barrage to move ahead and during these pauses they engaged the machine-guns in Crest Trench, which was found to be more strongly held than expected. As the attack closed, 200 Germans ran back towards the Switch Line and many were shot down by Lewis gun teams. However, one machine-gun proved more troublesome. In 10th (North Otago) Company, **Sergeant Donald Brown** and 9/77 Corporal Jesse Rodgers crawled towards it at considerable risk to their lives. When they were less than thirty metres away, they rushed in, killed the crew and captured the gun, thus completing the taking of Crest Trench.

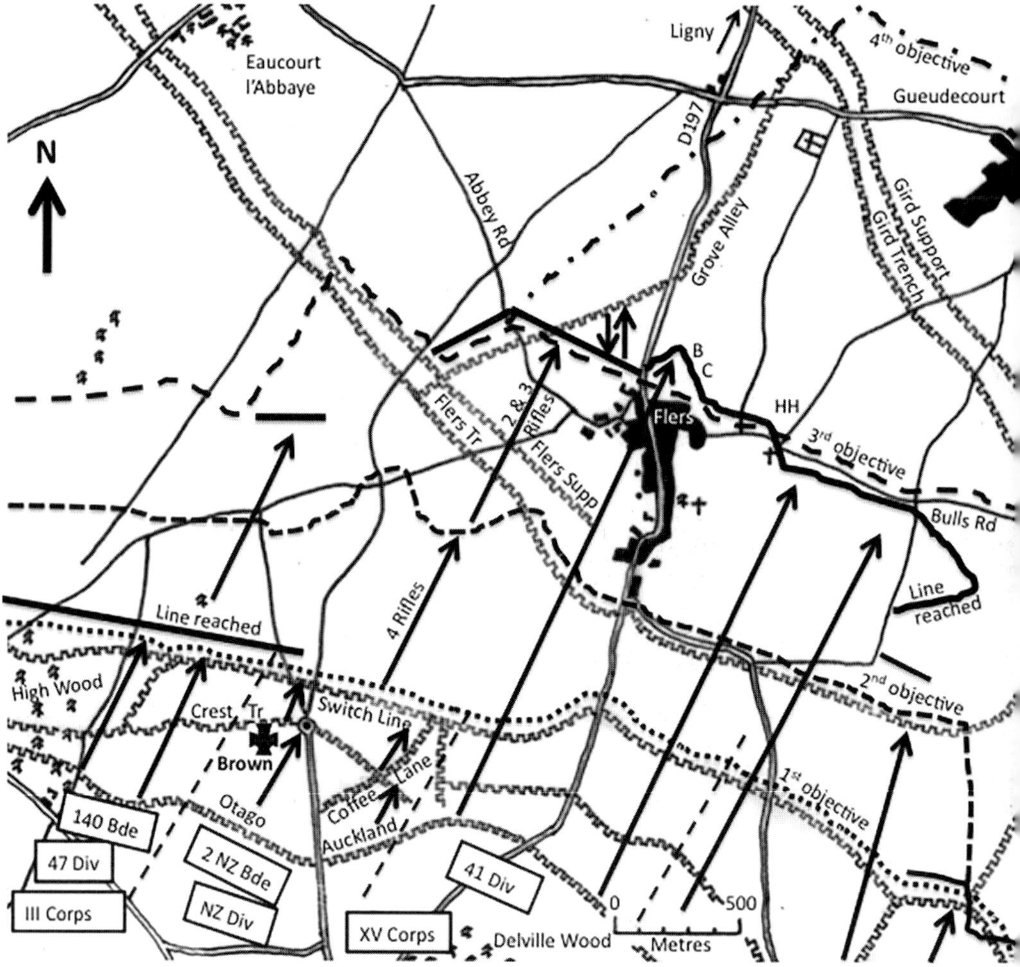

Drive north out of Longueval on the D197 towards Flers. As you leave the village turn left, signed for the New Zealand Forces Memorial, which is 1,200m to the north. Park at the Memorial, which has a track all round it to facilitate turning. Crest Trench, seized by 2nd Otago, ran along the crest line from the Memorial to High Wood to the west. Donald Brown's VC action was about 200m along this line west of the Memorial. A few abbreviations are used on the map - B = Box, C = Cox and HH = Hog's Head.

From where Donald Brown knocked out the German machine-gun post in Crest Trench, looking southeast.

The New Zealand Forces Memorial, close to where Donald Brown won his VC.

2nd Auckland Battalion kept up on the right, having also captured an outpost line, Coffee Lane, in front of Crest Trench. Once resistance had been dealt with in Crest Trench, the rear waves were left to mop up while 2nd Otago and 2nd Auckland Battalions chased the fleeing enemy down the slope towards the Switch Line. Just before it, 2nd Auckland Battalion overstepped the barrage and suffered casualties. On the left, 47th Division had been delayed in High Wood and a gap opened beyond 2nd Otago Battalion's left flank. It was raked by enfilade machine-gun and rifle fire from the corner of High Wood and the battalion suffered casualties. Despite this, the brigade's first objective was taken by 6.50 a.m. and a new trench was dug fifty metres in front of the Switch Line under heavy shellfire. In the final assault, Sergeant Brown and his comrade rushed another machine-gun and killed the crew. By then 10th (North Otago) Company had lost all its officers and Sergeant Brown, with Jesse Rodgers and Corporal R Douglas, assumed command. Having captured the trench, they consolidated the position and held it against counterattacks. Jesse Rogers received the MM for his part in this action and was later commissioned and received the MC. He died of wounds on 30th July 1917 and is buried in Trois Arbres Cemetery, Steenwerck, France (IV 22).

A soldier involved in this attack wrote:

...our platoon went over in the second wave, and I could see the Germans' heads above the trench firing at us when we got about half way across. Even when we joined the first wave I could see that our ranks were pretty thin. We lay down and watched for the third and fourth wave to join us before rushing them. The four waves combined made up about as many as one of the original waves. While we were lying down waiting for the rush, Fritz was rattling away with his machine-gun for all he was worth, and for a few seconds he ripped up the ground about a yard in front of me. It gave me a bit of a fright, and I wasted no time in wriggling back a few yards. I also yelled out to the man on my left to get back, but when I looked at his face I saw that he was dead. When we stood up and started to run, their fire slackened off a lot, and soon stopped altogether. Half of them put their hands up and ran towards us; some of them took to their heels, and a few of the fools kept firing at us. We all wanted to get at them with the bayonet, but some of us were faster than others, and those behind were so anxious to do something that they started firing at the Huns, at the risk of hitting their own men in front. I jumped into the Hun trench and found that it was so deep that I could not climb out at the other side, so I pulled a dead Hun into a sitting position at the side of the trench, stood on his shoulders, and managed to climb out... I was chasing one fellow and almost had him, but I soon found I was not too safe, as the fellows behind were firing, so I lay down, took steady aim, and shot him. Another poor beggar came stumbling towards me with a shower of bullets flying all round him. I knew that if I let him come too near me I would stand a good chance of getting hit by one of our own bullets, as he was drawing a lot of fire, so I gave him a bullet in the chest when he was about 15 yards from me....

A large calibre shell recently ploughed up awaiting collection, with the New Zealand Forces Memorial in the distance.

A company of 2nd Canterbury Battalion came up to help construct strongpoints and secure the left flank from attack from High Wood. During the night it connected the line with 140th Brigade (47th Division) on the left. Four Vickers machine-guns were positioned along the front of 2nd Otago Battalion. The operation cost 2nd Auckland Battalion 309 casualties. 2nd Otago Battalion lost fifteen officers and 445 men out of twenty officers and 816 men who went into action. At midnight it was relieved by 2nd Canterbury Battalion and pulled back to Savoy and Carlton Trenches, where it rested until 3.30 p.m. on 16th September. Having gathered some missing and slightly wounded, the battalion moved up to Worcester, Black Watch and Seaforth Trenches with seventeen officers and 466 men.

Meanwhile, 4th Rifles (3rd New Zealand (Rifle) Brigade) advanced on time at 7.20 a.m. and captured the second objective at 7.50 a.m. 2nd and 3rd Rifles followed close behind and set off at 8.20 a.m. for the third objective. 2nd Rifles collected eighty-five prisoners and took Flers Trench and Support. Thereafter machine-gun fire from the northwest of the village made progress costly. There was heavy fighting for Abbey Road but by 11 a.m. 2nd Rifles was on the third objective. 3rd Rifles on the left was held up by uncut wire in front of Flers Trench. About 10.30 a.m. tanks D11 and D12 crushed the wire, knocked out the machine-guns and assisted in the capture of one hundred prisoners. 3rd Rifles was then able to reach the third objective. There was no contact on the left with 47th Division and a defensive flank was formed. 1st Rifles had become involved in the fighting for Abbey Road and needed to reorganise before advancing at 11.30 a.m.

At 10.50 a.m. the Corps barrage lifted off the Gird Trenches in front of Gueudecourt, but 14th and 41st Divisions were in no state to follow up, despite the trenches appearing to be lightly manned and with little wire in front. Reinforcements were needed and 43rd Brigade began moving forward from reserve, but its leading elements were six kilometres back. Many field batteries were moving forward and could not support a renewed attack.

In 41st Division, 124th Brigade made little progress beyond Flers Trench. The situation on the left in Flers was unclear and it took the brigade commander's personal intervention to get the men moving again at 3.20 p.m. Bulls Road was reached and contact established with 122nd Brigade on the left. Attempts to press on to the Gird Trenches met with heavy machine-gun fire. 122nd Brigade reached the third objective by 3 p.m. Advanced posts were set up in Box, Cox and Hog's Head practice trenches. One tank reached Gueudecourt and knocked out a German gun before being hit and bursting into flames.

In the New Zealand Division, two companies of 1st Rifles attacked Grove Alley at 11.30 a.m. to establish a defensive flank. The exposed right flank suffered particularly heavily as it swung left. A footing was obtained in Grove Alley, but it was untenable, with hundreds of Germans advancing towards the unguarded right flank from the direction of Ligny. They withdrew back to the third objective after 2.00 p.m. and began to consolidate this line. The right flank was drawn back to protect Flers and connect with 41st Division, which had not advanced as far. 2nd Wellington Battalion (2nd New Zealand Brigade) was ordered up in support of 3rd New Zealand (Rifle) Brigade.

On the left, III Corps had a limited but important role: to protect Fourth Army's left flank. In this area the second and third objectives were in dead ground. 47th Division on the right secured the first objective, including High Wood, at some considerable cost. Only one of four tanks made any impression but it was hit by a shell and set on fire.

In the centre, 50th Division's start positions were forward of its flanking formations. 149th Brigade on the right took Hook Trench, but when the advance continued to the second objective resistance stiffened and the attackers came under enfilade fire from High Wood. Bombing parties fought towards the Wood to assist 47th Division and confused fighting followed with heavy losses. Later in the morning small parties reached the Starfish Line. Two tanks on the boundary with 150th Brigade were of great assistance. 150th Brigade reached the first objective without difficulty. By 10 a.m. seizure of the third objective was being reported, but it was not held strongly.

15th Division on the left of III Corps had two tanks to assist in taking the southwest of Martinpuich. There was only one objective on this flank. 45th Brigade on the right found the artillery had done its work well and most surviving Germans were happy to surrender. There was some resistance in Tangle Trench and the sunken Longueval – Martinpuich road. 46th Brigade on the left reached the first objective, Factory Lane, by 7 a.m., in contact with the Canadians on the left. When the artillery lifted at 9.20 a.m., both brigades sent forward strong patrols into the village.

Because of the check at High Wood, HQ III Corps decided to consolidate on the Starfish Line at 10.30 a.m. At 11.40 a.m., a hurricane bombardment of 750 Stokes mortar rounds into High Wood caused the defenders to begin surrendering as bombing parties of 47th Division worked their way forward. Several hundred prisoners were taken as well as machine-guns and two 10.5 cms howitzers. The survivors of 141st Brigade formed a composite battalion on the first objective. High Wood had finally fallen; the first attack was made on 14th July. It was 1 p.m., the Starfish Line was still 630 metres ahead and German artillery fire was falling heavily. At 3.30 p.m. two battalions of 142nd Brigade in reserve were ordered to continue the advance. There was no time for reconnaissance and at about 5.30 p.m. they set off from High Wood, but were halted in front of the Starfish Line by heavy machine-gun and shellfire. Many survivors hung on in shell holes overnight, but the second objective remained elusive, except on the right, where 1/6th London had reached the Cough Drop and were in contact with the New Zealanders on the right.

By 3.30 p.m. most of 149th Brigade (50th Division) had fallen back to Hook Trench (first objective) except for a party of about a hundred in the sunken road south of the Bow. On the left, at 1.50 p.m., 150th Brigade was ordered to push patrols into the north of Martinpuich and make contact with 15th Division on the left. The forward troops had been shelled out of Starfish Line and had fallen back on Martin Trench. At 5.45 p.m. the GOC of 50th Division ordered 151st Brigade in reserve to pass through and attack Prue Trench at 7.30 p.m.

Meanwhile, at 3 p.m., 15th Division had forced the Germans out of the northeast of Martinpuich. The northwest face of the village was occupied, facing Courcelette, in contact with the Canadians in Gunpit Trench. Contact was also made with 50th Division about the junction of Starfish Line with Martin Alley. 151st Brigade attacked towards Prue Trench at 9.40 p.m. under very heavy fire. Small parties reached Prue Trench, but were killed or wounded there. Others who reached the Starfish Line were driven out again.

Soon after 3 p.m. General Rawlinson, commanding Fourth Army, called off further attacks. At 3.45 p.m. divisions were ordered as far as possible to link up along the third objective, consolidate and relieve some of the forward troops. Some counterattacks were repulsed and some heavy German shelling had to be endured.

The Reserve Army was to protect the left flank. The Canadian Corps on the right was to secure points of observation over the 3rd Position about Courcelette, while on the left II Corps exerted pressure south of Thiepval. The attack by the

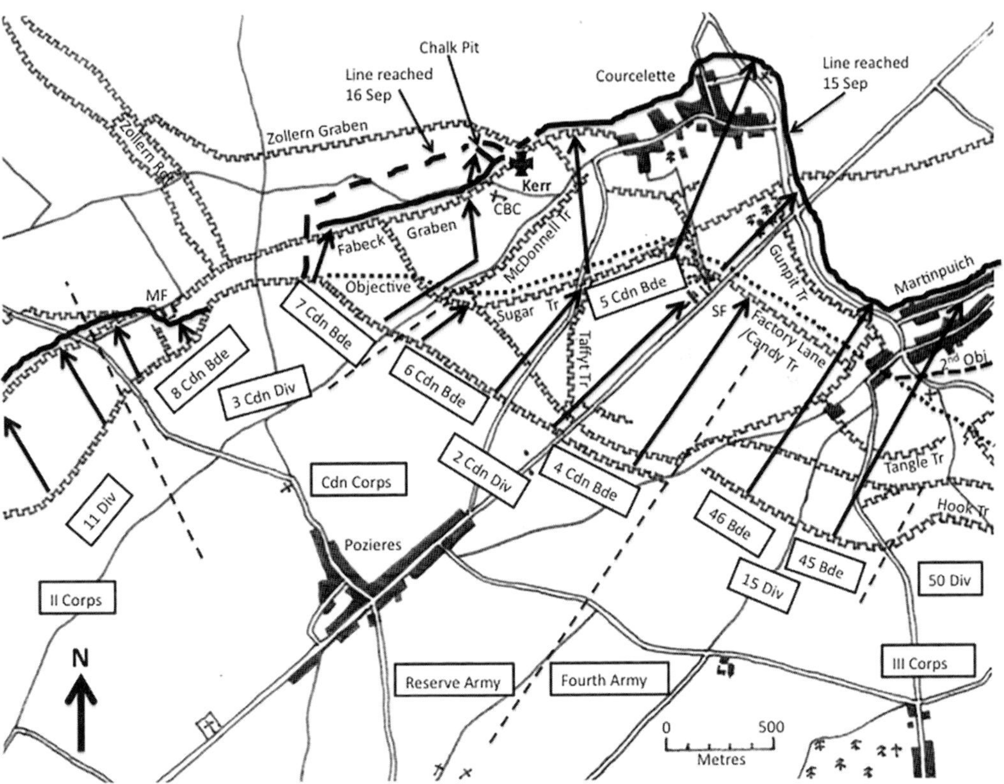

Drive northeast through Pozières on the D929 towards Bapaume. Almost at the limit of the village turn left onto an unclassified road signed for Courcelette. It is easy to miss, so approach slowly. Just under two kilometres later the road swings sharply right. Take the left turn here, signed for Courcelette British Cemetery. Take care making this turn, as oncoming traffic from Courcelette is prone not to waste any time rounding this corner. Follow the track for 500m and park at the cemetery. Continue along the track on foot for 100m, which is where Fabeck Graben crossed it. John Kerr's VC action was 175m to the northeast of this point. A few abbreviations are used on the map – CBC = Courcelette British Cemetery, MF = Mouquet Farm and SF = sugar factory.

Canadian Corps was made by 2nd Canadian Division on a frontage of 1,600 metres. On the right this involved an advance of 900 metres towards Courcelette, reducing to 360 metres on the left, where the flank was covered by 8th Canadian Brigade (3rd Canadian Division). There was only one objective initially, a continuation of Fourth Army's Green Line.

In 2nd Canadian Division, 4th Canadian Brigade on the right was led by 18th, 20th and 21st Battalions. 6th Canadian Brigade on the left was led by 27th and 28th Battalions, with 31st Battalion in support. Three tanks were to advance astride the Bapaume road as far as the sugar factory, which one tank was to attack while the others turned right along Factory Lane (known as Candy Trench to the Canadians). Over on the left flank, three more tanks were to head for Sugar Trench and follow it to the factory. Five infantrymen were allocated to each tank, to walk ahead and remove casualties from its path.

The Germans pre-empted the advance in 4th Canadian Brigade's area. German bombers advanced at 3.10 and 4.30 a.m. and it took prompt and energetic action to ensure the situation was restored in time for zero hour at 6.20 a.m. As soon as the advance commenced there was considerable resistance, but the Canadians moved quickly, covered by the creeping barrage and their own machine-guns. The German front line was overrun and by 7 a.m. 4th Canadian Brigade had reached Factory Lane, where any enemy refusing to surrender were dealt with quickly. 21st Battalion, assisted by 20th Battalion, cleared the sugar factory; 21st Battalion took 145 prisoners. 6 Canadian Brigade's advance was not quite so rapid, but it reached its objective just after 7.30 a.m. All battalions had suffered considerable losses, but consolidation proceeded and patrols were pushed forward. The tanks encouraged many Germans to surrender; but overall they failed to carry out their tasks. One inflicted great physical and moral damage and also laid a very useful telephone wire from the forward positions to the rear, but all six were out of action by the end of the attack. Only one reached its objective.

On the Canadian Corps' left, 3rd Canadian Division secured its portion of the objective to protect the main attack. On the far left, II Corps advanced 350 metre closer to Thiepval. HQ 2nd Canadian Division ordered posts to be pushed forward when the barrage lifted at 9.20 a.m. South of the Bapaume road this meant reinforcing posts established in the initial advance and contact was established with 15th Division on the right. North of the road it proved more difficult to make progress against Courcelette, though in the afternoon German counterattacks were forced back by heavy machine-gun and artillery fire.

At 11.10 a.m. HQ Canadian Corps issued orders for an attack at 6.00 p.m. on Fabeck Graben by 3rd Canadian Division (7th Canadian Brigade) and Courcelette by 2nd Canadian Division (5th Canadian Brigade, in Corps reserve). The boundary between the two assault brigades was Taffy Trench. There was some time for reconnaissance in the afternoon as the assault battalions made their way through Pozières under heavy shellfire. At 6.15 p.m., the barrage lifted and in 5th Canadian

Brigade 22nd and 25th Battalions advanced without difficulty through Courcelette. 26th Battalion followed and began the methodical clearance of dugouts, but this part of the operation took two days.

7th Canadian Brigade's start line was Sugar Trench. There was heavy machine-gun fire from the right, but Princess Patricia's Canadian Light Infantry on the right, despite initially losing direction over the broken ground, reached McDonnell Trench and went on to secure the east of Fabeck Graben. However, there was a gap of 180 metres at the junction with Zollern Graben before 5th Canadian Brigade's positions. On the left, 42nd Battalion (7th Canadian Brigade) secured its part of Fabeck Graben without difficulty. Before dark, in spite of heavy artillery and enfilade machine-gun fire from Mouquet Farm, 4th Canadian Mounted Rifles (8th Canadian Brigade) captured a further length of Fabeck Graben to the west and established blocks to secure the left flank.

By 8.15 p.m., 49th Battalion was advancing through the smoke and gathering darkness to pass through 7th Canadian Brigade to occupy a forward line within assaulting distance of Zollern Graben. It failed to achieve this, due to difficult ground and heavy machine-gun fire, but two companies seized the chalk pit forward of Fabeck Graben and a communication trench was dug to connect it. The positions held were consolidated for the night.

The Germans counterattacked repeatedly at Courcelette. 22nd and 25th Battalions were attacked fourteen times, seven during the first night against 22nd Battalion alone. The CO, Lieutenant Colonel TL Tremblay, wrote, *If hell is as bad as what I have seen at Courcelette, I would not wish my worst enemy to go there.* Up to 18th September, 22nd Battalion suffered 207 casualties, 25th Battalion another 222 and 26th Battalion 224 more. However, German losses were also heavy, including over 1,000 prisoners.

Overall, the results on 15th September fell short of expectations. The French had made no progress and, although the British had taken four kilometres of the German 3rd Position and captured High Wood, Flers, Martinpuich and Courcelette, they could not break through until the 3rd Position, covering Morval, Lesboeufs and Guedecourt, had been taken. Orders for 16th September were to press on and give the Germans no time to recover. The first priority was to complete the seizure of the third objective. The boundary between Fourth and Reserve Armies was shifted slightly west to rest on the Bapaume road. Throughout the night preparations were made and the artillery continued to batter the German defences. Some rain fell overnight, making the ground more difficult to negotiate. The 16th dawned fine but cloudy.

In XIV Corps, the Guards Division took the third objective relatively easily and many prisoners were taken with the assistance of 61st Brigade on the right, attached from 20th Division. 3rd Guards Brigade on the left had a harder time. Reorganisation during the previous night was more difficult than anticipated and it was not until 1.30 p.m. that the attack was made, without artillery support and in the face of heavy machine-gun fire. The survivors dug in 220 metres from the objective and that night, in pouring rain, the Guards Division was relieved by 20th Division. 1st Guards Brigade alone had suffered 1,776 casualties.

XV Corps attacked all along its front at 9.25 a.m. 14th Division attacked twice, but had little to show for it at the end of the day. 41st Division was unsure of the location of the forward troops and 64th Brigade set off from the southeast of Flers, almost 1,200 metres behind the barrage. It was hit by shrapnel and machine-gun fire from the outset. The troops pressed on to a few hundred metres from Gird Trench, where the attack petered out. The survivors rallied in Bulls Road. The New Zealand Division brought up 1st New Zealand Brigade under heavy shellfire. 1st Wellington Battalion pushed back a German attempt to advance down the Ligny road at 9 a.m. and then attacked to secure Grove Alley. Because of the failure of 64th Brigade on the right, further operations were suspended and the New Zealand Division's right was secured by 1st Canterbury Battalion and a trench was dug back to Box and Cox.

III Corps achieved a few minor gains, some of which were subsequently lost. In the Reserve Army, efforts continued to improve the position with a mind to the forthcoming operations to seize Thiepval. More would have been attempted had it not been for the adverse weather and Fourth Army being forced to postpone its operations.

Before daylight on 16th September, 1st Canadian Mounted Rifles (8th Canadian Brigade) established a line of posts from the Canadian Corps left boundary along the Courcelette road as far as Mouquet Farm. At 5 p.m., 3rd Canadian Division was ordered to seize Zollern Graben and Redoubt. Zollern Redoubt, on the crest of the ridge, was one of the main strongpoints in the German 2nd Position. From it the Germans dominated adjoining trenches with devastating enfilade machine-gun fire.

The Royal Canadian Regiment and 42nd Battalion in 7th Canadian Brigade attacked north from Fabeck Graben, in order to secure a line from where 9th Canadian Brigade could attack the Redoubt from the east. The barrage fell beyond the objective and the battalions were checked by machine-guns. 9th Canadian Brigade, rushed forward to follow on but had to be held back.

Meanwhile 49th Battalion and Princess Patricia's Canadian Light Infantry in 7th Canadian Brigade bombed inwards and closed the gap in Fabeck Graben around the

Looking along the line of Fabeck Graben in the direction in which John Kerr made his attack.

junction with Zollern Graben, taking sixty prisoners. Towards the end of this action **Private John Kerr**, of 49th Battalion, although wounded, ran alone along the top of the trench firing down into it. He shot several Germans at point blank range to bring the action to a rapid conclusion.

Later in the day, 2nd Canadian Mounted Rifles bombed some of the dugouts at Mouquet Farm and appeared to have secured it. However, that night 11th Division (II Corps) began to relieve the Canadians and realised that the garrison had merely taken refuge in tunnels. 34th Brigade finally secured the position on 26th September. Over the next few days 1st Canadian Division took over the area and continued pushing forward wherever possible. The Canadians acquitted themselves well in their first major Somme operation, but the cost had been heavy. In a week the Canadian Corps suffered 7,230 casualties.

Major operations were suspended until 21st September in order to synchronise the next advance with the French. In the meantime small operations went ahead to straighten and improve the line. Ammunition for the 18 Pounders was running low and the weather was increasingly wet, turning the ground into thick mud and limiting wheeled movement. The French also had problems bringing forward artillery ammunition and on 21st September it was decided to postpone the attack until 25th September.

2nd Otago Battalion took part in the Battle of Le Transloy on 1st October, during which an attack was made on a strongpoint near Eaucourt l'Abbaye. Sergeant Donald Brown was again involved in seizing an enemy machine-gun post that was holding up the advance. Moving forward on his own, armed only with a pistol, he attacked the post, killed the crew and captured the gun. This allowed the strongpoint to be captured, but Brown was shot in the head and killed.

Chapter Five

Morval and Thiepval Ridge

Battle of Morval – 25th–28th September

163 Pte Thomas Jones, 1st Cheshire (15th Brigade, 5th Division)

The Battle of Morval was fought to capture the objectives not taken during the Battle of Flers – Courcelette earlier in the month. In Fourth Army, XIV Corps on the right was assigned the capture of Morval and Lesboeufs. XV Corps in the centre was to take Gueudecourt, while III Corps on the left made some small advances. For XIV and XV Corps this involved an advance of 1,100 – 1,350 metres. To the west the Reserve Army also cooperated. The preparatory bombardment, which commenced at 7 a.m. on 24th September, caused great damage to the enemy, despite observation often being hampered by mist. The RFC conducted an aggressive air offensive on enemy battery positions and in the German rear areas. Jumping off trenches were dug in most places. Zero hour was set for 12.35 p.m. next day and the final objective was scheduled to be taken before 3 p.m.

25th September was fine and sunny with some haze. The assembly trenches were largely unaffected by enemy artillery fire. At 12.35 p.m. the creeping barrage crashed down ahead of the infantry and they advanced to the attack. In general, they advanced steadily and with few delays to their objectives. Most of the defenders were hit before they could organise themselves or fled. The German barrage fell too late and as a result British casualties were light.

On the right of XIV Corps, 56th Division formed a flank guard against Combles, while the other divisions (from right to left: 5th, 6th and Guards) attacked in line. 6th Division was already on the first objective.

56th Division only attacked with 168th Brigade. The northern end of Bouleaux Wood was cleared, but then the advance came under heavy fire from the railway embankment. On the right of 5th Division, the right battalion of 95th Brigade (1st East Surrey) was also held up by fire from the railway embankment but seized part of it. On the left of 95th Brigade, 1st Devonshire swung left to avoid uncut wire and worked down a trench from the north. On the left of 5th Division, the leading battalion of 15th Brigade (1st Norfolk) rushed the first objective in one bound, killing many of the enemy and taking a hundred prisoners. On the Battalion's left

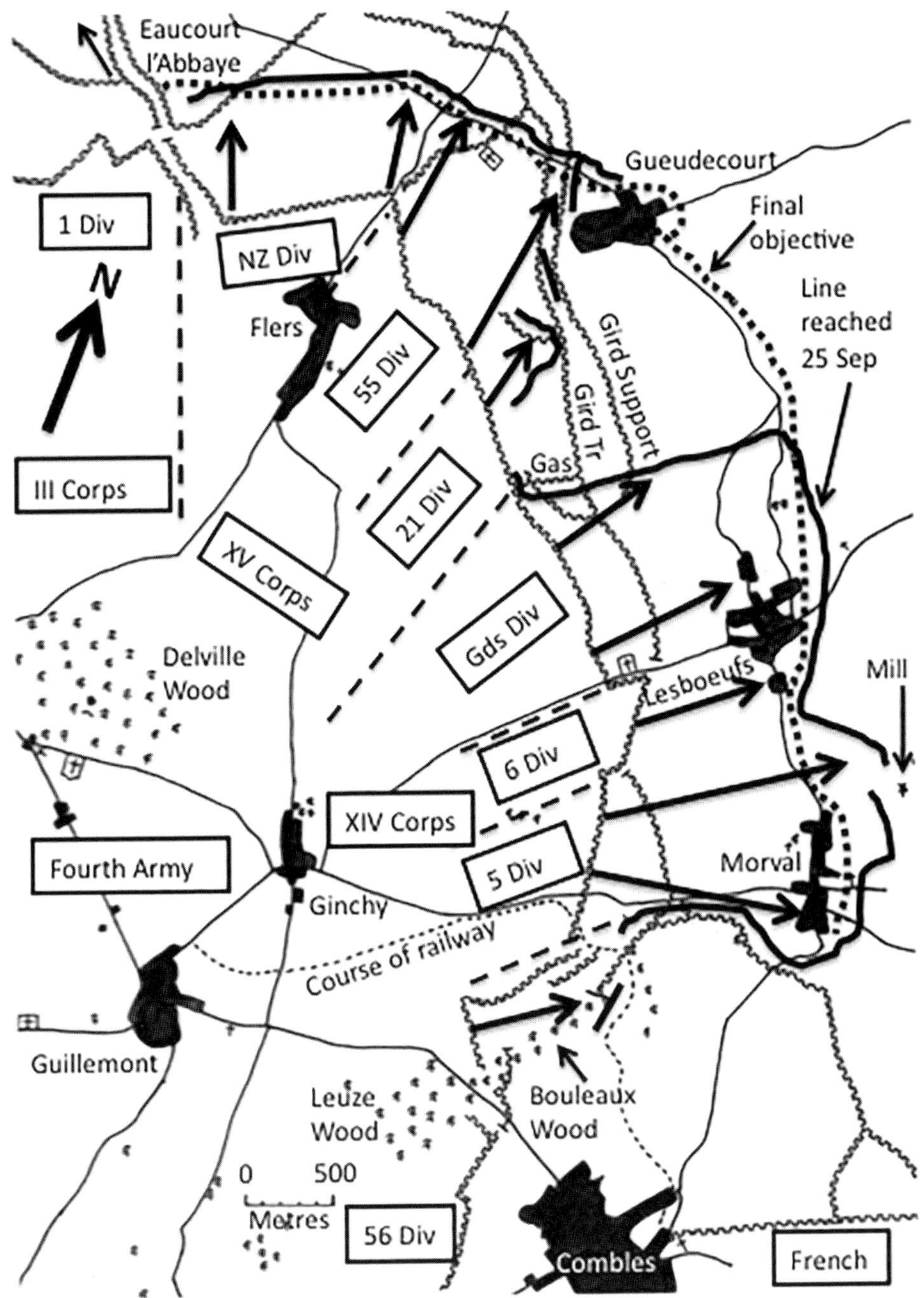

The Battle of Morval 25th–28th September.

excellent assistance was given by 6th Division with Stokes trench mortars and bombers.

While 6th Division stood fast and gave fire support to both flanks, to the north the right of the Guards Division encountered uncut wire and heavy fire. Casualties

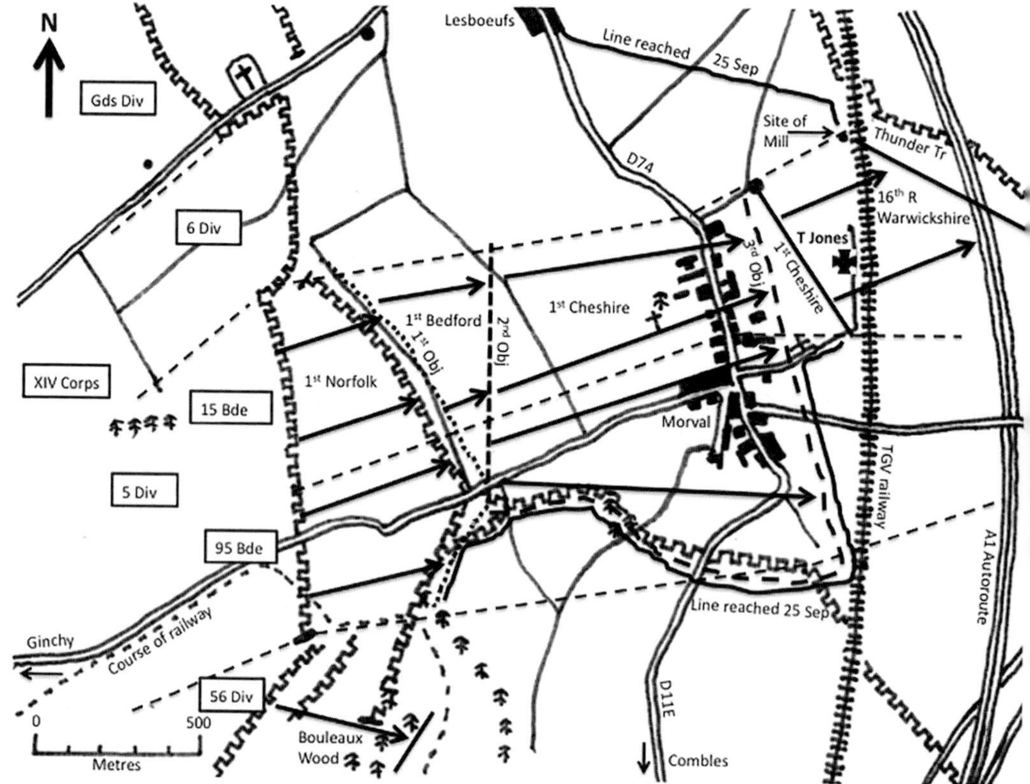

The attack in XIV Corps' area on 25th September. Enter Morval from the north on the D74 from Lesboeufs. Pass a Calvary on the left, where the road bends right into the village. 550m south turn left and park at the cemetery on the left after 175m. Walk in the same direction to the fence along the TGV railway line. The track swings left. Follow it for 150m. This is where Todger Jones captured the Germans.

were heavy, but the guardsmen cut the wire by hand and rushed the objective. The left came under fire from an unexpected trench in front of Gird Trench, which was rushed and many of the enemy were bayoneted. Except for the junction of Gas Alley with Gird Trench, the first objective was taken almost to time.

By 1.30 p.m., the first objective had been taken just about all along XIV Corps' front. However, there was no sign of the French on the right flank, who were scheduled to join up east of Morval. At 1.35 p.m. all three assault divisions continued their advance as planned. 5th Division's right had by this time taken the second objective and held where it was. On the left, in 15th Brigade, 1st Bedfordshire passed through 1st Norfolk and secured the second objective by 2.55 p.m. The battalions complained that the creeping barrage was too slow. The other divisions met with similar success and light casualties, except on the left of the Guards Division, where XV Corps had failed to take the Gird Trenches. A defensive flank was formed by 4th Grenadier Guards.

The final advance began at 2.30 p.m. Two battalions of 95th Brigade took the southern part of Morval, where the enemy did not provide much resistance. The northern part was taken by 1st Cheshire (15th Brigade) by 3 p.m., having passed through 1st Bedfordshire. The Battalion pushed patrols forward right up to the barrage and commenced consolidating about 200 metres in front of the village, assisted by a company of 1/6th Argyll & Sutherland Highlanders. To the north, Lesboeufs fell to the 6th and Guards Divisions with ease.

Across the front of XIV Corps the enemy was streaming back, withdrawing his batteries on the way. A heavy German barrage then fell on Morval and Lesboeufs. The front appeared to be wide open for further advance, but the GOC XIV Corps, Lord Cavan, was troubled by failures on his flanks and stood firm.

While B and C Companies, 1st Cheshire, were consolidating the line forward of Morval, they suffered constant sniping from old practice trenches east of the village. **Private Thomas Jones** turned to his officer and said, *They nearly got me, come on let's go and get them. There will be trouble for us if we don't*. The officer refused and told him to carry on digging. Then a few bullets whipped past Jones' head. One of the runners was killed (10026 Private George Kenworthy – Thiepval Memorial) and a man digging next to Jones was wounded in the leg. There appeared to be a white flag flying from the enemy trench, which further incensed Jones. Thoroughly fed up with the situation he threw down his shovel, grabbed his rifle and grumbling, *If I'm going to be killed, I'll be killed fighting not digging*, dashed forward to deal with the enemy.

As he crossed the 200 metres of open ground, the Germans hit his helmet and four bullets passed through the side of his tunic, but Jones was not seriously harmed. He pressed on towards the enemy trench, periodically stopping to engage the German snipers. He killed one up a tree and shot another two before reaching the trench. Jumping into it, he shot a German who lunged at him with a bayonet. His comrades watched in awe, expecting him to be killed at any moment. Two of his comrades came up and asked what was going on. When told that Jones had gone off on his own, they set off after him and a few minutes later another two followed.

Undaunted by the odds, Jones forced the Germans into their dugouts and he killed three as they tried to snipe him from the dugout entrances. Picking up a stick grenade, he tossed it into a dugout and three Germans rushed out with their hands up. One spoke English and Jones bluffed that his mates were on their way and if any harm came to him they would be cut to pieces. He sent the German back with the uncompromising message that they could surrender or be killed and that he preferred the latter. The German returned and told him that they preferred the former. Jones told them to come out without any arms or equipment. About eight dugouts surrendered, totalling perhaps 150 men and Jones gathered them in a hollow, hoping for support to arrive before they discovered the bluff. To occupy the time, he sent the prisoners back into their dugouts in pairs to collect their greatcoats, since the night would be cold. One big man made an attempt to escape as he went to his dugout, but Jones shot him dead and this stopped any further attempts. Swinging his rifle back to cover the rest, he found them with their hands up and Jones could not help *laughing like blazes*, since they refused to bring them down again.

From east of Morval cemetery looking north-northwest over the ground crossed by Todger Jones under heavy fire in order to bluff the German troops into surrendering in the hollow.

Looking over the parapet, Jones was relieved to see his comrades approaching, including his best mate, Bogson. Shocked to see so many prisoners, Bogson exclaimed, *Hello Todger what the ------- are you doing?* and then playfully slapped him 'across the earhole'. Together they marched the prisoners to the British lines, passing through a heavy barrage in which a number were killed. They were greeted with a huge cheer from the other soldiers, before being ordered to take the prisoners to the rear. It was only then that Jones had a wound attended to. The bullet that struck his helmet penetrated the front and was deflected from the back downwards into his shoulder, but much of the pace had been taken off it and the wound was not serious. No less than eleven officers from various units in the area witnessed Jones' exploits and recommended him for the VC. It was a truly remarkable achievement for one man.

Later 5th and 6th Divisions advanced to form spurs east and northeast of Morval. At 6 p.m., 16th Royal Warwickshire (15th Brigade, 5th Division) dug in 200 metres beyond the east of the village. A little later, 2nd York & Lancaster (16th Brigade, 6th Division) established posts from Morval Mill northwest to Lesboeufs. At daylight on 26th September, 16th Royal Warwickshire pushed forward and seized Thunder Trench. On the right 95th Brigade was held up by machine-gun fire. The Germans began to reoccupy Thunder Trench and came into contact with 16th Royal Warwickshire, who pushed them back fifty metres and established two trench stops. Later that day 15th Brigade was relieved by 71st Brigade. When 1st Cheshire was relieved late that night it had suffered 143 casualties, including twenty-three killed.

On the left of the attack, XV Corps had mixed results, but there were some significant advances. Orders were issued by Fourth Army for the continuation of the advance. XIV Corps was to surround Combles in cooperation with the French, prior to Morval and Lesboeufs being handed over to them. XV Corps was to complete the capture of its objectives by taking Gird Trenches and Gueudecourt. In addition, XV and III Corps were to gain as much ground as possible in preparation for an advance northwards either side of Eaucourt l'Abbaye.

By the time the offensive ended on 28th September, III Corps on the left had pushed forward up to 900 metres, XV Corps had secured Gueudecourt and the Gird Trenches to the northwest of the village and XIV Corps made some improvements to its positions, particularly on the right, where it assisted the French in taking Combles. Part of the front there was then handed over to the French, a complicated operation, but it was carried out successfully. Despite hold ups in places, the Battle of Morval represented the most successful operation since 14th July.

Battle of Thiepval Ridge 26th–30th September 1916

164 Pte Frederick Edwards, 12th Middlesex (54th Brigade, 18th Division) Thiepval, France
165 Pte Robert Ryder, 12th Middlesex (54th Brigade, 18th Division) Thiepval, France
166 Capt Archie White, 6th Yorkshire (32nd Brigade, 11th Division) Stuff Redoubt, near Thiepval, France
167 2Lt Tom Adlam, 7th Bedfordshire (54th Brigade, 18th Division) Thiepval, France

26th September 1916

Although the Battles of Flers-Courcelette and Morval had failed to seize all the objectives expected, it was thought that the Germans had used up their reserves. The British right wing had made slow but deliberate progress and Haig decided the time was right to push forward the Reserve Army on the left to secure Thiepval Ridge. The attack frontage extended for 5,400 metres from east of Courcelette to the original 1st July front line south of Thiepval. The preliminary bombardment opened on 23rd September and zero hour was set for 12.35 p.m. on 26th September.

The Canadian Corps on the right and II Corps on the left each deployed two divisions for the three-phase operation. The Canadian Corps' main objective was the trenches on the spur northwest of Courcelette. The right of II Corps faced two strong positions. 11th Division was to capture the Zollern Redoubt on the

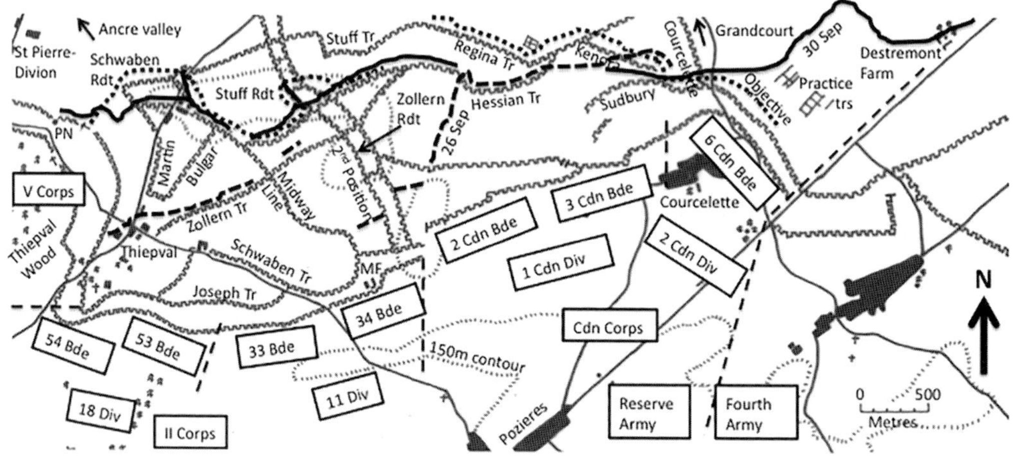

The Battle of Thiepval Ridge 26th-30th September 1916, showing the start positions and the lines reached.

2nd objective and Stuff Redoubt on the 3rd, both part of the old German 2nd Position. 18th Division on the left faced no less of a task, with Thiepval village on the 2nd objective and the notorious Schwaben Redoubt on the 3rd, which had already resisted two major assaults. Capture of the whole crest line would deny the Germans observation towards Albert and gain observation for the British over the upper Ancre valley. II Corps had six of the eight available tanks.

The Reserve Army used almost all its artillery and the guns of V Corps, north of the Ancre, were available for the river crossings and the German rear areas. Long range machine-gun fire was also coordinated between the two corps. Thick mist hampered the preparatory bombardment in the mornings and evenings, but otherwise it went ahead as planned. A preliminary operation on 24th September seized part of Mouquet Farm, but it could not be held against strong bombing attacks. The same afternoon, the projection of 500 lachrymatory gas shells into Thiepval village silenced the German trench mortars there. As the assault troops moved into their attack positions before dawn on 26th September they were largely unaffected by the enemy. 18th Division was particularly fresh, having been out of the line for three weeks whilst undertaking training.

On the right of the Canadian Corps, 2nd Canadian Division had 6th Canadian Brigade in the line and there was only one objective for the three assault battalions. The results were mixed. On the right the enemy fire was so intense that the battalion was forced to remain in its trenches. Conversely, the centre advanced swiftly and seized the objective in just ten minutes. The left suffered the same fate as the right flank, except where it was in contact with the centre battalion, which enjoyed the same success.

1st Canadian Division's 3rd objective was Regina Trench, just beyond the crest. It was uncertain if the wire had been cut in front of it, so the Division was ordered to halt on the 2nd objective while patrols went forward to check the wire and see if a further advance was possible. Despite heavy fire and many casualties,

3rd Canadian Brigade on the right seized the first objective in Sudbury Trench. The advance resumed at 1 p.m. and after some hard fighting most of the 2nd objective was secured. 2nd Canadian Brigade on the left was hit by flanking fire from Zollern and Stuff Redoubts in II Corps' area. Elsewhere there was some stiff fighting, but the objectives were taken. Patrols returning from Regina Trench brought mixed reports about the state of the wire. A flank was formed on the left from Hessian Trench back to Zollern Trench. The Canadians were almost on the crest by the end of the day.

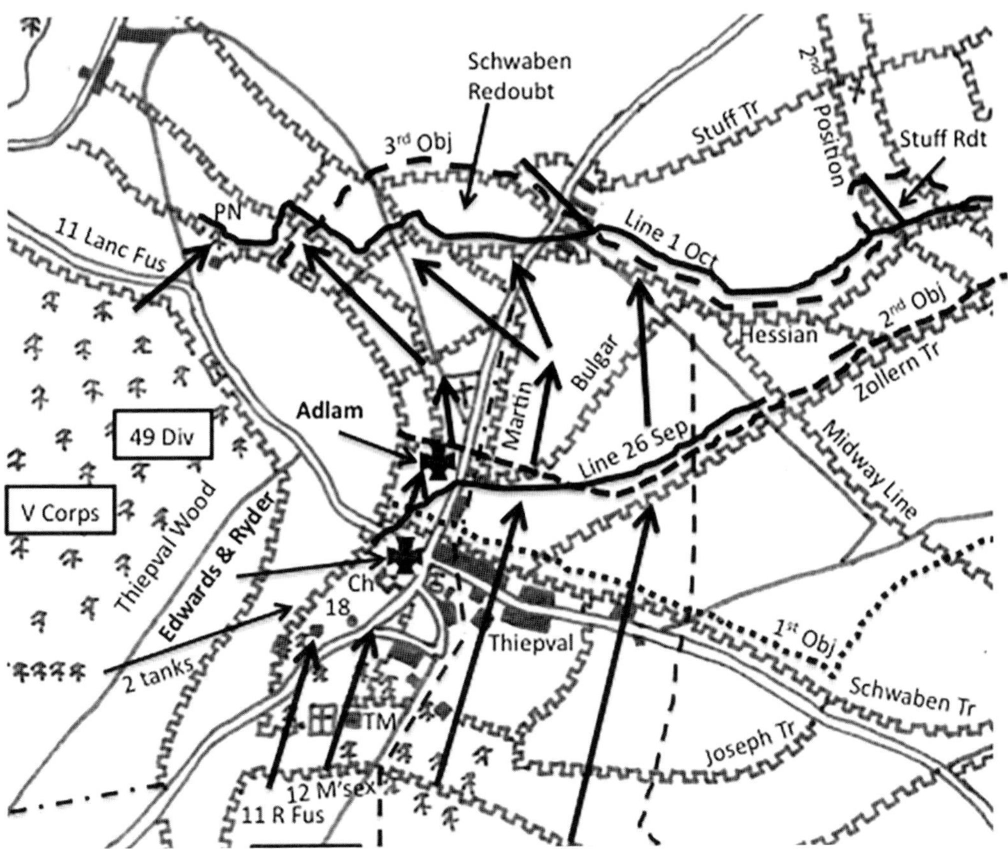

In Thiepval village park at the Visitors Centre and walk to the Thiepval Memorial, where a number of 1916 Somme VCs are commemorated. Returning to the car park, stand on top of the grassy bank and look north-northeast along the axis of 12th Middlesex's attack. Frederick Edwards' and Robert Ryder's VC actions were in the area between the farm (site of Thiepval Chateau) and the Church. A few abbreviations are used on the map – PN = Pope's Nose, Ch = Thiepval Chateau, TM = Thiepval Memorial and 18 = 18th Division Memorial. To overlook the site of Tom Adlam's VC action, keep Thiepval Church on your right as you walk north-northeast along the D151 to the crossroads with the D73. At the crossroads look just east of north towards the cemetery. Tom Adlam's action was in the field about 250m along this line.

On the right of II Corps, 11th Division's final objective was Hessian Trench, including Stuff Redoubt. Patrols were to push forward to Stuff Trench, the westward extension of Regina Trench in the Canadian Corps' area. 34th Brigade on the right faced Mouquet Farm and the old German 2nd Position, including Zollern Redoubt. Two tanks were allocated, but both ditched. The cellar exits at Mouquet Farm were seized thirty seconds before zero hour. At zero, 34th Brigade advanced quickly to the first objective. As the advance resumed, German resistance stiffened, particularly at Zollern and Stuff Redoubts, resulting in heavy casualties. Cohesion was lost, though some posts were established around Zollern Redoubt. Only a handful of men reached Zollern Trench on the 2nd objective, where they were isolated on both flanks. Despite the earlier operation against Mouquet Farm, resistance there continued until 5.30 p.m., when fifty-six survivors surrendered from the cellars.

On the left of 11th Division, 33rd Brigade had a slightly easier task on a frontage narrowing from 900 to 450 metres. Some casualties were suffered by catching up with the creeping barrage, but by 12.45 p.m. the first objective, Schwaben Trench, had been taken. At 1 p.m. a fresh battalion resumed the advance over the crest line and the 2nd objective, Zollern Trench, was taken. By 4 p.m. the final objective, Hessian Trench, had been reached, but not on the right, where it was protected by machine-gun fire from Zollern Redoubt. Both flanks were in the air, but casualties were relatively light overall. Some bombing attacks were repulsed.

On 18th Division's right, 53rd Brigade's first objective was Schwaben Trench. 8th Suffolk on the right was on the objective within twelve minutes. 10th Essex on the left kept pace and found a number of Germans ready to surrender in the sunken road running through Thiepval. They were encouraged by the arrival of a tank, which ditched shortly afterwards in Schwaben Trench. By 1.15 p.m. the 2nd objective, Zollern Trench, had also fallen to the leading battalions, which were in contact with the flanking brigades. Losses had so far been light, due in particular to the crushing effect of the creeping barrage. However, as the attackers continued the advance uphill towards the final objective, they were swept by heavy machine-gun and rifle fire and forced to take cover in shell-holes until dusk, when they withdrew to Zollern Trench. An attempt to bomb forward along Bulgar and Martin Trenches in the evening came to nothing.

On the left, 54th Brigade faced the toughest task of the day, the capture of the western part of Thiepval and the Schwaben Redoubt beyond. Because of the difficulty, the brigade's frontage was only 300 metres wide at the start and went down to as little as 200 metres at one point, increasing to 800 metres at the final objective. On the left in V Corps area, 49th Division assisted with enfilade fire. The attack was led by 12th Middlesex, with a company of 11th Royal Fusiliers on the left to advance along the German front line system, while another company followed to mop up the cellars and dugouts in the ruins of the village. Another company was ready to pass through to the final objective, with the fourth company available for whatever contingency arose. 6th Northamptonshire was in support, with 7th Bedfordshire in reserve. Two tanks were to set off from a small copse south of Thiepval Wood to arrive at Thiepval Chateau at the same time as the infantry and then move against the Schwaben Redoubt.

The attack began well, with the assault waves clearing their start positions before the German barrage came down. 11th Royal Fusiliers became embroiled in heavy fighting along the western edge of Thiepval, but eventually reached the 1st objective. 12th Middlesex was led by C Company (right) and B Company (left), supported by D Company, with A Company in reserve. As the village was approached the Battalion was hit by heavy fire from the Chateau. This was overcome with the assistance of one of the tanks appearing from the direction of Thiepval Wood, but it ditched shortly afterwards; the second tank failed to arrive on time and also ditched in the village. Had the tank not destroyed the machine-guns at the Chateau, it is likely that the advance would have petered out at that point. C Company pressed on, but veered to the east and the resultant gap had to be filled by a company of 11th Royal Fusiliers.

B Company became bogged down in close fighting in the ruins. At one point the advance was held up by a machine-gun. All the officers had become casualties, there was utter confusion and some men were preparing to retire. **Private Frederick Edwards** took the initiative. Dashing forward, he destroyed the gun position with grenades. B Company was held up again from a heavily defended trench. For want of leadership the attack was in danger of stalling, but **Private Robert Ryder** leapt up and charged the trench on his own, clearing it with his Lewis gun. Seeing this inspiring act of courage, the Company surged forward and the impetus of the advance was regained. Ryder went on to attack another enemy trench using bombs collected from his dead comrades. He was wounded in the left hand and leg and

12th Middlesex advanced from the left, parallel with the road into Thiepval village on the right. On the other side of the road, the farm is on the site of Thiepval Chateau. Frederick Edwards' and Robert Ryder's VC actions were in the area beyond the farm, around the church and houses.

was ordered to the rear. On the way he found two German prisoners whom he got to bandage his wounds before marching them back.

The 18th Division Memorial. 12th Middlesex attacked from left to right. In the left background is Thiepval Wood and the Ulster Tower.

The first objective, the road running southeast to northwest through the village, was not secured until 1 p.m. By then the two leading battalions were mixed up and running out of momentum. The enemy mostly fought to the death and many individual acts of courage were necessary to overcome them. 6th Northamptonshire suffered heavily from the German artillery and as its companies arrived they were also thrown into the battle. Elements of all three battalions in the village came under Lieutenant Colonel Francis Maxwell VC of 12th Middlesex, the only CO not to have become a casualty. He had his HQ at the Chateau. By dusk the village had been cleared and it was thought that the 2nd objective had been gained, except for the northwest corner. In reality the line reached by 54th Brigade was a little short of the 2nd objective. A defensive barrage was brought down 135m from the northern edge of the village and bombing fights continued all night. 54th Brigade suffered 840 casualties out of 2,290 men committed to the attack. Officer casualties were particularly heavy; 80% in 12th Middlesex, for example.

Thiepval Chateau before the war.

By nightfall both corps had enjoyed partial success, but the enemy still held the crucial crest of Thiepval Ridge. Orders for the next day were to complete the seizure of the original objectives.

27th September 1916

HQ Canadian Corps was unsure of its forward positions and Lieutenant General Byng's first priority was to join up with II Corps on his left. Heavy artillery fire

Leave Thiepval on the D151 north-northeast towards Grandcourt. After 2.85 kms turn sharp left uphill along a track signed for Grandcourt Road Cemetery and Stump Road Cemetery. The track is a little rough in places, but is passable with care. Either park at Stump Road Cemetery after 600m and walk the rest of the way or drive until the sunken lane flattens out on top of the plateau after another 750m. The whole distance can be driven, but unless it is dry turning at the top is not advised and you may face a long reverse on the return journey. On the top of the plateau, some 30m beyond the end of the sunken section, look west. About 150m along the line of the ridge towards La Grande Ferme is the centre of Stuff Redoubt, where Archie White performed his VC action.

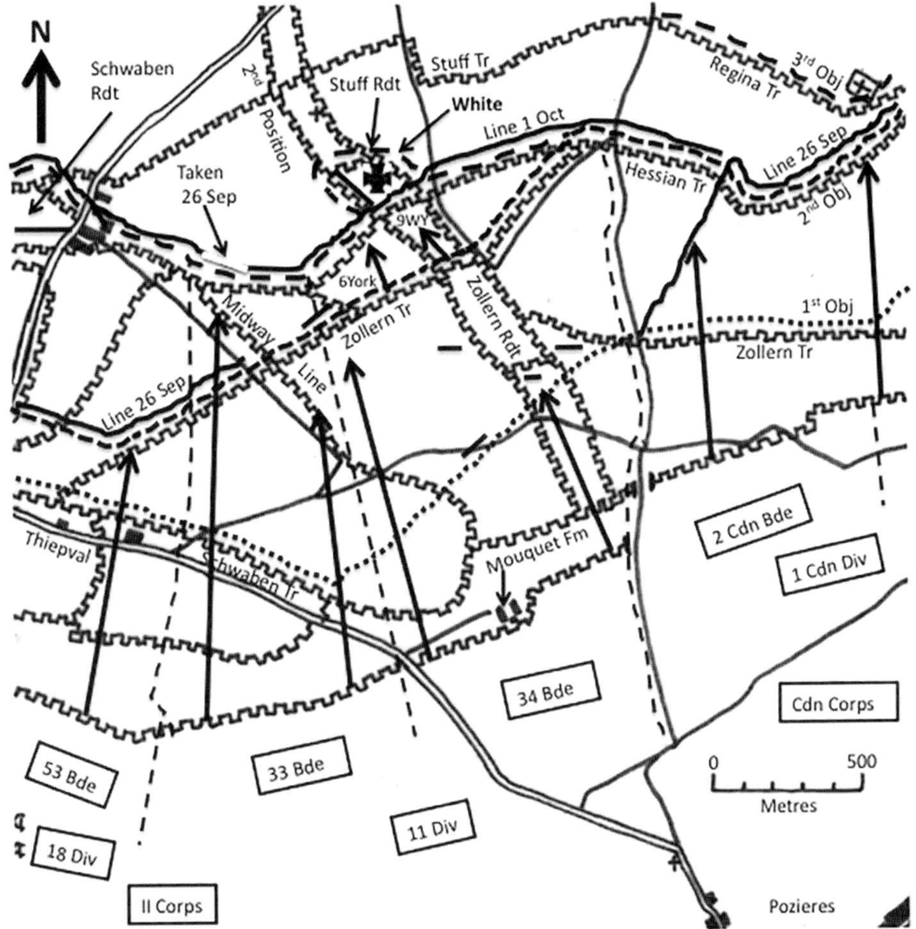

From the top of the sunken lane looking northeast over Stuff Redoubt towards the Schwaben Redoubt.

was received all night. On the afternoon of the 27th, the Germans began retiring in front of 6th Canadian Brigade (2nd Canadian Division) and the troops pushed forward to complete the capture of the previous day's objective.

In 1st Canadian Division, 3rd Canadian Brigade was forced to pull back 135 metres from Kenora Trench, but reoccupied it later when reinforcements arrived. About 6 p.m., a heavy counterattack was massing and a withdrawal was carried out again. An attack to recover the lost ground early the following morning failed. Early on the 27th, patrols of 2nd Canadian Brigade pushed west along Hessian Trench into II Corps' area. No opposition was encountered, but by the time a whole company was sent to occupy the trench the Germans had retaken possession. They were driven west towards Stuff Redoubt and northwards into Stuff Trench. The Canadians eventually established a block on the Corps left boundary in Hessian Trench. To the rear, contact had been established with 11th Division in Zollern Trench; but the area between Zollern and Hessian Trenches was swept by machine-gun fire from Stuff Redoubt all day, making it untenable. Later that evening 8th Canadian Brigade began taking over the line from 2nd Canadian Brigade.

At 10 a.m. on the 27th, 34th Brigade (11th Division) resumed the advance and occupied the abandoned Zollern Redoubt and Trench as far as Midway Line. However, attempts to continue to Stuff Redoubt and Hessian Trench were driven back by heavy machine-gun fire. A general attack across II Corps' front was ordered for 3 p.m. to complete the capture of the original objectives.

34th Brigade was exhausted, so two battalions of 32nd Brigade in reserve (9th West Yorkshire and 6th Yorkshire) were brought up to take Stuff Redoubt and Hessian Trench, but there was confusion over start times. The intention was to attack at 3 p.m. but at that time 6th Yorkshire received orders to postpone and accordingly remained on the start line, Zollern Trench. The postponement did not reach 9th West Yorkshire, which attacked alone from Zollern Trench on the right soon after 3 p.m. Despite heavy opposition and diverting to the left due to uncut wire, a footing

was gained in the south of Stuff Redoubt. At 4.06 p.m. C and B Companies, 6th Yorkshire attacked Stuff Redoubt and the west of Hessian Trench without artillery support. This surprised the Germans and the Battalion took Hessian Trench west of Stuff Redoubt with very few casualties, along with eighty prisoners. The Battalion was in contact with 33rd Brigade on the left and with 9th West Yorkshire on the right and went on to improve the gains in and around the Redoubt. However, there was still a gap on the right before the Canadians and 11th Manchester (34th Brigade) was ordered to bomb northwards from Zollern Redoubt in an attempt to link the two. This succeeded in making contact with the Canadians on the right and seizing a stretch of Hessian Trench, but a gap of about 450 metres remained on the left before the troops in Stuff Redoubt. During the evening, two companies of 8th West Riding went forward, one to each battalion in Stuff Redoubt.

On the left of 11th Division, 33rd Brigade concerned itself with joining up its flanks. During the morning bombers pushed east along Zollern Trench to link up with 34th Brigade. In the general attack at 3 p.m. the uncaptured portion of Hessian Trench was secured and a link was made with 6th Yorkshire. Patrols that evening reached the crest of the ridge and found no Germans.

During the reorganisation in Stuff Redoubt, **Captain Archie White** of 6th Yorkshire took command of a mixed force of the two assault battalions on the southern and western faces, having been unable to hold on to the north face. He held on for the next four days and nights against repeated counterattacks. Despite being constantly short of ammunition and supplies, he never wavered in his determination to hold the position and, if possible, improve it.

In 54th Brigade (18th Division), 7th Bedfordshire had taken over the front from the other battalions. It was ordered to take the northwest corner of Thiepval, an outstanding objective from the previous day, supported by 1/5th West Yorkshire (146th Brigade), which was to attack the final objective later. The relief was conducted with great skill in darkness over difficult and unknown ground.

From the D151 Grandcourt - Thiepval road looking north towards Stuff Redoubt.

The plan was simple. At 5.45 a.m., C and D Companies (right and left respectively), 7th Bedfordshire, were to charge the enemy position and clear it at bayonet point. Surprise was to be achieved by dispensing with artillery support. The left rushed on quickly but, on the right, C Company ran into determined resistance from machine-guns and snipers, which had to be cleared individually. At about 7 a.m., the right platoon of C Company was pinned down by fire from several strongpoints. The moment was critical, for if the advance faltered here the whole attack would have collapsed. **Second Lieutenant Tom Adlam** dashed forward, gathering up his men sheltering in shell-holes as he went. He then stripped off his equipment and using German grenades furiously bombarded the enemy. He was wounded in the leg, but continued throwing kneeling down. It is estimated that forty enemy were killed by his grenades alone. When they had been subdued,

From the crossroads in Thiepval looking north. The site of Tom Adlam's VC action was 250m into the field west of the D151 Grandcourt road.

Adlam led an attack over the open, overwhelmed the remaining Germans and made contact with D Company on the left. By 8.30 a.m., he had secured his objective and this helped the rest of the attackers to move forward again. Many Germans were despatched with the bayonet. By 11 a.m., the remainder of the village was secured and consolidation began in contact with 53rd Brigade on the right. Seventy prisoners were taken and few casualties were suffered, something of a miracle in a daylight attack with little artillery support. Without Adlam's intervention it is unlikely that the start positions for the attack on the Schwaben Redoubt would have been established.

GOC 18th Division, Major General Ivor Maxse, judged that further advance to the final objective was unlikely to succeed while Stuff Redoubt held out. He cancelled 1/5th West Yorkshire's advance until next day.

28th September 1916

The Canadian Corps continued to probe forwards. On the extreme right, progress towards Destremont Farm was met with heavy machine-gun fire and a protective barrage. They persevered and established a line facing northeast beyond the practice trenches. However, repeated attempts to fight northwards along Courcelette Trench came to nothing. The relief of 3rd Canadian Brigade by 5th Canadian Brigade was completed during the day. As a result, 2nd Canadian Division had two brigades in the line and extended its left boundary to the west. On the right, 6th Canadian Brigade was gradually handing over to 4th Canadian Brigade. Optimistic reports led to strong patrols being pushed forward to Regina Trench, but all attempts to enter it were defeated by uncut wire and heavy artillery. Beyond the Grandcourt Road, 3rd Canadian Division took over the line.

During the day, HQ Reserve Army issued orders for certain objectives to be achieved by 1st October in order to comply with future plans for Fourth Army

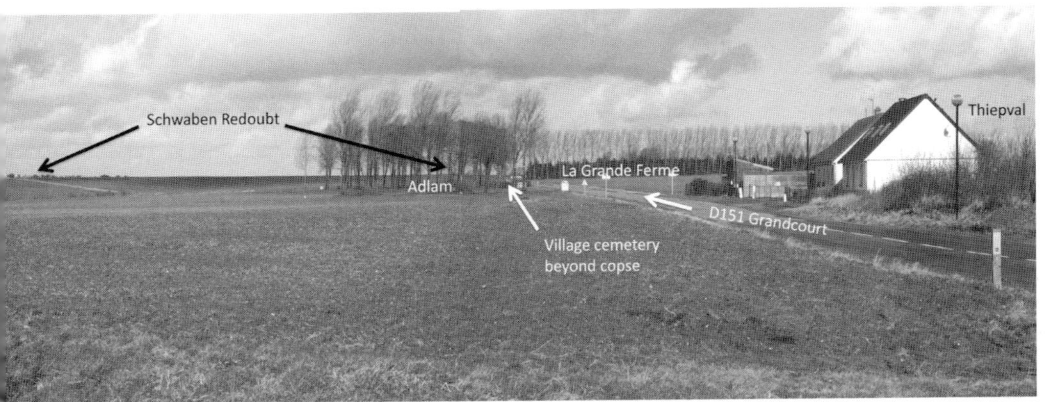

on the right. The Canadian Corps was to continue the line established beyond the practice trenches westwards to include Kenora Trench, while II Corps had to secure Stuff and Schwaben Redoubts and Stuff Trench.

In 11th Division, 32nd Brigade was expected to complete the capture of Stuff Redoubt and link up with the Canadians on the right in Hessian Trench. A dawn attack by 6th Yorkshire in Stuff Redoubt failed. An attack by a company of 8th West Riding at 6 p.m. was postponed due to heavy artillery fire and congestion in the trenches. However, White was not aware of this and with his men bombed their way from the right and took almost the whole of the north face of Stuff Redoubt. Unfortunately they were too weak to hold their gains and were driven back to their original positions.

18th Division began fighting for the Schwaben Redoubt. 53rd Brigade was tasked with its capture, with the attack commencing at 1 p.m. On the right, 8th Suffolk was to take the remainder of Midway Line, while 7th Queen's Royal West Surrey (attached from 55th Brigade) stormed the Schwaben Redoubt. Moppers up followed behind from 8th Norfolk. On the left, two fresh companies of 7th Bedfordshire (54th Brigade) attacked between the Redoubt and the German front system.

The attack started well. Bulgar Trench was taken and, after stiff resistance in Midway Line, 8th Suffolk was approaching the eastern end of the Schwaben Redoubt by 2.30 p.m., in contact with 11th Division on the right. On the left, 7th Queen's was new to the area and lost its bearings. It headed too far left and came under heavy fire from the Redoubt while advancing along Martin Trench. 7th Bedfordshire reached the northern edge of the cemetery, having lost heavily to fire from the Redoubt; the right platoon of the right company was completely knocked out. 7th Queen's pushed 7th Bedfordshire to the left and the Battalion struggled for several strongpoints in the original German front line system; with artillery support these were taken. The brigade commander directed that the main effort should be made against the Redoubt, as once it had been secured the German positions west of it would be easy to clear. Despite this, the troops of 54th Brigade were still distracted to the left where 7th Bedfordshire and 1/5th West Yorkshire continued to be involved in confused fighting in the frontline system.

At 3 p.m. the brigade commanders took stock and agreed to concentrate on the western face of the Redoubt by attacking inwards towards it. By 5 p.m. 7th Queen's had secured the whole of the south face and was in contact on the right with 8th Suffolk in Midway Line and the mixed up troops of 54th Brigade on the left. At this point it was decided that no more could be achieved and consolidation began. However, on the left 7th Bedfordshire and 1/5th West Yorkshire continued the attack. They took over a trench taken by 7th Queens that connected the Schwaben Redoubt with the front system. Further west another trench connecting the Schwaben Redoubt to the front system was held by 1/5th West Yorkshire. Blocks had been established by 8 p.m. to drive back German counterattacks from the northwest. At the same time, patrols of 11th Lancashire Fusiliers (74th Brigade,

25th Division) on the left flank secured a lodgement in the German front system at the Pope's Nose and linked up with the left of 54th Brigade. At 9.30 p.m. an isolated post of 1/5th West Yorkshire at the western tip of the Schwaben Redoubt was connected to the line held by 7th Bedfordshire and 7th Queen's on the south face, thus completing 54th Brigade's objective.

During this action, Tom Adlam again displayed great courage despite the wounds he had sustained the previous day. He was wounded again, this time in the right arm, and was finally ordered to leave the battlefield. During the night, 7th Royal West Kent (55th Brigade) began taking over from 54th Brigade and the relief was completed at 7 a.m. next morning. One of 7th Bedfordshire's casualties was Captain Arthur Percival (1887–1966), who was wounded in the fight for the south face of the Schwaben Redoubt. As Lieutenant General Arthur Ernest Percival CB DSO and Bar MC he commanded Imperial forces during the Japanese invasion of Malaya and the surrender of Singapore on 15th February 1942, the greatest catastrophe in British military history.

29th September 1916

At noon, 8th Canadian Brigade attacked in cooperation with 11th Division (II Corps) on the left. 2nd Canadian Mounted Rifles, covered by two Stokes trench mortars, got into Hessian Trench beyond the Corps boundary. Some ground was lost to counterattacks in the afternoon, but bombers managed to wrest it back.

Archie White's force in Stuff Redoubt repeated their attack of the previous morning and again succeeded in taking the north face of the Redoubt, but it could not be held due to lack of bombs and ammunition. Later that day they drove off a very strong German counterattack against the south face.

An attempt was made at noon by 32nd Brigade to clear Stuff Redoubt and Hessian Trench to the east, assisted by the Canadians on the right. 6th York & Lancaster attacked with three companies. Most of the trench was taken and contact was established with the Canadians, but about 200 metres of the trench east of Stuff Redoubt held out. 32nd Brigade had no fresh troops, so 7th South Staffordshire (33rd Brigade) was ordered to move forward to reinforce.

53rd Brigade at the Schwaben Redoubt was exhausted and spent the day reorganising and consolidating. The narrow 54th Brigade front saw continuous fighting. At 6.30 a.m. 7th Royal West Kent (55th Brigade) began taking over the west face of the Schwaben Redoubt as far as the German front system to the west. The Germans attacked during the relief and retook a trench junction northwest of the Redoubt. German bombing attacks preceded by a bombardment went on all day. There were heavy losses on both sides, but the Germans had little success. At 10 p.m. 7th Royal West Kent gained some ground, but could not hold it. The Battalion then relieved 74th Brigade in the German front line system overnight.

30th September 1916

5th Canadian Brigade was urged to make an attempt on Regina Trench, but its commander and the battalion COs protested that the brigade's strength was down to 1,134 and the artillery support was repeatedly falling short. The attack was postponed. Bombers in 8th Canadian Brigade cooperated in an 11th Division attack, which completed the capture of Hessian Trench.

A three-pronged bombing attack was arranged by 32nd Brigade to clear the rest of Hessian Trench and Stuff Redoubt at 12.05 p.m. 6th York and Lancaster attacked from the east along Hessian Trench, while 7th South Staffordshire (attached from 33rd Brigade), advanced from Zollern Trench up the old support line of the German 2nd Position. Archie White's party joined in from the south face of Stuff Redoubt. After a very stiff fight all the original 11th Division objectives were taken, with the exception of the north face of the Redoubt. That night 25th Division relieved 11th Division, which had suffered 3,615 casualties. 25th Division assumed command of the sector at 9 a.m. on 1st October. 6th Yorkshire was relieved by 10th Cheshire, having suffered 396 casualties.

18th Division was heavily engaged all day repulsing counterattacks and the west face of the Schwaben Redoubt was lost. At 4 p.m., an attack on the north face of the Redoubt was successful, but a strong counterattack drove it back to the junction with Stuff Trench. The struggle for the Schwaben Redoubt continued until 14th October, when it was finally cleared.

Chapter Six

Transloy Ridges and the Ancre

Battle of the Transloy Ridges 1st–18th October 1916 and Subsequent Operations

168 Lt Col Roland Bradford, 9th Durham Light Infantry (151st Brigade, 50th Division) Eaucourt l'Abbaye, France

169 2Lt Henry Kelly, 10th Duke of Wellington's (West Riding) (69th Brigade, 23rd Division) Le Sars, France

171 Sgt Robert Downie, 2nd Royal Dublin Fusiliers (10th Brigade, 4th Division) east of Lesboeufs, France

1st October 1916

With most of Thiepval Ridge captured on the left flank and Morval, Lesboeufs and Gueudecourt secured on the right, Haig decided the time was right to combine the actions of Third, Reserve and Fourth Armies. The target date to resume the offensive was 12th October. While preparations for this major attack were being made, Fourth Army continued its advance (Battle of the Transloy Ridge), supported by the Reserve Army, in order to keep the enemy under pressure. On 1st October, III Corps, supported by the New Zealand Division on the left of XV Corps, attacked to straighten the line at l'Abbaye de Eaucourt and to take the Flers Line as far as Le Sars. The bombardment commenced at 7 a.m. across the whole Army front, and the advance began at 3.15 p.m.

On the right, the Special Brigade RE fired thirty oil drums covering most of the New Zealand front in flames and thick smoke. Despite the cover this afforded, 2nd New Zealand Brigade (2nd Canterbury on the right and 2nd Otago on the left) suffered heavy casualties from machine-guns, but still secured its objectives. The 2nd Otago attack was launched from Goose Alley, with its left on Abbey Road, and advanced well beyond the objective. In this action, **Sergeant Donald Brown**, 2nd Otago, stormed a machine-gun post that was holding up the advance. This was the second part of his VC action, the first taking place during the Battle of Flers-Courcelette on 15th October. Brown was killed on 1st October and never knew he had received the coveted award.

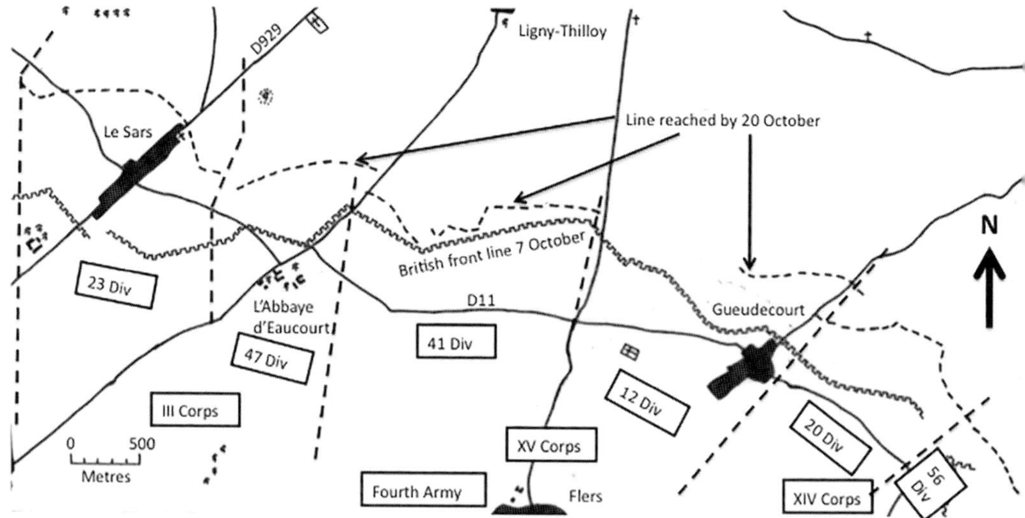

The area covered by the Battle of the Transloy Ridges. This map shows the situation from 7th to 20th October 1916.

III Corps' attack was made by three divisions. On the right, 47th Division attacked with three battalions and was held up on its left by uncut wire and machine-guns not subdued by the barrage. With the assistance of two tanks, the centre and right made progress, albeit with heavy losses, and on the right reached its objective, making contact with the New Zealand Division on the right on the Le Barque road. On the left, 23rd Division gained all its objectives, save for a section of Flers Support at the southwestern tip of Le Sars.

This picture was taken from the second option. Instead of taking the track to Ligny-Thilloy, turn right and continue along the D11 for 700m until it swings left. Park on the right, where two tracks join the road. Cross the road and walk along the track running northeast for 200m. Look northwest towards the Butte de Warlencourt. Donald Brown's VC action was about 300m along this line.

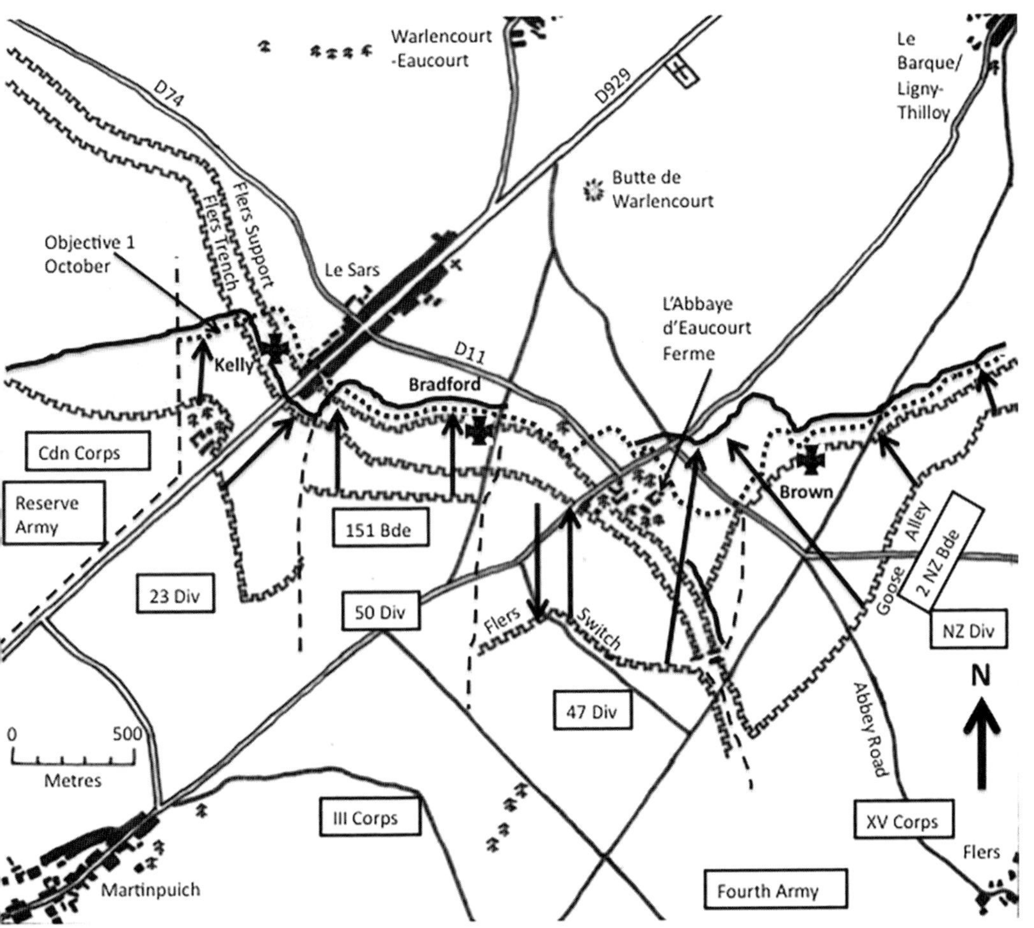

The site of the second part of Donald Brown's VC action is difficult to access as it is in the middle of completely featureless fields. The closest point on a track is some 250m away. However, it is possible to overlook the site from two places. The first option is to follow the D11 alongside l'Abbaye d'Eaucourt Farm in an easterly direction. As the road doglegs left then right at the farm, take the track straight on to the northeast towards Ligny-Thilloy and follow it for 600m to the crest. Stop and look due south for 400m, which is approximately where the action took place.

In the centre of III Corps was 50th Division's 151st Brigade. It attacked in line with three battalions; 1/6th Durham Light Infantry on the right, a composite battalion of 1/5th Border and 1/8th Durham Light Infantry in the centre and 1/5th Northumberland Fusiliers (attached from 149th Brigade) on the left. 1/9th Durham Light Infantry was in support. There was concern before the attack about the amount of uncut wire, but the artillery was diverted to the task. The centre and left battalions followed fifty metres behind the creeping barrage and had little trouble in occupying the Flers Lines as planned. However, at 2.35 p.m., on the right, the CO of 1/6th Durham Light Infantry, Major GE Wilkinson, was wounded and **Lieutenant Colonel Roland Bradford**, CO 1/9th Durham Light Infantry, was sent to assume command of both battalions. When the attack began, 1/6th

Drive through Martinpuich northeasterly along the D6E. At the end of the village the D6E turns left, but carry straight on towards l'Abbaye d'Eaucourt Farm along a tree-lined lane for 1,500m. Just after the entrance to a rough tree-lined track on the left, park alongside the road on the right, where there is grassy area just before an earth bank on the left. Walk along the rough track to the northeast for 450m and stand on top of the bank on the left. This is where the picture was taken, on 151st Brigade's start line for the attack on 1st October 1916.

Durham Light Infantry was exposed to flanking fire from the right, where 47th Division had failed to keep up. Despite this, it managed to gain a very precarious foothold in Flers Trench.

On arrival in the forward area, Bradford found the right flank wide open and under heavy machine-gun fire. A counterattack had driven the leading elements back from Flers Trench. He immediately set about rallying the troops and securing the flank. During this time he moved about freely under every sort of fire, disregarding the danger completely.

Continue along the track for another 400m to the D11 for the reverse view of the previous picture.

By 3.27 p.m.,151st Brigade was reporting the capture of the 1st objective. Part of the success was due to the almost perfect curtain of the creeping barrage. At 4.25 p.m. 1/8th Durham Light Infantry secured the 2nd objective and reported that the enemy was running away. About the same time 1/5th Northumberland Fusiliers gained touch with 23rd Division on the left. Casualties had been slight. At 4.40 p.m. 1/5th Border reported it was on the 2nd objective and in contact with 1/6th Durham Light Infantry on the right. By 5.45 p.m., HQ 151st Brigade was aware of the success on the left and in the centre, but was unsure of the situation on the right. However, five minutes later it was reported that the right had a lodgement in the 1st objective, but not the 2nd. At 7.20 p.m. the right reported the 1st objective was secure. 1/6th Durham Light Infantry had been driven out, but partly regained the lost ground. 47th Division on the right had still failed to reach the 1st objective, so this flank was in the air. 1/9th Durham Light Infantry was ordered to effect contact with 47th Division.

Bradford then organised a combined attack by 1/6th Durham Light Infantry and two companies of 1/9th Durham Light Infantry, which succeeded in securing Flers Trench by about 9.30 p.m. The other two companies of 1/9th Durham Light Infantry were working on the communications trench from the enemy front line to North Durham Trench. At 10 p.m. 151st Brigade proposed to take the German second line in 1/9th Durham Light Infantry's area at dawn on 2nd October and requested artillery support from 5 a.m. to 5.30 a.m.; at 1 a.m. this was overtaken by events when Flers Support was also taken, although there was still no contact with 47th Division.

By dawn on 2nd October Bradford had consolidated the position. The right flank of Flers Support was barricaded against German counterattacks and fierce bombing battles followed. One attack drove in the right flank for fifty metres, but it was recovered by bombing parties supported by Stokes trench mortars. At 10.25 a.m., two companies of 6th Northumberland Fusiliers were ordered to Flers Switch to support 1/9th Durham Light Infantry. During the early morning of 3rd October, 151st Brigade was relieved by 68th Brigade (23rd Division) and moved to Bécourt Wood.

Meanwhile, on 1st October, XIV and XV Corps on the right of Fourth Army made a few small gains, but further right the French failed to make any progress.

4th October 1916

General Rawlinson's next plan was to secure the low ridge running northwest towards Thilloy, including the prominent Butte de Warlencourt, on 5th October. Persistent rain set in for two days from 11 a.m. on 2nd October and plans to continue the advance on the 5th were postponed to the 7th. Around noon on 4th October, patrols from 47th Division found only a few Germans in Flers Trench, which was occupied with little opposition. At 6 p.m. 23rd Division made another attempt to secure the section of Flers Support that remained in enemy hands after 1st October. By then 69th Brigade had taken over the front from 70th Brigade.

10th West Riding was tasked to make the attack with two companies (A and C) from Flers Trench. The objective was the second Flers Line, from the Bapaume road westwards. At the same time 8th Yorkshire was to seize the remaining portion of the trench south of the Bapaume road and join with 10th West Riding across it. Troops were withdrawn from the first Flers Line for the bombardment, which was timed for 5.30–6.08 p.m. Stokes mortars were also to engage the objective. One sentry was to be left behind for each occupied dugout to prevent the Germans reoccupying Flers Trench from the north.

One hundred metres of open ground had to be crossed to the objective, which was not a great distance; but the recent weather had turned the area into a sea of mud. In addition the enemy wire was so close to the British line that the artillery could not cut it effectively without risking serious casualties. Nevertheless the attack

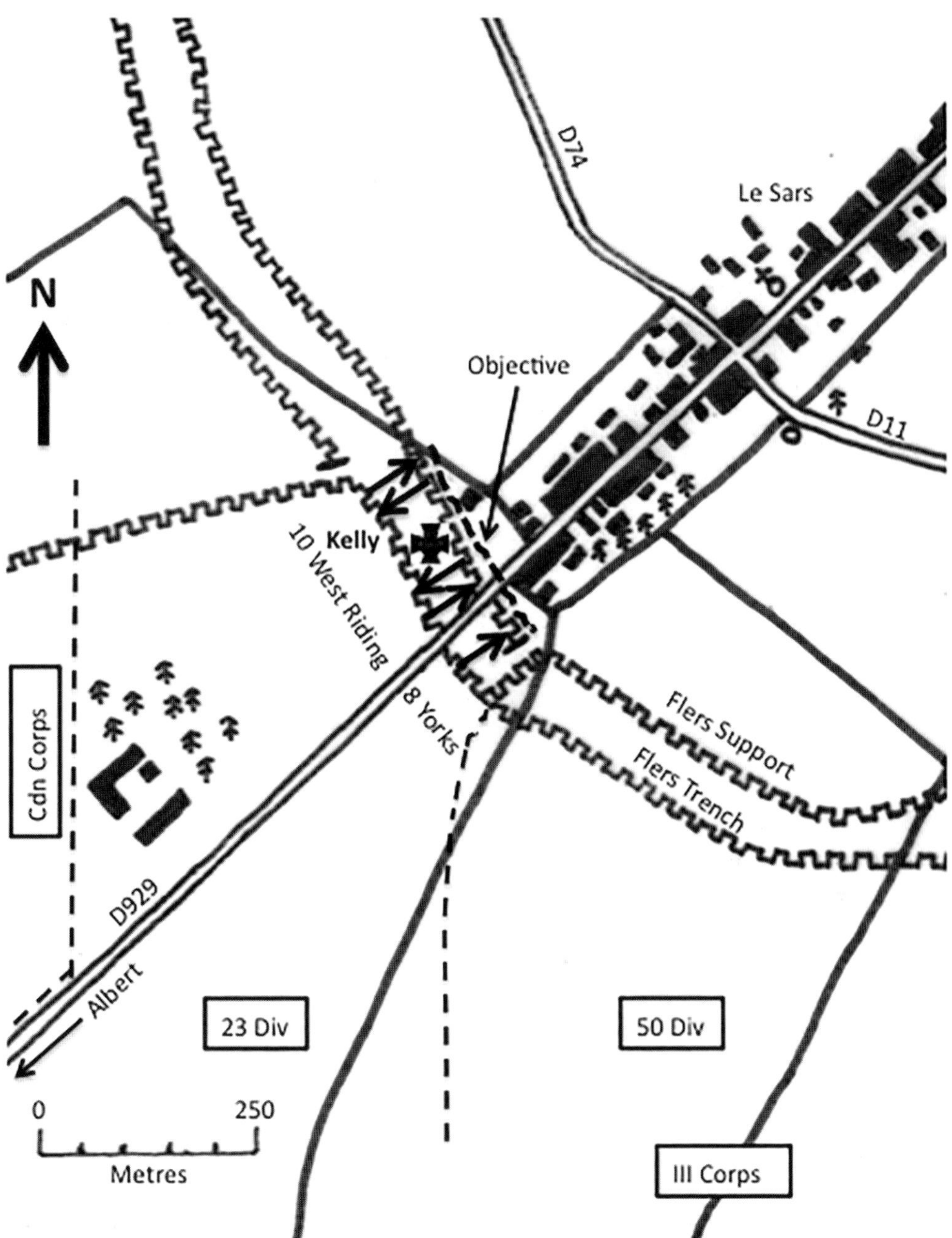

The area of the attack by 10th West Riding and 8th Yorkshire on 4th October. Approach Le Sars from the southwest on the D929. Just before the first building in the village on the right is a track. Turn here and park where you will not block farm vehicles. Walk back to the main road and turn left along the grass verge for just over 200m to where Flers Trench crossed the road. Turn back to face Le Sars. The attack by 10th West Riding on 1st October took place in the fields on the other side of the road. Beware traffic as this can be a fast stretch despite the speed limits in the village.

started at 6.08 p.m. and was pressed home with great courage and determination. Many casualties were caused by close range rifle and machine-gun fire as the men struggled forward through the mud and many did not even get to the wire. The preceding barrage does not seem to have been very effective.

Two platoon commanders were killed (Second Lieutenants Stafford and Harris) and **Second Lieutenant Henry Kelly** led two attacks from just in front of the wire. He managed to get into Flers Support with two men, where he remained bombing the enemy until his companions became casualties and he was forced to withdraw. Finding his Company Sergeant Major lying wounded in no man's land, he carried him sixty metres back to the British trench. Not content with this, he returned to rescue three other soldiers. An enemy counterattack was repulsed with heavy losses and later that night the Battalion was relieved, having suffered 110 casualties.

The atrocious weather conditions dashed Haig's hopes of completing his plans before winter, but he resolved to accomplish all that the weather would allow. Further operations were planned by Fourth Army to take Le Transloy Ridge, while the Reserve Army completed the capture of Thiepval Ridge.

There was an improvement in the weather after 4th October and the renewed offensive was set for the 7th. III Corps took Le Sars and there were small gains elsewhere. That night the rain returned, but it dried up for two days on the 9th and the next attack was set for the 12th. The ground was now sodden and reliefs were carried out with great difficulty. Incoming units had little time to learn the ground. The attack on 12th October started at 2.05 p.m. and there were mixed results. The Germans seemed ready to receive the attack and many assault battalions were weak. Air cooperation was limited by poor visibility. The Germans had sited their machine-guns further back, from where they were able to sweep the assault area more effectively.

In 10th Brigade (4th Division), 1st Royal Warwickshire on the extreme right of XIV Corps, in contact with the French, advanced 450 metres and dug in south of Hazy Trench. The new line was named Antelope Trench and a counterattack against it was repulsed. However, the left of 1st Royal Warwickshire failed, as did 1st

From Flers Trench looking northeast towards Le Sars. Henry Kelly's VC action was in the fields on the other side of the D929.

Royal Irish Fusiliers on the left in front of Rainy and Dewdrop Trenches, northeast of Lesboeufs.

The Germans had been given a respite by the weather and before the next move forward could be made the defences had to be bombarded methodically. The bombardment started immediately, with the target date for the attack the 18th October. A number of objectives were to be taken beforehand – Zenith, Mild and the rest of Cloudy Trenches in XIV Corps area; the Gird Lines southeast of the l'Abbaye de Eaucourt – Le Barque road by XV Corps; and Snag Trench by III Corps.

In XIV Corps, 2nd Seaforth Highlanders (10th Brigade, 4th Division) launched a surprise attack on Rainy Trench on 14th October. The objective was rushed and the gunpits immediately south of Dewdrop Trench taken, but the Battalion was forced back by a counterattack. 2nd Royal Dublin Fusiliers attacked the gunpits in front of Hazy Trench at the same time and was also repulsed. Bombing attacks by 12th Brigade along Spectrum Trench towards Dewdrop Trench on the evenings of 14th and 15th October also failed.

The attack on 18th October opened at 3.40 a.m., two hours before sunrise. By then the ground was a mass of overlapping, water-filled shell holes and flooded trenches. The advance was slow and arduous. Many weapons were clogged with mud as the men stumbled and fell into the morass. In XIV Corps, 4th Division's objective was Frosty, Hazy, Rainy and Dewdrop Trenches. The task fell to 11th Brigade. 1st Rifle Brigade reached the gunpits in front of Hazy Trench, but had to pull back again. 1st East Lancashire was halted in front of Dewdrop Trench by machine-guns that had not been located previously. In Spectrum Trench, bombing parties of 1st King's Own (12th Brigade) gained sixty metres towards Dewdrop Trench.

Elsewhere, 71st Brigade made a small gain in the northwest of Mild Trench. Late on 19th October, 1st Somerset Light Infantry (11th Brigade) found Frosty Trench abandoned and occupied it and then beat off a counterattack.

In XV Corps, 12th Division captured Grease Trench, but attempts to continue the advance resulted in heavy casualties. 30th Division suffered many casualties for little gain. At 8 a.m. a tank emerged from the ruins of Flers and reached the end of Gird Trench from where it shot up the defenders for twenty minutes; they fled

to the northeast. The tank commander climbed out and signalled the infantry to follow on, but they were too disorganised and exhausted to take advantage of the situation. The tank continued to the Le Barque road and then retired by the same route.

The sadly neglected and crumbling memorial to the German 11th Infantry Regiment. The inset is the other side of the memorial as it appeared in the 1920s when it stood in the remains of a shattered German cemetery. On this face the words Fricourt, Mametz, Montauban and La Boisselle can be made out, but the rest of the inscription had disappeared.

III Corps attempted to take Snag Trench again, using smoke and lacrymatory shells to disrupt German fire from the Butte and the Warlencourt Line. Snag Trench from the Le Barque road was taken and held against a counterattack. Attempts by the South Africans to go beyond Snag Trench were met by accurate machine-gun fire from the Butte, causing heavy casualties. By daylight on 19th October, the Germans only held a hundred metres of Snag Trench either side of the Nose. On 20th October, 6th King's Own Scottish Borderers (27th Brigade) attacked and held Snag Trench whilst a company of 11th Royal Scots pushed up the Tail for 225 metres.

23rd October 1916

On 17th October it was decided to exclude Third Army from the future operations. The Reserve Army's role was also restricted to an attack astride the Ancre around the 23rd. Fourth Army was to attack Le Transloy in cooperation with a French advance on the right towards Rocquigny. However, the results of the attack on 18th October were so disappointing that plans had to be revised again. Accordingly new objectives were set, to be achieved as the weather permitted:

21st October – Reserve Army to take Regina Trench, to complete the capture of Thiepval Ridge.

23rd October – Fourth Army to attack towards Le Transloy in cooperation with the French Sixth Army.

25th October
Reserve Army to attack astride the Ancre.
Fourth Army to secure the spur north of Gueudecourt, the Butte de Warlencourt and the Warlencourt Line.

26th October – Fourth and French Sixth Armies to carry out the main Le Transloy attack.

Even this amended plan was overambitious and unachievable given the conditions. After a few fine days, the weather reverted to heavy rain until 3rd November. To add to the difficulties, on 26th October the BEF was ordered to release a division to Salonika.

The preliminary Le Transloy operation by two divisions of XIV Corps began on 23rd October as planned. Zero hour had been set for 11.30 a.m., but was delayed until 2.30 p.m. due to thick mist. The objective was the German front defences and the establishment of a line beyond the crest of the spur, within assaulting distance of Le Transloy, in preparation for the main attack a few days later. The creeping barrage moved forward at forty-five metres per minute. Most battalions were down to two weak companies.

On the left was 8th Division. 23rd Brigade on the right gained Zenith Trench but, pressing on, it was shelled out of Orion. 25th Brigade in the centre suffered

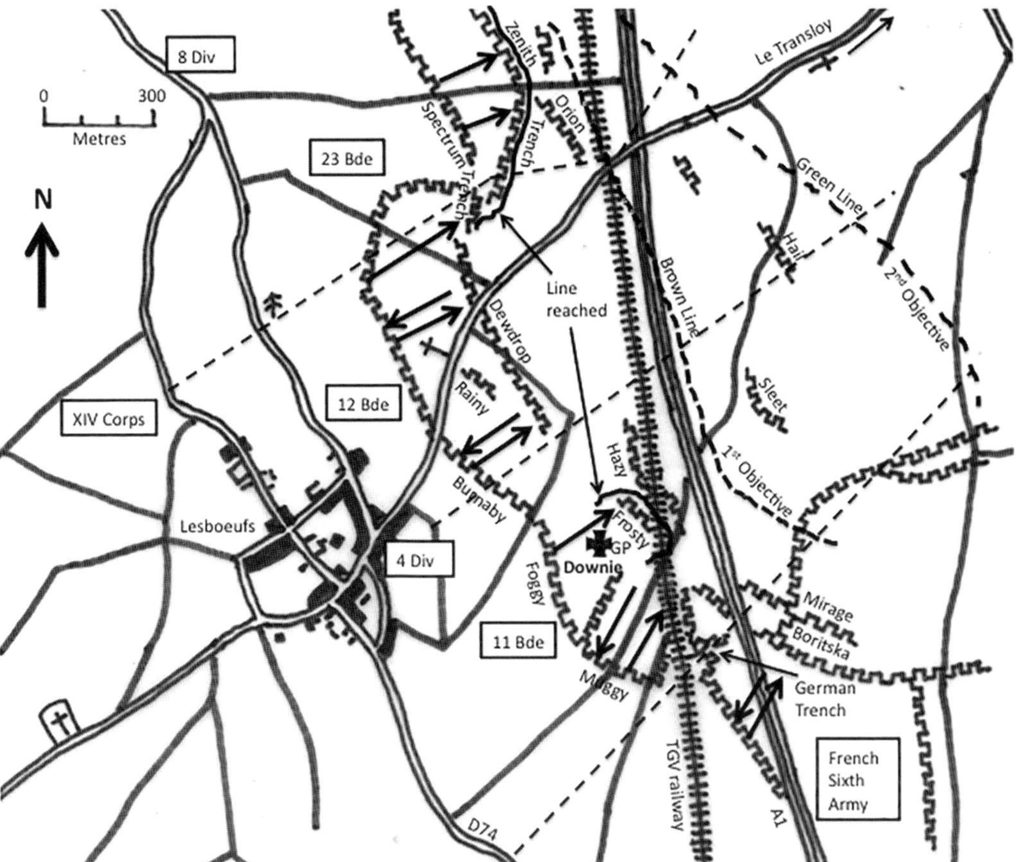

Leave Lesboeufs on the D74E/D19 road northeast towards Le Transloy. 150m before the cemetery on the left, turn right into a track and park. Walk along the track southeast for 300m and stop. The gunpits taken by Robert Downie were in the low ground 275m away half right.

almost total failure. 24th Brigade on the left captured most of Mild Trench and set up blocks on the flanks to repulse bombing attacks. 25th Brigade renewed the attack at 3.50 a.m. on 24th October, but was stopped by heavy small arms fire after sixty metres.

On the right, 4th Division deployed 11th Brigade on the right and 12th Brigade on the left. The first objective was the Brown Line, including portions of Boritska and Mirage Trenches within the boundaries, Hazy Trench and some gunpits. There was the usual creeping barrage and also a standing barrage on the first objective. The second objective, the Green Line, included Sleet Trench and the southern half of Hail Trench. Again there was a standing barrage on the objective and contact was to be established with the French on the right. The leading battalions were to take the first objective and the support battalions were to pass through thirty minutes after zero to the second.

The 12th Brigade attack failed, except for taking a section of Spectrum Trench. 11 Brigade attacked with two battalions. 1st Hampshire on the right and the French 152nd Division were halted by heavy fire from Boritska Trench and by scattered machine-gun posts in shell holes. Later the supporting battalion, 1st Rifle Brigade, arrived and a few posts were established northwest of the objective. After dark contact was established with 2nd Royal Dublin Fusiliers.

On 11th Brigade's left was 2nd Royal Dublin Fusiliers, attached from 10th Brigade, supported by 1st Royal Warwickshire. 2nd Royal Dublin Fusiliers had not moved into the assembly trenches until 6.30 p.m. the previous day and there was only time to issue verbal orders. However, they were in their attack positions by 6.30 a.m. and ready to advance half an hour later. The attack was led by D Company on the right from a new trench leading from Muggy Trench to Andrew's Post. C Company on the left attacked from the south end of Burnaby Trench and the north end of Foggy Trench. A Company was in support on the right in German Trench and B Company on the left in the south end of Foggy Trench. The attack began well, with the troops moving close behind the barrage and they escaped the enemy

From just east of the D74 south of Lesboeufs, looking northeast over the area attacked by 2nd Royal Dublin Fusiliers.

counter-barrage on the front line. They were within thirty metres of the gunpits when the enemy opened fire, forcing the attackers to dive for cover and continue the advance by crawling forward. Close range bombing fights and savage hand-to-hand fighting followed.

As **Sergeant Robert Downie**'s Company (C) approached the gunpits most of the officers were hit. The soldiers went to ground to avoid the terrible fire and the attack faltered. Completely oblivious to the storm of fire, Downie moved about calmly, reorganising the attack. At the critical moment he dashed forward calling, *Come on the Dubs!*, and the whole C Company line charged behind him. Downie accounted for a number of the enemy and then killed the crew of a machine-gun, capturing the weapon intact. The Germans were forced out of the gunpits and the strongpoint beyond it, leaving behind three more destroyed machine-guns. Although he had been wounded early on in the attack, Downie remained with his Company while a line was consolidated 180 metres beyond the gun-pits.

A and B Companies moved up and occupied the gunpits and a little later A Company went forward to occupy the new front line. However, this brought too many troops into the area and led to more casualties. The advance had also opened a gap of ninety metres on the right, resulting in both flanks being open. 1st Royal Warwickshire tried to press on but was halted by machine-gun fire from Dewdrop and Boritska Trenches. Further advance was clearly impossible. Three new lines were established; the most forward was newly dug, the second passed through the strongpoint and the third was in rear of it. A new trench was dug connecting the three lines on the right to act as a defensive flank and to protect against machine-gun fire from south of Dewdrop Trench. That night was very dark and heavy rain fell, making any task extremely arduous. By the time the Battalion was relieved early on the 25th, the new trench system had been dug down to a depth of one metre. Total casualties were 146.

The opposite view to the previous picture, taken from the track running southeast from the D74E/D19 Morval - Le Transloy road, as described in the map caption.

Meanwhile, 1st Royal Warwickshire, also attached to 11th Brigade from 10th Brigade, was due to advance through 2nd Royal Dublin Fusiliers, but the two battalions were badly mixed up. Heavy hand-to-hand fighting followed, but attempts to get ahead were halted by flanking fire. 12th Brigade failed to make progress against machine-guns in Dewdrop Trench, but managed to secure the German held portion of Spectrum Trench.

On 24th October the attack on Le Transloy was delayed for two days, and later was delayed again due to bad weather. On 31st October, General Foch asked Haig for a further delay until 5th November. In the meantime, XIV Corps attempted to make progress towards Le Transloy.

Battle of the Ancre Heights

170 Ppr James Richardson, 16th Battalion (Canadian Scottish) CEF (3rd Canadian Brigade, 1st Canadian Division) Regina Trench, Courcelette, France

As the next major phase of the Somme offensive approached, the Reserve Army embarked upon a reorganisation with the aim of concentrating forces ready for an attack between Beaumont-Hamel and Hébuterne. While this was going on, General Gough's main concern south of the Ancre was to capture Regina Trench and complete the seizure of Stuff and Schwaben Redoubts.

1st October 1916

At 3.15 p.m., the Canadian Corps attacked the section of Regina Trench on the higher ground to the west of Courcelette Trench. This was to be the start line for the forthcoming major attack to the north. Regina Trench was just over the crest and was consequently difficult for the artillery to engage. The Germans also used masses of concertina wire to supplement any gaps that were cut. As the troops waited for the attack to begin in the drizzling rain, they were hit by their own artillery in places.

In 2nd Canadian Division, 4th Canadian Brigade on the right advanced up to 360 metres, in conjunction with 23rd Division (III Corps, Fourth Army) on the right. However, on the left, 5th Canadian Brigade's attempt to seize 900 metres of Regina Trench west of the East Miraumont road was caught by the German barrage and heavy machine-gun fire in front of uncut wire. Kenora Trench was taken and held with a double block, but small groups of troops who reached Regina Trench were bombed back. In 3rd Canadian Division, parties of 8th Canadian Brigade managed to get through uncut wire and heavy machine-gun fire to enter Regina Trench. However, all gains were subsequently lost in bitter bombing fights.

Preparations were made to renew the attack, but due to the rain, high winds and poor visibility this could not take place until 8th October. In the meantime reliefs took place, with 3rd Canadian Division replacing 2nd Canadian Division, while the left brigade front was handed over to 25th Division (II Corps). 1st Canadian Division took over the right of the Canadian Corps.

The objectives were the Quadrilateral, where the Gird and Le Sars Lines intersected, Regina Trench across the whole frontage of the Canadian Corps and the high ground between Courcelette Trench and the West Miraumont road. Various advanced positions were linked and assembly trenches dug about 250 metres from Regina Trench. Much ground was gained in this process.

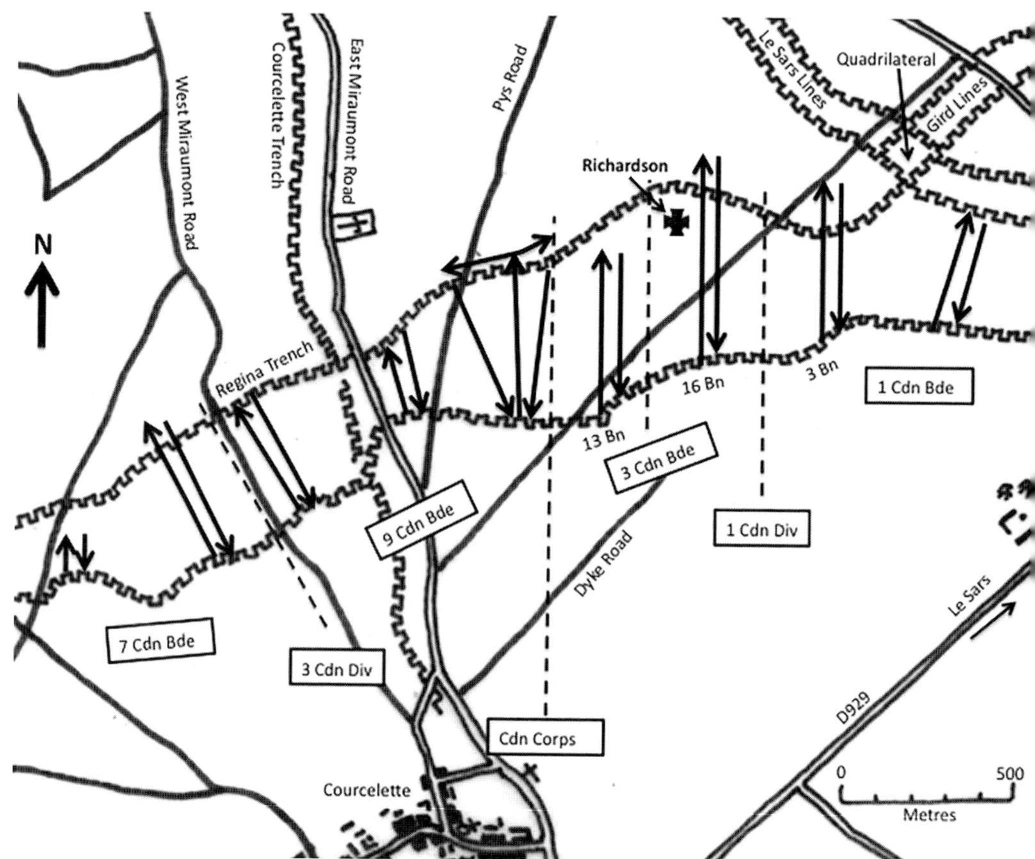

James Richardson's VC action took place in almost featureless terrain. Drive northwest from Le Sars on the D74 towards Pys. After 1,200m, at the crest of a hill, turn left and follow the long straight track for 1,125m, where there is a right turn in which to turn round. The track has a few bumps, but it is easily navigable with a little care. James Richardson's VC action was 250m slightly east of north from this point, towards the wind turbines right of Pys.

8th October 1916

The attack was launched at 4.50 a.m. while it was still dark and raining. On the right was 1st Canadian Division, attacking with 1st and 3rd Canadian Brigades, and on the left was 3rd Canadian Division, attacking with 7th and 9th Canadian Brigades.

On the extreme right, 1st Canadian Brigade advanced in four waves seventy metres apart. It reached the Le Sars road without delay, but southeast of the Quadrilateral the assault troops had to look for gaps in the wire. The forward trench of the Le Sars Line from Dyke Road to 360 metres beyond the Quadrilateral was cleared of resistance. At 1.20 p.m. a counterattack threatened, but it was checked by the artillery. However, while preparations were being made for the final advance, the Germans attacked behind a heavy barrage, coming down the trenches leading into the Quadrilateral from northeast and northwest. By dusk the assault troops had run out of bombs and were forced back to their start positions. During the night a forward trench was dug on the right, fifty metres from the Le Sars Line, and contact was established with 23rd Division on the right.

3rd Canadian Brigade attacked with 16th Battalion on the right and 13th Battalion on the left, covered by 3rd Canadian Machine Gun Company. 13th Battalion was stopped by wire and close range machine-gun fire. Only a small party reached the objective, whilst those stuck in no man's land were forced to retire that night.

16th Battalion had reached its assembly positions at 10 p.m. the previous evening. Nos.1 and 4 Companies formed the first two waves, with Nos. 2 and 3 Companies providing the third and fourth. Each wave was separated by fifty metres. There was a section of bombers on each flank of the second and fourth waves and four Lewis gun teams between the second and third waves with two more behind the fourth wave. Three parties of signalers were on the flanks and centre of the fourth wave, each with a field telephone connected to the front line. A company of 15th Battalion was in close support. Two sections of engineers were ready to assist in consolidating the objective and the Pioneer Battalion stood by to open a communications trench along an old German trench.

At 1 a.m. on 8th October, Nos.1 (right) and 4 (left) Companies advanced about one hundred metres and dug in while Nos.2 and 3 (left) Companies occupied the front line behind. Ahead was a slight slope, largely untouched by the artillery so far, with the German positions about 630 metres over the crest. As the barrage crashed down at 4.50 a.m., the advance began well, but in some places direction was lost in the darkness.

No.4 Company was led by Major George Lynch, Captain David Bell, CSM Mackie and **Piper James Richardson**. Bell fell back to command the second wave. The advance was easy because the ground was not cut up. CSM Mackie asked Richardson why he was not playing the pipes, but Major Lynch had told him not to. Mackie went ahead and discovered that the wire was not cut. As the rest of the Company arrived the Germans opened fire and threw bombs at them. Major Lynch was shot through the chest and there was nothing Mackie and Richardson could do for him (Adanac Military Cemetery, Miraumont – III F 31).

Richardson then asked, *Wull I gie them wund?* Mackie told him to go ahead and play while he did what he could to get the men through the wire. By then the second wave had arrived and no one had got through the wire. Captain Bell was killed there (Adanac Military Cemetery, Miraumont – VI C 19). While some men engaged the enemy, others tried to batter down the stakes supporting the wire or exploited the few small gaps. The enemy fire intensified and was extremely accurate. Fortunately most of the Germans had deployed behind the parados to avoid the Canadian grenades and consequently their bombs fell short. Richardson's pipes then struck up. Despite the heavy small arms fire, he played whilst striding up and down with great coolness for ten minutes. Richardson was not intended to be in the attack, but had pleaded to be included. His playing was just what was needed to inspire the troops and about one hundred of them forced their way through the wire and got into Regina Trench at about 9.00 a.m.

From 16th Battalion's left flank looking east.

On 16th Battalion's right the situation was not as critical, as there were gaps in the wire. A shower of grenades put a machine-gun out of action and bombing parties headed right to join up with 1st Canadian Brigade, but came up against stiff resistance.

In the centre and left there was hand-to-hand fighting and most of the bombers became casualties. Bombs ran short and captured supplies of German grenades were put to good use. The left flank was in the air and a block was established. The enemy trench beyond was well manned, with thick wire in front. Only two Lewis guns were in action, plus a captured enemy machine-gun. The only ammunition resupply was from casualties. With so few men and about 330 metres of front to hold, Lieutenant Hart chose to remain in Regina Trench rather than dig in ahead if it. However, a few men pressed on and reached some gunpits, but they were destroyed there.

A German counterattack against the left flank overwhelmed the post there. Lance Sergeant GH Slessor in charge was wounded, captured and died ten days later (Porte-de-Paris Cemetery, Cambrai – I A 10). After some hard fighting the block was retaken, but the attacks continued periodically all morning. Hart realised it was only a matter of time before the Germans succeeded. Attempts to get supplies of grenades from units on the right failed, because they too were running short. The telephone lines failed and only one runner in each direction to Battalion HQ got through, but this was sufficient for the artillery to bombard the trench to the left for a few hours in the early afternoon and prevent further attacks.

However, when 3rd Battalion (1st Canadian Brigade) on the right was forced back, it completely changed the situation. Hart consulted with the only other remaining officer, Lieutenant Bevan. They were down to seventy-five men with little ammunition, few bombs and both flanks were in the air. They decided correctly that they were unable to hold alone and had to pull back. Hart sent the men back in small groups; there were few casualties in the withdrawal, but one man who did not

make it was James Richardson. He had helped in the bombing parties and was later detailed to escort his wounded Company Sergeant Major and several prisoners to the rear. Richardson forgot his pipes and went back to get them. He vanished into the storm of shellfire and was not seen again. Consequently he was posted missing, presumed killed, until his remains were discovered in 1920.

By 6 p.m. on 9th October the remnants of the attacks were back in their start positions. They brought back twenty-five prisoners and two captured machine-guns. The action cost 16th Battalion 344 casualties, including 139 killed or died of wounds.

3rd Canadian Division had a similar experience. In 9th Canadian Brigade, many troops could not get through the wire, but small parties managed to enter Regina Trench on the flanks. However, they were either destroyed there or forced back. 7th Canadian Brigade's Royal Canadian Regiment found the wire well cut and got into Regina Trench. A strong party advanced 135 metres up the West Miraumont road, while bombers cleared westwards along the main trench. Efforts to reinforce the forward troops were halted by machine-guns and, after resisting three counterattacks, the survivors were forced back and abandoned Regina Trench. On the brigade's left, 49th Battalion lost direction and was halted in front of the objective.

The action on 8th October cost the Canadian Corps 1,364 casualties, more than double those on 1st October. Failure was largely due to the inability of the artillery to cut the wire and inflict significant damage on Regina Trench. Having been stopped by the wire and unsubdued defences, the assault troops were forced to make progress by bombing along the trenches instead. This required an enormous quantity of grenades and resupply in daylight proved inadequate. It was felt that the attack should have been delivered after noon to allow positions to be consolidated just before last light, when resupply and the digging of communications trenches could commence. This was the Canadian Corps' last act on the Somme. On 17th October it began moving to the First Army area, except for 4th Canadian Division, which remained under II Corps.

To the left of the Canadians, II Corps continued to battle for complete possession of the Schwaben and Stuff Redoubts. The latter was captured by 25th Division on 9th October. On 14th October, 39th Division wrested control of the Schwaben Redoubt from its defenders. Heavy counterattacks against both redoubts were repulsed.

Capture of Dewdrop & Boritska Trenches – 5th November 1916

172 Lt Eugene Bennett, 2nd Worcestershire (100th Brigade, 33rd Division) Near Le Transloy, France

While bad weather caused a number of postponements to the forthcoming Anglo-French offensive, Fourth Army made use of the delays to conduct further operations against Le Transloy. On 28th October, 33rd Division succeeded in taking Rainy and Dewdrop Trenches northeast of Lesboeufs, but on 1st November an attack against Boritska Trench by 100th Brigade (1/9th Highland Light Infantry and 2nd Worcestershire) foundered in waist deep mud and heavy shelling. On 2nd November, 17th Division cleared the remainder of Zenith Trench, but on 3rd November 100th Brigade made another unsuccessful attempt on Boritska Trench. Men arrived in the trenches already exhausted from slogging through the mud. During 4th November, 2nd Worcestershire moved through the French lines on the right and dug in on the left flank of the French 66th Infantry Regiment, at right angles to Boritska and Mirage Trenches.

The general offensive was fixed for 5th November. The previous night saw heavy rain and dawn broke with gale force winds. At 11.10 a.m. the attacking troops climbed out of their trenches and struggled forward. The creeping barrage had been slowed to just over twenty metres per minute to take account of the conditions. The III and I ANZAC Corps' attacks came to nothing. In XIV Corps, 17th Division, 19th Brigade pushed up the Lesboeufs – Le Transloy road, but made little progress. The brunt of the attack on the right was borne by two battalions of 100th Brigade, 33rd Division. On the left, 16th King's Royal Rifle Corps took Hazy Trench in a frontal attack. On the right, 2nd Worcestershire launched a successful flank attack against Boritska and Mirage Trenches from the more advanced French trenches. The two battalions joined up and dug a new line about 270 metres northeast of Boritska Trench. They were in touch with the French on the right and 19th Brigade on the left.

2nd Worcestershire's success was due mainly to the inspiring leadership of **Lieutenant Eugene Bennett**. The Battalion attacked from behind a sunken lane in lines of companies with D Company leading, followed by C, B and A Companies. Soon after first light a German plane swooped low over the Battalion and saw the troops in their attack formation. The officers urged the men to dig as deep as they could before the enemy artillery commenced. The barrage, which started twenty

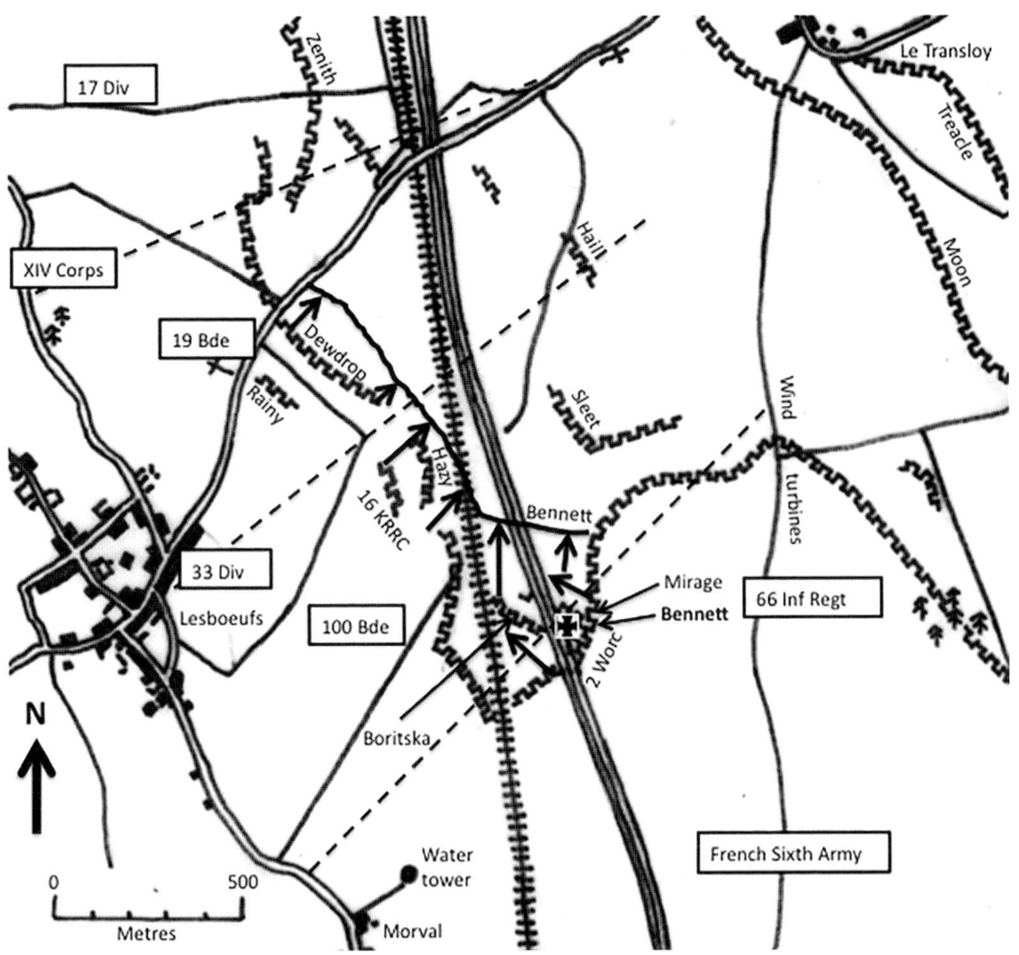

The topography around Boritska and Mirage Trenches has been altered by the A1 Autoroute and TGV railway line, which cut straight through them. Leave Le Transloy on the D19 southwest towards Lesboeufs. Pass the church on the left and after 100m turn left on an unclassified road. After 300m turn right. Follow the track for 1,300m to the top of a small hill and park on the left at the base of the third wind turbine. Look west across the sunken lane towards Lesboeufs church. This is the direction of the attack. There were other tracks in the area before the autoroute and railway came. The brigade war diary map suggests that the four waves were deployed closer to the Autoroute before the attack started, but it is possible that this sunken lane is the one out of which Eugene Bennett scrambled out of to inspire the troops to go forward.

A view from the opposite direction can be gained in Morval. Leave the village northwards on the D74 towards Lesboeufs. Where the road swings left at a Calvary, turn right. At the water tower there is a good view over the autoroute and railway to where the attack started near the middle wind turbine and in the other direction towards Lesboeufs church.

minutes later, mainly affected the two leading companies. D Company lost all its officers and C Company's commander was killed, leaving Bennett in command. The bombardment went on for hours and the troops sheltered as best they could in their shallow trenches.

The British barrage opened at 11 a.m. and the advance commenced thirteen minutes later. Having ensured that D Company started under its own NCOs,

Looking northwest from wind turbine lane across the ground over which 2nd Worcestershire attacked on 5th November 1916.

Bennett rejoined C Company. D Company advanced up the slope into a hail of shell and machine-gun fire. As C Company followed, Bennett and a number of other men were hit by a shell burst and collapsed into the sunken lane. While his wounds were being dressed by a French soldier, Bennett watched the rearmost companies go forward. Peering through the smoke he saw the attack break down; D Company's NCOs were all casualties and the soldiers did not know what to do. The other companies suffered from the fire of two machine-guns on the right flank and the survivors took cover with D Company.

The situation was critical and demanded drastic action. Bennett was sheltering in the sunken lane with a sergeant and another subaltern. The sergeant made a

From the base of the third wind turbine looking west across the only existing sunken lane in the attack area. Other lanes closer to Mirage and Boritska Trenches have disappeared under the autoroute and TGV railway. Most of the battlefield involved in Eugene Bennett's VC action is between the two and is inaccessible.

step in the bank and used it to spring forward, shouting, *The boys will go forward if there's someone to lead them*. He was hit and fell after covering only twenty metres. The subaltern followed and was killed. Bennett cut himself a step in the bank and ran forward still clutching the spade. Reaching the line of sheltering soldiers, he went on, urging them to follow. The whole Battalion rose and charged over the crest into the flank of the enemy trenches. Heavy casualties were caused by the machine-guns on the right, but the impetus of the attack could not be checked. As soon as Mirage and Boritska Trenches had been taken the Battalion swung right and pushed on about another 300 metres, where it made contact with 16th King's Royal Rifle Corps on the left and the French on the right. The line reached was consolidated and a new trench (Bennett) was dug along it under heavy fire. That night the Battalion was relieved by 1/6th Cameronians. Bennett marched out with only sixty men and one other officer.

Battle of the Ancre – 13th November 1916

173 Lt Col Bernard Freyberg, Queen's Royal West Surrey commanding Hood Battalion (189th Brigade, 63rd (Royal Naval) Division) Beaucourt sur Ancre, France

174 Pte John Cunningham, 12th East Yorkshire (92nd Brigade, 31st Division) Hebuterne Sector, France

The Battle of the Ancre, fought by the newly formed Fifth (formerly Reserve) Army, opened at 5.45 a.m. on 13th November 1916. The aim was to capture the area from Serre to St Pierre Divion, thereby reducing the German salient formed by the British advances to the south. The brunt of the fighting was borne by the four divisions of V Corps; from right to left: 63rd, 51st, 2nd and 3rd. To the north, 31st Division (XIII Corps) was to protect the open left flank, while to the south II Corps was to complete the reduction of the enemy front system south of the Ancre.

Each morning preceding the attack the artillery fired an intensive barrage coinciding with zero hour, hoping that on 13th November the Germans would

The final official act of the 1916 Battle of the Somme, was the Battle of the Ancre 13th-18th November, after which the offensive was shut down for the winter. Some objectives from 1st July remained in German hands. The four and a half months of fighting resulted in an approximate total of 1,265,000 casualties on all sides.

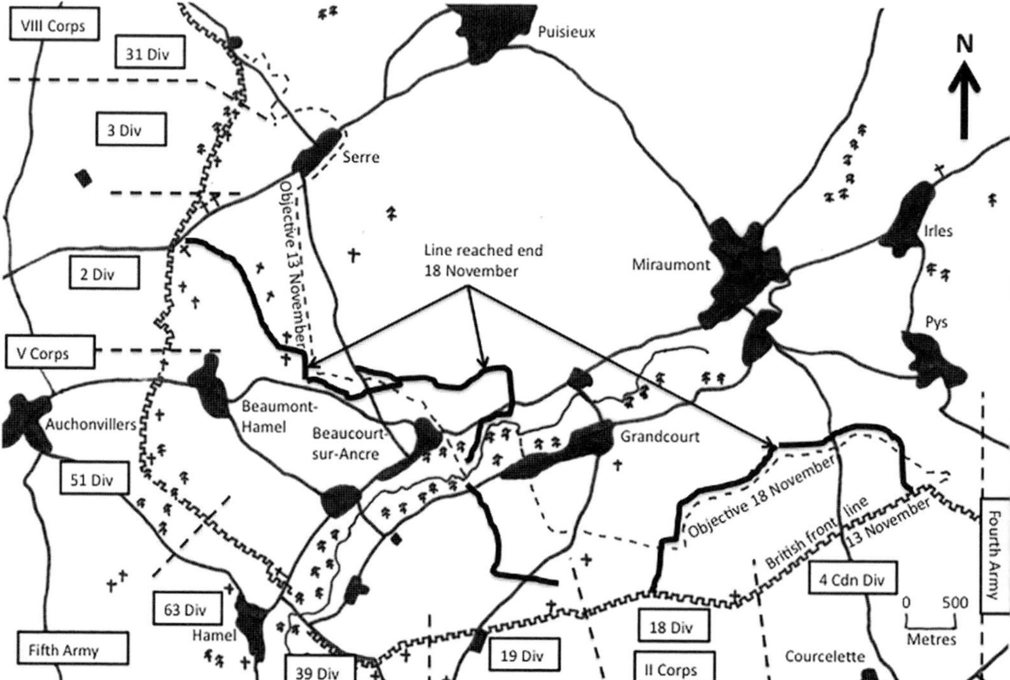

notice nothing until the attackers were upon them. The assault troops had been subjected to many delays and were in poor condition, having been out in the wet for weeks. However, the move into the assembly positions on the moonlit and foggy evening of 12th November proceeded without incident. At zero hour, about ninety minutes before sunrise, they set off into the thick fog close behind the creeping barrage. The rate of advance was only ninety metres every five minutes to allow for the muddy conditions. South of the Ancre, II Corps met with success almost everywhere. Casualties were light and many prisoners were taken.

On V Corps' right flank, 63rd Division (in its first major offensive action in France) deployed 189th and 188th Brigades (right and left respectively). Both brigades advanced with two battalions forward and two in support. In 189th Brigade, the Hood (right) and Hawke (left) Battalions led, supported by the Drake and Nelson Battalions respectively. In reserve were 1st Honourable Artillery Company and 7th Royal Fusiliers (190th Brigade). The leading battalions were to take the German front system of three trench lines before the support battalions passed through to beyond the Beaumont Hamel – Beaucourt Station road. The leading battalions were then to resume the advance and seize Beaucourt Trench. Finally, the support battalions were to capture Beaucourt village. Four tunnels under no man's land were to be opened, one by the explosion of a mine. The night before the attack was quiet and by 11 p.m. the assault troops were in position.

The Hood Battalion, advancing on a frontage of 270 metres, along with a company of 1st Honourable Artillery Company, took the front system at 6.05 a.m., despite the difficulty of finding and dealing with dugouts in the dark. Over 600 prisoners were taken. The success was due mainly to **Lieutenant Colonel Bernard Freyberg**, who pressed on very close behind the bombardment, although B Company suffered some casualties on the right from shells falling short. Freyberg went over the top that morning in his best uniform, *Polished to the knocker*, according to one who saw him, but it was no joy ride; his Adjutant and Signals Officer were killed alongside him by snipers. The Hood Battalion's success was the only one so far. While the first two waves held the enemy third line in anticipation of the support battalions continuing the advance, the third and fourth waves consolidated the enemy support and front lines respectively.

The Hawke Battalion and 188th Brigade to the left met very stiff

Looking back along the axis of the Hood Battalion's advance on 13th November, with the Royal Naval Division memorial on the left.

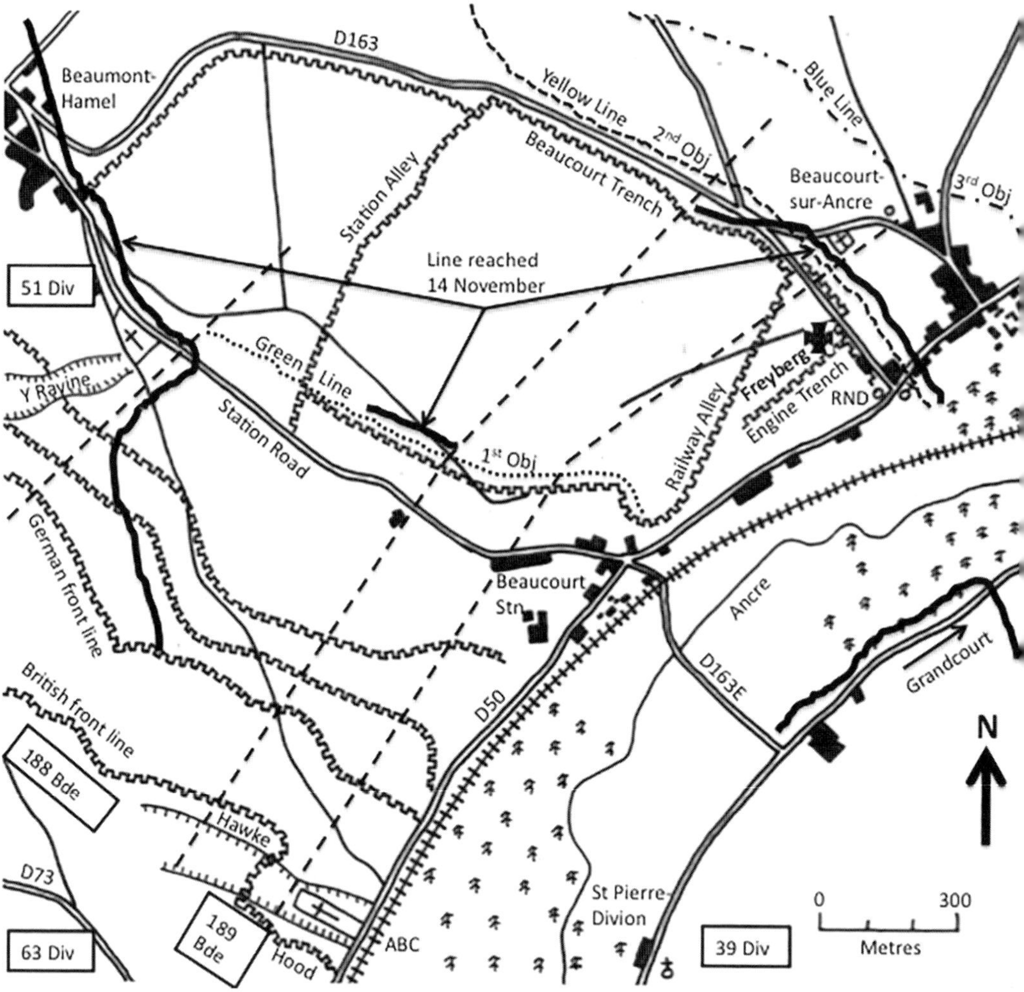

Approach Beaucourt-sur-l'Ancre on the D50 from the southwest. At the beginning of the village on the left is the Royal Naval Division memorial. Turn left and after 200m turn left again. Drive west along this track for about 350m. From here the whole of 189th Brigade's attack on 13th–14th November 1916 can be viewed.

From the track west of Beaucourt looking southwest from where 189th Brigade's attack commenced.

resistance and flanking fire from Y Ravine. As a result, most troops did not get beyond the enemy second line and in some places only the front line was taken in this initial phase. The planned echelon attack broke down and all battalions were soon involved in the fighting. Some of the troops also lost direction in the fog and dark and become intermingled. Freyberg went forward and personally untangled the mess prior to the next phase of the attack. Chief Petty Officer Tobin saw him calmly walking forward on his own over the rise. *Hello Tobin*, called out Freyberg, *I think we will get a VC today*. Freyberg should have halted here to allow the Drake Battalion to pass through to the second objective at Beaucourt Trench. However, delay would have meant losing the protection of the creeping barrage and very few of the Drake Battalion had arrived. So, at 7.45 a.m., he pressed on, with a combined force of about 450 men from the Hood (300) and Drake (120) Battalions and the Honourable Artillery Company, for Engine and Beaucourt Trenches.

On reaching the second objective, on the edge of Beaucourt, they ran into the combined fire of the British and German barrages. After two attempts to get through, they were halted. Brigade Headquarters forbade further advance until the situation elsewhere had been resolved. Freyberg's men dug in as best they could with their entrenching tools just short of the second objective, on a line from the railway embankment to Railway Alley, with the left flank thrown back. At about 9.30 p.m., 188th Brigade arrived and extended the line to the left as far as Station Alley. HQ 63rd Division then ordered all troops to consolidate where they were and prepare for another attack on 14th November.

Freyberg was wounded twice during the day. A spent 5.9″ shell splinter hit him in the chest, causing a bruise the size of a soup plate. A little later he was hit in the thigh. This was a more serious wound, but he kept it to himself until admitted to the General Hospital in Boulogne.

Further north 51st Division and the right of 2nd Division took Beaumont Hamel and secured the second objective. However, the attacks by the left of 2nd Division and 3rd Division failed completely.

Looking in the opposite direction to the previous picture towards the objective in Beaucourt beyond Beaucourt Trench.

92nd Brigade (31st Division) was to extend the defensive flank on the far left with an attack by two battalions of the East Yorkshires (12th left and 13th right). The plan was for the 13th Battalion to take the enemy reserve line and the 12th Battalion to take the support line, thus echeloning the defensive flank back towards the British front line. A planned smoke screen was abandoned because the wind was in the wrong direction, but some smoke bombs were fired to assist the advance. Two tanks scheduled to support the attack could not advance due to the state of the ground. During the night Lewis gun teams and snipers deployed into no man's land to support the attack. The artillery had done its work well and the wire was well cut.

13th East Yorkshire reached its objective, but the battalion on its right (2nd Suffolk in 3rd Division) could not get forward. As a result, 13th East Yorkshire was attacked from the right rear and about fifty men were cut off and forced to surrender. By 7 a.m. 2nd Suffolk was back on its start line and 92nd Brigade's right flank was completely in the air. Three major counterattacks were launched against this flank. 13th East Yorkshire managed to hold on to the second German line until 7 p.m. But, when it was clear that all attempts on the right flank by 3rd Division had failed, it was forced to pull back to the German front line. Late that night the Battalion had to withdraw to its start positions. Throughout the day very heavy German artillery fire thwarted attempts to bring up reinforcements and supplies in any meaningful quantities.

12th East Yorkshire attacked with its four companies in line; from the right A, B, C and D. The enemy front line was found hardly to exist due to the ferocity of the barrage. The first wave held it while the others pressed on. The support line was taken at some cost, but reinforcements were prevented from arriving by a heavy German barrage on the British front line and no man's land. Despite this the Battalion gained all its objectives within twenty minutes and with few casualties overall. Three hundred prisoners were taken, but about half of these

RND Memorial
Beaucourt-sur-l'Ancre

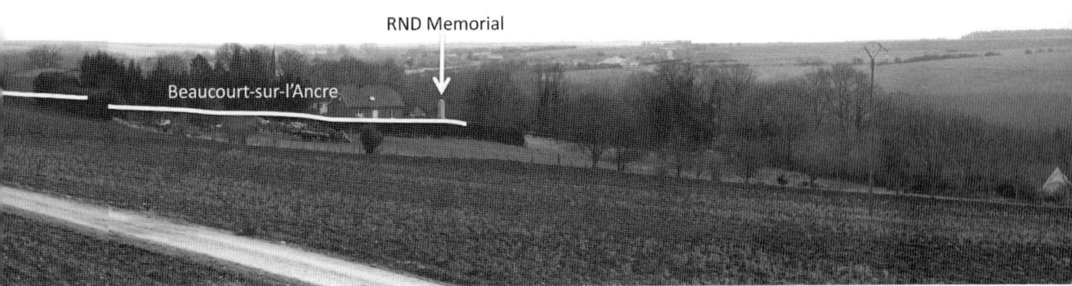

Drive through Serre from the southwest along the D919 towards Puisieux. In the village turn left and after 100m pass the water tower on the left. Continue to a farm on the left. Just beyond it is a track on the left leading to John Copse. There is usually space to park a car here for a few minutes. John Cunningham's VC action was 300m due north of this junction. A few abbreviations are used on the map; LCC = Luke Copse Cemetery, RHC = Railway Hollow Cemetery and QC = Queen's Cemetery.

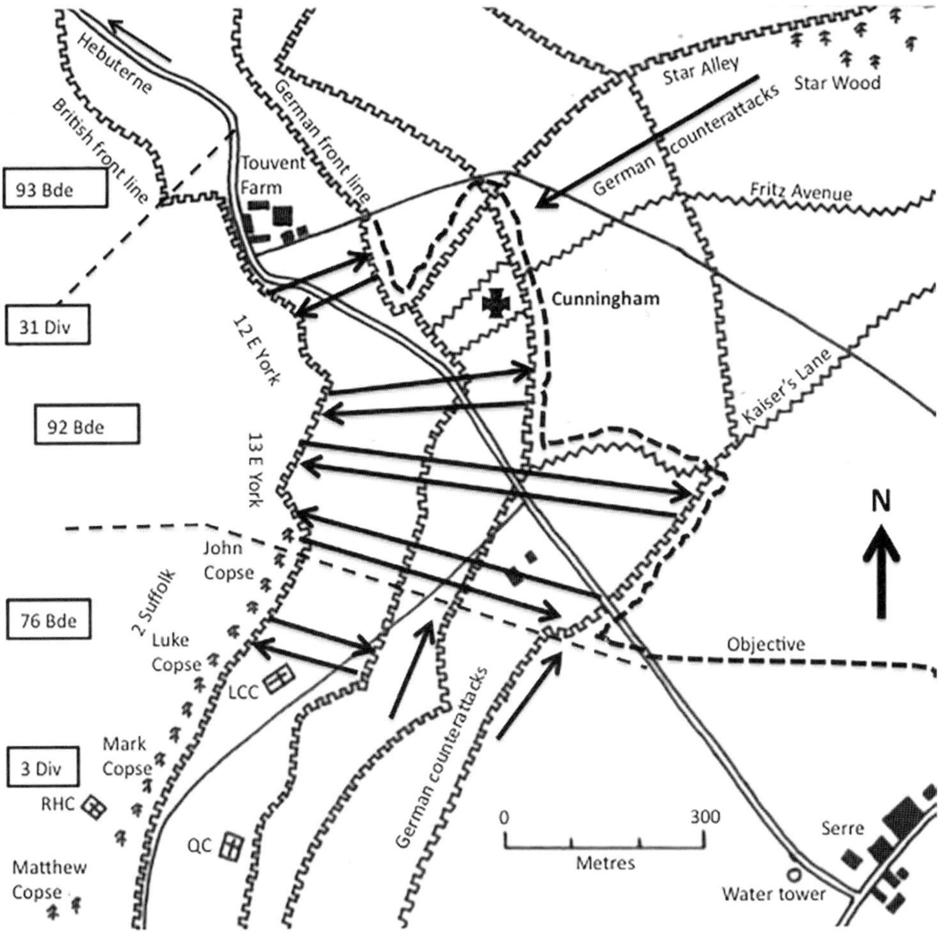
Hebuterne
British front line
German front line
Star Alley
Star Wood
German counterattacks
Touvent Farm
93 Bde
Fritz Avenue
Cunningham
31 Div
12 E York
Kaiser's Lane
92 Bde
13 E York
N
John Copse
2 Suffolk
76 Bde
Luke Copse
LCC
Objective
German counterattacks
Mark Copse
3 Div
RHC
QC
0
300
Metres
Serre
Matthew Copse
Water tower

From the track junction on the Serre - Hébuterne road looking north over the ground 12th East Yorkshire captured but was forced to relinquish later in the day due to the failure on its right.

became casualties of their own artillery fire as they moved back over no man's land. The German trenches had been severely damaged by the artillery and it proved impossible to make them defensible. Counterattacks from Star Wood from 9.30 a.m. onwards were beaten off by Lewis guns, but the enemy methodically nibbled away at the British gains. Fighting degenerated into small actions by bombers and snipers.

Soon after the initial attack, a bombing section proceeded up a communications trench, where it was soon in action against determined German opposition. All the section became casualties except for **Private John Cunningham**, who gathered the bombs from his fallen comrades and continued the fight. Although alone, he pushed the Germans back and when his supply of bombs ran out he went back and obtained more. Returning to the fray he came up against a party of ten Germans. Against the odds he killed them all and cleared the trench as far as the enemy line.

Some troops penetrated as far as the reserve line, but once 3rd Division's attack had failed to the south, it was only a matter of time before withdrawal became inevitable. By 3 p.m. the survivors had been forced back to the German front line and soon after it was learned that 3rd Division would not be renewing its attack. At 8.45 p.m. the survivors were in danger of being surrounded and by 9.30 p.m. the last of them were back in the British lines. 12th East Yorkshire lost 383 men in this attack.

At 6.20 a.m. on 14th November, 63rd Division renewed its attack. The objective was the Yellow Line on the left and Beaucourt on the right. On the left two battalions of 111th Brigade were checked about 200 metres short of Beaucourt Trench, but the front was extended 300 metres to the left and 13th King's Royal Rifle Corps began working around the flank of the village. At 7.45 a.m. 190th Brigade advanced against Beaucourt village, with 7th Royal Fusiliers in support. When the attacking troops reached Freyberg's position they had already been subjected to heavy fire and took cover. Three attempts by 1st Honourable Artillery Company to get into the village were driven back by machine-gun fire. Seeing that the situation was about to degenerate into total chaos, Freyberg led a fourth attack to divert attention from 13th King's Royal Rifle Corps. This time the impetus was unstoppable as men

from six battalions surged forward. After a short fight the village was taken and 500 prisoners captured. Shortly afterwards Beaucourt Trench also fell. Freyberg was slightly wounded in the advance when a bullet struck his helmet and he also became entangled in barbed wire while getting away from a grenade.

Consolidation began immediately under Freyberg's direction, with 1st Honourable Artillery Company on the right, 4th Royal Fusiliers in the centre and 13th King's Royal Rifle Corps on the left. Messages were sent to stop more troops coming into Beaucourt to avoid the counter-bombardment, during which Freyberg was wounded for a fourth time. A near miss by a shell killed two men and wounded two more in addition to Freyberg. Captain Montagu, commanding D Company, found him lying face down with a huge gash on his neck, revealing the vertebrae. After being bandaged Freyberg refused to be evacuated until he had personally explained the dispositions of the force to his successor, Lieutenant Commander Egerton. He also refused to expose anyone else to danger in removing him to safety during the shelling. When it eventually died down, Montagu supported Freyberg as he walked back to the aid post, where Surgeon McCracken bandaged him while Freyberg continued to issue orders to runners. He was then carried back to Brigade HQ where he explained the situation to the commander. On arrival at the field hospital he had so many wounds and was so pale from loss of blood that he was initially placed in a tent with those not expected to survive. Fortunately, a doctor on routine rounds checked his condition and moved him to another tent.

As a result of the Hood Battalion's lodgement at Beaucourt, St Pierre-Divion and Beaumont-Hamel also fell. Fighting went on until 18th November, when the Battle of the Somme came to an end. The final cost was 420,000 British and 195,000 French casualties, compared to between 520,000 and 650,000 Germans, who had lost another 330,000 men at Verdun. The British paid a terrible price on the Somme, but their sacrifice ensured the destruction of the cream of the old German Army and, although it was far from obvious at the time, had sown the seeds of ultimate victory in 1918.

Biographies

SECOND LIEUTENANT TOM EDWIN ADLAM
7th Battalion, The Bedfordshire Regiment

Tom Adlam was born at Waterloo Gardens, Milford, Salisbury, Wiltshire on 21st October 1893. His father was John Adlam (1861–1950), a wheelwright, living with his stepfather and mother, Seba and Mary Ann Burch, at Stratford-under-the-Castle, Wiltshire in 1881. Tom's mother was Evangeline née Phillips (1857–1916), a tailoress. She married John Adlam in 1882 at Alderbury. In 1901 the family was living at 14 Waterloo Gardens, Milford and in 1911 at 2 Farley Road, Waterloo Gardens, Salisbury. Tom had five siblings:

(Hazel Adlam).

- Gertrude Elsie Adlam (born 1884) married Claude Arthur Bryant (born 1887) in 1912 and they had four children – Robert J Bryant 1913, Gwendoline J Bryant 1916, Eric P Bryant 1918 and Mary E Bryant 1921.
- Ewart John Adlam (born 1886) was a junior clerk in a printing firm in 1901. He married Florence C Wratten in 1917 at Dartford, Kent and they had a daughter, Pauline C Adlam in 1927.
- Evelyn Violet Adlam (born 1887) married John Grant Purdie (born 1887 at Croy, Inverness-shire) in 1906 at Wandsworth, London. They had two children – Winifred Violet Purdie 1907 and Margaret Campbell Purdie 1910.
- Edward Percy 'Pearly' Wilfred Adlam (born 1890) became a tailor in Milford Street, Salisbury. He enlisted in 7th Royal Berkshire (33148) on 12th April 1915 and rose to corporal. His address at the time was 7 Farley Road, Waterloo Gardens, Salisbury. He qualified as a bomber and served in Salonika from 30th September 1916. He applied for a commission on 12th April 1918 and returned to England on 1st June, where he was granted fourteen days leave. He married Ada M Lewis in the 2nd quarter of 1918 at Salisbury. Following an attachment to the Wessex Reserve Brigade, he commenced officer training at No.2 Officer Cadet Battalion at Pembroke College, Cambridge on 20th September. He transferred

Bishop Wordsworth's School was founded in 1889 by Bishop John Wordsworth as The Bishop's School. After his death it was renamed Bishop Wordsworth's School. It became a grammar school in 1905 and expanded beyond its original premises in the cathedral close. Until 1928 it admitted boys and girls, when a separate girls' grammar school was established. Sir William Golding, author of 'Lord of the Flies', published in 1954 and Nobel Prize winner for Literature, was a teacher there between 1945 and 1962.

The Church of England Training School for Teachers in Winchester was first established in 1840. The purpose built college on West Hill was opened in 1862 by the Bishop of Winchester.

to No.13 Officer Cadet Battalion at Newmarket on 20th January 1919 and was commissioned in the Royal Berkshire Regiment on 17th March. He served until 1st September 1921. Edward was Mayor of Salisbury 1956–57.

- Dorothy Ethel Adlam (born 1900) married Ernest G Allingham in 1922.

Tom was educated at St Martin's Infants School, Bishop Wordsworth's School and the Pupil Teachers Centre, all in Salisbury. He then attended Winchester Training College 1912–14. Tom was a keen sportsman and played football regularly for Salisbury City FC with his brother 'Pearly' in the Southern League Second Division 1906–11. He became a teacher at Brook Street Council School, Basingstoke, Hampshire.

The beach and distinctive lighthouse at Dovercourt.

Tom enlisted in 4th Hampshire TF (1842) in September 1912 and served with 2/4th Hampshire early in the Great War. 1/4th and 2/4th Hampshire served in India from late 1914 and early 1915 respectively. 2/4th Hampshire sailed from Southampton on 13th December 1914, arriving at Karachi on 11th January

1915. Despite no hard evidence, it seems likely that Tom served in India before returning to Britain later in 1915. He was commissioned in the Bedfordshire Regiment on 16th November 1915 and posted to 9th (Reserve) Battalion, part of 6th Reserve Brigade stationed at Dovercourt, Essex.

St Mark's Church, South Farnborough, Hampshire, where Tom Adlam married Ivy Annette Mace on 21st June 1916.

On 21st June 1916, Tom Adlam married Ivy Annette née Mace (1891–1972), at St Mark's Church, South Farnborough, Hampshire. Her family lived at Guildford House, South Farnborough. Ivy and Tom had four children:

- Josephine Adlam, born on 22nd May 1918, registered at Cambridge. She married Bernard Hugh Swinstead (1909–72) in the 2nd quarter of 1937 at Alton, Hampshire and they had two children – Susan J Swinstead 1939 and Peter H Swinstead 1944.
- Stephanie Adlam, born on 11th June 1923, registered at Farnham, Surrey. She married Gerald E Melhuish in the 2nd quarter of 1944 at Alton.
- Roger Adlam, born on 16th August 1924, registered at Biggleswade, Bedfordshire. He died on 30th July 1981.
- Clive Adlam, born on 31st January 1929, registered at Alton, Hampshire. He married Doreen V Merton in the 1st quarter of 1956 at Chatham, Kent and they had three children – Caroline F Adlam 1959, Hazel K Adlam 1965 and Michael John Adlam 1968.

Tom Adlam receiving a gold watch from the Mayor of Salisbury, Councillor James Macklin, on 16th December 1916.

Tom was posted to 7th Battalion, joining C Company at Maricourt, France on 18th July 1916. **Awarded the VC for his actions at Thiepval, France on 27th/28th September 1916, LG 25th November 1916.** The VC was presented by the King at Buckingham Palace on 2nd December. On 16th December he was presented with a gold watch by the Mayor of Salisbury, Councillor James

Macklin, on behalf of the people of Salisbury. **Awarded the Italian Silver Medal for Military Valour, LG 26th May 1917.**

No.2 Officer Cadet Battalion, for which Tom Adlam was an instructor, was based at Pembroke College, Cambridge.

Tom was not fit to return to active duty and became an instructor at No.2 Officer Cadet Battalion, Cambridge. Appointed temporary lieutenant 19th April 1917. Promoted lieutenant 1st July 1917. Appointed acting captain 8th November 1918 – 16th November 1919, when he relinquished his commission and was granted the rank of captain.

He returned to military life, being commissioned as a lieutenant (on probation) in the Army Educational Corps on 11th December 1920, with seniority from 15th June 1920, and served in Ireland during the troubles. He was confirmed in this rank on 13th December 1921, backdated to the commissioning date and retained his seniority. On 12th February 1922 Tom unveiled the war memorial outside Salisbury Guildhall; Field Marshal Haig had been invited to perform the ceremony. The service was conducted by the Reverend WRF Addison VC, formerly Curate of St Edmund's, Salisbury. Tom transferred to the Regular Army Reserve of Officers on 20th February 1923 as a captain with seniority from 29th November 1922.

The family moved in with Ivy's parents at Guildford House, South Farnborough in 1923. Previously they had lived at Lynchford House, Farnborough. Tom was employed as an Assistant Master at Sandy Church of England School in Bedfordshire and was the first Chairman of the Sandy British Legion 1922–26. While there he was also the Scoutmaster and a member of Biggleswade Football Club. From 1926

Salisbury war memorial.

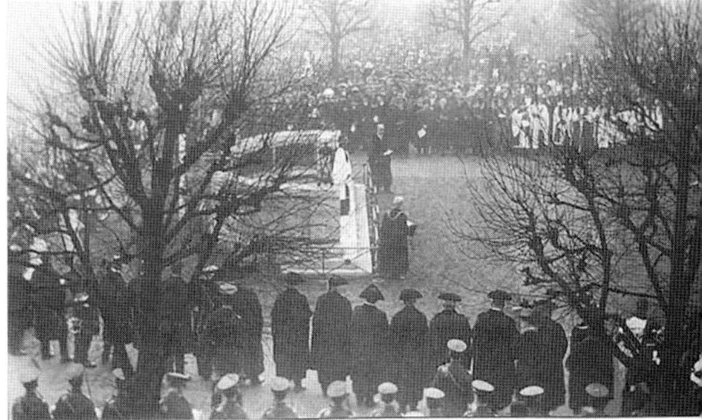

The dedication ceremony at Salisbury war memorial on 12th February 1922.

Tom was headteacher at Blackmoor Church of England School, Liss, Hampshire and the family lived at School House, Blackmoor.

On 24th August 1939 Tom was recalled as a captain (11792). He served with the Royal Engineers as a staff captain with the Movement Control Section at Avonmouth Docks, Somerset 1939–40. In February 1940 he was appointed Deputy Assistant Quartermaster General at Glasgow until August 1943, including a detachment to the United States. Appointed temporary major on 31st March 1941. Promoted war substantive major and temporary lieutenant colonel on 16th November 1943, to be Commandant at Dover, Kent and Tilbury, Essex 1943–46, including involvement with the Normandy invasion. He was not active from June 1946. On 24th May 1947 he was released from the Regular Army Reserve of Officers with the rank of honorary lieutenant colonel, having exceeded the age for liability for recall.

The Reverend WRF Addison VC, former Curate of St Edmund's, Salisbury, conducted the dedication service for the Salisbury war memorial on 12th February 1922.

He returned to Blackmoor Church of England School and, apart from his war service, remained in the post until 1952, when it closed and he retired. He bought the School and converted it into the family home. Tom became Clerk to Whitehill Parish Council and Secretary of the Blackmoor Flower Show Club. He was also employed on the Woolmer Estate by Lord Selbourne and later by the Blackmoor Estate Fruit Farm and Nursery. Tom pursued many interests, including reading, gardening, cricket and following sports. He was the wicketkeeper for his local team until he was seventy-one.

Tom attended every VC/GC Reunion and ceremony between 1920 and 1974. In 1933 he led the Remembrance Day Parade at the Cenotaph with Christopher Cox VC, also formerly of 7th Bedfordshire. In July 1966 he was one of twelve VCs invited by the Ministry of Defence to take part in the 50th anniversary commemoration of the Battle of the Somme. On 6th April 1970 Tom was one of '10 VCs on a VC10' on

Six VCs at Thiepval during the 50th anniversary of the Battle of the Somme commemorations in July 1966. From the left: Arthur Proctor, Robert Ryder, James Hutchinson, Archie White, Tom Adlam and Theodore Veale.

St Matthew's Churchyard, Blackmoor, Liss, where Tom and his wife are buried.

the inaugural flight of the Super Vickers VC 10 from London to Nairobi by East African Airlines. The ten VCs, five each from both World Wars selected by drawing names out of a hat, were guests of the company for a nine day holiday in Kenya, Tanzania and Uganda. In Kenya the schedule included Nairobi, Nyeri, Treetops (where Princess Elizabeth succeeded to the throne), Tsavo National Park and Mombasa. On 13th April the party flew over Ngorongoro Crater, the Serengeti and Lake Victoria to Uganda. In Kampala they were hosted by General Idi Amin and travelled up the Nile to Murchison Falls. Back in Nairobi they visited State House to meet President Kenyatta before flying back to Heathrow.

Tom Adlam died on holiday at Hayling Island, Hampshire on 28th May 1975 and is buried with his wife at St Matthew's Churchyard, Blackmoor, Liss, Hampshire. He is also commemorated at Bishop Wordsworth's School, Salisbury on a tablet and banner unveiled on 13th June 1933 by Major General George Henry Basil Freeth CB CMG DSO and on a memorial plaque unveiled on 27th September 1991.

In addition to the VC, he was awarded the British War Medal 1914–20, Victory Medal 1914–19, Defence Medal, War Medal 1939–45, George VI Coronation Medal 1937, Elizabeth II Coronation Medal 1953 and the Italian Silver Medal for Military Valour. The VC was held on loan by the Bedfordshire and Hertfordshire Regiment Museum, Luton from 1990. On 27th September 2003 the medals were presented to Salisbury Guildhall by his grandson, Sergeant Martin Adlam RAF, on loan from the family. Tom Adlam's portrait also hangs in Salisbury Guildhall.

Salisbury Guildhall, where Tom Adlam's VC is displayed.

CAPTAIN WILLIAM BARNSLEY ALLEN
1/3rd Field Ambulance Royal Army Medical Corps att'd 246th Brigade Royal Field Artillery

William Allen was born at 14 Botanical Road, Ecclesall, Sheffield, Yorkshire on 8th June 1892. His father, Percy Edwin Allen (1863–1952), was born as Percy Edwin Crofts. He was a steel merchant's clerk in 1881, living at 61 Albert Road, Ecclesall, Sheffield. By 1891 he was a silversmith's manager. His mother was Edith née Barnsley (born 1868). Percy and Edith married in 1889 and lived at 6 Victoria Avenue, Scarborough, Yorkshire. They had moved to 14 Botanical Road, Ecclesall, Sheffield by 1891 and to 42 Southgrove Road, Ecclesall by 1896. Edith had moved to Worksop, Nottinghamshire by 1901 and to 91 Endcliffe Vale Road, Sheffield by 1911. William had two sisters:

- Edith Dorothy Allen, born on 27th July 1890.
- Barbara D Allen, born on 13th September 1896.

William was educated at St Cuthbert's College (later Worksop College), Nottinghamshire 1902–09 and was a member of Mountgarrett House, then Mason House. He attended Sheffield Medical School, graduating in June 1914 (MB & ChB 1914), having been awarded the University Gold Medal for Pathology 1913, the Kaye Scholarship for the highest marks in physiology and anatomy and three bronze medals for academic distinction. He was also a member of Sheffield University OTC from 1911. William became a junior house doctor at the Royal

St Cuthbert's College (later Worksop College), attended by William Barnsley Allen 1902–09.

Sheffield University, where William Allen attended the Medical School.

The Dining Hall of St Cuthbert's College.

Royal Hospital, Sheffield, established in 1832 and closed in 1978. Most of it has since been demolished.

The Wesleyan Chapel at Gainsborough, Lincolnshire, where William Allen married Mary Mercer on 16th May 1916.

Hospital in Sheffield in June 1914 and was commissioned in 3rd West Riding Field Ambulance RAMC (Territorial Force) as a lieutenant on 8th August 1914. Promoted captain 1st April 1915 and went to France on 15th April, attached to 246th (West Riding) Brigade RFA.

William Allen married Mary 'Mollie' Young née Mercer (1894–1941) at the Wesleyan Chapel, Gainsborough, Lincolnshire on 16th May 1916, both giving their address as 27 Cecil Street. Mollie's brother, George Metcalfe Mercer (1884–1961), joined the RNR as a probationary sub-lieutenant and was confirmed in the rank on 1st July 1910. He was promoted lieutenant on 1st July 1912 and served in the Auxiliary Patrol in a number of ships and shore establishments, including HMS *David, Defiance, Indefatigable, Implacable, Drake, Victory, Orlando, President* and RMS *Aquitania*. He was awarded the DSC (LG 14th July 1916), demobilised in 1919 and retired on 1st January 1929 as a commander.

William and Mollie had a daughter, Patricia Josephine Laura Allen, born on 30th April 1920. She married Vivian H Faulkner (1916–55) in 1942 at Paddington, London. Vivian's previous marriage to Renée S Pickering in 1936 ended in divorce. Vivian and Patricia had at least one son – Timothy Vivian Faulkner, born 1943 at Windsor, Berkshire, was a director of Pads Ltd and Bondlens Ltd and was Company Secretary of Skin Deep Medical Ltd 2008–10. Patricia married Alban Clement Herbert Barchard (born 1906) in 1958 at Westminster.

William was awarded the MC for his actions south of Thiepval, Somme on 14th and 20th August 1916, when he went into no man's land under heavy shellfire to tend to a wounded artilleryman, repeating the procedure for others later, LG 26th September 1916. Awarded the VC for his actions near Mesnil, France on 3rd September 1916, LG 26th October 1916.

3rd Northern General Hospital, Sheffield, was established in the Teachers' Training College on Collegiate Crescent and Ecclesall Road, with a number of outstations in the city.

He was granted leave 5th-12th October 1916, travelling to 6 Victoria Avenue, Scarborough via Boulogne and Folkestone. On 12th October he was examined by a medical board at the Military Hospital, Scarborough. He was suffering from bronchial catarrh and debility and declared unfit for duty for seven days. On 18th October a medical board at 3rd Northern General Hospital, Sheffield found him unfit for duty for three weeks. At the time his address was 777 St Philip's Road, Sheffield. A medical board at Scarborough on 4th November declared him fit for general service.

Hyde Park, 2nd June 1917; William Allen, seated on the extreme right of the front row, awaits the presentation of his VC and MC by the King. Next to him is Frederick William Palmer, 22nd Royal Fusiliers, who was awarded the VC for actions north of Courcelette, France, on 16th-17th February 1917.

The VC and MC were presented by the King in Hyde Park on 2nd June 1917. **Awarded a Bar to the MC for his actions at Nieuport on 25th July 1917; during an intense bombardment of a town with HE and gas he left the ADS to search for wounded. Hearing there were some wounded in a remote part of town he went there, collected them and supervised their removal to the Dressing Station. He was seriously gassed, but performed his duties until evacuated to the**

RMS *St Denis* was built for the Great Eastern Railway in 1908 as the *Munich* on the Harwich - Hook of Holland service. She was requisitioned by the Admiralty and converted into the Hospital Ship *St Denis* with 231 sick berths. In October 1919, she resumed service with the GER, retaining the name *St Denis.* She was acquired by the London & North Eastern Railway when it was created in the 1923 railways groupings reorganisation. In 1940, during the evacuation from Holland, she was trapped by the advancing Germans and scuttled at Rotterdam. The Germans raised her and returned her to service. She was scrapped in 1950, having been renamed *Skorpion* and *Barbara* in the meantime.

The Swedish War Hospital at 16 Paddington Street, Marylebone, London was founded in 1911 as the Central Institute for Swedish Gymnastics. After the war, it was purchased by London County Council as the LCC College of Physical Education. It is now the Hellenic Centre.

CCS, LG 26th September 1917 (citation 9th January 1918).

The gas affected his eyes and chest and a large abscess formed in the pectoralis major, which was operated on five times. He arrived in Britain from France on HMHS *St Denis* on 13th August and was sent to the Swedish War Hospital, Paddington Street, London and then 3rd Northern General Hospital, Sheffield on 21st August. A medical board on 27th November granted him three weeks leave at 6 Victoria Avenue, Scarborough. He was to report to Southampton on 19th December, but on 7th December requested an extension to be home for Christmas for the first time since 1914; the leave was extended to 28th December.

William was appointed acting major on 4th January 1918. **Awarded the DSO for his actions on 11th-14th October 1918 with 1/3rd Field Ambulance west of Saulzoir on the River Selle line; he showed a high degree of fearless initiative in organising the collection of wounded under continuous hostile shellfire. By his untiring energy, inspiring example and contempt of danger he moved large numbers of helpless wounded from positions of danger before he was gassed, LG 2nd April and 10th December 1919.** He was wounded on 17th October and returned to Britain.

He transferred to a regular commission as a captain on 1st December, backdated to 8th February. Appointed acting major until 11th July 1919. **Mentioned in Sir Douglas Haig's Despatch dated 16th March 1919, LG 10th July 1919.** He was a captain on the Indian Army List RAMC with seniority from 8th February 1918 and served at Rawalpindi on the staff of the Prince of Wales and Duke of Connaught. From January 1923 he was in Aden until discharged on 26th September 1923, suffering from malaria and dysentery and granted the rank of major. He ceased to belong to the Reserve of Officers on 11th January 1933 on account of ill-health.

Upper Richmond Road, Putney, where William and Mollie were living before they separated.

In civilian life, William went into practice with Dr Louis Aimee Newton MRCS LRCP at 1 Pownall Gardens, Hounslow, Middlesex. The partnership was dissolved by mutual consent on 31st March 1931. William continued the business in his own name. In 1924 he set up the Bracklesham Bay Riding School.

William and Mollie were living at 105 Upper Richmond Road, Putney in 1923–24. She sued for divorce on 31st October 1924 on the grounds that William had committed adultery on many occasions with unknown women. Only one instance was cited, at the Craven Hotel, Charing Cross on 19th-20th September 1924 (Decree Nisi 8th April and Absolute 19th October 1925). Mollie was living at 105 The Mound, York at the time. She was granted custody of Patricia Allen. In 1926, Mollie married William B Wilson at York.

William married Gertrude née Craggs (1894–1953), a florist, at St Martin's Registry Office, Strand, London in the 4th quarter of 1925. A son, also William Barnsley Allen, was born on 4th May 1926. They lived at 1 Pownall Gardens, Hounslow, Middlesex and later at 'Perley's Marsh', Stock's Lane, Bracklesham Bay, Sussex. At the time of William's death in August 1933, Gertrude was a patient in a nursing home. William Barnsley Allen junior married June M Wuyts (born 1927) in 1948 at Chichester and they had two children:

- Nigel Barnsley Allen, born 1951, married Susan Clare Storr Bond (born 1957) and they had two children. He was managing director of NBA Sports Cars, Guildford, Surrey.
- Timothy Patrick Allen, born 1953.

William and June separated and June married Malcolm Martyn-Johns (born 1936) in 1961; they had a son. William junior was a company director living at 'Gaystones', Boughton Hall Avenue, Send, near Woking, Surrey at the time of his death on 7th April 1974.

William senior was probably suffering from sleeping sickness (encephalitis lethargica) from 1924, a disease only indentified in 1918. The symptoms include fever, headache, sore throat, double vision, disturbed eye movements, upper body weakness, tremors, neck stiffness, intense muscle pains, slowing of physical and mental response, drowsiness and lethargy. Behaviour and personality may also change. It is sometimes mistaken for epilepsy, hysteria or drug and alcolohol abuse. He also suffered a recurrence of malaria, dysentery and pleurisy. In July 1932 he crashed his car into a ditch near the junction of Bracklesham Drive and Bracklesham Lane and was charged with driving a motor vehicle while under the influence of alcohol. He was fined £1/-/- and his licence was suspended for five years. In his defence in court at Chichester, it was stated that he had, *...suffered as no other man in England had suffered*. His war wounds plagued him constantly and he took to drink and drugs to obtain relief.

William Allen telephoned Dr CR Sadler at 7.15 a.m. on 27th August 1933 from his home at 'Perley's Marsh', Stock's Lane, Bracklesham Bay. He died in bed within half an hour of the doctor's arrival and had been taking various drugs – veronal, opium and morphia. Death was attributed to an overdose. An inquest at Chichester on 28th August, conducted by the Deputy Coroner, Mr FB Tomkins, recorded a verdict of misadventure. William is buried in Earnley Cemetery, Bracklesham Bay. He left £4,548/3/3 to his widow.

In addition to the VC, DSO and MC & Bar, he was awarded the 1914–15 Star, British War Medal 1914–20 and Victory Medal 1914–19 with Mentioned-in-Despatches Oakleaf. His VC is held by the Army Medical Services Museum, Keogh Barracks, Mytchett, Surrey. William Allen is commemorated in a number of places:

- The 'Major Allen Award', established in 2001, is awarded annually to an Old Worksopian on leaving Worksop College to fund a gap year abroad or travel before proceeding to higher education.
- The 'Allen VC Room' is an anteroom in Sheffield University Officers' Training Corps, Somme Barracks, Glossop Road, Sheffield.

Somme Barracks, Glossop Road, Sheffield, home to Sheffield University Officers' Training Corps (Les Prosser).

William Barnsley Allen Court (University of Sheffield).

- 'William Barnsley Allen Court' (formerly Opal 2), University of Sheffield, accommodates almost 1,000 students. It was renamed on 1st September 2014 following a competition amongst the students; the winner was Graham Roberts.
- An Acer 'Crimson King' tree is dedicated to him in the RAMC Memorial Grove at the National Memorial Arboretum, Alrewas, Staffordshire.
- A German machine-gun in the Master Gunner's House at Scarborough Castle, North Yorkshire bears a plaque inscribed, *Presented to the town of Scarborough by the War Office in connection with the award of a Victoria Cross to Major W.B. Allen, V.C., D.S.O., R.A.M.C.*

2ND LIEUTENANT DONALD SIMPSON BELL
9th Battalion, Alexandra, Princess of Wales's Own (Yorkshire Regiment)

Donald Bell was born at Queen's Road, Harrogate, Yorkshire on 3rd December 1890. He was known as 'Donny'. His father was Smith Bell (1859–1938), a factory hand in 1871, a butcher by 1891 and a cattle dealer in 1911. His mother was Annie née Simpson (1861–1928). Smith and Annie married on 19th June 1883 at Harrogate. They are both buried in Grove Road Cemetery, Harrogate (Section G, Grave 1040). The family lived at various addresses in Harrogate, beginning with 1 Somerfield House, Parliament Terrace. By 1901 they had moved to 'Milton Lodge', 87 East Parade, Western Flats, Queen's Road and later to 23 St Mary's Walk. Donald had seven siblings:

- Ellen 'Nellie' Bell (1885–1968) married Henry Jackson (1880–1977) in 1907 and they had two sons – William Jackson 1908 and Donald Bell Jackson 1911.
- Minnie Bell (1887–1968) married Thomas James Wood (1884–1968) in 1915.
- William 'Willie' Bell (1889–1962) was a motor mechanic and driver. He enlisted in the Army Service Corps on 7th August 1914 (MS/1209) and was described as 5′ 7″ tall, weighing 164 lbs, with fair complexion, grey eyes, brown hair and his denomination was Wesleyan. He went to France on 16th August 1914 and served there until 11th January 1919, mainly with 4th Division Ammunition Column and 16th Division Motor Transport Company. He was appointed acting lance corporal on 21st September 1916 and promoted corporal on 7th January 1918. He transferred to the Reserve on 8th February 1919. Willie married Edith Thornton in 1923 and they had a son, Donald Simpson Bell, who eventually inherited his uncle's medals.
- Gertrude 'Gerty' Bell (born 1892) was a bookkeeper in 1911. She married John Arthur Umpelby (1887–1969) in 1920 and they had three children – Thomas Umpelby 1921, Doreen S Umpelby 1923 and John A Umpelby 1926.

- Annie Bell (born 1894).
- Dorothy 'Dollie' Bell (1897–1982) married Harold Angus (1897–1946) in 1921 and they had two daughters – Jean Angus 1923 and Ruth Angus 1927.
- Mary Bell, born and died in May 1905.

As a youngster Donald immersed himself in books and was intent on becoming a teacher. He was educated at:

- St Peter's School Harrogate, where Charles Hull VC was also a pupil.
- Harrogate Municipal Secondary School (later Harrogate Grammar School), where he was friendly with Archie White VC. He gained a First Division Pass in the London Matriculation Examination of June 1908.
- Westminster College, Horseferry Road, Westminster from 1909, where he trained to be a teacher. He was Captain of Athletics and excelled as a sprinter, winning the 100 yards at the Royal Polytechnic London in 1911. He was awarded colours for rugby, hockey, swimming, cricket and football. In July 1911 he passed the University of London Intermediate Arts Examination. The College moved to Oxford in 1959 and is now part of Oxford Brookes University. The site in Horseferry Road was damaged in the Blitz and is now the headquarters of Channel 4 Television.

Donald was a talented footballer. While at school he played full back for Starbeck Football Club. At Westminster he turned out as an amateur for Crystal Palace Football Club and was also offered a county rugby football place with Hertfordshire. He played football at various times for Mirfield, Bishop Auckland and Newcastle Football Clubs, the latter at the start of the 1911–12 season. To supplement his teacher's salary of £2/10/- per week, he became a professional footballer with Bradford Park Avenue, making five first team appearances in the 1912–13 and 1913–14 seasons; the first was against Wolverhampton Wanderers at Molineux on 13th

Crystal Palace football ground in 1905 (Wikipedia).

April 1913. Donald also toured Denmark with the YMCA football team in 1913. He was a member of the Harrogate Claro Tent of the Independent Order of Rechabites.

Donald Bell while playing for Bradford Park Avenue.

From 1911, Donald was an assistant master at Starbeck Council School near Harrogate and was a junior class teacher at Wesley Methodist Church in Harrogate. He was very popular with his pupils, teaching them football techniques if the class had been well behaved. Years later Archie White recalled, [He was] *a deviation from the ordinary … six feet high and over fourteen stone, he had the build of a hammer-thrower; he could never have been a runner. Yet he had a unique gift of acceleration; he could start from zero on the centre line, be in top gear in two strides, and cover thirty, forty or fifty yards at the speed of a sprinter on a running track. This is what made him so valuable as a footballer.*

Donald enlisted in the 9th West Yorkshire (15722) in November 1914. He wanted to join the cavalry, but his athletic prowess was noticed by the recruiters, who thought he would be wasted on a horse. He was quickly disillusioned with Home Service and eager to get overseas. By chance in early 1915 he met Lieutenant Archie White, 6th Yorkshire, a friend from Harrogate, also destined to win the VC on the Somme. Archie White was astonished that Donald was not an officer and introduced him to the CO of 6th Yorkshire, Lieutenant Colonel EH Chapman, who recommended him immediately for a commission. Donald was promoted through the ranks to sergeant and was commissioned into 11th (Reserve) Battalion, Yorkshire Regiment on 10th June 1915. He transferred to the 9th Battalion on 18th June and went to France on 25th November.

While home on leave, Donald married Rhoda Margaret née Bonson (1887–1952) at the Wesleyan Chapel, Kirkby Stephen, Westmorland on 5th June 1916. There were no children. Margaret was a dressmaker from Westmorland who was living with her uncle, George Bonson and his wife Annie, at Altrincham Road, Wilmslow, Cheshire at the time. Donald returned to the front, having spent only two days with his wife.

Starbeck School near Harrogate.

Awarded the VC for his actions at Horseshoe Trench, near La Boisselle, France on 5th July 1916, LG 9th September 1916. The only other professional footballer to win the VC was William Angus, who played for Celtic. Donald was killed in action

Donald Bell's grave in Gordon Dump Cemetery.

Gordon Taylor OBE, Chief Executive of the Professional Footballers Association and former player with Bolton Wanderers, Birmingham City, Blackburn Rovers and Bury, who bid successfully for Donald Bell's medals at auction in 2010.

The Professional Footballers Association is the proud owner of Donald Bell's VC.

a few days later at 'Bell's Redoubt', Contalmaison, France on 10th July 1916, while attached to the 8th Battalion. He was buried where he fell and the grave was marked by a wooden cross and surrounded by a rail fence. In 1920 he was reinterred in Gordon Dump Cemetery, Ovillers-la-Boisselle, near Albert (IV A 8). The damaged helmet he wore during his VC action is held by the Green Howards Museum, Richmond, Yorkshire. He left £41/5/- to his wife.

The VC was presented to his widow by the King at Buckingham Palace on 13th December 1916; she was accompanied by her sister-in-law, Minnie Bell. Rhoda received £100 from the Daily Mail and moved to 'Charnwood', Altrincham Road, Wilmslow. She never remarried.

In addition to the VC, he was awarded the 1914–15 Star, British War Medal 1914–20 and Victory Medal 1914–19. The medals were kept by the family until 1964 when his nephew, also Donald Simpson Bell, loaned them to the Green Howards Museum, Richmond, Yorkshire. On 25th November 2010, the medals and memorial plaque were sold at auction by Spinks and purchased for £210,000 on behalf of the Professional Footballers' Association by Gordon Taylor, the chief executive. They are held by the Professional Footballers' Association, 20 Oxford Court, Bishopgate, Manchester and in 2014 were on loan to the National Football Museum, Urbis Building, Cathedral Gardens, Manchester.

Donald Bell is commemorated in a number of places:

- The Professional Footballers' Association and Green Howards dedicated a memorial on the spot where he fell at Bell's Redoubt, Contalmaison on 9th July 2000.
- Starbeck Council School, Harrogate, Yorkshire.
- Harrogate War Memorial.
- St Peter's Church, Harrogate.
- St Paul's Parish Church, Harrogate.
- Bradford Town Hall, Yorkshire.
- Victoria Gardens, Harrogate.

Donald's cousin, Second Lieutenant James Marsden Simpson (1888–1916), was a civil engineer working for the Land Valuation Department. He enlisted in 5th West Yorkshire on 22nd May 1913 (1420) and was promoted lance corporal on 30th July. He attended annual training at Aberystwyth that year. Promoted corporal 20th July 1914, embodied on 5th August and was promoted sergeant on 31st October. He went to France on SS *Invicta* on 16th April 1915 from Folkestone to Boulogne. He was commissioned on 11th September 1915 and was serving in 173rd Tunnelling Company RE when he died on 9th May 1916. He is buried in Noeux-les-Mines Communal Cemetery, France (I L 4). His mother was the sole executrix to the will and his estate was valued at £358/10/1.

Harrogate War Memorial, with St Peter's Church on the right.

Bradford Town Hall.

CAPTAIN ERIC NORMAN FRANKLAND BELL
9th Battalion, The Royal Inniskilling Fusiliers (Co Tyrone) att'd 109th Trench Mortar Battery

Eric Bell was born at Alma Terrace, Enniskillen, Co Fermanagh, Ireland on 28th August 1895 (1896 according to his commissioning application). His father, Edward Henry Bell (1860/61–1920), born at Devonport, Devon, was a shoemaker. He enlisted in the 108th Regiment on 2nd May 1878 (1815 later 2996) and joined at Colchester. On enlistment he was 5′ 5½″ tall, with fair complexion, grey eyes, brown hair and his denomination was Wesleyan. He gained 2nd Class Education on 9th September and was promoted lance corporal 14th December and corporal 5th July 1879. Awarded Good Conduct Pay on 2nd May 1880. Promoted lance sergeant 28th August and sergeant 23rd March 1881. He was posted to 2nd Royal Inniskilling Fusiliers on 1st July. He gained 1st Class Education on 12th April 1882 and attended the Musketry Instructor Course at Hythe the same year. In 1883 he attended the Field Defences Course at Chatham. Promoted colour sergeant 26th March 1884 and was awarded 2nd Good Conduct Pay on 2nd May that year.

Eric's mother was Dora Algeo née Crowder (1866–1919), born at Manorhamilton, near Enniskillen, Co Fermanagh, Ireland. She married Edward Bell on 19th April 1885 at St Nicholas, Church of Ireland, Carrickfergus, Co Antrim, Ireland. Edward was posted to Malta on 31st December 1885 and returned to Britain on 15th May 1886. On 1st July 1888 he joined the permanent staff of 1st Royal Guernsey Light Infantry and rejoined 1st Royal Inniskilling Fusiliers on 24th March 1889. He was posted to the 2nd Battalion on 10th December 1890 and departed for India two days later. Promoted sergeant major 23rd January 1891. At Secunderabad on 18th July 1892 he received a serious cut to the right wrist in a sword fighting accident. Edward returned to Britain on 26th October 1894 and on 24th February 1895 was posted to Egypt. On 17th July he was commissioned as Quartermaster with the honorary rank of lieutenant in 2nd Battalion and went with it to Thayetmayo in Burma. He took part in operations on the North-West Frontier in 1897–98 with the Peshawar Column and the 5th Brigade Tirah Expedition, during which he contracted dysentery. His health deteriorated and he was on the sick list at Chakrata August – October 1896, Meerut December 1896 – February 1897 & May – August 1897, Landi Kotal April – May 1898 and Dalhousie in September 1898. A Medical Board on 31st January 1899 found he was suffering from congestion of the liver and general debility as a result of several severe bouts of malaria and sent him home for six months. He transferred to 2nd Liverpool in Dublin on 5th July and later served with the 5th Battalion.

A Medical Board in Dublin on 26th April 1900 found him permanently unfit and he was put on half pay from 26th May. However, another Medical Board on 28th March 1901 found him fit for Home Service and he returned to duty on 17th April. It was not to last, as on 27th November a Medical Board found him unfit for six months and he was put on half pay again on 11th December. A final Medical Board on 23rd May 1902 found he was still suffering the results of malaraia and he was retired on 23rd July. Edward and Dora lived with their family at:

- 10 Alder Street, Seaforth, Lancashire in 1901.
- 114 Huskisson Street, Liverpool.
- 18 Prince's Avenue, Toxteth, Liverpool.
- 22 University Road, Bootle, Liverpool.
- 128 Hill Street, Liverpool by 1911.

In addition to Eric they had four other children:

- Alan George Frankland Bell (born 1887 Enniskillen, Co Fermanagh) was a mechanical engineer in America at the outbreak of the war. He returned and was commissioned in 11th Royal Inniskilling Fusiliers on 22nd February 1915. Having been wounded by a large piece of shell driving band in his right forearm on 12th August 1916 at Hill 63 in Belgium, he embarked on SS *St Denis* 16th August and was treated at Hall Walker Hospital, Sussex Lodge, Regent's Park, London. Medical Boards on 28th August at Caxton Hall, London and 23rd October at 1st Western General Hospital, Liverpool found him unfit and sent him on leave. A Medical Board on 3rd November at Liverpool found him fit for light duties in three weeks, extended his leave to 24th November and later to 3rd February 1917. At the next Medical Board on 20th February he was found unfit and granted leave to 19th March, extended to 6th May. He recovered sufficiently to attend a course at Brocton Camp, Staffordshire in June and a Medical Board on 21st June found him fit for Home Service. Promoted lieutenant 1st July. On 21st August he was downgraded to light duties and on 23rd October was sent on leave to 22nd December. A Medical Board on 11th January 1918 found him fit for light duties and on 11th February for General Service. He returned to the front and was severally wounded serving with 9th Battalion at Neuve Eglise, France on 4th September, with gunshot wounds to the right forearm and left chest. He embarked on 15th September at Boulogne, arriving at Dover next day, to be admitted to Hall Walker Hospital and later to Savoy Hospital, Blackpool, Lancashire. Medical Boards on 4th October at Prince of Wales's Hospital, Marylebone, London and 7th March 1919 found him unfit for service and granted leave until 6th May. On 17th May he was found fit for Home Service and reported to 3rd Battalion at Plymouth, Devon on 31st May. He was later found fit for General Service and was demobilised on 25th November 1919 while serving with 348 Motor Transport Company ASC at Omagh, Ireland. In February 1920 he was living at 12 Hereford Street, Wavertree, Liverpool and in October 1929 at 2 Chambers Street, Donegall Pass, Belfast. He is understood to have returned to America.

- Dora Irene Frankland Bell (born 1889 at Bundoran, Donegal, Ireland). She migrated to New Zealand in 1920 and married George Bruce Bolt (1893–1963) in 1933 at Khandallah, Wellington. It was George's second marriage; his first wife, Mary, died in 1928. George was a pioneer of aviation in New Zealand. He designed and built gliders, the first of which flew in December 1911, and won the glider Distance Challenge Cup at Hagley Park in March 1913 with a record flight of 1,224 feet. He became an apprentice mechanic with Leo and Vivian Walsh's New Zealand Flying School at Mission Bay, Auckland and made his first solo flight in a powered aircraft in July 1916, gaining the aviator's certificate in 1917. In July 1919, he became the School's chief pilot. In January 1919 he set an altitude record of 6,500′ and in May completed a record long distance flight from Auckland to Russell. In December he made the first experimental airmail flight from Auckland to Dargaville. In May 1921 he started an airmail service from Auckland to Whangarei six days a week, but it was not a financial success. To finance the struggling Flying School, he took passengers on joyrides and in March 1923 dropped a display parachutist over Ellerslie Race Course. Also in 1923, George was an instructor for ex-service pilots forming the nucleus of the New Zealand Air Force (Territorial). In 1930 he became chief pilot for Dominion Airlines and visited Britain to purchase a Saunders-Roe Windhover flying boat and a Desoutter II land-plane. In Europe he gained experience handling large aircraft and was seconded to the Dutch airline KLM. In New Zealand he flew the Desoutter in a regular passenger service between Gisborne and Hastings. When Dominion Airlines went into liquidation, he was appointed commercial pilot, chief engineer and advanced flying instructor for Wellington Aero Club. George became technical adviser to Cook Strait Airways in 1935 and became its chief pilot. In November 1939 he was appointed chief engineer at the Royal New Zealand Air Force station at Ohakea. By 1943, he was a wing commander and director of aeronautical production. In 1944, he returned to civil aviation as chief engineer of Tasman Empire Airways for the next sixteen years. He was awarded the OBE in 1953 and retired in 1960. The son from George's first marriage, Richard Bruce Bolt (born 1923), joined the Royal New Zealand Air Force in 1942. He flew Halifax and Lancaster bombers on operations in Europe, including with the Pathfinder Force. He became New Zealand's Chief of the Defence Staff 1976–80 as Air Marshal Sir Richard Bolt KBE CB DFC AFC.
- Haldane Frankland Bell (born 1891 at Bundoran, Donegal, Ireland) was a clerk in 1911. He was in Australia at the outbreak of war and left on 19th December 1914 to return to Britain. He was commissioned in 2nd Royal Inniskilling Fusiliers on 16th

April 1915 and promoted lieutenant on 17th March 1916. Haldane received two gun shot wounds at La Boisselle, France on 11th July and was treated at 44 Casualty Clearing Station and the No.2 British Red Cross Hospital at Rouen. He embarked on NZHS SS *Marama* on 30th July at Havre for Southampton, arriving next day, and was treated at 1st Western General Hospital, Liverpool. A Medical Board on 23rd October at Liverpool found him unfit and he was treated at Croxteth Hall Auxiliary Hospital, Liverpool until 12th January 1917. A Medical Board on 2nd March found him fit for light duties and he transferred to Swan Hydro Red Cross Hospital, Harrogate, Yorkshire until 4th March. Haldane was on the strength of 3rd (Reserve) Battalion in Londonderry, Ireland from 7th March. He was in hospitals at Belfast and Omagh 7th March 1917 – 9th April 1918, including the Military Convalescent Hospital, Holywood 15th August 1917 – 28th January 1918. Medical Boards on 16th April, 23rd May and 26th June 1917 kept him on light duties. While on leave in Liverpool in July 1917 he had a breakdown and was admitted to 1st Western General Hospital and later to Hesketh Park Hydro, Southport, Lancashire. Medical Boards on 3rd August at 1st Western General Hospital and on 24th August at Dublin kept him on light duties. On 25th October he was found fit for Home Service, but a Medical Board on 28th February 1918 found him permanently unfit for General Service. A Final Medical Board on 9th April found him permanently unfit for further service and he was discharged on 6th May 1918. Haldane trained at the Royal Horticultural Society Gardens, Wisley, Surrey. He migrated to Australia on 20th March 1920 from Tilbury on the Overseas Settlement Scheme. He married Elie May Wilcher (married twice previously) (1893–1928) in 1923 and they lived in Maribyrnong, Victoria and Melbourne Ports, Victoria. Haldane left Australia on 25th April 1956 for Canada and lived at 85 Botfield Avenue, Toronto, Ontario.

George Bruce Bolt, a pioneer of aviation in New Zealand, who married Edward's sister, Dora Irene Frankland Bell.

Edward's nephew, Air Marshal Sir Richard Bolt KBE CB DFC AFC.

- Lorna Mary Frankland Bell, born in 1893 at Thayetmayo, Burma. She died very young.

When war broke out Edward was recalled on 5th August 1914. On 13th September he was appointed Quartermaster of 9th Royal Irish Fusiliers and on 9th December became the Adjutant. On 31st March 1915 he transferred as Adjutant of 12th (Reserve) Battalion, Royal Irish Fusiliers and on 22nd August became Adjutant of 1st Garrison Battalion, Royal Irish Regiment at Mudros and later in Egypt and the Libyan Desert. A Medical Board on 19th July 1916 found him unfit for General Service and another on 1st September sent him on leave until 30th November. Having recovered, he embarked at Southampton on 26th January 1917, disembarked at Alexandria on 10th February and rejoined his unit next day. He left his unit again on 16th May and was admitted to hospital in Cairo. He embarked at Alexandria on 7th August, disembarking at Folkestone on 16th August and was attached to 3rd Garrison Battalion, Royal Irish Regiment from 2nd October. He was promoted captain the same day with seniority from 13th September 1914. He was graded unfit for General Service on 5th September and at various medical boards thereafter and was treated at 1st Western General Hospital, Liverpool and 2nd Western General Hospital, Manchester. Edward retired on 20th April 1918. He died at sea aboard RMS *Arawa* en route for Auckland, New Zealand on 5th December 1920; he was emigrating for health reasons.

Eric was educated at:

- People's Elementary School, Arpley Street, Warrington.
- St Margaret's School, Upper Hampton Street, off Prince's Road, Toxteth, Liverpool from 18th August 1902. It closed in 2010.
- Bedford Road Community Primary School, Bootle, Lancashire, 1904–06.
- Liverpool Institute. The Headmaster, Henry V Whitehouse, wrote, *Eric Bell was always a charming creature, with a strong artistic feeling. He was an example of honourable boyhood, but rather retiring by nature. If he had stayed longer in the school he would have become a power for good in all possible ways; by force of*

St Margaret's School, Upper Hampton Street, Toxteth (Liverpool City Group).

Bedford Road School, Bootle in the early 1900s (Liverpool City Group).

character rather than by strength of limb. A soldier was the last thing I ever expected him to be, but once he was a soldier I felt quite certain that he would do his duty finely. There are only a few of the hundreds of old pupils from this and other schools whose death was a more personal grief to me. The Institute was later attended by Beatles Paul McCartney and George Harrison.
- School of Architecture, Liverpool University, where he trained as an architect and worked as an assistant to Professor Sir Charles Reilly, who wrote, *Eric was one of the few men I know who could have won such an honour without being spoilt by it. He was as modest as he proved to be brave. He had the sensitive temperament of the real artist.*

Sir Charles Reilly (1874–1948) was Roscoe Professor of Architecture at the University of Liverpool 1904–33, where he championed university training for architects. In 1906 he was appointed first Chairman of the Royal Institute of British Architects' board of architectural education. He established the Department of Civic Design at the University of Liverpool, the first place in Britain where town planning and architecture were taught.

Eric was a gifted artist, working in oils and pen and ink. While at the School of Architecture examples of his work were published in several journals. He was also a talented musician and spoke French and German fluently. Despite his talents and rapid progress, he was described as being reserved and unpretentious.

Eric was commissioned in 6th Royal Inniskilling Fusiliers on 22nd September 1914. He transferred to 8th Battalion then 9th Battalion on 12th November, in which his father was Adjutant. Eric went to France on 5th October 1915, where he attended a trench mortar course. Promoted lieutenant and attached to 109th Brigade Trench Mortar Battery.

Awarded the VC for his actions at Thiepval, France on 1st July 1916, LG 26th September 1916. He was killed during his VC action and is commemorated on the Thiepval Memorial. His will was administered by his father – value £198/12/6. As Eric never married, the VC was presented to his father by the King at Buckingham Palace on 29th November 1916.

In addition to the VC, he was awarded the 1914–15 Star, British War Medal 1914–20 and Victory Medal 1914–19. The VC passed down through his sister Dora to her stepson, Sir Richard Bolt, who said, *The VC has been a source of pride and inspiration in my own family, but I now wish to ensure that it is kept in*

Sir Wilfred Stokes (1860–1927) with his 3" Mortar. During the war he worked for the Inventions Branch, Ministry of Munitions. The Stokes Mortar, which also had a 4″ version, was amongst the first truly man-portable mortars. It was first used at Loos in September 1915 and, with modifications, remained in service until replaced by the Ordnance ML 3″ Mortar in the early 1930s.

appropriate hands... the Royal Inniskilling Fusiliers Museum ... is where Bell's VC should be. The VC was presented to the Patron of the Royal Inniskilling Fusiliers Museum at Enniskillen Castle, Co Fermanagh, Viscount Brookeborough by Colonel Stewart Douglas, Regimental Colonel of the Royal Irish Regiment on 15th February 2001. Viscount Brookeborough said, *I am honoured to accept Captain Bell's Victoria Cross into the Royal Inniskilling Fusiliers collection and would like to express the thanks of the Regimental Trustees to Sir Richard for his outstanding generosity in presenting this highest of decorations for gallantry to be displayed with the treasures of Eric Bell's old Regiment.*

The dedication of Enniskillen War Memorial in 1921. On 8th November 1987 it was the scene of an IRA bomb outrage during a Remembrance Sunday ceremony. Eleven people were killed and sixty three injured. The condemnation that followed marked a turning point in the Troubles.

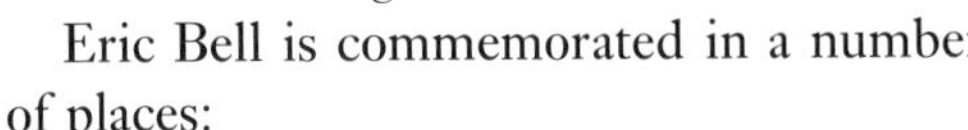

Eric Bell is commemorated in a number of places:

- Memorial Board at William Gladstone Primary School, Thompson Road, Seaforth, Liverpool.
- Memorial at Bedford CP School, Quarry Road, Bootle, Liverpool.
- A memorial stone at Ulster Tower, Thiepval, France to all ranks of the 36th (Ulster) Division, dedicated on 1st July 1991, names the Division's nine VCs, including Eric Bell.
- Bootle War Memorial.
- Enniskillen War Memorial.
- Regimental Memorial, St Anne's Cathedral, Belfast, Northern Ireland.

LIEUTENANT EUGENE PAUL BENNETT
2nd Battalion, The Worcestershire Regiment

Eugene Bennett was born at Church School House, Cainscross, Stroud, Gloucestershire on 4th June 1892. His father was Charles Bennett (1853–1919), a railway clerk in 1871. He was a schoolmaster in 1881. His mother was Florence Emma Sophia née Ody (c.1863–1950), a barmaid at her father's public house, the Royal Table Inn, Barton Hill Road, Bristol, Gloucestershire, in 1881, living at 72 Barton Hill Road (Royal Table), Bristol St Philip & Jacob Out, Gloucestershire on 13th April 1882. Charles and Florence married at St Werburgh, Bristol, registered at Barton

Cainscross, Gloucestershire.

Royal Table Inn, Barton Hill, Gloucestershire.

Regis, Gloucestershire. Charles was Headmaster of the National School (later St Matthew's School), Cainscross, Stroud, Gloucestershire to 1894. From 1894 until his retirement he was Chief Secretary of Stroud and Mid-Gloucestershire Working Men's Conservative Association Benefit Society, living at Bath Road, Rodborough, Stroud. He was also leader of the orchestra accompanying the Stroud Choral Society and was organist at Cainscross Church to 1894 and Rodborough Church from 1895. In 1915 he was Chief Secretary of the Mid-Gloucester Friendly Society. The family later moved to 'Fromehurst', Frome Park Road, Stroud. He died on 27th September 1919 following an operation in London, registered at St Thomas. Eugene was too ill to attend his funeral in Stroud. Eugene had five siblings:

- Leonora Florence 'Dora' Bennett (1883–1958) was a pupil teacher at a board school in 1901. She married Sidney Joseph Burford (1883–1952), a chartered accountant, in 1911 and they had two children – Sidney CL Burford 1912 and George J Burford 1913.
- Alexander George Amos Bennett (1885–1945) passed the Civil Service Open Competitive Examination in October 1903 and joined the Civil Service as a Second Division Clerk on 8th February 1904. He was assigned to the Inland Revenue on 31st August 1905 and later transferred to the Bank of England. Alexander served in the Civil Service Rifles 28th November 1905 – 31st March 1908 as a private. He married Amy Dora Husbands (1887–1930) on 12th July 1911 at Grove Chapel, Cosham, Bristol and they had two children – Alfred Charles Leopold Bennett 1914 and Denise Alexander Bennett 1924. They were living at 74 Broxholm Road, West Norwood, London when he attested on 10th December 1915. He enlisted on 10th July 1917 as a gunner (61474) in the Royal Horse Artillery at the Depot, Woolwich, Kent. He was described as 5′ 8¾″ tall and weighed 135 lbs. By 26th January 1918 he was training with No.1 Group, No.3 Royal Field Artillery Officer Cadet School, Weedon, Northamptonshire. He transferred to the Royal Garrison Artillery Cadet School at Trowbridge,

Wiltshire, because he had no previous experience of riding, and was posted to the RGA Cadet School on 4th February 1918 and the School of Gunnery on 8th June 1918. Alexander was commissioned on 14th July 1918 and relinquished his commission on 6th January 1919.

- Harold Stanley Bennett (1889–1915) entered the Civil Service in 1908 and was appointed Assistant Surveyor of Taxes, Inland Revenue Department, on 24th September 1909. He lived at 270 Edward Rd, Edgbaston. He was commissioned in the Special Reserve of Officers in the Royal Garrison Artillery on 6th January 1915. He passed an examination in gunnery at Cardiff, Glamorgan on 23rd April and was cycling back to Nells Battery, Barry Island when, going through Penarth on Albert Road, a laundry van ran out of a side street and knocked him off, fracturing the base of his skull. He died at 3rd Western General Hospital in Cardiff (Officers' Nursing Home) at 12.40 a.m. on 25th April. A Coroner's hearing on 27th April at City Hall, Cardiff exonerated the van driver of blame. He is buried in Rodborough (St Mary Magdalene) Churchyard, Stroud, Gloucestershire.
- Leopold Charles Bennett (1891–1914).
- Theodore John Bennett (1893–1918) was training to be a chartered accountant when war broke out. He enlisted on 7th December 1914 in D Company, 18th Royal Fusiliers (3696) and served at Woodcote Camp, Epsom, Surrey. He was commissioned on 19th May 1915 in the Special Reserve of Officers in 1/5th Worcestershire Regiment. He embarked for France on SS *Normania* on 1st October 1915 and joined the Battalion on 6th October. He was admitted to 6 Field Ambulance with pleurisy 13th-16th November. On 13th December he was posted to 5th Brigade Machine Gun Company and on 17th December was seconded to the Machine Gun Corps (Infantry). He left the unit sick on 13th August 1916, suffering from varicocele and appendicitis, embarked on 20th August at Boulogne for Dover and was sent on leave on 18th September. He was readmitted to hospital on 5th October and his appendix was removed on the 16th. Theodore transferred to the Machine Gun Corps on 31st October. A medical board at Norton Barracks, Worcester on 17th January 1917 extended his leave to 17th February. On 22nd February he was examined again and found to be suffering from gastric catarrh, weakness and abdominal pain. Further medical boards found he was suffering from dyspepsia, insomnia and general nervous debility, until a board at Bristol on 19th March 1917 passed him fit for General Service. He joined the MGC Training Centre at Grantham, Lincolnshire on 23rd March and applied for a commission in the Indian Army on 7th December 1917 while serving with 162nd Machine Gun Company. He was seconded to the Indian Army on probation on 8th February 1918 and admitted to the Indian Army as a lieutenant on probation on 20th February, with seniority from 19th February 1917. He was killed in action in Palestine on 7th September 1918, attached to 1/17th Indian Infantry (Loyal Regiment) and was originally buried in Bahkara Military Cemetery. His remains were moved to Jerusalem War Cemetery, Israel

(L 62) in 1920. The CWGC record him as attached to 1/17th Indian Infantry from 1/5th Worcestershire rather than MGC.

A cousin on his mother's side, John Harold Standrick (1893–1918), served as a captain in 2/18th London Regiment (London Irish Rifles). He was killed on 21st February 1918 and is buried in Jerusalem War Cemetery, Palestine (S 76). He was awarded a posthumous MC, LG 18th July 1918.

Jerusalem War Cemetery, Israel, while it was being developed just after the end of the war. Eugene's brother, Theodore, and his cousin, John Harold Standrick, are buried there.

Eugene was educated at Uplands Council School, from where he won a scholarship to Marling School, Stroud 1905–08. He was employed at the Bank of England as an assistant in the Accountant's Department 1909–14.

He enlisted in 28th London (Artists' Rifles) (1253) in October 1913 and was embodied on 4th August 1914. The battalion guarded German prisoners at Olympia initially and moved to the Tower of London for public duties in September. It joined 2nd London (later 47th) Division for training at Bricket Wood near Watford on 17th October. The Battalion embarked at Southampton on SS *Australind* on 27th October and disembarked at Boulogne, France next day. Eugene underwent officer training with the battalion, which had become an Officer Training Unit at Bailleul, November-December 1914. He was commissioned in the Worcestershire Regiment and posted to 2nd Battalion on 1st January 1915.

Eugene was involved in the Battle of Neuve Chapelle in March and was the only officer in his company to survive. He was wounded at Festubert in May when his trench was mined and he had to be dug out; returned to duty from hospital on 20th June. Promoted lieutenant 7th August.

Marling School, Stroud.

The Bank of England.

SS *Australind* (4251 tons) a cargo ship built by Charles Connell & Co in 1904 for the Australind Steam Ship Co Ltd. In 1928 she was sold to Andre Grosos & M Potet of Le Havre and renamed *Colbert*. In 1933 she was sold to Societe Baltique-Ocean-Mediterranee, also of Le Havre, and renamed *Scandinavie*. She was scrapped the following year.

Awarded the MC for his actions east of Cambrin on the night of 10th/11th November 1915. The Battalion had just taken over the line when shortly after last light the Germans exploded a mine, destroying sixty metres of trench held by D Company. The Germans illuminated the scene with a searchlight, but he led rescue parties over the debris and set about digging out those trapped. The enemy were firing from only thirty metres away, but work continued until the survivors had been rescued. A bombing fight for the crater went on all night but by dawn it had been secured, LG 14th January 1916. He was Mentioned in Sir John French's Despatch dated 30th November 1915, LG 1st January 1916. The MC was presented by the King at Buckingham Palace on 10th May 1916. Appointed acting captain 26th September – 6th November 1916.

Awarded the VC for his actions near Le Transloy, France on 5th November 1916, LG 30th December 1916. He was wounded in the same action and evacuated to England. The VC was presented by the King at Buckingham Palace on 5th February 1917. Eugene was attached to the War Office in September (Army List November 1917 – April 1918) and was at Aldershot before returning to France. He sustained severe shell splinter wounds on 18th October 1918 and was treated at No.8 Stationary Hospital, Wimereux near Boulogne. He was in hospital until October 1919 and relinquished his commission on account of ill health caused by wounds on 11th June 1920; he was granted the rank of captain. Eugene was a member of the VC Guard at the Interment of the Unknown Warrior on 11th November 1920.

On 26th July 1922, he married Violet Regina née Fuerst (born 1902) at Kingston, Surrey. Her father changed the family name to Forster by deed poll on 16th

February 1916, LG 18th February 1916. She was a songwriter. They lived at various addresses – 3 Pump Court, Temple, London 1924; 18 Manor Gardens, London 1920s; 8 York Gate, Regent's Park, London 1928–40; Homefield, Aldwick, Sussex; 30 Elm Tree Road, London 1945 and 48 Hanover House, London 1954. The family was twice bombed out in Marylebone, London during the Second World War. Violet went missing for a few days in 1949 and was found in a distressed condition on Hampstead Heath. Violet and Eugene had two children:

- Anne Bennett, born 2nd September 1923, registered at Marylebone.
- Jonathan Bennett, born on 24th July 1931, registered at Marylebone. He died of meningitis at Eton in early 1946.

Violet's father, Joseph Frank Forster (formerly Fuerst) (c.1861–1921), was born in Germany. He was a chemical and general merchant in partnership with his brothers, Jules and Albert Francis Fuerst, trading as 'Fuerst Brothers' at 17 Philpot Lane, London and as 'Fuerst Brothers and Company' at 2 & 4 Stone Street, New York, USA. The partnership was dissolved on 15th February 1895 and re-established as two separate companies. The London firm was a partnership of Joseph and Jules Fuerst and the New York firm was solely under Albert Francis Fuerst. The London firm dissolved by mutual consent on 19th February 1917. Joseph was living with his brother Jules at 25 Craven Street, St Martin in the Fields, London in 1891. Joseph married Eva Alice née Joseph (1873–1934) in 1895 at Paddington, London and by 1901 they were living at 52 Hamilton Terrace, Marylebone, London. By 1916 they had moved to 30 Hamilton Terrace. When Eva died on 26th October 1934, she was living at 8 York Gate, Regent's Park, London.

Eugene returned to the Bank of England until 1921 and then studied law; called to the Bar (Middle Temple) October 1923. On 28th April 1930, Eugene was opposing barrister to Brett M Cloutman VC in a case at Southwark County Court. He held various appointments:

- Deputy-Umpire under the Unemployment Insurance Act 1920 on 16th June 1930.
- Prosecuting Counsel to the Post Office, South East Circuit 1931–35.
- Metropolitan Stipendary Magistrate at West London Magistrates Court 28th May 1935 – 1946 and at Marlborough Street Court 1946–61.
- Governor of Regent Street Polytechnic.

Eugene served in the Air Training Corps as an Acting Pilot Officer (108266) RAFVR from 10th September 1941. After November 1942 he appears in the Air Force List index but there is no other entry. He resigned his RAFVR (Training Branch) commission on 25th March 1946.

When he retired in 1961, fifty-three West End street traders, many of whom Bennett had fined, presented him with a picnic set and an ice bowl, with red roses for his wife. Eugene and Violet retired to Vicenza, Italy in 1961 and lived at 'Villa Violetta', via Roma, Marostica, Vicenza, Italy. He died at his home on 4th April 1970 and was cremated at Vicenza, where his ashes are interred in Niche 116 of the Mausoleum there.

In addition to the VC and MC, he was awarded the 1914 Star with 'Mons' clasp, British War Medal 1914–20, Victory Medal 1914–19 with Mentioned-in-Despatches oakleaf, George VI Coronation Medal 1937 and Elizabeth II Coronation Medal 1953. His VC is held by the Worcestershire Regiment Museum, Foregate Street, Worcester. He is commemorated in a number of places:

- The 'Bennett Prize' established at Marling School in 1917 is presented annually for 'outstanding service to the school'.
- A framed portrait, which formerly hung in Marlborough Street Court, was presented by his widow to the Headmaster of Marling School and hangs in the school hall.
- A window dedicated to his memory in the cloisters of Worcester Cathedral.
- His armorial bearings were placed in the Hall of the Middle Temple, an honour normally reserved for the Masters of the Bench appointed as Master Readers.

2ND LIEUTENANT ARTHUR SEAFORTH BLACKBURN
10th Australian Infantry Battalion AIF

Arthur Blackburn was born at Woodville, Hyde Park, South Australia on 25th November 1892. His father was Canon Thomas Blackburn BA (1844–1912), born at Islington, Liverpool, Lancashire. He was a merchant's apprentice in 1861. In 1870 he married Jessie Ann Wood (1847–85) in Wandsworth. Jessie was related to the poet William Wordsworth (1770–1850) through her mother. By 1871 Thomas was a curate at Swanscombe, Kent and spent six years in Honolulu, Hawaii before moving to Port Lincoln, South Australia in 1882, where he was appointed Rector of St Thomas's Church. Jessie died there in May 1885. Thomas served as Rector of St Margaret's, Woodville for twenty-seven years. He was also a renowned entomologist and his collection was recognised by the Royal Geographical Society of Australasia. He sold the collection to museums and the proceeds provided for his children. Thomas published, *Memoirs on the Coleoptera of the Hawaiian Islands* and *True and False Issues Between Christianity and Science*. He collapsed in May 1912 and died a week later, on 18th May.

Arthur's mother was Margaret Harriette Stewart née Browne (1864–1904), known as Harriette. She married Thomas Blackburn on 8th September 1886 at St Thomas's Church, Port Lincoln. Arthur had six siblings from his father's two marriages:

- Thomas Wordsworth Gavin Blackburn (1872–1970), born at Dartford, Kent. He studied music at Adelaide University and married Bridget Delia Learhinan (1874–1964) from Co Clare, Ireland in 1904. They had moved to Vancouver, British Columbia, Canada by 1908, where he was an insurance agent and managed the 'Old Country Lunch and Tea Rooms'. Thomas and Bridget had two children – Dorothy May Blackburn, born 1908, married John Young in 1934 and Gladys Mary Blackburn (1912–84), who married Glendon John McLeod (1911–83) c.1940.
- Charles Bickerton Blackburn (1874–1972), born at Greenhithe, Kent was godfather to his half-brother Arthur. He was educated at the Universities of Adelaide (BA 1893) and Sydney (MB & ChM 1899, MD 1903). Charles became junior resident medical officer at the Royal Prince Alfred Hospital, Sydney 1899, senior resident 1900, medical superintendent 1901–03, honorary assistant physician 1903–11, honorary physician 1911–13 and honorary consultant 1935–72. He was also in private practice 1903–1965. In addition he held a number of other appointments in Sydney; honorary physician at the Royal Hospital for Women in Paddington, honorary pathologist at the Royal Alexandra Hospital for Children and honorary consultant at the Prince Henry Hospital. He served as a lieutenant colonel pathologist with 14th Australian General Hospital in Cairo 1916–19 (OBE 1919) and with 113th Australian General Hospital at Concord during the Second World War. At the University of Sydney he was lecturer in clinical medicine 1913–34, Dean of Medicine 1932–35, Deputy Chancellor 1939–41 and Chancellor 1941–64. Charles was President of the New South Wales branch of the British (Australian) Medical Association 1920–21, President of the Association of Physicians of Australasia 1933–35, a founder and first president (1937–38) of the Royal Australasian College of Physicians and was on the council of the Australian Red Cross Society and appointed a life member in 1960. He was knighted in 1936 and appointed KCMG in 1960. Charles married Vera Louisa Le Patourel (1880–1936) in 1910. Vera's grandfather, Henry Le Patourel (1807–91), was the brother of James Le Patourel, the great great grandfather of Herbert Wallace Le Patourel VC. They had three children:
    - Vera Bickerton Blackburn (1911–91) moved to England and married a scientist, Philip (later Sir Philip) Malcolm Game (1911–83), in 1939. Philip had been married previously to Anne Muriel Isabella White (1914–38). Vera and Philip had three children – Thomas P Game 1943, John C Game 1946 and Margaret AV Game 1951.

- Charles Ruthven Bickerton Blackburn (born 1913), was a doctor, He married Nell Freeman in 1940 at North Sydney and had a daughter, Nell Bickerton Blackburn. His wife Nell died in 1967 and he married Ann Janet Woolcock (1937–2001) in 1968 and they had two children – Agnes and Simon Blackburn. Charles was appointed Professor of Medicine at the University of Sydney.
- Thomas Arthur Blackburn (1915–32), died on 22nd December 1932 at Yaouk, New South Wales. The coroner concluded, "Injuries accidentally received through a gun shot wound caused by a shot accidentally fired by himself".

Arthur Blackburn's brother, Charles Bickerton Blackburn, served during both World Wars as a doctor.

- Edward Forth William Blackburn (1875–1937) was born at Greenhithe, Kent. He married Edith Lillian Fletcher (1880–1969) in 1906 at Woodville, South Australia. Edward was a manager of the Bank of New South Wales at Perth, Wagin and Williams in Western Australia, Moama in Victoria and Mudgee in New South Wales. He and Edith had two children:
  - Lillian Elizabeth Blackburn (1907–96) married Richard Vernon Finlay (1913–92) in 1946 and had a child.
  - Jessie Mary Blackburn (c.1912–2002) was a dental nurse who never married.
- John 'Jack' Stewart Blackburn (1887–1969) enlisted as a sapper on 5th September 1914 in 3rd Field Company, Australian Engineers AIF (434) and served until returning to Australia on 23rd October 1918. The war cost him his sight. He ran a stationary shop and his work for the Blind Institute earned him the MBE. He married Mildred Alice George in 1919 and they had two children:
  - Harold Stewart Blackburn (1919–98) married Marcia Constance Jack (1918–2002) in 1945. Both were State Medical Officers for Kingsborough and Bruny Island, Tasmania. They had seven children, including Elizabeth 'Liz' Helen Blackburn, born in 1948. She graduated BSc 1970, MSc 1972 and PhD 1975 before studying molecular and cellular biology at Yale University. Her study of the telomere, a structure protecting the end of chromosomes, led to the co-discovery of telomerase, the enzyme that replenishes the telomere, for which she was awarded the 2009 Nobel Prize for Physiology or Medicine with Carol W Greider and Jack W Szostak. She married John W Sedat in 1975 and had a son, Benjamin David Sedat, 1986. Her biography, *Elizabeth Blackburn and the Story of Telomeres: Deciphering the Ends of DNA* by Catherine Brady was published in 2007.

- Suzanne Blackburn (1922–2005) moved to England, where she married Anthony G Oram in 1959 and had three children.

Arthur Blackburn's niece, Elizabeth Helen Blackburn, who was awarded the 2009 Nobel Prize for Physiology or Medicine with Carol W Greider and Jack W Szostak.

- Harry Kenneth Baines Blackburn (1889–1963) enlisted on 22nd February 1916 in 4th Australian Infantry Battalion AIF (5423) until returning to Australia on 24th January 1919. He enlisted again as a private on 28th April 1942 (N225830), giving his date of birth as 15th June 1893. He was discharged from 9th Battalion, Volunteer Defence Corps, on 20th July 1943. Harry was an accountant.
- Margaret Browne Blackburn (1891–1969) was a nurse in England during the Great War and was a matron in New South Wales by 1943. She never married.

Arthur's paternal grandmother, Elizabeth Hannah Blackburn (née Williams), was the daughter of Sir John Bickerton Williams (1792–1855), the first person to be knighted by Queen Victoria. Arthur's maternal grandfather, John Stewart Browne (1814–88), was born at Tallantire Hall, Cumberland. He emigrated to Port Lincoln, South Australia and became a mounted police constable in 1843. He was later Chief Clerk in the General Post Office, Clerk to the Government Resident at Port Lincoln, Clerk to the Returning Officer of Flinders, South Australia in 1846, Government Resident and Sub-Protector of Aboriginals, Clerk and Librarian to the Legislative Council 1854 and Stipendiary Magistrate 1856, serving at Kapunda and Mount Gambier, before returning to Port Lincoln by 1870.

Arthur Blackburn was educated at Pulteney Street Church of England School, Adelaide, South Australia from 1903. In 1906 he moved to the

Pulteney Street Church of England School, Adelaide.

Collegiate School of St Peter's, Adelaide. On the right is the chapel where Arthur Blackburn married Rose Ada Kelly on 22nd March 1917 (National Library of Australia).

HMAT A11 *Ascanius* (10,048 tons) was completed in 1910 as a passenger ship for the Ocean Steam Ship Co Ltd of Liverpool. She was requisitioned as a troopship in 1914 for the Australian Imperial Force. In 1940 she was again requisitioned by the Admiralty as a troopship. On 30th July 1944 she was damaged by U-621 in the English Channel and there were a number of casualties. After the war, she moved Jewish emigrants from Marseilles to Haifa. In 1949 she was sold to an Italian company and renamed *San Giovannino*; she was broken up at La Spezia in 1952.

Collegiate School of St Peter's, Adelaide and in 1910 to Adelaide University, where he graduated in law (LL.B) in 1913. He served his articles with the firm of Fenn & Hardwick in Adelaide under its senior partner, C Burton Hardy, who was attacked one evening by two men. Arthur chased them away and Hardy presented him with a silver cigarette case as a token of his gratitude. Arthur was called to the Bar on 13th December 1913 and served as a barrister and solicitor with the firm of Nesbit & Nesbit in Adelaide.

Mena Camp, near the pyramids, outside Cairo, Egypt.

Arthur served in the South Australian Scottish Infantry from 1911 and enlisted in 10th Australian Infantry Battalion (31) as a private at Morphettville, South Australia on 19th August 1914. He embarked with the battalion on HMAT A11 *Ascanius* for the Middle East on 20th October, disembarked at Alexandria, Egypt on 8th December and moved to Mena Camp. On 28th February 1915, the Battalion embarked at Alexandria for Lemnos.

On 25th April, Arthur landed on the Gallipoli peninsula with the Battalion scouts from HMS *Prince of Wales*. He and 638 Lance Corporal Philip de Quetteville Robin set off inland and penetrated further than any other Australian in the whole campaign. They spotted large numbers of Turks and withdrew to pass on the information. Robin was killed on 28th April and is commemorated on the Lone Pine Memorial.

Arthur was promoted lance corporal on 27th April and later took charge of the Battalion Post Office for a month. He was commissioned in the field on 4th August as a platoon commander in A Company. 10th Battalion withdrew from Gallipoli on 21st November and moved to Lemnos later that month. On 27th December the battalion embarked on *Serang Bee* for Gebel Habieta, Egypt and on 15th January 1916 paraded for The Prince of Wales and General Sir Archibald Murray.

Arthur was promoted lieutenant on 20th February at Ismailia and was admitted to hospital on 11th March suffering from neurasthenia. He proceeded with the Battalion to France, sailing on the *Saxonia* on 28th March, arriving at Marseilles via Malta on 2nd April. He was granted leave 29th April – 7th May.

Awarded the VC for his actions at Pozières, France on 23rd July 1916, LG 9th September 1916. Appointed temporary captain on 1st August. He was evacuated to No.3 London General Hospital, Wandsworth from Boulogne suffering from pleurisy on 7th September and reverted to lieutenant. Arthur was invested with the VC by the King at Buckingham Palace on 4th October. However, his health did not improve and on 16th October he began the return journey to Australia on the Hospital Ship *Karoola*, arriving at Melbourne on 1st December. He was discharged on medical grounds with a pension of £4/5/- on 10th April 1917.

However, his military career was not over. He was a lieutenant on the Reserve of Officers from 1st October

HMS *Prince of Wales*, a pre-Dreadnought battleship launched in 1902 and completed in March 1904, served in the Mediterranean until 1909, when she was transferred to the Atlantic Fleet as Flagship, Vice Admiral. In 1912, she transferred to the Home Fleet as Flagship, Vice Admiral, 3rd Battle Squadron and later as Flagship, Rear Admiral, Second Fleet at Portsmouth. When war broke out, *Prince of Wales* was Flagship 5th Battle Squadron at Portland. On 20th March 1915, she moved to the Dardanelles and supported the ANZAC landings on 25th April. Later, she was part of the 2nd Detached Squadron in the Adriatic and in February 1917 was ordered home and placed in reserve as an accommodation ship. *Prince of Wales* was sold for scrap in 1920.

RMS *Saxonia* (14,281 tons) of the Cunard Line operated on the Atlantic and Mediterranean routes from 1900. In August 1914 she was requisitioned and used initially as an accommodation ship for German prisoners. In March 1915 she resumed service as a troopship. After the war *Saxonia* returned to service on the North Atlantic route between Liverpool and New York until scrapped in 1925.

1920 and transferred to 43rd Battalion, Citizens' Military Forces on 30th October 1925. He was promoted captain on 1st July 1928 and transferred to 23rd Light Horse Regiment. On 1st July 1930 he transferred to 18/23rd Barossa Light Horse Regiment on amalgamation.

On his return to Australia Arthur proposed to Rose Ada Kelly (1894–1981) and they married on 22nd March 1917 at St Peter's College Chapel, King William Road, North Adelaide. They lived at various addresses in Adelaide – 59 Northcote Terrace, Medindie in 1920; 45 Flinders Street; 5 Salisbury Terrace, Collinswood 1924–28 and 1933; 20 Park Terrace, Gilberton 1928; 77 Church Street, Walkerville 1937 and later at 'Green Gables', Crafers. Rose was President of the 2/3rd Machine Gun Battalion Women's Club. She and Arthur had four children:

No.3 London General Hospital, Wandsworth, where Arthur Blackburn was treated in September and October 1916.

Hospital Ship *Karoola* (Australian War Memorial).

- Richard 'Dick' Arthur Blackburn (26th July 1918–1st October 1987) graduated from the University of Adelaide, winning the John Howard Clark Prize for the highest place in the final examination. He was selected as the Rhodes Scholar for South Australia in 1940, but was unable to take it up because of the outbreak of war. He served as a trooper in 18/23rd Barossa Light Horse Regiment under his father in the 1930s. He enlisted in the Australian Army at Walkerville on 14th May 1940 (SX2747) and served in North Africa and Papua New Guinea, reaching the rank of captain before being discharged on 7th November 1945 from 2/9th Division Cavalry Regiment. Dick took up his Rhodes Scholarship at Magdalen College, Oxford after the war and was awarded the Eldon Scholarship. He attended Eldon Law School and was called to the Bar in Britain (Inner Temple) in 1949. Back in Australia he was appointed Bonython Professor of Law at Adelaide University in 1950 and Dean of the Faculty of Law in 1951. In 1957 he become a partner in the law firm of Finlaysons, while continuing part time at Adelaide University until 1965. In 1966 he was appointed a judge of the Supreme Court of the Northern Territory and presided over the first significant case concerning aboriginal land rights, which led to the Aboriginal Land Rights Act 1976. A number of other senior legal appointments followed: Judge of the Supreme Court of the Australian Capital Territory 1971; Judge of the Federal Court of Australia 1977–84; Chief Judge of the Supreme Court 1977; and Chief Justice 1982 (knighted 31st December 1982 for services to the law). Dick also continued a part time military career. In 1957, he was commissioned as lieutenant colonel to command the Adelaide University Regiment. Having been promoted colonel in 1962, he took command of 1st Battalion, Royal South Australian Regiment until 1965 (OBE 1965). He was Patron of the St John Council for the Australian Capital Territory 1981–84 (CStJ 1981). In 1984 he became Chancellor of the Australian National University and after retiring was elected Honorary Fellow of St Mark's College in 1986. His service to the Australian legal community is commemorated by the annual Sir Richard Blackburn Memorial lectures in Canberra. Dick married Bryony Helen Carola Dutton (1919–2005) on 1st December 1951. She was married previously to William R Curkeet, an American serviceman, in 1942 and lived in Madison, Wisconsin. Dick and Bryony had two children – Charlotte Bryony Blackburn 1952 married Alistair Calder in 1976 and Tom Dutton Blackburn 1955 also became a lawyer.

Arthur's son, Sir Richard Arthur Blackburn.

- Robert Stewart Blackburn (3rd January 1921 – 6th September 2003) became a dentist, practising at Victor Harbour, South Australia. He enlisted in the Australian Army at Collingwood, Terowie, South Australia on 3rd July 1942 (SX20311) and reached the rank of captain. He saw active service in Borneo in 1945 and was discharged on 25th January 1946 from 2/6th Dental Unit. He married Shirley O'Gorman (1919–c.92) in 1943 and had three children – Julie Blackburn 1944 married Dudley Hill, Susan Blackburn 1947 married Daniel Del-Rosi and Michael Stewart Blackburn 1949 married Dodi Norton-Wilson.
- Rosemary 'Wody' Neville Blackburn (6th January 1925 – 7th February 1994) become a university lecturer and women's adviser to South Australian Liberal Premier, David Tonkin. She married Dr Dugald Craven Wighton (1919–88) in 1948. Dugald enlisted on 11th November 1940 in the Royal Australian Air Force as a pilot (407597) and flew Mustang P51-K aircraft with 84 Squadron at Ross River airfield until discharged as a flight lieutenant on 1st February 1946. Rosemary and Dugald had five children: Helen Craven Wighton 1949 married Andrew Cambell; Mary Craven Wighton 1951 married Alexander Conrad Hope; David Blackburn Wighton 1954; James Dugald Wighton 1956 married Susan Bassett; and Henrietta Elizabeth Wighton 1960 married Charles Roderic Simpson.
- Margaret Alison Blackburn (born 4th July 1929) moved to England and married Dr Alexander James de Burgh Forbes (born 1923) at Oxford in 1952. In her

father's absence she was given away by Cecil Noble, a friend of her father's from army days. Margaret and Alexander had five children: Sarah Margaret Forbes 1954; Emma Caroline Kingston Forbes 1955 married Ian Hartley McClintock; Alexander Stewart Forbes 1958 married Wendy Kilgariff; David James Forbes 1960 married Teresa Santana; and Anna Rose Forbes 1960 married Jonathon Rose. Alexander was born at Hobart, Tasmania and graduated from the Royal Military College, Duntroon in 1942 (NX138171), serving in 2nd Australian Mountain Battery as a lieutenant. He was awarded the MC for services at Genga and Gillman Rivers, South West Pacific, in January/February 1945 (LG 21st June 1945) and was invested by the Governor General at Government House, Adelaide on 20th November 1947. Alexander was in Australia's victory contingent in the London Victory Celebrations of 1946. He studied at the University of Adelaide and Magdalen College, Oxford. Alexander was Liberal candidate for Barker, South Australia in 1956 and held the seat until retirement in 1975. He served as Minister for the Army 1963–66, Minister for the Navy 1963–64, Minister for Health 1966–71 and Minister for Immigration 1971. During his time as Minister for Immigration he ordered the deportation of singer Joe Cocker when cannabis was found in his band's hotel room. In November 1973, Prime Minister Gough Whitlam accused Forbes in Parliament of drinking excessively during a reception for the New Zealand Prime Minister. Forbes demanded he withdraw, which Whitlam eventually did, but outside the chamber the two men exchanged angry words. Alexander was alleged to have abused privileges by spending $16,000 on twenty-nine flights for himself and his family under the Gold Pass scheme. However, he was appointed CMG for his services to Parliament in 1977 and in 2001 was awarded the Centenary Medal for service to the Commonwealth Parliament and as Chairman of the Commonwealth Serum Laboratories.

Arthur returned to the legal profession, becoming a principal in the firm of Fenn & Hardy and served as a member of the Citizens' and Business Men's Committee. He was appointed Justice of the Peace on 29th August 1918 and represented the District of Sturt in the South Australian House of Assembly as a Nationalist member 6th April 1918 – 16th April 1921. In 1925 he entered into partnership with Lieutenant Colonel WF McCann MC, who was also at Pozières, as barristers and solicitors in Adelaide. In 1933 Arthur was appointed City Coroner until 1947.

On 11th November 1918 he became a Freemason, joined St Peter's Collegiate Lodge. He was later Worshipful Master of both the United Services and Gawler Lodges and Grand Registrar of the Grand Chapter for three years in the late 1930s. Arthur joined the Returned Soldiers' Association, forerunner of the Returned and Services League (RSL), in 1917. He was elected a State Vice-President in May 1917, was appointed the Association's Legal Adviser and elected President of South Australian RSL 1919–20. He was elected President again 1946–50 and remained on the State Board until 1954.

On 1st July 1939, Arthur was appointed to command 18th Light Horse Australian Machine-Gun Battalion. He rejoined the AIF on 28th May 1940 (SX6962) and was appointed to command 2/3rd Machine Gun Battalion, 2nd AIF on 18th June at Wayville Camp. Promoted lieutenant colonel on 1st July. The Battalion marched twenty-six miles to Warradale Camp, near Glenelg, South Australia on 30th October and moved to Woodside, in the Adelaide Hills, in January 1941. Arthur then marched the Battalion to Victor Harbour and back (192 miles) to improve fitness in preparation for active service.

The battalion embarked on the *Ile de France* (codenamed MM) at Sydney on 10th April 1941. The Governor General, Lord Gowrie VC, went aboard to bid farewell. The Battalion disembarked at Port Tewfik on 14th May and took part in operations in Syria. After the surrender of Damascus on 21st June, he was appointed a member of the Allied Control Commission for Syria. He was attached to HQ I Australian Corps 30th July–13th September and his duties included the welfare of Vichy French prisoners. Having rejoined 2/3rd Machine Gun Battalion, he embarked at Suez on RMS *Orcades* for the Far East on 1st February 1942. Promoted colonel on 14th February.

The battalion landed briefly at Oosthaven, Sumatra on 15th February with orders to assist in the demolition of Palembang airfield, but the Japanese had already secured it. General Wavell cancelled the operation and the battalion re-boarded the *Orcades*. The Battalion landed at Tandjong Priok, Java on 19th February to assist the Dutch. On 22nd February, Arthur was appointed temporary brigadier to command

SS *Ile de France* was the first liner built for the French Compagnie Generale Transatlantique after the First World War. She was completed in 1927 and her maiden voyage was from Le Havre on 5th June to New York. Her entirely art deco fittings caused something of a sensation. *Ile de France* was the last ship to leave France before the outbreak of the Second World War, carrying mainly American passengers anxious to get out of Europe. In New York she was laid up until taken over by the British Admiralty and used for troop and prisoner of war movements. In 1945, she was returned to the CGT and was used to return American and Canadian troops. In 1947, she commenced a two-year refit. She was scrapped in 1960, having been used in the making of the film *The Last Voyage*, during which she was partially sunk.

Troops of 2/3rd Machine Gun Battalion, commanded by Arthur Blackburn, in Syria (Australian War Memorial).

2nd AIF, named 'Blackforce' after him, which came under the local Dutch commander, Major General Schilling. Arthur's troops were dispersed on five widely scattered airfields and he tried to concentrate them as a strike force, but was denied. He was summoned to see General Wavell on 25th February and was told to give every assistance to the Dutch forces. Wavell then left for India to meet Major General HDW Sitwell, who finally agreed to Arthur's request to concentrate his troops.

In early March, in the face of the advancing Japanese, the Dutch on his left withdrew to protect the main city of Bandung. On 4th March Arthur learned that the Dutch had decided to abandon Bandung. He agreed to cover the Dutch withdrawal from Batavia, despite having no air cover or tanks. As the front extended Blackforce was outflanked, but by then the Dutch had completed their withdrawal from Batavia and the remaining Australians withdrew early on 5th March. Blackforce had delayed a Japanese division for three days, causing heavy casualties and tying down large numbers of troops that could have been used elsewhere. The Japanese were closing in on the only port suitable for an evacuation. The Dutch declared Bandung an open city and saw little point

RMS *Orcades* (23,400 tons) was a passenger liner built in 1937 for the Orient Line for the Britain to Australia route. She was used as a troopship during the Second World War. On 10th October 1942, 220 nautical miles southwest of Cape Town, she was attacked by U-*172*. An epic two and a half hours battle followed, during which U-*172* had to fire seven torpedoes to sink *Orcades*. Most of the survivors were picked up by the *Narwik*, but forty-five were lost. Her Captain, Charles Fox, was awarded the CBE and Lloyd's War Medal for Bravery at Sea.

continuing the fight. However, the British and Australians thought otherwise. Arthur called on Major General Sitwell, GOC British Troops Java, on 6th March and told him of his plans to continue the fight. He handed Sitwell a message to be sent to Australia detailing his situation and asking to be evacuated from the south coast, but did not realise that the radios had already been smashed.

On the night of 7th March, Arthur started to shift Blackforce southeast of Bandung, covering the British withdrawal to Tjikadjang and blowing bridges behind them. Before leaving Bandung, Arthur was the last man to have a drink at the Harmony Club. The Dutch ordered all troops to surrender. Arthur wanted to keep fighting, but did not want to be in breach of international law. Sitwell concluded there were more points in favour of surrendering than not. Arthur was more concerned about supplies and the next stand. The British were ordered to lay down their arms on 8th March, but the order did not apply to Blackforce. Arthur found a route to the south coast at Pameungbeuk and hoped to evacuate his force, but was unaware his message to Australia had not been received; there were no ships on the way. He considered taking to the mountains to continue fighting and had ammunition and food for thirty days, but no shelter at the height of the rainy season, or medical supplies. On 11th March, he reluctantly decided that he had to capitulate and ordered the troops to destroy their arms and equipment. They were taken prisoner on 12th March and held at Singapore, Moji in Japan, Pusan in Korea and Mukden in Manchuria.

Having been liberated, Arthur returned by air to Perth, Western Australia from Colombo, Ceylon on 13th September 1945. He was treated at 121 Australian General Hospital 14th October – 29th November and returned to the Melbourne Depot on 1st December. As a mark of respect, sixty-two men of 2/3rd Machine Gun Battalion who served with him on Java assembled at the end of Salisbury Terrace, Adelaide and marched to his house. This was followed by a civic reception at Adelaide Town Hall the following day, attended by fellow VCs Roy Inwood and Phil Davey. Arthur's appointment was terminated on 18th July 1946. He was appointed CBE for his gallant and distinguished services in Java in 1942, LG 30th May 1946, but it was not until 6th October 1949, that he was invested by the Governor of South Australia, Lieutenant General Sir Willoughby Norrie KCMG CB DSO MC, at Government House, Adelaide.

Arthur was reappointed to the AIF on 11th October 1946 as temporary brigadier (SX500503) for duty as a witness at the War Crimes Trials in Tokyo. He embarked in Sydney for Kure, Hiroshima, Japan on the *Kanimbla* 15th October – 1st November 1946. He was attached to No.2 War Crimes Section, Supreme Commander for the Allied Powers, for the duration of the trials and returned by air to Australia on 22nd December. His appointment was terminated on 10th January 1947.

In 1946 Arthur commissioned a RSL newspaper, *Back – Like the Diggers*. He welcomed Field Marshal Montgomery to Adelaide in 1947, during which Monty was made a Life Member of the RSL. Arthur served as a conciliation commissioner in the Commonwealth Court of Conciliation & Arbitration 1947–54, Chairman of the Services Canteen Trust Fund 1947–60, member of the Television Broadcaster's Board overseeing the introduction of the new media in South Australia, Chairman of the Civilian Internees' Trust Fund and the Prisoners of War Trust Fund. Arthur was one of 25,000 former servicemen inspected by Queen Elizabeth II at a rally on Adelaide University Oval in March 1954; he introduced her to a party of VC and GC winners.

After the 1955 Black Sunday bushfires in the Adelaide Hills, Arthur helped form a community fire brigade in Stirling and was its chairman and chief fundraiser. The same year he became a member of the National Airlines Commission and a company director. He was appointed CMG for services as the Commonwealth Conciliation Commissioner, Chairman of the Civilian Internees Trust Fund and the Prisoners of War Trust Fund, LG 1st January 1955. Arthur attended the VC Centenary Celebrations at Hyde Park, London on 26th June 1956, travelling on RMS *Orcades* with other Australian VCs.

Arthur was diagnosed with prostate cancer in 1956. The treatment was initially successful, but in 1959 secondary cancers developed. He died suddenly at Crafers, South Australia on 24th November 1960 and was buried with full military honours at West Terrace Cemetery, Adelaide, South Australia.

In addition to the VC, CMG and CBE he was awarded the 1914–15 Star, British War Medal 1914–20, Victory Medal 1914–19, 1939–45 Star, Pacific Star, Defence Medal 1939–45, War Medal 1939–45, Australia War Service Medal 1939–45, George V Silver Jubilee Medal 1935, George VI Coronation Medal 1937, Elizabeth II Coronation Medal 1953 and Efficiency Decoration (Australia). His service in Syria June-July 1941 qualified him for the Africa Star, but he does not appear to have been issued it. His medals passed initially to his eldest son, Dick, and then to his son, Tom, in October 1987. They were presented to the Australian War Memorial by the family and are held in the Hall of Valour at the Australian War Memorial, Treloar Crescent, Campbell, Canberra, Australian Capital Territory, Australia. Arthur is commemorated in a number of places:

- Headquarters of the South Australia branch of the Veteran's Affairs Department at Blackburn House, Grenfell Street, Adelaide.
- Blackburn Avenue, Glenelg North, Adelaide.
- Blackburn Street, Kilburn, Adelaide.
- Blackburn Street, Bittern, Melbourne, Victoria, on the Victoria Cross Estate built in 1916–18.
- Blackburn Close, Wodonga, Victoria.
- Named on the Victoria Cross Memorial, Campbell, Canberra dedicated on 24th July 2000.
- Named on the Victoria Cross Memorial, Queen Victoria Building, George Street, Sydney, New South Wales.

- Named on one of eleven plaques honouring 175 men from overseas awarded the VC for the Great War. The plaques were unveiled by the Senior Minister of State at the Foreign & Commonwealth Office and Minister for Faith and Communities, Baroness Warsi, at a reception at Lancaster House, London on 26th June 2014, attended by The Duke of Kent and relatives of the VC recipients. The Australian plaque is at the Australian War Memorial.
- The Secretary of State for Communities and Local Government, Eric Pickles MP, announced that Victoria Cross recipients from the Great War would have commemorative paving stones laid in their birthplace as a lasting legacy of local heroes within communities. The stones would be laid on or close to the 100th anniversary of their VC actions. For the 145 VCs born in Australia, Belgium, Canada, China, Denmark, Egypt, France, Germany, India, Iraq, Japan, Nepal, Netherlands, New Zealand, Pakistan, South Africa, Sri Lanka, Ukraine and the United States of America, individual commemorative stones were unveiled at the National Memorial Arboretum, Alrewas, Staffordshire by Prime Minister David Cameron MP and Sergeant Johnson Beharry VC on 5th March 2015.

14603 SERGEANT WILLIAM EWART BOULTER
6th Battalion, The Northamptonshire Regiment

William Boulter was born at 51 Bull Head Street, Wigston Magna, Leicestershire on 14th October 1892. His father was a Liberal party supporter and gave William the second name Ewart in honour of William Ewart Gladstone becoming Prime Minister for the fourth time in July 1892.

His father was Frederick 'Fred' Boulter (1866–1940), a winder (hosiery) in 1881 and a stocking framework knitter by 1892. On 6th May 1897, he and other local hosiers formed the Wigston Hosiery Society (Wigston Cooperative Hosiers Ltd from 1930) as a co-partnership, with an office at the Wigston Working Men's Club on Long Street. He was elected to the committee and late in 1898 premises were rented in Bull Head Street. In February 1903, he was elected chairman. In 1906 a factory was opened on Paddock Street and in 1909 Fred became the manager, a position he held until he retired in 1937. In 1913 a larger factory was opened in Paddock Street. He was also President of the Cooperative Productive Federation Ltd and was its Treasurer for many years.

William's mother was Mary Ann née Dore (1864–1940) a domestic servant. Fred and Mary married at the Independent Chapel (later Wigston Magna Congregational Church), Long Street, Wigston Magna on 4th August 1890. The family was living at 51 Bull Head Street in 1891, Welford Road in 1901, 38 Harcourt Road in 1911 and by 1916 at 9 Central Avenue; all addresses in Wigston Magna. William had five siblings:

Bull Head Street, Wigston Magna, where William Boulter was born.

William Ewart Gladstone, whose second name was given to William Boulter in honour of Gladstone becoming Prime Minister for the fourth time in July 1892 (Elliot & Fry).

- George Boulter (born 1890) was a hosiery operative in 1911. He worked at the Wigston Hosiery Society factory, where his father was manager. On 8th August 1917 he was conscripted into the Royal Navy (J75666), trained on HMS *Victory I* until 26th November and was assigned to HMS *Cyclops* in the Home Fleet on auxiliary and repair ships at various depots and at Scapa Flow, including the hired drifter, *Mary Swanston*, until demobilised on 7th July 1919. He married Mabel Elizabeth Rawlings (1892–1919), a hosiery machinist, in 1915. After the war he returned to the Wigston Hosiery Society factory as a driver and chauffeur to its senior members. The marriage of a George Boulter to Clara Taylor was registered at Leicester in the 3rd quarter of 1922.

The Wigston Hosiery Society factory on Paddock Street (Derek Seaton).

Fred Boulter seated second from left with the Committee of the Wigston Hosiery Society 1920 (Midlands Cooperative Society).

- Albert Boulter (1894–1959) was a boot and shoe operative in 1911. He served in 2nd Leicestershire in Mesopotamia as a sniper, where he was wounded, and later in India. On return his father helped him set up his own hosiery business. Later he worked for Nathaniel Corah & Sons Ltd at St Margaret's Works, Canning Street, Leicester. He married Ada Marshall Hastings (1896–1998), a silk winder, in 1921. They had three children – Betty Boulter 1922, Marian Boulter 1924 and Ralph Boulter 1936.
- Harold Boulter (1896–1980) was a boot and shoe operative in 1911. He enlisted in the Royal Army Medical Corps (103331) on 29th October 1915 and was in 35th Company at Millbank, London in October 1916. He served in Mesopotamia 25th December 1916–31st December 1918 and then went to Russia until 5th September 1919. He returned to Britain on 25th September and was demobilised on 19th November. He was awarded a disability pension of 8/- per week due to malaria. He worked in various grocery shops in Leicester and then for Wigston Cooperative Stores (later Wigston Cooperative Society) and went on to become manager of the Wigston Fields store. In the 1940s he became a buyer for the Cooperative grocery stores, working from the warehouse of the Wigston Cooperative Society Ltd and was a member of the Society's board. He married Gladys A Glover (born 1900) in 1925 and they had two children – Winifred E Boulter 1926 and Fred A Boulter 1932.
- Mabel Boulter (1898–1975) was a fancy hosiery learner in 1911. She married Thomas Alfred Getliff (1899–1973) in 1927. They had three children – twins Anne Getliff and Trevor E Getliff 1930 and Raymond A Getliff 1938.
- Sarah May Boulter (1904–89) married William Eric Crosby Clark (1907–55) in 1933.

William was educated at Bell Street Infants' School, Wigston Magna and Great Wigston Board School, Long Street (Long Street Council School from 1903), where he was noted for his sporting abilities. On 13th May 1993, HRH The Duke of Gloucester GCVO opened the Leicestershire Record Office in the former school. William worked as a grocer's assistant at the Wigston Cooperative Stores from 1904. From late 1911, he was a draper's assistant in the Leicester Cooperative Society store on Leicester High Street. In 1912 he moved to the Kettering Industrial Cooperative Society as a draper's assistant at the Newland Street store. He lodged with Henry and Elizabeth Shuffle at 38 Princes Street and played for Kettering Thursday Football Club and was a member of the Old Adult School.

Great Wigston Board School, now the Leicestershire Record Office (Derek Seaton).

William was engaged to Florence May Lusher (born 1895) before the war and she appeared with him during a number of receptions after the award of the VC. Their relationship did not survive after the war.

William enlisted in 6th Northamptonshire on 4th September 1914, which trained initially at Shorncliffe before moving to Colchester and later Codford on Salisbury Plain. He was described as 5′ 6¼″ tall and weighed 131 lbs. Promoted lance corporal 29th September. He was charged with being absent from duty for twelve hours at Colchester on 1st November and was admonished, but forfeited one day's pay. Promoted corporal on 18th November. He was charged with being absent from parade at Colchester on 23rd March 1915 and reprimanded. Promoted lance sergeant on 13th April. On 26th June, King George V inspected 18th Division, including 6th Northamptonshire, near Stonehenge. George was charged with being absent from duty at Codford for over fifteen hours on 5th July and was reprimanded again and forfeited two days' pay.

The Battalion marched from Codford to Warminster on 25th July and then travelled by train to Southampton for the crossing to Boulogne the following day. William was promoted sergeant the same day. He was charged with being late for church parade on 24th October and was once again reprimanded.

Awarded the VC for his actions at Trônes Wood, France on 14th July 1916, LG 26th October 1916. He was recommended by his CO, Lieutenant Colonel George Ripley, a man much respected by William. Ripley died on 16th October 1916 of wounds received at Thiepval on 26th September, never knowing that his recommendation had been successful (Cottingham [St Mary Magdalene] Churchyard). William was evacuated to Southampton on 18th July. He was treated at Lichfield Military Hospital, Staffordshire (the only hospital in Lichfield was a specialist venereal disease establishment at Whittington Barracks, which does not appear to be appropriate) 19th July – 7th September and at 5th Northern General Hospital, Leicester until 21st October. When the wound was virtually healed, X-rays revealed a piece of decayed bone, which required further surgery to remove it. He convalesced at the British Red Cross VAD Hospital at Green Hill, Belper,

5th Northern General Hospital, Leicester, now part of Leicester University.

British Red Cross VAD Hospital, Green Hill, Belper.

Derbyshire followed by sick leave at home. While having dinner with the family on 26th October a telegram arrived announcing he had been awarded the VC.

William Boulter's visit to Kettering on 28th October 1916 (Northampton Chronicle & Echo).

William attended a civic reception at Kettering on 28th October and the following day visited the Old Adult School there. On 30th October he was received by Wigston Magna. On 2nd November Kettering Industrial Cooperative Society hosted him at a tea party at which he was presented with a gold watch and chain, followed by musical entertainment. On 4th November an estimated 20,000 greeted him during his visit to Northampton, during which he was presented with a marble timepiece by the Co-Operative Society at a ceremony at Abingdon Park. The Corporation of Northampton presented him with another watch and an illuminated address. On 7th November he was the guest of the Cooperative Wholesale Society in London and was presented with a smoker's cabinet. On 9th December, he was received by Wigston Magna, including a visit to Glen Parva Barracks, and was presented with a bronze shield.

William was next posted to the Bedfordshire Command Depot at Ampthill, commanded by the Duke of Bedford, on 10th November. While there he applied for a commission on 18th January 1917 and commenced officer training at No.13

The 200 bedroom Imperial Hydropathic at St Anne's-on-Sea opened in 1910. During the First World War it became the Imperial Hospital and in 1920 it was renamed the Majestic. It was regularly used by stars appearing at nearby Blackpool. It was demolished in 1975 and the site used for flats.

William leaving Buckingham Palace after his investiture on 17th March 1917. The white band on his hat indicates that he was an officer cadet.

Officer Cadet Battalion, Newmarket on 9th March. He was given special leave to travel to London in order to receive his VC from the King at Buckingham Palace on 17th March. He was commissioned in the Northamptonshire Regiment on 27th June and joined 7th Battalion in France on 30th August. He contracted trench fever and acute bronchitis on 16th October and by December was convalescing at Nice, in the south of France. The bronchitis flared up again and he was evacuated to England on 26th February 1918, where he was admitted to No.2 Western General Hospital, Manchester. He was cared for in a part of the hospital reserved for officers on the High Street, 3rd April – 14th May. On 2nd October he was admitted to the Imperial Hospital at St Anne's-on-Sea, Lancashire with trench fever.

College of Technology, Sackville Street, Manchester.

His last medical board on 11th November found him unfit for General Service. Despite this he continued to serve, assuming duty with the Ministry of Labour's No.3 District, College of Technology, Sackville Street, Manchester on 28th November and was promoted lieutenant on 27th December. According to the Army List he was employed by the Ministry of Labour until August 1919, but was demobilised on 24th April 1919. He relinquished his commission, retaining the rank of lieutenant, on 1st September 1921.

In 1920 William joined the staff of the Northampton Chamber of Commerce journal and allied publications at their offices at Barclays Bank Chambers in St Giles' Square. He ran a Leicester hosiery business in 1921. In 1922, he was joined by Leslie William Hurren to form Boulter & Hurren Ltd on Market Street, Leicester. They appeared in court on 9th September 1925 for giving false information about an employee,

William Boulter (right) chatting with Sam Meekosha VC before the VC contingent marched to Buckingham Palace for the Garden Party on 26th June 1920.

Mademoiselle Lea Irma Jacquart, engaged to increase business in France. She had been most successful, resulting in the firm taking on five men. However, they failed to obtain a Home Office permit under the Aliens Act. An informant in France attempted to blackmail them into sending her back and when they refused, he reported them to the police. The magistrates fined them £15 each, but the Mayor of Leicester, Councillor Herbert Simpson, despite being obliged to enforce the law, saw no reason why Mademoiselle Jacquart should be deported and applauded Boulter's and Hurren's refusal to accede to blackmail. In 1927 William moved to London to manage a large hosiery manufacturers, Messrs TH Downing & Co Ltd, at 3A Wood Street.

William and Rene at their wedding on 14th April 1927 (Associated Newspapers).

On 14th April 1927 William married Alice Irene 'Rene' née Toone (1897–1988) at the Register Office, St Giles, London. At the time, she was living at her late father's home, Wigston Hall, with her half sister Edith Birkett and her husband Thomas Birkett. He was living at 54/55 Tavistock Square, Bloomsbury, London. The reception was held at the Coventry Restaurant on Rupert Street and they honeymooned at Worthing. There were no children.

In July 1933, William joined John Lewis & Co Ltd on a one month trial, resulting in him being appointed Superintendent of the Department of Shoes and Trunks at the East House store on Oxford Street, London on 28th September. He was soon promoted to Sales Manager for several departments. In November 1933 John Lewis gained control of Messrs Lance & Lance Ltd in Weston-super-Mare and Boulter was appointed to manage all the ground floor departments of the store on 11th April 1934. He returned to Oxford Street later in the year, moving to the West House store as Sales Manager of the Furnishing Department. He returned to Lance & Lance Ltd in Weston-super-Mare as acting General Manager in August and September 1935 and then went back to Northamptonshire to join Messrs B Toone & Co Ltd, boot and shoe manufacturers in Desborough. His

John Lewis' West House store on Oxford Street, London, just before the Second World War (John Lewis Partnership).

wife's grandfather had set the company up and the governing director at the time was Thomas Birkett, his wife's brother-in-law. In 1936, he joined Knight & Co, auctioneers, surveyors, valuers and estate agents, of 14 Cromwell Place, South Kensington, owned by Cyril Wilson Black, who married Dorothy Joyce Birkett, his wife's niece. The same year he and Rene moved into a flat at 10 Wimbledon Close, The Downs, Wimbledon, Surrey. Rene continued to live there for thirty-two years after William died until her own death on 20th January 1988 at the Royal Marsden Hospital, Fulham Road, London.

Sir Cyril Wilson Black JP DL (1902–91) was a prominent Baptist involved with Billy Graham's 1955 and 1966 Crusades. He was Deputy Lieutenant for Greater London, Conservative MP for Wimbledon 1950–70, Chairman Surrey County Council 1950–64 and Mayor of Merton 1966–67. He was knighted in 1959. Amongst his many business interests, he was Chairman of Beaumont Properties 1933–80, the Temperance Permanent Building Society 1939–73, MF North Ltd 1948–81 and London Shop Property Trust 1951–79. He was also a director of a number of other companies and was at one time President of Wimbledon Football Club.

William was commissioned as an acting pilot officer (62809) in the RAFVR Training Branch on 1st February 1941. He was confirmed in the rank of pilot officer on 1st February 1942 and later that year was promoted flight lieutenant. He commanded an Air Training Corps Squadron in Wimbledon, Surrey. Another officer in the Squadron was his civilian employer, Flying Officer Cyril Black. On 12th May 1942, William was outside Buckingham Palace when he bumped into another RAF officer. Both apologised before realising they both wore the crimson ribbon of the VC. They grinned, shook hands and introduced themselves, the other man being Squadron Leader John Dering Nettleton VC, who had just been invested. William resigned his RAFVR commission on 25th July 1944 due to ill health.

After the Second World War he assumed responsibility for acquiring furniture for the flats managed by the companies on whose boards Cyril Black sat. He was also a company director for several prominent firms. Away

William photographed outside Buckingham Palace on 12th May 1942 with Squadron Leader John Dering Nettleton VC, just after the latter's investiture (Associated Newspapers).

from his business life, William was a member of Malden Golf Club, Surrey and Captain of the Golf Society in 1950, winning a trophy in 1951 and 1952. He was also a member of the Ypres League, attending the annual parades on Horse Guards Parade, London. At the League's parade on 4th November 1938 he was one of three VC wreath layers with Douglas Belcher and Alfred Wilcox. In 1953 he became President of the 6th Battalion Association of the Northamptonshire Regiment.

William was a heavy smoker and developed lung cancer. He became seriously ill in April 1955 and was admitted to Wimbledon Hospital, where he died on 1st June 1955. He left £6,917/1/1 gross, £6,553/6/10 net to his widow. William was cremated at Putney Vale Cemetery, London on 6th June and his ashes were scattered in the Garden of Remembrance between two cherry trees close to the lily pool opposite the East Lodge. The funeral was attended by the Mayor and Mayoress of Wimbledon, his former employer Cyril Wilson Black MP and Brigadier John Lingham CB DSO MC, representing the Northamptonshire Regiment.

In addition to the VC, he was awarded the 1914–15 Star, British War Medal 1914–20, Victory Medal 1914–19, George VI Coronation Medal 1937 and Elizabeth II Coronation Medal 1953. Rene left his medals to the Regiment, except for the Elizabeth II Coronation Medal 1953, which was retained by the family. On 3rd July 1988, 220 members of the Regimental Association paraded with the band and drums of 5th (Volunteer) Battalion, The Royal Anglian Regiment at Gibraltar Barracks and marched to the Church of the Holy Sepulchre in Northampton. The Deputy Supreme Allied Commander Europe, who was also Colonel of the Royal Anglian Regiment and Northamptonshire Regimental Association, General Sir John Akehurst KCB CBE, took the salute, following which the five medals were handed over by William's nephew, Peter Birkett. An escort from 2nd, 5th and 7th Battalions took the medals into the church for the Comrades to view. Afterwards they were displayed during a lunch party at Simpson Barracks at which Peter Birkett and other members of the family were guests. The VC is held by the Northamptonshire Regiment Museum, Abington Park Museum, Northampton.

William Boulter is commemorated in a number of places:

- In 1997 Wandsworth Borough Council named seven roads and paths at Putney Vale Cemetery as memorials to the seven VCs buried, cremated or commemorated there, including Boulter's Path.
- In 2008, a Blue Plaque was erected at his former home at 9 Central Avenue, Wigston by the Greater Wigston Historical Society in conjunction with Wigston Civic Society.
- A framed wall display consisting of photographs, the VC citation and a set of replica medals hangs in the Malden Golf Club members' bar.
- A small display at Kettering Museum, Northamptonshire, presented by Tanky Turner of the Northamptonshire Regiment in 2007.

LIEUTENANT COLONEL ROLAND BOYS BRADFORD
1/9th Battalion, The Durham Light Infantry

Roland Bradford was born at Carwood House, Witton Park, Bishop Auckland, Co Durham on 23rd February 1892. His father was George Bradford (1845–1911), born at Churnside, Berwickshire. He was a miner at the Earl of Durham's Lambton Collieries before gaining his certificate as a mining engineer. About 1885 he was appointed manager of Messrs H Stobart's Bishop Auckland Collieries and was also manager of the local school at Witton Park. He then developed a small colliery of his own, possibly Carterthorne Pit, near Evenwood, south of Bishop Auckland. Later he was chairman of a steel company near Darlington and of Newport and Abercarne Collieries in South Wales. He also inspected coal properties in Canada and Spain. After leaving Stobart's about 1894, he lived at Morton Palms Farm, four miles from Darlington, Co Durham. In 1898, he moved to Milbanke House, Milbank Road, Darlington. Although heavily involved in his business interests, he found time to shoot and fish and was keen on sport of any kind, something he passed on to all his children. Roland's mother Amy Marion née Andrews (1859–1951), was born at Willesborough, Kent. George and Amy married in the 2nd quarter of 1885 registered at East Ashford, Kent. Amy moved to Folkestone, Kent in 1917 and purchased a property in Ravenlea Road, which she named 'Milbanke'. Roland had four siblings:

- Thomas 'Tommy' Andrews Bradford, born on 23rd March 1886, was a land agent and farmer. He captained the Durham County Cricket XI and in 1909

Carwood House, Witton Park, where Roland Bradford was born in 1892.

George Bradford senior was Chairman of Newport and Abercarne Collieries.

Lambton Colliery, where George Bradford senior gained his certificate as a mining engineer.

scored 207 runs in ninety minutes against Philadelphia. He joined 4th Volunteer Battalion, Durham Light Infantry and was commissioned in 8th Durham Light Infantry on 7th April 1906. Promoted lieutenant 1st April 1906 and transferred to the Territorial Force when it replaced the Volunteers in 1908. Promoted captain on 8th February 1910. He went to France on 8th April 1915 and was wounded near Ypres on 25th April while commanding D Company in a desperate fight when surrounded on three sides. On 25th July 1915 he was withdrawn from front line service suffering from rheumatism, flat feet and trench fever. He was later appointed a staff captain, brigade major and in 1917 received a regular commission in the York & Lancaster Regiment. He was twice Mentioned in Despatches and awarded the DSO, LG 1st January 1916. Thereafter he undertook a number of training appointments, including No.7 Officer Cadet Battalion at Moore Park, Fermoy, in Ireland, No.1 School Cannock Chase, NCO School Berkhampstead and II Corps School in France from 9th September 1918. He transferred to the General Reserve of Officers as a captain on 4th April 1919 with seniority from

Morton Palms Farm near Darlington (Hugh Mortimer).

3rd October 1917. In the 3rd quarter of 1915 he married Honor Rebe Blackett (1886–1943) at Chester-le-Street, Co Durham. She was the daughter of Colonel William Cuthbert Blackett CBE DL of Acorn Close, Sacriston, Co Durham, where Thomas and Honor were living in August 1923. They had a son, George James Roland B Bradford 1919, who was an actor before becoming an antiques dealer. Thomas became Chairman of the Durham County Conservative Association and sought election to Parliament as Conservative candidate for the Seaham Division of Durham in October 1922, but lost to Sidney Webb, the Labour candidate. He tried again at the General Election in December 1923 as the Conservative candidate for the Durham Division, but was defeated by 3,200 votes. He became a colliery proprietor and was knighted (LG 2nd January 1939). He was also a JP and DL Durham 15th January 1926 and Sheriff of County Durham 27th March 1942. Tommy was commissioned as a lieutenant Special List (98034) in March 1941 with seniority from 1st September 1939. He married Kathleen 'Kitty' Mernie Vernon Percy (née Ross) (1898–1981) on 10th July 1945 at Durham. She was the widow of Lieutenant Colonel Joscelyn Edward Seymour Percy DSO (1898–1943), whom she married in 1923 and they had four children. Percy commanded 9th Durham Light Infantry 1940–42 and 151st Brigade in 1942. He died at sea on 8th August 1943 and is commemorated on the Brookwood Memorial. Tommy and Kitty lived at Aden Cottage, Whitesmocks, Durham. He relinquished his appointment as Honorary Colonel 11th Durham Light Infantry in September 1949. Thomas died in 1966.

Thomas Andrews Bradford while serving in the York & Lancaster Regiment.

- George Nicholson Bradford, born on 23rd April 1887, joined HMS *Britannia* as a cadet on 20th February 1902. He was appointed midshipman and drafted to HMS *Revenge* on 15th January 1904, HMS *Exmouth* on 18th May 1904 and HMS *Terrible* in March 1907, before he was commissioned as sub lieutenant on 30th April 1907.

Moore Park Camp, Fermoy, Ireland, where Tommy Bradford was an instructor with No.7 Officer Cadet Battalion.

Further drafts followed to HMS *Bullfinch* 25th July 1907, HMS *Blenheim* 7th January 1908 and the destroyer HMS *Chelmer* on 29th January 1909 under Lieutenant Loftus William Jones RN, who went on to win the VC aboard HMS *Shark* on 31st May 1916. Off Lowestoft at 3.20 a.m. on 3rd March 1909, HMS *Doon* rammed the trawler *Halcyon. Doon* was proceeding to Dover accompanied by HMS *Chelmer*. Five of the trawler's crew jumped aboard *Doon*, leaving four in the sinking ship. Bradford launched the whaler from HMS *Chelmer* and rescued three of the men. He was about to be hoisted aboard when he received a signal from *Doon* that there was a boy on board the sinking trawler. Bradford immediately pulled over to the sinking *Halcyon*, jumped aboard and, rushing to the forepeak, located the boy and picked him up. Bradford jumped aboard the whaler just before the trawler up-ended and sank a few minutes later. Promoted lieutenant 30th July 1909. He was drafted to HMS *Vanguard* on 1st March 1910, HMS *Amazon* in January 1912 and HMS *Orion* on 27th January 1914. Promoted lieutenant commander 30th July 1917 and assigned to HMS *Hindustan*

George Nicholson Bradford VC.

Commander Loftus William Jones VC RN (1879–1916), who as a lieutenant commanded HMS *Chelmer* 1908–10. On 31st May 1916, he was commanding HMS *Shark*, leading a division of destroyers to attack the German Battle Cruiser Squadron at Jutland. A shell hit the bridge, knocking out the steering gear and soon afterwards another shell disabled the engines. Another destroyer came between her and the enemy, but Jones warned her off to avoid almost certain destruction. Jones was wounded in the leg, but went aft to help connect and man the after wheel. Meanwhile the forecastle gun had been blown away and soon afterwards the after gun. He went to the midships gun and assisted in keeping it in action, all the time under very heavy fire from enemy light cruisers and destroyers at short range. The gun crew was reduced to three. An able seaman was badly wounded in the leg and minutes later Jones was hit by a shell, taking off his leg above the knee. He continued to give orders to the crew, while a chief stoker improvised a tourniquet. He realised the ship could not survive and a German destroyer was closing. He ordered the survivors to put on lifebelts and almost immediately Shark was torpedoed and sank. Jones' body washed ashore in Sweden a few days after the battle. He is buried in Kviberg Cemetery, Gothenburg. His VC was purchased by Lord Ashcroft in 2012 and is displayed at the Ashcroft Gallery at the Imperial War Museum.

HMS *Chelmer* was launched in December 1904 and completed in June 1905. She was assigned to the East Coast Destroyer Flotilla of the 1st Fleet based at Harwich until 1909, when she was assigned to the China Station. In November 1914 she redeployed to the 5th Destroyer Flotilla in the Mediterranean Fleet and on 25th April 1915 supported the landings at ANZAC on the Gallipoli Peninsula. She remained in the Mediterranean for the rest of the war and in 1919 returned to Britain to be laid up. In June 1920 she was sold for breaking at Hayle, North Cornwall.

while training for a special operation in early 1918. This turned out to be the Zeebrugge Raid on 23rd April 1918, for which he was awarded the VC. George was killed during his VC action, having landed on the Mole from HMS *Iris II* on St George's Day, which was also his birthday. He is buried in Blankenberge Town Cemetery, Belgium (A 5). His VC was sold at a Spinks auction on 8th December 1988 for £17,500 to Lord Ashcroft and is held in the Ashcroft Gallery at the Imperial War Museum.

The Mole in the background, with blockships in the foreground across the entrance to the canal leading to the U-boat base, following the Raid on Zeebrugge on 23rd April 1918.

- James 'Jimmie' Barker Bradford, born on 11th December 1889. He was a gifted musician and excelled in boxing, wrestling and swimming. He occasionally hunted with the Hurworth Hounds. He was employed at R & W Hawthorn, Leslie & Company's Engineering Works, Newcastle-upon-Tyne. as a mechanical engineer and was living at 164 Westmoreland Road in 1911. Later he became a director of Dinsdale Wire and Steel Works, Co Durham. James joined the Royal Naval Volunteer Reserve as an able seaman in 1911 before transferring to the Northumberland Hussars as a trooper (2187) on 1st April 1912. He was embodied on 5th August 1914, embarked at Southampton on 4th October and disembarked at Zeebrugge, Belgium next day. While with B Squadron on 7th July 1915 he was confined to camp for seven days with loss of pay for disobeying Divisional Orders by walking horses at a pump. He was commissioned in 18th Durham Light Infantry on 9th September and was slightly wounded on 10th May 1916. He received gun shot wounds to the arm and right ankle on the Somme on 1st July 1916 and was treated at No.14 General Hospital, Wimereux, near Boulogne, from 3rd July before being evacuated to Britain. James married Annie 'Nancy' Wall (born 1894) in the 3rd quarter of 1916 at Darlington and returned to France early in 1917. He was awarded the MC for his actions in the Hébuterne Sector on 3rd March 1917 (LG 17th April 1917); he led his men into the enemy trench, capturing many prisoners and two machine-guns. He killed three of the enemy and later repelled a determined counterattack. James was wounded in the left shoulder and left thigh on 10th May 1917 and died on 14th May at No.41 Casualty Clearing Station (Duisans British Cemetery, Etrun, France – IV G 33). His MC was sent to his wife by post at her request rather than being presented.

In 1906 two new ferries came into service on the Mersey, the *Iris* and the *Daffodil*. Each could carry 1,735 passengers. When King George V and Queen Mary went to Wallasey to lay the foundation stone of the Town Hall on 15th March 1914, they crossed the Mersey on *Iris*. As HMS *Iris II* and HMS *Daffodil* they were commandeered by the Royal Navy for the Zeebrugge Raid because of their double hulls and shallow draft. They were towed to the target by HMS *Vindictive* and cast off close to the Mole. Iris attempted to come alongside the Mole to disembark her Royal Marines. When the first attempt failed, two officers, George Bradford and Lieutenant Hawkins, climbed ashore under heavy fire and attempted to secure the ship. Both were killed and Bradford received a posthumous VC. *Iris* returned under her own steam, but with a fire under the bridge and water in the engine-room. Of the men aboard, 188 were killed and sixteen were missing. *Iris* and *Daffodil* returned to the Mersey on 17th May 1918. They were reconditioned and added the prefix Royal to their names in recognition of their gallant action. *Royal Iris* was sold in October 1931 to Palmer Brothers and used as a cruise boat from Dublin under the same name and later at Cork. In 1947 she was renamed *Blarney* having been purchased by the Cork Harbour Authorities.

- Amy Isabelle Bradford (3rd May 1901 – 1962), was known as 'Baby' and later 'Ginger'. Like her brothers she was very keen on sport and was still playing competitive squash aged forty-nine. Her marriage to Harry Leslie H Cremer (1893–1976) was registered in the 3rd quarter of 1922 at St Martin, London. Harry was an articled clerk in a paper mill in 1911 and later owned Chartham Paper Mills, Kent. They had five children:

James Barker Bradford.

- David George Bradford Cremer (1924–2009) joined the Royal Navy and was aboard HMS *Prince of Wales* when she was sunk off the coast of Malaysia on 10th December 1941. In 1942 he was a midshipman on HMS *Duke of York* and a sub-lieutenant on HMS *Scylla* in 1944; Scylla was flagship for the Eastern Task Force landing on Gold, Juno and Sword Beaches during the Normandy invasion. He was later a lieutenant on HMS *Hornbill* and with 787 Squadron RN at West Raynham, Norfolk in 1948. He also served on HMS *Peregrine* and *Gannet* 1951, promoted lieutenant commander 1954. Served at HMS *Dryad* 1956, on HMS *Ark Royal* 1958, HMS *Hermes* 1960 and at HMS *Dryad* again 1962. He married Ada Florence Elizabeth Mary Mead (1928–2006) in 1948. They had two children – David Anthony Bradford Cremer (1950–96) and Peter L Bradford Cremer 1955.
- Roland Paul Bradford Cremer, born 1926, married Ann Partington in 1956 and they had three children – Martin L Bradford Cremer 1958 and twins Patrick J Bradford Cremer and Richard J Bradford Cremer 1960.
- Jonathan L Bradford Cremer, born 1933, married Gerda Hillenbrand (born c.1937) in 1956 at St Pancras, London. They had five following children – George Michael Bradford Cremer 1957, Christopher Roland Bradford Cremer 1959, Andrew J Bradford Cremer 1961, Arianne Alison Bradford Cremer 1967 and Dominique Joanna Bradford Cremer 1969.

R & W Hawthorn, Leslie & Company's Engineering Works, Newcastle-upon-Tyne.

No.14 General Hospital, Wimereux, near Boulogne, was based around Chateau Mauricien, a former hotel.

- Waveney JR Bradford Cremer (twin with Joanna), married John C Brooks in 1971.
- Joanna R Bradford Cremer (twin with Waveney), born 1938.

The four Bradford brothers just before the war. From left to right: Roland, Thomas, George and James. By the time peace came, only one was still living.

Roland's paternal grandparents were Thomas Bradford (c.1810–85) and Isabella née Nicholson (c.1806–81), both born in Scotland. They married at Aytoun, Lamberton Toll, Berwickshire in 1841. Thomas was a farmer of 240 acres, employing three labourers and a boy at Vigo, Birtley, Co Durham in 1881. In addition to George, they also had Bessy Bradford c.1844 and James Bradford c.1847.

Roland's maternal grandparents were George Andrews (c.1823–1905) and Ellen née Barker (c.1833–1917), both born in Kent. Their marriage was registered in the 3rd quarter of 1854 at East Ashford, Kent. George was an accomplished boxer and amongst his opponents were renowned fighters Tom Sayers and Jem Mace. He was a farmer, living with his family at Shed End Villa, Willesborough, Kent in 1871. By 1881 the family had moved to Dunns Hill House, Willesborough Street, Willesborough and he was running a farm of 120 acres, employing five men and a boy. In addition to Amy they also had:

Tom Sayers (1826–65) was a bare-knuckled prize-fighter. His final bout against American champion John Camel Heenan is considered to be the first world championship. It went to forty rounds and ended in chaos when the spectators invaded the ring; the referee declared a draw. Sayers is buried in Highgate Cemetery, London.

- Agnes Jane Andrews (1857–1926) married Harold Allen (born 1856) in 1881 at East Ashford. He was a building surveyor and they were living at 13 Holmdale Road, Hampstead, London in 1901. They had four children – Harold Colin Allen 1882, Agnes Mabel Allen 1884, John Gordon Allen 1885 and Kenneth Beale Allen 1890.

Darlington's Queen Elizabeth Grammar School (later Queen Elizabeth Sixth Form College), where Roland was educated June 1900 - July 1901 and was a member of the OTC.

Roland was a member of the Church Lads' Brigade at Holy Trinity Church, Darlington. There is a memorial there to the three Bradford brothers killed during the war.

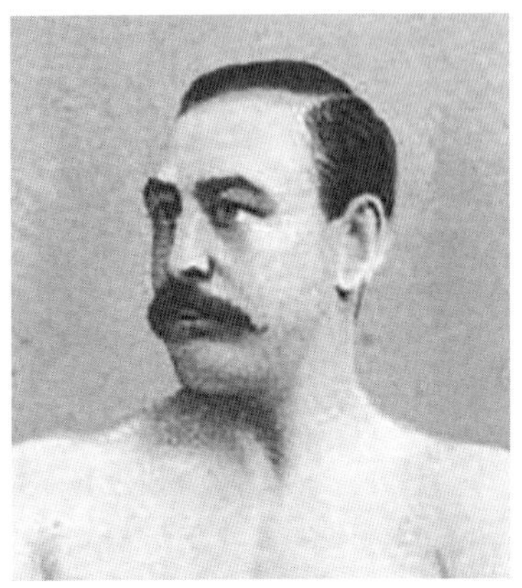

Jem Mace (1831–1910) was Champion of England in 1861. Bare-knuckle boxing was outlawed and in 1869 he went to America and toured with John Camel Heenan giving exhibitions. He won several titles in America and lived in Australia 1877–82, where his exhibitions led to the acceptance of glove boxing. In 1883 he went back to America and continued as an exhibition boxer until 1909, then aged seventy-eight. He was also a professional runner, publican, circus proprietor and racehorse owner. He kept a bar in New York and ran a hotel in Melbourne. Jem married three times and had at least fourteen children by five women. He gambled away a fortune, died penniless and was buried in an unmarked grave in Anfield Cemetery, Liverpool until 2002, when Merseyside Former Boxers Association erected a memorial headstone.

Epsom College.

- Fanny Elizabeth Andrews (1860–1945) married Edward Robert Olive (1857–1924) in 1884 at East Ashford. He was a clergyman and they were living at 57 Park Road, Sittingbourne, Kent in 1901.
- Mary L Andrews (1866–1917).
- Bertha Eliza Andrews (1868–1943).

Roland was educated in Darlington at Bondgate Wesleyan School, Queen Elizabeth Grammar School (later Queen Elizabeth Sixth Form College) June 1900 – July 1901 and Polam Grange School. He went on to Epsom College, Surrey 1907–09, where he captained his House Rugby XV and was a forward in the College XV in his final year. He was also in the Epsom Cadet Corps as a lance corporal and section leader. Roland was a member of the Church Lads' Brigade attached to Holy Trinity Church, Darlington.

Roland was commissioned in 5th Durham Light Infantry (Territorial Force) on 16th April 1910. He attended Brigade Territorial Camps at Richmond, Surrey in July 1910 and Featherstone Park, Haltwhistle, Northumberland in July 1911. At the latter he was appointed aide de camp to Colonel Bush. He enjoyed military life so much at the annual camps that he changed his mind about studying for a medical degree and opted for life in the army instead. He was commissioned in 2nd Durham Light Infantry on 22nd May 1912. His batman throughout his service was Private/Lance Corporal King.

Roland was posted to Lichfield, Staffordshire, where he decided to learn to ride. He purchased a horse in the spring of 1914, entered a point-to-point with no experience and won against good competition. He subsequently joined the Atherstone and South Staffordshire Hounds and also hunted with the East Essex Hounds.

He sailed from Southampton for France on 9th September 1914 with the battalion, landing at St Nazaire the following day. The battalion was in action shortly after on the Aisne Front. Promoted lieutenant 24th September. Mentioned in Field Marshal Sir John French's Despatch dated 14th January 1915, LG 17th February 1915, **Awarded the MC for services rendered in connection with operations in the field, LG 18th February 1915. It is not known what this was for, but there are a number of possible actions in the Battalion war diary. The two most likely are:**

> 20th September – the enemy attacked the flank and Roland Bradford was the only officer left in his company until relieved on 25th September.
>
> 13th October – the Battalion advanced near Vieux Berquin, Ferme Labis and Les Trois Fermes. Thirteen men were killed and sixty-one wounded. On the third night of continuous fighting Roland Bradford's platoon was almost surrounded in the Bois Grenier area and he skilfully extracted it from a most awkward situation.

Roland was appointed temporary captain on 3rd March 1915 and transferred to 1/7th Durham Light Infantry as its adjutant on 3rd May.

Promoted captain and brevet major on 1st January 1916. Appointed brigade major in February and second-in-command 1/9th Durham Light Infantry in April. Appointed temporary major 8th May. He received his MC on 24th May. **Mentioned in Field Marshal Sir Douglas Haig's Despatch dated 30th April 1916, LG 15th June 1916.** Appointed acting lieutenant colonel and CO 1/9th Durham Light Infantry on 4th August. He was wounded by a shell splinter on 15th September 1916 at Mametz Wood, but went forward with the attack and carried a wounded man back under heavy fire to the assembly trench. The wound still required dressing two months later. Roland proved to be an excellent commander and took an exceptional interest in the welfare of his men. In the trenches he made a point of spending a few hours each day talking to them and knew them all by name.

Awarded the VC for his actions at l'Abbaye de Eaucourt, France on 1st October 1916, LG 25th November 1916. The Battalion returned to the front to fight at the Butte de Warlencourt and the Gird Line on 5th November and some months later Roland escorted the Duke of Connaught round the Butte, explaining the November operations. **Mentioned in Field Marshal Sir Douglas Haig's Despatch dated 13th November 1916, LG 4th January 1917.**

Roland wrote to Lord Northbourne, Honorary Colonel of 1/9th Durham Light Infantry, seeking welfare support for his men and warm clothing for the winter. He also requested music for the band he had started. Lord Northbourne obliged with the music and food parcels. As Christmas 1916 approached, Roland organised a football tournament within the battalion and wrote to Lord Northbourne seeking medals for the winners and runners up. The design was to include the Durham Light Infantry badge and the inscription, *9th D.L.I. Football Tournament, December, 1916*. The medals arrived on 2nd February 1917 and were presented to the teams in the field.

In the line Bradford started a custom of the men singing verses of *Abide With Me* each evening. He also organised a Battalion Concert Party, 'The Green Diamonds', after the identification patch on their uniforms. Its first performance was at Maricourt. It performed on 22nd April 1917 at Ronville, outside Arras, against a ruined wall, with the audience sitting in shell holes. Roland became concerned at the frequency of skin disease amongst his men. The MO said exposure to sunlight would help remedy the condition, so Bradford ordered them to sit naked in the sun for an hour each day. They were reluctant to comply, so he stripped off and ordered them to follow suit. Thereafter the difficulty was getting them to put their clothes back on, but skin complaints gradually decreased.

Roland was wounded again on 16th January 1917. He led an attack near Guémappe on 23rd April, achieving his objectives and capturing over 300 prisoners, two howitzers, and many machine-guns, with the minimum of casualties amongst his own men.

The VC was presented by the King in Hyde Park on 2nd June. He was the fourteenth out of 350 recipients of gallantry medals to receive his award that day; thirteen was omitted from the programme. Appointed temporary lieutenant colonel 18th August. On 15th September, his Battalion penetrated the enemy's second line and captured Chérisey. He was slightly wounded while talking to one of his company commanders on 4th November. A bullet pierced the officer's helmet and splinters struck Bradford in the face. He confirmed the other officer was unhurt before walking to a dressing station to have the wound dressed. Roland returned to the front and next day was appointed to command 186 Brigade as temporary brigadier-general, the youngest in the Army, aged twenty-five. However, he remained in command of 1/9th Durham Light Infantry for a few days whilst awaiting his successor. Divisional Headquarters grew impatient and telephoned his unit with orders for him to report immediately. He assumed command of 186th Brigade on 10th November and was appointed acting brigadier-general on 13th November. **Mentioned in Field Marshal Sir Douglas Haig's Despatch dated 7th November 1917, LG 28th December 1917.**

Roland Bradford's grave in Hermies British Cemetery.

186th Brigade was involved in the attack on Anneux and Graincourt and the penetration of the Hindenburg Line on 20th November, followed by action against the Marquoin Line and Bourlon Wood. On 30th November, Roland was visiting his Brigade's positions alone near Graincourt during a German counterattack on Bourlon Wood. He was killed by a shell fragment in the back about one mile southwest of Graincourt, near Lock 7 on the Canal du Nord, France. He is buried in Hermies British Cemetery (F 10).

Roland never married and probate was granted to his brother, Thomas Andrews Bradford. He left £10,042/3/-. Roland left a generous legacy to his faithful batman of five years, Lance Corporal King.

In addition to the VC and MC, he was awarded the 1914 Star with 'Mons' clasp, British War Medal 1914–20 and Victory Medal 1914–19 with Mentioned-in-Despatches Oakleaf. The VC is held by the Durham Light Infantry Museum, Durham Art Gallery, Aykley Heads, Durham. Roland is commemorated in a number of places:

- A marble plaque was unveiled by by Lord Daryngton on the east wall of the north transept of St Cuthbert's Church, Church Row, Market Place, Darlington, during a memorial service on 19th July 1925, conducted by the Bishop of Durham, the Right Reverend Herbert Hensley Henson DD.

- Bradford Crescent, Gilesgate, Durham is one of nine roads named after Durham and Durham Light Infantry VCs.
- The Roland Bradford VC Trophy is awarded to the winners of the annual Ex-Servicemen's Bowls Tournament in northeast England.
- The Territorial Army Centre in Neasham Road, Darlington was named 'The Bradford Armoury' on 5th October 1963 by Sir Thomas Bradford.

St Paul's Church, Witton Park, Etherley, Bishop Auckland.

- A brass plaque and rose window at St Paul's Church, Witton Park, Etherley, Bishop Auckland. The window was destroyed by vandals and redesigned by Patricia Hudson Moses in 1992, when it was also dedicated to Rosetta Heslop, whose son donated it.
- A commemorative stone honouring the eleven Durham Light Infantry soldiers awarded the VC was unveiled in the grounds of the Durham Light Infantry Museum on 8th September 2001 by Brigadier Robin MacGregor-Oakford MC. The stone was funded by the Durham Light Infantry veterans' group, 'The Faithful Inkerman Dinner Club'. The ceremony was attended by the Regiment's sole surviving VC holder, Captain Richard Annand.
- The 'General Bradford Memorial Fund', established in the early 1920s, raised £3,000 for the Darlington Memorial Hospital in Hollyhurst Road, opened by HRH Prince George on 5th May 1933. The walls of the entrance hall to the administration building are lined with eleven marble tablets that form the 1914–18 War Memorial. There are 700 names and Panel 1 carries the three Bradford brothers' names. In 1997 the entrance hall was to be sold, but a spokesman for the National Health Service Executive assured the public that right of entry would not be revoked.
- Memorial plaque in Holy Trinity Church, Woodland Road, Darlington to the three Bradford brothers killed during the war, unveiled on 11th November 1921 by Thomas Bradford DSO and dedicated by the Bishop of Durham, the Right Reverend Herbert Hensley Henson DD. Panels on the rood list the names of seventy-five men of Holy Trinity Church who died in the war. Panel 1 carries the names of the three Bradford brothers.
- The Fellowship of the Services Bradford VC Mess 428, meets at the Darlington Ex-Servicemen's Club.
- Twenty two Berberis shrubs, representing the twenty-two members of the Church Lads' Brigade who were awarded the VC, were planted in the Church Lads & Church Girls Brigade Memorial Plot at the National Memorial Arboretum, Alrewas, Staffordshire.

8/3504 SERGEANT DONALD FORRESTER BROWN
2nd Battalion, Otago Regiment, New Zealand Expeditionary Force

Donald Brown was born on 23rd February 1890 in Dunedin, New Zealand. His father was Robert Brown (c.1847–1922), a draper. His mother was Jessie née McFarlane (c.1849–1915). Robert and Jessie married at Dunedin in 1872. They were both born in Lanarkshire, Scotland. The family lived at Wharf Street, Oamaru and Jessie is also known to have lived at Thames Street. Donald had nine siblings:

- Margaret McFarlane Brown (1875–1962) married the Reverend James Crawford Patterson MA (1870–1933) in 1911.
- James Brown 1877.
- Robert Brown 1878, married Susanne Thomson in 1906. Robert and his brother Charles were executors to Donald's estate and received his campaign medals.
- Thomas Morland Brown (1880–1912) married Vanora Rose Balfour in 1910.
- Leonard Snodgrass Brown born and died 1881.
- Charles Osbourne Brown (1882–1967).
- Elizabeth Cecilia Beatson Brown (1884–1962) married Angus Oswald Hugo in 1924.
- Jessie McFarlane Brown (1885–1934).
- John Ebenezer Kelly Brown (1886–1945) married Isabell Wilson Hills in 1915.

Donald was educated at South School, Dunedin and Waitaki Boys' High School, Oamaru, in 1908. He was known to be a good footballer in his youth. He then

Oamaru breakwater.

Thames Street, Oamaru.

Waitaki Boys' High School, Oamaru.

HMNZT 37 *Maunganui* (7527 tons), a passenger steamship built for the Union Steamship Co of New Zealand. Her maiden voyage was on 15th February 1912 from Wellington to Melbourne, Australia. In 1914 she became a troopship. After the war she was on the Auckland - Sydney - Vancouver route and later serviced San Francisco until 1936. In 1937 she ran the New Zealand - Sydney route until 1940, when she was requisitioned as a hospital ship. In 1945 she was laid up at Wellington and by 1949 was owned by the Hellenic - Mediterranean Line and refitted at Piraeus as a migrant vessel, the *Cyrenia*, for emigrants from Genoa in Italy, Valetta in Malta and Piraeus in Greece to Australia. She was scrapped in February 1957.

Donald Brown's grave in Warlencourt British Cemetery, situated alongside the busy D929 Albert-Bapaume road.

worked on his farm at Totara for three years, selling it before enlisting in the New Zealand Expeditionary Force on 19th October 1915 at Totara, Oamaru. He was described as 5′ 7″ tall, weighed 168 lbs, with dark complexion, grey/green eyes, dark brown hair and his religious denomination was Presbyterian. Donald was promoted corporal and embarked for Egypt aboard HMNZT 37 *Maunganui* with the 9th Reinforcements on 8th January 1916. On arrival in Egypt on 8th February he was assigned to 2nd Battalion Otago Regiment and arrived at Marseilles, France on 11th May. He was promoted sergeant before 20th May.

Awarded the VC for his actions on 15th September at Crest Trench, near Flers, France and on 1st October 1916 at l'Abbaye de Eaucourt, France, LG

The obelisk and sundial at Caroline Bay, Timaru, carrying the names of eleven New Zealand VCs, including Donald Brown.

Arthur William de Brito Savile Foljambe, 2nd Earl of Liverpool GCB GCMG GBE MVO PC DL JP (1870–1941), was a Liberal politician, who held the honorary title of Viscount Hawkesbury between 1905–07. He was educated at Eton and after Sandhurst served with the Rifle Brigade in the Boer War, leaving the army in 1906. He succeeded to the earldom in 1907. He was the 16th and final Governor of New Zealand 1912–17; and its first Governor-General, 1917–20. During the First World War he conferred his name on a New Zealand regiment, The New Zealand Rifle Brigade (Earl of Liverpool's Own).

14th June 1917. Captain WGA Gibson-Bishop MC, commanding 10th (North Otago) Company, recommended him for the DCM for his actions on 15th September. The CO, Lieutenant Colonel GS Smith, told Brown's father in a letter dated 3rd November that he hoped the recommendation would be upgraded to a VC, but it was not until the officers of the battalion started agitating that any progress was made. This was the first VC awarded to a New Zealander on the Western Front.

Donald was killed in action at l'Abbaye de Eaucourt on 1st October 1916 and is buried in Warlencourt British Cemetery, near Bapaume, France (III F 11). A memorial service was held on 13th June 1917 at Waitaki High School. The following day another memorial service was held at Columba Presbyterian Church, which Donald used to attend.

As Donald never married, the VC was presented to his father by the 2nd Earl of Liverpool, Governor-General of New Zealand, at Oamaru on 30th August 1917.

In addition to the VC, Donald was awarded the British War Medal 1914–20 and Victory Medal 1914–19. The VC is held privately. In 1962 it was displayed at the North Otago Pioneer Gallery and Museum, which no longer exists. In the mid 1980s the VC was loaned to Waitaki Boys' High School to display during a special ANZAC service and also to the National War Museum at Waiouru.

Donald is commemorated in a number of places:

- Brown Quarters, Linton Military Camp, near Palmerston North, New Zealand.
- An obelisk in the centre of the War Memorial Wall, Caroline Bay, Timaru, bears the names of eleven New Zealand VCs, including Donald Brown.

Dunedin Cenotaph in Queens Gardens (The Castle Cruiser).

The New Zealand Post 60¢ stamp commemorating Donald Brown, issued in April 2011.

- Victoria Cross winners' plaque at Dunedin Cenotaph in Queens Gardens, formerly at Dunedin Returned Servicemen's Association.
- An issue of twenty-two 60c stamps by New Zealand Post entitled 'Victoria Cross – the New Zealand Story' honouring New Zealand's twenty-two VC holders was issued on 14th April 2011.
- Named on one of eleven plaques honouring 175 men from overseas awarded the VC for the Great War. The plaques were unveiled by the Senior Minister of State at the Foreign & Commonwealth Office and Minister for Faith and Communities, Baroness Warsi, at a reception at Lancaster House, London on 26th June 2014 attended by The Duke of Kent and relatives of the VC recipients. The New Zealand plaque was unveiled on 7th May 2015 to be mounted on a wall between Parliament and the Cenotaph in Wellington. The ceremony was attended by Defence Minister Gerry Brownlee, Defence Force Chief Lieutenant General Tim Keating and Corporal Willie Apiata, New Zealand's only living VC.
- The Secretary of State for Communities and Local Government, Eric Pickles MP announced that Victoria Cross recipients from the Great War would have commemorative paving stones laid in their birthplace as a lasting legacy of local heroes within communities. The stones would be laid on or close to the 100th anniversary of their VC actions. For the 145 VCs born in Australia, Belgium, Canada, China, Denmark, Egypt, France, Germany, India, Iraq, Japan, Nepal, Netherlands, New Zealand, Pakistan, South Africa, Sri Lanka, Ukraine and the United States of America, individual commemorative stones were unveiled at the National Memorial Arboretum, Alrewas, Staffordshire by Prime Minister David Cameron MP and Sergeant Johnson Beharry VC on 5th March 2015.

LIEUTENANT COLONEL JOHN VAUGHAN CAMPBELL
3rd Battalion, Coldstream Guards

John Campbell was born in London on 31st October 1876. His father was Captain The Honorable Ronald George Elidor Campbell (1848–79), born at Stackpole Court, Saint Petrox, Pembroke. He was commissioned in the Coldstream Guards on 25th December 1867, promoted captain on 22nd March 1871 and appointed Adjutant 1st Battalion, 19th August 1871 – 29th October 1878. He married Katharine Susannah née Claughton (1848–1934) on 17th December 1872 at St George's, Hanover Square, London. Having applied for special service in South Africa, Ronald was seconded as a staff officer to Colonel Sir Evelyn Wood VC and took part in the Zulu War. On 28th March 1879, he led an assault on a Zulu position on Hlobane Mountain, accompanied by Lieutenant Henry Lysons and Private Edmund Fowler of 2nd Cameronians. Campbell was shot through the head and killed while approaching the entrance to a cave. Lysons and Fowler captured the stronghold and were awarded the VC. Sir Evelyn Wood wrote, *Without wishing to take away in the slightest degree from the bravery evinced by Lieutenant Lysons and Private Fowler, I should add that if Captain Ronald Campbell*

Sir Evelyn Wood VC (1838–1919) began his career in the Royal Navy during the Crimean War, including serving on land at Sebastopol and Inkerman, where he almost lost an arm and was recommended unsuccessfully for the VC. In the army he returned to the Crimea and spent time in Florence Nightingale's hospital at Scutari. He served in the Indian Mutiny and was awarded the VC for rescuing a merchant from robbers who were about to hang him. Wood attended Staff College in 1863, but also studied law and was called to the Bar (Middle Temple) in 1874. He was involved in the Third Anglo-Ashanti War, Zulu War, First Boer War and the Mahdist War in Egypt. During the Zulu War he commanded the 4th column as it crossed the Zulu frontier. Following the massacre of other forces at Isandlwana, he pulled back to fortified positions at Kambula. Having failed to take Hlobane on 28th March 1879, he recovered and defeated the Zulus at Kambula and also took part in the final battle at Ulundi, following which he headed the peace negotiations. During the First Boer War, he became Governor and C-in-C in Natal and led the peace negotiations after, which brought him political and royal favour. He reorganised the Egyptian Army and also held senior appointments in Britain as Quartermaster-General 1893, Adjutant-General 1897, Commander II Corps and GOC CinC Southern Command 1901–04. On 8th April 1903, he was promoted field marshal. Wood's sister, Kitty, married Captain William O'Shea, but was also the lover of the Irish nationalist politician Charles Parnell, which caused a public scandal. Wood retired in December 1904 and was appointed Constable of the Tower of London in 1911. He died in 1919 and is buried in Aldershot Military Cemetery.

Lieutenant Henry Lysons and Private Edmund Fowler were awarded the VC for their part in the action on Hlobane Mountain on 28th March 1879, in which Captain Ronald Campbell was killed.

The Empress Eugenie (1826–1920) was born in Granada, Spain, and was the wife of Napoleon III, 1853–71. In 1856, she gave birth to an only son, Napoleon Eugene Louis Jean Joseph Bonaparte, the Prince Imperial. Following the French defeat in the Franco-Prussian War 1870–71, Napoleon III was overthrown and he and Eugenie took refuge in England. Following his death in 1873 and the Prince Imperial in 1879, she moved to Farnborough, Hampshire. The house is now an independent RC girls' school. She died in 1920 and is interred in the Imperial Crypt at St Michael's Abbey, Farnborough, with her husband and son.

had survived, I should have recommended him for the Victoria Cross before the others, as in the assault of such a cave, as I have attempted to describe, the greatest danger is necessarily incurred by the leader. Wood requested the War Office to publish a memorandum in the London Gazette, stating that Captain Campbell would have been recommended for the VC if he had lived. However, General Wolseley, the Adjutant General, did *not wish the question raised.* Katherine accompanied the Empress Eugenie when she went to South Africa to visit the site where Louis Napoleon, the Prince Imperial, had been killed. Katherine was

The cross marks the grave of Ronald Campbell and Llewellyn Lloyd, with Hlobane Mountain in the background. On the right is a memorial to the Zulu force involved in the battle on 28th March 1879 (Tony Scott).

John Campbell's father, Captain The Honorable Ronald George Elidor Campbell.

also able to visit her husband's grave on the slopes of Hlobane Mountain.

John had three siblings:

- Maud Campbell, born 1873, died unmarried 1900.
- Guy Ronald Campbell (1874–1950), born at the Tower of London, was educated at New College, Oxford (MA). He married the Honorable Vere Annesley (1879–1975), eldest daughter of the 11th Viscount Annesley, in 1901. Guy was Rector of Wilton, Salisbury, Wiltshire 1912–43. They had three children:
    - Hester Maud Vere Campbell CBE (1904–82) married the Honorable Eric Rupert Walter Barrington in 1929. They divorced in 1938.
    - Margaret Helen Campbell (1907–75) married Bruce Delacour Hylton Stewart in 1937 and they had a son, Richard Anthony Stewart, in 1945.
    - Colin Arthur Ronald Campbell (1910–76) was commissioned in 2nd Oxfordshire & Buckinghamshire Light Infantry on 30th January 1930 and last appears in the Army List in September 1933. On 24th August 1939 he was commissioned as a lieutenant and appointed Adjutant of 5th Wiltshire TA, with seniority from 14th July 1930. He was appointed acting captain on 3rd September 1939 and by January 1946 had been released to the Unemployed List.
- Robert Campbell (1878–1945) was commissioned in the Cameron Highlanders 8th March 1899 and promoted lieutenant 5th March 1900. He was appointed Adjutant on 21st November 1904 and promoted captain on 23rd October 1905. Robert served in France 9th December 1914 – 3rd March 1915, 13th June 1916 – 3rd January 1918 and 18th October 1918 until the end of the war. He was promoted major 1st September 1915. As an acting lieutenant colonel he commanded 8th Argyll and Sutherland Highlanders 12th July 1916 – 3rd January 1918, 2nd Royal Scots Fusiliers 23rd October 5th November 1918 and 5th Cameron Highlanders thereafter. He was awarded the DSO (LG 1st January 1917) and a Bar (LG 26th July 1917). The latter was awarded for conspicuous gallantry and devotion to duty when, at a critical moment, the enemy pierced the line and were consolidating a position to the rear. He skilfully and energetically counter-attacked, forcing the enemy to surrender with heavy loss, then rendered valuable assistance to another unit, bringing enfilade fire to bear upon the enemy. His promptness and energy saved a very awkward situation. Mentioned in Despatches twice (LG 4th January and 21st December 1917) and transferred to the Regular Army Reserve

The Prince Imperial in Royal Artillery mess dress in 1875.

of Officers Class 2 on 19th September 1923. Robert married Mary Emelda Wood (died 1979) in 1926 and they had two sons:

- Robin John Ronald Campbell, born 1927, was commissioned in the Seaforth Highlanders on 15th July 1948. Promoted lieutenant 15th July 1950, temporary captain 29th June – 14th July 1954, captain 15th July 1954 and major 15th July 1951. Mentioned in Despatches for services in Malaya, LG 24th October 1950. He transferred to the Queen's Own Highlanders when it formed after amalgamation and was Specially Employed with East Africa Land Forces 17th January – 30th June 1960. He was seconded to 4th King's African Rifles 9th October 1962 -5th April 1964. He married Alison Barbara Rose Cave-Browne in 1954 and they had two sons – Ian Robert Campbell 1956 and James Farquhar Robin Campbell 1958.
- Alan Campbell, born 1929, was commissioned in the Cameronians on 22nd December 1948 (397835) and transferred to the Queen's Own Highlanders on its formation on 15th May 1968. He was promoted lieutenant colonel on 30th June 1976 and was appointed Senior Instructor of the School of Transport 26th April 1976 – 9th April 1979. Mentioned in Despatches for his services in Malaya, LG 21st October 1952). He married Sylvia Ann Hermon in 1963 and they had five children: Alexander Campbell 1964, Theresa Ann Campbell 1965, James Campbell 1967, Andrew Campbell 1969 and Nicholas Campbell 1971.

John's paternal grandfather, John Frederick Vaughan Campbell, Earl of Cawdor (1817–98), was created 1st Viscount Emlyn in 1838. He was Conservative MP for Pembrokeshire 1841–60, JP Pembrokeshire 1841–1860, Lord Lieutenant and Custos Rotulorum (Keeper of the Rolls) Carmarthenshire 1861–98 and Deputy Lieutenant Inverness-shire. He married Sarah Mary née Compton-Cavendish (1813–81), daughter of General Henry Frederick Compton-Cavendish (1789–1873), in 1842. She was Maid Of Honour to Queen Victoria 1837–42. In addition to Ronald they had five other children:

- Victoria Alexandrina Elizabeth Campbell (1843–1909) married Colonel Francis William Lambton (c.1834–1921) in 1866 and had eight children, including:
  - Alexander Frederick Lambton (1869–99) was commissioned in 1st Highland Light Infantry on 22nd August 1888. He took part in the occupation of Crete 1898 (Mentioned in Despatches LG 24th January 1899) and was killed in action at Magersfontein, South Africa on 11th December 1899.
  - Cuthbert Archibald Lambton (c.1873–1946) married Margaret Alice Hamilton Fergusson (1889–1969), paternal aunt of Thomas Riversdale Colyer-Fergusson VC, in 1913.
  - Edward Lambton (1877–1916) served as a captain in the Pembroke Yeomanry during the Great War as Inspector of Assiut Barrage Circle of Irrigation,

Egypt. He died on 28th March 1916 at the Red Cross Hospital, Giza and is buried in Cairo War Memorial Cemetery (F 16).

- Ronald Robert Lambton (1879–1901) was commissioned in 3rd Middlesex and transferred to 1st Durham Light Infantry. He served in South Africa from October 1899 in the Natal Field Force and was at the Battle of Colenso and operations on the Tugela January – February 1900. He was severely wounded at Vaal Krantz, but recovered to take part in the advance through Northern Natal into the Transvaal (Mentioned in Despatches by Lord Kitchener 8th December 1901). He died on 17th September 1901 at Tagus Drift of wounds received near Vryheid with Major Gough's Column and is buried there.

Frederick Archibald Vaughan Campbell, 3rd Earl Cawdor.

- Muriel Sarah Campbell (1845–1934) married Courtenay Edmund Boyle (1845–1901) in 1876. He was born at Newcastle, St Andrew, Jamaica.
- Frederick Archibald Vaughan Campbell (1847–1911), who became Viscount Emlyn 1860–98 and 3rd Earl Cawdor of Castlemartin in 1898, married Edith Georgiana Turnor (c.1844–1926) in 1868. He was Conservative MP for Carmarthen 1874–1885, Ecclesiastical Commissioner 1880–1911, Honorary Commissioner of Lunacy 1886–1893, Chairman Great Western Railway 1895–1905, Lord Lieutenant Pembrokeshire 1896–1911, Chairman Carmarthen Quarter Sessions and Member of Carmarthen County Council, Magistrate and Deputy Lieutenant of Inverness-shire and Carmarthenshire, Militia ADC to Queen Victoria 1899–1901, Edward VII 1901–1911 and George V 1911, President of the Royal Agricultural Society 1901, Member of the Privy Council 1905 and 1st Lord of the Admiralty March – December 1905. They lived at Cawdor Castle at Nairn, Stackpole Court, in Pembrokeshire and Golden Grove, Carmarthenshire. When he died his estate was valued at £52,973 net. Frederick and Edith had ten children, including:
  - Mabel Marjorie Campbell (1876–1966) married Major Sir Henry Bernard de la Poer Beresford-Peirse (1875–1949) in 1904 and had three children.
  - Lilian Katherine Campbell (1879–1918) married the Reverend Richard Windham de la Poer Beresford-Peirse (c.1877–1952) in 1910 and they had four children.
  - Eric Octavius Campbell (1885–1918) was commissioned in the Seaforth Highlanders on 20th December 1905. He was promoted lieutenant 28th March 1911 and appointed Adjutant 10th May 1914 – 5th December 1915. Promoted captain 13th November 1914, brevet major 3rd June 1916, acting major 3rd-5th December 1916 and 28th July 1917, having been acting lieutenant colonel 8th June – 27 July 1917 and temporary lieutenant colonel

Reverend Thomas Legh Claughton.

20th October 1917 to command 8th Seaforth Highlanders. Previously he was staff captain 6th December 1915 – 2nd January 1916, when he was appointed brigade major until 24th September 1916 and 22nd January – 27th May 1917. He was awarded the DSO & Bar and died on 4th June 1918. He is buried in the Cawdor Plot of Stackpole Elidor (St Elidyr and St James) Churchyard, Pembrokeshire.

- Rachael Anne Georgina Campbell (1853–1906) married Edward (later Sir Edward) Stafford Howard (1851–1916) in 1876. Edward was MP for Cumberland East 1876–85, MP for Thornbury, Gloucestershire 1885–86 and was briefly Under Secretary of State for India April-June 1886. He was Senior Commissioner of HM Woods and Forests and Deputy Lieutenant Gloucestershire (CB 1900, KCB 1909). Rachael and Edward had three children: Ruth Evelyn Howard (1877–1962), Algar Henry Stafford Howard (1880–1970) and Alianore Rachel Howard (1886–1974). Edward married Catherine Meriel Stepney in 1911 and had two more children: Margaret Catherine Stepney Howard (1913–1953) and Stafford Vaughan Stepney Howard (1915–1991).
- Alexander Francis Henry Campbell, Viscount Emlyn (1855–1929), was commissioned in the Royal Carmarthen Artillery (Militia) on 6th September 1873 and transferred to 12th Lancers in 1876 and 3rd Royal Scots in 1878. He married Constance Pleydell Bouverie (1854–87) in 1879. Alexander married Rosa Rebecca Blyton (1860–1929) in 1888. Alexander died on 5th March 1929 at 41 Boulevard des Moulins, Monte Carlo, Monaco.

John's maternal grandfather, the Right Honorable Reverend Thomas Legh Claughton (1808–92), was educated at Rugby and Trinity College, Oxford (BA 1831, MA 1833). In 1828, his poem, *Machina Vi Vaporis Impulsa* gained the university prize for Latin verse. In 1829 he won the Newdigate Prize for another poem, *Voyages of Discovery to the Polar Regions* and in 1832 won the prize for a Latin essay, *De Stoicorum Disciplinâ*. Thomas was ordained in 1834, appointed public examiner 1835 and select preacher to the University 1841, 1850, 1863 and 1868. In 1841 he became vicar of Kidderminster, Worcestershire and was Professor of Poetry at Oxford 1852–57. In April 1867 he became Bishop of Rochester and in 1877 Bishop of St Albans, until resigning in 1890. Thomas married Julia Susannah née Ward (c.1819–1902), daughter of the Reverend William Humble Ward, 10th Baron Ward of Birmingham, in 1842. In addition to Katherine they had eight other children:

- Amelia Maria Claughton (1843–94) married Captain the Honorable Augustus Henry Archibald Anson VC, 84th Regiment (1835–77) in 1863. He was awarded the VC for his gallantry at Bolandshar on 28th September 1857 during the Indian Mutiny. Amelia's second marriage was to George John Douglas Campbell, 8th Duke of Argyll (1892) KG KT PC (1823–1900) in 1881. He was a Liberal politician and a writer on science, religion, and politics. His first marriage in 1844 was to Lady Elizabeth Georgiana Sutherland-Leveson-Gower (1824–78), daughter of the 2nd Duke of Sutherland. Elizabeth had been Mistress of the Robes. George and Elizabeth had thirteen children, including Lord John Lorne, who married Queen Victoria's daughter, Princess Louise. George was Master of the Household of Scotland, Sheriff of Argyllshire, Vice Lord Lieutenant, Chancellor of the University of St Andrews, FRS 1851, Lord Privy Seal 1852–55, 1859–66 and 1880–81, PC 1853, Rector of the University of Glasgow 1854, Postmaster General 1855–58 and Honorary Lord Lieutenant Argyllshire 1862 until his death. He supported the Northern cause in the American Civil War and was appointed Secretary of State for India 1868–74; his refusal to support the Emir of Afghanistan against the Russians helped lead to the Second Afghan War. He resigned

Augustus Henry Archibald Anson VC.

George Douglas Campbell, 8th Duke of Argyll.

Potchefstroom Station.

as Lord Privy Seal in 1881 in protest at Gladstone's Land Bill. After Amelia's death without issue, George married Ina McNeill in 1895.

- Hyacinth Ann Claughton (1844–45).
- William Claughton (1846–60).
- Thomas Legh Claughton (1847–1915) was Rector of St Andrew's, Worcester and Canon of Worcester. His birth was registered as Thomas Ash Claughton. He married Henrietta Louisa Horatia St John-Mildmay (1852–1927) in 1876. They had three children.
- Piers Leopold Claughton (1850–1939) was Rector of Hutton, Brentwood, Essex from about 1882 and moved into the Rectory, where he lived with his sister Lucy for the rest of their lives. He died there on 2nd January 1939, leaving £1,825/13/2 to William Thomas Alban Claughton, Professor of Music.
- Lucy Eleanor Claughton (1852–1939) died within hours of her brother Piers on 2nd January 1939, leaving £10,123/6/2 to the Reverend Guy Ronald Campbell and John Vaughan Campbell VC.
- Robert Dudley Claughton (1854–55).
- Gilbert Henry Claughton (1856–1921) was created baronet on 4th July 1912. He died unmarried without an heir and the baronetcy became extinct. He left £44,729/0/8 to the Reverend Guy Ronald Campbell and Robert Henry Hoare.

John Campbell was educated at Eton in the Reverend Raymond Coxe Radcliffe's House 1890–94 and the Royal Military College Sandhurst. He was commissioned on 5th September 1896 and promoted lieutenant 6th April 1898. He served in Britain until 20th October 1899 and then in the South African War with 2nd Coldstream Guards in No.6 Company. He acted as Adjutant from 30th November 1900 and was appointed officially on 29th December until 13th July 1903. The battalion was sent to Potchefstroom, where he also became the Acting Assistant Provost Marshal from 18th December 1900 and Station Staff Officer from 27th April 1901. The battalion formed the nucleus of a composite force hunting the Boer commander Hertzog and his followers. During his time in South Africa, John took part in various operations:

> Advance on Kimberley and at Belmont, Enslin, Modder River and Magersfontein.
>
> Orange Free State at Poplar Grove, Driefontein, Vet River and the Zand River, February – May 1900.
>
> Transvaal at Johannesburg, Pretoria and Diamond Hill, May – June 1900.
>
> In Transvaal east of Pretoria, including at Belfast, July – October 1900.

Wellington Barracks Chapel, London, also known as the Guards Chapel. Only the apse survived when it was hit by a V1 in June 1944.

In Transvaal west of Pretoria, November 1900.

In Cape Colony south of the Orange River in 1900.

In the Transvaal, November – December 1900.

In Cape Colony, December 1900 – May 1902.

Mentioned in Lord Roberts' Despatch dated 4th September 1901, LG 10th September 1901 and Lord Kitchener's Despatch dated 23rd June 1902, LG 29th July 1902. He was awarded the DSO in recognition of his services on operations west of Pretoria and at Belfast November – December 1900, LG 27th September 1901. The DSO was presented by Edward VII on 18th December 1902.

John returned to Britain on 7th October 1902 and was promoted captain on 27th June 1903. He married Amy Dorothy née Penn (1877–1927) on 18th July 1904 at Wellington Barracks Chapel, London and they lived at Benwell Lane, Painswick, Gloucestershire. John and Amy had two children:

- John Ronald Campbell was born on 18th September 1905. He married Ethel Mildred Bibby (née Hague-Cook) in 1935, daughter of Thomas Reginald Hague-Cook MP, of Portman Square, London. She had married Captain Frank Brian Frederic Bibby (1893–1929) in 1919. He was of the Bibby shipping line family and his estate was valued at £900,072. Ethel was Master of Foxhounds for North Shropshire 1929–31. John and Ethel had a daughter, Cynthia Joan Bibby (1921–1971). He was commissioned in the Coldstream Guards on 3rd September 1925 and transferred to the Reserve on 21st December 1936 as a captain. Recalled as a captain from the Reserve of Officers on 24th August 1939 (33632). He was a major in 1st Coldstream Guards when he was killed in action on 30th May 1940 and is buried in Veurne Communal Cemetery Extension, West-Vlaanderen, Belgium (A 2). Ethel died in 1967.
- Diana Marion Campbell, born on 11th October 1909. She married James George Charles Carney (died 1955) in 1939. James was the son of George Carney, who once worked with the actor Charlie Chaplin. Diana and James had a son, John James G Carney (1940–95). He joined the Junior Leaders' Regiment RA (Pat Porteous VC was CO at the time), but purchased his discharge when he obtained his Actors' Equity card in the early 1960s. He appeared in repertory, films and television. Notable film appearances include 'The Charge of the Light Brigade' 1968, 'Hamlet' 1969, 'A Clockwork Orange' 1971, 'Burke & Hare' 1971, 'Hawk the Slayer' 1980, 'Sword of the Valiant' 1984, 'Top Secret!' 1984 and 'The Shooting Party' 1985. He appeared in a number of television series, including 'Dixon of Dock Green', 'UFO', 'Z-Cars', 'Doctor Who', 'The Sweeney', 'Blake's 7' and 'Shoestring'. Diana died in November 1975.

One of John Penn's factories.

Amy's father, John Penn MP (1848–1903), was a marine engineer and head of John Penn & Sons, Greenwich and Deptford. In 1881 he was employing 838 men and 132 boys. He was Conservative MP for Lewisham 1891–1903 and a Director of the Great Eastern Railway. John Penn married Amy Florence née Lucas (1857–1931), daughter of Sir Thomas Lucas, in 1876. They had another daughter, Marion Joan Penn, in 1880. The marriage ended in divorce and Amy married Lieutenant Colonel Aubrey Maurice Maude (1852–1943) in 1885 and they had two children: Christian George Maude (1884–1971) and Nancy Maude 1886. Christian was commissioned in the Northumberland Fusiliers in 1904 and served on operations in Mohmand on the North West Frontier in 1908. He was Adjutant of 1/24th London (The Queen's) 1912–15 and then served on the staff of 13th Infantry Brigade in Flanders March 1915 – June 1917 and April – November 1918 (MC, LG 14th January 1916). He was with the Egyptian Expeditionary Force July 1917 – April 1918 and was Mentioned in Despatches five times (LG 1st January & 15th June 1916, 15th May 1917, 14 June 1918 and 5 July 1919). He was also awarded the OBE. Christian married Patience Kemp (1898–1935) in 1920, daughter of George Kemp (Lord Rochdale). They had two children before the marriage ended in divorce. Christian married Hester Joan Egerton (1903–93) in 1931 and they had three children.

Brigadier-General JV Campbell VC addressing 137th (Staffordshire) Brigade on Riqueval Bridge after its men had stormed across the St Quentin Canal and broke the Hindenburg Line on 29th September 1918.

John Campbell was Master of the Tanatside Harriers 1909–26. He was promoted Major 21st June 1913 and went to France on 11th May 1915. He was appointed temporary lieutenant colonel on 29th July to command 3rd Coldstream Guards. Appointed brevet lieutenant colonel 1st January 1916. **Awarded the VC for his actions at Ginchy on 15th September 1916, LG 26th October 1916.** The

Cawdor Castle.

VC was presented by the King at Buckingham Palace on 14th November 1916. He was appointed temporary brigadier general 16th November 1916 and commanded 137th Brigade until 10th November 1918, except for 4th–5th October 1918, when he temporarily commanded 3rd Brigade (1st Division) when the previous commander, Brigadier General Sir William AI Kay CMG DSO, was killed (Vadencourt British Cemetery, Maissemy, France – III B 4). John commanded 3rd (Guards) Brigade, 11th November 1918 – 28th March 1919 and relinquished his rank of temporary brigadier general on 23rd February 1920. **For his services during the war he was also awarded the CMG (LG 1st January 1918), the French Croix de Guerre (LG 21st August 1919) and the French Officier de l'Legion d'Honneur (LG 21st August 1919). Mentioned in Sir John French's Despatch dated 30th November 1915 (LG 1st January 1916) and Sir Douglas Haig's Despatches dated 7th November 1917 and 16th March 1919 (LG 11th December 1917 and 5th July 1919).**

John was promoted lieutenant colonel 29th November 1917 and appointed brevet colonel and ADC to the King 3rd June 1919, an appointment he held until 10th November 1933. Promoted colonel 30th June 1920 and commanded 165th (Liverpool) Infantry Brigade until 1923, when he was appointed Colonel Coldstream Guards and Regimental District and Commander 169th (3rd London) Infantry Brigade 14th October 1923 – 15th February 1927. John went on to half pay on 15th February 1927 and retired with the honorary rank of brigadier on 31st October 1933.

Amy died in 1927 and John married Margaret Emily Robina Tennyson-Smith (1909–85) on 6th February 1937 at Poole. They settled in Stroud, Gloucestershire. Margaret's parents were Dr Albert Tennyson-Smith OBE (1870–1953) and Catherine Maud King née Alcock (1864–1941), who married in 1895. In addition to Margaret they had three other children:

- Lieutenant John Alan Tennyson-Smith (1896–1917) 10th Queen's Own (Royal West Kent Regiment) was killed in action on 7th March 1917 and is buried in Dickebusch New Military Cemetery, Belgium (G 2).
- Brenda King Tennyson-Smith (1898–1916).
- Enid Mary Tennyson-Smith (1902–66) married Walter G Sykes in 1924. They had three children: Walter J Sykes 1926, Christopher D Sykes 1928 and Elizabeth M Sykes 1931.

John Campbell was a member of the Honourable Corps of Gentlemen-at-Arms 1934–44 and was in charge of the British Equitation Team during the 1936 Olympic Games. He was a member of the Guards' and Turf Clubs. He served as an honorary flight lieutenant in the Royal Air Force Volunteer Reserve, 28th August 1939 – 4th February 1940. He commanded 8th Gloucestershire (Dursley) Battalion, Home Guard from 1st February 1941 until his death.

John Campbell died suddenly at Woodchester, near Stroud, Gloucestershire on 21st May 1944. He was cremated at Cheltenham Crematorium and his ashes were scattered into the River Findhorn from Banchor Bridge on the Cawdor estate, near Nairn, Scotland. A memorial service was held at the Guards Chapel, Wellington Barracks, London on 2nd June 1944, only sixteen days before it was destroyed by a V1. His will was administered by Major Arthur Horace Penn.

In addition to the VC, he was awarded the CMG, DSO, Queen's South Africa Medal 1899–1902 with six clasps (Belmont, Modder River, Driefontein, Johannesburg, Diamond Hill & Belfast), King's South Africa Medal 1901–1902 with two clasps (South Africa 1901 & South Africa 1902), 1914–15 Star, British War Medal 1914–20, Victory Medal 1914–19 with Mentioned-in-Despatches Oakleaf, George V Coronation Medal 1911, George V Silver Jubilee Medal 1935, George VI Coronation Medal 1937, French Legion d'Honneur and French Croix de Guerre. The VC is held by HQ Coldstream Guards at the Guards Museum, Wellington Barracks, Birdcage Walk, London.

John Campbell is commemorated on a memorial plaque in Cawdor Parish Church, near Nairn and is named on the Eton College Cloisters For Valour Memorial. The hunting horn he used to rally his men at Ginchy is displayed at the Guards Museum, Wellington Barracks.

LIEUTENANT COLONEL ADRIAN PAUL GHISLAIN CARTON DE WIART
4th Dragoon Guards (Royal Irish) attached 8th Battalion, The Gloucestershire Regiment

Adrian Carton de Wiart was born in Brussels, Belgium on 5th May 1880. His father was Léon Constant Ghislain Carton de Wiart (1854–1915), Knight of the Belgian Order and Grand Cross of the Egyptian Orders of Osmaniah and Medjidieh. He qualified as a Doctor of Law in Brussels in 1877. Adrian's mother was Ernestine-Zéphirine-Émilie née Wenzig (1860–1943). Léon and Ernestine married in Brussels on 15th October 1879. The family moved to Alexandria, Egypt in 1883, where Léon become a leading barrister. Later

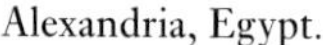
Alexandria, Egypt.

Cairo Electric Railway at the Heliopolis Palace Hotel.

he was called to the English Bar and became a naturalised British subject on 9th October 1900 (Certificate A11679). He moved back to Egypt and served as a board member of the Cairo Electric Railways & Heliopolis Oases Society from 1906. Léon and Ernestine divorced in January 1886 and he married secondly Mary I James (born c.1845), an Englishwoman, in 1888. When they met she was the travelling companion to a Turkish princess. Ernestine married Demosthenes Gregory Cuppa later in 1886 in London. Adrian had four siblings:

1

1

THE

Cairo Electric Railways and Heliopolis Oases Company

SOCIÉTÉ ANONYME

CAPITAL porté à 30 MILLIONS de francs Par décision du Conseil d'administration du 20 Novembre 1906, prise en exécution de l'Art. 6 des statuts

Registered 23rd January 1906 and authorized by decree of H.H. the Khedive on 14th February 1906 published in the Journal Officiel of the Egyptian Government on 24th February 1906

SIÈGE SOCIAL: LE CAIRE

CAPITAL: 15,000,000 DE FRANCS

... ACTIONS DE CAPITAL DE 250 FRANCS CHACUNE ... ACTIONS DE DIVIDENDE SANS DÉSIGNATION DE VALEUR

IN 60.000 ORDINARY SHARES OF 250 FRANCS EACH AND 60.000 FOUNDERS SHARES WITHOUT INDICATION OF VALUE

TITRE AU PORTEUR DE 1 ACTION DE CAPITAL DE 250 FRANCS

NUMÉRO DU TITRE 46133 SHARE WARRANT NUMBER

SHARE WARRANT TO BEARER FOR 1 ORDINARY SHARE OF 250 FRANCS

Nous Certifions que le porteur du présent titre est propriétaire de UNE action de capital entièrement libérée de THE CAIRO ELECTRIC RAILWAYS AND HELIOPOLIS OASES COMPANY (SOCIÉTÉ ANONYME) portant le numéro indiqué ci-dessus et soumise aux stipulations des statuts de la Compagnie et aux résolutions des assemblées générales. 15 MARS 1906.

This is to Certify that the bearer of this warrant is the proprietor of ONE fully paid up ordinary share numbered as above in the capital of THE CAIRO ELECTRIC RAILWAYS AND HELIOPOLIS OASES COMPANY (SOCIÉTÉ ANONYME) subject to the articles of association of the Company and to the resolutions of the general meetings of the Company. 15 DAY OF MARCH 1906.

ADMINISTRATEURS.

Share certificate of the Cairo Electric Railways and Heliopolis Oases Company.

- Maurice Edmond Carton de Wiart (born 7th August 1895 in Cairo) was educated at Eton. He was commissioned in 1/6th Lancashire Fusiliers on 3rd December 1914 and transferred to the Welsh Guards in November 1915. He left 1st Welsh Guards in France on 30th June 1916 with shell shock and was evacuated to Britain on 2nd July. Having been sent on leave until 16th August, he was treated at King's College London and Shafford Military Hospital, St Albans. He was rejected for service with the Egyptian Army in January 1917 on the grounds of being too young to withstand the unhealthy stations in the Sudan. Medical Boards in September and November found him unfit for any service for two and one months respectively. A Medical Board in June 1918 found him permanently unfit for service and he was placed on the Retired List (Special Reserve) on 4th July on account of ill health contracted on active service. In November 1918 he went to Egypt and was employed by the Economic Section of the Occupied Territory Administration (South) and was subsequently appointed ADC to General Sir AW Money on a local commission 24th December 1918 – 31st July 1919. He left Port Said on 2nd August with General Money when he relinquished his appointment and arrived at Southampton on 10th August. Carton de Wiart assumed his appointment was also finished. Early in September he sought employment with the Polish Army through the Polish legation in London. However, the War Office ordered him to proceed to Egypt via Dover and Marseilles at the end of his leave. He embarked at Dover on 12th September and reported next day to HQ Central Area Lines of Communication in Paris for instructions, stating he was awaiting orders to proceed to Warsaw on a six months contract arranged through the War Office. This is odd, as he clearly left Britain with orders to proceed to Egypt and the War Office was not involved with his arrangements with the Poles. As he was not being paid, he was eventually unable to pay his hotel bill and was evicted. On 8th October he was ordered to proceed to Egypt on 10th October and failed to comply, so was returned to Britain under arrest on 21st October. He was detained in the officers cubicles at Great Scotland Yard next day and on 4th November was attached to 1st Grenadier Guards under open arrest at the Tower of London. On 17th November he was taken back to Paris under escort and tried by General Court Martial on 5th December for disobeying a lawful command. He was found guilty and reprimanded. Having reported to the War Office on 19th December, he was informed he would be unemployed from the next day.
- Marie-Ghislaine Carton de Wiart (26th October 1889 – 31st May 1891).
- Beatrice Carton de Wiart (13th March – 4th June 1891).
- Edith Carton de Wiart (4th August 1893 – 17th May 1897).

An influenza epidemic in Egypt in 1891 may explain the deaths of Marie and Beatrice so close together. Amongst Adrian's cousins were:

- Henri Victor Marie Carton de Wiart (1869–1951) was elected to the Belgian House of Representatives in 1896 as a member of the Catholic Party's reform-oriented left wing. He served as Minister of Justice 1911–18, introducing child welfare legislation in 1912. He was Prime Minister 20th November 1920 – 16th December 1921 and was created comte (count) in 1922. He was Minister of Social Welfare and Hygiene 1932–34 and was later President of the Supreme Court of the Belgian-Luxembourg Economic Council. From 1928 to 1935 he was the Belgian Delegate at the League of Nations. In 1945 he reorganised the Catholic Party as the Social Christian Party and was minister without portfolio 1949–50 until becoming Minister of Justice again in 1950.

Henri Victor Marie Carton de Wiart, Prime Minister of Belgium November 1920 - December 1921, was created Comte in 1922.

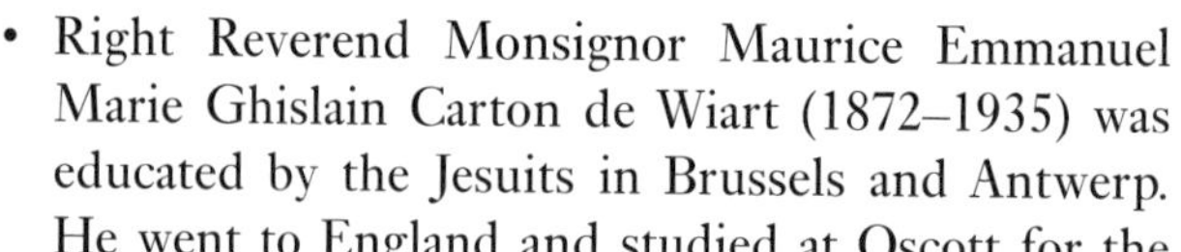

- Right Reverend Monsignor Maurice Emmanuel Marie Ghislain Carton de Wiart (1872–1935) was educated by the Jesuits in Brussels and Antwerp. He went to England and studied at Oscott for the priesthood. Ordained 1895. 1896, secretary to Bishop Riddell of Northampton for eleven years. 1908, Assistant Diocesan Treasurer in Westminster. 1909, succeeded Bishop Johnson as Treasurer and filled the office for the rest of his life. 1916, Domestic Prelate. 1926, honorary Canon of the Westminster Chapter. In 1933 the Pope conferred on him the distinction of Protonotary Apostolic. Honorary Canon of Louvain, honorary Chaplain at the Grotto of Our Lady of Lourdes, Belgian Knight of the Order of Leopold, Officer of the Belgian

St Andrew's Hospital, Dollis Hill, where Monsignor Maurice Emmanuel Marie Ghislain Carton de Wiart was Administrator and from where he took charge of one of the first nursing parties deployed from Britain to France.

Order of the Crown, Belgian Military Medal for civilians and the Gold Medal of Reconnaisance Francaise. As Administrator of St Andrew's Hospital, Dollis Hill, in 1914, he took charge of one of the earliest nursing parties from Britain to France; OBE.

- Comte Edmond Constant Marie Ghislain Carton de Wiart (1876–1959) was Political Secretary to King Léopold II 1901–09. He married Louise de Moreau in 1910.

Balliol College, Oxford.

Adrian spoke English, French and Arabic. When his father hired an Italian governess in Egypt, she tried to teach him Italian. Adrian thought this was 'overdoing things' and revolted. The governess did not remain with the family much longer. His education commenced at a day school in Cairo run by French priests. He recalled it was, *memorable only because I was allowed to ride there every day on my charger*. He was frequently ill in Egypt and had to leave the school to be taught by an inefficient tutor. He was at the Oratory School Edgbaston from 1891, where he overcame disdain for foreigners by a natural aptitude for English games. He became Captain of the Cricket and Football XIs and won the Raquets, Tennis and Billiards tournaments. He passed the entrance examination for Balliol College Oxford at the second attempt and studied law there from January 1899. He failed his first year examinations, but was allowed to return. However, his days at Oxford were numbered when the Boer War broke out.

Adrian enlisted in the Middlesex Yeomanry on 25th January 1900 under the name of Carton because he was underage, not a British citizen and his father did not know. He served in South Africa with Paget's Horse and was hospitalised with fever while serving in Orange River Colony. Returning from hospital he joined a local corps and was wounded in the stomach and groin while trying to cross a river in full view of a Boer detachment. While being questioned about it afterwards, he was asked if there were many Boers, to which he replied, *No, but the few were very good shots*. Having been evacuated to the same hospital, his identity was discovered. His parents were notified and he was sent back to England to be invalided out of the Army on 22nd October.

Back at Balliol, he could not settle and in December went to Egypt and persuaded his father to let him leave. He returned to South Africa, enlisted in 2nd Imperial

Lieutenant General Sir Henry Hildyard, General Officer Commanding-in-Chief South Africa, under whom Adrian Carton de Wiart served as ADC.

The Mall, Rawalpindi, before the First World War.

Murree Hills.

Light Horse and was commissioned on 23rd February 1901. On 14th September he received a Regular Army commission in 4th Dragoon Guards and joined the Regiment at Rawalpindi, India in March 1902. There he attended a musketry course at Changla Gali in the Murree Hills, on successful completion of which he went with the advance party of the Regiment to Muttra. Adrian was very happy there, as it offered opportunities to indulge in the sport of pig-sticking. His horse fell while on a pig-sticking expedition and he suffered several cracked ribs and a damaged ankle when the horse rolled on him. While convalescing he went shooting in the Murree Hills, where a native servant caused him some annoyance. Adrian threw stones at the miscreant, who withdrew out of range and laughed at him. Enraged at this, Adrian snatched up a shotgun and fired upon the servant, *peppering him in his tail.* The servant reported him to the magistrate's office and he was arrested the following morning and fined heavily.

Adrian moved with the regiment to Middelburg, Cape Colony, South Africa in 1904 and was promoted lieutenant on 16th July. He was appointed ADC to Brigadier

General Thomas Hickman, GOC Middelburg District 20th July – 31st October 1905. He then became ADC to Lieutenant General Sir Henry Hildyard, General Officer Commanding-in-Chief South Africa 1st November 1905 – 18th March 1908. Adrian became a naturalized British citizen on 25th April 1907. He returned to Brighton, England with the regiment in 1908.

Princess Eleonora Fugger von Babenhausen, Adrian Carton de Wiart's first mother-in-law.

Adrian Carton de Wiart married Countess Friederike Maria Karoline Henriette Rosa Sabina Franziska Pauline, née Fugger von Babenhausen on 27th October 1908 in Vienna, Austria. She was born at Klagenfurt, Kärnten, Austria on 27th October 1887 and they were living at 1 San Remo, Hove, Sussex in 1911. Friederike was the daughter of Karl Georg Ferdinand Jakob Maria, 5th Fürst (Prince) Fugger von Babenhausen (1861–1925), chamberlain to Emperor Franz Joseph I, and Fürstin (Princess) Eleonora Aloysia Maria zu Hohenlohe-Bartenstein und Jagstberg (1864–1945). As Nora Fugger she wrote her memoirs, *The Glory of the Habsburgs: The Memoirs of Princess Fugger*, in 1932. Her brother, Leopold Heinrich Karl Friedrich Maria Graf Fugger von Babenhausen (1893–1966), served on the staff of the Condor Legion during the Spanish Civil War 1937–39 and ended the Second World War as Generalmajor der Luftwaffe. Leopold's marriage to Vera Aloysia Emma Theresia Maria Josefine Gräfin Czernin von Chudenitz und Morzin was annulled in 1936. Vera married Dr Kurt Alois Josef Johann von Schuschnigg, Chancellor of Austria, in 1938. Following the annexation of Austria by Germany, Schuschnigg resigned and was detained in Dachau, Flossenbürg and Sachsenhausen concentration camps until liberated by US forces in April 1945. The family emigrated to the United States in 1947. Adrian and Friederike had two daughters:

- Anita Carton de Wiart, born on 25th July 1909 in Bavaria, Germany. She married Walter H Thompson in 1933 at Hambledon, Surrey and had two daughters, Maureen Thompson in 1934 and Deirdre Thompson in 1937. Deirdre married William Tetbert Vivian Loyd in 1962. He was commissioned in the Life Guards (National Service List) on 15th June 1957 (453071) and transferred to the Regular Army on 8th August 1959.
- Maria-Eleanora Carton de Wiart (26th September 1911 – c.1984). She married William Roger Holmes Walker (1897–1967) in 1937 in Surrey. They had two children: Roger Carton de Wiart Walker (1938–96), who married Kathleen M Simms; and Sonja Ann Walker, born in 1940, who married as Woolland.

Adrian was promoted captain 26th February 1910 and temporary major 15th February 1911. He was appointed Adjutant of the Gloucester Yeomanry 1st January 1912 – 22nd July 1914. His father was financially ruined in January 1914 and this left Adrian short of money as well. He sold his horses to pay his debts and served with the Somaliland Camel Corps from 23rd July on operations against Sayyid Mohammed Abdullah Hassan, the 'Mad Mullah'. **Awarded the DSO for his actions on 19th November against Dervish forces at Shimber Berris, Somaliland. He stormed a seemingly impregnable fort, during which he lost an eye and was also wounded in the elbow and ear. Although the fort was not taken, the enemy withdrew during the night, LG 15th May 1915. Mentioned in Lieutenant Colonel Thomas Astley Cubitt's Despatch dated 9th February 1915, 2nd August 1916.** He was evacuated to Berbera and then Aden by P&O steamer to a hospital run by nuns. The missionary eye specialist could do nothing and he was moved to Egypt, where he was advised to have the eye removed. He refused and was returned to England for treatment at King Edward's Hospital in London before admittance to Sir Douglas Shield's Nursing Home at 17 Park Lane, where the eye was removed on 3rd January 1915.

Contemporary depiction of Sayyid Mohammed Abdullah Hassan, the 'Mad Mullah'.

As a result of his injuries he was declared unfit for service, but within two weeks demanded to be seen by a Medical Board. The Board decided that if he could wear a glass eye, his case would be reviewed. He obtained one, went before the Board, was declared fit, left the building and hailed a taxi. As he got in, he removed the glass eye threw it out of the window and donned a black patch, which he wore for the rest of his life.

Adrian rejoined 4th Dragoon Guards in Flanders in March 1915, but it was not for long. He was evacuated to England as a result of wounds received at Zonnebeke on 22nd April. A doctor in Belgium refused to remove some fingers hanging on by threads to his left hand, so Adrian pulled them off. The hand was amputated in London. He received his DSO from the King while a patient at Sir Alfred Fripp's Hospital on Park Lane, London on 29th June. Now minus a hand and an eye, he again managed to persuade a Medical Board he was fit for active service and returned to France early in 1916. He was appointed temporary major 15th February – 25th March and temporary major and second in command of 7th Loyal North Lancashire 26th March – 17th July. While in this appointment he

Lieutenant Colonel Thomas Astley Cubitt (later General Sir Thomas Cubitt KCB CMG DSO) (1871–1939) was commissioned in the Royal Artillery in 1891. He served in a number of campaigns in Africa and in July 1914 was appointed Deputy Commissioner in Somaliland, where he mounted a series of campaigns against the Dervishes. Later he commanded a battalion, a brigade and finally 38th (Welsh) Division on the Western Front and was Governor of Bermuda 1931–36. He was known as a fire-eater who used very picturesque language.

was given command of 8th Gloucestershire in June. Appointed temporary lieutenant colonel while CO 8th Gloucestershire 18th July – 9th December.

Awarded the VC for his actions at La Boisselle, France on 2nd/3rd July 1916, LG 9th September 1916. He was wounded in this action and later in the head at High Wood. He was taken to the dressing station at Corbie before being evacuated to England. When he returned to France a few weeks later, he retrieved the stick he lost near High Wood when he was wounded. He was wounded by shrapnel at Grandcourt in September and evacuated again. Back in France, he was gassed on 8th/9th November.

The VC was presented by the King at Buckingham Palace on 29th November. Appointed brevet major 1st January 1917. He returned to France and commanded 8th North Staffordshire for a short time in the line opposite Hébuterne. Appointed GOC 12th Brigade, 11th January – 23rd November, vice Brigadier General JD Crosbie DSO. Appointed temporary brigadier general 12th January 1917 – 26th April 1918. He commanded 12th Brigade during the Battles of Arras and Third Ypres, until wounded by shrapnel in the hip on 23rd November and evacuated to England.

Appointed brevet lieutenant colonel on 3rd June and promoted major 18th July. Appointed temporary commander 115th Brigade 6th-7th April 1918 and temporary commander 105th Brigade 7th-20th April. Having been wounded in the left leg on a reconnaissance near Martinsart on 20th April, he was evacuated to England and relinquished the temporary rank of brigadier general on 26th April. **Awarded the CMG, LG 3rd June 1918.** He returned to France in October and was appointed GOC 113th Brigade, 8th November 1918 – 4th February 1919 as temporary brigadier 8th November 1918 – 31st December 1920. He was wounded nine times during the war but, despite this, he wrote, *Frankly I had enjoyed the war*.

Awarded the Belgian Croix d'Officier de l'Ordre de Couronne (LG 21st April 1917), the Belgian Croix de Guerre (Belgium) (LG 11th March 1918) and the CB (LG 3rd June 1919). He was mentioned in General/Field Marshal Sir Douglas Haig's Despatches dated 13th November 1916, 9th

April & 9th November 1917, 7th April 1918 and 16th March 1919 – LG 4th January, 15th May & 11th December 1917, 20th May 1918 & 5th July 1919 respectively. The reputed award of the Belgian Order of Leopold and the French Commandeur de Legion d'Honneur were not found in the London Gazette, but the latter forms part of his medal group

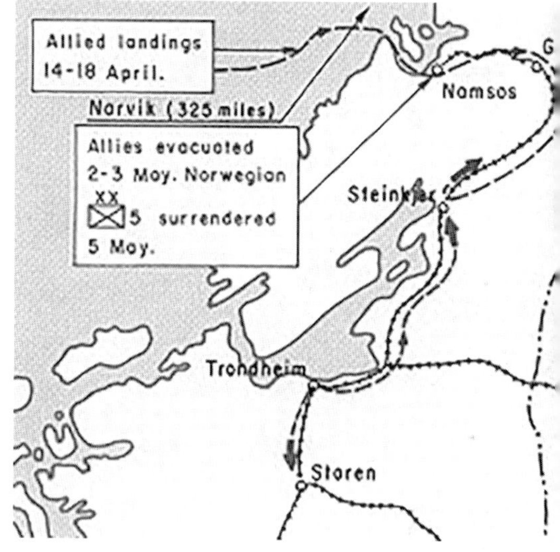

The area of Norway where the Central Norwegian Expeditionary Force operated in April and May 1940.

Adrian was appointed second-in-command of the British Military Mission to Poland and succeeded as its commander when General Louis Botha went home due to ill health in 1919. Appointed brevet colonel and ADC to the King 27th July 1920 – 1924. Appointed local major general 1st January 1921 – 31st March 1923. Promoted colonel 21st June 1922. He relinquished the local rank of major general on 31st March 1923 and went on to half pay on 1st April. He transferred to the Regular Army Reserve of Officers and was granted the honorary rank of major general on 19th December. He settled at Prostyn in the Prypet Marshes, Poland, on an estate loaned by Prince Charles Radziwill, his last Polish ADC.

Castello di Vincigliata at Fiesole, near Florence, where Adrian Carton de Wiart was held prisoner with other senior officers. It is now a very sought after wedding venue.

On 4th May 1937 Adrian attained the age limit and ceased to belong to the Reserve, but in July 1939 he was summoned back to Britain to be appointed to head the Military Mission to Poland 25th August – 7th October 1939. He managed to escape through Romania and on returning to Britain was appointed acting major general on 28th November 1939 and GOC 61st Division until April 1940. He commanded the Central Norwegian Expeditionary Force April – 5th May 1940 and managed to extract his force with great skill. He returned to resume command of 61st Division from 14th May and took it to Northern Ireland. Appointed temporary major general on 15th November 1940. On 6th April 1941 he was appointed to the Military Mission to

The main participants in the Cairo Conference. Standing next to Adrian Carton de Wiart is Lord Louis Mountbatten. Seated from left to right: Chiang-Kai-Shek, leader of the Chinese Nationalists; President Franklin D Roosevelt; Winston Churchill; and Chiang-Kai-Shek's wife, Soong Mayling.

Adrian Carton de Wiart relaxing during a quiet moment in Cairo.

Yugoslavia, but the Wellington bomber carrying him crashed in the sea off Libya and he had to swim ashore, where he was captured by the Italians. He was held for four months at Villa Orsini, Sulmona and from October 1941 at Castello di Vincigliati, at Fiesole, near Florence, along with General Richard O'Connor, General Philip Neame VC, Air Vice Marshall Owen Boyd and Brigadiers John Combe, Reginald Miles and James Hargest.

Adrian attempted to escape a number of times and on one occasion eluded capture for eight days while covering 150 of the 200 miles to Switzerland. He was released by the Italians in August 1943 and sent to Lisbon to help negotiate the Italian surrender. He returned to England on 28th August and relinquished the temporary rank of major general on 25th September. He was appointed Head of the Special Military Mission to Nationalist Chinese leader Chiang-Kai-Shek and promoted War Substantive major general and temporary lieutenant general on 9th October. Adrian left Britain on 18th October for India, attended the Cairo Conference en route and arrived in Chungking in December. He broke his back in an accident in Rangoon on his way back to Britain in 1946 and spent seven months in hospital.

Awarded the Polish Cross of Valour (Krzyz Walecznych), LG 11th April 1941 and KBE, LG 1st January 1945. Mentioned in War Office Despatches

dated and LG 20th December 1940 and 9th December 1943. A number of other awards were not found in the London Gazette: French Croix de Guerre, Chinese Order of Cloud and Banner and the Polish Order of Military Virtue (Virtuti Militari).

Adrian Carton de Wiart's memoirs.

Adrian reverted to retired pay as honorary lieutenant general on 4th October 1947. His rise from private to lieutenant general was the greatest rank difference of any VC recipient. He became an Honorary MA of Oxford University and a Fellow of Balliol College Oxford in December 1947 and an Honorary LLD of Aberdeen University. His wife died in Vienna on 4th July 1949. His autobiography, *Happy Odyssey*, was published in 1950. Evelyn Waugh based Brigadier Ben Ritchie-Hook in his *Sword of Honour* trilogy on Carton de Wiart. Ian Fleming, author of the James Bond books, said of him, *one arm, one eye, and rather more surprisingly only one Victoria Cross.*

Adrian married Ruth Myrtle Muriel Joan Sutherland (née McKechnie) (1903–2006), also on her second marriage, on 18th July 1951 at Tiverton, Devon. Joan, as she was known, had divorced Lieutenant Colonel Arthur Henry Carr Sutherland (1891–1962) OBE MC TD (also Chevalier Legion d'Honneur) Black Watch in 1943, having married him in 1928. It was Arthur Sutherland's second marriage, having married Ruby Miller in 1919.

Arthur and Ruby's son, David George Carr Sutherland (1920–2006), served with the Special Boat Squadron and was attached to the Special Air Service in the Second World War; MC and Bar. Arthur married for a third time in December 1943, Elizabeth Warburton-Lee (née Swinton) (1900–81). She was the widow of Captain Bernard Armitage Warburton Warburton-Lee VC RN, who died of wounds following his VC action on HMS *Hardy* in Ofot Fjord, near Narvik, Norway on 10th April 1940.

Adrian and Joan moved to Aghinagh House, Killinardrish, Co Cork, Ireland. Adrian died there on 5th June 1963 and he is buried close to the eastern wall of Killinardish Church, but just outside the churchyard, in the grounds of Aghinagh House. He left £15,000 to Joan. A requiem mass was held at Westminster Abbey, London in July 1963.

Adrian Carton de Wiart's grave, just outside Killinardrish Churchyard, in the grounds of Aghinagh House.

Adrian Carton de Wiart's medal group. Only the Chinese Order of the Cloud and Banner appears to be missing.

He is also commemorated:

- On a memorial beside the door of Thiepval Church in France.
- The Secretary of State for Communities and Local Government, Eric Pickles MP, announced that Victoria Cross recipients from the Great War would have commemorative paving stones laid in their birthplace as a lasting legacy of local heroes within communities. The stones would be laid on or close to the 100th anniversary of their VC actions. For the 145 VCs born in Australia, Belgium, Canada, China, Denmark, Egypt, France, Germany, India, Iraq, Japan, Nepal, Netherlands, New Zealand, Pakistan, Sri Lanka, South Africa, Ukraine and the United States of America, individual commemorative stones were unveiled at the National Memorial Arboretum, Alrewas, Staffordshire by Prime Minister David Cameron MP and Sergeant Johnson Beharry VC on 5th March 2015.

Adrian was President of the Military Historical Society. The 'Carton de Wiart Society' inaugural dinner was held at the Oratory School on 26th April 2013 to celebrate the Centenary of the Oratory School CCF. It is open to all Old Oratorians who have served in HM Forces and friends of the school with military connections.

In addition to the VC, he was awarded the KBE, CB, CMG, DSO, Queen's South Africa Medal with four clasps ('Cape Colony', 'Orange Free State', 'Transvaal' & 'South Africa 1901'), Africa General Service Medal 1902–56 with clasp 'Shimber Berris 1914–15', 1914–15 Star, British War Medal 1914–20, Victory Medal 1914–19 with Mentioned-in-Despatches Oakleaf, 1939–45 Star, Africa Star, Italy Star,

Burma Star, War Medal 1939–45 with Mentioned-in-Despatches Oakleaf, George VI Coronation Medal 1937, Elizabeth II Coronation Medal 1953, Belgian Order of the Crown, Polish Order of Military Virtue, Polish Cross of Valour, Belgian Croix de Guerre, Nationalist Chinese Order of Cloud and Banner, French Commander Legion of Honour, French Croix de Guerre with Bronze Palme.

During the Second World War his house in London was bombed and his medals were thought to have been destroyed. Official replacements were issued and he added the Second World War decorations to them. After his death the original set was found and Lady Carton de Wiart placed them in the custody of the Ogilby Trust before they were transferred to the National Army Museum, where they remain. The replacement and more complete set was handed over to the 4th/7th Dragoon Guards and was later stolen from its museum in Halifax. The following medals are missing from the National Army Museum group: KBE, Africa General Service Medal 1902–56, British War Medal 1914–20, 1939–45 Star, War Medal 1939–45 and Elizabeth II Coronation Medal 1953.

1352 SERGEANT CLAUD CHARLES CASTLETON
5th Australian Machine Gun Company AIF

Claud Castleton was born on 12th April 1893 at 5 Morton Road, Kirkley, South Lowestoft, Suffolk. His father was Thomas Charles Castleton (1867–1944) a bricklayer/builder living at Carlton Colville, Lowestoft in 1881. His mother was Edith Lucy née Payne (1868–1923), born at Bishop's Stortford, Hertfordshire. Thomas and Edith married on 4th September 1887 at Christ Church, Lowestoft, Suffolk. The family lived at 62 Whapload Road, Lowestoft before moving to 5 Morton Road, Kirkley, South Lowestoft by 1891. They had moved to Rose Cottage (believed to be No.18), Wilson Road, Kirkley by 1901. Thomas died at his home at 20 Rochester Road, South Lowestoft in 1944.

Claud had a brother, Frank William Castleton (1887–1952), who was a law clerk in 1911 and later Town Clerk of Folkestone, Kent. He married Lily Elizabeth Shanks (1886–1930) in 1919 at Depwade, Norfolk and they had a daughter, Dorothy Helen Elizabeth Castleton, born in 1925. The family lived at 7 West View, Canterbury Road, Folkestone.

Claud was educated at Morton Road School, Kirkley, South Lowestoft from 25th October 1897 and Lowestoft Municipal Secondary School from 2nd August 1905 (renamed Lowestoft County Grammar School after the Second World War

The Whapload Road area of Lowestoft, with Christ Church on the left.

Lowestoft Municipal Secondary School, now Ormiston Denes Academy. These buildings were constructed in 1909–10 at the end of Claud Castleton's time there (Ormiston Denes Academy).

Christ Church, Lowestoft, where Claud's parents married in 1887.

HMAT *Ceramic* loading in 1915. SS *Ceramic* was built in Belfast for the White Star Line 1912–13. She worked the Liverpool - Australia route following her maiden voyage on 24th July 1913. In 1914, she was requisitioned as HMAT *Ceramic* and survived a number of U-boat attacks. She returned to the White Star Line to resume civilian service in November 1920. When White Star merged with Cunard in 1934, *Ceramic* was sold to Shaw, Savill & Albion, but carried on working the same route. In February 1940 she was again requisitioned as a troopship. In the South Atlantic on 11th August she collided at speed with the cargo ship *Testbank*. Both ships were damaged but remained afloat. *Testbank* made Cape Town under her own power. *Ceramic*'s passengers were transferred to RMS *Viceroy of India* and she was assisted to Walvis Bay in South West Africa by a tug. After emergency repairs she went to Cape Town for renovation before resuming service. On 3rd November 1942 *Ceramic* left Liverpool for Australia carrying 641 passengers and crew and 12,362 tons of cargo. She sailed with Convoy ON 149 until it dispersed and continued unescorted. At midnight on 6th/7th December, she was hit by a torpedo from U-*515* in mid-Atlantic. A few minutes later two more hit the engine room. However, she remained afloat and was abandoned in good order. Three hours later, U-*515* fired two more torpedoes, which sank her immediately. It was a stormy night and the heavy sea capsized some lifeboats. U-*515* returned to look for *Ceramic*'s Master, Herbert Elford, to ascertain the ship's destination. One lifeboat was sighted around noon, but with the storm raging, the U-boat crew seized the first available survivor, Sapper Eric Munday RE. Despite searches by neutral craft, no other survivors were picked up. Munday spent the rest of the war at Stalag VIII-B in Silesia (Australian War Memorial).

D Company, 18th Battalion AIF in 1915 (Australian War Memorial).

and is now Ormiston Denes Academy). He joined the Lowestoft Young Men's Christian Association in September 1910. Claud returned to Morton Road School as a student teacher 1st September 1910 – 31st August 1911 and transferred to London Road School until September 1912. He emigrated to Melbourne, Australia in October, where he worked on a sheep farm and also prospected for gold before moving to Tasmania. He also travelled throughout Victoria, New South Wales and Queensland. His intention had been to work his way home via New Zealand, India and Africa; but when war broke out he was in Port Moresby, New Guinea (later Papua New Guinea). With another white man, he was in charge of a group of native

Camp Heliopolis.

No.1 Australian Casualty Clearing Station at Gallipoli (Australian War Memorial).

A light and airy ward at No.4 Auxiliary Hospital, Abbassia, Cairo, Egypt. It would have seemed a world apart from the filth and dangers encountered on the Gallipoli Peninsula (Australian War Memorial).

HMT *Royal George* (11,146 tons) on the right, with her ill-fated sister ship HMT *Royal Edward* (formerly RMS *Cairo* and later SS *Royal Edward*) in the background at Avonmouth. HMT *Royal Edward* was sunk in six minutes by UB-*14* on 13th August 1915 en route to Gallipoli with reinforcements; 461 survivors were picked up by other ships, but 935 perished. *Royal George* was built as SS *Heliopolis* on the Clyde in 1907 for the Egyptian Mail Company. On her maiden voyage (10th March - 26th April 1907) she carried 2,246 Spanish migrants to Hawaii as contract labourers; the first ship to participate in this emigration. *Heliopolis* operated on the Marseilles – Alexandria route until 1909. In 1910, she was bought by the Canadian Northern Steamship Company, renamed SS *Royal George* and worked the Avonmouth - Quebec - Montreal route. *Royal George* was requisitioned by Canada when war broke out, making her first sailing on 3rd October 1914 to Plymouth. In 1915 she was involved in the Gallipoli campaign and continued throughout the rest of the war as a troopship. *Royal George* returned to Cunard after the war, which had bought the Canadian Northern Steamship Company's ships in 1916, and worked the North Atlantic until being retired in 1920 and used as a depot ship at Cherbourg, France. She was scrapped in 1922.

Alexandria harbour.

troops on coastal defence duties. He also worked for a cable and wireless station before returning to Australia, where he enlisted in the AIF in Liverpool, Sydney on 11th March 1915. He was described as 5′ 7½″ tall, of fair complexion, with blue eyes and brown hair. Claud embarked on HMAT A40 *Ceramic* at Sydney with 18th Battalion on 25th June, disembarking at Alexandria, Egypt and moving to Camp Heliopolis.

Claud Castleton's grave in Pozières British Cemetery.

He was engaged in operations at Gallipoli from 16th August with D Company until reporting sick with dysentery at No.1 Australian Casualty Clearing Station on 15th September. He was taken by hospital ship to No.4 Auxiliary Hospital, Abbassia, Cairo, Egypt on 27th September and discharged at Helwan on 22nd October. Claud returned aboard HMT *Royal George* on 8th November. Promoted corporal at Mudros on 7th December and returned to active service next day.

Following the evacuation of Gallipoli, Claud went to Alexandria from Mudros on 9th January 1916 and moved to Tel el Kebir. He reported sick with malaria and was admitted to 1st Australian Stationery Hospital on 27th January until discharged to duty at Ismailia on 16th February. Appointed temporary sergeant on 20th February

Pozierès from the northeast on the D929. The water tower carries the names of the seven Pozierès area VCs. Rather confusingly, William Short is shown as 8th Battalion, implying he was part of the AIF, which of course he was not.

and was posted to 5th Australian Machine Gun Company on 8th March. He was promoted sergeant on 16th March and embarked at Alexandria for Marseilles, France, next day, arriving on 23rd March.

Awarded the VC for his actions at Pozières, France on 29th July 1916, LG 26th September 1916. Claud Castleton was killed during his VC action. His body was recovered from no man's land and eventually was buried in Pozières British Cemetery, France (IV L 43). In addition to the VC, he was awarded the 1914–15 Star, British War Medal 1914–20 and Victory Medal 1914–19. Claud never married and the VC was presented to his father by the King at Buckingham Palace on 29th November 1916. It is held in the Hall of Valour, Australian War Memorial, Treloar Crescent, Campbell, Canberra, Australia. Claud is commemorated in a number of places:

- Bronze plaque and framed scroll erected by his parents in South Cliff Congregational Church, Lowestoft (now St Nicholas' Catholic Church). The benefactors of the original church were the Colmans, the mustard people of Norwich.
- War Memorial in St Margaret's Church, Lowestoft.
- Memorial and portrait in Lowestoft Town Hall.

Claud Castleton's former home at 18 Wilson Road, Kirkley, Lowestoft (John Greenacre).

The memorial plaque at 18 Wilson Road (John Greenacre).

- Plaque at his former home at 18 Wilson Road, Pakefield (formerly Kirkley), Lowestoft, Suffolk.
- Victoria Cross Memorial, Campbell, Canberra, dedicated on 24th July 2000.
- Victoria Cross Memorial, Queen Victoria Building, George Street, Sydney, New South Wales.
- Named on one of eleven plaques honouring 175 men from overseas awarded the VC for the Great War. The plaques were unveiled by the Senior Minister of State at the Foreign & Commonwealth Office and Minister for Faith and Communities, Baroness Warsi, at a reception at Lancaster House, London on 26th June 2014 attended by The Duke of Kent and relatives of the VC recipients. The Australian plaque is at the Australian War Memorial.
- Castleton Avenue (A1145), Carlton Colville, Lowestoft, Suffolk, a 1.3 mile long link road.
- Castleton Meadows, Carlton Colville, a housing development off Holystone Way, north of Castleton Avenue, built in 2007.
- Castleton Close, on the Gunton Estate, Lowestoft, a 1960s council housing estate.
- Castleton Crescent, Gowrie, Canberra, Australian Capital Territory.
- Castleton Street, Hamilton, Brisbane, Queensland, renamed by Brisbane City Council on 16th December 1938.

- Castleton Street, White Box Rise Estate, Wodonga, Victoria, on the former Bandiana Army Camp.
- In 2014, Campbelltown City Council, Sydney, New South Wales approved forty-four VC road names, including Castleton, for the Airds-Bradbury Renewal Project. Road suffixes will be allocated during each stage of construction.

A cousin, 3556 Lance Corporal Edward Samuel Castleton (1895–1916), was killed in action on 19th June 1916 with 4th Suffolk and is buried at Gorre British and Indian Cemetery (I B 19). A distant cousin, 5309 Private Reginald Robert Frank Castleton, 2/1st Buckinghamshire Battalion, Oxfordshire & Buckinghamshire Light Infantry, was killed in action on 26th June 1916 and is buried in Laventie Military Cemetery, La Gorgue, France (II A 6).

LIEUTENANT GEOFFREY ST GEORGE SHILLINGTON CATHER
9th Battalion, Princess Victoria's (Royal Irish Fusiliers)

Geoffrey Cather was born at 55 Christchurch Road, Streatham Hill, London on 11th October 1890. His father was Robert Gabriel Cather (c.1860–1908), born in Coleraine, Ireland. He was a partner in Joseph Tetley & Co, tea merchants. His mother was Margaret Matilda née Shillington (1865–1939), born at Portadown, Co Armagh, Ireland. The family was living at Holmcroft, Bycullah Road, Enfield, Middlesex in 1891 and 'Red Roofs', Blue House Lane, Limpsfield, Surrey in 1901. Margaret later moved to 26 Priory Road, West Hampstead, London and by 1919 she was living at 35 Circus Road Mansions, St John's Wood, London.

Geoffrey had a brother, Dermot Patrick Cather (1894–1985), born at Enfield, Middlesex. He joined the Royal Navy as a midshipman on 15th January 1912 and was promoted acting sub lieutenant 18th May 1914, sub lieutenant 15th Nov 1914, acting lieutenant 15th June 1916, lieutenant 27th February 1918 backdated to 15th May 1916, lieutenant commander 15th February 1924 and commander 31st December 1929. He was a captain when he retired on 21st May 1944. He married Elizabeth Joyce Shillington Scales in 1930 at Cambridge. From 1931 they were living at 8 Coombe Villas, Saltash, Cornwall and moved to Mayfield, Wyton, St Ives, Huntingdonshire before 1949. He was living at 14 Hampden Close, Tollgates, Battle, Sussex in 1962 and at 6 Hampden Close, Tollgates in 1979.

Geoffrey's paternal grandfather was the Reverend Robert George Cather (c.1820–79), a minister of the Irish Methodist Church, born in Londonderry, Ireland. He married Margaret and they moved to England after having four daughters in addition to Robert:

- Annie S Cather (c.1849–1938) was a Post Office civil servant in London.
- Margaret E Cather (c.1851–1931) retired as a Principal Post Office Clerk before 1901.
- Harriet IG Cather (c.1855–1937) was a clerk in the Office of the Crown Agents for the Colonies.
- Mary Jane Cather (c.1857–1885).

Geoffrey's maternal grandfather was Thomas Primus Shillington JP (1831–89) of Tavanagh House, Thomas Street, Portadown, Co Armagh, Ireland, son of Thomas Shillington (1767–1830), a grain purchaser of Portadown and owner of Shillington's Quay on the River Bann. Thomas Primus Shillington was appointed Master Extraordinary in the Irish Court of Chancery in June 1859. He married Mary Jane née Graham (c.1831–1915) and they had three children in addition to Margaret, including:

- David Graham Shillington (1872–1944), a timber and coal merchant in the family business (T Shillington & Son of Portadown), was a member of the Orange Order and a company commander in 4th (Portadown) Battalion, Armagh Regiment, Ulster Volunteer Force. He enlisted as a private (14679) in the Royal Irish Fusiliers, on 15th September 1914 and was commissioned as a captain in 9th Royal Irish Fusiliers on 16th September. He commanded D Company, 9th Royal Irish Fusiliers until he left the unit on 19th December 1915 suffering from debilitation, insomnia and neurasthenia. He embarked on SS *St Andrew* at Rouen on 30th December and disembarked at Southampton next day. He

Shillington's Quay.

rejoined the Battalion on 23rd June 1916 and was left out of the battle on 1st July. He commanded B Company later in July and August and on 21st August was appointed second-in-command of the Battalion. He fell ill again in late 1916 and returned to Britain in February 1917, where he was treated at Harrogate, Yorkshire, for nervous exhaustion before being attached to 4th Royal Irish Fusiliers in Belfast and then to 10th Reserve Battalion at Newtownards on 16th March. A Medical Board at Belfast on 8th June declared him fit for General Service. Promoted major 2nd July. Later transferred to the Royal Irish Rifles and served with 20th Reserve Battalion. He was demobilised on 4th June 1919 and relinquished his commission on 1st September 1921. He was a founder member and later President of the Portadown Royal British Legion. David was elected the Stormont MP for Co Armagh 1921–1929 and Central Armagh 1929–1941, becoming Minister of Labour in Northern Ireland 1937–1938. Appointed Privy Councillor 1937. He was also Deputy Lord Lieutenant County Armagh, Justice of the Peace and District Master of the Portadown Loyal Orange Lodge No.1 from 1926 until his death. He married Sarah Louisa Collen in 1895 and they had three sons and two daughters including:

- Thomas Graham Shillington (1897–1917) was commissioned, aged seventeen, on 7th January 1915. He went to France as a platoon commander in B Company, 9th Royal Irish Fusiliers and was promoted lieutenant 12th January 1916. He understudied Geoffrey Cather as Adjutant in March 1916. He received gunshot wounds to the left thigh and right calf on 1st July at Hamel, France. His mother received a telegram on 12th July stating her husband had been wounded, but the War Office corrected this on 16th July to her son being the casualty. He embarked at Boulogne on 4th July on SS *St Andrew*, arriving at Southampton on 6th July. He was treated at Bathurst House Hospital, Belgrave Square, London. He was also listed as a prisoner of war and had to point out that this was Lieutenant TC Shillington. He was posted to 10th Reserve Battalion on 26th September, declared fit for General Service on 26th October and rejoined the Battalion in December. Appointed temporary captain 23rd February 1917. Commanded A Company from April. Attended the Adjutant's Course at Second Army Central School in May. He received a gunshot wound to the throat at Langemarck on 17th August and was admitted to No.3 Australian Casualty Clearing Station on 18th August 1917, where he died. Thomas is buried at Brandhoek New Military Cemetery No.3, Vlamertinghe, Ieper (II E 31).
- John Graham Shillington (born 18th December 1900) was commissioned in the King's Own Scottish Borderers on 16th July 1920 (18073). Promoted lieutenant 16th July 1922. Appointed Adjutant 5th King's Own Scottish Borderers and promoted captain 15th December 1934 – 15th December 1938. Promoted major 1st August 1938 and was OC C Company, 1st King's Own Scottish Borderers in 1939, serving in France and Flanders with the

BEF. Acting lieutenant colonel 14th July 1941. Temporary lieutenant colonel 14th October 1941 – 14th November 1944 and 10th April 1945. CO 6th King's Own Scottish Borderers 14th October 1941 – 16th July 1944 and October 1944 – May 1945. Wounded by mortar fragments on 16th July 1944. Awarded the DSO, LG 19th October 1944. He retired as honorary lieutenant colonel on 4th July 1947 on account of disability. He was appointed Secretary of the Territorial and Auxiliary Forces Association for Co Antrim and Belfast; OBE (LG 12th June 1958).

Sir Graham Shillington OBE, Chief Constable of the Royal Ulster Constabulary 1970–73.

- Robert Edward Graham Shillington (later Sir Graham Shillington OBE DL) (1911–2001). After 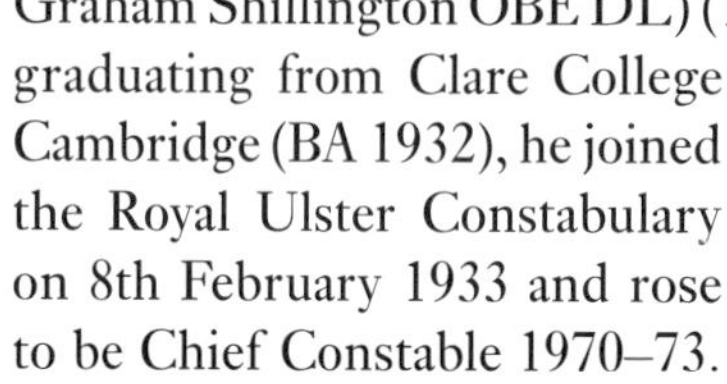 graduating from Clare College Cambridge (BA 1932), he joined the Royal Ulster Constabulary on 8th February 1933 and rose to be Chief Constable 1970–73. MBE 1952, OBE 1959.

The Thiepval Memorial, where Geoffrey Cather is commemorated.

Geoffrey was educated at Hazelwood Preparatory School in Limpsfield from September 1900 (also attended by Percy Howard Hansen VC) and Rugby School from September 1903. He suffered from scarlet fever in 1906 and was temporarily removed from the school. His academic record was not great and he left in June 1908 following the death of his father. He was then employed by Tetley's in London, travelling to America and Canada in 1911 and returning to the London branch in May 1914.

He enlisted in 28th London Regiment (Artist's Rifles) in January 1909 and served as a private until February 1911, when he resigned in order to go to America on business. He enlisted in 19th Royal Fusiliers (2nd Public Schools Battalion) on 3rd September 1914 (196) and was commissioned in 9th Royal Irish Fusiliers on 22nd May 1915, serving alongside his uncle and cousin, Major David Graham Shillington and Lieutenant Thomas Graham Shillington. Geoffrey went to France on 5th October 1915. Promoted lieutenant and appointed Adjutant on 7th December 1915.

Rugby School (Greer's).

Awarded the VC for his actions near Hamel, France on 1st July 1916, LG 9th September 1916. He was killed in the same action. His body was identified and his ID discs were removed by fellow officers, but his remains could not be identified later and he is commemorated on the Thiepval Memorial. His mother administered his will; estate valued at £255/4/9.

As he never married, the VC was presented to his mother by the King at Buckingham Palace on 31st March 1917. In addition to the VC, he was awarded the 1914–15 Star, British War Medal 1914–20 and Victory Medal 1914–19. The medals were presented to the Regiment in 1979 by his brother, Dermot. They are held by the Royal Irish Fusiliers Museum, Sovereign's House, The Mall, Armagh, Co Armagh, Northern Ireland. Geoffrey Cather is commemorated in a number of places:

- A plaque at Hazelwood School was in the school chapel until the building was destroyed in a hurricane in October 1987. It was remounted on the wall of the main school building.
- Limpsfield War Memorial, Surrey.
- Regimental Memorial in St Anne's Cathedral, Belfast, Northern Ireland.
- A memorial stone at Ulster Tower, Thiepval, France to all ranks of the 36th (Ulster) Division, dedicated on 1st July 1991, names the Division's nine VCs, including Geoffrey Cather.

CAPTAIN NOEL GODFREY CHAVASSE
Royal Army Medical Corps att'd 1/10th (Scottish) Battalion, The King's (Liverpool Regiment)

Noel Chavasse was born at 36 New Inn Hall Street, St Peter-le-Bailey Rectory, Oxford on 9th November 1884. He was the younger twin with Christopher. The twins were very frail at birth and contracted a form of typhoid fever as infants. However, during their long recovery they spent much time outdoors and this helped them develop considerable athletic ability.

His father was Francis James Chavasse (1846–1928), a rather diminutive man, who graduated from Corpus Christi College, Oxford with a First in Law and Modern History in 1869. He was ordained in the Church of England at Manchester in 1870 and was a curate at St Paul's, Preston until 1873. He was then Vicar of St Paul's, Upper Holloway until 1877 and Rector of St Peter-le-Bailey, Oxford until 1889, when he became Principal of Wycliffe Hall, living with his family at Wycliffe Lodge, 52 Banbury Road, Oxford. Francis was consecrated the second Bishop of Liverpool, succeeding Bishop John Charles Ryle on 25th April 1900. The family lived at 19 Abercromby Square, Liverpool, just a few doors away from Robert Alexander and family, father of Ernest Wright Alexander VC. Francis was effectively the founder of Liverpool Cathedral, although the project started under his predecessor. On 19th July 1904 King Edward VII and Queen Alexandra laid the foundation stone. The Lady Chapel was opened in 1910, but the Cathedral

New Inn Hall Street, Oxford.

Noel's father, Francis James Chavasse, 1846–1928.

Abercromby Square, Liverpool, home to the Chavasse family while Noel's father was bishop there.

Liverpool Cathedral under construction.

was not completed until 1978. Francis retired in 1913 and moved to St Peter's House, Oxford, where he was elected an honorary fellow of Corpus Christi College. He was a major influence in the creation of St Peter's Hall (later St Peter's College). He died on 11th March 1928 and is buried in Founder's Plot at Liverpool Cathedral. Christ Church at Norris Green was dedicated to him.

Noel's mother was Edith Jane née Maude (1851–1927). She and Francis were married at Overton-on-Dee near Wrexham on 27th September 1881. The service was conducted by the Reverends LT Chavasse and S Maude (her brother). She was a devout and compassionate woman who took a great interest in missionary work. Noel had six siblings:

St Peter's Hall, later St Peter's College, Oxford.

The seven Chavasse children.

- Dorothea Chavasse (1883–1935) married the Reverend George Foster-Carter (1876–1966), Rector of St Aldate's, Oxford in 1908. They had four children:
  - Aylmer Francis Foster-Carter (1911–79) was a chest physician. He married Ethna Josephine McDermott (1914–2005) in 1947 and they had two children: Aidan G Foster-Carter 1947 and Clare F Foster-Carter 1950. Aylmer was a physician and expert on tuberculosis.
  - Lois Marguerite Foster-Carter, born 1916. She was commissioned as subaltern in the ATS (W/242314 – 350580) on 29th June 1945.
  - Pamela Mary Foster-Carter (1918–67).
  - Felicity J Foster-Carter, born 1923. She was a Franciscan Tertiary who moved to Singapore in 1955, teaching scripture and carrying out pastoral work at St Margaret's Primary School. She moved to mission schools in Singapore and Malaysia and was appointed Assistant Boarding Mistress before retiring to Oxford in 2000 where she lived with her sister Lois. She wrote, *All Things to All People – An Exciting Life in Singapore and Malaysia* in 2011.
- Christopher Maude Chavasse (1884–1962) was Noel's elder twin by twenty-eight minutes. He was educated at the same schools as Noel. While at Trinity College, Oxford he gained blues for lacrosse and athletics. Christopher became a curate at St Helens, Lancashire and an army chaplain in 1914. He was commissioned as chaplain to the forces 4th Class on 20th August 1914 and was chaplain to No.10 General Hospital at St Nazaire. He was at the bedside of William Rhodes-Moorhouse VC when he died at No.6 or No.7 Casualty Clearing Station at Merville on 27th April 1915 and about the same time he was at the execution of a soldier, which affected him deeply. Christopher became Senior Chaplain of 62nd Division in 1916. For attending to the wounded under fire at Bullecourt in April or May 1917 he was recommended for the DSO, but received the MC, LG 25th August 1917. In 1918, he became Deputy Assistant Chaplain General of IX Corps as temporary chaplain 2nd Class, 30th September 1918. He was also awarded the French Croix de Guerre, LG 7th October 1919. Christopher was wounded some time during the war and last appears in the Army List in June 1920. After the war he was Vicar of St George's, Barrow-in-Furness until 1922, when he returned to Oxford as Rector of St Aldates and later St Peter-le-Bailey. He helped found St Peter's Hall at Oxford with his father and was appointed its first master in 1929. He was a tenacious opponent of proposals to revise the Book of Common Prayer and risked advancement in the Church. Christopher was Proctor in Convocation for Oxford University 1936–39. He was a chaplain in the Territorial Army Reserve 2nd May 1930 and, as chaplain to the forces 3rd Class, 29th November 1931, was attached to Oxford UOTC until 9th November 1944 (OBE, LG 23rd June 1936 and TD 1940). On 18th August 1939, he and his wife were sailing off Northern Ireland aboard a whaler near the Giant's Causeway when it was capsized by a huge wave. Christopher's leg was crushed against a rock and he was rushed to Portrush Cottage Hospital in

Rochester Cathedral, where Christopher was Bishop 1940–60.

Christopher Maude Chavasse (1884–1962) when Bishop of Rochester.

a baker's van. The leg was saved, but continued to trouble him and in February 1942 it was amputated at St Nicholas Hospital, Pyrford, Surrey. He said, *The boys were becoming too good for me at tennis. Now I can always claim: 'If only I had my other leg, I'd show you!'* Christopher was consecrated Bishop of Rochester on 25th April 1940 and chaired the commission that produced the report *Towards the Conversion of England* in 1945. He wrote a number of publications, including *The Meaning of the Lessons and of the Psalms*, *A Letter from the Catacombs*, *Christ and Fairies*, *Five Questions before the Church* and *This is Our Faith*. He was appointed Deputy Lieutenant of Kent in 1959 and retired the following year to 14 Staverton Road, Oxford. He became an honorary fellow of St Peter's College in 1949 and Trinity College in 1955. St Peter's was fully incorporated into the University in 1961. Frost Crescent, Wayfield Road, Wayfield, Chatham, Kent, was named Chavasse Terrace in his honour. Christopher married Beatrice Cropper née Willink (1896–1977) in 1919 at Toxteth Park, Liverpool and they had five children:

- Noel Willink Chavasse, born 1920, was awarded the MC during the Second World War. He married Janet Eleanor Davidson in 1951.
- Michael Louis Maude Chavasse (1923–83) graduated from Trinity College, Oxford. He enlisted in the Royal Armoured Corps in October 1941 and was commissioned in the Buffs (Royal East Kent Regiment) in 1942, seeing service in Italy with the Royal Norfolk Regiment 1943–45. He was called to the Bar, Inner Temple, in 1949 and was Recorder of the Crown Court 1972–77 and a QC and Circuit Judge. He married Rose Ethel Read (born 1925) in 1951, daughter of Vice Admiral Arthur Duncan Read CB and the Honorable Rosamond Vere née Monckton. They had three daughters. His publications include *A Critical Annotation of the RIBA Standard Forms of Building Contract* 1964 and *Rights of Light* with Bryan Anstey 1959.

Christopher Chavasse with members of St Peter's Hall in 1929–30.

  - John Chavasse, born 1925, married Mary née Vaughan in 1965 and they had three children.
  - Anna Chavasse, born 1927, married Richard Charles Chalinor Watson (born 1923) in 1955. He was the son of Colonel Francis William Watson and Alice Madeline née Collings-Wells, the sister of John Stanhope Collings-Wells VC DSO. They had two children. Richard was commissioned in the Indian Army Artillery and served as a captain in South East Asia 1942–45. He became a curate in Stratford, East London 1952–53 and was Tutor and Chaplain at Wycliffe Hall, Oxford 1954–57. In 1957, he became Chaplain of Wadham College and Oxford Pastorate and from 1962 was Vicar of Hornchurch, Essex until 1970. He was also Examining Chaplain to the Bishop of Rochester 1956–61, Examining Chaplain to the Bishop of Chelmsford 1962–70, Assistant Rural Dean of Havering 1967–70, Rector of Burnley, Lancashire 1970–77 and Suffragan Bishop of Burnley 1970–87.
  - Susan M Chavasse, born 1931.
- Edith Marjorie Chavasse (1886–1987) was a twin with Mary. She worked for Dr Barnardo's and represented England at Hockey.
- Mary 'May' Laeta Chavasse (1886–1989) was a twin with Edith. She was a nurse at Liverpool Merchant's Mobile Hospital, Étaples (No.6 British Red Cross Society Hospital) and was

Mary 'May' Laeta Chavasse.

Francis Bernard Chavasse.

Aidan Chavasse.

Mentioned in Sir Douglas Haig's Despatches in May 1917. She joined the Queen Alexandra's Imperial Military Nursing Corps in the Second World War and served aboard the Elder Dempster Company Hospital Ship *Aba*. She was later a nurse in Oxford.

- Francis Bernard Chavasse (1889–1941), known as Bernard, graduated from Balliol College, Oxford and became a doctor (MRCS (Eng) 1915, LRCP (London) 1915). Commissioned in the RAMC on 1st May 1915. He was appointed Medical Officer of 17th King's, captain 1st May 1916, and was awarded the MC for tending the wounded at great personal risk for four days while wounded himself at Hooge, Belgium during the Third Battle of Ypres, LG 9th January 1918. Later served with 11th Casualty Clearing Station. Appointed acting major on 6th November 1918. After the war he was Honorary Ophthalmic Surgeon at the Liverpool Eye and Ear Infirmary and lecturer in Ophthalmology at Liverpool University living with his family at 39 Rodney Street, Liverpool. He edited a new edition of Claud Worth's *Worth's Squints* regarding binoculars reflexes and the treatment of strabismus. Bernard challenged Worth's theory, applied his own ideas to new developments in physiology and pathology and almost rewrote the book. The seventh edition, published in 1939, became *Worth's and Chavasses's Squint*. Bernard went on to invent several surgical instruments, but his best-known device was the eponymous lens. He died in a car accident in 1941. Francis married Anita née Reeves-Thomas in 1923 and they had three children:
    - Edgar FJ Chavasse, born 1924.
    - Evadne Chavasse (1928–97) married Donald Louis Nicholas (1909–73) in 1950 and had three children.
    - Thomas A Chavasse, born 1932, married Barbara AJ Beyer (born 1938) in 1960 and had two children.
- Aidan Chavasse (1891–1917) was commissioned on 22nd August 1914 and promoted lieutenant on 1st January 1915. He served in 17th King's. On the night of 3rd/4th July 1917, he was with a patrol of eight men on Observatory Ridge, near Hooge, Belgium, when they met a German patrol. In the ensuing encounter, Aidan was wounded by a bullet in the right thigh. Lance Corporal W Dixon

MM was with him, but was unable to move Aidan alone. As it was getting light and they were only ten metres from a German sap, Aidan sent Dixon back. Next night he and Aidan's brother Francis went out, but found no trace of Aidan, nor on the next night. He was listed as missing until early 1918, by when there had been no notification through the Red Cross and he was presumed dead officially. He is commemorated on the Ypres (Menin Gate) Memorial, Belgium.

Noel's paternal grandfather was Thomas Howard Chavasse FRCS (1800–84). He married Catherine Margaret Grant (1807–42) in 1827 and they had eight children: Ludovick Thomas Chavasse 1829–92, Nicholas Horace Chavasse 1830–1918, Jane Ann Chavasse 1832–63, Catherine Henrietta Chavasse c.1834–1915, Howard Sidney Chavasse 1835–63, Margaret Elizabeth Chavasse 1838–1927, Charles Edward Chavasse c.1841–93 and Emily, born and died 1842. In 1844, he married Miriam Sarah née Wyld (1817–84). The family was living at Wylde Green House, Sutton Coldfield, Warwickshire in 1851 and 1861. Thomas and Miriam had four more children in addition to Francis:

- Miriam Sarah Chavasse (1848–1935) married (as Miriam Theresa Chavasse) the Reverend Percival Ewen Wilson (1853–1948) in 1879 at Aston, Warwickshire.
- Ada Martha Chavasse (1850–1922) married the Reverend Henry Charles Squires (c.1847–1910) in 1878. They had five children: Herbert C Squires 1880–1964, Elsie C Squires 1883–1946, Francis 'Frank' Chavasse Squires 1885–1915, Winfred C Squires 1888–1962 and Mildred Christian Squires 1892–1963. Captain Francis Chavasse Squires was Adjutant of 1/23rd Sikh Pioneers when he died on 7th July 1915 (Maala Cemetery, Aden – C 137).
- Thomas (later Sir Thomas) Frederick Chavasse FRCS LRCP (1854–1913) was a Doctor of Medicine, Master of Surgery and Consulting Surgeon to the General Hospital, Birmingham. Thomas published various papers on surgical subjects in the *Transactions of the Royal Medical Chirurgical Society*, *Transactions of the Pathological Society* and the *Lancet*. He married Frances Hannah Ryland (1848–1928) in 1885 and they had six children – Gwendoline L Ryland Chavasse 1885, Arthur Ryland Chavasse 1887–1916, Frederick Ryland Chavasse 1889, Francis Ryland Chavasse 1890, Frances Gladys Ryland 'Gaggie' Chavasse 1893 and Esmé Margaret Ryland Chavasse 1895. Frances Gladys Ryland Chavasse was engaged to Noel in April 1916. Captain Arthur Ryland Chavasse RAMC BA MA MB MRCS LRCP was serving at No.2 General Hospital when he died of pneumonia on 12th March 1916 (Ste Marie Cemetery, Le Havre – 19 T 3).
- Joseph Hodgson Chavasse (1856–1906) married Mary Elizabeth Gilman (1859–92) in 1880 and they had a son, Thomas John Chavasse, in 1881. Joseph married Alice Maria Nation (1867–1962) in 1895.

Noel's maternal grandfather was Canon Joseph Maude (1805–74), Curate of Newport, Isle of Wight in 1851 and later Vicar of Chirk, Denbighshire. He married

Mary Fawler/Fowler née Hooper (1820–1913) in 1841 and they had six more children in addition to Edith:

- Samuel Maude (1845–1912). He was Curate of Holy Trinity, St Pancras, in 1881, Vicar of Needham Market in Suffolk in 1891, before moving to Lyncombe, Guildford Road, Woking, Surrey by 1911.
- Mary Julia Maude (1847–1934).
- Margaret Esther Maude (1848–49).
- Joseph Hooper Maude (1852–1927) was a Clerk in Holy Orders. He married Louisa Frederica Grey Fuller (1864–1938) in 1884 and had two children: Cecily Margaret Evadne Maude 1887–1958 and Louis Edward Joseph Maude 1891–1916, who served as a lieutenant in 11th King's Own Yorkshire Light Infantry and was killed in action on 1st July 1916 (Gordon Dump Cemetery, Ovillers-la-Boisselle, France – Special Memorial B 7).
- Daniel Edward Maude (1855–56).
- Grace Fawler Maude (born and died 1858).

Noel and Christopher were identical in looks and manner, so were often made to wear a different item of clothing or a coloured ribbon to identify them in class and on the sports field. They took great amusement in swapping these items to cause confusion. They were very close to each other and also with their twin sisters.

Christopher (left) with Noel at an athletics event.

Until they were twelve, Noel and Christopher were educated by their governess and a tutor. They then went to Magdalen College School in Oxford 1896–1900, where they won numerous athletics trophies and produced a number of small publications for their classmates. In 1900 they moved to Liverpool College, where Noel won the Earl of Derby's History Prize in 1901 and the Routhwaite Prize for Reading and Recitation in 1902. The twins were very active in debating, often taking opposing sides. They continued to excel at sports, with Noel taking first place in Neat Diving for Beginners in 1900. Both played for the Cricket 2nd XI in 1902 and the Rugby 1st XV in 1904. Noel broke the school records for the 100 yards, quarter mile and mile races in 1903. The same year a knee injury prevented him playing rugby. Instead, during his games afternoons and summer vacations, he helped to organise sports and annual camps for Holy Trinity Certified Industrial School for Boys, Grafton Street, Liverpool. He also led Bible reading and singsongs. Also attending the College at the time was the future VC Ronald Niel Stuart.

Magdalen College School in Oxford on the right, where Noel and Christopher were educated 1896–1900.

Trinity College, Oxford.

At Trinity College, Oxford 1904–09 (BA 1907, MA 1909), the twins shared rooms in Kettle Hall. Noel was a member of the medical section of Oxford University OTC January-May 1909 as a lance sergeant, but gave it up due to his studies. Noel and Christopher gained blues in 1907 for running against Cambridge. Noel gained a first in Physiology in 1909, but Christopher failed his exams. Noel was awarded a post-graduate exhibition in medicine at Oxford, but deferred it until his brother passed his examinations. Instead he decided on a course at Liverpool University (Royal Southern Hospital) to be at home and able to help his brother prior to the examinations.

Royal Southern Hospital, Liverpool.

Rotunda Hospital, Dublin.

At Liverpool University 1910–12, he qualified as MBChB MRCS LRCP. The placement part of the course was at the Rotunda Hospital, Dublin, in the summer of 1911. On 15th March 1912 the committee of the University's Medical Faculty awarded him their premier prize, the Derby Exhibition. During his time at Oxford Noel spent his weekends learning the skills of orthopaedic surgery

The Great Britain team at the opening ceremony of the Olympics in 1908.

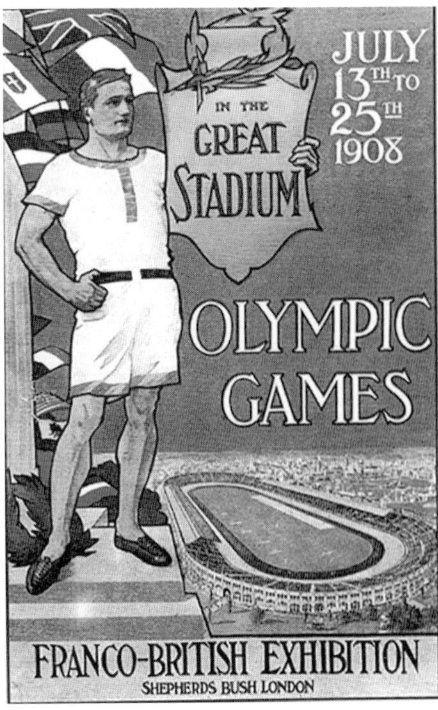

Poster advertisement for the London Olympics of 1908. The athletics events were at the White City in July as shown, but the Games lasted for a record 187 days. Great Britain emerged with the largest number of medals – 146, including fifty six Gold, with the USA next, with forty seven medals, including twenty three Gold.

at the surgeries of his friend and mentor, Dr Robert Jones. He was registered as a doctor with the General Medical Council on 22nd July 1912.

As talented athletes, Noel and Christopher were both invited to trials for the British team for the Fourth Olympic Games in London, 13th-25th July 1908. Noel pulled a muscle and could not take part and Christopher also pulled out. They wrote to the authorities explaining that they could not run due to injuries, but would be fit for the Games. Their times for the quarter mile and 100 yards were included, some of which were the best in England since 1906. They were invited to run in front of King Edward VII and the French President, but had to decline. However, their times were good enough and on 2nd June, PL Fisher, Secretary of the Amateur Athletic Association, invited them to take part in the Games. They were both entered in the 400 metres. Noel came third in Heat VII and Christopher was second in Heat VIII, but neither time was good enough to go through to the next round. Strangely, the press made no mention of twin brothers running in the same event.

After university Noel researched blood plasma at the Radcliffe Infirmary, Oxford. He became a house physician and resident house surgeon to Mr Douglas Crawford at the Royal Southern Hospital in Liverpool 4th October 1912 – 31st March 1913, which was extended for a further six months. He specialised in orthopaedics under Sir Robert Jones, the leading orthopaedic surgeon of the day.

On 2nd June 1913, Noel was commissioned in the RAMC (TF) and was attached to 10th King's as its medical officer. On 2nd August 1914 the Battalion went to

Hornby Camp, Lancashire for annual training camp, but was ordered to return to Liverpool next day. Noel and his brothers did not want to wait to get to the front, so on 5th August they travelled to the War Office in London to volunteer for immediate service overseas. The battalion was recalled on 7th August and Noel was ordered to Chester Castle next day to perform medical examinations on recruits. He rejoined the battalion in early September at King's Park, Edinburgh, where the unit formed part of the Forth Defences. The battalion moved to Tunbridge Wells, Kent on 10th October, where it kitted out and undertook exercises prior to going overseas.

The Liverpool Scottish Battalion Headquarters in Liverpool.

Noel embarked with the battalion at Southampton on SS *Maidan* on 1st November. The ship missed the tide and did not put in to Le Havre until the following night. The Battalion disembarked on the morning of 3rd November. It arrived at St Omer on 5th November and then spent two very cold weeks at Blendecques in training. On 20th November it reached Bailleul and on the 22nd crossed the border into Belgium.

Noel quickly developed a strong concern for the health and condition of the men and obtained whatever he could for them. He earned a reputation for being able to get hold of the impossible. He was one of the first doctors to use anti-tetanus serum on wounded men. This was a great success and very few developed tetanus as a result. The battalion moved into the front line for the first time on 27th November,

A remarkable picture taken under fire by a wounded soldier of the Liverpool Scottish, Private FA Fyfe, a pre-war newspaper photographer, during the attack at Bellewaarde and Hooge on 16th June 1915. A number of wounded and dead can be seen. It was in this area that Noel earned his MC (FA Fyfe).

near Kemmel. Noel's first patient was Captain Arthur Twentyman, who was hit in the chest by a bullet next day and died of his wound on 29th November (Rue-Petillon Military Cemetery, Fleurbaix – II A 63).

Noel returned to Britain for a few days' leave in early February 1915. Over the next few months the battalion was in the Ypres Salient and at St Eloi. Noel's dressing station was in the infantry barracks in Ypres 10th March – 2nd April. On 16th June, the Battalion took part in Second Army's attack on Bellewaarde as part of 9th Brigade, 3rd Division. Of the twenty-three officers and 519 other ranks who went into action, twenty-one officers and 379 other ranks became casualties. Noel scoured the ground between the opposing lines to provide aid to the wounded. In his search for one officer he visited all hospitals in the area by bicycle in the hope of finding him, but to no avail. **Awarded the MC for clearing no man's land of the wounded at Hooge during this attack, LG 14th January 1916.**

The CO, Major GA Blair, submitted a list of recommendations for awards, but it never reached Divisional Headquarters and was probably destroyed in a fire at Brigade Headquarters. However, believing that the recommendations had been approved, he announced them at a church parade in a barn near Ouderdoum. None of those who subsequently received awards for 16th June resulted from recommendations made by the battalion. Noel had been told earlier of his award and was absent from the parade. He was found later weeping in a wood. **The Battalion was involved an attack on Sanctuary Wood on 30th September, for which he was Mentioned in Sir John French's Despatch of 30th November 1915, LG 1st January 1916.**

The battalion transferred to 166th Brigade, 55th (West Lancashire) Division under Major General Sir H Jeudwine on 1st January 1916. Noel was arrested as a spy by a vigilant Military Policeman because his uniform was unusual; he was wearing RAMC uniform with Corps insignia and a Glengarry cap with the Liverpool Scottish badge, but the battalion wore the khaki Balmoral. Early in April 1916, he was chosen from hundreds of other officers to receive his MC from the King, but his leave was postponed. As a result he was not formally decorated with the MC until 7th June, almost a year after the action at Bellewaarde.

Noel had a few days' leave in Britain and returned to the Battalion at Busselboom, Belgium on 9th July. **He was awarded the VC for his actions at Guillemont, France on 9th August 1916, LG 26th October 1916.** He was promoted captain in August, backdated to 1st April, and in November was transferred temporarily to a field hospital. He attended the start of a six day course on hygiene and sanitation in December, but he and the battalion were sent for rest at C Camp, Brandhoek, for Christmas, following which he completed the course.

Noel was granted fourteen days leave to attend his VC investiture at Buckingham Palace on 5th February 1917. The medal was taken back to Liverpool for safekeeping by his sister Marjorie. A miniature version was carried by Noel. On 20th July the Battalion left St Omer and moved by train to Poperinghe for a short rest before marching up to the lines in front of Wieltje. Up to 24th July the Battalion suffered

Noel Chavasse with the stretcher-bearers of the Liverpool Scottish in Flanders shortly before the opening of the Third Battle of Ypres in July 1917.

145 casualties from a mustard gas attack, combined with heavy shelling. It was relieved that day and rested at Derby Camp, between Poperinghe and Ypres, where it re-equipped and prepared for the forthcoming offensive.

Gladys in later life.

Awarded a Bar to the VC for his actions at Wieltje, Belgium 31st July – 2nd August 1917, LG 14th September 1917. His was the only Great War double VC. He was very seriously wounded by a shell exploding in his dugout at 3 a.m. on 2nd August and was eventually taken to No.32 Casualty Clearing Station at Brandhoek. On the way the ambulance stopped briefly at 46th Field Ambulance, commanded by Lieutenant Colonel Arthur Martin-Leake VC and Bar. He was seen by Dr Colston who wrote, *An ambulance came up late tonight and in it was Captain Chavasse VC RAMC of the King's Liverpool Battalions* [sic] *of the 55th Division. His face was unrecognizable, all blackened from a shell burst very near and he seemed to be unconscious. As he had an abdominal wound besides I did not take him out of the Ambulance which was sent on direct to 32 CCS, where he will probably die.* Despite a successful operation to remove shell fragments, his condition worsened on 4th August and he died of wounds at 1 p.m. He was nursed in his final hours by Sister Ida Leedam, who had worked with Noel at the Royal

Southern Hospital in Liverpool. Noel was buried next day; his brother Bernard did not manage to get there until 6th August. Noel is buried in Brandhoek New Military Cemetery – III B 15. His CWGC gravestone is unique, as it carries two Victoria Crosses. His will was administered by his father; he left £603/8/4.

The Bar to the VC was presented privately to his father by Lieutenant General Sir William Pitcairn Campbell KCB, GOC Western District, in late 1917. Noel became engaged to his cousin, Frances Gladys Ryland Chavasse in April 1916. She became a volunteer worker with the Church Army at Euskirchen, Germany, where she met the Reverend James 'Pud' Ferguson Colquhoun (c.1881–1937). Their marriage was registered in the 4th quarter of 1919 at Bromsgrove, Worcestershire. Christopher Chavasse was one of the officiating clergy. James had been chaplain to 12th York & Lancaster and later was Senior Chaplain of 31st Division. Gladys ran a canteen for troops and was evacuated from Dunkirk in 1940 and was Mentioned in Despatches for gallant and distinguished services at Monte Cassino, Italy. She visited Noel's grave every year until she was knocked over in France in September 1962 and killed; she was very deaf and probably never heard the car.

Noel is related distantly to three other VCs:

- Captain Charles Hazlitt Upham VC and Bar – his aunt by marriage was the wife of Noel's second cousin.
- Lieutenant Neville Josiah Coghill VC – his paternal aunt, Anne Georgina Coghill, was married to Pye Henry Chavasse, Noel's great uncle.
- John Stanhope Collings-Wells VC DSO – Noel's niece, Anna Chavasse, married Collings-Wells' nephew, Richard Charles Chalinor Watson.

In addition to the VC & Bar and MC, he was awarded the 1914 Star with 'Mons' clasp, British War Medal 1914–20 and Victory Medal 1914–19 with Mentioned-in-Despatches oakleaf. The VC passed to his brother, Christopher, who left it to the trustees of St Peter's College, Oxford in the 1930s. It was displayed on the main staircase, but the insurers became concerned about the location and a replica set replaced the originals, which were locked in a bank vault for about fifteen years. They were presented on permanent loan to the Imperial War Museum on 22nd February 1990 in the presence of Queen Elizabeth The Queen Mother, Colonel-in-Chief RAMC. In November 2009 the medals were purchased by Lord Ashcroft, reputedly for £1.5 million. They are now held by The Michael Ashcroft Trust in the Lord Ashcroft Victoria Cross Collection and are displayed in the Ashcroft Gallery of the Imperial War Museum; Christopher's medals are displayed alongside Noel's.

Noel is commemorated in a considerable number of places, including:

- Chavasse House, 208 (Liverpool) Field Hospital, Territorial Army Centre, Sarum Road, Liverpool, Lancashire. The unit also holds a competitive twenty-one kilometres march annually, with the winner receiving a medal inscribed, "Chavasse March" "208 R.A.M.C.".

- 207 (Manchester) Field Hospital (Volunteers) Officers' Mess, The Castle Armoury, Castle Street, Bury, Lancashire, was dedicated to him in February 2009.
- A memorial plaque at Forbes House, Liverpool, dedicated in 1979, was the idea of Great War Liverpool Scottish veteran, Brigadier Tom Robbins.
- A bronze bust of Noel is next to the Liverpool Book of Remembrance in Liverpool Cathedral.
- He was one of six VCs commemorated on a set of stamps published by the Royal Mail to commemorate the 150th Anniversary of the Victoria Cross on 21st September 2006. The other VCs were Jack Cornwell, Agansingh Rai, Charles Lucas, Albert Ball and Charles Upham.

The commemorative Chavasse VC stamp issued by the Royal Mail in September 2006.

- A tree and plaque in the RAMC Memorial Grove at the National Memorial Arboretum, Alrewas, Staffordshire, as part of a tribute to every VC & GC recipient within the Corps. The Grove was dedicated on 18th October 2000.
- RAMC Great War Book of Remembrance in Westminster Abbey. His entry wrongly records that he was awarded the DSO.
- Blue plaque unveiled on 30th September 2005 at Magdalen College School, Oxford by the Oxfordshire Blue Plaques Board.
- Blue plaque on the wall of the former Bishop's Palace, 19 Abercromby Square, Liverpool.
- A memorial unveiled opposite 19 Abercromby Square, Liverpool, in July 2008, depicts Noel helping a wounded soldier accompanied by a stretcher-bearer. Fifteen other VCs associated with Liverpool are included on the memorial.
- Portrait painting in the Dining Room and portrait photograph in the Snooker Room of the Officers' Mess, Defence Medical Services Training Centre, Keogh Barracks, Aldershot, Hampshire.
- Named on the Army Medical Services VC & GC Roll of Honour in the Army Medical Services Regimental Headquarters at the former Army Staff College, Camberley, Surrey.

Basil Rathbone (1892–1967) served as a private with the London Scottish until commissioned in 2/10th King's early in 1916; he was the intelligence officer. 2/10th amalgamated with 1/10th King's early in 1918. Basil became adept at daylight reconnaissance, using camouflaged suits, fresh foliage and hands and face blackened with burnt cork. After the war he had a full career on stage and in films. His most famous role was as Sherlock Holmes in fourteen films between 1939 and 1946.

- As the son of a sitting bishop, his name is on the House of Lords memorial.
- Chavasse Trophy – awarded annually by Oxford University Athletic Club to the winning college in the inter-college athletics competition based on aggregated points from the two 'cuppers' competitions. 'Cuppers' in Hilary Term is dedicated to Noel Chavasse and in Michaelmas Term to his brother, Christopher. They both competed for Oxford in the 1906 and 1907 Varsity matches.
- Chavasse VC House, Colchester, Essex, a Personnel Recovery Centre funded by Help for Heroes and The Royal British Legion for wounded, injured and sick service personnel was opened on 8th May 2012.
- Chavasse Ward, MOD Hospital Unit Frimley Park, Surrey established in February 1996. The other military ward is named after Martin-Leake VC and Bar.
- Liverpool College has memorials to Noel and Aidan.
- Noel is named in the rolls at Liverpool Town Hall's Hall of Remembrance. For an unknown reason his brother Aidan is missing.
- The Merseyside Branch of the Western Front Association and the King's (Liverpool) Regiment published a limited edition first day cover on the 80th Anniversary of his first VC.

Members of the British Olympic Association, including the Chairman, Lord Colin Moynihan, conducted a memorial service at Noel's grave at Brandhoek on 11th November 2011. Dr Jacques Rogge, President of the International Olympic Committee, also attended, as did representatives of the Belgian, French and German National Olympic Committees and several Olympic medalists.

72132 ACTING CORPORAL LIONEL 'LEO' BEAUMAURICE CLARKE 2nd Battalion (Eastern Ontario Regiment), Canadian Expeditionary Force

Leo Clarke was born on 1st December 1892 at Waterdown, near Hamilton, Ontario, Canada. He was known as Nobby as a child and later as Leo. His father was Henry 'Harry' Trevelyan Clarke (1868–1938), born at Boxted, Essex. His mother was Rosetta 'Rose' Caroline Nona née Bodily (1869–1924), born at Colchester, Essex. Henry and Rose emigrated to Canada and married in Manhattan, New York, USA on 20th February 1892. They returned to England with their family prior to 1901, when they were living at Thrift Farm near Boxted, Essex. The family returned to Canada in 1904 and were living at 785 Pine Street,

Winnipeg, Manitoba by 1911. Leo had five siblings:

Waterdown, Hamilton, Ontario.

Portage Street, Winnipeg.

- Harry V Clarke, born in April 1894 at Wentworth, Ontario, was a press man in a printing firm. He married Bessie Henbrey Rogers (1894–1975) in 1918 at Winnipeg, Manitoba. They were living at 526 Craig Street, Winnipeg in 1921. By 1957, Harry was a Departmental Manager at Eatons Department Store, living at 773 Spruce, Winnipeg. He retired to Okanagan, British Columbia. They had a son: Robert Harry Rogers Clarke c.1919.
- Charles 'Charlie' Edward Clarke was born on 8th December 1895 in Essex. He enlisted in 32nd Battalion (81291) on 10th February 1915, giving his occupation as box maker. He had served previously for six months with 101st Edmonton Fusiliers and was described as 5′ 7″ tall, with fair complexion, grey eyes, brown hair and his religious denomination was Church of England. He transferred to 2nd Battalion. Charles later married and had a son, Leo Clarke.
- Muriel Rosamond Clarke (1898–1991), born at Chelmsford, Essex, married Guy Edmund Smith (1892–1975) in 1920 at Winnipeg, Manitoba and they had a son, Henry Clarke Smith. Guy was a painter, born at Biggleswade, Bedfordshire. He served in 79th Cameron Highlanders of Canada before enlisting in the Canadian Expeditionary Force on 13th July 1915. He was described as 5′ 7″ tall, with fair complexion, grey eyes, fair hair and his religious denomination was Church of England.
- Jack Trevelyan Clarke, born 1901 in Chelmsford, Essex.
- Arthur Roy Clarke (May 1907 – 1990) at Winnipeg, Manitoba. He married Winnifred McCartney (c.1906–86) c.1932. They had a son, Allan Clarke 1938.

Leo's paternal grandfather, Beaumaurice Stracey Clarke (1813–97), was born at Trumpington, Cambridge. He was the son of Edward Daniel Clarke (1769–1822), a naturalist, mineralogist and traveller, whose portrait hangs in the National Portrait Gallery in London. Beaumaurice was a chaplain with the East India Company and became known as the 'Fighting Parson' during the Indian Mutiny. He was appointed

Argyle School, Winnipeg.

Leo's great grandfather, Edward Daniel Clarke (1769–1822), a naturalist, mineralogist and traveler.

Vicar of Boxted in 1871 and by 1891 was Rector of Basildon, Essex. Beaumaurice married Georgiana née Brooking (1826–94) in 1845 at Madras, India. In addition to Henry, they had sixteen other children; nine were born in India, of whom four died before they moved back to Britain. A surviving child, Gertrude Clarke (1862–1946), married Captain Arthur John Mullins RGA (1861–1944) in 1890 at Billericay, Essex. He was commissioned on 27th July 1880, seconded for service with the Indian Staff Corps and promoted to major by January 1899.

Leo's maternal grandfather, Henry James Bodily (1830–1903), was Curate of St Mark's at Victoria Docks, London in 1881 and by 1891 he was Vicar of Little Burstead, Essex. He married Rosetta née Cole (c.1833–90) in 1855 at Wigton, Cumberland. In addition to Rosetta they had seven other children.

Gladstone School, Winnipeg.

Leo's education commenced in England and continued at Argyle and Gladstone Schools, Winnipeg, Manitoba. He then worked as an engineer and was engaged in a survey for the Canadian Northern Railway in the north of the country in 1914.

Leo enlisted in 27th Battalion (City of Winnipeg) CEF in Winnipeg on 25th February 1915. He was described as 5′ 7½″ tall, with dark complexion, grey-green eyes, dark brown hair and his religious denomination was Presbyterian. The Battalion embarked for Britain on SS *Carpathian* on 17th May, where it underwent training; Leo transferred to 2nd Battalion to be with his younger brother Charles. He went to France on 13th October.

Leo received a gunshot wound to the right side and was admitted to No.2 Canadian Field Ambulance on 8th December. He was transferred to No.2 Canadian Casualty Clearing Station before being discharged on 11th December. He contracted influenza and was admitted to No.3 Canadian Field Ambulance on 10th April 1916, to the North Midland Division Casualty Clearing Station on 25th April and rejoined his unit on 2nd May. Leo was appointed acting corporal on 6th August.

Awarded the VC for his actions near Pozières, France on 9th September 1916, LG 26th October 1916. Leo was appointed acting sergeant and admitted to hospital on 18th September, rejoining his unit on 24th September. He was in the newly captured Regina Trench, between Pys

The Canadian Northern Railway (CNoR) station at Sudbury, Ontario. CNoR was established in 1899 by the amalgamation of all railway companies owned by Sir William Mackenzie and Sir Donald Mann. It began to compete with the Canadian Pacific Railway (CPR) by building a line linking the Prairie Provinces with the east, completed in December 1901. The company bought the Great Lake steamships and expanded its lines into northern Quebec and Nova Scotia. In 1905, CNoR reached Edmonton, capital of Alberta. In 1910, it joined the trans-Atlantic business by founding the Canadian Northern Steamship Company. That year construction started on the line west of Edmonton to Vancouver, but CPR had a better route and numerous problems followed. The line from Montreal to Vancouver was finally completed in January 1915, but it struggled to compete with CPR. In exchange for funds the federal government gained control and CNoR was nationalised in September 1918. In December CNoR and Canadian Government Railways were managed together as Canadian National Railway but did not formally merge until January 1923.

Ambulance crews of No.3 Canadian Field Ambulance in July 1916 (Canadian War Museum).

The crew of No.22 Ambulance Train (Greaves).

and Courcelette, on 18th October 1916, which was still under heavy artillery fire. A shell exploded nearby and he was buried, but his brother Charles was close by and rushed to dig him out. Charles' shovel struck Leo's helmet and he then scooped the earth out with his hands. Leo looked up at him and smiled, but he was very seriously injured. The explosion had crushed his back and he was paralysed from the waist down. The enemy barrage continued and prevented him being removed until evening. He was taken to No.22 Ambulance Train at 8 p.m. and moved to No.1

Étretat from the cliffs to the west. Many of the principal buildings in the town were taken over by No.1 General Hospital, which was based there from December 1914 to January 1919.

Étretat Churchyard during the war. The graves now have CWGC headstones.

An ambulance convoy in Rue Monge, Étretat in May 1917.

General Hospital at Étretat, north of Le Havre, arriving at 11 p.m. His lower limbs were paralysed and he was weak, restless and groaning. In the morning, he was restless and his skin was blue due to lack of oxygen. Leo Clarke died at 11 a.m. on 19th October. A post-mortem revealed dark congested patches in the lungs with pus and an enlarged spleen, but the spinal cord appeared normal. He is buried at Étretat Churchyard, Seine-Maritime, near Le Havre, France (II C 3A).

As Leo never married, the VC was presented to his father by the Governor-General of Canada, the 9th Duke of Devonshire, at the corner of Portage and Main Streets, Winnipeg on 7th March 1917 before a crowd of 30,000. This was the first VC presented in Canada. In addition to the VC, he was awarded the 1914–15 Star, British War Medal 1914–20 and Victory Medal 1914–19. As he died on operational duty, his next of kin were eligible for the Canadian Memorial Cross. His medals were donated by his family to the Canadian War Museum at Vimy Place, Ottawa, Ontario in December 2009, where they are held. Leo is commemorated in a number of places:

The Canadian Memorial Cross was established on 1st December 1919 to be awarded to the mother, widow or next of kin of a member of the Canadian Forces who lost their life on active service. From October 2001 it was awarded for any service related death.

A funeral procession in Étretat during the war.

- Leo Clarke VC, Frederick Hall VC and Robert Shankland VC all lived on Pine Street, Winnipeg, Manitoba; Clarke at 785, Hall at 778 and Shankland at 733. In honour of them, Pine Street was renamed Valour Road in 1925, through By-Law 11673 and a bronze plaque was mounted on a street lamp at the corner of Portage Avenue and Valour Road by the Women's Canadian Club of Winnipeg. A new site, Valour Road Plaza, at Sargent Avenue and Valour Road, was dedicated on 5th November 2005. It features Tyndall Stone monuments supporting steel silhouettes of three soldiers. Bronze plaques to the three VCs were dedicated on 27th May 2012.
- Memorial plaque, erected by the Ontario Heritage Foundation, unveiled in front of the Royal Canadian Legion Building at the corner of Hamilton Street North and White Oak Drive, Waterdown, Ontario on 19th September 1971.
- A wooden plaque bearing fifty-six maple leaves each inscribed with the name of a Canadian-born VC holder was dedicated at the Canadian Forces College, Toronto, on Remembrance Day 1999.
- Named on a Victoria Cross obelisk to all Canadian VCs at Military Heritage Park, Barrie, Ontario, dedicated by The Princess Royal on 22nd October 2013.
- Named on one of eleven plaques honouring 175 men from overseas awarded the VC for the Great War. The plaques were unveiled by the Senior Minister of State at the Foreign & Commonwealth Office and Minister for Faith and Communities, Baroness Warsi, at a reception at Lancaster House, London on 26th June 2014 attended by The Duke of Kent and relatives of the VC recipients. The Canadian plaque was unveiled outside the British High Commission in Elgin Street, Ottawa on 10th November 2014 by

Leo Clarke's headstone in Etretat Churchyard.

Victor Christian William Cavendish, 9th Duke of Devonshire (1868–1938), was the 11th Governor-General of Canada, 1916–21. He presented Leo Clarke's VC to his father in Winnipeg on 7th March 1917. Cavendish inherited the title in 1908 and held various government posts prior to and after his elevation. His last political appointment was Secretary of State for the Colonies, 1922–24.

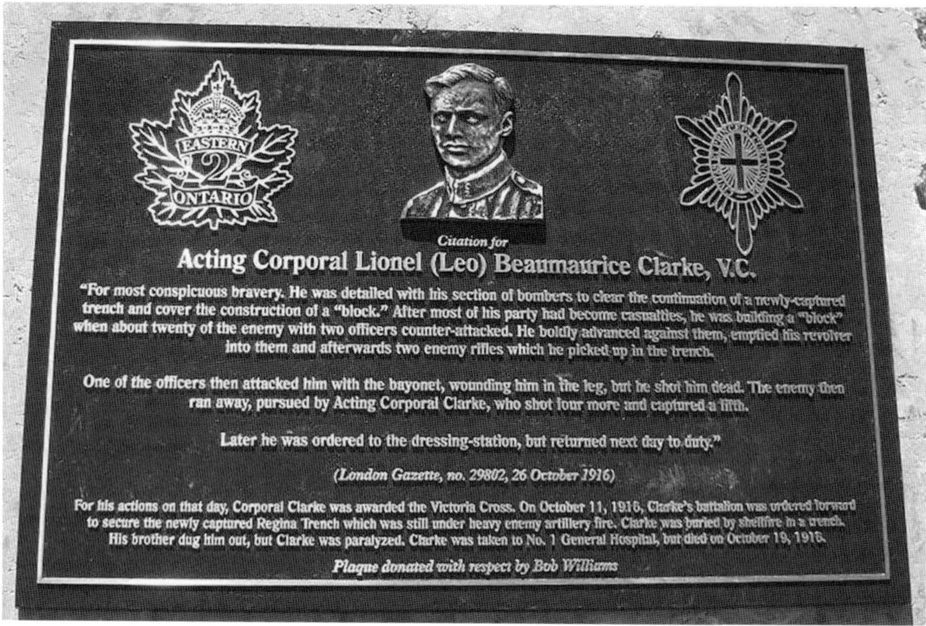

Leo Clarke's memorial plaque in Valour Road Plaza, Winnipeg.

The memorial plaque, placed by the Ontario Heritage Foundation in front of the Royal Canadian Legion Building, Hamilton Street, Waterdown, Ontario in 1971.

The Princess Royal in the presence of the British High Commissioner, Howard Drake, Canadian Minister of Veteran Affairs, Julian Fantino and Canadian Chief of the Defence Staff, General Thomas J. Lawson.

- His VC action was featured in Issues 795 & 1329 of the Victor comic, dated 15th May 1976 and 9th August 1986 respectively.
- The Secretary of State for Communities and Local Government, Eric Pickles MP, announced that Victoria Cross recipients from the Great War would have commemorative paving stones laid in their birthplace as a lasting legacy of local heroes within communities. The stones would be laid on or close to the 100th anniversary of their VC actions. For the 145 VCs born in Australia, Belgium, Canada, China, Denmark, Egypt, France, Germany, India, Iraq, Japan, Nepal, Netherlands, New Zealand, Pakistan, South Africa, Sri Lanka, Ukraine and the United States of America, individual commemorative stones were unveiled at the National Memorial Arboretum, Alrewas, Staffordshire by Prime Minister David Cameron MP and Sergeant Johnson Beharry VC on 5th March 2015.
- Two ninety-four cent postage stamps in honour of the 94 Canadian VC winners were issued by Canada Post on 21st October 2004 on the 150th Anniversary of the first Canadian VC's action, Alexander Roberts Dunn VC.

MAJOR WILLIAM LA TOUCHE CONGREVE
The Rifle Brigade attached HQ 76th Brigade

William Congreve was born at Burton Hall, near Neston, Cheshire on 22nd March 1891 and was known as Billy. His father was General Sir Walter Norris Congreve VC KCB MVO (1862–1927), nicknamed 'Squibs' due to the family connection with rocketry. His soldiers knew him affectionately as 'Old Concrete'. He was commissioned in (King's Own) 2nd Stafford (Light Infantry) Militia on 7th January 1880. In 1881 the unit became 3rd Battalion, The Prince of Wales's (North Staffordshire Regiment). Walter resigned his Militia commission on 29th March 1884. He was commissioned as a lieutenant (because of seniority due to Militia service) through Sandhurst in The Rifle Brigade on 7th February 1885. He joined the 1st Battalion at Belgaum, India in the spring of 1885 and transferred to the 4th Battalion at Meerut later that year, until returning to Britain with the Battalion in 1889. Walter went back to India in spring 1894 to the 3rd Battalion, which was mobilised for the Chitral Relief Force in 1895, but was in the Reserve Brigade at Rawalpindi and saw no action. In early 1896 he returned to Britain on posting to the Rifle Depot. In January 1898 he was appointed District Inspector of Musketry, Aldershot District Command, under the Area Commander, General Sir

Billy Congreve was born at Burton Hall, more usually known as Burton Manor, in Cheshire. It was built about 1805 for Richard Congreve. Much of it was re-modeled in 1904 for Henry Neville Gladstone, son of former Prime Minister William Ewart Gladstone. It later became an adult education college for Liverpool City Council, which closed in 2011. The Friends of Burton Manor have been restoring the Grade II listed buildings since.

Redvers Buller VC. On 24th October 1899 he was posted to 2nd Battalion, which had been ordered from Crete to Natal. He sailed from Southampton, arriving at Cape Town on 18th November. In South Africa he was attached to the staff of 4th Infantry Brigade and on 14th December became Press Censor at General Buller's Headquarters. Next morning he was Galloper to General Buller and was awarded the VC for his actions in saving the guns at Colenso on 15th December 1899. On recovering from his wounds, he became Adjutant of Kitchener's Horse and was appointed Brigade Major of 18th Infantry Brigade 4th March – 4th November 1900. He was then Deputy Assistant Adjutant General at Headquarters 5th November until appointed Assistant Military Secretary and Private Secretary to General Officer Commanding-in-Chief South Africa, Lord Kitchener, 30th November 1900 – 16th October 1902. On 16th November 1902, he was appointed Assistant Military Secretary and ADC to HRH The Duke of Connaught, Commander-in-Chief Ireland. On 7th May 1904, he accompanied the Duke to London in his new appointment of Inspector General of the Forces, until he was appointed second-in-command of 3rd Rifle Brigade on 1st December 1905. He was on half pay from 8th July 1908 until appointed Commandant of the School of Musketry at Hythe, Kent on 5th September 1909. Two years later he was promoted

General Sir Walter Norris Congreve VC KCB MVO was known as 'Squibs' or affectionately to his soldiers as 'Old Concrete'. He was awarded the VC for his actions in the Second Boer War in 1899 (Rifle Brigade).

Saving the guns at Colenso on 15th December 1899. It was for this action that Walter Congreve was awarded the VC, as were Major William Babtie, Lieutenant The Hon Frederick Roberts, Captain Harry Schofield, Captain Hamilton Reed and Corporal George Nurse (Sidney Paget).

The funeral of General Sir Walter Norris Congreve, Governor of Malta, on 4th March 1927.

brigadier general and took command of 18th Brigade, which he took to France in August 1914. Promoted major general on 18th February 1915, he took command of 6th Division on 27th May. On 15th November, as a temporary lieutenant general, he took command of XIII Corps. Walter suffered from cholera in August 1916 and was wounded on 12th June 1917 while inspecting a battery below Vimy Ridge

HMS *Chrysanthemum*, a sloop launched in November 1917, was involved in convoy duties before joining the Mediterranean Fleet as a target towing ship from Malta. She carried General Sir Walter Norris Congreve's body on its final journey for burial at sea. When the Spanish Civil War broke out in 1936, she rescued British nationals from Barcelona. In 1938, she became a drill ship of the RNVR and RNR and was a familiar site moored alongside the Thames embankment in London until she was decommissioned and sold in 1988. That year she was used in the filming of a boat chase in Tilbury Docks for the film *Indiana Jones and the Last Crusade*. She was scrapped in 1995.

and had his left hand amputated. On 3rd January 1918 he was given command of VII Corps then X Corps, but was worn out and was sent home in May for a rest on half pay until 16th August 1919. He then assumed command of British Forces in Palestine and on 14th October also British Forces in Cairo, Egypt, until 15th April 1923. During this time he was responsible for the evacuation of British troops from Syria when it was handed over to France following the Treaty of Versailles. Promotion to general followed on 25th November 1922 and on 16th April 1923 he was appointed General Officer Commanding-in-Chief Southern Command, stationed at Salisbury, Wiltshire. He was appointed ADC General

The memorial to General Sir Walter Norris Congreve on the southwest coast of Malta, overlooking the tiny island of Filfola. He chose to be buried at sea in this area as it was a favourite fishing spot.

Reconnaissance Française or Medal of French Gratitude, created on 13th July 1917 by the French government to express its gratitude to those who, without obligation, came to the aid of the injured, disabled and refugees or performed an act of exceptional dedication in the presence of the enemy. The last award was made in 1959.

The Belgian Médaille de la Reine Elisabeth (Queen Elisabeth Medal) was created on 15th September 1915 to recognise exceptional service to Belgium in the relief of suffering of its citizens. Recipients who worked in hospitals received a variant with a red enamelled cross in the suspension wreath.

to King George V on 29th March 1924. His last appointment was Governor and Commander-in-Chief of Malta on 20th June 1924 until his death there on 27th February 1927. He was buried at sea from HMS *Chrysanthemum* between Malta and Filfola on 4th March. Walter and his son William are one of only three father and son VC pairs and the only pair in the same Regiment.

Billy's mother, Cecilia Henrietta Dolores née La Touche (1867–1952), was born in India. Walter and Cecilia were married at St Jude's Church, London on 3rd June 1890. They purchased Chartley Castle, Staffordshire in 1911. She served as a nurse in Belgium and France during the Great War and was awarded the Reconnaissance Française and the Belgian Médaille de la Reine Elisabeth for being one of the last nurses to leave Antwerp with the wounded in 1914. She was also awarded the French Croix de Guerre for her coolness and bravery when the hospital where she was nursing at Rosières-aux-Salines, near Nancy, was shelled and bombed by aircraft in 1918.

Bill's paternal grandfather was William Congreve (1831–1902), born at Newcastle upon Tyne, Northumberland. He joined the 4th (King's Own) Regiment as an ensign in 1849 and later transferred to the 29th Regiment, rising to captain. He was Brigade Major, Chatham Garrison, when his son Walter was born. He resigned in 1866 and became Chief Constable of Staffordshire until 1888. During his tenure there was much unrest in the industrial areas, including the 1874 election riots at Wednesbury, Stoke-on-Trent and Wolverhampton. He married Fanny Emma née Townshend (c.1837–1924) at St Mary, Great Budworth in 1862 and they had eight children in addition to Walter. The family lived at The Hollies, Castle Church, Staffordshire and later at Congreve Manor, Staffordshire and Burton Hall, Burton Road, Cheshire.

Billy's maternal grandfather was Captain Charles William Blount La Touche (1835–67). He was from an old Huguenot family, descended from David Digues De La Touche, who went to Holland after the Revocation of the Edict of Nantes and served under Prince William of Orange (later William III of England), distinguishing himself at the Battle of the Boyne in 1690. He settled in Dublin, where he established the first bank in Ireland. Charles served as a captain and political agent in the Bombay Staff Corps at Kathiawar. He distinguished himself on several occasions during the Indian Mutiny, in particular at Sumnassa on 3rd November 1857, where he, Lieutenant Henry Hebbert and four Sepoys (all 17th Bombay Native Infantry), rescued a comrade from the enemy under very heavy fire. Lieutenants La Touche and Hebbert were recommended for, but did not receive, the VC. The four Sepoys were awarded the Indian Order of Merit 3rd Class. Had Charles received the VC, his daughter, Cecilia, would have had the unique distinction of being the daughter, wife and mother of VCs. Charles married Rosa Wilhelmina 'Minna' née Müller (c.1845–1930), born in Valparaiso, Chile, on 26th July 1866 at Saint James, Westminster. Charles was killed in action at Macherba, Kathiawar, India on 29th December 1867. Rose married the Reverend James William Rynd BA (born c.1838) in May 1871 at Barnet, Hertfordshire. He was Rector of Basted, Kent in 1881. They had eight children: Evelyne Elsye Rynd 1872, Minna Henrietta Augusta Rynd c.1874, Charles William Rynd 1874, Winifred L Rynd 1876, Reginald Fleming Rynd and Francis Fleetwood Rynd 1877, Leonora Charlotte Maude Rynd c.1880 and Denys Ashley Fearon Rynd 1883.

Amongst Billy's aunts and uncles were:

- Winifred Mary Congreve (1872–1938), married Captain John Steuart Mackenzie Shea (1869–1966) in 1902. He was commissioned in the Royal Irish Regiment 11th February 1888 and transferred to the Indian Army, rising through the ranks to retire in 1932 as General Sir John Shea GCB KCMG DSO. On 9th December 1917 he received the keys of the city of Jerusalem.
- Dorothy Lee Congreve (1874–1953) married Major Arthur Montague King (1869–1915), 4th Rifle Brigade, in 1897. He was commissioned on 3rd May 1893 and served on the North West Frontier 1897–98 in the Tochi Valley and in South Africa 1901–02. He was appointed Adjutant with the Militia 26th Mar 1902 – 25th March 1907 and was promoted major on 23rd December 1909. Arthur was killed at St Eloi on 15th March 1915 (Ypres (Menin Gate) Memorial). Billy managed to reach his uncle's body on 4th May and recover some items from it but, as it was within thirty metres of the German lines, he was unable to bring it back for proper burial.
- Francis Lane Congreve (1881–1962) was serving with his battery at Ciry on the Aisne front in September 1914 when Billy visited him. He was commissioned on 19th December 1900, promoted lieutenant 19th December 1903, captain 6th January 1913, major 20th July 1915, acting lieutenant colonel 6th June 1918 – 7th June 1919 and lieutenant colonel on 26th February 1929. He was an adjutant with the Territorial Force 1st February 1910 – 31st January 1914 and with a regular unit 5th January – 19th July 1915. He served in South Africa 1901–02 and in France and Belgium from 16th August 1914 until the end of the war. During the First World War he was awarded the DSO and MC and was Mentioned in Despatches four times (LG 19th October 1914, 4th January 1917, 23rd December 1918 and 7th July 1919). He married Evelyn Gertrude Knaggs in 1909 and they had two daughters, Gweneth Isolda Congreve 1911–25 and Frances Hope Congreve 1914.
- Leonora 'Nora' Charlotte Maude Rynd (born c.1880) married Lieutenant Murray MacGregor Lockhart RN (born 1871) in 1902, son of Sir William Stephen Alexander Lockhart (1841–1900). Murray served in the Royal Navy until 18th October 1909 and was recalled in 1914 to be Divisional Naval Transport Officer (MID, LG 7th June 1918 and OBE, LG 4th July 1919). They had three children.

Billy is related to the Restoration playwright, William Congreve (1670–1729) and Sir William Congreve (1722–1828). Sir William was Superintendent of the Royal Laboratory, Woolwich and invented the Congreve Rocket used by the British in the Napoleonic Wars and War of 1812. 'The Star Spangled Banner', the American national anthem, comes from a poem, *Defence of Fort McHenry*, by Francis Scott Key after witnessing the bombardment of the Fort by the Royal Navy. The poem was set to the tune of a popular British song at the time, which with various lyrics

The Restoration period playwright and poet, William Congreve (1670–1729). He is buried in Poet's Corner in Westminster Abbey (Sir Godfrey Kneller).

A Royal Navy ship firing rockets at the time of the War of 1812.

was also popular in America. It was recognized for US Navy use in 1889 and by President Woodrow Wilson in 1916, but did not become the national anthem officially until 3rd March 1931. 'The Star Spangled Banner' mentions Congreve's rockets, fired from HMS *Erebus*:

Sir William Congreve, inventor of the Congreve rocket, succeeded his father, Lieutenant General Sir William Congreve, as second Baronet Congreve in 1814. He had a very varied career. In 1803 he joined the London and Westminster Light Horse. He published the Royal Standard and Political Register newspaper until turning to inventing. The British came up against rockets used by Indian forces in the late 18th Century. In 1801 the Royal Arsenal began its own development, but it was not successful. In 1804, Congreve began experimenting and by the following year solid fuel rockets were sufficiently advanced to be used operationally by the Royal Navy at Boulogne. In 1807, 300 rockets were used in the bombardment of Copenhagen. They were then in general use for the rest of the Napoleonic Wars at sea and on land. During the War of 1812, Congreve's rockets achieved immortality at the siege of Fort McHenry, being described in a poem that eventually became the US national anthem; ***And the rocket's red glare, the bombs bursting in air.*** In 1814, Congreve became Comptroller of the Royal Laboratory at Woolwich, a post previously held by his father. Because of his expertise, Congreve organised the fireworks displays in London for the Peace of 1814 and the Coronation of George IV in 1821. In 1812 he became MP for the rotten borough of Gatton and in 1818 became MP for Plymouth. Later he was chairman of the Equitable Loan Bank and director of the Arigna Iron and Coal Company, Palladium Insurance Company and Peruvian Mining Company. Charged with fraud in 1826 in connection with the Arigna Company, he fled to France and died in Toulouse in May 1828 (James Lonsdale).

Oh, say! can you see by the dawn's early light
What so proudly we hailed at the twilight's last gleaming;
Whose broad stripes and bright stars, through the perilous fight,
O'er the ramparts we watched were so gallantly streaming?
And the rocket's red glare, the bombs bursting in air,
Gave proof through the night that our flag was still there:
Oh, say! does that star-spangled banner yet wave
O'er the land of the free and the home of the brave?

Billy is also distantly related to three other VCs in addition to his father:

Fenton John Aylmer VC KCB, through his paternal great grandmother, whose sister, Elizabeth Frances Bayly, married William Josiah Aylmer, paternal great uncle of Fenton John Aylmer VC.

John Augustus Conolly VC, through Billy's great great aunt, Mary La Touche, who was Conolly's maternal aunt.

Frederick Francis Maude VC, through his marriage to Maude's great niece, Pamela Cynthia Maude.

Billy had two brothers:

- Commander Sir Geoffrey Cecil Congreve DSO RN (1897–1941) served as a lieutenant (15th June 1918) in the Royal Navy during the First World War and was ADC to the GOC-in-C Egypt and Palestine 1920–21. He married Helena Madeline Mary Allhusen (1897–1956) at St James's Church, Piccadilly on 14th October 1922. Among the guests were Princess Christian and Princess Helena Victoria. Geoffrey and Helena had three children: Ann Henrietta Congreve 1923, Marygold Elizabeth Congreve 1926 and Carola Congreve 1929. On the death of his father, he was created Baron Congreve on 30th June 1927; the title became extinct on his own death. Geoffrey retired from the Royal Navy on 25th August 1928, but was recalled in the Second World War as a commander with seniority from 19th July 1937 and served at the Signal School from 23rd August 1939. Geoffrey was awarded the DSO (LG 26th September 1940) and was Mentioned in Despatches (LG 26th July 1940) for the Norwegian Campaign whilst commanding HMS *Aston Villa* (FY 261) (took command 17th January 1940), an anti-submarine trawler in 16th Anti-Submarine Striking Force. She was heavily damaged on 30th April 1940 by German dive-bombers in Kroken Bay, Namsos Fjord, Norway and was scuttled on 3rd May. He then commanded a Dutch vessel, *Jupiter*, 10th August – 21st October and on 12th May 1941 was appointed to the shore based HMS *Quebec*, the Combined Operations Training Centre at Inveraray, under

HMS *Aston Villa*, an anti-submarine trawler taken over by the Admiralty on 29th September 1939 and commanded by Sir Geoffrey Congreve. During the Norwegian Campaign she was damaged by German dive-bombers on 30th April 1940 and scuttled on 3rd May in Kroken Bay, Namsos Fjord. Sir Geoffrey was awarded the DSO and was also Mentioned in Despatches for this action.

Commodore Warren. On 28th July 1941, he was observing Operation Chess, a raid by sixteen men of 12 Commando at Ambleteuse, from a landing craft when he was hit by a stray machine-gun bullet and killed. His death was registered at Dover in addition to the CWGC. Geoffrey appears to have been the only casualty; the commandos remained ashore for an hour, no prisoners were taken and there were no casualties in the withdrawal. He was cremated at Golders Green Crematorium, Middlesex. Helena married Reginald James Tyler, a retired Ceylon police officer, at the King's Chapel of the Savoy on 21st October 1942. He was the father of Richard Michael Townsend Tyler (1916–2009) through his first marriage. Richard married Helena's daughter, Henrietta, in 1944 and they had four children. Richard was commissioned in the Royal

HMS *Quebec*, the Combined Operations Training Centre at Inveraray, where Sir Geoffrey Congreve was based until his death off the French coast on 28th July 1941 during Operation Chess.

Engineers on 7th September 1940 (145254) and served in 7th Armoured Division Support Group, commanded by Brigadier Jock Campbell, who went on to win the VC. Richard was hit in the thigh by shrapnel during the Battle of Sidi Rezegh in late 1941. The leg was amputated. Following convalesce in South Africa he returned to Britain and went into an architect's partnership with Tom Bird DSO MC, whom he met in a Cairo military hospital. He was involved in alterations to Salisbury Cathedral and many other ancient and classical building projects, including Forde Abbey in Dorset, Wrotham Park, Knebworth House and Lord Burton's Dochfour, overlooking Loch Ness.

- Major Arthur Christopher John Congreve (1903–92) accompanied his father on a visit to the trenches at Hooge in August 1915 aged twelve and dressed in his Boy Scout uniform. He was in France for the summer holidays, helping his mother at the Anglo-American hospital at Ris-Orangis, south of Paris. He was commissioned in the Rifle Brigade on 30th August 1923 and was promoted lieutenant 30th August 1925, captain 1st September 1936 and major 30th August 1940. On 1st March 1926, he was appointed ADC to his father, Governor and Commander-in-Chief Malta. He was Assistant Provost Marshal 15th April 1937 – 30th October 1939 and served throughout the Second World War. He retired in 1946. Arthur married four times:
    - Rosemary Minna Robinson Thurburn (1906–93) in 1927. They had a daughter, Audrey Melissa Congreve, in 1928. They divorced in 1933.
    - Janet Henrietta Cross (née Curtis) (born 1908), widow of Commander William Kenneth Ramsden Cross RN and elder daughter of Vice Admiral Berwick Curtis CB CMG DSO, in 1943. They divorced prior to 1951.
    - Jessie Violet Betty Onslow (née Gillam) (1909–93), daughter of Brigadier General Reynold Alexander Gillam CMG DSO, in 1951. She was the widow of Captain Richard Francis John Onslow MVO DSC RN (1896–1942), who was commanding HMS *Hermes* with the Eastern Fleet when she was attacked by Japanese carrier-based aircraft on 9th April 1942 off the coast of Ceylon. *Hermes* was hit by forty 250 lbs bombs. He was one of 306 of the ship's company lost and is commemorated on the Plymouth Naval Memorial. Arthur and Jesse divorced in 1956.
    - Audrey née Lester, daughter of Dr Alexander Lester, of Bermuda, in 1956. They had three children – Simon Congreve 1957, Nicola Congreve 1958 and Tristram Alexander Congreve 1964.

Billy was educated at Miss Linton's Day School in Farnborough, Summerfields School in Oxford 1899–1902, Eton May 1903 – July 1907, and then by RK Cardew in a crammer in London in preparation for Sandhurst September 1907 – December 1908 and Messrs Carlisle and Gregson from January 1909. In his early years he suffered from rheumatic fever and convalesced with family friends, Edward Hudson (founder of Country Life magazine) and his wife at Lindisfarne Castle. The Hudsons were childless and, had William survived, he would have

Eton College, attended by Billy Congreve from May 1903 until July 1907. Thereafter he was taught by tutors in a crammer in London in preparation for entering Sandhurst. This was a common practice at the time.

inherited the estate. He joined the Royal Military College Sandhurst later in 1909. Having passed out in second place, he was commissioned into the Rifle Brigade on 4th March 1911. He joined the 3rd Battalion at Moore Park Camp, Tipperary, Ireland and was promoted lieutenant on 1st February 1913.

3rd Rifle Brigade sailed for Holyhead, Anglesey aboard SS *Patriotic* on 17th August 1914 and moved to Cambridge and Newmarket. It embarked at Southampton on the Canadian Pacific Steamship SS *Lake Michigan* on 10th September 1914 and arrived at St Nazaire on the 12th. Billy became ADC to Major General Hubert Hamilton, GOC 3rd Division, on 23rd September vice Lieutenant RT Hammick RA. One of his first tasks as ADC on 27th September was to accompany a VIP guest on a visit to the front:

SS *Lake Michigan*, launched by Swan Hunter in 1901 and operated by Canadian Pacific Steamships from 1903. She was sunk by U-100 on 16th April 1918.

This afternoon who should turn up at HQ but Winston Churchill. He wanted 'to see things', so HH handed him over to my tender care with orders to take him up to the observation station above Chassemy [overlooking the River Aisne]. *He was dressed as a Trinity Brother – blue coat, brass buttons, etc. We went up in his car to just short of Chassemy…. The car was a beauty, a 60–hp Rolls-Royce. Half-way there WC asked me, 'Are you quite sure there are no parties of Germans inside our lines?' …. I said I was sure there were none. However, this did not satisfy him and I had to get his revolver out from his coat pocket, a very fierce looking weapon which he held ready for action on his knee. I was a bit scared of that revolver, as it was one of those patent beasts that you 'pull the trigger and the gun does the rest' sort of thing. However, it didn't get going. When I got the car behind the Brenelle ridge, I told them to wait while I went up to see if things were fairly quiet. Only a few shells were coming over, so I took him up to the observation station from where one gets an excellent view over the river. There wasn't much to see, but a few of their shells came gurgling over, and I was glad when they were safely over and bursting well behind us, for I am by no means used to them yet myself. One sees a column of mud and smoke and then the crash of the explosion. We got away without any excitement, after he had grandiloquently exclaimed: 'Now I have been under fire in five continents.' …*

When Hubert Hamilton was killed by shrapnel on 14th October 1914 (Cheriton (St Martin) Churchyard, Folkestone, Kent), Billy continued as ADC to his successors, Major Generals CJ Mackenzie until 29th October, FDV Wing until 21st November and JAL Haldane thereafter. He was promoted captain on 6th June 1915 and appointed General Staff Officer Grade 3 with HQ 3rd Division on 15th July vice Brevet Lieutenant Colonel ARC Sanders. Appointed Brigade Major of 76th Brigade on 10th December vice Temporary Major Viscount RG Howick, Northumberland Fusiliers. **Awarded the French Croix de Chevalier of the Legion d'Honneur on 15th October 1915 for his work during the Second Battle of Ypres, LG 24th February 1916.** It was presented by General de Boiselle, GOC of the French XXX Corps, at a joint parade on 6th November. **Awarded the MC for his actions at Hooge in November 1915, LG 14th January 1916.**

Awarded the DSO for his actions at the Bluff, St Eloi, Belgium on 27th March 1916, LG 16th May 1916. An unknown number of Germans occupying No.5 Crater started firing on the attackers from behind. Billy realised that some Germans were willing to surrender while others were not. He thought bluff might work and instructed an officer and four men to follow him, including his orderly. With his revolver drawn he dashed for the Crater under fire, but was not hit. At the rim of the crater, he looked in, *Imagine my surprise and horror when I saw a whole crowed of armed Boches! I stood there for a moment feeling a bit short of shy, and then I levelled my revolver at the nearest Boche and shouted, 'Hands up, all the lot of you!' A few went up at once, then a few more and then the lot; and I felt the proudest fellow in the world as I cursed them.* He captured two officers and seventy-two soldiers and was recommended for the VC by Brigadier General RJ Kentish, commanding 76th Brigade on 6th April, but it was downgraded to the DSO on 22nd April.

Crater No.5 at St Eloi is now a pond in a private garden and can only be glimpsed through the gateway. The crater is in the dip to the left of the chalet. Billy Congreve would have approached it from the right rear on 27th March 1916. On the same day and in the same area, Captain Reverend Edward Noel Mellish, attached to 4th Royal Fusiliers, 9th Brigade, 3rd Division, won the VC.

Billy Congreve married Pamela Cynthia née Maude (16th July 1893 – 20th October 1975) on 1st June 1916 at

St Martin in the Fields, London. She was living at 15 Queen Anne's Gate, London, at the time, the London residence of Edward Hudson. They honeymooned at Beaulieu for a few days before he returned to the front; Pamela never saw Billy again. Billy and Pamela had a daughter, Mary Gloria Congreve (21st March 1917 – 1992). She married Augustus William Stephenson (1909–2000) on 19th April 1939 at St Martin in the Fields, London. He was the son of Sir Guy Stephenson CB and Gwendolen Talbot. Pamela and Augustus had a son, Martin Guy Stephenson 1942. The marriage ended in divorce in 1956 and, later that year, Mary married Byrne Warman (c.1910–60) at Hitchin.

Billy Congreve and Pamela Cynthia Maude at their wedding in London on 1st June 1916.

Pamela Maude's father was Cyril Francis Maude (1862–1851). He was educated at Charterhouse and moved to the USA in 1883 for a career in the theatre. He was noted for being a quietly humorous actor. He returned to London to become co-manager of the Theatre Royal, Haymarket, with Frederick Harrison 1896–1905. In 1906 he became lessee and manager of The Playhouse Theatre, Northumberland Avenue. Cyril starred in several films in the 1930s, including *Grumpy*, and in 1947 appeared in *While the Sun Shines*. In 1905 he succeeded Sir Henry Irving as President of the Actors' Orphanage Fund (later the Actors' Charitable Trust), establishing the first orphanage for actors' children at Croydon, Surrey and inaugurating fundraising events, which attracted royal patronage, and secured committee members from among leading actors of the day.

St Martin in the Fields, where Billy and Pamela were married, in the centre at the rear of Trafalgar Square.

Cyril married Maud Isabel Winifred M née Emery (1862–1924), daughter of Samuel Anderson Emery and granddaughter of John Emery, both well-known actors of their day, in 1888 at Kensington, London. She made her first appearance in Liverpool in 1870 and played the lead in many West End productions until 1923, often alongside her husband. In addition to Pamela, Cyril and Maud also had:

Pamela Maude's father, Cyril Francis Maude, was an actor and theatre manager, who was also President of the Actors' Orphanage Fund.

Pamela Congreve with her daughter, Mary Gloria Congreve, born on 21st March 1917 (Tatler).

- Margery Kathleen Maude (1889–1979) became a well-known actress, appearing on Broadway 1913–65 and in a number of films and on television. She married Joseph Warren Burden in 1917 in New York and they had three children.
- John Cyril Maude (1901–86) was educated at Eton and Christ Church, Oxford. He was called to the Bar (Middle Temple) 1925 and became a King's Counsel in 1943. During the Second World War he was a Civil Assistant at the War Office before being commissioned in the Intelligence Corps on 8th June 1940. Promoted War Substantive captain 8th September 1940 and honorary major 14th November 1942. He worked in the War Cabinet offices from 1942 and was transferred to the Unemployed List from October 1945. He was elected MP for Exeter in the 1945 general election and stood down in 1951. He was a judge at the City of London Court 1954–65 and at the Central Criminal Court 1965–68. He was chairman of the Old Vic Trust 1951–54 and of the British Drama League 1952–54. He married Rosamund Murray (1904–63) of Boston, Massachusetts in 1927. They divorced in 1955 and he married Maureen Constance Buchanan (born 1907) in the same year, daughter of the Hon Arthur Ernest Guinness. Maureen was married twice previously: first, to Basil Sheridan Hamilton-Temple-Blackwood in 1930, son of the 4th Marquis of Dufferin and Ava of Clandeboye, Co Down. Basil was Parliamentary Under Secretary of State for the Colonies 1937–40 and Director of the Empire Division, Ministry of Information 1941–42. He then served as a captain in the Royal Horse Guards and was killed in action on 25th March 1945 in Burma (Rangoon Memorial).

Secondly, she was married to Harry Alexander Desmond Buchanan in 1948. The marriage ended in divorce in 1954.

In addition to their children, Cyril and his wife also raised a niece, Winifred Isabel Emery (1890–1972), after she was abandoned by her parents, Frederick Arthur Emery (1864–1930) and Gertrude Turner (1861–1969) in 1895. Winifred married Leslie Noel Gascoyne (1886–1969) and had three sons, including David Emery Gascoyne (1916–2001), the novelist and poet.

Back in France, Billy was appointed brevet major on 3rd June 1916. **Awarded the VC for actions at Longueval, France 6th-20th July 1916, LG 26th October 1916.** He was the first officer to be awarded the VC, DSO and MC. Billy Congreve was killed in action at Longueval, France, on 20th July 1916 and is buried in Corbie Communal Cemetery Extension – I F 35. His father bade his son farewell with a kiss and placed a posy of poppies, cornflowers and daisies in his hand. The other chief mourner was Private Cameron, Billy's batman. Other men carried wild poppies and cornflowers to lay on his grave.

Probate was granted to his widow – he left £170/15/6. She received all three gallantry medals from the King at Buckingham Palace on 1st November 1916. Billy was Mentioned in Sir John French's Despatches dated 14th January and 30th November 1915, LG 17th February 1915 and 1st January 1916 respectively. He was also Mentioned in Sir Douglas Haig's Despatches dated 30th April and 13th November 1916, LG 15th June 1916 and 4th January 1917 respectively.

Pamela married Major (later Brigadier) The Honorable William Fraser DSO MC Gordon Highlanders (1890–1964) at St George's, Hanover Square on 22nd December 1919. He was the son of Lord Alexander William Fraser, 18th Earl of Saltoun, and had been Billy's best man. William was commissioned on 27th July 1910 and served in Egypt and India before France and Belgium in the First World War: 5th October – 5th November 1914; 15th March 1915 – 21st June 1916; and April 1917 to the end of the war. Initially he was machine-gun officer of 2nd Gordon Highlanders and was wounded during First Ypres. He held various appointments, including staff captain 27th Infantry Brigade November 1915 – April 1916, then brigade major 151st Infantry Brigade until late June. He commanded 1/6th Gordon Highlanders at Ypres and Cambrai in 1917. As an acting lieutenant colonel he was Commandant of a School of

Billy Congreve's grave in Corbie Communal Cemetery Extension is next to the entrance and stands slightly apart and at an angle to the other graves.

Instruction in France February – September 1918. In addition to the DSO and MC, he was Mentioned in Despatches three times (LG 1st January 1916, 21st December 1917 and 9th July 1919). After the war he was an instructor at Sandhurst April 1919 – January 1921, followed by adjutant of his battalion and then the brigade major in Eastern Command until January 1929, when he transferred to the Grenadier Guards. In February 1931, he became Military Attaché in Brussels and The Hague until February 1935 and then commanded 1st Grenadier Guards for a year. In August 1938 he was appointed Military Attaché at the British Embassy in Paris. In February 1940 he took command of 24th Infantry Brigade and took it to Norway, where he was wounded. After the evacuation from Norway, the brigade became part of the London defences. In June 1941, he took command of 8th Infantry Brigade until March 1942 and that October he took command of 228th Infantry Brigade in the Shetlands until it disbanded in September 1943. He retired in 1944 with the honorary rank of brigadier. After the war he was Chief of the UN Relief and Rehabilitation Administration in Paris.

William and Pamela's son, David William Fraser (1920–2012), was educated at Eton, but left when war broke out. The Army did not need him immediately, so in January 1940 he went up to Christ Church College, Oxford. While there he was arrested for throwing eggs at a communist anti-war march. He enlisted as a private in 8th Royal Berkshire and was made a junior NCO. At Sandhurst he was slightly injured in a German bombing raid. He was commissioned in the Grenadier Guards on 4th April 1941 and served with 2nd (Armoured) Battalion. He was one of the first to reach Brussels in September 1944 after the breakout from Normandy and at the Royal Palace found the Queen Mother (Elisabeth), who shook every one of them by the hand. On patrol in Holland in a scout car he spotted the barrel of a machine-gun protruding through a hedge. He was about to open fire when he realised it was a group of Dutch children playing soldiers; the image haunted him for the rest of his life. He was a company commander in 3rd Battalion in Malaya during the Emergency in 1948–49, attended Staff College, was Brigade Major of 1st Guards Brigade October 1952 – October 1954 and commanded 1st Grenadier Guards 1960–62, including a deployment to Cameroon (OBE). As a brigadier he commanded 19th Brigade in the UK Strategic Reserve December 1963 – November 1965, including in Sarawak during the Indonesian Confrontation. He commanded 4th Division in Germany October 1969 – October 1971, was Vice Chief of the General Staff April 1973 – August 1975 (KCB), ADC General to Queen Elizabeth II 1977–80 and, as a general, was UK Military Representative to the NATO Military Committee October 1975 – October 1977. His final appointment was Commandant of the Royal College of Defence Studies 1978–80 (GCB), following which he became a prolific author. He was also Colonel of the Royal Hampshire Regiment 1981–87, Deputy Lieutenant Hampshire 1982 and Vice Lord Lieutenant Hampshire 1988–96. He married Anne Balfour in 1947 and they had a daughter, Antonia Isabella Fraser, in 1949.

General Sir David William Fraser as a major in the 1950s.

The marriage was dissolved and he married Julia FO de la Hey in 1957. They had four children: Arabella Katherine Fraser 1958, Alexander James Fraser 1960, Lucy Caroline Fraser 1965 and Simon William Fraser.

In addition to the VC, DSO and MC, Billy Congreve was awarded the 1914 Star, British War Medal 1914–20, Victory Medal 1914–19 with Mentioned-in-Despatches Oakleaf and the French Legion of Honour. His daughter, Mary, sold his medals for £26,000 on 30th June 1983 at Sotheby's to buy a house in Spain. They are held by the Royal Green Jackets (Rifles) Museum, Peninsula Barracks, Winchester. Billy is commemorated on:

- A panel of the Rifle Brigade Memorial in Winchester Cathedral.
- A panel at Stow-by-Chartley Church, Staffordshire.
- A plaque in Corbie Abbey, close to where he is buried.
- On the Eton College Cloisters For Valour Memorial.

3055 PRIVATE THOMAS COOKE
8th Australian Infantry Battalion AIF

Thomas Cooke was born on 5th July 1881 at Kaikoura, Marlborough, New Zealand. His father, Thomas Cooke (c.1855–1943), born in England, was a carpenter who emigrated to New Zealand. He was known as Tom and appears as such in some official records. His mother was Caroline Anne née Cooper (1861–1941). She married Thomas on 2nd March 1881 at Kaikoura. Thomas junior had three sisters:

- Catherine Cooke (5th February 1883 – 1918), married Charles Albert Oldman (1877–1950) in 1904. They had seven children: Albert Dudley Oldman 1904–88; Hugh Charles Oldman 1906; Thelma Catherine Oldman 1908–2003; Robert Frank Oldman 1909–93; Geoffrey Ernest Oldman 1910–99; Hilda Annie Oldman 1912–2002, married Arthur James Burge in 1937, who served as a sergeant in the New Zealand Engineers during the Second World War; and Jack Stanley Oldman 1913. Charles married Helen Catherine Gulliver

Cradwick in 1920 and they had a son, Patrick Charles Oldman, in 1923. Patrick served as Aircraftman 1st Class RNZAF (431964) and died on active service on 18 April 1944 (Bourail New Zealand War Cemetery, New Caledonia – Plot 8, Grave 2).

- Flora Cooke, born on 12th May 1885, died unmarried in 1905.
- Ethel Cooke, born on 2nd May 1887, died in 1918.

Thomas was educated at Kaikoura Demonstration High School. Afterwards he was employed as a carpenter and builder in Wellington. He played cornet in Jupp's Band and the Wellington Garrison Band. Thomas married Maud Elizabeth née Elliott (born 1881) on 4th June 1902 and they had three children:

- Ethel Maud Cooke, born in 1903. She married George Wilson in 1925.
- Reginald Thomas Arthur Cooke, born on 1st November 1904. He died in 1925.
- Florence Mildred Cooke (1907–95). She married Ernest James McQuade (1896–1980) in 1929.

In 1912 they moved to Melbourne, Victoria, Australia, where Thomas continued working as a builder. The family settled at 51 Gardiner Street, Richmond and Thomas joined the Ancient Order of Foresters.

Thomas enlisted in the Australian Imperial Force on 16th February 1915 in Melbourne. He was described as 5′ 6″ tall, weighed 145 lbs, with dark complexion, light brown eyes, black hair and his religious denomination was Church of England. He was posted to Broadmeadows Camp before moving to 1st Depot Battalion at Seymour, Victoria. Appointed acting corporal 25th November 1915 – 23rd February 1916 while with the 7th Reinforcement Group for the 24th Battalion, with which

Wellington Garrison Band February 1905 (Sir George Grey Special Collections, Auckland Libraries).

Broadmeadows Camp in 1915.

HMAT A73 *Commonwealth* was built for Wilhelm Lund's Blue Anchor Line in 1902 for the Australia route. The fleet was taken over by P&O in 1910. She served as a troopship until 23rd June 1917 and was sold for scrap in 1923.

he sailed for the Middle East from Melbourne on HMAT *Commonwealth* on 26th November 1915. He disembarked at Alexandria, Egypt and was posted to 6th Training Battalion at Heliopolis, until transferring to 8th Battalion at Serapeum on 24th February 1916, having relinquished his acting rank.

While he was abroad, his family lived c/o Mrs W Richardson, Sugarloaf Road, Brooklyn, Wellington, New Zealand and also at 139 Ohiro Road, Brooklyn. The battalion embarked at Alexandria on HMT *Megantic* on 26th March and disembarked at Marseilles, France on 31st March. It travelled north for operations in France and Flanders.

Awarded the VC for his actions at Pozières on 24th/25th July 1916, LG 9th September 1916. He was killed during his VC action and is commemorated on the Villers-Bretonneux Memorial, France. On 20th September his wife wrote to the Minister of Defence at St Kilda Road, Melbourne asking why she had read about the award of the VC in newspapers, but no official had been in contact with her beforehand. The VC was presented to her by The Earl of Liverpool, Governor-General of New Zealand, at Wellington on 2nd February 1917.

In addition to the VC, he was awarded the British War Medal 1914–20 and Victory Medal 1914–19. The VC is held on loan by the Army Museum, State Highway 1, Waiouru, New Zealand. Thomas Cooke is commemorated in a number of places:

SS *Megantic* (14,878 tons) was built for the White Star Line in 1908 for the Canadian route. Her maiden voyage from Liverpool to Montreal was on 17th June 1909. When war broke out she was briefly on the Liverpool - New York route until requisitioned as a troopship in 1915. She was attacked by U-*43* in 1917, but managed to escape. After a refit in 1919, she returned to the Canadian service. Dr Crippen was returned to Britain from Canada after his arrest on the *Megantic*. She was laid up in 1931 and sold for scrap in 1933.

Arthur William de Brito Savile Foljambe, 2nd Earl of Liverpool GCB GCMG GBE MVO PC DL JP (1870–1941), served in the Boer War and in 1907 succeeded to the earldom. In 1912 he became the last Governor of New Zealand and the first Governor-General, serving until 1920.

The port of Marseilles.

The Villers-Bretonneux Memorial, where Thomas Cooke is commemorated. The views from the tower are stunning.

- Cooke Street, Canberra, Australian Capital Territory.
- Cooke Street, Bittern, Melbourne, Victoria, on the Victoria Cross Estate built in 1916–18.
- A memorial at Victoria Cross Park, Campbell, Canberra, dedicated on 24th July 2000, commemorates the ninety-six Australians who have been awarded the Victoria Cross.

The 8th Infantry Battalion panel bearing Thomas Cooke's name.

Kaikoura War Memorial (Francis Vallance).

- Victoria Cross Memorial, Queen Victoria Building, George Street, Sydney, New South Wales.
- Named on one of eleven plaques honouring 175 men from overseas awarded the VC for the Great War. The plaques were unveiled by the Senior Minister of State at the Foreign & Commonwealth Office and Minister for Faith and Communities, Baroness Warsi, at a reception at Lancaster House, London on 26th June 2014 attended by the Duke of Kent and relatives of the VC recipients. The Australian plaque is at the Australian War Memorial in Canberra and the New Zealand plaque is mounted on a wall between Parliament and the Cenotaph in Wellington.
- Kaikoura War Memorial.
- In 2010 a new barracks was named after him at Linton Military Camp, near Palmerston North.
- The Secretary of State for Communities and Local 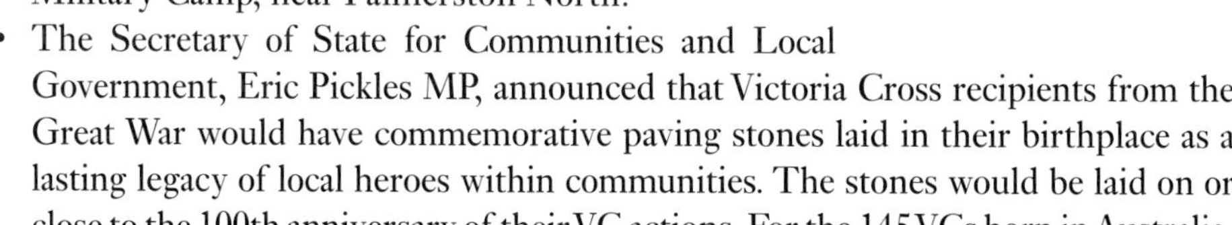 Government, Eric Pickles MP, announced that Victoria Cross recipients from the Great War would have commemorative paving stones laid in their birthplace as a lasting legacy of local heroes within communities. The stones would be laid on or close to the 100th anniversary of their VC actions. For the 145 VCs born in Australia, Belgium, Canada, China, Denmark, Egypt, France, Germany, India, Iraq, Japan, Nepal, Netherlands, New Zealand, Pakistan, South Africa, Sri Lanka, Ukraine and the United States of America, individual commemorative stones were unveiled at the National Memorial Arboretum, Alrewas, Staffordshire by Prime Minister David Cameron MP and Sergeant Johnson Beharry VC on 5th March 2015.

A rather grainy newspaper photograph of Maud Cooke with her children Ethel, Reginald and Florence at about the time of Thomas' death.

Maud married Thomas Ebenezer Clapperton in 1920. He served as a private in the Canterbury Infantry Battalion (6/599) in the war and was from Loch Maben, Dumfriesshire, Scotland. Maud and Thomas lived at 59 Mein Street, Newtown, Wellington.

SECOND LIEUTENANT GABRIEL GEORGES COURY
3rd (attached 1/4th) Battalion, The Prince of Wales's Volunteers (South Lancashire Regiment) (Pioneers)

Gabriel Coury was born at 16 Croxteth Grove, Toxteth, Liverpool, Lancashire on 13th June 1896. He was born on St Anthony's feast day and the name sometimes appears amongst his middle names. His father, Raphaél Coury (c.1859–1903), was Turkish of Armenian origin and was born in Alexandria, Egypt. He was a merchant trading throughout the Ottoman Empire in cotton and silk. With his brother, Basile, he set up the firm Coury & Company, General Merchants, at 62 The Albany Building, Old Hall Street, Liverpool, Lancashire. Gabriel's mother, Marie née Dagher (1873–1957), was born in Beirut, Lebanon. She was a French Maronite Christian, but became naturalised British on 26th June 1906. One of her sponsors was James Philip (later Colonel Sir James) Reynolds (1865–1932), President of the Liverpool Cotton Association. The family lived at 139 Granby Street, Liverpool. In 1891 Basile retired and handed the business to Raphaél before returning to Egypt. Raphaél's family moved to 16 Croxteth Grove, Toxteth in 1893 and later to The Mount, Waterloo Park, Liverpool where he died on 10th March 1903. Marie wound up the family firm and moved to 22 The Esplanade, Waterloo, by 1906. By 1929, she was living at 43 Canning Street, Liverpool and had moved to Flat 4, 64 Holland Park Avenue, Kensington, London in 1932 with her son Ernest and daughters Louisa and Aimeé. They had moved to 47 Fitzgeorge Avenue, West Kensington by 1934. Marie Coury died on 17th November 1957, leaving £949/5/8 to her son Charles. Gabriel had six siblings:

Granby Street, Liverpool.

- Sophie Victorine Coury born 1888.
- Charles John Raphaél Coury (1889–1970), born in Alexandria, Egypt, became a ring trader with Bazett

The Esplanade, Waterloo.

Hooper & Co on the floor of the Liverpool Cotton Exchange in Old Hall Street. He married Winifred Ridgway (1892–1976), a ladies' hairdresser, in 1911.

- Aimeé Zenobia Coury (c.1892–1950), born in Alexandria, Egypt, did not marry.
- Louisa Andree Coury (1894–1983) was editor of 'Queen' magazine before it merged with 'Harper's Bazaar' as 'Harper's and Queen' in 1970. She had her own publishing house and was the last member of the family to live at 47 Fitzgeorge Avenue, West Kensington.
- Maurice Nicholas Coury (1898–1926) enlisted in the King's Regiment on 13th October 1914, giving his age as eighteen, but on 9th November he was discharged, having been 'irregularly enlisted'. In January 1915, he enlisted in 3rd Lancashire Fusiliers and was commissioned on 26th March. He served in Flanders as Draft Conducting Officer April – June 1915, but had to resign his commission due to ill-health on 30th June 1915 and received the Silver War Badge in November 1916. He worked for Reiss Brothers.
- Ernest Joseph Coury (1901–39) suffered from Hodgkin's disease and lived with his mother at 47 Fitzgeorge Avenue, West Kensington until admitted to St Joseph's Nursing Home, Hackney, where he died on 3rd August 1939.

Liverpool Cotton Exchange.

Gabriel was educated at St Francis Xavier's School, Salisbury Street, Liverpool 1901–07, Hodder Place (preparatory boarding school for Stonyhurst) May 1907 – January 1909 and then Stonyhurst College until April 1913. He was fluent in French, served in the Officer Training Corps and was a better sportsman than scholar, particularly in cricket and shooting. By the time he left school, Coury & Company had been wound up and he took a position with Reynolds & Gibson, Cotton Brokers and Merchants, at Tithebarn Street and 30 Exchange Street East, Liverpool.

On 11th September 1914, Gabriel enlisted in 2/6th King's (2482) and trained at Blackpool, Canterbury, Margate and Upstreet Camp in Kent. He was commissioned in 3rd South Lancashire (Special Reserve) on 25th

St Francis Xavier's School, Liverpool, where Gabriel Coury was educated 1901–07.

Stonyhurst College.

Tithebarn Street, Liverpool.

April 1915 and went to France on 15th August, attached to 1/4th Battalion on 11th September. The Battalion became Pioneers in October. **Awarded the VC for his actions near Arrow Head Copse, near Guillemont, France on 8th August 1916, LG 26th October 1916.**

He was appointed temporary lieutenant on 9th August 1916 and seconded to the RFC on 28th August as an Observer, joining 13 Squadron at Savy Aubigny on photo-reconnaissance and artillery spotting missions. His first operational flight was on 3rd September. On 23rd September, he was flying with Lieutenant McKain when they made a forced landing at 4 Squadron's base due to an engine fault. Gabriel was appointed flying officer observer on 15th November, with seniority from 28th August.

Colonel James Reynolds DSO, senior partner of Reynolds and Gibson, welcomed him to the Liverpool Cotton Exchange on 14th November and a civic reception was hosted by the Lord Mayor at Liverpool Town Hall the following day. The VC was presented by the King at Buckingham Palace on 18th November. At the same Investiture, four other VCs were presented and Albert Ball, who was later awarded a posthumous VC, received the DSO and two Bars. After the investiture, Gabriel was escorted to the Cotton Exchange for a hero's welcome. He returned to duty in France on 25th November and was granted two weeks leave on 17th February 1917.

On 4th April, his aircraft dropped two bombs, resulting in three large explosions in gun pits. Two days later, over Étaing, he was directing artillery fire and dropped bombs on Brebières. His squadron, and the RFC in general, suffered heavy losses against the German Albatross D111 in what became known as 'Bloody April'.

Gabriel was recommended for a gallantry award on 17th April, but it was not approved. On 23rd April he was flying with Lieutenant Trollope in a BE2c near Plouvain when they were attacked by an Albatross. Gabriel returned fire, causing the German to break off the engagement. A week later, aboard an RE8 piloted by Lieutenant Black, they were attacked at 5,000 feet by a single-seat Albatross. Gabriel emptied a drum at the German before the RE8 went into a spin, spiraling down to 500 feet under fire from the Albatross until the German broke off the attack. There were many other engagements and missions.

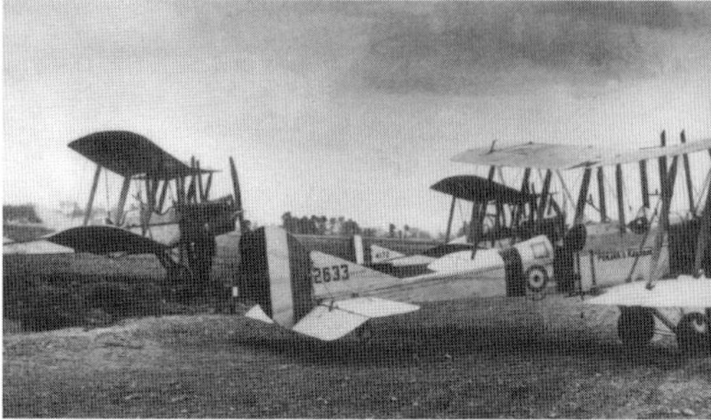

The Royal Aircraft Factory BE2 was a single-engine, two-seat biplane in service with the RFC and RAF 1912–19. Initially intended for reconnaissance and as a light bomber, it was also used as a night fighter, but was unable to take on superior German fighters in daylight. It had a good reputation for reliability and was very stable, making it ideal for artillery observation and air photography. The BE2c entered service just before war broke out and was essentially a redesigned aircraft.

Gabriel returned to Britain on 18th May 1917 to undertake pilot training at No.1 School of Military Aeronautics, Reading, Berkshire. He was promoted lieutenant on 1st July and posted to 66 Training Squadron at Yatesbury, Wiltshire, on 23rd July. Re-appointed flying officer 20th September with seniority from 28th August 1916. He was posted to 7th Aircraft Acceptance Park at Kenley Common, Croydon, where he test flew new aircraft and ferried them across the Channel to operational RFC units at the front. On 2nd October, he was allocated to mail carrying duties.

The Royal Aircraft Factory RE8 was also a two-seat biplane used for reconnaissance and as a light bomber. It was intended to replace the slow and vulnerable BE2, but was more difficult to fly and less reliable. It was in service, mainly for reconnaissance and artillery spotting, from mid 1917 to the end of the war.

On 22nd November he volunteered to ferry an aircraft from Kenley to France in bad weather because there was a shortage at the front. His wing tip hit a flagpole, the aircraft crashed and burst into flames, burning his face, arms and legs. He was treated at the Royal Herbert Hospital, Shooters Hill, Woolwich, during which time he was on the Non-Effective Personnel list. Having been discharged from hospital in January 1918, he was assessed as 30% disabled by a medical board and assigned to light duties on Home Service. He transferred to the newly formed Royal Air Force on 1st April as a lieutenant in the Aeroplane and Seaplane Branch (later Aeroplane Branch).

On 13th April, Gabriel was passed fit for flying duties and began ferrying aircraft to the front again. In May he was diagnosed with neurasthenia, but the requirement to ferry aircraft was considered more important and he continued flying. However, in June he crashed an aircraft at Kenley and was in hospital for three months. A medical board on 21st August found him unfit for flying duties, but fit for Home Service ground duties and on 5th September he transferred to the Administrative Section of the Medical Branch as a Medical (Administrative) Officer. Appointed acting captain on 30th September. He contracted Spanish Flu in February 1919 and was admitted to Mount Vernon Hospital, Northwood, London when pneumonia and pleurisy set in. On 1st March he was moved to Central Hospital, Hillingdon Hall, Hampstead and, on being discharged on 28th April, was assessed as being 20% disabled. Part of his convalescence was at Swanage, Dorset. Gabriel was demobilised from No.1 Dispersal Unit, Heaton Park, Manchester on 30th April, relinquishing his rank of acting captain. He was assigned the new rank of flying officer on 1st August 1919 and relinquished his Special Reserve commission on 1st April 1920.

Royal Herbert Hospital, Shooters Hill, Woolwich.

On 7th January 1918 Gabriel married Katherine ‘Kitty’ Mary Christina née Lovell (1889–1975) at St Mary’s Roman Catholic Church, Clapham, London. She was a volunteer with a medical/welfare group during the Great War. A silver bowl presented by the officer patients of the Royal Herbert Hospital, Woolwich on the occasion of the wedding was sold at a Dix Noonan Webb auction on 22nd September 2006.

Heaton Park, Manchester from where Gabriel Coury was demobilised on 30th April 1918.

Kitty lived at 56 Gayton Road, Hampstead while Gabriel was overseas. By April 1919 they were at 43 Canning Street, Liverpool. They also lived at 'Cora Linn', 2 Merton Grove in Bootle, 38 Brooke Road in Waterloo and 5 Argyle Road, 10 Albert Road and 32 Queens Road in Southport. After the Second World War, Gabriel moved to 103 Brunswick Road, Liverpool. Kitty and Gabriel had three daughters:

- Joan Marie Louise Coury (11th December 1918 – 28th October 2011). She was educated at a convent in Bexhill, Sussex and Carisbrooke House (Convent of Our Lady of the Sacred Heart), Isle of Wight. She was in Prague during Hitler's invasion of Czechoslovakia in October 1938. Joan married Peter Drury Bird (1920–2014) in 1940. He served in 102 Squadron, Bomber Command (742789) at Topcliffe, Yorkshire and was commissioned on 22nd May 1942 (123832). He was promoted flying officer on probation (War Substantive) 22nd November 1942, flying officer (extended service) 18th December 1945, flight lieutenant 1st July 1946 backdated to 22nd November 1945, squadron leader 1st January 1951, wing commander 1st July 1960 and group captain 1st July 1967. Peter was a Freemason, Royal Naval Anti-Aircraft Lodge No.3790 at 1 Warwick Road, Ealing. He was Air Attaché at the British Embassies in Oslo, Athens and Tel Aviv. He commenced the latter appointment on 5th June 1967 at the start of the Six-Day War. Later he was an Escort Officer at the Foreign Office. They had three children: Susan Christina Joan Drury Bird 1941, Simon Drury Bird 1943 and Stephanie Louise Drury Bird 1950.
- Carmen Katherine Mary Coury was born on 9th October 1921. She was educated privately at Birkdale, Lancashire before joining Joan at Carisbrooke House and later went to the Ursuline Convent, Blundell Sands, near Southport. She married Reginald Charles Walden (1906–94) in 1944 and they divorced c.1948. In 1957, Carmen married George Alfred Reeve (1918–2006), who was previously married to Eva Winifred Archer (1914–90) in 1938. There were no children to either marriage.
- Margaret Mary Coury, born on 28th August 1923, was educated in the same schools as Carmen. She married Peter Willie Shepherd (1922–97) in 1948. He was a manager with the Central Electricity Generating Board. They had two children – 'Steve' Paul Pater Shepherd 1951 and Sarah Louise Shepherd 1954.

One of Kitty's brothers, Henry Stuart Cuthbert Anthony Lovell (1888–1923), was a tea plantation manager in Ceylon. His son, Stuart James Lovell (1916–44), was serving as a flight lieutenant (107258) with 183 Squadron when he was killed in action on 29th January 1944 (Brest (Kerfautras) Cemetery – 46 11 2). His other son, Wing Commander (40402) Anthony Desmond Joseph Lovell (1919–45) DSO & Bar, DFC & Bar and US DFC, died in service on 17th August 1945 (Portrush Cemetery, Co Antrim, Northern Ireland – F 1153).

Gabriel returned to work for Reynolds & Gibson, including in Egypt 1927–32, as cotton agent and shipper. He was commissioned as a lieutenant RASC (Regular

Army Emergency Commission) on 9th September 1940 (141249) and served with 913 Company RASC at Eccles, Manchester. Appointed temporary captain 28th March 1942. Gabriel took part in the Normandy landings and served in France, Belgium, Holland and Germany until demobilised in August 1945.

After the war the government took control of the raw cotton market, putting many firms out of business. Gabriel opened a fish and chip shop (The Frying Pan) by converting part of his home at 103 Brunswick Road, Liverpool. He opened a second fish and chip shop at 58 Everton Road and his wife opened a confectionery and tobacco shop at 5 Everton Road. He then opened a cafe in West Derby Road (Three Jolly Gentlemen) and gained concessions for catering and confectionery in the cafés and kiosks in Sefton, Otterspool, Calderstones and Reynolds Parks. The latter was formerly the home of Sir James Reynolds, senior partner in Reynolds and Gibson, who presented the estate to Liverpool in 1929. In 1952 he transferred the management of the business to his wife and returned to the cotton trade as manager and senior salesman of George Way & Company.

Gabriel Coury was a heavy smoker and developed carcinoma of the bronchus and cerebral metastases. He was admitted to Walton Hospital, Rice Lane, Liverpool, but returned to his home at 103 Brunswick Road, where he died on 23rd February 1956. He is buried in the family grave in the churchyard of St Peter and St Paul's Roman Catholic Church, Crosby, Merseyside. Lieutenant Colonel Donald Farmer VC attended the funeral. Gabriel was estranged from his wife by the time he died and she was living at Hill Brow, 73 Hornsey Lane, Highgate, London. He left £1,285/5/9, but the net value of the estate was nil. Kitty died on 6th August 1975 at Dresden House, Albany Villas, Hove, Sussex.

In addition to the VC, he was awarded the 1914–15 Star, British War Medal 1914–20, Victory Medal 1914–19, 1939–45 Star, France & Germany Star, Defence Medal, War Medal 1939–45, George VI Coronation Medal 1937 and Elizabeth II Coronation Medal 1953. On 12th November 1961, the VC (but not the other medals) was presented by Gabriel's widow to Brigadier HH Whalley-Kelly on behalf of the Regimental Museum at the Grosvenor Hotel, Victoria, London. The VC is held by the Queen's Lancashire Regiment Museum, Fulford Barracks, Preston. On 23rd February 1982 the Museum was broken into and the VC displays of Gabriel Coury and John Lucas were stolen. However, the displays contained copy VCs, the originals being in safe custody.

His Victory Medal was owned by a private collector until offered for sale at Thomson Roddick & Medcalf in Carlisle in March 2006. The 1914–15 Star and Victory Medal were regained by the family. Gabriel's miniature medals group was sold at a Sotheby's auction in London on 17th September 1992. The VCs of Gabriel Coury and Maurice Dease were loaned to Stonyhurst College for the visit of Princess Anne on 24th September 2014 in her capacity as patron of the Woodland Trust's First World War Centenary Woods Project. She planted a tree alongside 301 oak saplings planted by Stonyhurst College CCF; each tree represents a serviceman who died in the Great War and other conflicts.

Gabriel Coury is very distantly related to Neville Joshua Aylmer Coghill VC, Noel Godfrey Chavasse VC & Bar and Maurice Dease VC through the Lovell family. He is also commemorated on:

- A memorial to Captain Noel Chavasse VC & Bar MC, unveiled in Abercromby Square, Liverpool, in July 2008, opposite No.19, where the Chavasse family lived and close to No.13 where Ernest Alexander's VC father lived. The names of fifteen other VCs associated with Liverpool are also inscribed on the memorial, including Gabriel Coury.
- The Great War Honours Board at St Francis Xavier's College, Beaconsfield Road, Woolton, Liverpool.
- A portrait by Thomas Baines in the Elizabethan Refectory at Stonyhurst College.
- Stonyhurst College CCF has seven platoons organized into two companies, each platoon named after one of the seven College VCs, including Coury Platoon.
- A propeller held at The Shuttleworth Collection, Old Warden Aerodrome, near Biggleswade, Bedfordshire.

12/21 PRIVATE JOHN CUNNINGHAM
12th Battalion, The East Yorkshire Regiment

John Cunningham was born at Swaby's Yard, off Manley Street, Scunthorpe, Lincolnshire on 28th June 1897. He was known as Jack. His father was Charles Cunningham (c.1860–1949), a licensed pot hawker who moved around the northeast of England a great deal. His mother was Mary Ann née Cunningham (1863–1932). Charles and Mary were married on 10th September 1881 at Westgate, Rotherham, Yorkshire. The family was living in Hull, Yorkshire at the following addresses:

- 12 Chapel Terrace, Carlton Street in February 1900.
- 4 Williams Place, St James Street in 1915.
- 18 Stainforth Place, Hessle Road in May 1922.
- 59 Edgar Street, Hessle Road when Mary died in 1932.
- Charles was living at 6 Fredericks Terrace, Strickland Street when he died in 1949.

John had four siblings:

- Thomas Cunningham (born c.1884) appeared in an article in the Liverpool Echo on 20th May 1918 - "Brother of Private John Cunningham, the Hull VC, Thomas

Cunningham (34), was "handed over" for having failed to join the Army." Nothing more is known of him.

- Matthew Cunningham (1900–51) was born in a van off Carlton Street, Hull. He enlisted in 2/4th East Yorkshire on 2nd February 1915 at the Central Hull Recruiting Office (3426). He was described as nineteen years old and 5′ 3½″ tall. He was discharged on 30th April when his true age was discovered. He married Emily Mulvy (born 1898) in 1917 and they had two children - Matt Cunningham 1920 and Charles H Cunningham 1922.
- Benjamin Cunningham born 1905.
- Mary Ann Cunningham married William Moore in 1916 and was living at 11 Charles Terrace, Albert Street, Walmgate, Yorkshire in 1949.

The Hessle Road area of Hull.

Wheeler Street School, Hull.

John was educated at St James' Day, Wheeler Street (later Newington High) and Chiltern Street Schools in Hull. He was keen on boxing and football. After school he took up hawking and was so employed for the rest of his life.

John enlisted at the Central Recruiting Office, Hull on 14th September 1914, described as 5′ 7″ tall, weighed 148 lbs, with fresh complexion, grey eyes, auburn hair and religious denomination was Church of England. He embarked with his Battalion on 15th December 1915 for Egypt arriving on 28th December. The Battalion moved to France on 8th March 1916. **Awarded the VC for his actions opposite the Hebuterne Sector, France on 13th November 1916, LG 13th January 1917.** He was presented with an illuminated address by Hull City Council on 1st February 1917 at the Guildhall, Hull. The VC was presented by the King in Hyde Park on 2nd June 1917.

John Cunningham married Eva née Harrison (1897–1971) on 10th June 1917 at Hull Registry Office. Their courtship lasted only a few days, but they knew each other from school and John had been a frequent visitor to the Harrison's home. Eva was working in munitions at the time. They had two children:

- Annie Cunningham born in the 3rd quarter of 1919. Her death was registered in the following quarter.
- John Cunningham born in the 3rd quarter of 1920.

While John was away, Eva was living at 75 Walker Street, Hessle Road, Hull and received a separation allowance of 12/6. Back at the front, John was posted to 10th Battalion on 11th February 1918 following the disbandment of 12th Battalion. He was shot in both feet and the chest on 13th April. He was evacuated to Britain on 17th April on the strength of the Depot at Beverley. His injuries left him with a permanent limp and as a result he was discharged on 26th June 1918. He was awarded Silver War Badge No.417229 on 2nd July and a disability pension of £1/7/6 per week. On discharge he was described as fresh complexion with grey eyes, auburn hair and his character was honest, sober, hardworking and thoroughly reliable. In May 1922, a man impersonating him was serving in 2 Platoon, No.1 Company of King's Own Royal Lancaster Regiment at The Barracks, Bowerham, Lancaster. He claimed to have served in the Duke of Wellington's Regiment August 1914 - September 1916. It is not known what action was taken against him.

The family lived at 72 Walker Street, Hessle Road, Hull and 38 Vine Street, Norton, Malton, Yorkshire. John returned to hawking brushes and household hardware in Hull, but had difficulty settling to married life and became physically abusive to Eva. He appeared in court at Hull on a number of occasions:

- 16th July 1919 - for persistent cruelty to his wife after allegedly giving her a black eye, dragging her by the hair and kicking her two days before the birth of their daughter Annie. John pleaded not guilty, claiming his wife left him "three times a week". The magistrate granted Eva a separation order with £1/5/- per week maintenance.
- 12th November 1920 - for failing to pay maintenance. In his defence he stated he was living solely on an army pension of £2 per week and was unable to afford £1/5/-.
- 23rd November 1920 - he was remanded for hitting a soldier over the head with a bottle during a street brawl; he appeared in the dock wearing his VC on 29th November and was remanded on bail.
- 13th September 1921 - for quarrelling and striking with a man. He pleaded guilty and was bound over to keep the peace for six months.
- 19th March 1922 - for failing to comply with a maintenance order in respect of his wife and child. He owed £10 and as he didn't have the money, he was imprisoned for six weeks.
- 6th February 1923 - he was fined two guineas for beating a horse with a thick stick, breaking the stick against the horse's legs. He was living at 9 Jobb's Place, Porter Street, Hull at the time. The court judged he was intoxicated at the time. An angry crowd gathered and John may have suffered injury but for the timely intervention of the police. He was fined 2 Guineas and ordered to control his temper in future.
- 30th March 1929 - for being drunk and disorderly on Good Friday evening. He was fined 7/6d or six days imprisonment. He did not offer any defence and admitted to ten previous convictions.

- November 1929 - two fellow hawkers, William Winter of Sheffield and Frederick William Downes of Drogheda, Ireland were accused of stealing a roll of linoleum from John valued at £4/10/- while he was attending the VC Dinner at the House of Lords on 9th November 1929. They pleaded not guilty, stating they had purchased the goods from Cunningham, but the magistrate did not believe them, saying he had no doubt that Cunningham was a man of truth and sentenced them both to twenty-eight days hard labour.
- May 1933 - with Charles Cunningham, a distant relative, he was charged with breaking a window, found guilty and fined £1.

Hull's Victoria Cross Winners Memorial.

Eva lived at a number of temporary addresses in Hull and Nottingham. In 1922, John's disability pension was reduced to £1/4/- and he tried to commute part of it to raise £80 to pay for a horse and cart, but was refused. John was presented to George VI and Queen Elizabeth during a Royal visit to Hull in October 1937. He kept his VC in his wallet with a French coin he had used as an identity disc during the war. The coin was inscribed 'J. Cunningham, VC. 12SB/EYR'. He lost his wallet while selling goods from his cart at Market Weighton, Yorkshire. He reported the loss immediately and when he returned to his cart half an hour later his wallet had been returned minus the money and his identity disc. The identity disc was discovered in some change by Mr HA Gill, Endyke Lane, Hull who notified the Hull Daily Mail and an article was published on 2nd August 1950. One of Cunningham's brothers claimed it.

John Cunningham died penniless after a long illness at 5 Beaufort Terrace, Hull on 20th February 1941. The cause of death was congestive cardiac failure and bilateral phthisis. The informant was Pauline Cook also of 5 Beaufort Terrace, but his next of kin was recorded as living at 75 Walker Street, Hull. It is not known who this was. He was buried in the family plot at Western Cemetery, Hull, Yorkshire (Section 180, Grave 17509) with his mother, father and brother Matthew. Eva married James Tyre (1890–1962) in the 1st quarter of 1942 at Hull.

Pauline Cook also went under the alias Cunningham. She was charged at Hull Police Court on 17th April 1944 with 'keeping a disorderly house'. The prosecutor stated that during standard surveillance of her house in Great Thornton Street over a period of fifteen days, thirty-nine men and two women were observed using the house. She was fined £10 or fifty-one days in detention. The Magistrate advised her to accept the detention in order that a thorough medical examination could be carried out, *"because you never know what you have got"*.

In addition to the VC, John was awarded the 1914–15 Star, British War Medal 1914–20, Victory Medal 1914–19 and George VI Coronation Medal 1937. His VC alone is held by the Prince of Wales's Own Regiment of Yorkshire Museum in York. John is commemorated on:

- A memorial plaque at Chiltern Street School, Hull, Yorkshire.
- The Hull Victoria Cross Winners Memorial, which also commemorates 2nd Lieutenant John Harrison VC MC, Boatswain John Sheppard VC CGM and Sergeant William Bernard Traynor VC.

34314 CORPORAL JOSEPH JOHN DAVIES
10th Battalion, The Royal Welsh Fusiliers

Joseph Davies was born at 7 Nock Street, Tipton, Staffordshire on 28th April 1889. His father, John Davies (c.1855–1915), served in 7th Regiment of Foot (Royal Fusiliers) for twelve years, including during the 1878–80 Afghanistan War, in which he was wounded. He was with the 2nd Battalion at Kandahar, one of four battalions garrisoning the city and relieved by Major General Roberts' famous march from Kabul to Kandahar in August 1880. He became a miner later. His mother was Ann/Annie née Bullock, born c.1856 at Bilston, Staffordshire. She married another soldier, David Allen, in the 1st quarter of 1877 at

Kandahar just after the relief in 1881.

Dudley, Staffordshire. Ann and David had two children – David Allen 1877, who was a cotton spinner in 1891 and Eliza Allen 1878. Ann is reputed to have married John Davies after David Allen, but their marriage was registered in the 1st quarter of 1876 at Wolverhampton. According to the 1911 Census, John and Ann had been married for thirty-six years, indicating the marriage in 1876 is correct. At present there is no explanation for this. In 1901, John was a coal miner pikeman and the family was living at 5 Nock Street, Tipton and had moved to 29 Walker Street, Toll End, Tipton by 1909. At some time they also lived at 48 Cross Street, Wednesbury, Staffordshire.

Ann was living with her parents and the two children from her marriage to David Allen at 8 Nock Street, Tipton in 1881. By 1891 she was living with her children at 19 Alexander Street, Tyldesley with Shakerley, Lancashire, together with her sister, Elizabeth Bullock. Joseph had at least six siblings from the marriage of John and Ann:

- Phoebe Jane Davies 1890–1902.
- Alice Davies (1893–1977) married Joseph Gibbs (1894–1982) in 1914. They had ten children: Alice Gibbs 1914, Thomas Gibbs 1918, Joseph H Gibbs 1920–21, Sarah Gibbs 1921, Annie Gibbs 1923, Joseph J Gibbs 1925, Evelyn Gibbs 1927, Albert Gibbs 1929, Henry Gibbs 1930 and Frederick Gibbs 1931.
- Martha Gladys Davies (born 1895) was a polisher in an iron holloware foundry in 1911. She married Thomas Evans in 1915 and they had at least three children: Nellie Evans 1923, Dorothy M Evans 1925 and Hilda Evans 1927.
- Elizabeth Davies 1898.
- Robert Davies 1900.
- John Thomas Davies (c.1902–1955) married Ellen Goddard (1904–68) in 1924 and they had two children: Irene Davies 1925 and Frederick Davies 1926–80.

Joseph was educated at Greatbridge Council School Tipton. He was then employed as a planer at Old Park Works, Wednesbury. He married Lucy Mason (1890–1952) on 8th June 1908 at St Mary & All Saint's, Walsall and they were living at Wednesbury in 1914. A child was born and died before 1911. She was a harness stitcher in 1911, living with her parents.

Abbassia Barracks, Cairo.

Joseph enlisted in the Welsh Regiment on 19th August 1909 (10236) and reported to the Depot at Cardiff on 25th August. On enlistment he was described as 5′ 4¾″ tall, weighing 119 lbs, with fresh complexion, grey eyes and brown hair. He was awarded the 3rd Class Certificate of Education on 1st October and was posted to the 1st Battalion at Bordon, Hampshire on 19th November. He served in Egypt with the battalion from 18th January 1910, based at Alexandria initially. While there, he passed the swimming test on 6th June and the battalion moved to Cairo on 11th February 1912. He was appointed Armourer's Assistant December 1912 – 5th December 1913. The battalion was in Khartoum, Sudan February 1913 – February 1914. On 21st July 1913, he was confined to barracks for seven days for urinating on his bedding. On 30th November he was confined to barracks for five days for falling out of the line of march to get water without permission. On 27th January 1914, he departed Egypt with the battalion, arriving in Bombay, India on 6th February. The battalion moved to Meerut and on 28th March moved again to Chakrata. Joseph was employed as a regimental policeman for two months before returning to the armoury on 14th August. At this time he was assessed as very good character, steady, sober, reliable and clean; a good worker. He left India via Karachi on 18th November and arrived in England on 24th December.

Joseph and Lucy's marriage ended in divorce, with Benjamin Andrews (1885–1952) being cited as correspondent. Lucy married Andrews at Walsall Registry Officer on 6th July 1914, although her divorce from Joseph Davies was not finalized until 1917. Benjamin Andrews served in 1st Duke of Wellington (West Riding) Regiment from 15th September 1904 (8162) at Halifax, York and Lichfield before departing for India on 28th February 1906. There he served at Lebong, Sitapur and Ambala, until returning to Britain on 12th October 1912. He transferred to the Reserve on 15th October and the following year signed on for another year on the 1st Class Reserve. He was recalled on 5th August 1914 and arrived in France on 14th August. A gun shot wound to his left arm resulted in a compound fracture of the ulna on 15th November and he was evacuated to Britain on 3rd December, where he was treated at the Red Cross Hospital in Tewkesbury until 13th February 1915. He was readmitted to hospital in Halifax on 21st June and was discharged on 15th May 1916, unfit for further service; awarded Silver War Badge 94985 on 23rd December. Lucy and Benjamin went on to have twelve children between 1915 and 1932.

1st Welsh was based at Hursley Park until it went to France on 16th January 1915. Joseph was wounded at Ypres on 10th March and evacuated to Britain, where he was held on the strength of the Depot. He returned to France on 8th May and was appointed unpaid lance corporal on 7th July. He transferred to the Royal Welsh Fusiliers (34314) on 11th August and was posted to Gibraltar on 23rd August to join 1st Garrison Battalion. Promoted lance corporal 30th September, acting corporal 10th January 1916 and corporal in April. He was posted to the 10th Battalion in France on 8th May.

Awarded the VC for his actions at Delville Wood, France on 20th July 1916, LG 26th September 1916. Appointed acting sergeant the same day. Having received a gun shot wound to the left shoulder on 8th August, he was evacuated to Britain and put on the held strength of the Depot from 29th August while in hospital in Bristol. He returned to the 10th Battalion on 1st October. The day before, the VC ribbon was presented to him by Brigadier General RJ Kentish DSO, on his last day in command of 76th Brigade, at Enquin-les-Mines. Promoted sergeant 1st October.

The VC was presented by the King at Buckingham Palace on 7th October 1916. Joseph's arm was again in a sling and the King had to pin the medal to it. **Awarded the Russian Cross of St George 1st Class, LG 15th February 1917; it was presented by General Campbell in Manchester.**

Joseph was posted to the 3rd (Reserve) Battalion on 27th June and transferred to the Military Provost Staff Corps (T1950) as a sergeant on 19th September, due to being unfit for active duty because of a severe shoulder wound. Appointed acting staff sergeant 15th March 1918, but reverted to sergeant on 7th May on transfer to shipyard labour. Joseph was transferred to the Class P Reserve (men whose services were of more value in civilian life due to their trade rather than in the Army) on 4th June and discharged on 14th December 1918, surplus to military requirements.

However, that was not quite the end of Joseph's military career. He re-enlisted in the Herefordshire Regiment (Territorial Army) on 13th November 1920 (4103165) and was promoted sergeant on 13th January 1921. He was discharged on 12th November 1922.

On 23rd June 1919, Joseph married Elsie Thomas (5th August 1898 – 1978) at the Hereford Registry Office, Herefordshire. He was living at 20 Commercial Road, Hereford and was a machinist in a factory at the time, possibly the Royal Ordnance Factory at Rotherwas in Hereford. Elsie was a laundress. They lived initially at 8 Bath Street, Hereford, then in Birmingham, where Joseph was a commissionaire for Birmingham Corporation Gasworks. They are also known to have lived at three addresses in Poole, Dorset – 11 North Road at Parkstone, Milne Road at Waterloo and 2 Trinidad House, Rossmore Road at Parkstone. Elsie and Joseph had two daughters:

- Elsie Victoria Davies, registered as Elsie V Thomas in the 1st quarter of 1919 at Hereford. The birth entry was corrected in 1962 to Elsie Victoria Davies, registered in the 4th quarter of 1918 at Hereford. She served in the ATS as a sergeant during the Second World War. She married as Howard (no record found) and was living at 7 French Road, Poole in 1976. They had a son, Robert John Howard, in 1948.
- Joyce Irene Davies, registered in the 2nd quarter of 1924 at Hereford.

Elsie's brother, Robert Leslie Thomas (1893–1966), enlisted in the Army Service Corps on 20th April 1915 at Hereford but was discharged on 10th March 1916 due to myopic degeneration. Elsie's sister, Winifred Thomas (1896–1931), married Hubert

The Royal Navy Cordite Factory, Holton Heath, established in the First World War, was reactivated in the Second World War. It was later used as an Admiralty Research Establishment, closing in the 1990s. Parts of it are now a nature reserve, an industrial estate and a housing estate.

James Jones (1892–19) in 1914. He served as a sergeant in 1st King's (Shropshire Light Infantry) (9373) and was awarded the DCM (LG 15th March 1916) for bringing in a man who had been gassed.

During the Second World War, Joseph was not fit enough for the Home Guard and instead served as RSM of Poole Cadet Force. He was also Chief ARP Warden at Oakdale, Poole and worked at the Royal Navy Cordite Factory at Holton Heath throughout the war.

Joseph Davies died at Bournemouth Royal National Hospital, Dorset on 16th February 1976. He was cremated at Bournemouth Crematorium and his ashes scattered on Evening Hill, overlooking Poole Harbour.

In addition to the VC, he was awarded the 1914–15 Star, British War Medal 1914–20, Victory Medal 1914–19, Defence Medal 1939–45, George VI Coronation Medal 1937, Elizabeth II Coronation Medal 1953 and the Russian Cross of St George 1st Class. The VC is held by the Royal Welch Fusiliers Museum, Caernarfon Castle. Joseph is commemorated in a number of places:

- Davies Court, Hightown, Wrexham, Clwyd.
- A memorial at Greatbridge School, Tipton was unveiled by Lieutenant Colonel Sir John Norton Griffiths. Griffiths was the man who did most to establish mining on the Western Front and was the MP for Wednesbury until 1918. Unfortunately, when the old school was demolished in 2004 the memorial disappeared and it does not appear in the new school.
- Tipton Society Blue Plaque at the Nag's Head Inn, Tipton – the public house was previously named 'The Fusilier' in his honour.
- A memorial plaque in Delville Wood, France to him and Private Albert Hill VC was unveiled by Major General BP Plummer, Colonel Royal Welch Fusiliers, on 26th May 2001. A Hornbeam tree was planted alongside it by members of both families.
- A poem was written in his honour by Lance Corporal CE Lee.

11213 SERGEANT ROBERT DOWNIE
2nd Battalion, The Royal Dublin Fusiliers

Robert Downie was born at 611 Springburn Road, Springburn, Glasgow, Lanarkshire on 12th January 1894. His father was Francis Downie (c.1857–1913), born in Ireland. He worked as a machine oiler and iron planer at Hyde Park Locomotive Works, Glasgow.

His mother was Elizabeth 'Lizzie' Jane née Taylor (1856–1924), a factory hand spinner of Small's Wynd, Dundee at the time of her marriage to Francis on 14th February 1876 at St Andrew's Roman Catholic Chapel, Dundee. The family was living at 569D Springburn Road,

St Rollox, Glasgow in 1881, at 611 Springburn Road in 1891, at 19 Centre Street, Springburn in 1901, at 38 Carleston Street, Springburn when Francis died in 1913 and at 7 Carleston Street when Lizzie died in 1924. Robert had fifteen siblings, including:

- David Downie (1876–1917) was an apprentice blacksmith in 1891. He married Elizabeth Downie and they lived at 105 Habarn Street, Glasgow. David enlisted in 1st Royal Scots Fusiliers in Glasgow (7674) and was promoted to sergeant. He died of wounds on 11th April 1917 and is buried in Duisans British Cemetery, Ètrun, France (III G 4).
- John Downie (born 1878) was a message boy in 1891.
- Mary Jane Downie, born 1880.
- Catherine Downie, born 1882.
- Richard Downie (1887–1917) married Hannah Downie and they lived at 33 Carleston Street, Springburn, Glasgow. He enlisted in 4th Seaforth Highlanders in Glasgow (204408) and died on 20th July 1917. He is buried in Étaples Military Cemetery, France (XXV K 5).
- Elizabeth Downie, born 1889.
- Francis Downie, born 1890.
- Ann 'Annie' Downie (1893–1960) married Duncan Joseph McGregor in 1916 and they had a son, Duncan McGregor c.1917.
- Thomas Downie, born 1895.
- Ellen 'Helen' Downie, born 1896.
- Isabella 'Bella' Downie, born 1898.
- Amelia 'Emily' Downie, born 1899.

One of the other brothers was killed, but cannot be identified; and another served in the Royal Navy, but was discharged on medical grounds.

Robert was educated at St Aloysius' School, Springburn. He was employed at Hyde Park Locomotive Works, as was his father, owned by North British Locomotive Company Ltd, then

The Springburn Road area of Glasgow.

The Cathedral Church of St Andrew, Dundee (Alexander Wilson).

York Cottage, Sandringham.

the largest locomotive company in Europe and the third biggest in the world. He enlisted in 2nd Royal Dublin Fusiliers on 8th February 1912.

Robert Downie later in life.

On 4th April 1914 Robert Downie married Ivy Louise (1896–1970) at Gravesend, Kent, where his battalion was based. They had three children:

- Robert F Downie, born on 18th April 1915, registered at Gravesend, Kent.
- Annie Downie, birth registered in the 1st quarter of 1916 at Gravesend. She died on 27th May 1970 and is buried with her parents.
- Elizabeth Downie, born in 1917, registered at Camlachie, Glasgow. She died on 16th April 1919.

One of Ivy's sisters, Clara Elizabeth Sparkes (1902–93), married Henry 'Harry' T Medhurst (born 1900) in 1922 at Gravesend, Kent. Henry was the son of Winnifred Blanche Margaret Carter, sister of Nelson Victor Carter VC.

Robert went to France with the Battalion on 23rd August 1914. **Awarded the VC for his actions east of Lesboeufs, France on 23rd October 1916, LG 25th November 1916. Awarded the MM, LG 11th November 1916.** He was presented with a gift of money by the Springburn Branch, United Irish League, on 4th January 1917. The VC was presented by the King at York Cottage, Sandringham on 8th January. Robert was wounded five times and gassed on several occasions during the war and was demobilised in March 1919.

Post war Robert worked for Glasgow Corporation as an electrician on the trams. He served in the Home Guard during the Second World War. In the 1950s he worked

Robert Downie being welcomed home by his father.

Glasgow Celtic Park in the 1920s.

the turnstiles for Glasgow Celtic. He lived at 33 Carleston Street, Springburn and died there on 18th April 1968. He is buried in St Kentigern's Cemetery, Glasgow (Section 21, Lair 506) with his wife and daughter Annie.

In addition to the VC and MM, he was awarded the 1914 Star with 'Mons' clasp, British War Medal 1914–20, Defence Medal, George VI Coronation Medal 1937 and Elizabeth II Coronation Medal 1953. The VC is held privately.

2442 PRIVATE FREDERICK JEREMIAH EDWARDS
12th Battalion, The Duke of Cambridge's Own (Middlesex Regiment)

Frederick Edwards was born at St George's, Queenstown (Cobh), Co Cork, Ireland on 3rd October 1894. His birth was registered as Jeremiah Frederick Edwards and he was known as Patsy.

His father was Henry James (1870–1902), a fishmonger. He enlisted into the Middlesex Regiment (1668) at Hounslow on 4th February 1886, when he was described as 5′ 7″ tall, weighing 117 lbs, with a florid complexion, brown hair and eyes and his religious denomination was Church of England. He was posted to the 1st Battalion on 15th February and passed his 4th Class Education Certificate on 2nd March 1886. He transferred to the Royal Garrison Artillery on 15th October 1887 at Portsmouth (63523) and served in the South Irish Division. Appointed bombardier on 1st November, passed his 3rd Class Education Certificate on 14th December, reverted to gunner on 9th January 1888 and was granted Good Conduct Pay on 4th February. Appointed bombardier again on 1st April 1889, served in the Irish Division from 1st July and passed his 2nd Class Education Certificate on 15th October. Having attended a course in gunnery from 30th December 1889 to 28th March 1890, he was promoted bombardier on 3rd February 1890, corporal on 9th July and sergeant on 1st October 1890. On 7th February 1891 he extended his service to complete twelve years and was posted to 34th Company RGA on 14th May and 17th Company RGA on 1st August 1891. He was stationed at Templemore Barracks, Queenstown, Ireland in 1893–94. On 1st April 1895 he was posted to 27th Company RGA and appointed Company Quartermaster Sergeant on 23rd June 1896. He re-engaged to complete twenty-one years service on 22nd December 1897

Queenstown, now Cobh, Co Cork, where Frederick Edwards was born.

and was posted to 9th Company RGA on 8th March 1898 at Trimulgherry, India, where he was stationed with his family. On 1st January 1902 he was posted to 72nd Company RGA and died of alcoholism at Trimulgherry on 2nd May.

Frederick's mother was Anne/Annie née Cavanagh. She married Henry on 9th July 1892 at St Colman's Cathedral, Queenstown. In addition to Frederick they had five other children:

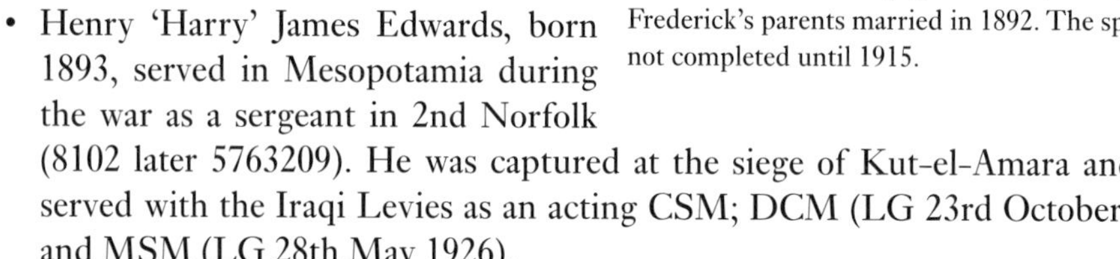

St Colman's Cathedral, Queenstown, where Frederick's parents married in 1892. The spire was not completed until 1915.

- Henry 'Harry' James Edwards, born 1893, served in Mesopotamia during the war as a sergeant in 2nd Norfolk (8102 later 5763209). He was captured at the siege of Kut-el-Amara and later served with the Iraqi Levies as an acting CSM; DCM (LG 23rd October 1916) and MSM (LG 28th May 1926).
- Michael Patrick Edwards (1896–1922) was born as Michael John Edwards. He joined the army as a Boy in 1911 and went on to serve during the war as a gunner (32596 later 1405265) with 51st Siege Battery RGA. He served in Waziristan after the war and died there on 23rd June 1922. His remaining credits from the Army were divided equally between his mother and brothers Frederick and Henry, receiving £14/5/11 each.
- Charlotte Edwards, born in 1898.
- Arthur Edwards, born in 1899.
- Bertie Edwards, born in 1901.

Frederick was educated at the Royal Hibernian Military School, Dublin and was initially employed by the Western Electric Company at Woolwich, London. He enlisted in the Royal Garrison Artillery in Dublin on 30th October 1908 as a Boy (29910) and was described as 4′ 10″ tall, weighing 76 lbs, with fresh complexion, grey eyes, brown hair and his religious denomination was Roman Catholic. He joined at No.3 Depot RGA at the Citadel, Plymouth, Devon next day and gained his 3rd Class Education on 18th December and 2nd Class on

The Royal Citadel at Plymouth was built in the 1660s and is still a military base. Currently it is home to 29 Commando Regiment, Royal Artillery, part of 3rd Commando Brigade.

P&O's SS *Sunda* was transferred to a Japanese company in 1914 as the *Hokokuo Maru* and was lost in December 1915 after leaving Singapore.

Frederick Edwards with his mother while on leave, just after the award of the VC.

23rd July 1909. He served at Portsmouth and with 88th Company RGA at Victoria Barracks, Hong Kong from 9th September 1910. He became a trumpeter on 16th September. In September 1912, he served ten days in detention for being drunk on duty and was discharged for misconduct in February 1913. As a result he was embarked on SS *Sunda* on 5th February, but when the ship arrived early in England the NCO detailed to disembark him arrived late. Edwards departed and did not report to Woolwich.

On 31st August 1914, he re-enlisted in the Middlesex Regiment (G/2442) and was posted to 12th Battalion as a drummer. He was promoted corporal and went to France on 25th July 1915. **Awarded the VC for his actions at Thiepval, France on 26th September 1916, LG 25th November 1916.** The VC was presented by the King at Buckingham Palace on 5th February 1917. He returned to his old school in Dublin and was presented with a solid silver flask and a cheque to invest in War Bond certificates.

Frederick transferred to 2nd London (G8/81451) in February 1918 when 12th Middlesex disbanded and to the Royal Fusiliers (6080039) on 13th April 1918. He was taken prisoner near Amiens on 24th April 1918. He was demobilised on 20th March 1919, but sources also quote 20th March and 31st March 1920 and 20th March 1921.

Post war he is said to have worked in a family business, which went bankrupt. He returned to work for Western Electric Company at Woolwich. In January 1924 he was assaulted by Bert Ward for taking too much interest in his sixty year old mother; Ward was fined £1/10/-. Frederick fell on hard times and pawned his VC in 1928. A national newspaper bought it back for him, but he was forced to pawn it again. He worked as a temporary messenger in Holborn Town Hall and was Mace Bearer to the Mayor of Holborn, London in 1930 until he suffered a stroke in 1954. Thereafter he could only say *Jinnah* and this became his nickname. He moved into the Royal Star and Garter Home, Richmond on 27th April 1955.

Frederick may have served in the Royal Fusiliers in the Second World War. He married a lady with the initials GH. The only marriage of a Frederick J Edwards matching these details was in the 3rd quarter of 1948 at Holborn to Grace Helen Malcolm (1906–70).

Frederick Edwards died at the Royal Star and Garter Home for Disabled Ex-Servicemen at Richmond, Surrey on 9th March 1964 of acute coronary thrombosis following an attack of bronchitis. He was given a funeral with full military honours and an escort from the Middlesex Regiment. His life-long friend, Bob Ryder VC, was present, together with Ted Veale VC and Mr Justice PV Storkey VC. The service was conducted by Reverend Father FJ Davys, whose great-uncle, Surgeon Major Reynolds, was awarded the VC for his actions at Rorke's Drift in 1879. Frederick was buried in the Star & Garter Plot, Richmond Cemetery, on 16th March 1964 (Section 22, Grave 87).

Frederick Edwards, seated, with his friend and fellow VC, Robert Ryder, on Horse Guards Parade, London in 1963.

In addition to the VC he was awarded the 1914–15 Star, British War Medal 1914–20, Victory Medal 1914–19, George VI Coronation Medal 1937 and Elizabeth II Coronation Medal 1953. He may have been awarded the Defence Medal for his service in the Second World War.

Frederick eventually sold his medals for £180. They were owned by a Canadian before appearing on the market in 1965, but the Middlesex Regiment could not afford the asking price at the time. They were auctioned by Glendining's on 26th October 1966 and the Regiment purchased them with private subscriptions for £900. When the Middlesex Regiment Museum at Bruce Castle, Tottenham closed in 1992, the collection went to the National Army Museum, Royal Hospital Road, Chelsea, London, which is where his VC is now held.

10947 COMPANY SERGEANT MAJOR WILLIAM JOHN GEORGE EVANS
18th Battalion, The Manchester Regiment

George Evans, as he was known, was born in Kensington, London on 16th February 1876, although the record of his baptism on 19th March 1876 gives his date of birth as 6th March. His father, Daniel Jones Evans (1854–88), was a pub barman at 3 Commercial Road, Kirkdale, Lancashire in 1871. By 1876 he was a brakeman, living at 42 Hellier Street, Hammersmith, London. His mother was Mary Georgina née Atkinson (c.1853–76). Daniel and Mary were married on 10th April 1875 at St John's Church, Walworth, Surrey. Her death was registered in the 1st quarter of 1876 at Fulham, London, when George was only six weeks old. Daniel Evans married Caroline Elizabeth Burnett (1856–80) in the 3rd quarter of 1877 at Fulham. He married for the third time, Ruth Ann Hoskins (1861–1944) in the 1st quarter of 1881 at Fulham. They lived at 8 The Grove, Hammersmith. Daniel was a grocer at the time of his death on 3rd April 1888 at his home at 147 Stanley Road, Croydon, Surrey. He left £485/3/- to his widow. By 1901, Ruth was a lodging housekeeper at Melbourne House, Cromer, Norfolk and in 1911 was housekeeper for her son, Bernard, at 4 Blakemore Road, Streatham, London. George had four half-brothers from the father's third marriage, but two did not survive infancy:

- Daniel John Evans, born 1883, was a butcher in 1901, living with his mother at Melbourne House, Cromer, Norfolk.
- Bernard Edward Evans, born 1887, was a boarder at Mount St Mary's College, Eckington, Derbyshire in 1901 and by 1911 was a banker's clerk, living at 4 Blakemore Road, Streatham, London. He died in 1953.

George was educated in various London schools and was employed as a labourer before he enlisted in 1st Scots Guards (343) on 5th March 1894. He was promoted lance corporal on 6th April 1895, but reverted to private on 19th December 1896. He transferred to the Depot on 15th February 1898 and served in the South African War 24th October 1899 – 17th April 1900. Having returned to Britain to 3rd Scots Guards on 18th April, he was seconded to the Imperial Representative Corps accompanying the future King George V on the Australian Commonwealth inauguration tour, 12th November 1900–22nd April 1901. George then served in England until 14th April 1902 and in South Africa until 21st July. He returned to Britain and was discharged to the Reserve on 26th August. His Reserve liability ended on 4th March 1906.

St Chad's Church, Cheetham, Manchester, where George Evans married Clara Bates on 21st September 1903 (Oratory Church of St Chad).

George served for three years with the Derby Borough Police Force and then the Manchester Police. He married Clara née Bates (born 1875) from Derby on 21st September 1903 at St Chad's, Cheetham, Manchester. She was a tobacconist's assistant in 1901, visiting 10 Corden Street, Derby. They lived at 62 Woodlands Road, Manchester. By 1911 they were living at 5 Johnson Street, Cheetham and at 36 Greenhills Road, Cheetham Hill in 1918. They later lived at 203 Langworthy Road, Salford and were at 5 Tremaine Road, Anerley, in southeast London, in 1937. George and Clara had four children, whose births were registered at Derby, except George, who was registered in Manchester:

- Daniel James Evans, born 4th May 1904.
- Constance Evans, born 9th April 1906.
- Violet May Evans, born 16th May 1910.
- George Evans, born 4th August 1912.

In 1910 George became an Inspector with the National Society for the Prevention of Cruelty to Children and the following year was working for the Society in Prestwich, Manchester. He enlisted in 18th Manchester (3rd City) as a sergeant on 4th January 1915 and was appointed CSM on 18th March. He went to France on 7th November with the battalion. While he was away, his wife deputised for him in the NSPCC.

Awarded the VC for his actions at Guillemont, France on 30th July 1916, LG 30th January 1920. He became known as the 'Children's VC' due to his work with the NSPCC. George was taken prisoner later on, 30th July 1916, and was held in various camps in Germany, where he is reputed to have lost six stones in weight due to the poor diet. He was exchanged through Holland on 6th June 1918 and stayed there until 19th November, when he was repatriated. He was demobilised to the Class Z Reserve on 19th February 1919. His VC was the last gazetted for the Great War and it was presented by the King at Buckingham Palace on 12th March 1920.

George resumed work for the NSPCC in Hackney and Sydenham, London. He worked for the Society for twenty-seven years and is understood to have helped over 12,500 children in that time. George was a Freemason with the Wilton Lodge No.1077, East Lancashire; the Lodge was erased in 2007. He was presented to the Prince of Wales outside the Town Hall in Albert Square, Manchester on 7th July 1921, together with fellow VCs Harry Coverdale, John Readitt, and George Stringer.

Manchester Town Hall in Albert Square, where George Evans was presented to the Prince of Wales in 1921.

George Evans died suddenly at his home at 5 Tremaine Road, Anerley, London on 28th September 1937. Masonic rites were observed during his funeral and he is buried in Elmers End Cemetery, Beckenham, Kent. A memorial service was held at the same time at the Regimental Chapel, Manchester Cathedral. Clara is understood to have died in Derby in 1944. George's grave was completely refurbished in 2009 by his only grandchild, Dilys Fisher, her husband James and their children William and Jonathan.

The Duke of Lancaster Regiment Chapel in Manchester Cathedral, formerly dedicated to the Manchester and King's Regiments (Disabled Holidays Info).

In addition to the VC, he was awarded the Queen's South Africa Medal 1899–1902 with four clasps (Belmont, Modder River, Orange Free State, South Africa 1902), 1914–15 Star, British War Medal 1914–20, Victory Medal 1914–19 and George VI Coronation Medal 1937. In 2002 his grand daughter, Dilys Fisher, loaned the medals to the Imperial War Museum, where they are displayed in the Lord Ashcroft Gallery. George is commemorated in a number of places:

- Guards Chapel, Birdcage Walk, London.
- Manchester Cathedral in the Book of Remembrance of the Manchester and King's Regiments.
- A plaque at Lewisham Civic Centre bears the names of eight local men awarded the VC – Harold Auten, George Evans, Philip Gardner, Sidney Godley, Alan Jerrard, George Knowland, Noel Mellish and John Pattison. It was unveiled in May 1995 by the only survivor, Captain Philip Gardner VC.

4073 PRIVATE WILLIAM FREDERICK FAULDS
1st South African Infantry

William Faulds was born on 19th February 1895 at 34 Market Street, Cradock, Eastern Cape, South Africa. He was known as Mannie. His father was Alexander Faulds (c.1852–1901), a carpenter, born at Barrhead, Renfrewshire, Scotland. His mother was Wilhelmina Ernestina née Neseman (1862–1929), born at Cradock, South Africa. Alexander and Wilhelmina were married on 2nd February 1881 at the Wesleyan Chapel Church, Cradock. Mannie had six siblings:

- Margaret Wilhelmina Faulds (1881–1967) married Charles Ernest Hayes Dennett (1871–1918) in 1907 at Grahamstown.

- Augustus Conrad Faulds (1883–1951) served in Gorringe's Flying Column, a colonial unit during the Boer War, 17th January – 17th June 1901 as Trooper Conrad Augustus Faulds. He married Maud Ann Edmunds (1889–1982) in 1914. Two of Mannie's brothers served in the South African Infantry in the First World War. One is known to be Paisley below and because Douglas was only fifteen when war broke out, it seems likely that Augustus was the other. Augustus and Maud had a son, Raymond Alexander Faulds (1915–95).
- Ida Neseman Faulds (born 1885) married Samuel Rowson in 1910.
- Effie Gladys Faulds (born 1887) married Edward George Mullett Cowley (1880–1940) in 1927. He was born in Stourton, Wiltshire.
- Alexander Paisley Faulds (born 1891). He served in 1st South African Infantry during the First World War. He married Alma Florence Weir in 1919 and they had at least one child, Ulyth Faulds, in 1921.
- Douglas Ernest Faulds (1899–1968) married Winifred May Dickens (1896–1980) in 1926 at Grahamstown. They had two children, Olwen Faulds 1930 and Bruce Faulds 1933.

Mannie was educated at Cradock and worked at the Midland Motor Garage there. He enlisted in the Cradock Commando on 19th October 1914 and served in South West Africa until discharged on 12th January 1915. He enlisted in 1st South African Infantry at Potchefstroom on 23rd August 1915 and served in Egypt. He went to France with his Battalion on 16th April 1916.

Awarded the VC for his actions in Delville Wood on 16th and 18th July 1916, LG 9th September 1916. He was the first South African born soldier serving with South African forces to win the VC. He was promoted lance corporal on 20th August and corporal and lance sergeant on 18th October. The VC was presented by the King at York Cottage, Sandringham, Norfolk on 8th January 1917. Promoted sergeant on 12th April and on 19th May, he was commissioned. He went to Egypt, where he served in the Transport Department until returning to France. **Awarded the MC for his actions at Hendicourt on 22nd March 1918 – in the retirement**

York Cottage, Sandringham, Norfolk where Mannie Faulds received his VC from the King.

he commanded one of the platoons forming the rear guard. He handled his men most ably, exposing himself freely and although the enemy pressed hard, by fearless and able leadership, he checked them, and enabled the remainder of the battalion to withdraw with only minimal losses, LG 29th November 1919. He was wounded and taken prisoner on 24th March.

Mannie after being commissioned.

Mannie was promoted temporary lieutenant on 9th November 1918 and repatriated to England on 19th November. Promoted lieutenant on 16th March 1919, shortly before returning to South Africa for demobilisation on 10th April.

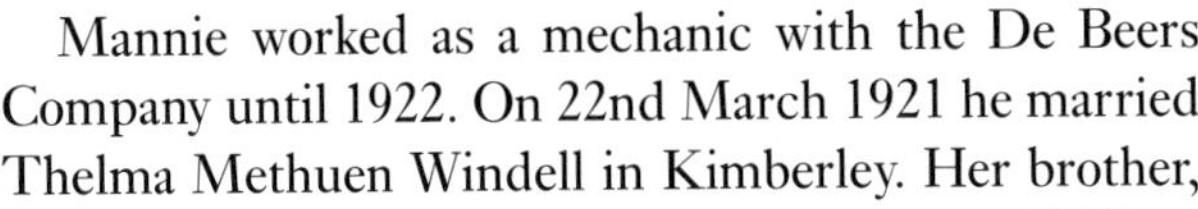

Mannie worked as a mechanic with the De Beers Company until 1922. On 22nd March 1921 he married Thelma Methuen Windell in Kimberley. Her brother, 16591 Private Neville Girling Windell (1888–1918), served in East and South West Africa before going to France with 2nd South African Infantry, where he died on 24th March 1918 (Pozières Memorial). He was in the same action with Mannie at Delville Wood and was reputedly awarded the French Croix de Guerre. Mannie and Thelma had two children:

- Selwyn Herbert Faulds (16th September 1924 – 22nd April 1980) was born at Benoni.
- Veronica Joy Faulds, born on 22nd November 1928 at Kimberley.

Mannie joined the part time Kimberley Regiment as a lieutenant in 1922 and was later promoted captain. He commanded guards of honour during royal visits and commanded the King's Guard of VC holders at the coronation of King George VI. In civilian life he was appointed to a position in Jagersfontein and later at Bulawayo, Rhodesia.

Mannie served for five years during the Second World War, enlisting as a private in the Mechanical Service Corps and served in Abyssinia and Egypt. He was commissioned later and was a lieutenant in East Africa in 1941. After the war Mannie became the Rhodesian Government Industrial Inspector in 1945 in Salisbury (now Harare). He died at Salisbury General Hospital, Rhodesia on 16th August 1950 and was buried in an unmarked grave at Salisbury Pioneer Cemetery, Remembrance Drive. In 1972 a headstone was erected through the efforts of the Cradock Branch of the South African Legion. Thelma died in February 1952.

In addition to the VC and MC, he was awarded the 1914–15 Star, British War Medal 1914–20, Victory Medal 1914–19, 1939–45 Star, Africa Star, Defence Medal, War Medal 1939–45, Africa Service Medal 1939–45 and George VI Coronation Medal 1937. His VC was held by the National Museum of Military History, Erlswold

Way, Saxonwold, Johannesburg, South Africa until it was reported stolen in October 1994; it has not been recovered. Mannie is commemorated on:

The South African Memorial in Delville Wood on the day of its dedication (South African National Museum of Military History).

- The South African Memorial, Delville Wood, France.
- One of eleven plaques honouring 175 men from overseas awarded the VC for the Great War. The plaques were unveiled by the Senior Minister of State at the Foreign & Commonwealth Office and Minister for Faith and Communities, Baroness Warsi, at a reception at Lancaster House, London on 26th June 2014 attended by the Duke of Kent and relatives of the VC recipients. The South African plaque was unveiled at Castle of Good Hope in Cape Town on 11th November 2014 by the British High Commissioner, Judith Macgregor, in the presence of Tsepe Motumi, Director General of the Department of Military Veterans.
- The Secretary of State for Communities and Local Government, Eric Pickles MP, announced that Victoria Cross recipients from the Great War would have commemorative paving stones laid in their birthplace as a lasting legacy of local heroes within communities. The stones would be laid on or close to the 100th anniversary of their VC actions. For the 145 VCs born in Australia, Belgium, Canada, China, Denmark, Egypt, France, Germany, India, Iraq, Japan, Nepal, Netherlands, New Zealand, Pakistan, South Africa, Sri Lanka, Ukraine and the United States of America, individual commemorative stones were unveiled at the National Memorial Arboretum, Alrewas, Staffordshire by Prime Minister David Cameron MP and Sergeant Johnson Beharry VC on 5th March 2015.

LIEUTENANT COLONEL BERNARD CYRIL FREYBERG
The Queen's (Royal West Surrey Regiment) commanding The Hood Battalion, Royal Naval Division

Bernard Freyberg was born at 8 Dynevor Road, Richmond Hill, Surrey on 21st March 1889. He was known as 'Tiny' because of his large size. His father was James Thomas Freyberg (c.1829–1914) who had a number of varied occupations including decorator, upholsterer, estate agent, auctioneer and surveyor. His first marriage was to Jane Wood (1828–77) in 1852 at St James, Westminster. Bernard's mother was Julia Kate née Hamilton (1852–1936)

RMS *Aorangi*, launched in 1883 in Glasgow for the New Zealand Shipping Company, was the vessel that took the Freyberg family to New Zealand to begin a new life.

and their marriage was registered in the 3rd quarter of 1880 at Kensington, London. They were living at 88 Beaufort Street, Chelsea in 1881. The family emigrated to New Zealand, embarking at Plymouth on RMS *Aorangi* on 17th October 1891 and arriving at Wellington on 3rd December 1891 via Tenerife, Cape Town and Hobart. The move was prompted when James' partner went bankrupt. James found work with the forestry department and the family lived in a few different houses in Hawker Street on the slopes of Mount Victoria. Bernard had eight siblings from the two marriages:

- Rose Freyberg (1853–1931) married John Beaumont Lester (1851–94) in 1880 at St Matthew, Earls Court, London. He was a warehouseman in 1891 and they were living at 31 Halford Road, Richmond, Surrey. By the time he died, he was a director and secretary of a public company, living at 26 Halford Road. Rose was living at 167 Sheen Road, Richmond in 1901. They had four children:
    - Mary Monica Lester (1881–1968) married Charlie Lionel Patton-Bethune (1882–1957) in 1916. He was commissioned in the Cameron Highlanders on 18th April 1900 and was serving with the Chinese Regiment in 1908. They had two children including Michael Lisle Patton-Bethune (1918–40) who was a Sergeant in the Royal Air Force Volunteer Reserve (754290) before being commissioned as Pilot Officer (74340) on 26th September 1939. He was killed on active service on 16th May 1940 and is commemorated at Golders Green Crematorium.
    - Hugh William Lester (1884–1972) emigrated to Australia.
    - John Beaumont Lester (1893–1916) was a Lance Corporal in the Inns of Court Officer Training Corps. He married Leontine Isabella Emmeline Rowson (1890–1980) in 1915. John was serving as a Captain in 18th King's

Royal Rifle Corps when he was killed on 15th September 1916 (Bulls Road Cemetery, Flers, France - Special Memorial 14).
  - Eric Stanley Lester 1895.
- Jessie Freyberg (1854–1927) married Frank Hawker Kingdon (1860–1958) in 1886. He was ordained priest on 19th December 1886 and was Vicar of St John's, Penzance then St Maddern, Madron, Cornwall in May 1887 and Vicar of Holsworthy, near Bridgewater, Devon on 5th April 1888. They had five children:
  - Mary Joyce Kingdon (1887–1965) married Chadwick Nind Aytoun (1888–1970) in 1918. He was a Cadet in the OTC and was commissioned in the Royal Garrison Artillery on 14th December 1914. He served in 103rd Siege Battery RGA and rose to Acting Major on 1st November 1918, retaining the rank of Major on demobilisation on 18th June 1919.
  - Robert Claude Hawker Kingdon (1890–1917) was registered as an Eastern Cadet in the Colonial Office on 22nd October 1913. He was commissioned in the Royal Field Artillery and was serving in 123rd Battery when he was killed on 19th April 1917 (Ecoivres Military Cemetery, Mont St Eloi, France - VI D 25).
  - Bridget Mary Kingdon born 1892 studied physical culture and was commissioned in the Women's Royal Air Force 1st October 1918–22nd October 1919. She became a teacher of symmetrical dancing in Colombo, Ceylon.
  - Jane Edith Mary Kingdon born 1896.
  - Frank Denys Kingdon (1898–1971) was commissioned in the Royal Field Artillery on 31st August 1917. While serving with 29th Battery, he organised a stretcher party when two of his men were killed and several others wounded and got them to safety under heavy shellfire. He was later observing under heavy enfilade fire, passing valuable information to his Battery. As a result, he was awarded the MC, LG 2nd December1918. Frank married Florence Helen Constance Williams (1903–87) in 1931. He was appointed to the Sudan Government and was awarded the Order of the Nile, 4th Class, LG 10th June 1932. When Sudan became independent in 1956 he was Acting Governor.
- Herbert Freyberg (1855–1924) married Laura Jane Grimwade (1853–1946) in 1880 at Holy Trinity, Tulse Hill, London. Herbert was a Captain in 1881, living at 200 Earls Court, Kensington and by 1901 he was a surveyor and they had moved to 2 Woodville Road, Ealing. By 1906 they were living at 28 York Street, Portman Square, London, by

Wellington College.

1911 at Constable's Cottage, Felixstowe, Suffolk where he was an architect as well as a surveyor and at the time of his death in 1924 at 8 Gray's Inn Square, London. He was a Temporary Captain and Group Adjutant, County of London Volunteer Regiment, East Group until relinquishing the appointment on 6th July 1917. Temporary Major 3/6th Battalion 7th July. Herbert and Laura had two sons:

- Geoffrey Herbert Freyberg (1881–1966) was commissioned in the Royal Navy as a Sub-Lieutenant on 15th November 1900, rising to Commander on 30th June 1915. He was Mentioned for his services at Jutland, LG 15th September 1916, and was awarded the OBE for valuable services as Navigating Officer of HMS *Valiant*, LG 31st July 1919.
- Launcelot Percy Freyberg (1885–1916) was commissioned in the Royal Navy as a Sub-Lieutenant on 3rd May 1906 and was a Lieutenant Commander on HMS *Russell* when she struck two mines laid by U-73 off Malta on 27th April 1916. HMS *Russell* sank with the loss of 125 of her crew, including Launcelot who is commemorated on the Chatham Naval Memorial.

Bernard Freyberg in a swimming competition in 1914.

SS *Maunganui*, launched in 1911 to carry the Royal Mail, worked the San Francisco - Sydney route and was a troopship in both World Wars. She was subsequently sold twice and broken up in 1957.

The Carrancistas were one of many factions involved in the Mexican Civil War. They followed Venustiano Carranza from 1913 and the Government army 1914–20.

- Percy Freyberg, (1859–1931) married Florence Mary Charter (c.1853–1937) in 1884 at Kensington. He was a surveyor by 1901 and they were living at 47 Warwick Road, Ealing.
- Oscar Freyberg (1881–1915) volunteered with his brother Paul in 1900 and served as a Private in South Africa during the Boer War with the New Zealand South African 'Rough Riders'. He was commissioned in the Volunteer Naval Brigade in Wellington and studied to become a lawyer. At the outbreak of war in 1914, he joined the Royal Naval Volunteer Reserve as a Sub-Lieutenant. Early in the war he may have had the original idea for fast motor launches with a gun mounted forward to tackle the growing submarine threat. If so it was developed within the Admiralty and the Motor Launch Patrol was born. Many of the boats were built in America and this led to claims that the idea originated there as well. Oscar and served with the Collingwood Battalion, Royal Naval Division. He was killed in action during the Third Battle of Krithia, Gallipoli on 4th June 1915, when the Battalion was all but destroyed (Helles Memorial).
- Paul Milton Freyberg (1884–1917) studied law and volunteered with Oscar to serve in South Africa during the Boer War. He was also commissioned in the Volunteer Naval Brigade and served during the Great War as a Rifleman in 4th Battalion, 3rd New Zealand Rifle Brigade (12374). He was wounded at Basseville, near Bullecourt, France and died at Boulogne on 18th June 1917 (Boulogne Eastern Cemetery, France - IV A 7).
- Cuthbert Freyberg (1886–1973) enlisted as a Gunner in D Battery, New Zealand Artillery (2/91) on 1st August 1914 at Wellington and served in Samoa. He was commissioned Temporary Sub-Lieutenant in the Royal Naval Volunteer Reserve on 11th November 1916 and served in the Royal Naval Auxiliary Patrol, Motor Boat Service until he transferred to the Army and was appointed Temporary 2nd Lieutenant on probation for duty with the Royal Flying Corps 14th March 1917. Temporary Lieutenant, West Yorkshire Regiment 14th September 1918. After the war, he returned to New Zealand where he became a solicitor and married Helen Mary Stuart. They lived at 97 North Street, Palmerston North, Manawatu-Wanganui. Cuthbert may have served again in the Second World War.
- Claud Victor Freyberg (born 1888) became a civil servant. His mother was determined that one member of the family should remain and he did not enlist for war service.

Bernard was educated by his mother and at Wellington College 1897–1904, where he was also a Sergeant in A Company of the Cadet Corps. He was known as 'Freyberg Tertius' and was not a scholar. His passion was swimming and he won the junior and senior swimming championships at the College. In the period 1900–11, he won fourteen gold medals and nine silver medals for swimming. In 1905 he competed in the Australian championships in Sydney and Brisbane and in the New Zealand championships at Nelson in 1906, in which he won the 100, 440 and 880 yards and the mile races. He also won the 100 yards freestyle in the New Zealand senior championship in 1910. He also played water polo, rugby, rowed, boxed and sailed.

Royal Naval Division troops at Antwerp in October 1914.

Despite being ranked bottom of the fourth form, Bernard had ambitions of becoming a doctor, but his father could not afford to support him while training. James realised for a relatively small payment of £100, his son could take up an apprenticeship for dental surgery. Bernard was removed from school in December 1904, just in time to enrol for the dental apprenticeship, as a reformed and expensive four-year degree course was enforced from January 1905. He was apprenticed to JS Fairchild and later to Arthur Hoby, both dental surgeons in Wellington, from December 1904. He attended dental school at Otago University March - May 1910 and was admitted to the Dentists' Register on 22nd May 1911, remaining on it until 30th July 1936, when he was removed at his own request.

He became an assistant and locum to Arthur L Yule at Morrisville for just under a year and managed a branch for him in the final months. He was then employed for two years in the surgery of Stuart Mackenzie at Levin. Bernard served in D Battery, New Zealand Field Artillery Volunteers in Wellington 1905–07 and was

The poet Rupert Brooke was one of Bernard Freyberg's platoon commanders. He died just before the landings on Gallipoli and was buried on Skyros on 23rd April 1915.

commissioned in 6th (Territorial) Hauraki Regiment on 18th January 1912 (later backdated to 20th November 1911). He attended the first Territorial camp held in the Auckland district early in 1912 and then attended a machine-gun course at Paeroa. He also volunteered as a mounted Special Constable at Wellington during the national dock and shipping strike in 1913. He answered the Government's call for volunteers and served as a stoker on TSS *Manganui*, making the Wellington - Sydney trip on several occasions and often worked a double-shift in an effort to obtain his stoker's certificate.

Bernard grew restless and frustrated with his life and career. A former swimming friend advised him *'to cut adrift and find his feet in a wider world'*. He handed in his notice and travelled during March and April 1914 on RMS *Tahiti* from Wellington, via Tahiti to San Francisco, California, arriving on 20th April.

It is understood he then served as a Captain Volunteer with the Mexican Carrancistas, on the staff of General Filipe Angeles, under General Carranza and Francisco 'Pancho' Villa June–July 1914, during the Mexican Civil War. Another version says he was attracted by advertisements for volunteers to serve and he signed up as an armed guard for the National Film Unit, which was filming the war in Mexico. He deserted in late July/early August on hearing of the coming war in Europe. With a price on his head for desertion, he walked and hitchhiked 300 miles to catch a steamer out of Tampico, Mexico. He arrived in New York in early August and travelled aboard the White Star liner SS *Cedric* via Queenstown, Ireland on 14th August, arriving at Liverpool, England on 24th August. He caught a train to London intending to enlist in the New Zealand Expeditionary Force at Parliament Chambers, 13 Victoria Street.

HMS *Dartmouth*.

The enlistment officer, Major FM Lampen, told him the quota for officers for the New Zealand Force had been filled and there was no immediate prospect of a commission. A London-based New Zealand press representative advised him to try the newly formed Royal Naval Division. Bernard approached Winston Churchill, First Lord of the Admiralty, as he crossed Horse Guards Parade from the Admiralty to Downing Street. Churchill tried to brush him aside, but faced with a very determined young man, was forced to stop and listen to him. With Churchill's encouragement, Freyberg applied immediately and was granted a temporary commission as a Lieutenant RNVR on 8th September 1914 with seniority backdated to the end of August.

Bernard was allocated to the Hood Battalion to command A Company. He was known as 'Khaki Jack' as he arrived in khaki, whereas most officers were still wearing naval blue. His fellow officers in A Company, the 'Argonauts', were the cream of British society; Arthur Asquith, Rupert Brooke, Denis Browne and Patrick Shaw-Stewart.

The Hood Battalion trained at Betteshanger Camp in Kent on the estate of Lord Northbourne until it embarked, with 2nd Brigade RND from Dover to Dunkirk on 2nd October 1914 and thence by train to Antwerp. They were under-equipped, having little personal kit, bandoliers or haversacks and only 120 rounds of rifle ammunition per man in their pockets. The Hood Battalion deployed to trenches between Forts 5 & 6 in the inner ring of defences around Antwerp on 5th October. The Battalion was forced to withdraw three days later. Bernard caught his hand in the electrified barbed wire system, resulting in severe burns and flesh damage to his right hand. It was bandaged hastily as his Company pulled back across the Scheldt. He was hospitalised at Ostend on 10th October. 2nd Brigade RND embarked in three ships at Ostend for Dover on 13th October and returned to Betteshanger Camp.

In mid-November, the Battalion moved to a hutted camp at Blandford, Dorset where the Division was reorganised. Days after Winston Churchill inspected the Division in February 1915, orders were received for deployment to the Mediterranean. The Division was reviewed on 25th February by the King and on the evening of 27th February, it marched to Shillingstone to entrain for Avonmouth Docks. The Hood Battalion embarked on the Union Castle liner SS *Grantully Castle* the following morning and sailed in the evening. It arrived at Malta on 8th March and Mudros Bay, Lemnos on 11th March.

On 18th March the Battalion sailed into Turkish waters around Gallipoli, as a feint to make the Turkish forces disclose their dispositions and strength. *Grantully Castle* returned to Lemnos. The feint warned the Turks and gave them time to prepare to meet the coming landings. The Hood Battalion left for Port Said, Egypt, arriving on 27th March for two weeks preparatory training. It re-embarked on *Grantully Castle* at Port Said for Lemnos on 10th April, arriving on 16th April. The ship diverted to Trebuki Bay on the southern tip of Skyros because the harbour was congested with other ships. Bernard was one of the grave-diggers and pallbearers at Rupert Brooke's funeral on Skyros on 23rd April.

A fleet of fourteen transport ships and naval escorts proceeded into the Gulf of Saros on 24th April as a diversion to the main landings on the Gallipoli peninsula. With *Grantully Castle* anchored off the Bulair shore, a platoon of Freyberg's A Company was to land and light flares at intervals along the beach to fool the Turks into thinking a large-scale night landing was imminent. Freyberg, instead proposed one or two swimmers could accomplish the task with less risk and asked for his friend, Lieutenant Arthur Asquith (son of the Prime Minister, Herbert Asquith) to accompany him, but the request was turned down. Freyberg made the swim on his own covered in thick, dark grease to protect him from the cold water and make him inconspicuous. At 9 p.m., the steam pinnace of HMS *Dartmouth* towed him to within three miles of the shore. He was rowed in another mile and at 12.40 a.m. on 25th April, he started swimming ashore, towing a waterproof canvas bag containing three oil flares and five calcium lights, a knife, signalling light, and a revolver. After seventy-five minutes in bitterly cold water he reached the shore and lit the first flare. He swam east for about 300m to light a second flare and hid among the bushes. Nothing happened, so he crawled up a slope to some trenches and discovered they were dummies. After crawling just over 300m and listened for some time, he discovered nothing, returned to the beach, lit the last flare and swam off. He was picked up by Lieutenant Nelson in a cutter after 3 a.m. The destroyer HMS *Kennet* searched the shore with 12 Pounder and machine-gun fire, but there was no response. **For his gallant actions during this feint operation he was awarded the DSO, LG 3rd June and 2nd July 1915.** The feint worked for a time and the German Commander of Turkish Forces, General Liman von Sanders, was sufficiently convinced to redeploy troops and moved himself at Bulair to supervise.

Grantully Castle and *Royal George* were off Cape Helles on 30th April and the Howe and Hood Battalions disembarked during the night. They were involved in the Second Battle of Krithia 6th-8th May. Bernard was wounded in the abdomen on 8th May and evacuated to Egypt. He returned to duty in mid-June and was appointed Temporary CO of the Hood Battalion 25th June - 19th July. He was wounded again on 25th July and evacuated to Egypt until returning on 19th August. Bernard was in the rear party at Helles on 9th January 1916 and was evacuated to Mudros. He departed there on 27th February for Marseilles and then to England for ten weeks leave to recover from his wounds. He went to France to

St Martha's Church, Chilworth, Surrey, where Bernard married in 1922 and he was buried in 1963.

rejoin the Battalion on 1st May and transferred to the Royal West Surrey Regiment as a Captain and Temporary Lieutenant Colonel on 19th May, but remained to command the Hood Battalion. Bernard was slightly wounded in July.

Awarded the VC for his actions at Beaucourt sur Ancre, France on 13th November 1916, LG 15th December 1916. He was seriously wounded in the same action and spent three months recovering in London, during which he met the dramatist JM Barrie, who became one of his greatest friends. Bernard returned to France on 23rd February 1917, resuming command on 25th February. Appointed Temporary Brigadier-General and Commander 173rd Brigade 21st April - 19th September. Appointed Brevet Major 3rd June. He was wounded in five places by a shell-burst in an attack on St Julien, Ypres on 19th September and reverted to Major on relinquishing command on 15th November.

Appointed Brevet Lieutenant Colonel on 1st January 1918. The VC was presented by the King at Buckingham Palace on 2nd January and Bernard returned to France on 11th January. Appointed Temporary Brigadier-General and Commander 88th Brigade on 22nd January.

Bernard was wounded at the Forest de Nieppe on 3rd June, with shell fragments in the leg and head, but returned to duty; this was the ninth time he was wounded during the war. **Awarded a Bar to the DSO; the success of his Brigade at Gheluvelt on 28th September and on the following days was largely due to his inspiring example. He was always where the fighting was hardest, encouraging and directing his troops, LG 1st February 1919. Awarded a second Bar to the DSO at Lessines on 11th November for rushing the Dendre river bridge with nine men of 7th Dragoon Guards (including the OC, Major Wickham Frith Chappell who was awarded a Bar to his DSO for this action) one minute before the Armistice to prevent it being blown up, taking 106 prisoners, LG 8th March and 4th October 1919.** On 13th December, he was with 29th Division when it crossed the Rhine over the Hohenzollern Bridge to begin the occupation.

Awarded the CMG for services in the military operations in France and Flanders, LG 3rd June 1919. He was also Mentioned in Despatches, LG 13th July 1916, 22nd May 1917, 11th December 1917, 20th December 1918 and 5th July 1919. Awarded the French Croix de Guerre, LG 19th June 1919.

Bernard commanded the Guard of Honour for the return of the King of the Belgians to Brussels on 22nd November 1918. He served in the Army of Occupation on the Rhine and relinquished command of 88th Brigade on 15th March 1919 when he was seconded as a Captain Grenadier Guards for service on the staff with seniority from 25th September 1917. Attended Staff College from April 1919 and was accepted for Balliol College Oxford in December, but the War Office would not release him. He was a company commander in 1st Grenadier Guards at the Tower of London in January 1920 and commanded the VC Guard at the interment of the Unknown Warrior on 11th November 1920. He suffered ill health from unhealed wounds and undertook a six-week sea journey to New Zealand in May 1921 to recover and also to visit his mother. Appointed GSO2 44th Division (TA) 20th December 1921–19th December 1925. Appointed Brevet Colonel 1st January 1922.

Bernard Freyberg, standing right, at a Corps briefing in April 1945.

Although continuing with his military career, Bernard wished to enter politics. He was the unsuccessful Liberal candidate for Cardiff South in the 1922 General Election. On 3rd May 1922, he was made Honorary Doctor of Law (LLD) at St Andrews University.

On 14th June 1922, Bernard Freyberg married Barbara McLaren née Jekyll (14th June 1887 - 24th September 1973), at St Martha's Church, Chilworth, Surrey. They honeymooned in Bodnant, North Wales and at the Palazzo Barbarigo in Venice, Italy, home of Barbara's aunt, Caroline Eden. Barbara was the widow of 2nd Lieutenant The Honourable Francis Walter Stafford McLaren RFC (1886–1917), Liberal MP for Holland and Boston. Francis was the son of Sir Charles Benjamin Bright McLaren, 1st Baron Aberconway. Barbara and Francis were married on 14th June 1911, registered at St George, Hanover Square, London and they had four children - Martin Jekyll McLaren 1914, Guy LI Jekyll McLaren 1916, Elsie McLaren and Florence McLaren. Francis was killed in a flying accident in Scotland on 30th August 1917 and is buried at Busbridge (St John the Baptist) Churchyard, Surrey.

Barbara and Bernard had one son, Paul Richard Freyberg (27th May 1923 - 26th May 1993), registered at birth as Christian P Freyberg. He was educated at Eton and joined the New Zealand Division in 1940, serving in Greece the following year. He was commissioned and served with the Long Range Desert Group in North Africa 1941–42. He transferred to the Grenadier Guards (231225) 27th March 1942 and spent the remainder of the war in Tunisia and Italy. He was taken prisoner at Anzio, but escaped to the Vatican. Awarded the MC, LG 19th April 1945. After the war he saw service in Palestine 1947–48, Cyprus 1956 and 1958, and British Cameroons in 1961. Paul married Ivry Petronelle Katherine née Guild (born 1931) on 23rd July 1960. As a Lieutenant Colonel, Paul commanded the Honourable Artillery Company Infantry Battalion 1965–68 and was awarded the OBE, LG 12th June 1965. A series of staff appointments followed - Defence Policy Staff 1968–71, Director of Volunteers, Territorials & Cadets 1971–75 and as a Colonel on the General Staff 1975–78 when he retired. Paul succeeded his father as 2nd Baron Freyberg in 1963. He was a member of Boodle's and the Royal Automobile Clubs and wrote a biography of his father, *'Bernard Freyberg VC: Soldier of Two Nations'* in 1991. Paul and Ivry had four children:

Bernard Freyberg as Governor-General of New Zealand.

- Annabelle Pauline Freyberg, born 1961, married Andrew Barrow in 2000 and had a son.
- Venetia Rose Freyberg, born 1963, married Robert Phillips in 1991 and had two children.
- Christina Gabriel Freyberg, born 1967.
- Valerian Bernard Freyberg, born 1970, succeeded his father as 3rd Baron Freyberg in 1993, becoming the youngest hereditary peer in the House of Lords. He married Harriet Rachel Atkinson in 2002. Valerian was a sculptor and a member of the Design Council.

Barbara's father was Colonel Sir Herbert Jekyll KCMG (c.1847–1932), born in Scotland. He lived at Munstead House, Godalming, Surrey and married Agnes née Graham (1861–1937) in 1881 at St George, Hanover Square, London.

Bernard made two attempts to swim the English Channel in August 1925, when he failed by just 450m, and in August 1926. He returned to the Grenadier Guards in January 1926 and was promoted Major on 3rd June 1927. A staff appointment as GSO2 HQ Eastern Command followed on 31st October and he was promoted Lieutenant Colonel to command 1st Manchester at Shorncliffe near Folkestone 4th February 1929 - 3rd February 1931. While in command he wrote '*A Study of Unit Administration*'. Promotion to Colonel followed and appointment as Assistant Quartermaster-General Southern Command 6th March 1931 - 8th September 1933, then GSO1 Staff Duties Branch War Office 9th September 1933 - 15th October 1934.

Lady Freyberg in Cairo, Egypt, February 1942 (Alexander Turnbull Library).

He was promoted Major General on 16th July 1934 and went on Half Pay on 16th October awaiting an appointment. In January 1935 he was appointed GOC in the Presidency and Assam District of the Eastern Command of India, but a medical board detected an irregular heartbeat and it was cancelled. **Awarded the CB, LG 1st January 1936.** He retired on 16th October 1937 unfit for further service, became a director of Birmingham Small Arms in 1938 and supervised the erection of fifteen houses on properties inherited by his wife. Bernard tried politics again, but failed to gain the Conservative candidacy for Ipswich. He was offered the candidacy for Spelthorne, Middlesex in 1940, but was unable to stand because of renewed military commitments.

When war broke out, he was recalled on 3rd September 1939 for a home service only appointment as GOC Salisbury Plain Area, but was upgraded for active service in temperate climates on 11th October. On 16th September he offered his services to the New Zealand government and in early November met Peter Fraser, New Zealand's deputy prime minister in London. As a result, he was appointed GOC 2nd New Zealand Expeditionary Force on 22nd November. After a short visit to France, he went to New Zealand to consult with the government. He subsequently served in Egypt, Greece, Crete, North Africa, Lebanon and Italy. He was C-in-C Crete during the German invasion in 1941. **Awarded the KBE, LG 1st January 1942.** Appointed Temporary Lieutenant General 1st March 1942 and was wounded in the neck by a shell splinter on 28th June. **Received his knighthood on 27th July 1942.** Appointed temporary Commander XIII Corps 10th-16th August 1942. **Awarded the KCB in recognition of supreme gallantry and magnificent achievement on operations in the Middle East, LG 24th November 1942.**

Bernard was appointed Commander X Corps 30th April - 15th May 1943 and accepted the surrender of Italian and German forces in North Africa under the Italian Field Marshal Messe on 13th May 1943. Promoted Major General 23rd September 1943, backdated to 2nd November 1939. Appointed Commander New Zealand Corps on 3rd February 1944. He was injured in an out of action plane crash on 3rd September and returned to duty on 14th October.

Awarded a third Bar to the DSO for his conduct of the advance to Trieste in May 1945, LG 5th July 1945. He relinquished command of 2nd New Zealand Expeditionary Force on 22nd November 1945 and was promoted Lieutenant General on 28th November with seniority from 8th May 1943.

Bernard was Mentioned in Despatches three times - LG 15th December 1942, 24th June 1943 for gallant and distinguished services in the Middle East 1st May - 22nd October 1942, and 29th November 1945. Awarded KJStJ, LG 1st January 1946 and GCMG, LG 1st February 1946. Bernard also received a number of foreign awards:

- **Greek Military Cross 1st Class, LG 10th April 1942.**
- **Greek Grand Commander of the Order of the Phoenix, LG 20th June 1944, for assisting 3rd Greek Mounted Brigade in training and during the Battles of Rimini, Bellaria and Rubicone in Italy 1944, while GOC 2nd New Zealand Expeditionary Force. This was corrected to Grand Commander of the Royal Order of George I (Basilikon Tagma toy Georgioya), LG 8th February 1945.**
- **American Commander of the Legion of Merit, LG 2nd August 1945.**

Bernard was made Honorary Doctor of Civil Law, Oxford University in October 1945 and retired from military service on 10th September 1946. Barbara served throughout the war in the Welfare Branch of the New Zealand Division in Egypt, Italy and London. She was Mentioned in Despatches for her services in Cairo, Egypt in 1941, LG 15th December 1942. Awarded the OBE for the promotion and direction of the welfare of New Zealand forces in the Middle East, LG 16th July 1943. Created Dame of Grace of the Venerable Order of St John of Jerusalem, LG 1st January 1946 and Dame Grand Cross of the Most Excellent Order of the British Empire, LG 1st January 1953 for services to New Zealand.

Bernard was appointed Governor-General of New Zealand 17th June 1946 - 15th August 1952. **Created Baron Freyberg of Wellington and Munstead on 7th June 1951.** He was made Honorary Doctor of Law, Victoria University College of Wellington, New Zealand on 3rd July 1952. Returning from New Zealand, Bernard was appointed Deputy Constable and Lieutenant Governor of Windsor Castle 1st March 1953.

He was a Freemason - Household Brigade Lodge No.2614, New Zealand Lodge No.5175 and Westminster Lodge No.308 (NZ) from 1922. Bernard commanded the VC contingent at the VC Centenary Parade in Hyde Park on 26th June 1956 and attended the dedication of the Brookwood Memorial by the Queen on 25th October 1958, during which he laid a wreath.

On the afternoon of 4th July 1963, Bernard collapsed at Windsor Castle and was admitted to King Edward VII Hospital, Clewer, Berkshire. His Gallipoli stomach wound had opened up. Bernard Freyberg died without regaining consciousness that evening. The cause of death was a ruptured abdominal aorta, atherosclerosis and Parkinsonism.

The evening before his funeral on 10th July, the coffin was brought to St George's Chapel, Windsor where it lay overnight, draped with the Union and New Zealand flags. Next day, the coffin was carried out of the Chapel to Handel's *'Toll for the Brave'*. The Windsor Castle Guard presented arms as the hearse left. The funeral was held at St Martha-on-the-Hill, Chilworth, near Guildford, Surrey where he and Lady Freyberg had married in 1922. Bernard is buried in the churchyard. His wealth at death was £34,620 and probate was granted on 23rd December 1963.

In addition to the VC, Bernard was also awarded the Knight Grand Cross of the Order of St Michael & St George, Knight of the Order of the Bath, Knight of the Order of the British Empire, Knight of Justice of the Order of St John of Jerusalem, DSO & 3 Bars, 1914 Star with 'Mons' clasp, British War Medal 1914–20, Victory Medal 1914–19 with Mentioned-in-Despatches oakleaf, 1939–45 Star, Africa Star with '8th Army' clasp, Italy Star, Defence Medal, War Medal 1939–45 with Mentioned-in-Despatches oakleaf, New Zealand War Service Medal 1939–45, George V Jubilee Medal 1935, George VI Coronation Medal 1937, Elizabeth II Coronation Medal 1953, US Legion of Merit, French Croix de Guerre with Bronze Palm, Greek Military Cross and Greek Grand Commander of the Royal Order of

George I with Swords. His medals are held privately. Bernard was related distantly to four other VCs:

- John Graham - 3rd cousins.
- Robert Sherbrooke - 3rd cousins.
- Francis Grenfell.
- Walter Lorrain Brodie - Bernard's son Paul married Ivry Guild, whose uncle Reginald Mackenzie Guild married Brodie's sister, Mary Wilson Brodie.

Bernard Freyberg is commemorated in numerous places including:

- The Freyberg Scholarship funded by the New Zealand MOD to encourage graduate study into areas relevant to national security.
- Freyberg Place, a public space in Auckland with a bronze statue of him.
- Freyberg Avenue in Christchurch.
- Malus domestica Freyberg – a golden-green dessert apple originated by JH Kidd at Greytown, Wairarapa Valley, New Zealand in 1934.
- Narcissus Freyberg – a large-cupped Daffodil originated by Mrs BT Simpson in 1963.
- Freyberg Cup - a number of cups were established by the New Zealand Division or donated by Bernard himself for various sports and challenges during the Second World War. There were cups for the ten-man relay race, team athletics, inter-unit rugby and inter-unit football. The cup for rugby is in the National Army Museum, Waiouru. In 2007, the New Zealand Army Rugby Committee reinstated the Freyberg Cup to be contested annually for inter-unit rugby.
- Freyberg Cup donated by him in 1941 to be competed for by the Maadi Camp Rowing Club (MCRC) on the Nile against local Egyptian rowing clubs. At a regatta on 20th November 1943, the MCRC won against the Cairo Rowing Club (CRC). The MCRC gifted the Freyberg Cup to the CRC for future competitions and in return the CRC donated a cup to the MCRC, which on return to New Zealand became the Maadi Cup, contested by boys' eights in the New Zealand Secondary Schools' Rowing Championships.
- Freyberg Cup awarded by the Royal New Zealand Yacht Squadron to the winning Division B yacht in the Round Rangitoto leeward course.
- Freyberg Cup established by the Kohimarama Yacht Club, Auckland awarded to the winner of the Optimist Division 2 Handicap race held each half season.
- Freyberg Cup donated in 1951 by Bernard to the Wellington and Hutt Valley Agricultural & Pastoral Association for the best rider aged 14–20 at the annual Show held at Maidstone Park, Upper Hutt.
- Freyberg Rosebowl donated by Bernard in 1951 to the Centenary Golf Tournament for the Interprovincial Team Tournament. Control of the trophy and tournament

transferred to the New Zealand Golf Association (now New Zealand Golf) in 1952.

- Freyberg Masters Tournament inaugurated in 1986 by the New Zealand Golf Association (now New Zealand Golf) for teams of five male amateurs aged 40 or over.
- Freyberg Shield established in 1954 by the New Zealand Amateur Swimming Association (now Swimming New Zealand) for the highest points scoring region at the New Zealand Age Group Championships and New Zealand Open Championships.
- Freyberg Shooting Competition contested annually by Regular and Territorial Force battalions of the Royal New Zealand Infantry Regiment. It comprises rifle, machine-gun, pistol and a section shoot.
- Freyberg Trophy donated to the New Zealand Army in 1964 by Sir Eugen Millington-Drake KCMG is awarded annually to the unit shooting team attaining the highest overall score in the Freyberg Shooting Competition.
- Sir Bernard Freyberg Cup established in 1950 is awarded to the winning club in the Men's Single Sculls at the New Zealand Rowing Championships.
- Freyberg High School, Roslyn, Palmerston North, North Island (NI) opened in 1955. The School's icon is a Salamander, the nickname given to Bernard by Winston Churchill. The School also has a Lord Freyberg Memorial Gymnasium.
- Freyberg Community School, Te Atatu South, Auckland, NI opened in 1963 as Freyberg Memorial Primary School. Lady Freyberg presented a photograph of Bernard to the school in 1970. The school was renamed Freyberg Memorial Community School and is now Freyberg Community School.
- A number of New Zealand schools have Freyberg Houses:
    - Apanui School, Whakatane, Bay of Plenty.
    - Avondale Intermediate School, Auckland, NI.
    - Central Hawke's Bay College, Waipukurau, NI.
    - Hutt International Boys' School, Silverstream, Upper Hutt, NI.
    - Kaiapoi Borough School, North Canterbury, SI.
    - Opotiki College, Bay of Plenty, NI.
    - Papakura High School, Auckland, NI.
    - Rangitikei College, Marton, NI.
    - Rangitoto College, Mairangi Bay, North Shore City, NI.
    - Tauranga Boys' College, NI.
    - Tauranga Girls' College, NI.
    - Tokoroa Intermediate School, NI.
    - Waikohu College, Te Karaka, Gisborne, NI.
    - Wellington East Girls' College, NI.

2815 SERGEANT ALBERT GILL
1st Battalion, The King's Royal Rifle Corps

Albert Gill was born at 83 Hospital Street, off Summer Lane, Birmingham on 8th September 1879. His father was Henry 'Harry' Gill (c.1854–1921), an iron galvaniser. His mother was Sophy/Sophia née Ashton (1861–99). Their marriage was registered in the 2nd quarter of 1878 in Birmingham. The family was lodging with Joseph Saunders and his family at 6 Court, 28 Bridge Street West, Birmingham in 1881. By 1891 they were living at 5 Court, New John Street West, Birmingham and Henry was a tube drawer. The family also lived at Dugdale Street at some time. Henry was a brass caster in 1901, boarding at 2 Back 84 Monument Road, Birmingham and was living with his son Albert in 1911. Albert had two brothers:

- Harry Gill (1878–1947) was a tube drawer brass, boarding at 60 Steward Street, Birmingham in 1901. His marriage to Margaret Fidoe/Fido (1882–1964) was registered in the 4th quarter of 1905. They were living at 62 Steward Street, Ladywood, Birmingham in 1911. Harry and Margaret had six children: Harry Albert Gill 1906–51, Elsie Margaret Gill 1907–91, Beatrice Maud Gill 1909–91, Lily May Gill 1910–2006, Selina Sophia Gill 1914–20 and Margaret R Gill 1916.
- Samuel Gill (1889–99).

Albert worked for the Post Office for seventeen years, initially as a town sorter at Birmingham Head Post Office, Pinfield Street and later as a delivery postman in Hockley. He married Rosetta 'Rosie' née Furze (1882–1925) in the 2nd quarter of 1910. She was born at Torquay, Devon and was living with her grandparents at Queen Street, Torquay in 1891. By 1901, she was working as a nursemaid at 193 Albany Street, St Pancras, London. They were living at 1 Back of 17 Aberdeen Street, Birmingham in 1911. Albert and Rosie had two children:

The Summer Lane area of Birmingham (Newsteam).

- Albert JH Gill, birth registered in the 2nd quarter of 1911 and death in the 2nd quarter of 1915.
- Henry birth, registered in the 1st quarter of 1914 and death in the 1st quarter of 1915.

Albert is understood to have served in the Army prior to the First World War as he appears to have been a reservist in 1914 and went to France on 9th November 1914 to join the 1st Battalion. Almost nothing is known of his previous service. **Awarded the VC for his actions at Delville Wood, France on 27th July 1916, LG 26th October 1916.** He was killed during the VC action and is buried in Delville Wood Cemetery (IV C 3).

Birmingham Head Post Office, where Albert Gill worked.

On 16th August 1916, Gill's company commander wrote to his widow, *The Adjutant has handed me your letter of 8 August, as I was your late husband's Company Commander. I am afraid that it is quite true that your husband was killed in action on 27 July. He was shot in the head, and must have died at once. He could have known nothing about it. I would have written to you before had I known your address, as your husband was one of the most valued men in my company – a man whom anyone would be proud to call friend. He was killed when rallying his men under terrible fire, and had he lived he would certainly have got the D.C.M. I was quite close to him, despite the very trying circumstances. The battalion had just taken a wood, and the Germans were counter-attacking heavily. I am glad to say we drove them back, and we have since received the thanks of everyone, from Sir Douglas Haig down. It was entirely owing to the heroic example and self-sacrifice of men like your husband that we did so well. He was loved by his platoon, of which I am sorry to say only four or five men remain. That day's work will always remain fixed in my memory as the one in which I lost so many gallant comrades. I lost all the officers and sergeants in my own company, and very many of the men. You should be justly proud of your husband in his life and death. He had one of the finest natures I have ever known. No words of mine can express my sympathy with you in your terrible sorrow. May the memory of his heroic end support you.*

Albert Gill's grave in Delville Wood Cemetery.

The VC was presented to his widow by the King at Buckingham Palace on 29th November 1916. In addition to the VC, he was also awarded the 1914 Star, British War Medal 1914–20 and Victory Medal 1914–19. The medals were sold at Sotheby's to Spink's on 19th July 1965 for £800. They were later owned by A Strutt of the Military Historical Society. On 29th March 2000 they were sold by Dix Noonan Webb for £69,000 and purchased by Lord Ashcroft. Albert's Army Temperance Association Medal was included in the sale. The medals are held by the Lord Ashcroft VC Collection and are displayed in the Imperial War Museum's Lord Ashcroft Gallery.

The Army Temperance Association Medal.

The Secretary of State for Communities and Local Government, Eric Pickles MP, announced that Great War VCs would have commemorative paving stones laid in their birth places on or close to the 100th anniversary of their VC actions. Albert Gill's stone was dedicated at the Walk of Heroes, Hall of Memory, Centenary Square, Birmingham on 7th December 2015. Albert is also commemorated on his brother Harry's gravestone in the Church of England Cemetery, Warstone Lane, Birmingham (Section I, Plot 1822). Rosetta married Walter Curtis C Reed (1875–1919) in the 3rd quarter of 1917 at Birmingham. She married for the third time, Robert Price in the 1st quarter of 1920 at King's Norton, Warwickshire.

CAPTAIN JOHN LESLIE GREEN
Royal Army Medical Corps att'd 1/5th Battalion, Sherwood Foresters (Nottinghamshire and Derbyshire Regiment)

John Green was born at 'Coneygarths', High Street, Buckden, near St Neot's, Huntingdonshire on 4th December 1888. He was known as Leslie to avoid confusion with his father, John George Green BA JP (1855–1941), a farmer of 165 acres. He was commissioned in the Huntingdonshire Rifles Militia in January 1879 and promoted lieutenant 7th September 1880. On 14th April 1886 he was promoted captain in 5th King's Royal Rifle Corps (Militia) and was qualified as an Instructor of Musketry. He resigned on 4th May 1895. Leslie's mother was Florence May née Toussaint (1863–1928), born on 24th May 1863 at Kasauli, Punjab, India. John and Florence were married on 24th November 1886 at St Stephen's Church, Twickenham, Middlesex. John was living at The Hoo, Brickden at the time. The family was living at Mill Street, Buckden in 1891, St Ives Footpath,

Buckden in 1901 and at 'Birchdene', Houghton, Huntingdonshire in 1911. By 1927, John and Florence were living at St Mark's Lodge, Cambridge. Florence died at Kingston upon Thames in June 1928, leaving £69/4/7 to her husband. John left £16,249/8/11 when he died at Surbiton, Surrey in December 1941. Leslie had five siblings, but two died very young, before 1911:

- Charles Kenneth Green, whose birth and death was registered in the 4th quarter of 1890 at St Neot's.
- Dora Margaret Green (born 1893).
- Edward Alan Green (1895–1915) was commissioned in 5th South Staffordshire on 31st March 1914 and was appointed acting lieutenant on 20th November. He was killed in action on 13th October 1915. His body was never recovered and he is commemorated on the Loos Memorial. In the Army List he appears as AE Green.

Leslie's paternal grandfather, Francis 'Frank' Green (1822–1908) was born at Christchurch, Hampshire and was the son of John George Green (1789–1882), Gentleman Usher to Queen Victoria. Frank was a Commissioner of the Peace and a landowner, living at Field House, Silver Street and later at 'Coneygarths', High Street, Buckden. Frank married Louisa La Page née Norris (c.1830–1910) of Halifax in 1864.

Leslie's maternal grandfather, Reverend Charles Thomas Toussaint (1835–69), was born at Jaffna, Northern Province, Ceylon, son of Charles Cornelis Toussaint

The barracks at Kasauli, Punjab, where Leslie's mother was born in 1863.

Dud Corner Cemetery and the Loos Memorial, where Leslie's brother, Edward Alan Green, is commemorated.

and Everardina Dorothea de Vos. The family was of Dutch and Belgian origin. In 1865 Charles was appointed a junior chaplain in the Church of England in Bengal Province and became chaplain at Kasauli. He married Hannah Julia née Lewin (1827–1912). Hannah was born at Serdhannah, West Bengal, India, daughter of Benjamin Lewin, lieutenant in the service of Her Highness Begum Sombroo, and Joanna Redgrove. Charles and Hannah married in 1857 at St Paul's Church, Landour, West Bengal. In addition to Florence, they had five more daughters: Cornelia Catherine Toussaint (1858–1945), Dora Lewin Toussaint (c.1859–1943), Isabella Mary Aitchison Toussaint (born 1861), Gertrude Shackell Toussaint (c.1866–1952) and Elizabeth Monk Toussaint (born 1868). One of the daughters refused an offer of marriage from Rudyard Kipling.

Felsted School in Essex, attended by Leslie 1902–06.

St Bartholomew's Hospital, London.

Leslie was educated at St Catherine's School, Haslewood Avenue, Hoddesdon, Hertfordshire before attending Felsted School in Essex September 1902 – December 1906. He gained a scholarship to Downing College, Cambridge (BA Natural Science 1910) and went on to train as a doctor at St Bartholomew's Hospital in London (MRCS & LRCP 1913). Leslie was an all-round sportsman, excelling at rowing, golf and tennis. He became house surgeon at Huntingdon County Hospital and also went to West Africa as a surgeon on an Elder Dempster Line ship.

Rudyard Kipling as a younger man.

Leslie was commissioned as acting lieutenant on 28th September 1914. He went to France on 2nd March 1915 and was attached successively to 1/5th South Staffordshire, 1/2nd North Midland Field Ambulance and 1/5th Sherwood Foresters in July or August. Promoted captain 1st April.

Leslie married another doctor, Edith May Nesbitt née Moss MB BS (born 1889), in London on 1st January 1916. There were no children. She was a medical student at College Hall, Byng Place, London in 1911 and was on the staff of a Nottingham hospital at the time of her husband's death. She married William Hemsley Emory (born c.1886 in Washington DC, USA) in 1919 at St Giles, London.

Awarded the VC for his actions at Foncquevillers, France on 1st July 1916, LG 5th August 1916. Leslie was killed during his VC action and is buried in Foncquevillers Military Cemetery (III D 15). His will was administered by his father – estate valued at £234/2/6. The VC was presented to his widow by the King at Buckingham Palace on 7th October 1916; it is believed to be the first presentation of a posthumous VC to a relative by the monarch instead of being sent by post.

In addition to the VC, he was awarded the 1914–15 Star, British War Medal 1914–20 and Victory Medal 1914–19. His widow presented the medals to the RAMC and they are held at the Army Medical Services Museum, Defence Medical

Downing College, Cambridge.

St Mary's Church, Buckden.

Leslie Green's grave in Foncquevillers Military Cemetery.

Services Training Centre, Keogh Barracks, Mytchett, Surrey. Leslie Green is commemorated on memorials at:

- Downing College, Cambridge.
- Buckden, with his brother Alan. In 1920, an offer by their father to erect a memorial at his expense to the men of the village killed in the war, was rejected by Buckden Parish Council, but he went ahead anyway on land he owned next to 'Coneygarths'. The memorial was repaired and rededicated on 1st July 1986, the 70th anniversary of Leslie's death.
- Buckden War Memorial at St Mary's Church.

- Felsted School, Essex to both of the school's VCs (WRP Hamilton 1879 & JL Green 1916). The plaque was lost in the 1960s when the school was modernised. A new plaque was dedicated on Remembrance Sunday 1986.
- RAMC Memorial Grove at the National Memorial Arboretum, Alrewas, Staffordshire.
- Former RAMC College, Millbank, London.

15280 PRIVATE ALBERT HILL
10th Battalion, The Royal Welsh Fusiliers

Albert Hill was born at Hulme, Manchester, Lancashire on 24th May 1895. His father, Thomas Hill (1844–1907), was a coal miner. His mother, Elizabeth née Pegg (born 1848), was a charwoman. Their marriage was registered in the 4th quarter of 1869 at Lichfield, Staffordshire. The family was living at John Street, Cannock, Staffordshire in 1901 and moved to 7 Peacock Street, Denton, near Manchester in 1907. By 1916, Elizabeth was living at High Street, Denton. Albert had at least eight siblings:

- Sarah Ann Hill born 1870.
- Ellen Hill born 1874.
- Thomas Hill, born 1876, was a coal miner hewer. His marriage to Sarah Maria Bradbury (born 1877) was registered in the 3rd quarter of 1900 at Cannock. They were living at 19 Mount Pleasant Road, Denton, Manchester in 1911 and had four children: Sarah Ann Hill 1901, William Hill 1905, Annie Elizabeth Hill 1907 and Albert Hill 1910.
- Enoch Hill (1879–1958) was a coal miner in 1901. His marriage to Hannah Maria Buckley (1882–1969) was registered in the 3rd quarter of 1903 at Cannock. They were living at Piggott Street, Wimblebury, Staffordshire in 1911. Hannah had a daughter, Ellen Elizabeth Buckley, born in 1900. Enoch and Hannah had four children: Andrew Thomas Hill 1905, Dorothy Hill 1906, Mildred Hill 1908 and Leslie Hill 1910.
- William Hill, born 1881, was a coal miner in 1901. His marriage to Amanda Hill (born 1887) was registered in the 1st quarter of 1908 at Ashton. Amanda was a ring spinner in 1911 and they were living at 75 Ashton Road, Droylsden, Lancashire. They had at least three children: John Thomas Hill 1908, Doris Hill 1910 and Amanda Hill 1911.
- Mary Ann Hill born 1885.
- Elizabeth Hill born 1889.

- Joseph Hill (1896–1916) was a felt hatter machine hand in 1911. He enlisted in 10th Royal Welsh Fusiliers with his brother Albert at the outbreak of the Great War (No.24810). He was killed in action on 20th July 1916 and is commemorated on the Thiepval Memorial.

It is understood there was another brother whose name is not known. In a 1916 newspaper article, a married daughter aged twenty-one was present with Albert Hill's mother when a reporter called at the family home. The youngest known sister at that time would have been twenty-six or twenty-seven years old.

Albert was educated at Trinity Wesleyan School, Denton, Manchester. He was employed at the Alpha Mill and then as an apprentice hat maker with Messrs Joseph Wilson & Sons Ltd, of Wilton Street, Denton, Manchester as a planker. Planking involved rolling felt domes, which were rudimentary hats, with a hatter's pin on a plank to remove knots and impurities and gradually shrink and thicken the material. The process was repeated a number of times, in between which the domes were dipped in a hot water and a mild acid solution. In the previous century mercury nitrate was used in hat making, exposing hatters to its toxic fumes daily, resulting in them being 'as mad as a hatter'.

Albert enlisted on 3rd August 1914 and went to France on 27th September 1915, with his brother Joseph, sailing from Dover on SS *Onward*. The battalion moved into the line at Hooge on 15th October.

Awarded the VC for his actions at Delville Wood, France on 20th July 1916, LG 26th September 1916. The VC ribbon was presented by Brigadier General R J Kentish DSO at Enquin-les-Mines at the same time as that of Corporal Joseph Davies, on 30th September 1916. The VC was presented by the King at Buckingham Palace on 18th November 1916. Albert was feted on his return to Denton on 12th October 1916 and was thereafter known as 'Denton's VC' or the 'Hatters VC'.

Alpha Mill was badly damaged by a fire on 22nd April 1915 and on 16th March 1920 an explosion blew the roof off. It is seen here in a derelict state in 1932, before it was demolished.

SS *Onward* was built in 1905 for the South Eastern & Chatham Railway Company for the Folkestone - Boulogne service and had an eventful life. On 4th May 1905, she carried King Edward VII to Calais and on 1st June 1908, was involved in a head on collision with the steamer *Queen*. Once repaired, she carried the first motorcar over the English Channel. In the First World War she was a troop transport on her normal route. She caught fire on 24th September 1918 in Folkestone harbour and had to be scuttled to save her. She was bought by the Isle of Man Steam Packet Company in 1920 and rebuilt as *Mona's Isle*. On 29th June 1936 she struck Devil's Rock and limped into Dublin for repairs. In 1939 she was fitted out as an Armoured Boarding Vessel and made the first return trip during the evacuation of Dunkirk 27th-28th May 1940, bringing back 1,420 men from Dunkirk quayside. She was hit a number of times by German shore batteries on the return and a strafing German fighter killed twenty-three and wounded sixty. Commander John CK Dowding was awarded the DSO for his handling of his ship and Petty Officer LB Kearley-Pope the DSM for remaining at his 12 Pdr gun despite multiple wounds. Dowding was Commodore of the ill-fated PQ17 Convoy to Russia in July 1942. *Mona's Isle* made a second trip to Dunkirk, rescuing another 1,200 men. In 1941 she was transferred to the Tyne, using her guns to thicken up the anti-aircraft defences. She was involved in three collisions, one resulting in her being in dock for three months. After D-Day she was used as a cross-Channel transport. *Mona's Isle* returned to the Isle of Man route in 1946 and was broken up in 1948.

William Murrell Lummis (1886–1985) was a clerk in a magistrates' clerk's office in Coddenham before enlisting in 11th Hussars as a trooper in 1904. He met survivors of the Charge of the Light Brigade and in 1912 began to create an accurate roll of the men who served in the Regiment during the Crimean War. In August 1914 he was the RQMS and served on the Western Front throughout the war. He was commissioned in 1916 and transferred to 2nd Suffolk. He was awarded the MC for his actions on 21st- 23rd August 1918 and commanded the battalion on 23rd October 1918 is its final action of the war. After the war, he was Adjutant and Quartermaster of the Army School of Education in India and rejoined his Regiment in 1925 until retiring on 9th December 1930. Lummis was ordained deacon and had several livings before becoming a canon in 1955. His research broadened to the other four regiments involved in the Charge of the Light Brigade and, aged 98, he appeared on the BBC's Timewatch, recounting memories of meeting survivors of the Charge of the Light Brigade. Lummis is probably best known for his Victoria Cross archive, started in the 1890s. He built up the service records and final resting places of Victoria Cross holders, but was aware of shortcomings and encouraged David Harvey to continue and develop the work, which resulted in Harvey's *Monuments to Courage* in 1999. Lummis became chaplain to the VC & GC Association. The Crimean War Research Society awards the Canon Lummis Trophy annually for original research.

Awarded the French Croix de Guerre, LG 9th December 1916. For seven days in 1917 Albert was orderly to Lieutenant William Murrell Lummis MC, Acting Quartermaster of 2nd Suffolk. Lummis wrote, *Pte Hill was one of those quiet, unobtrusive fellows who make such dependable soldiers in action. He was worked up to fury against the enemy on the morning of the attack of the 76th Inf. Bde. on Delville Wood, by the news that his brother had been KIA.* Lummis retired as a captain in 1930, studied theology, was ordained and became a canon and an early researcher into the Victoria Cross. His VC files are now in the National Army Museum in Chelsea.

St George's Church, Hyde, Cheshire.

Albert was demobilised on 16th February 1919 and returned to his pre-war job. On 14th February 1920 he married Doris May née Wilson (born 1899) at St George's Church, Hyde, Cheshire. They both gave their address as 3 Perrin Street, Hyde and

RMS *Scythia* was the first of the new smaller Cunard liners built after the First World War, making her maiden voyage in 1921. She operated from Liverpool and Queenstown to New York and Boston. She was requisitioned in 1939 and was used for evacuees and as a troopship. In late 1942 she took part in the Operation Torch landings in North Africa, but on 23rd November was hit by an aerial torpedo. She got into Algiers harbour with only five casualties out of 4,300 men aboard. Having been repaired in New York, she ferried US troops to Europe and after the war took many of them home, some with their GI brides. Having brought troops back from the Far East, she completed a number of voyages taking Canadian war brides and their children from Liverpool to Halifax in 1946. In 1948 she was used by the International Refugee Organisation, taking refugees from Europe to Canada and did not return to trans-Atlantic commercial service until 1950. When she was broken up in 1958, she was the longest serving Cunard liner until 2005, when she was surpassed by the *QE2*.

later lived at 45 High Street, Denton, near Hyde. She was a cardroom operative. They emigrated to the United States, departing Liverpool on 12th May 1923 aboard RMS *Scythia* for Boston, Massachusetts, arriving on 21st May. They settled at Central Falls for ten years before moving to Pawtucket, Rhode Island c.1933. At Pawtucket, they lived at 41 Thornley Street, 117 Maryland Avenue and 175 Broad Street. Doris was a matron in a hospital in 1940 at Rhode Island. They were naturalised on 4th December 1944. Doris and Albert had four children:

Slater Mill on the Blackstone River in Pawtucket was based on cotton spinning mills first established in England. It was the first water-powered cotton spinning mill in North America to utilise the Arkwright system. It was established by Samuel Slater, from Belper, Derbyshire, in 1793.

- Joan Hill, born 1921 at Stockport, Cheshire was a carder in a thread mill at Rhode Island in 1940. She married as Garside and moved to Palmetto, Florida.
- Lawrence 'Larry' Hill (15th January 1925 – 1980), born at Rhode Island, USA. He is understood to have served in Burma during the Second World War. He married Patricia Savage (c.1931–69) and they had nine children, including David and Patricia.
- Hazeldean Hill (1929–2012), born at Rhode Island, married Joseph P Cheetham. She was a secretary at Pawtucket School Department until retirement, when they moved to Fairway Drive, Attleboro, Massachusetts around 1990. They had at least four children: William A Cheetham, Dennis Cheetham, Debra Cheetham and Dawn Cheetham.
- Joyce Hill, born 1924 at Rhode Island, USA. She married as Ervey and died before 2012.

Albert was employed as a bricklayer's labourer with HM Soule Construction Company. He tried to enlist during the Second World War, but was advised to do defence work instead. He attended the Coronation of Queen Elizabeth II on 2nd June 1953 and during his stay in Britain went back to Denton on 3rd July.

Albert Hill died at Pawtucket Memorial Hospital, Rhode Island on 17th February 1971 and is buried in Highland Memorial Park, Rhode Island Avenue, Johnston, Rhode Island (Ref 10075, Buttonwood Division, Section K, Lot 196, Grave 1). In addition to the VC, he was awarded the 1914–15 Star, British War Medal 1914–20, Victory Medal 1914–19, George VI Coronation Medal 1937, Elizabeth II Coronation Medal 1953 and French Croix de Guerre 1915 with Bronze Palme.

Albert Hill's turfstone in Highland Memorial Park, Johnston, Rhode Island.

His VC is held by the Royal Welch Fusiliers Museum, Caernarfon Castle. Albert is commemorated in a number of places:

- Hill Court, Hightown, Wrexham, Clwyd.
- Blue Plaque at Denton Gardens of Remembrance, Stockport Road, Denton, Manchester unveiled by Councillor Jill Harrison in March 1996.
- A memorial plaque in Delville Wood, France, to him and Corporal Joseph Davies VC was unveiled by Major General BP Plummer, Colonel Royal Welch Fusiliers, on 26th May 2001. A Hornbeam tree was planted alongside it by members of both families.
- Blue Plaque to all Tameside VCs at the main entrance to Ashton Town Hall, Tameside unveiled by Councillor Philip Wilkinson on 20th April 1995. The other VCs are – John Buckley, William Thomas Forshaw, James Kirk, Andrew Moynihan, Arthur Herbert Procter, Harry Norton Schofield and Ernest Sykes.

LIEUTENANT JOHN VINCENT HOLLAND
7th Battalion, The Prince of Wales's Leinster Regiment (Royal Canadians)

John Holland was born at Athy, Co Kildare, Ireland on 19th July 1890. His father was also John Holland MRCVS (c.1847–1921), born at Castlecomer, Co Kildare, Ireland. He was a veterinary surgeon at Model Farm, Athy and a member of the Kildare Hunt. His mother was Katherine née Peppard (1864–1951), born at Maryborough, Queen's County, Ireland. John and Catherine married c.1889. John junior had seven siblings:

- Michael William Holland MRCVS (1892–1934) became a veterinary surgeon and never married.
- Frances Holland (died 1968) became a nurse and never married.
- James Kevin Holland (1894–1933) became a doctor and was commissioned as a lieutenant RAMC on 1st June 1917. He served in Mesopotamia July 1917 – July 1918, North Persia & South Russia July 1918 – April 1919, North Russia August – October 1919, Malta 1920–21 (invalided) and 1921–22, Constantinople 1922–23 and Malta 1923–24. He was Adjutant with the Territorial Army 26th October 1926 – 28th October 1929 and went to India in 1930, where he died on 6th September 1933. He was promoted major on 1st June 1929. James married Annie J Osbourne and had three sons, one of whom emigrated to Australia. Another son, 1799510 Sergeant William James Kevin Holland RAFVR, died on 5th March 1945 aged nineteen, serving with 114 Squadron and is commemorated on the Malta Memorial.
- Edward Holland (c.1898–1979) became a doctor. He married Marian and had four children, three of whom emigrated to Australia.
- Ellen 'Nellie' Holland (c.1900–87) never married.
- Martin Cyprian Holland (1901–78) became a farmer and never married.
- Catherine 'Kathy' Holland (1904–77) married Hugh Cogan (died 1978). They had a son, Rory Cogan, who emigrated to the United States.

Leinster Street, Athy.

Model Farm, Athy (Buildings of Ireland).

John was educated at Clongowes Wood College, Clane, Co Kildare 1906–09 and Liverpool University, where he studied to be a vet, but did not complete his studies. He travelled extensively in South America (Brazil, Argentina, Chile and Bolivia) and was engaged in ranching, railway engineering and hunting. John was working on the Central Argentine Railway at Rosario in Santa Fe Province when war broke out and he returned to Britain immediately.

Clongowes Wood College.

He enlisted in 2nd Life Guards on 2nd September 1914 and trained at Combermere Barracks, Windsor until commissioned in 3rd Leinster on 13th February 1915. He was nicknamed 'Tin-Belly' because of his service with the Life Guards. John went to France on 9th June and was attached to 2nd Royal Dublin Fusiliers. Having been wounded at Ypres on 26th June, he was evacuated to Britain. Promoted lieutenant on 31st July and returned to France in time for the Battle of Loos as bombing officer of 7th Leinster. He returned to the 3rd Battalion in Cork in early 1916 and went back to France again in July.

Liverpool University.

Awarded the VC for his actions at Guillemont, France on 3rd September 1916, LG 26th October 1916. He was also awarded 'The Parchment Certificate of the Irish Division'.

John Holland married Frances Grogan (1896–1960) at the Cathedral in Queenstown (now Cobh, Co Cork) on 15th January 1917. She lived at 34 Elm Road, Seaforth, Liverpool, Lancashire. Her father, Joseph Grogan JP (1855–1928) of Belview Terrace, Rosleaugue and the Manor House, Queenstown,

Combermere Barracks, Windsor in 1909.

had a business that included servicing Royal Naval vessels at Queenstown. John and Frances had two children:

Cobh (Queenstown) Cathedral, Co Cork, where John Holland married Frances Grogan on 15th January 1917.

- Niall Vincent Holland, born on 14th July 1918 at St Asaph, Denbighshire. He was educated at Penryn Preparatory School, Edgbaston, Birmingham and the Royal Military College Sandhurst, where he gained a half blue for Army cricket as a bowler. He was commissioned in the Indian Army and served with 4/5th Mahratta Light Infantry in Assam, Burma during the Second World War. On one occasion he led a feint attack during the monsoon season even though he had been ill for three days and was barely able to walk. He was awarded the MC for his actions at Sangskaku 21st-26th March 1944. Niall was killed on 15th June 1944 as a major and is buried in Imphal War Cemetery, India (6 G 9).
- Norman Joseph P Holland, born at Colwyn Bay, North Wales on 10th January 1922. He was also educated at Penryn Preparatory School, Edgbaston, Birmingham and served for six years as a gunner in the Royal Artillery in North Africa, Sicily and Europe during the Second World War. He emigrated to Australia under a free ex-service scheme in 1947 and became a Commonwealth Reconstruction and Training Scheme student at university in 1948 (1st Class Hons BA, PhD). He was commissioned in the RAAF during the Korean War, but did not see active service. Norman married Kathleen 'Kay' Mary Smith (1923–2011) in Hobart in 1949. She was born in West Ham, London. Norman went on to become a lecturer at the University of Queensland and the Australian Catholic University until retirement in 1987. Kay and Norman had six children: Mary Clare Holland 1949 became a Dominican nun; Niall Holland 1951 became a doctor (MB GS FRNZCGP) and was President of the Royal New Zealand College of General Practitioners; Gabrielle Holland 1953

John Holland with his wife Frances.

became a guidance officer and school principal at Rockhampton in Queensland; Denise Holland (1956–90) also became a principal, at Toowoomba in Queensland; Bernard Holland 1958 became a principal of a school at Brisbane, in Queensland; and Andrew Holland 1963 became a bank manager in Brisbane, Queensland. Norman married secondly Deirdre McNamara in 1993.

The main gate to Kinmel Park Camp at Rhyl.

The VC was presented by the King at Buckingham Palace on 5th February 1917. Promoted captain 18th March. Became an instructor with No.16 Officer Cadet Battalion at Kinmel Park, Rhyl (Army List April 1917 – December 1919). Seconded to the Indian Army as a lieutenant 31st October 1919, with seniority from 13th November 1916. He relinquished his Leinster Regiment commission on appointment to the Indian Army as a captain on 27th November 1920 with seniority from 13th November 1919. John was attached to 2/26th Punjabis and later served with 10th Duke of Cambridge's Own Lancers (Hodson's Horse). He retired on 15th September 1922.

John joined the Colonial Service in Kenya until 1936, then returned to Britain, where he worked in a number of civil service departments, including the Passport Office and Land Settlement. The family settled at Colwyn Bay, North Wales. John was appointed a captain Royal Artillery Territorial Army Administrative Officer

SS *Orcades* (1947–73), a P&O liner, started service as a Royal Mail Ship and carried many migrants to Australia and New Zealand. She replaced the 1937 *Orcades* lost during the Second World War. *Orcades* was almost identical to P&O's RMS *Himalaya*. During the 1956 Melbourne Olympics she was used as floating accommodation.

St Mary's Cathedral, Hobart, where John Holland's funeral took place on 1st March 1975.

in June 1939 with seniority from 24th March 1939, but resigned that commission on 19th September 1939. He served in the Indian Army in the Second World War until 1941, when he was invalided out and took up a position with the Ministry of Food, being granted the honorary rank of captain on reversion to the Retired List on 16th January 1943.

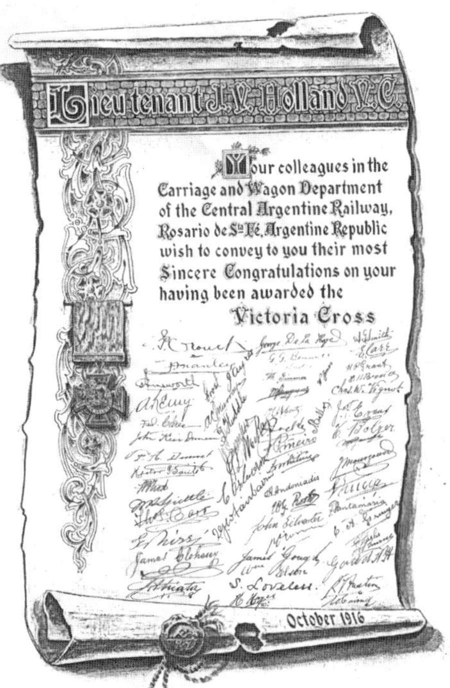

Signed certificate from his former colleagues on the Central Argentine Railway.

John and Frances were invited to live in Tasmania by their youngest son, Norman, in 1955. They settled at Gellibrand House, New Town. John attended the VC Centenary Celebrations at Hyde Park, London on 26th June 1956, travelling on SS *Orcades* with other Australian VCs.

John Holland died at St John's Park Hospital, Hobart, Tasmania on 27th February 1975. His funeral, with full military honours, on 1st March 1975, included 200 marching troops, six majors to carry his coffin and four young officers carried his medals. The coffin was transported through the streets of Hobart on a gun carriage draped in the Southern Cross, accompanied by a military band and led by a motorcycle police escort. Following a requiem Mass at St Mary's Cathedral, conducted by Archbishop Dr Gilford Young, he was buried in Cornelian Bay Cemetery with his wife (RC Section N-D, Lot 63). He is also commemorated on a memorial in Guillemont church.

In addition to the VC, he was awarded the 1914–15 Star, British War Medal 1914–20, Victory Medal 1914–19, Defence Medal, War Medal 1939–45, George V Silver Jubilee Medal 1935, George VI Coronation Medal 1937 and Elizabeth II Coronation Medal 1953. The VC is held privately.

3/5027 PRIVATE THOMAS HUGHES
6th Battalion, The Connaught Rangers

Thomas Hughes was born at Coravoo in the parish of Donaghmoyne, five miles from Castleblayney, Co Monaghan, Ireland on 10th November 1885 (20th November has also been seen). His father, Patrick Hughes born c.1854, was a farmer living with his family at Coravoo, Donaghmoyne, Castleblayney in 1901 and 1911. His mother was Alice née Walshe, born c.1860. Patrick and Alice married c.1882. Thomas had eight siblings:

- Mary Hughes, born c.1883, married as Christy c.1904 and had a daughter, Mary Jane Christy, born c.1905.
- Francis Hughes, born c.1888.
- Patrick Hughes, born c.1892.
- Kate Jane Hughes, born c.1894.
- Annie Hughes, born c.1896. She had a son, Michael.
- Margaret Hughes, born c.1898.
- Peter Paul Hughes, born c.1900.
- Alice Hughes, born c.1903.

Thomas was educated at Aughnafarcon National School, Broomfield, Castleblayney. He went to the Curragh, Co Kildare to train as a jockey as he was not very tall and lightly built. Later he was a groom for Irish horse trainer Lawrence Rooney, based at Cannock Chase, Staffordshire. He was living at 361 Hill View, Rawnsley, Hednesford, Staffordshire at the time of his enlistment.

He enlisted on 24th November 1914 at Hednesford, Staffordshire and was described as 5′ 6¼″ tall and his religious denomination was Roman Catholic. He joined 3rd (Reserve) Battalion at Kinsale on 1st December and went to France on 2nd May 1915 to join 1st Battalion. For an unknown reason he returned to the Depot on 27th September and was posted to the 3rd (Reserve) Battalion on 14th December. Thomas returned to France to join 6th Battalion on 7th February 1916.

The main street in Castleblayney.

The Silver War Badge was issued to service personnel honourably discharged, usually due to wounds or sickness. The first issue was in September 1916. It was intended to be worn on civilian clothes on the right breast. About 1,150,000 were issued, each with a unique number engraved on the back.

Contemporary sketch of Thomas Hughes receiving his VC from the King in Hyde Park on 2nd June 1917.

Awarded the VC for his actions at Guillemont, France on 3rd September 1916, LG 26th October 1916. He returned to Britain for Home Service on 14th September. The VC was presented by the King in Hyde Park on 2nd June 1917. Thomas was fined eight days pay for absence 28th November – 5th December. He was discharged no longer fit for war service on 12th February 1918 and awarded Silver War Badge No.325002C.

On his return to Ireland he helped run the family farm at Coravoo with his sister Annie, her son Michael, and another man. The people of Castleblayney, Lord Francis Hope and other prominent citizens made a presentation of money to him, with which he purchased the hill farm of Thomas Gilmours at Fincarn, Donaghmoyne, Castleblayney. Thomas became increasingly dependant on drink and in 1924 was fined for being in possession of illegal alcohol.

Thomas never married, but is understood to have had an illegitimate son, Ken Hughes, who was born in England and served in the Royal Navy as an air mechanic. Thomas died at his home at Fincarn on 4th January 1942. He is buried in Taplagh Graveyard, also known as Broomfield Old Cemetery, Broomfield, Co Monaghan. The cause of death was haemoptysis (coughing up blood) and secondary heart failure. A family source told a pupil researching local history that Thomas died at the Famine Workhouse in Carrickmacross, Co Monaghan, a County Home for the infirm, aged and destitute. He is also commemorated on a memorial in Guillemont church.

In addition to the VC, he was awarded the 1914–15 Star, British War Medal 1914–20, Victory Medal 1914–19 and George VI Coronation Medal 1937. He left the VC to his sister Annie, who sold it to a London dealer for £420 when she got into financial difficulties. Members of the Connaught Rangers Association purchased the VC from the same dealer on 4th December 1959 for £500 and presented it to the Sandhurst Military Museum, because the Connaught Rangers had disbanded in 1922. The VC later passed to the National Army Museum, Royal Hospital Road, Chelsea, London, where it is held.

14951 SERGEANT DAVID JONES
12th Battalion, The King's (Liverpool Regiment)

Hutchinson Street in 1966 (Liverpool Picture Book).

David Jones was born at 3 Hutchinson Street, West Derby, Liverpool, Lancashire on 10th January 1892. His year of birth appears frequently as 1891, but he does not appear with the family in the 1891 Census and was nine years old in the 1901 Census. He was baptised on 22nd January 1892 at St Peter's Church, Liverpool. His father, also David Jones, born at Oxton, Cheshire in 1866, was an iron moulder who became a cotton porter at Liverpool Docks by 1891. Later, he was employed as a carrier by the grocery firm of Cooper & Co. His mother was Jessie née Ginochio, born 1865 at Liverpool. David and Jessie married on 23rd February 1885 at St Nicholas Parish Church, Liverpool. They lived initially with her widowed mother at 3 Hutchinson Street, Liverpool. By 1901 the family was living at 25 Elmore Street, Everton and by 1911 had moved to 29 Aigburth Street, Liverpool. David and Jessie had eight children; nothing is known of one of them. David Junior's known siblings were:

- Marguerite Ellen Jones (1888–1965) married John H Comer in 1947.
- Joseph Jones, born 1890, was a clerk at a cotton brokers in 1911.
- William Jones, born 1894, was a wooden hoop maker in 1911.
- John Alfred Jones (1896–1862), a groceries and prisons boy in 1911, married Martha Tipping (registered as Tippin) (1894–1977) in 1915. They had five children: David Jones 1815, Lilian Jones 1916, John A Jones 1918–22, Ellen Jones 1920, Hilda Jones 1921–2009, Gladys Jones 1927, Walter Jones 1932 and Margaret Primrose Jones 1935.

St George's Dock and Our Lady and St Nicholas Church, where David Jones' parents married on 23rd February 1885, the Anglican parish church of Liverpool. On 11th February 1810 the spire collapsed into the nave, killing twenty-five people gathering for morning service. A new tower and lantern were built and until 1868 it was the tallest building in the city. In an air raid on 21st December 1940 the main body of the church was destroyed. The rebuilt church was dedicated on 18th October 1952.

- Samuel Wilkinson Jones (1898–1939).
- Walter George Jones, born 1907 at Liverpool.

David's paternal grandfather, also David Jones (c.1834–82), was an engraver. He married Thirza Pope (c.1836–60) on 31st December 1855 in Liverpool. They had two children:

- William James Jones (1856–1914), a boilermaker, married Mary Elizabeth Nicholson (1855–1905) in 1880 and had three daughters: Thirza Elizabeth Jones (1881–1961), Sarah Jane Jones 1883 and Emma Eleanor Jones 1884.
- Emma Jane Jones (1858–1941) married George Deaville (1860–1949) on 24th December 1877 at St Nicholas Church, Liverpool. They had six children: Thirza Deaville 1878, Minnie E Deaville 1882, David Deaville 1885, Joseph William James Deaville 1888, Matilda Deaville 1890 and George Deaville 1894.

He married Matilda née Smith (c.1836–75) in 1861 at St Nicholas's Church, Liverpool. The family had moved to Newbury's Lane, Oxton, Cheshire by 1871. In addition to David they also had: Caroline Ann Jones (1863–72) and Joseph Jones 1874. By 1881 he was boarding with his two sons, David and Joseph, at 12 Clare Street, Islington, Liverpool.

David's maternal grandfather, Peter or Pietro Ginochio (or Genochio), was born c.1822 at Genoa, Italy. He emigrated to Liverpool and worked as a plaster-moulder and journeyman marble mason. He died between 1864 and 1871. David's maternal grandmother, Sarah Ann née Wilkinson (c.1823–97), married Ludovicus 'Louis' Gasparino (c.1807–1851) in 1840 in Liverpool. He was born at Palermo, Sicily and his surname also appears as Gasparini, Gaspernie and other variations. They had six children:

- John Samuel Gasparino (1841–42).
- Maria Rose Anna 'Mary' Gasparino (1844–1904), was a lady's maid in 1871. She married Bernardo Mutti (c.1830–81), a musician born in Italy, in 1872 (she was registered as Mary Gaspernei or Gaspernel). His surname has also been seen as Mulli, Motti, Mutto and other variations. They had four children: Margaret Phyllis Mutti 1874–1944, Peter Paul Mutti 1876–1973, Theresa Dominic Mutti, born and died 1877, Mary Louisa Mutti 1879–81 and Francisco Bernardo Mutti, born and died c.1881. As Maria Mutti she married Peter Morri (c.1842–95) in 1885. He was an organ grinder, born in Italy. It is possible he was Bernardo's brother. They had a son, Joseph Motti (1887–1967).
- Cecilia Gasparino, born 1846.
- Margarita Elena 'Margaret Ellen' Gasparino (1848–1932), married William Faulds in 1869, but the marriage ended in divorce in 1894 on the grounds of her adultery. She was housekeeper to John Fearon Goodacre (1847–1909) from at least 1881 and they married in 1895.
- Elizabeth Gasparino 1850–51.
- Joseph Gasparino, born 1851–52.

Following Louis' death in 1851, Peter Ginochio married Sarah Ann Gasparino née Wilkinson at St Joseph's, Liverpool, in 1856. In addition to Jessie they also had:

- Elizabeth Anne Ginochio (1857–1913) married Michael Danahy (c.1857–95) in 1880. She married John Vermiglio (c.1860–1940) in 1898. He was an ice-cream seller with at least four children from a previous marriage: Victoria Vermiglio c.1885, Joseph Vermiglio c.1890, Dominic Vermiglio c.1893 and Albert Vermiglio c.1895.
- Catherine 'Catherino/Catharina' Ginochio (1859–87) married Angelo Diodati (born c.1851 in Italy), a musician, in 1880. They had two children: Marian Sunta Diodati 1881 and Vincenza Diodati 1884.
- Angelo Steven Ginochio (1864–66).

In 1861, Peter and Sarah Ann were living at Nash Grove, Liverpool with Peter's nephew, Louis Carvanaro, and his wife Mary and son Andrew. By 1881, Sarah Ann was living as a widow with the remainder of her family at 24 Spring Place, Liverpool, before moving to 3 Hutchinson Street, Liverpool.

The headquarters of 9th King's (Liverpool Regiment), Territorial Force, in Everton Road. David Jones was a member of the Battalion between 1909–13.

Heyworth Street Council School, Everton, in 1967 (Liverpool City Group).

David was educated at Heyworth Street Council School, Everton. It amalgamated with Steers Street School to form Everton Park School in 1971. Everton Park School itself amalgamated with St George's to form The Beacon Primary School on Heyworth Street, Everton in 1998. David became a trainee motor mechanic with J Blake Motor Company in Liverpool. He also enlisted in

Heyworth Street, Everton, in 1951.

David Jones' grave in Bancourt British Cemetery, near Bapaume,

9th King's (Liverpool Regiment) Territorial Force on 8th June 1909 (1207) and served until 7th June 1913. David enlisted again on 29th August 1914, joining 12th King's.

On 27th May 1915, he married Elizabeth Dorothea née Doyle (1890–1967) at St Cecilia, Tuebrook (the current church was built in 1930). She was living at 55 Silverdale Street, Tuebrook at the time and they moved to 87 Heyworth Street, Everton. There were no children.

An advertisement for J Blake Motor Company in 1916. Joseph Blake opened a carriage building firm in Liverpool in 1871 and became involved with motor vehicles later. Blake's was responsible for transporting Royal Mail around the Liverpool area between 1908–20 and in 1910 became Merseyside's first Ford dealer. The company expanded and was owned by Albany Garages Ltd, later Albany Lease Ltd. It went into liquidation in 1998.

David's battalion was inspected by the King at Knighton Down, Larkhill on Salisbury Plain on 24th June. Knighton Down is where part of the Beatles film, 'Help' was shot in May 1965. The Battalion moved to France on 24th July. He returned home on leave in November. **Awarded the VC for his actions at Guillemont, France on 3rd September 1916, LG 26th October 1916.** It had been assumed that David Jones died without knowing he had been awarded the VC. However, one of his comrades, Francis Coxhead, reported that the CO, Lieutenant Colonel Vince, told David on 6th October, almost three weeks before it was gazetted. He was killed in action near Gueudecourt, France, on 7th October 1916 during the Battle of the Transloy Ridges. He was buried close to where he died and his body was later exhumed and reinterred at Bancourt British Cemetery, near Bapaume, France (V F 20).

The VC was presented to his widow by the King at Buckingham Palace on 31st March 1917. The King asked her to wear it over her right breast, which she did, but was embarrassed when soldiers saluted her. She married William John Woosey (1891–1957), a plumber, on 19th July 1920 at St Anne's Catholic Church, Liverpool. They lived at 138 Portelet Road, Tuebrook and had a son, Gordon Woosey in 1921. Elizabeth died at St Vincent's Hospice, Liverpool in 1967 and is buried in Ford Cemetery (PO 28).

In addition to the VC, he was awarded the 1914–15 Star, British War Medal 1914–20 and Victory Medal 1914–19. His widow presented the VC to his former employer, Joseph Blake & Co (Ford Motor Dealers), as she was not willing to present it to the amalgamated King's

The outside memorial at Heyworth Street Council School.

St Nathaniel's Church, Oliver Street, Liverpool, just before it was pulled down. It was founded in 1869, burned down in 1900, rebuilt and reopened in 1904, closed in 1980 and demolished in 1993.

Everton Library, St Domingo Road, Liverpool, in 1949. It was built in 1896 and is being restored by the Heritage Works Buildings Preservation Trust in partnership with Hope Street Ltd, Liverpool City Council and the Heritage Lottery Fund for reopening in 2016 as an international creation centre for arts, culture, heritage and enterprise (Liverpool City Group).

and Manchester Regiment. The VC was on loan to the Museum of Liverpool from August 1994 and in 2009 was presented to it by the Trustees of Joseph Blake & Co. The campaign medals are not with it.

David Jones is commemorated in a number of places:

- Two memorials were erected at Heyworth Street Council School; one of brass inside the school and another of granite at the front of the school, facing Heyworth Street. The plaque inside the school was moved to Everton Park CP School in the 1970s. The plaque outside was moved to Everton Library, St Domingo Road, Liverpool in the 1980s.
- Memorial tablet in St Nathaniel's Church, Edge Hill, Liverpool. The church was demolished in 1993.
- Victoria Cross Memorial, Liverpool Town Hall.
- Named on Panel 66 of the First World War Memorial Roll, Hall of Remembrance, Liverpool Town Hall.
- Memorial Plaque, Guillemont Church, France.
- A memorial unveiled opposite 19 Abercromby Square, Liverpool in July 2008, depicts Captain Noel Chavasse VC & Bar MC RAMC helping a wounded soldier accompanied by a stretcher-bearer. Fifteen other VCs associated with Liverpool are included on the memorial, including David Jones.

11000 PRIVATE THOMAS ALFRED JONES
1st Battalion, The Cheshire Regiment

Thomas Jones was born on 25th December 1880 at 39 Princess Street, Runcorn, Cheshire. He was known as Todger, a combination of Thomas and Dodger, a name he acquired as a result of his soccer dribbling skills. His father, Edward Jones (1843–1932), was a fitter at the Hazlehurst Soap Works, Runcorn, where he worked for sixty two years. He was also a preacher at the Ellesmere Street Free Church in Runcorn and a member of the Oddfellows friendly society. Todger's mother was Elizabeth née Lawson (1849–1927). Edward and Elizabeth married on 18th April 1868 at Frodsham Parish Church, Cheshire. The family was living at 24 Princess Street, Runcorn in 1871 and 39 Princess Street by 1881. Todger had eight siblings:

- Joseph Edward Jones (1868–1923) was a construction labourer in a chemical works in 1911, living with his family at 27 Egerton Street, Runcorn. He married Annie Molyneux (1872–1931) in 1890. They had six children: Annie Lilian

Jones 1890–1970, Joseph Edward Jones 1893–1962, Thomas Clifford Jones 1894, Sarah Maud Jones 1897, Charles Leonard Jones 1906–26 and Mary Beatrice Jones 1911.

- Emma Jones (1870–1956) was known as Emily. She married David Lightfoot (1867–1947), a chemical labourer, in 1890. By 1911 he was a pipe fitter and the family was living at 51 Princess Street, Runcorn. They had four children: Charles Edward Lightfoot 1891–1961, Frank Leonard Lightfoot 1893–1964, George Frederick Lightfoot 1897 and Florence Elizabeth Lightfoot 1901.
- Frederic Jones (1873–1925) was a chemical labourer in 1891. He married Mary Elizabeth Caldwell (1874–1901) in 1894 and they had a son, Peter Caldwell Jones 1894–1962. In 1904, Frederic married Elizabeth Louisa Thornton (1882–1951). They were living at 6 Princess Street, Runcorn in 1911 and had five children: Ivy Elizabeth Jones 1904–97, Charles Edward Jones 1907–95, George Frederick Jones 1909–85, Lilian Jones 1911 and Emily Jones 1914–87.
- Peter Jones (1875–1926) was steward of the Liberal Club in Widnes.
- Lilly Jones 1878–79.
- Charles Arthur Jones (1884–1917) was a toilet soap labourer. He served as a private in 10th Cheshire (15088) and was shot in the head by a sniper on 6th October 1915. He was treated at No.25 General Hospital, Boulogne before being evacuated to North Western General Hospital, Hampstead on the 22nd, where he underwent the first of four operations. He was transferred to the Regimental Depot on 14th April 1916 and was discharged from the Army on 16th June as no longer fit for war service, with a pension of 12/6 per week. He was awarded Silver War Badge No.86821. He took employment as a weigher and lived with his parents until he died at home on 30th July 1917. He is buried in Runcorn Cemetery, Cheshire with his sister Lilly (11 400).

Runcorn in the 1920s (Britain from Above).

Frodsham Parish Church (St Lawrence), Cheshire, where Todger Jones' parents married in 1868.

- Sarah Maude Jones (born 1887) married Richard H Williams in 1915.
- Walter Jones (1890–1937) was an apprentice boiler maker in 1911. He married Hilda Bayes née Wheat (1891–1958) in 1915 and they had a daughter, Gladys Jones, in 1917.

Todger's paternal grandfather was Edward Jones, born c.1811 at Halkin, Flintshire, where he was a lead miner. Having moved to Runcorn, he was a labourer in a soap works, living with his family at Nelson Street. He married Fanny née Dunbabin (c.1815–72) in 1837. In addition to Edward, they had five other children: John Jones c.1837–77, William Jones c.1840, Thomas Jones 1844, Joseph Jones 1848 and Henry Jones 1854.

His maternal grandfather, Peter Lawson (c.1818– 95), was a labourer. He married Martha (c.1806–83) c.1834. In addition to Elizabeth they had three other children: James Lawson c.1834, Thomas Lawson c.1836 and Peter Lawson c.1839.

Todger was educated at Runcorn National School 1885–94, later known as Runcorn All Saints Parish Church School and is now All Saints CE Primary School, Church Street, Runcorn. He was an apprentice fitter at the Hazlehurst Works in Runcorn and was later an engineering fitter at the Salt Union Works at Weston Point, Runcorn.

The Territorial Force Efficiency Medal was awarded for twelve years service in the Territorial Force. It replaced the Volunteer Long Service & Good Conduct Medal when the Territorial Force was formed in 1908. It was replaced in turn by the Territorial Efficiency Medal when the Territorial Force became the Territorial Army in 1920.

He enlisted in the Runcorn Volunteers on 15th January 1900, a company of 2nd (Earl of Chester's) Volunteer Battalion. It became 5th (Earl of Chester's) Battalion, The Cheshire Regiment on 24th April 1908 on the formation of the Territorial Force. He was noted for his marksmanship and was awarded the Territorial Force Efficiency Medal in 1912. When he resigned from the Territorial Force in 1913, he went on to the National Reserve.

Todger was recalled on 5th August 1914 and was attested at Runcorn on 31st August 1914. He wanted to go to the Royal Engineers, but remained with the Cheshire Regiment. He was described as 5′ 6″ tall, weighed 126 lbs and was of good physical development. Having spent some time training at Birkenhead, he went to France on 16th January 1915. On 24th December 1915 he was awarded twenty-eight days Field Punishment No.1 for over-staying his leave in England by four days and also forfeited four days' pay.

Awarded the VC for his actions at Morval, France on 25th September 1916, LG 26th October 1916. The VC was presented by the King at Buckingham Palace on 18th November. He received a civic reception in Chester

A newspaper picture from 1916, which purports to show Todger Jones (right) leading some of his prisoners to the rear.

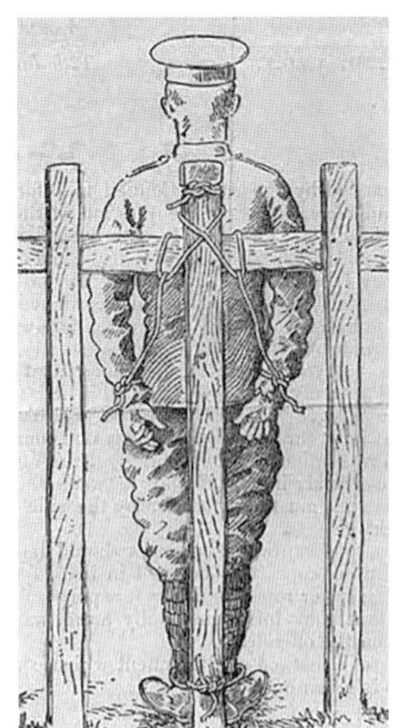

Field Punishment No.1 was introduced in 1881 when flogging was abolished in the army. Commanding officers could award it for up to twenty-eight days and courts martial up to ninety days. The punishment consisted of being tied hand and foot to a fixed object, such as a wheel or fence, for up to two hours per day. Sometimes the arms were stretched out and the soldiers called it 'crucifixion'.

A hero's welcome in Runcorn.

and was presented with a gold wristwatch, a silver teapot, a case of cutlery and a pair of field glasses. In November 1916 the Buffalo Lodge at the Saddle Inn, Grosvenor Road, Chester presented him with a silver cigarette tube and case. The same month the Salt Union Company of Runcorn presented him with a silver teapot.

Todger was wounded and gassed on 4th August 1918 and admitted to hospital at St Omer the following day. **Awarded the DCM for his actions at Beugny near Bapaume, France on 28th September 1918; he went forward five times with messages through an intense barrage, he also led forward stragglers to their positions, LG 5th December 1918.** He was discharged on 28th May 1919.

Todger with the helmet, complete with bullet hole, that he wore at Morval. It is now displayed in the Cheshire Military Museum.

Todger's son, Thomas William Jones Abram, with his wife Minnie and daughter Edna c.1941 (Percy Dunbavand).

Todger Jones being presented to King George V at Runcorn on 8th July 1925. On his left is Thomas Taylor and on his right is Thomas Moffat, survivors of the action at Rorke's Drift in January 1879, for which eleven VCs were awarded.

During the Second World War Todger served in the Home Guard (Percy Dunbavand).

Todger was to marry Robina Abram (1895–1983), but the plan fell through. However, they had a son, Thomas William Jones Abram, born on 8th April 1915 at 26 Shaw Street, Runcorn. He married Minnie Edna Nash (1918–95) in 1939 and they had two children: Edna Abram 1941–96 and Lynda Abram 1947. During the Second World War he served in the Royal Navy. Thomas William Jones Abram died on 1st May 1986 at 6 Cedar Avenue, Runcorn. Robina Abram married Joseph Griffiths (c.1895–1962) in 1918 and they lived at 18 Larch Close, Runcorn.

Todger returned to his pre war job at the Salt Union Works, which was later taken over by ICI, and remained there for a total of thirty-six years, until retiring in 1949. He lived at Old Cross Street and in 1920 he was presented with a gold medallion by Sir Frederick Norman at the Runcorn Liberal Club. On 8th July 1925 he was presented to King George V during his visit to Runcorn.

The Victoria Memorial Hospital, Runcorn, known locally as the Cottage Hospital, where Todger died on 30th January 1956.

The VC memorial in Victoria Park, Widnes, Cheshire.

Thomas Jones' grave in Runcorn Cemetery.

In the Second World War he was an ARP Warden and later served in the Home Guard. He was a member of the Liberal Club in Runcorn, winning prizes for billiards, and also served as Honorary Secretary of Runcorn Reserves Football Club.

Thomas Jones was admitted to Victoria Memorial Hospital (Cottage Hospital), Runcorn on 4th January 1956 and died there on 30th January. The causes of death were pulmonary embolism, auricular fibrillation and arteriosclerosis. The informant when the death was registered was his niece, Florence Anderton, of The New Inn, Runcorn. He is buried in Runcorn Cemetery. The headstone was renovated in 1986, largely due to the efforts of Western Front Association member Stan Ellison.

In addition to the VC and DCM, he was awarded the 1914–15 Star, British War Medal 1914–20, Victory Medal 1914–19, Defence Medal, Territorial Force Efficiency Medal, George VI Coronation Medal 1937 and Elizabeth II Coronation Medal 1953. On 16th May 1956, his sister, Emily Lightfoot, donated the medals to the Cheshire Regiment Museum and they are currently held at The Soldiers of Cheshire, Cheshire Military Museum, The Castle, Chester, Cheshire. She also presented an Iron Cross that Todger took from one of his prisoners at Morval. The Museum also displays the bullet-holed helmet he was wearing during the VC action. Todger is commemorated in a number of places:

- A white marble VC was placed on his grave by the Regiment on 17th June 1956 during a short service conducted by the chaplain of the local British Legion.
- A memorial tablet to him is set into the floor of the Regimental Chapel in Chester Cathedral, Cheshire.
- On 3rd August 2014, a bronze statue by David Annand was unveiled in the Memorial Garden, Runcorn.
- A memorial to him, Thomas Mottershead VC and Thomas Wilkinson VC in Victoria Park, Widnes, Cheshire.
- Todger Jones Memorial Cup awarded annually for a bowls competition in Runcorn. The original trophy is in the Cheshire Regiment Museum, but in 1997 the competition between the Runcorn and Halton Royal British Legion branches was revived.
- Todger Jones VC Cup, awarded annually to the winner of the Runcorn Darts League.
- Memorial on the wall of the Halton Community Partnership Trust, the Old Police Station, Bridge Street, Runcorn, Cheshire.
- Thomas Jones Way and Morval Crescent in Runcorn are named after him and the battle in which he won his VC.
- An illuminated scroll presented to him by Runcorn Urban District Council is displayed in the Mayor's Parlour in Runcorn Town Hall.

SECOND LIEUTENANT HENRY KELLY
10th Battalion, The Duke of Wellington's (West Riding Regiment)

Henry Kelly was born at 12 Lewis Street, St George, Manchester, Lancashire on 17th July 1887. His father Charles Kelly (c.1865–1904), born at Sandyford, Dublin, Ireland, was a labourer and by 1901 was a gas stoker. His mother was Jane née McGarry, born in 1868 at Lambeth, London. Charles and Jane married in the 2nd quarter of 1887 at Manchester. The family was living at 5 Hulis Street in 1891, 5 Clegg Street in 1901, 53 Princess Street, Moston in 1911 and 4 Cicero Street, Moston in 1914. Henry had ten siblings, one of whom did not survive infancy:

- Margaret 'Maggie' Kelly, born c.1889, was a telephonist in 1911.
- Louisa Kelly, born c.1890, was a machinist mantles in 1911.

- Jane Kelly, born c.1893, was a finisher mantles in 1911.
- Charles Kelly, born 1893, was a warehouseman in 1911.
- Thomas Kelly, born c.1896, was a telegraph messenger in 1911.
- Joseph Kelly, born c.1900.
- James Kelly, born c.1902.
- Mary Kelly, born c.1904.

Henry's maternal grandfather, Henry McGarry, born c.1838 in Co Limerick, Ireland, was a bricklayer's labourer in 1871, living with his family at 4 King Street, Manchester, Lancashire. He married Mary née Hickey (born c.1845 at Co Limerick, Ireland) in 1865 in Kensington, London. In addition to Jane they also had a son, Thomas McGarry, born c.1866.

Henry was educated at St Patrick's School, Manchester and the Xaverian Brothers College, Victoria Park, Manchester. He then worked as a sorting clerk at Newton Street Post Office, Manchester. When his father died in 1904, Henry was the sole provider for his mother and her children. Henry was working as a sorting clerk and telegraphist in 1911.

The Xaverian Brothers College, Manchester.

Newton Street Post Office, Manchester.

Henry served in the East Lancashire Engineers (TF) and was time expired according to his enlistment documents in 1914. He enlisted in 12th Manchester on 5th September 1914 (5987), described as 5′ 8″ tall, weighing 147 lbs, with ruddy complexion, blue eyes, brown hair and his religious denomination was Roman Catholic. Promoted lance corporal 19th September, corporal 13th November and unpaid lance sergeant 18th November. Appointed acting sergeant on 16th February 1915 and was commissioned in 11th (Reserve) Battalion West Riding Regiment on 12th May. He went to France in May 1916 and joined 10th Battalion. Promoted temporary lieutenant 11th September 1916 and was appointed acting captain 23rd October – 26th December 1916 while commanding a company.

Awarded the VC for his actions at Le Sars, France on 4th October 1916,

LG 25th November 1916. The VC was presented by the King at Buckingham Palace on 14th February 1917. Temporary captain while commanding a company 21st September – 16th December. The battalion went to Italy in November. Appointed acting captain 8th March 1918.

Awarded the MC for his actions at South Avenue, 1000 yards south of Asiago, Italy on 21st/22nd June 1918; he commanded a raiding party of his company and two platoons of another, killing up to eighty enemy, taking thirty-one prisoners, a flamethrower and two machine-guns for the loss of one killed, eighteen wounded and three missing, LG 24th September 1918. Promoted captain 21st September 1918. **Awarded a Bar to the MC for his actions near Casa Polesi, four miles southwest of Vazzola, on the north bank of the Piave River, on 27th October 1918; he took all his objectives in an attack across the Piave against Austrian positions, capturing many machine-guns and several hundred prisoners, LG 2nd April 1919 and 10th December 1919.** Temporary major 19th July 1919 while second-in-command of No.9 Rest Camp in France until demobilized on 7th January 1920.

Henry returned to the Post Office. In 1922 he went to Ireland and took part in the civil war, serving as a major for the General Chief of Staff for Operations in the Irish Free State Army. While in Ireland he studied at the National University, Dublin and qualified as a chartered surveyor (BA & BSc). He returned to England and the Post Office again until 1925, when he opened a number of grocery shops with his brothers on Rochdale Road and Upper Charlton Road. He also joined the Catholic association, the Knights of St Columba, and became the first Grand Knight of Council 105, 1925–27.

Henry Kelly married Eileen Guerin (1898–1985) of Killarney, Co Kerry, Ireland at Manchester in September 1926. They had two children:

- Eileen Kelly, born in the 1st quarter of 1928 at Manchester North.
- Henry Kelly, born in the 1st quarter of 1931 at Manchester South. He was commissioned in the Duke of Wellington's Regiment on 14th August 1954. Promoted lieutenant on 11th September 1955 and was attached to the Federation of Malay Forces on 23rd September. He was appointed temporary captain on 1st July 1957 and left the Army in 1959/60.

The Spanish Royal and Military Order of Saint Ferdinand.

Competition in the grocery trade resulted in Henry appearing in the Manchester Bankruptcy Court on 17th July 1931. His liabilities were £4,593, with a deficiency of £397. Failure to the business was caused by lack of capital, losses through fire, accidental loss of takings, and ill-health. Henry went into the licensed victualler business, keeping various hotels in Manchester, including the Crown Hotel. In 1932 he moved to North Wales and continued in the licensed trade.

Henry fought in the Spanish Civil War as Commandante Generale International Brigade against the Fascists 1936–8. **Awarded the Royal and Military Order of Saint Ferdinand in 1937 (Real y Militar Orden de San Fernando), commonly known as the Laureate Cross of Saint Ferdinand.**

On 13th December 1940 he was commissioned in the East Surrey Regiment as a lieutenant. Promoted captain 17th December 1940 and transferred to the Pioneer Corps with seniority as lieutenant backdated to 13th December 1940. He served in 73rd Company 29th January – 2nd February 1941, 123rd Company 8th February – 5th March and then with 75th Company. He transferred to the Cheshire Regiment on 6th October 1941 and worked as District Claims Officer, Curzon Street, London District. His duties included investigating claims for war damage, necessitating journeys around London.

He was accused of making fraudulent claims for travel expenses in the period October 1943 to February 1944 and was tried by General Court Martial at Chelsea on 5th October 1944; he denied the charges. Major FCB Covell, prosecuting, alleged that on ten dates Kelly claimed train and bus fares when he had travelled in a War Department vehicle. On another occasion Kelly is alleged to have claimed on a day when he was ill and did not make a journey. Kelly stated that typists had made an error in transcribing expenses forms from the rough draft. He also said he worked on Sundays and did not want his Colonel to know, so entered his claims for Sundays on other dates. The total value of claims amounted to £2/10/-. He was found guilty, severely reprimanded and resigned his commission on 30th November 1944.

Henry returned to North Wales and worked as an auctioneer, valuer and estate agent for a few years before retiring and moving back to Manchester. Henry died at Prestwich Hospital, Manchester on 18th January 1960 and is buried in the Roman Catholic Section of Southern Cemetery, Wythenshawe, Manchester (Plot 1, Grave 1372) with his wife and her sister. His address at the time was 178 Hall Lane, Baguley, Manchester.

In addition to the VC and MC & Bar, he was awarded the 1914–15 Star, British War Medal 1914–20, Victory Medal 1914–19, Defence Medal, George VI Coronation Medal 1937, Elizabeth II Coronation Medal 1953 and the Spanish Royal and Military Order of Saint Ferdinand. The VC is held by the Duke of Wellington's Regiment Museum, Bankfield Museum, Boothtown Road, Halifax, Yorkshire.

101465 PRIVATE JOHN CHIPMAN KERR
49th Battalion (Edmonton Regiment), Canadian Expeditionary Force

John Kerr was born on 11th January 1887 at Fox River, Cumberland County, Nova Scotia, Canada. His father, Robert Kerr (1834–98) was a lumberman born in Cumberland County, Nova Scotia. His mother was Elizabeth née Green, born 1847. Robert and Elizabeth married on 30th July 1868 at Amherst, Cumberland. The family was living at Parrsboro Shore in 1891 and at Port Greville, Cumberland County 1901. John had seven siblings:

- Ebenezer Ernest Kerr (1869–84).
- Catherine Kerr (1870–84).
- Gertrude Kerr (1873–1917).
- Robert Gesner Kerr, born 1877, married Eva Mae/May Loring (1880–1969) in 1907. They had a son, Robert Loring Kerr, in 1908.
- Roland J Kerr (1881–1917) (also seen as Charles Roland Kerr), served as 461137 Private Roland J Kerr, 43rd Battalion (Manitoba Regiment) CEF and died on 26th October 1917 (Ypres (Menin Gate) Memorial, Belgium).
- Ernest Kerr, born 1885.
- Sarah Isabel Kerr, born 1891.

RMS *Olympic* (45,324 tons), the lead White Star Olympic class liner, was in service 1911–35; the others in the class were *Titanic and Britannic*. While a troopship she was known as "Old Reliable". She was the world's largest liner until overtaken by RMS *Titanic* (46,328 tons) and later by SS *Imperator*. On her maiden voyage in June 1911 from Southampton to New York she was captained by Edward Smith, who captained *Titanic* the following year. *Olympic* received *Titanic*'s distress call and set off at full power, but was still 100 nautical miles away when the rescue effort was completed. On 24th September 1915, she commenced her first voyage as a troopship from Liverpool to Mudros. On 12th May 1918, en route to France with US troops, she sighted a U-boat, opened fire and turned to ram it. It dived, but *Olympic* struck the submarine and sliced through U-*103*'s hull. The crew abandoned her, but *Olympic* continued to Cherbourg; USS Davis picked up the survivors. During the war, *Olympic* carried about 200,000 personnel and travelled 184,000 miles. In 1934, White Star merged with Cunard, allowing funds to be granted for completion of RMS *Queen Mary* and RMS *Queen Elizabeth*. *Olympic* left New York for the last time in April 1935 and was broken up in 1936–37. She completed 257 Atlantic round trips, carried 430,000 passengers and travelled 1,800,000 miles.

Halifax, Nova Scotia.

John's paternal grandfather was Ebenezer Kerr (1796–1870). He married Lavinia Caroline née Gesner (1809–90) in 1827 and in addition to Robert, they had twelve other children – James Kerr 1828, Anna Maria Kerr 1830, John Kerr 1832, Ebenezer Kerr 1836, Famicha Kerr 1838, Harriet Elizabeth Kerr c.1839, Henry Gesner Kerr 1843–1915, Lavinia Caroline Kerr 1845–1913, Joseph Norman Kerr born and died 1846, Sarah Catherine Kerr 1849, Julia Charlotte Kerr 1850 and Aleida Yates Kerr 1852–1920.

John was educated at Fox River School, Cumberland and St John Commercial School. He left home in 1906 to work in the Kootenay area of British Columbia as

An 1846 engraving of St John Evangelist, Charlotte Street, Fitzroy Square, where John Kerr married Gertrude Bridger in 1917. The church was badly damaged by a V1 flying bomb on 25th March 1945.

Bexhill-on-Sea, where John Kerr was serving at the time of his marriage at the Canadian Training School.

a lumberman. In 1911 he was lodging at 43 Slocan Riding, Kootenay. He moved to Spirit River, 300 miles north of Edmonton, Alberta, in 1912 and bought a 65 hectare homestead and farmed it with his brother, Roland, until war broke out. They left the homestead with a note on the door, *"War is hell, but what is homesteading?"* and then walked fifty miles to the railhead. They enlisted in 66th Battalion CEF on 25th September 1915 at Edmonton, Alberta. John was known as Chip to his comrades. He was described as 6' tall, weighing 191 lbs, with dark complexion, grey eyes, dark brown hair and his religious denomination was Church of England. He was in hospital at Edmonton 2nd March–18th April for a hernia operation.

66th Battalion embarked at Halifax on 1st May 1916 aboard RMS *Olympic* and disembarked in England on 6th May. John joined a draft to 49th Battalion on 4th June and went to France to join the Battalion on 8th June. He was soon in Belgium and in action at Sanctuary Wood near Ypres. **Awarded the VC for his actions at Courcelette, France, on 16th September 1916, LG 26th October 1916.**

He received a gun shot wound to the right hand on 18th September 1916 and was admitted to 2nd Canadian General Hospital at Le Treport before being evacuated to Britain on 21st September aboard HS *Asturias*. He was transferred to the strength of the Canadian Casualty Assembly Centre at Folkestone and was treated at Lewisham Military Hospital from 23rd September. He transferred to the Canadian Convalescent Hospital at Bromley on 30th November until discharged on 8th December and reported to the Canadian Casualty Assembly Centre at Hastings next day. The VC was presented by the King at Buckingham Palace on 5th February 1917.

Following Medical Boards at Hastings, Sussex on 5th and 10th March, he joined the Alberta Regiment Depot at Hastings. On 24th March, he became orderly to GOC Canadian Troops London Area, but this appointment only lasted until 31st March when he was posted to 224th Battalion (Forestry). On 12th May he was posted to the Base Depot Canadian Forestry Corps and joined HQ Canadian Troops London

The Peace River ferry at Dunvegan, Alberta.

The Turner Valley oilfields near Calgary.

John Kerr's grave marker in Mountain View Cemetery, Vancouver, British Columbia.

The Canadian Volunteer Service Medal 1939–45 was awarded to members of the armed forces who voluntarily served on active service from 3rd September 1939 to 1st March 1947 and completed eighteen months. In 2001 it was extended to certain civilian categories, including merchant mariners, Corps of Canadian Fire Fighters who served in Britain during the Blitz, Overseas Welfare Workers, Ferry Command aircrew and British Commonwealth Air Training Plan Instructors. In 2003 it was extended to members of the Royal Canadian Mounted Police who voluntarily served during the War. A silver bar with a maple leaf was awarded for sixty days service outside Canada. Other bars were awarded for Dieppe, Hong Kong and Bomber Command.

Area as a clerk. Appointed Acting Corporal 26th May–15th September, when he was posted to the OTC at Bexhill on Sea until 27th December. A Medical Board at Smith's Lawn, Sunningdale on 10th January 1918 concluded he had deformities of the left foot and right forefinger; the former was mainly due to a pre-war accident. On 9th January he was posted to the Canadian Discharge Depot at Buxton and on 23rd February embarked for Canada from Liverpool on SS *Missanabie* (sunk by UB-*87* on 9th September 1918 off Ireland). He arrived at St John, New Brunswick on 17th March and was admitted to No.13 Casualty Unit on 23rd March. He attended another Medical Board at Edmonton on 6th April.

John Kerr married Clarissa Gertrude Bridger (26th February 1898–5th December 1981) on 7th November 1917 at St John The Evangelist, Fitzroy Square, London. She was born at Edmonton, Middlesex and was known as Gertrude. At the time, she was living at 42 Seaton Street, Hampstead Road, London and he at the Canadian Training School, Bexhill-on-Sea, Sussex. John and Gertrude had four sons and a daughter, including:

- Leslie Walter Kerr (c.1919–42) served as a Sergeant Pilot in the RCAF (R/61046) and died on 16th July 1942. He is buried in the same grave as his father at Vancouver (Mountain View) Cemetery.
- Rod Kerr.

Mount Kerr in Jasper Park, Alberta is the peak in the centre background.

Gertrude's father was Walter Bridger (1873–1954), a butcher living at 135 Lever Street, Finsbury, London in 1891. He married Clarissa née Bird (1875–1958) at Poplar, London in 1897 at Islington, London. The family was living at 241 Hoxton Street, Hackney, London in 1902 and later moved to Picton, 6 Kings Avenue, Birchington, Kent. In addition to Clarissa, they had five other children - Ethel Rosie May Bridger 1899, Jessie Violet Bridger 1900–02, Walter George Bridger 1902–67, Richard Bridger 1909 and Ruby E Bridger 1909–94.

The Port Greville War Memorial, Cumberland County, Nova Scotia (Nova Scotia's Electric Scrapbook).

On his return, John was greeted by a crowd of 10,000 near the Canadian Pacific Railway depot and the streets were blocked for hours by people waiting for the train to arrive. He was met by Mayor Harry Evans and the city aldermen. His wife Gertrude accompanied him to the Legislative Building, where they were met by Lieutenant Governor Robert Brett, Premier Charles Stewart, ministers of the cabinet and members of the legislature. He was presented with $700 in gold. In his reply John said, *"You don't go in for heroics at the front. If a man is chosen for the job, he does it and that is all there is to it unless someone sees him doing his duty and rewards him for it. Nobody thinks of gaining distinction. If a man saves his hide, he thinks himself well off."*

John was discharged on 20th April 1918 no longer fit for war service (he had lost 31 lbs since he enlisted) and returned to the Spirit River homestead, but sold it six years later and then worked in the oil fields at Turner Valley near Calgary. He returned to Spirit River, where he worked as a forest ranger patrolling the Peace River and ran the government ferry at Dunvegan, Alberta.

At the outbreak of the Second World War, John re-enlisted in the Army and transferred to the RCAF in the hope of going overseas. However, he remained in Canada as a Service Policeman and Sergeant-of-the-Guard at Sea Island, British Columbia. He retired to Port Moody, British Columbia and took up salmon fishing. In 1955, he jumped into the icy waters of Burrard Inlet, Loco to refloat his fishing boat. John was presented to Queen Elizabeth II and Prince Philip at Westminster during their Royal Tour of Canada in 1959.

John Kerr died at his home in Port Moody, British Columbia on 19th February 1963. He is buried in the Veteran's Division, Abray Section, Mountain View Cemetery, Fraser Street, Vancouver, British Columbia with his son Leslie in Block 5, Plot 6, Lot 9. His grave marker is erroneously located at Block 5, Plot 8, Lot 12 where his wife is buried.

In addition to the VC, he was awarded the British War Medal 1914–20, Victory Medal 1914–19, Canadian Volunteer Service Medal 1939–45, War Medal 1939–45, George VI Coronation Medal 1937 and Elizabeth II Coronation Medal 1953. His widow presented his medals to the Canadian War Museum, Vimy Place, Ottawa, Ontario in 1975, where they remain. John also received the unofficial French Médaille Commémorative des Batailles de la Somme 1914–18 & 1940.

John Kerr is commemorated in a number of places:

- Chip Kerr Park at Port Moody, British Columbia was named after him on 1st January 2006.
- Plaque near the ferry he ran at Dunvegan, Alberta.
- Mount Kerr (2560m/8399') in Jasper Park, Alberta is one of six peaks of nineteen in the Victoria Cross Range named after Canadian VCs. It was named after him in 1951.
- A war memorial was dedicated to him and those who served during two World Wars and the Korean War, at Port Greville, Cumberland County, Nova Scotia on 22nd July 2001. Her Honour, Myra A Freeman, Lieutenant Governor of Nova Scotia, unveiled the monument, accompanied by Loring Kerr, nephew of John Kerr, who wore his uncle's medals.
- A wooden plaque bearing fifty-six maple leaves each inscribed with the name of a Canadian-born VC holder was dedicated at the Canadian Forces College, Toronto on Remembrance Day 1999.
- Named on a Victoria Cross obelisk to all Canadian VCs at Military Heritage Park, Barrie, Ontario dedicated by The Princess Royal on 22nd October 2013.

- Named on one of eleven plaques honouring 175 men from overseas awarded the VC for the Great War. The plaques were unveiled by the Senior Minister of State at the Foreign & Commonwealth Office and Minister for Faith and Communities, Baroness Warsi, at a reception at Lancaster House, London on 26th June 2014 attended by The Duke of Kent and relatives of the VC recipients. The Canadian plaque was unveiled outside the British High Commission in Elgin Street, Ottawa on 10th November 2014 by The Princess Royal in the presence of British High Commissioner Howard Drake, Canadian Minister of Veterans Affairs Julian Fantino and Canadian Chief of the Defence Staff General Thomas J Lawson.
- The Secretary of State for Communities and Local Government, Eric Pickles MP announced that Victoria Cross recipients from the Great War would have commemorative paving stones laid in their birthplace as a lasting legacy of local heroes within communities. The stones would be laid on or close to the 100th anniversary of their VC actions. For the 145 VCs born in Australia, Belgium, Canada, China, Denmark, Egypt, France, Germany, India, Iraq, Japan, Nepal, Netherlands, New Zealand, Pakistan, South Africa, Sri Lanka, Ukraine and United States of America, individual commemorative stones were unveiled at the National Memorial Arboretum, Alrewas, Staffordshire by Prime Minister David Cameron MP and Sergeant Johnson Beharry VC on 5th March 2015.
- Two 49 cents postage stamps in honour of the 94 Canadian VC winners were issued by Canada Post on 21st October 2004 on the 150th Anniversary of the first Canadian VC's action, Alexander Roberts Dunn VC.

John Kerr was related to Greg J Kerr (born 1947), who represented Annapolis West in the Nova Scotia House of Assembly 1978–93 for the Progressive Conservatives. He served in the Executive Council of Nova Scotia as Minister of Culture, Recreation and Fitness 1980–81, Minister of the Environment 1981–83, Minister of Finance 1983–93, Minister of Housing 1988–89 and Minister of Tourism and Culture 1992–93. He was not re-elected in 1993 and was unsuccessful in the 2006 election for the House of Commons. In 2008, he was elected as Conservative MP for West Nova and became Parliamentary Secretary to the Minister of Veterans Affairs. Following a stroke in 2014 he decided to stand down at the next election.

2053A PRIVATE JOHN LEAK
9th Australian Infantry Battalion, AIF

Details of John Leak's birth, family and early life are uncertain. It is claimed he was born in Portsmouth on 1st March 1896, but no documentary evidence can be found. The year was calculated from his headstone, which gives his age as 76 when he died in 1972. Family sources indicate the date was 1st March. On enlistment, the age he gave indicates he was born in February 1892. Other sources indicate that his parents were from South Wales, which they left in 1886, but others indicate John was born in Queensland about 1894. No documentary evidence to support either claim has been found. Indeed, in interviews, John provided different places of birth. When he was invested at Buckingham Palace in November 1916, the *Cardiff Times* stated he claimed his mother was from Mountain Ash and that his father, James, from Brynmawr, had moved to New South Wales. However, although the family was described as being well known in these places, nobody could be found who knew them. When John married in Australia in 1927, his name was William JE Leak and gave his age as twenty-eight, indicating he was born about 1899. He gave his birthplace as Peak Hill in Canada, which has not been identified. His parents were given as James Leak, which was consistent with his first marriage registration in Wales, and his mother as Sarah Wilson; his mother's name was not required for his first marriage record. In summary, there is nothing definite about John's birthplace and date, his family or his early life. Indeed he may not have been born as a Leak.

Australian reinforcements about to board HMAT A55 *Kyarra* (6,953 tons) in 1917. The scene would have been similar when John Leak boarded her with 5th Reinforcement Group on 16th April 1915. *Kyarra* was built in Scotland for the Australian United Steam Navigation Company in 1903. She worked the route between Freemantle, Western Australia and Sydney, New South Wales, carrying cargo and passengers. On 6th November 1914 she was requisitioned and converted into a hospital ship and in March 1915 became a troop transport. On 5th May 1918 she was sailing from Tilbury to Devonport when she was sunk by UB-57 off Anvil Point, near Swanage; six lives were lost (Australian War Memorial).

John is reputed to have had a brother, George or James Leak, who emigrated to Saskatchewan, Canada. John nominated him as his next of kin when he enlisted. Nothing is known about John's education, but he emigrated to Australia as a young man and reputedly became a bullock teamster in Queensland. However, this is questionable as he would not have been old enough to have the experience to be a teamster.

Mudros harbour on Lemnos was the main logistics base for the Gallipoli operation.

John enlisted on 28th January 1915 at Rockhampton, Queensland. He was described as 5′ 6″ tall, weighed 133 lbs, with sallow complexion, brown eyes, black hair and his religious denomination was Church of England. He was based

Kingstonian (6,454 tons) was torpedoed and damaged in the Mediterranean off San Pietro Island, Italy by UB-*68* on 11th April 1918. She was beached in Carloforte Bay, but was torpedoed by UB-*48* on 29th April and the damage caused resulted in her being a total loss.

at Enoggera Barracks, Brisbane before embarking on HMAT A55 *Kyarra* for the Middle East with the 5th Reinforcement Group on 16th April. Having disembarked at Alexandria, Egypt, he moved to camp at Heliopolis before taking part in operations on the Gallipoli peninsula with 9th Battalion from 22nd June. He was evacuated sick to Mudros on 31st August and was transferred to St David's Hospital, Malta on 30th September. From there he was evacuated to Britain on 8th October. John

Dieppe (1,210 tons), a passenger ferry built in 1905 for the London, Brighton and South Coast Railway on the Newhaven-Dieppe route, was requisitioned as a troopship and later as a hospital ship. In 1933 she was sold to WE Guinness and converted to a private yacht, *Rosaura*. In 1934, the Prince of Wales and Wallis Simpson cruised aboard her, as did Winston Churchill and his wife Clementine in the Mediterranean. She was requisitioned again in the Second World War as an armed boarding vessel, HMS *Rosaura*, and was sunk by a mine off Tobruk on 18th March 1941 with the loss of seventy-eight lives.

returned to Alexandria aboard the *Kingstonian* on 4th March 1916 and rejoined 9th Battalion on the 9th. The battalion embarked at Alexandria on the *Saxonia* on 27th March, landing at Marseilles, France on 3rd April.

Awarded the VC for his actions at Pozières on 23rd July 1916, LG 9th September 1916. He was wounded near Pozières on 21st August with a gunshot to the back and was evacuated to Britain from Calais aboard the Hospital Ship *Dieppe* on 13th September. John's condition had improved sufficiently for him to be granted leave on 9th October until posted to Wareham, Dorset on 27th October. He was presented with the VC by the King at Buckingham Palace on 4th November.

John appears to have been adversely affected by his experiences at the front and this was reflected in his disciplinary record. On 3rd January 1917 he was awarded fourteen days detention for entering the Staff Sergeants' Mess at Wareham to demand drinks and refused to leave when ordered. He was absent 23rd February – 2nd March, which resulted in him being awarded four days' detention and forfeiting fifteen days' pay. On 23rd March he transferred to 69th Battalion at Fovant, near Salisbury, Wiltshire. He went absent from Hurdcott, close to Fovant, 29th – 30th July, but was admonished and just forfeited two days' pay. On 11th August he was posted to the Overseas Training Depot at Perham Down, near Tidworth, Hampshire and absented himself again 20th– 24th August; he forfeited seven days' pay as a fine and another four days to cover the days of absence.

John embarked at Southampton for Le Havre on 9th October and returned to 9th Battalion on 15th October. On 1st November the battalion was in reserve trenches south of Zonnebeke near Ypres, when warned to move to the front line. Just before his platoon was due to move, John could not be found. Six days later he was arrested at Calais among soldiers going on leave. He had no leave pass and claimed his papers had been stolen. He was tried by Field General Court Martial on 23rd November for desertion and pleaded not guilty. He told the court, *When I got back to the line this time after returning from England, I found I could not stand shellfire. On the night of 30th October I was in a ration party up the line and we were shelled with gas shells and had to put our box respirators on and finding we could not see in the dark we removed the eye pieces and I was affected by the gas. I saw my Company Commander next morning as I wanted to go and see the Medical Officer. He said if I could smoke a cigarette I was not too sick and there was no sick parade in the line. He told me to go and lie down for a bit.* He was found guilty. The court took his record, including the VC and previous offences, into account and Leak was allowed to make a plea in mitigation. He concluded with, *I volunteered to return to France and rejoined the 9th Battalion*

An early camp at Wareham, Dorset.

There were a number of camps at Fovant during the First World War. Some of the units based there left their mark by carving their regimental badges into the chalk down to the south of the camps and a few of these still exist.

in October 1917. I never had any leave in England except fourteen days sick furlough and had to pay all my own expenses when I went to Buckingham Palace. He was sentenced to penal servitude for life; for Australian forces this was the most severe punishment available. However, under the Army Suspension of Sentences Act, penal servitude could be suspended to allow the soldier to return to active service, but the threat of the sentence remained and was reconsidered quarterly.

St Denis (2,570 tons) was built at Clydebank in 1908 for the Great Eastern Railway for the Harwich - Hook of Holland service and was originally named the *Munich*. She was requisitioned during the First World War as a hospital ship and renamed *St Denis*. After the war she was acquired by the London & North Eastern Railway in 1923 and continued on the Hook of Holland route. In 1940, while involved in the evacuation of Amsterdam, she became trapped and was scuttled. The Germans salvaged her and she was eventually scrapped in 1950.

John rejoined 9th Battalion from detention on 23rd December. He was gassed on 7th March 1918 near Hollebeke, Belgium and evacuated to 55th General Hospital at Aubergue, Wimereux, near Boulogne, on 11th March. From there, he boarded the Hospital Ship *St Denis* to England the same day and was admitted to the Military Hospital at Boscombe, Hampshire. He recovered at the Convalescent Depot, Hurdcott from 26th March. He was absent yet again 25th – 29th April, forfeiting seven days pay as a fine and another four days' for the days of absence. He was posted to Longbridge Deverill Depot, Wiltshire on 23rd May. On 5th June he was awarded seven days

Field Punishment No.2 for insolence to an NCO.

John embarked at Folkestone, Kent for France on 19th June and rejoined 9th Battalion on 26th June. On 30th August, he reported sick with bronchitis and was sent to hospital. On 5th September he was in 1st Australian General Hospital with a fractured ulna and transferred to No.2 Convalescent Depot, Rouen on 12th September and to No.11 Convalescent Depot at Buchy next day. John returned to the battalion on 13th October and was granted leave in England on 8th December. His suspended sentence was reviewed in March, June, and September and on Christmas Day was remitted.

Five days later, John Leak married Beatrice May Chapman (born 1897) at St John the Baptist Church, Cardiff. He applied to the Australian Government for assisted passage for his wife, but was refused. He was posted to Weymouth for recuperation on 15th January 1919 and embarked on HMAT *Ascanius* on 26th March for Australia. He travelled to Rockhampton, Queensland on 9th April and was received formally at the Soldiers' Rest and Recreation Rooms next day. John Leak was discharged in Brisbane, Queensland on 31st May 1919.

Folkestone became the main port of departure and arrival to/from France for most soldiers.

Soldiers at No.2 Convalescent Depot, Rouen, celebrating Christmas 1917.

1st Australian General Hospital.

St John the Baptist Church, Cardiff, where John Leak married Beatrice May Chapman on 30th December 1918.

Beatrice remained in Wales and was living with her parents at 18 Shakespeare Street, Roath under her maiden name until 1935. The marriage of a Beatrice M Chapman to Leonard H Williams, registered in Cardiff in the 1st quarter of 1936, may explain why there is no further trace of her as Leak.

Meanwhile, in Australia John was registered to sell firewood from The Commonage in the Allora district of Queensland. He eventually owned three leases in the region on Portions 179, 182 and 184 at The Commonage, Berat via Allora. The land was poor, but he managed to raise a few sheep and did some market gardening. He was well respected in the community and was eventually granted government assistance. He was living at the Diggers' Rest Home, Bishopscourt, White Hills, Bendigo in 1922.

Although there is no record of his marriage to Beatrice being annulled, John Leak married Ada Victoria Bood-Smith (c.1908–64) on 12th January 1927 at Coolgardie, in Western Australia. He gave his name as William JE Leak, aged twenty-eight. Ada and John had eight children: Ada Victoria Leak 1927–28, Myrtle Marie Leak 1928–2001, John William Leak 1929–2000, Margaret Alice Leak 1930, Katherine 'Kathy' Leak 1932, Alfred Leak 1933–93, Raymond Leak 1934 and Patrick James Leak 1946.

John moved frequently, working in Queensland, New South Wales, South Australia and then to Esperance, in Western Australia, about 1932, where he became a garage proprietor and mechanic. He was living at Waverley Ridge, Crafers, South Australia in retirement in 1963. Ada died on 27th September 1964 and is buried in Stirling District Cemetery, Adelaide, South Australia (14 A).

John suffered medical problems for most of his life as a result of the war. In later years, he suffered from bronchitis

John Leak with Beatrice Chapman and her family (Australian War Memorial).

HMAT A11 *Ascanius* (10,048 tons) was launched in 1910 in Belfast for the Ocean Steam Ship Company of Liverpool. She was a troopship from October 1914. After the war she was used as a refrigerated cargo ship between Liverpool and Australia. She was a troopship again in the Second World War and in 1949 was sold to an Italian company and renamed *San Giovannino* until she was scrapped at La Spezia in 1952.

and emphysema and died following a heart attack at Redwood Park, Crafers, Adelaide, South Australia on 20th October 1972. He is buried with his wife.

In addition to the VC, he was awarded the 1914–15 Star, British War Medal 1914–20, Victory Medal 1914–19, George VI Coronation Medal 1937 and Elizabeth II Coronation Medal 1953. In February 1967 a gunsmith and second-hand dealer named Harris appeared in court in Carlton, Victoria for having three forged VCs. The Leak forgery carried the number 2653 instead of 2053 and was smaller and lighter than the original. Harris was fined $A40 plus costs and the forgeries were destroyed by the Department of Defence. The whereabouts of John Leak's VC is not known. He is commemorated in a number of places:

- Victoria Cross Memorial, Campbell, Canberra dedicated on 24th July 2000.
- Plaque at the Cenotaph, Allora, Queensland, unveiled on 11th November 2009 by Allora Sub-Branch Returned and Services League President, Eric Taylor.
- Victoria Cross Memorial, Queen Victoria Building, George Street, Sydney, New South Wales.
- Monument on Sir Raymond Huish Drive, Rockhampton, Queensland, dedicated on 20th April 2012.

- Named on one of eleven plaques honouring 175 men from overseas awarded the VC for the Great War. The plaques were unveiled by the Senior Minister of State at the Foreign & Commonwealth Office and Minister for Faith and Communities, Baroness Warsi, at a reception at Lancaster House, London on 26th June 2014 attended by The Duke of Kent and relatives of the VC recipients. The Australian plaque is at the Australian War Memorial in Canberra.
- Leak Street, Bittern, Melbourne, Victoria, on the Victoria Cross Estate, built in 1916–18.
- Leak Street, Wodonga, Victoria.

MAJOR STEWART WALTER LOUDOUN-SHAND
10th Battalion, Alexandra, Princess of Wales's Own (Yorkshire Regiment)

Stewart Loudoun-Shand was born at Dichory, Ceylon on 8th October 1879. The family name of Shand was changed to Loudoun-Shand by deed poll in August 1911. His father was Major John Loudoun Loudoun-Shand (1845–1932), born at Barony, Lanarkshire. He moved to Ceylon in 1864, where he planted tea, mainly in the Dimbula and Dichorya districts. He was Chairman of the Planters' Association of Ceylon 1879–80, Planting Member of the Legislative Council in 1882 and 1884 and Honorary Life Member of the Ceylon Association in London. In addition to tea planting, John was a director of colonial merchants Shand, Haldane and Co, Chairman of the Teluk Piah Rubber Estate Limited and Chairman of Marudu Rubber Limited. Stewart's mother was Lucy née Lawson (1851–1930), born at Elgin, Moray. She travelled to Ceylon in 1872 and married John on 29th November 1873 at Christ Church, Colombo. She was living with her family at Henry Cottage, Elgin in 1881. The family was living at 'Ardoch House', Thurlow Park Road, West Dulwich in 1891 and 'Craigellie', 27 Alleyn Park, Dulwich, London in 1901. Stewart had ten siblings:

- William Edward Loudoun Loudoun-Shand (1874–1938) became a planter in Ceylon and Malaya. He served in the Malay States Volunteer Rifles and was a sergeant major in the Ceylon Planters Rifles, including with the Ceylon Planters Rifle Corps, 2nd Ceylon Contingent (No.7502) in the Boer War 1899–12th August 1902. William was commissioned as a temporary lieutenant in the Royal Field Artillery on 30th March 1915. He found life at the front arduous and on 4th February 1916 left his unit and on 15th February was evacuated to Britain from Dieppe to Dover. Having been sent on leave 3rd March–17th April, a number of medical boards followed and it was concluded his health would not allow him to serve on active service. As a result he was forced to relinquish his commission due to ill health on 30th June. He applied for a commission again in 1917, but was turned down until his varicose veins could be treated. William married Maud Williams (c.1885–1968) in 1911 at Croydon, Surrey and settled at 88 Beulah Hill, London. They had two daughters. Margaret Maud Loudoun-Shand (1916–99) married former Lieutenant Colonel Desmond Hamilton Mappin (1914–71) of the Royal Deccan Horse in 1949 and had three children: Sarah 1951, Victoria 1952 and Lucinda 1954. Jean H Loudoun-Shand (born 1919) married Roy D Marshall in 1947 and had a daughter, Janet, in 1951.

- Frances Lucy Loudoun-Shand (c.1876–1954) died unmarried.
- Alice Mary Loudoun-Shand (c.1878–1924) married Heathfield Macmahon Mahon (1877–1953) in 1905. There were no children. Heathfield married Nora H Priday later in 1924.
- Clementina Margaret 'Daisy' Loudoun-Shand (1879–1916) worked as a hospital sick nurse. She married Commander Ivor Mackenzie RN in 1911 and died at Lugano, Switzerland on 3rd January 1916.
- Alexander John Loudoun-Shand (1881–1963) was an officer in the Mercantile Marine. He married Vivien Irene Gilray Norman in 1910 and they had a son, John Jeffrey Erskine Loudoun-Shand, in 1915. They emigrated to Australia, where Alexander served as a commander in the Royal Australian Navy and was Director of the Royal Australian Naval College.
- Clare Babbington 'Bosun' Loudon-Shand (1883–1958) joined the Mercantile Marine in 1901, went to Rhodesia in 1908 and later ran a tea plantation at Delta, Pussellawa, Ceylon. He was commissioned in 11th Loyal North Lancashire Regiment on 6th February 1915. Promoted lieutenant 30th March, temporary captain 1st October 1915 and acting major 22nd December 1918 – 21st April 1919. He transferred to the Army Service Corps on 3rd May 1915. Mentioned twice (LG 4th January 1917 and 21st February 1919). Relinquished his commission as a temporary captain on 16th August 1919. Later he became colonel of the volunteer Ceylon Planters Rifle Corps. He married Dorothy Duke (born c.1889) in 1911 and they had a son, Stewart Gordon 'John' Loudoun-Shand c.1912, who moved to Kenya and married twice.
- Rolland Erskine Loudoun-Shand (1887–1904).
- Eric Gordon Loudoun-Shand (1893–1972) played rugby for Oxford University in the Varsity Match against Cambridge University in 1913 (Cambridge won) and for Scotland against England at Twickenham on 15th March 1913 (England won 3–0). He attested in 5th Buffs (Territorial Force) at Ashford (No.1584) on 17th August 1914 and was commissioned in 8th King's Royal Rifle Corps on 22nd August. Promoted lieutenant on 1st November 1914 and captain and temporary major 24th November 1915. Rather ironically he contracted German measles and was evacuated to Britain on 3rd July 1915. On 21st August 1916 he received a gun

shot wound resulting in a fracture and was evacuated to Britain on 1st September, arriving at Southampton from Rouen. He was serving in an officer cadet battalion at some time in 1918. Transferred to the General List and appointed ADC to GOC 14th Division and temporary captain 17th May 1918. He was admitted to 44 Field Ambulance on 30th August 1918 with debility and was treated there and at 43 Field Ambulance before returning to duty on 15th September. He relinquished his commission on 21st June 1919, having been Mentioned in Despatches (LG 4th January 1917) and awarded the MC (LG 3rd June 1919). Eric captained the Oxford University Rugby XV in the 1919 Varsity Match against Cambridge with his badly injured arm (Cambridge won). The arm was eventually amputated, but he joined the Royal Engineers in the Territorial Army as a lieutenant on 23rd August 1919. His surname appears in the Army List at this time as plain Loudoun. He last appears in the Army List in August 1921. Meanwhile, he joined the Defence Force during the industrial crisis as a lieutenant in 14th London on 10th April 1921 and relinquished this commission on 7th July 1921. Eric married Dorothy Feldtmann (1904–85) in 1923 and they lived at 172 Bromley Road, Shortlands, Kent and The Glebe House, Limpsfield, Surrey. They had a son, Keith Nigel Loudoun-Shand, in 1927, who married Gerardine CE Francis in 1959 and had three daughters: Henrietta 1961, Sophia 1969 and Emma 1972. Eric was accepted for enrolment in the Officers' Emergency Reserve on 9th September 1938.

A group of Ceylon Planters Rifle Corps in 1896 (Justin Kirby).

Eric Loudoun-Shand meets the King at the 1919 Varsity Match (Bystander).

- There were two other sisters.

Stewart was educated at Dulwich College 1891–97 and was then employed by William Deacon's Bank. He enlisted in the London Scottish Rifle Volunteers on the outbreak of the Boer War, but only served for five months because he was debarred from overseas service due to his age. He transferred to the Pembroke Yeomanry as Stewart Walter Shand for service with the Imperial Yeomanry (4121) on 26th January 1900. He served in South Africa as a lance corporal with 30th Company, 9th Battalion, Imperial Yeomanry 14th March 1900 – 8th July 1901 and was wounded. Having been discharged at Tenby on 7th August 1901, he took up a mercantile appointment at Port Elizabeth, Cape Colony for three years. His father then arranged an appointment for him in Ceylon as a tea merchant, working with his brother William until the outbreak of the Great War.

Dulwich College.

Port Elizabeth Market Square.

Stewart had a medical examination in Columbo on 23rd October 1914 and was declared fit for service in the infantry and cavalry. He returned to Britain and was commissioned as a lieutenant on 28th November. Promoted captain 14th June 1915 and went to France on 9th September. Promoted major 28th December. He was wounded on 2nd March 1916, but returned to duty on the 10th.

Awarded the VC for his actions near Fricourt, France on 1st July 1916, LG 9th September 1916. He was killed during his VC action and is buried in Norfolk Cemetery, near Bécourt, France (I C 77). His will was administered by his father – he left £439/11/11. In addition to the VC, he was awarded the Queen's South Africa Medal 1899–1902 (clasps

Stewart Loudoun-Shand's grave in Norfolk Cemetery.

'Cape Colony', 'Orange Free State' & 'South Africa 1901'), 1914–15 Star, British War Medal 1914–20 and Victory Medal 1914–19. He never married and the VC was presented to his father by the King at Buckingham Palace on 31st March 1917. It was purchased privately by Michael Ashcroft's VC Trust in 2005 and is part of the Lord Ashcroft Victoria Cross Collection at the Imperial War Museum.

Stewart is also commemorated on:

- The family grave in West Norwood Cemetery & Crematorium, West Norwood, London.
- The Dulwich College War Memorial.
- The Secretary of State for Communities and Local Government, Eric Pickles MP, announced that Victoria Cross recipients from the Great War would have commemorative paving stones laid in their birthplace as a lasting legacy of local heroes within communities. The stones would be laid on or close to the 100th anniversary of their VC actions. For the 145 VCs born in Australia, Belgium, Canada, China, Denmark, Egypt, France, Germany, India, Iraq, Japan, Nepal, Netherlands, New Zealand, Pakistan, Sri Lanka, South Africa, Ukraine and the United States of America, individual commemorative stones were unveiled at the National Memorial Arboretum, Alrewas, Staffordshire by Prime Minister David Cameron MP and Sergeant Johnson Beharry VC on 5th March 2015.

14/18278 PRIVATE WILLIAM FREDERICK MCFADZEAN
14th Battalion, The Royal Irish Rifles (Young Citizen's)

William 'Billy' Frederick McFadzean was born at Lurgan, Co Armagh, Ireland on 9th October 1895. His father was William McFadzean JP (born c.1867 in Co Louth, Ireland). William senior was a linen yarn salesman in 1901. His mother was Annie née Pedlow (born c.1869 in Co Down). William and Annie married c.1895. The family lived at 9 Jocelyn Gardens, Ormeau, Co Down in 1901; 29 Cregagh Town, Belfast by 1911; and later moved to 'Rubicon', 372 Cregagh Road, Belfast. Billy had four siblings:

- John Bowden McFadzean (born c.1898).
- Robert James McFadzean (born c.1900).
- Mary Gordon McFadzean (born c.1901).
- Henry Bowden McFadzean (born c.1907).

Billy was educated at Mountpottinger Boy's School 13th April 1904 – 12th August 1908 and the Trade Preparatory School, Municipal Technical Institute, Belfast. He was apprenticed in the linen trade with Spence, Bryson & Co of 41 Great

The Municipal Technical Institute, Belfast.

1st Battalion (Ballynafeigh and Newtownbreda Young Citizen Volunteers), East Belfast Regiment, Ulster Volunteer Force on parade on 6th June 1914. Billy McFadzean is understood to be the man to the right of the sergeant wearing a sash.

Victoria Street, Belfast. He played as a junior for the Collegians Rugby Football Club. Billy was a member of 1st Battalion (Ballynafeigh and Newtownbreda Young Citizen Volunteers), East Belfast Regiment, Ulster Volunteer Force, known as the 'Chocolate Soldiers', because most men had a commercial background and came from reasonably well-off families.

He enlisted in 14th Battalion, Royal Irish Rifles on 22nd September 1914 and joined C Company. He was bigger than the average recruit, standing six feet tall and weighing thirteen stones. The battalion trained at Finner Camp, Co Donegal before moving to Randalstown Camp in the grounds of Lord O'Neill's Shane Castle Estate, Co Antrim. The battalion moved to England for further training at Seaford, East Sussex and Liphook, Hampshire. Billy accompanied the battalion to France on 5th October 1915. He wrote, *You people at home make me feel quite proud when you tell me 'I am a Soldier Boy of the McFadzeans'. I hope to play the game and if I don't add much to the lustre to it I will certainly not tarnish it.*

Ulster Tower, Thiepval, France, shortly after it was built in the 1920s. It is a copy of Helen's Tower at Clandeboye, close to where 36th (Ulster) Division trained prior to departing for England.

Awarded the VC for his actions near Thiepval Wood, France on 1st July 1916, LG 9th September 1916. Billy was killed during his VC action, but his body was not identified after

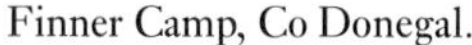

Finner Camp, Co Donegal.

Memorial at the Old Town Hall, Lurgan (Robert Taylor).

the war and he is commemorated on the Thiepval Memorial. It is possible he is buried in Connaught Cemetery, a few yards from where he died.

As he never married, the VC was presented to his father by the King at Buckingham Palace on 28th February 1917. When handing over the VC the King said, *Nothing finer has been done in this war for which I have given a Victoria Cross than the act committed by your son to save many lives in giving his own so heroically.*

In addition to the VC, he was awarded the 1914–15 Star, British War Medal 1914–20 and Victory Medal 1914–19. His VC was donated by his brother and sister to the Royal Ulster Rifles Regimental Museum on 1st March 1980. It is held by the Royal Ulster Rifles Museum, Waring Street, Belfast. Billy McFadzean is commemorated in a number of places:

- McFadzean Room, Royal British Legion Home, Lurgan, Co Armagh.
- Two plaques at St John's Presbyterian Church, Newtownbreda, Belfast.
- A memorial stone at Ulster Tower, Thiepval, France to all ranks of the 36th (Ulster) Division, dedicated on 1st July 1991, names the Division's nine VCs, including Billy McFadzean.
- War Memorials at St John's Presbyterian Church, Newtownbreda and Lurgan, Co Armagh.
- Two plaques at St John's Presbyterian Church, Newtownbreda, one of which was unveiled by Colonel Barlow DSO, General Staff Officer, Northern District Irish Command, following a commemoration service on 1st July 1917.
- Regimental Memorial at St Anne's Cathedral, Belfast.
- Memorial at the Old Town Hall, Lurgan, Co Armagh.
- Plaque in Castleneagh Council Offices, Northern Ireland.
- A black marble panel on McFadzean's former home on Cregagh Road, Belfast.
- A song was written in his honour, 'The Ballad of Billy McFadzean VC'.
- A series of posters depicting ten VC and GC holders, including Billy McFadzean, were displayed on the walls of the London Underground in 2004.
- First Lurgan Presbyterian Church.
- Collegians RFC.

13301 LANCE SERGEANT FRED MCNESS
1st Battalion, Scots Guards

Fred MackNess was born at Wilson's Place, Bramley, near Leeds, Yorkshire on 22nd January 1891. His surname was misspelled when he enlisted. His father, John Francis MackNess (c.1842–1908), was born in Scotland and in 1861 was serving in the Royal Engineers at Brompton Barracks, Gillingham, Kent. In 1881 he was a tanner, in 1891 a labourer and in 1901 caretaker of Bramley National School. Fred's mother, Mary née Webster (1852–1920), married John on 2nd August 1873 at St Peter's Parish Church, Leeds. The family lived at Waterslacks, Bramley. In 1911 Mary was living with two of her children at 39 Town End Yard, Bramley. Fred had four siblings:

- Francis Joseph MackNess (1874–1950) was a clicker boot maker. He married Peace Nicholson (1876–1935) in 1898 and the family was living at 13 Bath Place, Bramley in 1911. They had two sons: Donald MackNess 1901 and James Morris MackNess 1903.
- James William MackNess (1876–1952) was a boot knitter. He married Elizabeth Pullan (1878–1952) in 1899 and the family was living at 8 Eightlands Place, Bramley in 1911. They had eight children, including: Harold MackNess 1899–1900, Ethel MackNess 1900–05, Rowland MackNess 1902–03, Ida Mary MackNess 1905–89, Amy MackNess 1906–92, Maud MackNess 1907, Walter MackNess 1911 and Hilda MackNess 1913–89.
- Sarah MackNess, born in 1878, was a boot upper machinist.
- Isabella MackNess (1881–96).

St Peter's Parish Church, Leeds, where Fred McNess' parents were married. In 2012 it became Leeds Minster, or the Minster and Parish Church of Saint Peter-at-Leeds.

Fred's paternal grandfather, William MackNess (c.1802–72), was born at Huntingdon. He married Marjory née Moon (1811–65) at St James, Piccadilly, London in 1831. She was born at Blackford, Perthshire, Scotland. William was a waiter, living with his family at 89 South Street,

Bramley National School, also known as Good Shepherd School, was built in 1896 and is now a veterinary practice (Leeds Library).

Bramley around the turn of the last century.

Welbeck Abbey in Nottinghamshire was an Augustinian monastery prior to the Dissolution, when it was granted by Henry VIII to Richard Whalley. It was later owned by the Earl of Shrewsbury and Duke of Newcastle until it became the seat of the Earls and Dukes of Portland. Archduke Franz Ferdinand, whose assassination sparked the outbreak of the First World War, stayed at Welbeck in November 1913 and was almost killed when a shotgun was discharged accidentally. During the First World War, the kitchen block was used as a hospital. From 1951 until 2005 Welbeck was leased to the Army as a sixth form college for future officers in the technical corps.

PRO REGE ET LEGE

BRAMLEY — PRESENTED TO — YORKSHIRE

Sergt. F. McNess V.C.

The Committee, whose names are appended, desire on behalf of the subscribers to your estimonial und, to express their great appreciation of the gallant conduct you displayed on eptember 15th 1916, during the European War 1914-1919, for which is ajesty the ing awarded you the highest of all coveted honours . The citizens of Leeds, and of "Our Village" in particular, feel proud that one so intimately connected with them, upheld the noblest traditions of the ritish mpire, and congratulate you on the distinction so worthily won.

Chairman.

Treasurer. Secretary.

COMMITTEE

C. Akeroyd. F. J. Butler-Fleming. J. H. Boan. T. Cook.

R. Gawthorp. W. L. Haley. F. Halliday. T. Jubb.

F. L. Lunn. J. Spetch. H. Tallant. E. Wade Wilton.

The illuminated address presented to Fred McNess in 1920 (Bramley War Memorial).

Colonel Henry Fludyer (1847–1920) was commissioned in the Scots Fusilier Guards (later Scots Guards) in1866 and was with the 1st Battalion at Tel-el Kebir in Egypt in 1882. He served with the 2nd Battalion during the Gordon Relief Expedition in 1885. Henry Fludyer commanded 2nd Scots Guards and was later Officer Commanding Scots Guards and Regimental District. In 1909 he was appointed Gentleman Usher to Edward VII and continued in the appointment under George V until 1919 although he served as an Extra Gentleman Usher to the King for another year. Between 1914 to 1916 he resumed command of the Scots Guards.

King George's Hospital, Stamford Street, Waterloo, London, where part of a rib was used to reconstruct Fred's jaw. In 1914 it was a newly built warehouse for HM Stationery Office and was commandeered to be converted into a hospital. It was reputedly the largest hospital in the country. The King opened it at the end of May 1915, the project having suffered from labour disputes and strikes. Convoys of wounded were brought by train to Waterloo Station nearby and transferred by tunnels to the hospital. The flat roof was converted into a roof garden with flower beds and shrubs, where patients could exercise. On Christmas Day 1916, either the King, the Queen or one of their children visited every ward. The Hospital closed on 15th June 1919, having treated 71,000 patients. Today, it is the Franklin-Wilkins Building of King's College London.

Decorated members of C Company, 1st Battalion, Scots Guards. Standing, left to right: Sergeant Leitch Croix de Guerre; Sergeant Goldie MM; CSM McDonald DCM; CSM Pyper DCM; Sergeant Rhodes MM. Seated, left to right: Sergeant Fred McNess VC; RSM Cutler MC; and Sergeant J McAulay VC DCM. Lieutenant Boyd-Rochfort VC also served in the same company. The photograph was taken after January 1918, when John McAulay's VC was gazetted, but before June 1918, when Fred McNess was discharged.

Perth in 1861. Mary died at King Street, Broughty Ferry, Forfarshire in 1865 and by 1871 William was living at St Mary's Lane, Huntingdon. In addition to John, William and Mary had seven other children: Isabella MackNess c.1833, Eliza Mary MackNess (c.1834–1905) and James MackNess 1838 were born in England and William MackNess c. 1839, Frederick MackNess c.1843, Francis MackNess c.1845 and Charles Helmore MackNess c.1851 were born in Scotland.

His maternal grandfather was Joseph Webster (c.1825–92), a journeyman tanner who was blinded c.1864. He married Sarah née Priestley (c.1827–1901) in 1846. The family was living at 9 Pratts Buildings, Headingley, Yorkshire in 1851, at Watson's Buildings, Headingley in 1871 and at 1 Watson's View, Headingley by 1881. In addition to Mary they had five other children: Fredrick Webster 1847, Benjamin Webster 1852, Annie Elizabeth Webster 1856, Thomas Webster 1859 and Emma Webster 1862.

Fred was educated at Bramley National School before being employed as a carter's assistant by Mr Joseph Henry 'Harry' Boan. He enlisted in 3rd Reserve

Battalion, Scots Guards on 30th January 1915. On 7th February 1916 he was appointed unpaid corporal and went to France on 6th April to join the 1st Battalion. Promoted corporal and acting lance sergeant on 25th August. **Awarded the VC for his actions at Ginchy, France on 15th September 1916, LG 26th October 1916.** After the VC action he was treated by Captain Noel Chavasse VC before being evacuated to 9th General Hospital at Rouen. He was moved to Welbeck Abbey and later to King George's Hospital in London, where part of a rib was used to reconstruct his jaw.

On 9th December 1916 he was summoned from hospital and driven to Buckingham Palace, accompanied by a RAMC Sergeant, to be presented with his VC. At the Palace he was escorted to the King by Colonel Fludyer, Scots Guards. The King spent twenty minutes talking with Fred and expressed concern about his wounds.

Fred was later promoted to sergeant. In July 1917 he received official welcomes at Leeds and Bramley. He was presented with a bronze clock and sidepieces by Colonel JW Smith-Neill, Scots Guards at Wellington Barracks, London, in October 1917. He remained in hospital until being discharged unfit for further service on 14th June 1918 and was awarded the Silver War Badge (386975) on 8th June.

When he returned to Leeds and Bramley in January 1920, he was presented with an illuminated address and £400, which he used to start a shoe repair business at 95 Woodhouse Lane. He received specialist training to assist with his new venture, but the business was forced to close when most of the staff were called up in the Second World War. He then worked for Leeds City Engineers Department as a filing clerk. Fred tried to re-enlist in the Second World War, but was turned down due to his injuries and his age.

John Archibald Boyd-Carpenter PC (1908–98) was a barrister and politician. He joined the Scots Guards in 1940 and held various staff appointments; including with the Allied Military Government in Italy. He was elected Conservative MP for Kingston-upon-Thames in 1945 and held the seat until 1972, when he was appointed a life peer as Baron Boyd-Carpenter of Crux Easton. During his career he held a number of ministerial appointments: Financial Secretary to the Treasury 1951–54; Privy Counsellor 1954; Minister of Transport and Civil Aviation 1954–55; Minister of Pensions and National Insurance 1955–1962; Chief Secretary to the Treasury and Paymaster-General 1962–64. He was the first Chairman of the Civil Aviation Authority at the time of the collapse of the Court Line airline in 1974. As Minister of Pensions and National Insurance he overturned the decision to cease paying Fred McNess' pension to his widow.

Fred McNess married Dorothy Smith (1893–1981) on 4th October 1919 at Dover, Kent. She was born at Egerton, Kent and was a nurse who helped care for him. They lived at 39 Eightlands Lane, Bramley and 6 Springbank Crescent, Headingley, Leeds, until moving to 37 Petersfield Road, Boscombe, Bournemouth, Dorset in January 1956. Fred and Dorothy had a daughter, Winifred Barbara Mollie

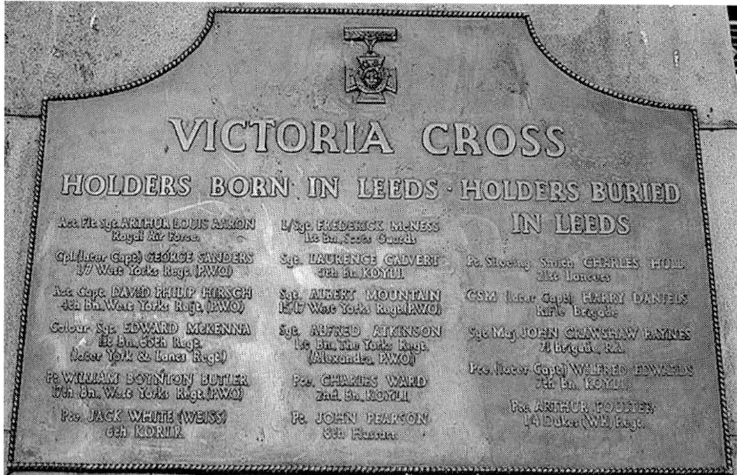

The commemorative plaque for VCs born or buried in Leeds at Victoria Gardens, The Headrow, Leeds.

McNess, born in 1920. She married Leslie Morris in 1943 at Repton, Derbyshire and had two children, John L Morris 1944 and Christine A Morris 1948.

Fred suffered from depression and headaches. On 4th May 1956, while his wife was out, he committed suicide by cutting his throat at 37 Petersfield Road, Boscombe. He was cremated at Bournemouth Crematorium and his ashes were scattered there.

The Ministry of Pensions and National Insurance ceased paying his Army pension to his widow on the grounds that he had taken his own life. She was living on only £2 per week, but the Scots Guards intervened and awarded her £10 per month from Regimental funds. She appealed against the Ministry decision and the Regiment also wrote directly to the Minister responsible, John Boyd-Carpenter, a former Scots Guard. On 18th June 1957 Boyd-Carpenter replied positively to the Scots Guards that the appeal had been successful. The pension was backdated to Fred's death and Dorothy received a new pension book on 15th July. She moved to 11 Cecil Court, Charmiston Road, Bournemouth and attended the 1956 VC Centenary celebrations six weeks after her husband's death. Dorothy married Sydney T Maddock in 1963 at Bournemouth. Sydney had previously married Bertha J Gadsby (1894–1961) in 1920 and they had a son, Frederick R Maddock 1926.

In addition to the VC, he was awarded the British War Medal 1914–20, Victory Medal 1914–19, George VI Coronation Medal 1937 and Elizabeth II Coronation Medal 1953. The medals were presented to the Regiment after Dorothy's death. The VC is held by Regimental Headquarters Scots Guards at the Guards Museum, Wellington Barracks, Birdcage Walk, London. Fred is commemorated with sixteen other VCs born or buried in Leeds on a plaque at Victoria Gardens, The Headrow, Leeds. A painting of his VC action by David Rowlands was commissioned by the Sergeants' Mess, 1st Scots Guards. On the fiftieth anniversary of his death, his name was added to the book of remembrance at Bournemouth Crematorium and a rose bush was planted there.

12639 PRIVATE JAMES MILLER
7th Battalion, The King's Own (Royal Lancaster Regiment)

James Miller was born at Taylor's Farm, Hoghton, near Preston, Lancashire on 13th March 1890; he was baptised on 4th May and this is often quoted as his date of birth. The farm is now New Wicken House and is in Withnell, due to a boundary change. His father was George Miller (1852–1922), a mason's labourer. His mother was Mary née Gardner (1855–1915). George and Mary were married during the 2nd quarter of 1878 at Chorley. The family was living at 107 Bolton Road, Withnell, near Chorley in 1891, 13 Sunny View, Bolton Road, Withnell in 1901 and 1 Ollerton Cottages, Withnell in 1911. James had fourteen siblings, but five did not survive infancy:

- Joseph Miller, a twin with Annie (1880–1936), was a cotton spinner. He married another cotton weaver, Isabella Fletcher (1882–1968), in 1906. They were living at 4 Garden Street, Abbey Village, Withnell in 1911 and later at 280 Livesey Branch Road, Blackburn, Lancashire.
- Annie Miller, a twin with Joseph (1880–1951), married Walter Drain (1876–1955) in 1899. The family was living at 26 Mount Pleasant, Withnell in 1911. They had nine children: George Frederick Drain 1900–60; Annie Drain 1902–68; Mary Drain 1904; Thomas Drain 1906–91; Elizabeth Drain 1909; Joseph Miller Drain 1911–12; Alice Drain 1913–70; James Miller Drain 1920–43, was serving as a gunner (1457861) with 67th (2/5th East Surrey Regiment) Anti-Tank Regiment RA when he was killed in action on 28th October 1943 (Naples War Cemetery, Italy – III O 10); and Harry Drain 1922–69.
- Thomas Gardner Miller (1881–1958), a platelayer with the London & North Western Railway in 1911, married Annie Harwood (born c.1879) in Blackburn in 1915 and they had a son, George Miller, in 1916. He was living at 5 East View, Abbey Village at the time of his death at 21 Station Terrace, Withnell.
- William Miller (1883–1918) was a labourer at a paper mill. He married Teresa Crook (1881–1951) in 1907. They were living at 11 Ollerton, Withnell in 1911. William served as a Lance Sergeant in 1/4th King's Own (Royal Lancaster Regiment) (12650) and was killed in action on 9th April 1918. He is buried in Vieille-Chapelle New Military Cemetery, Lacouture, France (III E 20). William and Teresa had at least two children, Frances Miller 1908 and Lucy Miller 1910.
- Sarah Alice Miller, born 1884, was a willow winder at Wiggins Teape paper mill in 1911. It is understood that she married James Arnold (born c.1880) in 1915. They had four children: James Miller 1915, Mary E Miller 1919, Alex M Miller 1921 and Margaret A Miller 1925.

- George Edmond Miller (1886–1918) was a cotton reacher in 1901 and out of work in 1911. He enlisted in 1/4th Loyal North Lancashire (40866) and died in service on 25th December 1918. He is buried in Tournai Communal Cemetery Allied Extension, Hainault, Belgium (IV K 3).
- Cicely Jane Miller (1887–1914) was a cotton winder in 1901. She married James Henry Miller (1886–1947) in 1908 at St Paul's Church, Withnell. He was a police constable in 1911 and the family was living at 763 Oldham Road, Rochdale. Cicely and James had at least one son, William Miller 1910, and may have had two daughters.

Withnell Fold was a model village and paper mill constructed in 1843–44 by Thomas Blinkhorn Parke (1823–1885). The mill supplied newsprint for a number of Lancashire newspapers and in 1890 combined with Wiggins Teape & Company, a stationary firm, which had been supplied by the mill since 1847. It closed in 1967 (Douglas Law).

- Fred Miller, born 1891, was a size wheeler at Wiggins Teape paper mill in 1911.
- Alexander 'Alex' Miller (1894–1917) was a sheet catcher at Wiggins Teape paper mill in 1911. He enlisted in the Royal Army Service Corps (R4/090022) and was serving with 3rd Base Remount Depot when he was killed on 11th February 1917. He is buried in Janval Cemetery, Dieppe, France (I F 2).

Bowerham Barracks, Blackburn.

James Miller's platoon while training at Tidworth, Hampshire, on Salisbury Plain. He is in the back row, fourth from the right. Next right is Emmanuel Snape, whose son provided the picture (Frank Snape).

James was educated at Abbey Village Primary School, Bolton Road, Chorley and was a popular local footballer. He was employed at Wiggins Teape paper mill at Withnell Fold. near Blackburn.

In September 1914 James enlisted at Bowerham Barracks, Blackburn. He went to France with his Battalion on 17th July 1915 and saw action at Lens and Loos in the autumn. The Battalion moved to the Somme in April 1916 and was in action at La Boisselle 3rd-7th July 1916. During his last leave he told his sister he did not think he would survive the war and hoped he would die a hero.

James Miller's grave in Dartmoor Cemetery at Bécordel-Bécourt.

Awarded the VC for his actions at Bazentin-le-Petit, France on 30th/31st July 1916, LG 9th September 1916. He was killed during his VC action and is buried in Dartmoor Cemetery near Bécordel (I C 64). James never married and the VC was presented to his father by the King at Buckingham Palace on 29th November 1916.

In addition to the VC, he was awarded the 1914–15 Star, British War Medal 1914–20 and Victory Medal 1914–19. The VC was presented by his family to the King's Own Royal Regiment in September 1989 and it is held by the King's Own Royal Regiment (Lancaster) Museum, City Museum, Market Square, Lancaster.

James Miller is commemorated in a number of places:

- St Paul's Church, Withnell, where a portrait of him hangs inside the church; his name is inscribed on his mother's headstone and a memorial Celtic Cross was erected by public subscription and dedicated on 14th July 1917. The memorial was restored and re-dedicated in August 1988 with help from the Royal British Legion and others.
- Memorial stone at Wiggins Teape Paper Mill at Withnell Fold.
- Regimental Memorial at The Priory, Lancaster, Lancashire.
- The story of his gallantry was recorded in the poem, 'The Message', by Colour Sergeant Ellis Williams of the King's Own, in October 1916.

The memorial Celtic Cross to James Miller in St Paul's Churchyard, Withnell (L Bennett).

3970 PRIVATE MARTIN O'MEARA
16th Australian Infantry Battalion AIF

Martin O'Meara was born on 6th November 1885 at Lorrha, Rathcabbin, Co Tipperary, near Birr, King's County (now Co Offaly), Ireland. His father, Thomas O'Meara of Lissernane, Rathcabbin, was a labourer. His mother was Margaret née Connors (died 1916). Thomas and Margaret had nine children, seven of whom were living in December 1916. The following are known: Thomas, John, Keogh and Alice. A Hugh O'Meara signed the receipts for Martin's British War Medal and Victory Medal on 24th June 1924 and may be another brother. One brother and one sister, whose names are not known, married and emigrated to the United States.

Martin was educated at Lorrha National School, Nenagh, Co Tipperary. He worked as a tree feller in Ireland before moving to Liverpool for a time and then emigrated to South Australia c.1911, working his passage as a stoker. He worked initially at Pinjarra and moved to Collie, Western Australia, where he worked at Bowling Pool Timber Mill as a sleeper layer. He never married.

Blackboy Hill Camp, Greenmount, Western Australia.

Martin enlisted in the Australian Imperial Force on 19th August 1915 at Blackboy Hill Camp, Greenmount, near Perth, Western Australia. He was described as 5′ 7″ tall, weighing 140 lbs, with dark complexion, brown eyes and brown hair and his religious denomination was Roman Catholic. His next of kin was his sister, Alice O'Meara, of Rathcabbin. He embarked at Fremantle, Western Australia for the Middle East with the 12th Reinforcement Group aboard HMAT A31 *Ajana* on 22nd December, disembarking at Alexandria, Egypt. He moved to Tel El Kebir, where he joined 16th Battalion on 7th March 1916. The Battalion embarked at Alexandria for Marseilles, France on 1st June.

Awarded the VC for his actions at Pozières, France on 9th-12th August 1916, LG 9th September 1916. He was wounded on 12th August 1916 (gunshot to the abdomen) and was admitted to 3rd Casualty Clearing Station at Puchevillers

HMAT A31 *Ajana* (7,759 tons) was launched in 1912 for the Australind Steam Shipping Co Ltd of London as a refrigerated cargo vessel. She was leased by the Commonwealth from November 1914. On 14th April 1917, she was attacked by a U-boat in the English Channel and escaped. On 29th July 1917 she was chased by another U-boat off Ireland and escaped again. *Ajana* was sold to the New Zealand Shipping Co in April 1920 and renamed *Otarama*. She was sold again in 1928 to D&E Fratelli Bozzo, Genoa and renamed *Amaranto*. She was scrapped in 1932.

SS *St Andrew* (2,495 tons) was built in 1908 for the Fishguard service. After service as a hospital ship during the war, she returned to her peacetime route. In 1932 she was renamed *Fishguard* and was scrapped in 1933.

and moved to No.11 Stationary Hospital at Rouen on 16th August. Evacuated to England aboard HMHS *St Andrew* from Rouen on 18th August and admitted to 3rd London General Hospital next day. He was granted two weeks' convalescent leave in Ireland, arriving there on 18th October. Lorrha and neighbouring parishes raised money for him, which he left for the restoration of Lorrha Abbey, but there were insufficient funds and it was used to repair the parish church instead.

Patients arriving at 3rd London General Hospital in Wandsworth. Before the war it was the Royal Victoria Patriotic School for orphans. By May 1917 the Hospital had almost 2,000 beds, many in hutted wards behind the main building. It closed in August 1920, having treated 62,708 patients, and became an orphanage again until the Second World War, when the children were evacuated. During the war, MI6 used it as a clearing, detention and interrogation centre. Post-war it became a teacher training college and later a school. By the 1970s the building was badly run down. In 1980 the Greater London Council sold it for £1 on condition it was properly restored and it is now apartments (Daily Graphic).

The passenger ferry *Princess Victoria* (1,687 tons) was launched in 1912 for the Stranraer/Larne route for the Portpatrick & Wigtownshire Railways Joint Committee. Having been a troopship between 1914–19, she returned to her usual service until scrapped in 1934.

He embarked at Folkestone, Kent for France on 4th December aboard SS *Princess Victoria*. On 3rd January 1917, he was admitted to 4th Australian Field Ambulance with a sprained ankle. He was wounded by shrapnel in the face on 9th April 1917 and admitted to hospital at Rouen. The wound was not serious and he rejoined the Battalion on 25th April, taking part in operations at Bullecourt and Messines. He was granted leave to be decorated with the VC by the King at Buckingham Palace on 21st July.

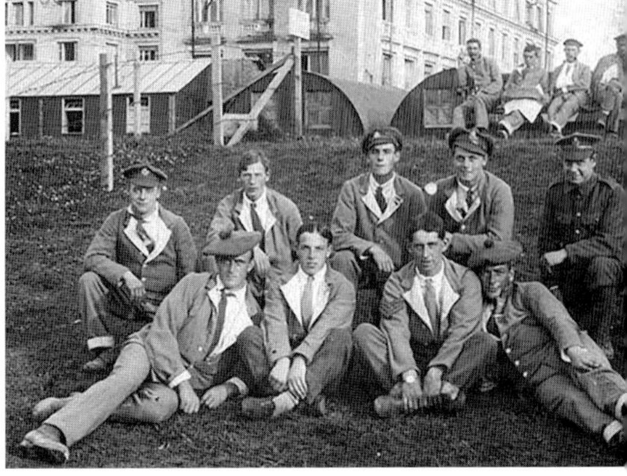

No.2 Canadian General Hospital.

On 8th August he was wounded with shrapnel to the buttock near Polygon Wood, near Ypres and admitted to No.2 Canadian General Hospital before being evacuated to England on 18th August and admitted to Bath War Hospital, Somerset. He transferred to 1st Convalescent Depot, Sutton Veny, Wiltshire on 19th November.

Martin embarked at Southampton, Hampshire for France on 10th January 1918 and rejoined the Battalion on 18th January, taking part in operations at Hèbuterne

Bath War Hospital, Combe Park, Bath, Somerset.

and Villers Bretonneux. Promoted corporal on 13th March and acting sergeant on 22nd March before proceeding to Second Army Musketry School the following day. He rejoined the Battalion on 30th March and reverted to corporal at his own request on 15th April. He was detached from the Battalion 12th July – 2nd August to SOS School (not identified). Promoted sergeant on 30th August and returned to England, posted to Codford Depot, Wiltshire on 1st September.

RMS *Arawa* (9372 tons) was built for Shaw, Savill & Albion of London. Taken over as HMNZT *Arawa*, on 1st November 1914 it assembled with the first convoy at King George's Sound, Albany, Western Australia, to transport the First Detachment of the Australian and New Zealand Imperial Expeditionary Forces. On 9th November, she picked up a faint signal from an unknown warship, details of which were passed to the escorting cruisers and HMAS *Sydney* was despatched to the Cocos Islands, where she discovered the German warship SMS *Emden*. In 1928 she was sold to A Bernstein and renamed *Konigstein*. In 1940 she was sold to Van Heyghen Bros and renamed *Gandia*. On 22nd January 1942 she was torpedoed and sunk in the North Atlantic.

He returned to Australia aboard HMNZT *Arawa* on 15th September, disembarking at Fremantle on 10th November. There was a deliberate policy by the Australian government to return VC winners early. On 19th December, OC 24th Australian Auxiliary Hospital, Stromness reported that Martin was, *...suffering from Delusional Insanity, with hallucinations of hearing and sight, is extremely homicidal and suicidal, and requires to be kept in restraint. He is not hopeful of his recovery in the near future. Admitted to Claremont Mental Hospital (insane patient), 3 January 1919.* He was formerly discharged from the Army at Perth, Western Australia on 30th November 1919 and spent the rest of his life in mental hospitals.

Martin O'Meara during one of his periods of convalescence (Australian War Memorial).

In addition to the VC, he was awarded the British War Medal 1914–20 and Victory Medal 1914–19. His VC was presented to Major F Warner on behalf of the 16th Battalion (Cameron Highlanders) Citizens Military Forces by TL Axford VC at Crystal Park, Perth, Western Australia in 1940. It was donated to the Army Museum of Western Australia in 1986, where it is held in Artillery Barracks, Burt Street, Fremantle.

Martin was in Lemnos Hospital at Shenton Park 1926–35, but died at Claremont Mental Hospital, Perth, Western Australia on 20th December 1935, having never recovered from the chronic mania caused by his war experiences. His funeral, with full military honours, was conducted by Father John Fahey DSO. The mourners

The closed Claremont Mental Hospital, Perth, Western Australia, where Martin O'Meara died in 1935.

included Clifford Sadlier VC, James Woods VC and Thomas Axford VC. Senator Sir George Pearce, former wartime Defence Minister, was a pallbearer. Martin is buried in the Roman Catholic Section at Karrakatta Cemetery, Perth, Western Australia (HA Plot 93). His will was completed on 16th November 1917 whilc at Bath War Hospital, but the two beneficiaries, HE Luesh and CC Hore (formerly of 6th Battalion), could not be traced after his death.

Martin is commemorated in a number of places:

Martin O'Meara's grave in Karrakatta Cemetery, Perth (Gavin Fitzpatrick).

- The wards at Hollywood Private Hospital, Western Australia, were named after sixteen VCs and GCs, including one for Martin O'Meara.
- O'Meara Place in Canberra, Australian Capital Territory.
- O'Meara Street, Wodonga, Victoria.
- Omeara [sic] Street, Crib Point, Melbourne, Victoria.
- O'Meara Way, Alexander Heights, Perth, Western Australia.
- Named on the Victoria Cross Memorial, Campbell, Canberra dedicated on 24th July 2000.

State War Memorial, King's Park, Perth, Western Australia (Study Perth).

The unveiling of the memorial to Martin O'Meara at Lorrha, Co Tipperary, Ireland, on 19th June 2013 (Lorrha & Dorrha Parish).

- Named on the Victoria Cross Memorial, Queen Victoria Building, George Street, Sydney, New South Wales.
- Memorial plaque at the State War Memorial, King's Park, Perth, dedicated on 26th January 1996.
- Named on a bronze memorial plaque in a set of eleven country-related plaques honouring the 175 men from overseas who won the Victoria Cross during the Great War. The plaques were unveiled by Senior Minister of State in the Foreign & Commonwealth Office and Minister for Faith and Communities, Baroness Warsi at a special reception at Lancaster House, London on 26th June 2014. The reception was attended by HRH The Duke of Kent and relatives of the VC recipients. The Australian plaque is at the Australian War Memorial in Canberra.
- Memorial dedicated at Lorrha, Co Tipperary, Ireland on 19th June 2013.
- Memorial plaque at Blackboy Hill Memorial site, Greenmount, Western Australia.
- A one-act play, *Under Any Old Gum Tree*, about the life of Martin O'Meara, written by Noel O'Neill, was performed at Old Mill Theatre, South Perth on 1st February 2014, Collie Senior High School on 30th March and the Irish Club of Western Australia on 29th April.

12/18645 PRIVATE ROBERT QUIGG
12th Battalion, The Royal Irish Rifles (Central Antrim)

Robert Quigg was born at Ardihennon, Carnkirk, Giant's Causeway, near Bushmills, Co Antrim, Ireland on 28th February 1885. His father was also Robert Quigg (born c.1859), at various times employed as a farm labourer, boatman and tourist guide on the Giant's Causeway. His mother was Matilda née Blue (born c.1860), known as Tillie. Robert and Matilda married on 2nd June 1862 at Billy Parish Church, Co Antrim. In 1901 the family was living at 8 Ballymoy, Dunseverick, Co Antrim and in 1911 at 13 Cankirk, Dunseverick. Robert junior had five siblings, all of whom survived him:

- Alex Quigg (c.1887–1965) married Mary.
- Matilda 'Tilly/Tillie' Quigg (born c.1891), married as McDermott.
- Isabella 'Bella' Quigg (born c.1893) was a dressmaker in 1911 and married as Gibson.
- Elizabeth 'Eliza' Quigg (born c.1896) married W Reynolds.
- Frances Quigg, married as Tose.

Robert was educated at Giant's Causeway National School. He was employed as a farm labourer by Mr David Forsyth of Turfahum and later on the MacNaghten estate at Bushmills. He was a member of the Orange Order, Aird LOL 1195 and played in the flute band. He was also a member of the Royal Black Institution and the William Johnston Memorial Royal Black Preceptory 559. Robert commanded the Bushmills Volunteers of the Ulster Volunteer Force in 1913.

Dundarave House, home of the Macnaghten family, near Bushmills.

Robert enlisted in September 1914 and volunteered to be Lieutenant Sir (Edward) Harry MacNaghten's (1896–1916) servant. Sir Harry was commissioned in 12th Royal Irish Rifles on 12th September 1914. On 4th May 1916 he was also appointed to the Black Watch, but remained serving with 12th Royal Irish Rifles. Robert went to England with the division in July 1915 and to France on 6th October 1915. **Awarded the VC for his actions at Hamel, France on 1st July 1916, LG 9th September 1916.** The VC was presented by the King at York Cottage, Sandringham on 8th January 1917. As the King pinned the VC on Robert Quigg's chest, he remarked, *You're a very brave man Quigg*. Robert is reputed to have replied, *You're a brave wee man yourself, Sir*; he was using 'brave' in the Ulster-Scots sense, meaning decent. The King asked if he was married, to which he replied, *No Sir, but after what has happened to me I suppose I soon will be.*

Sir Harry MacNaghten.

On his return to Bushmills, Robert received a tremendous welcome. Lady McNaghten presented him with a gold watch in recognition of his bravery in trying to rescue her son. Unfortunately, he had to sell it for £100 when he suffered financial difficulties. He was also presented £200 in Exchequer Bonds at a reception at Hamill Hotel, Bushmills on 11th January 1917. **Awarded the Russian Medal of St George 4th Class, LG 15th February 1917.**

Robert later served as a sergeant in Mesopotamia and Egypt. He claimed to have been awarded the Croix de Guerre, but there is no documentary evidence for this. Following the Partition of Ireland, he served in the Royal Ulster Rifles (2/25667 & 7007261), including in Iraq. On 23rd May 1926, he fell fifty feet from the window of the Sandes Soldier's Home in Clifton Street, Belfast and was very seriously injured. He was not expected to survive, but did recover. However, his injuries were such that he was discharged on medical grounds on 18th October 1926.

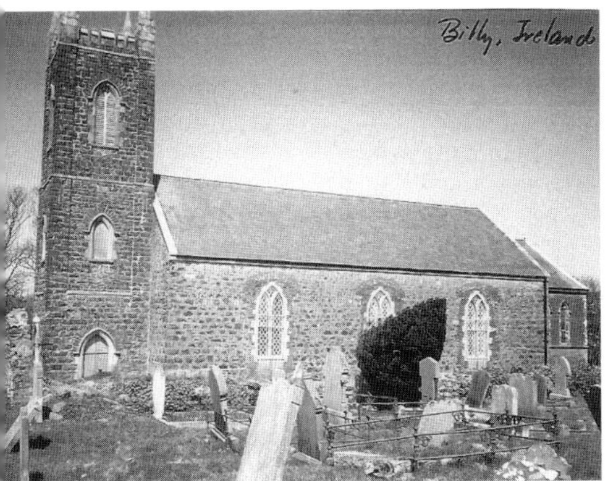

Billy Parish Church (Lynn Hansen).

The Giant's Causeway Amphitheatre, where Robert Quigg and his father before him were guides.

The Regiment employed him as a civilian at the Royal Ulster Rifles Depot at Armagh until he retired in 1934. He then became a guide at the Giant's Causeway, following in his father's footsteps. The local war memorial was modelled on him. Robert never married and lived the rest of his life in a cottage on the McNaghten estate. He met Queen Elizabeth II in 1953 in Coleraine, just after she had acceded to the throne, and was one of five Northern Irish VCs presented with a silver tankard in May 1954 at Ulster Hall.

Robert Quigg died at Dalriada Hospital, Ballycastle, Co Antrim, Northern Ireland on 14th May 1955 and is buried in Billy Church of Ireland Parish Churchyard, Bushmills. A granite headstone, erected by the Royal British Legion, was unveiled by Lord Rathcavan, Lord Lieutenant of Co Antrim, on 16th November 1958.

In addition to the VC, he was awarded the 1914–15 Star, British War Medal 1914–20, Victory Medal 1914–19, General Service Medal 1918–62 with clasp 'Iraq', George V Silver Jubilee Medal 1935, George VI Coronation Medal 1937, Elizabeth II Coronation Medal 1953 and the Russian Medal of St George 4th Class. The VC is held by the Royal Ulster Rifles Museum, Waring Street, Belfast.

28930 PIPER JAMES CLELAND RICHARDSON
16th Battalion (Canadian Scottish), Canadian Expeditionary Force

James Richardson was born on 25th November 1895 at the Police Station, Bellshill, Glasgow, Lanarkshire, Scotland. His father, David Richardson (1867–1955), was apprenticed at the hardware firm of W & R Moffat for six years. He joined the Lanarkshire Police in 1886, living at Mount Vernon, Old Monkland, Lanarkshire. He

was a sergeant by 1901, living at Blantyre Police Station, and rose to police inspector and Fire Chief for the Rutherglen District. He married Mary Dall née Prosser (1866–1956), a mill worker, on 14th August 1891 at 69 High Street, Peebles. The family emigrated to Canada in 1913 and lived at Princess Avenue, Chilliwack, British Columbia, where David was appointed Chief of Police until retiring from the Force in 1920. He became janitor at Chilliwack High School. Known as 'Chief', he was a prominent Freemason, supported the St Andrew's and Caledonia Society, was a member of Cooke's Presbyterian Church and a founding member of the Chilliwack Lawn Bowling Club. Mary was active in the

Bellshill Police Station, Glasgow, where James Richardson was born on 25th November 1895.

Blantyre Police Station, home to the Richardson family in 1901.

Chilliwack, British Columbia c.1910.

Chilliwack High School, where David Richardson was janitor after retiring from the Police Force in 1920.

Cooke's Presbyterian Church, Chilliwack.

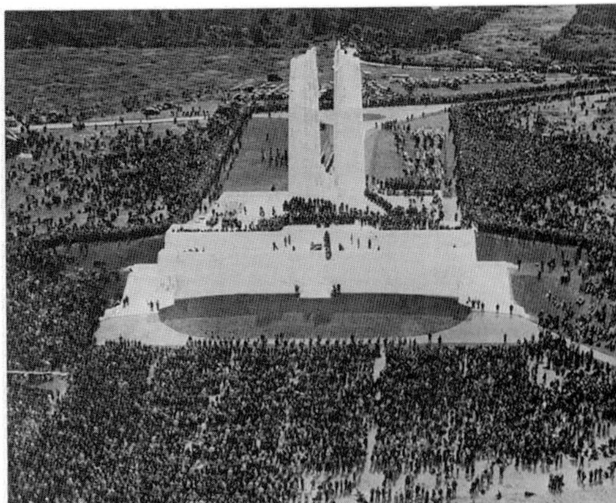

On 16th July 1936, five liners departed Montreal for France. They carried 6,400 Canadian veterans and family members, whilst another 1,365 came from Britain for the dedication of the Canadian National Vimy Memorial on 26th July. Edward VIII led the ceremony in one of his few official engagements as king. Over 50,000 Canadian, British and French veterans and their families attended, including James Richardson's parents, sister Alice and brother David.

Women's Missionary Society of Cooke's Presbyterian Church. David and Mary went on the 1936 Vimy Pilgrimage, with their daughter Alice and son David, and attended the dedication of the Vimy War Memorial on 26th July. They also visited the grave of their son, James, at Adanac Military Cemetery. In 1939 David and Mary were presented to King George VI and Queen Elizabeth during their visit to Chilliwack. James had seven siblings, all born in Scotland:

- Mary Prosser Richardson, born on 23rd February 1893.
- Alice Preston Richardson, born on 1st December 1897.
- David Mitchell Richardson, born on 16th December 1899, served in the Navy.
- Alexandra Prosser Richardson, born on 13th July 1902.
- Isabella Melrose Richardson, born on 12th December 1904.
- Robert Richardson, born on 21st January 1907.
- Janet Thomson Richardson, born on 20th September 1910.

James' paternal grandfather, James Cleland Richardson (c.1834–93), an agricultural labourer, was born at Rowland, Peebleshire. He married Allison née Preston (c.1834–1912) on 27th May 1864 at Peebles. The family was living at Windylaws Cottage, Eddleston, Peebleshire in 1871. By 1881 they had moved to 2 Harcus Cottages, Eddleston. In 1891 James was a stableman living with his family at 7 Albert Street, Edinburgh. When he died on the street opposite 76 Grassmarket, Edinburgh on 31st October 1893, his address was 40 Lorne Street, Leith. Allison was living with her son, David, at 136 Duke Street, Leith, Midlothian in 1901. In addition to David they also had Isabella Melrose Richardson c.1866 and Robert Preston Richardson 1871.

James' maternal grandfather, James Prosser (c.1820–73), was a railway surface man. He married Mary née Dall (c.1827–83) on 11th August 1851 at Lindores, Newburgh, Fife. They were living at Craigs Land, Lochee, Angus in 1861. Mary was a housekeeper in 1881, living with her family at School Brae, Peebles, Peebleshire. In addition to Mary they also had:

- Margaret Prosser (c.1853–81), a weaver, married Peter Small (born c.1852), a printer/compositor, in 1876. They were living at 44 Ure Street, Forfar in 1881 and had three children.
- Janet Prosser, born c.1855, was a woollen weaver in 1881.
- Elexa (also seen as Alexa and Alexandrina) Prosser, (1857–1944), a tweed weaver, married David Mitchell (1858–1930), a house painter, in 1878 and they had a daughter, Blanche Mitchell c.1887. They were living at 69 High Street, Peebles in 1901. David was also a piper.
- Elizabeth Prosser, born 1860.
- Richard Prosser (c.1863–82) was a tailor in 1881.
- Thomas Prosser, born 1869.

Auchinwraith Public School, Blantyre, where James was educated.

James was educated at Bellshill Academy in Glasgow, Auchinwraith Public School at Blantyre and John Street School, Bridgeton, Glasgow. While living in Rutherglen, Lanarkshire he was a member of the Boy Scouts. He learned to play the bagpipes and won several contests. On 1st July 1914, he won three first prizes at the Scottish Sports Day held in Victoria, British Columbia.

He worked as an apprentice electrician in a False Creek factory at Vancouver, British Columbia. While working there in 1914 the alarm was raised about a boy drowning in the creek. He ran to the spot, dived under the water and brought up the boy, but was too late to save his life.

He served for six months in the Cadet Corps of 72nd Battalion (Seaforth Highlanders), joining the pipe band. At the outbreak of the war he volunteered for the Canadian Expeditionary Force and was taken on strength on 23rd September 1914 at Valcartier, Quebec. He was described as a driller, 5′ 8″ tall, weighing 137lbs with fair complexion, blue eyes and brown hair. He was assigned to 16th Battalion (Canadian Scottish), as a piper. The Battalion sailed for Britain on 3rd October 1914, went to France on 9th February 1915 and was involved in stemming the German offensive at St Julien, Belgium in April. On 22nd April, the battalion advanced through Kitcheners Wood in a night counterattack. After advancing about thirty yards on the other side of the wood, a party of about fifty men started to dig in, but James kept going on his own. After about forty yards he reached a farmhouse, around which Germans were sheltering from the heavy fire. He dropped down to avoid being seen and saw an officer coming towards him waving his men on. James shot him and ran back. He was able to tell the sergeant major that the farmhouse was occupied and the artillery dealt with it.

James Richardson's grave in Adanac Military Cemetery.

At Festubert, in May, he carried despatches and saved the life of a wounded comrade. **Awarded the VC for his actions at Regina Trench, near Courcelette on 8th October 1916, LG 22nd October 1918.** James was missing presumed killed in action on 9th October 1916 near Courcelette, France. His body was recovered by a farmer in 1920 and is buried in Adanac Military Cemetery, near Albert, France (III F 36).

The recommendation for the VC was made by Major Cyrus W Peck, but in a letter to James' father in January 1917 he believed it had not gone through because of a technicality. As a lieutenant colonel, Cyrus Peck was awarded the VC for his gallantry at Cagnicourt, near Bapaume, France, on 2nd September 1918; he was also awarded the DSO & Bar. James' VC was not gazetted until late in 1918. The reason for the delay is not known.

James Richardson's parents and sister Alice at his grave in July 1936.

In addition to the VC, he was awarded the 1914–15 Star, British War Medal 1914–20 and Victory Medal 1914–19. As he never married, the VC was presented to his father by the Lieutenant Governor of British Columbia, Sir Francis Stillman Barnard, at the Ritz Hotel, Victoria, British Columbia on 3rd April 1919. It is held at the Canadian War Museum, 1 Vimy Place, Ottawa, Ontario. James is commemorated in a number of places:

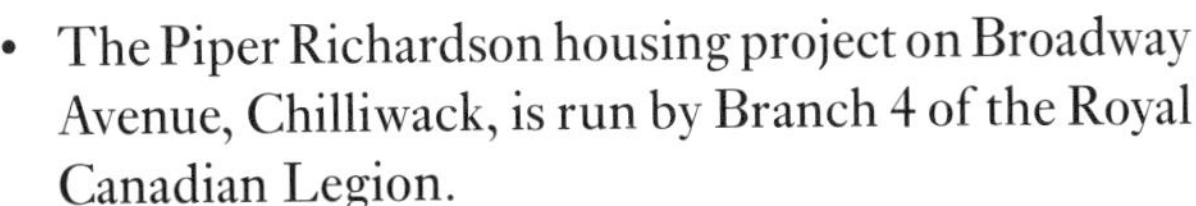

- The Piper Richardson housing project on Broadway Avenue, Chilliwack, is run by Branch 4 of the Royal Canadian Legion.
- Named on the Chilliwack War Memorial, dedicated on 9th April 1923.
- Named on the First World War Honour Roll at Cooke's Presbyterian Church, Wellington Avenue, Chilliwack.

- His statue was unveiled at the Chilliwack Museum, 45820 Spadina Avenue, Chilliwack on 11th October 2003.
- A memorial to the fourteen Lanarkshire VCs was dedicated on 19th April 2002 in Hamilton, Lanarkshire, following a public appeal by the *Hamilton Advertiser* and South Lanarkshire Council. The VCs commemorated are: Frederick R Aikman, William Angus, Thomas Caldwell, Donald Cameron, John Carmichael, William C Clamp, William Gardner, John B Hamilton, David R Lauder, David MacKay, William J Milne, John O'Neill, William Reid and James C Richardson.
- Named on memorial paving to the three VCs from Bridgeton, Glasgow: John Simpson Knox, James Cleland Richardson and Henry May – unveiled on 23rd August 2010. The inscribed pavers form part of the Bridgeton Burns Club Memorial.
- His VC action was featured in the *Victor* comic on 4th September 1965, 28th June 1975 and 11th May 1985.
- Two 49 Cent postage stamps in honour of the ninety-four Canadian VCs were issued by Canada Post on 21st October 2004 on the 150th Anniversary of the first Canadian VC's action, Alexander Roberts Dunn.
- Named on one of eleven plaques honouring 175 men from overseas awarded the VC for the Great War. The plaques were unveiled by the Senior Minister of State at the Foreign & Commonwealth Office and Minister for Faith and Communities, Baroness Warsi, at a reception at Lancaster House, London on 26th June 2014 attended by The Duke of Kent and relatives of the VC recipients. The Canadian plaque was unveiled outside the British High Commission in Elgin Street, Ottawa on 10th November 2014 by The Princess Royal in the presence of British High Commissioner Howard Drake, Canadian Minister of Veterans Affairs Julian Fantino and Canadian Chief of the Defence Staff General Thomas J. Lawson.

Cyrus W Peck VC DSO & Bar recommended James for the VC.

Sir Francis Stillman Barnard, Lieutenant Governor of British Columbia, who presented James' VC to his father in 1919.

A mud-stained set of broken bagpipes was presented to Ardvreck School by former Major Edward Yeld Bate when he retired from his teaching post at the school at Crieff, Perthshire in 1931. Bate found the bagpipes on the battlefield at Courcelette in spring 1917. Tomas Christie, also a piper, wondered if he could trace the family of whoever owned them. He was curious about the unusual tartan, which was not

James Richardson's statue at Chilliwack Museum (Tom Sauriol) .

The Canadian War Museum in Ottawa, where James Richardson's VC is held (Canadian War Museum).

The memorial to Lanarkshire's fourteen VCs in Hamilton.

Chilliwack War Memorial.

associated with any Scottish Regiment. He was contacted by Pipe Major Roger McGuire of the Canadian Scottish Regiment, who realised the significance of date, place and tartan. 16th Battalion had been formed from four Highland regiments. There was a company from Vancouver's Seaforth Highlanders, from which James Richardson had enlisted, and other companies from the Gordon Highlanders, Cameron Highlanders and Canadian Highlanders. These Regiments wore different tartans and the 16th Battalion needed one in common, so the CO decided it would be his wife's family tartan, Lennox. Roger McGuire went to Scotland in January 2002 to investigate. The cover on the pipes' bag was soiled with mud and the ivory speckled with brown stains that might be blood, but inside the cover the Lennox tartan was pristine. The broken pipes were without doubt from 16th Battalion and pointed to

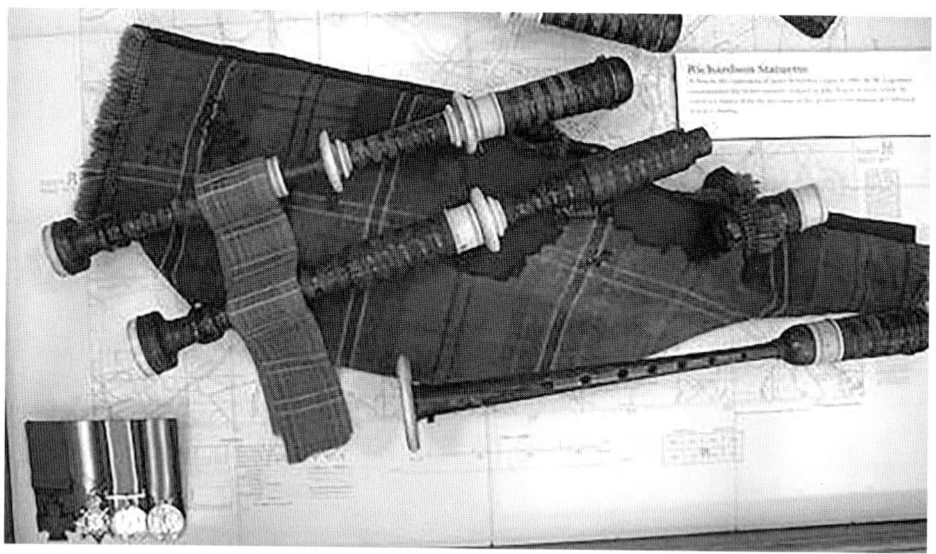

James Richardson's pipes on display at British Columbia's Legislature in Victoria.

Piper James Richardson. However, another 16th Battalion Piper, John Park, was killed on the same day at Courcelette (Vimy Memorial). Andrew Winstanley of The Canadian Club and Roger McGuire investigated further. Because they came from different units before joining 16th Battalion, James Richardson and John Park used different models of Henderson pipes. One difference was the diameter of the opening of the ivory sole at the base of the chanter. Photographs taken at Valcartier and on Salisbury Plain show the opening of John Park's chanter is too small to be a match with the Ardvreck School pipes, but it matches James Richardson's perfectly. An anonymous donor put up the funds to purchase the pipes and on 9th October 2006 they were handed over by the Headmaster of Ardvreck School to James' grandnephew, Dan Richardson. On 8th November 2006, The Canadian Scottish Regiment (Princess Mary's) handed them to Premiere Gordon Campbell, at the British Columbia Legislature in Victoria, where they are on public display.

68 DRUMMER WALTER POTTER RITCHIE
2nd Battalion, Seaforth Highlanders (Ross-shire Buffs, The Duke of Albany's)

Walter Ritchie was born at 81 Hopefield Road, Glasgow on 27th March 1892. His father, also Walter Ritchie (born 1855), was a journeyman iron fitter in 1884, an ornamental iron fitter in 1901 and caretaker of the Canal Boatmen's Institute at 162 Port Dundas Road, Glasgow in 1916. His mother was Helen 'Ellen' Montieth née Murphy (1858–1935), a muslin manufacturer's warehousewoman, living with

her parents at 161 Stirling Road, Glasgow at the time of her marriage to Walter on 18th July 1884. The family lived in Glasgow at 244 Parliamentary Road in 1884, 55 Cedar Street by 1887, 39 Raglan Street by 1890, 162 Port Dundas Road when Walter won the VC in 1916 and later at 435 Dobbie's Loan. Walter junior had five siblings:

- Janet Ritchie (born c.1882).
- John Ritchie (born c.1885).
- Arthur Ritchie (1887–1871) was a message boy in 1901 and later a turner. He married Jeanie Thomson, a widow, on 9th September 1912. They had five children recorded in his service records: Angus 1907, Alice 1910, Arthur 1912, Walter 1913 and Jeanie in 1914. He enlisted in the Royal Garrison Artillery (SR/6284 and later 281284) on 16th July 1915 and served in Britain until 14th December 1918.
- Elizabeth McLarty Mitchell Ritchie (1890–1971) was a mantle cutter. She married Robert Millar on 30th June 1916. He was a tube works clerk (born c.1889). They had a daughter, Isabella Walker Millar, in 1917.
- Thomas James Ritchie (1898–1964) was a journeyman electrician. He enlisted in 2/1st Lovat Scouts (3381 later S/25705) on 10th November 1915. He was only 5′ 5″ tall. He transferred to 3rd Cameron Highlanders on 6th September 1916 and served in Salonika from 24th September. He transferred to the Argyll & Sutherland Highlanders on 7th October. He returned to the Cameron Highlanders and was posted to the 10th Battalion (Lovat Scouts) on 27th September 1917. Thomas suffered from malaria and was admitted to 82nd Field Ambulance on 26th October, 27th Casualty Clearing Station on 29th October and 48th General Hospital on 2nd November. Following convalescence and time at based depots, he was posted to the Depot in Britain on 6th July 1918. His service records were annotated, 'not to be posted to a theatre where malaria was prevalent'. Thomas served in France 25th September 1918 – 21st April 1919, transferred to the Class Z Reserve on 20th May and was demobilised on 31st March 1920. He married Mary Campbell Macintyre on 27th May 1922 by declaration at 435 Sauchiehall Street, Glasgow. She was a typist (born c.1903) of 128 North John Street. They emigrated to Vancouver, British Columbia, Canada after having a daughter in Scotland, Catherine Macintyre Ritchie, in October 1922. He married again, Phyllis E Thomas (1920–2004) and had a child.

Walter was educated at Normal School (later Dundas Vale) in the Cowcaddens area of Glasgow and also at St Mary's Episcopal Church, Renfield Street, Glasgow. Thereafter he was employed as a blacksmith's apprentice and was a member of 44th Glasgow Company, Boys' Brigade.

Walter enlisted in 8th Cameronians (TF) underage. He transferred to Regular service in 2nd Seaforth Highlanders on 17th August 1908 and was appointed drummer on 19th September 1909. Walter went with the Battalion to France on 23rd August 1914. He was wounded near Armentières on 13th October and evacuated to England on the 17th. He returned to France on 26th May 1915 and was slightly wounded again just before the Battle of the Somme.

The Canal Boatmen's Institute at 162 Port Dundas Road, Glasgow, where Walter's father was caretaker and the family lived.

Awarded the VC for his actions north of Beaumont Hamel, France on 1st July 1916, LG 9th September 1916. The VC was presented by the King at Buckingham Palace on 25th November 1916. **Awarded the French Croix de Guerre, LG 9th December 1916, which was presented to him by Lieutenant General Sir Aylmer Hunter-Weston.**

Walter was slightly wounded in the knee during the Somme offensive. On a brief visit to Glasgow, The Boatmen's Institute, where his father worked, awarded him a gold watch and £23. Back at the front, Walter was wounded twice in 1917. By the end of the war he had been wounded five times and gassed twice. He was serving as a lance corporal with 3rd Seaforth Highlanders at Newton Camp, Cromarty when

1st Seaforth Highlanders Warrant Officers and Sergeants in the 1920s with their Colonel-in-Chief, The Prince of Wales. Walter Ritchie is standing on the extreme left. At least seven other gallantry awards, DCM or MM, can be seen.

he married in February 1919. His remaining service was with 1st Battalion. In order to complete twenty-one years service, he re-engaged in Belfast in July 1921, by which time his number was 2809134. Walter was a member of the VC Guard at the Interment of the Unknown Warrior on 11th November 1920. He rose to drum major and was discharged on 16th August 1931.

Walter Ritchie married Mary née McLagan (1895–1977) at All Saints & St Regulus, Cromarty on 7th February 1919. She was born at 2 Gowan Brae, Blairgowrie, Perthshire and was serving as a WAAC cook at Newton Camp, Cromarty at the time. They had two sons:

- Arthur Henry Ritchie, born 5th October 1919 at Montrose, served in the Royal Corps of Signals in the Second World War. He died in 1984 at Montrose.
- James Dugmore Ritchie, born 1923 at Montrose (not confirmed).

Walter became a recruiting officer in Glasgow and was later a schools attendance officer and Grand Janitor of the Royal Arch Halls in Edinburgh. He served in the Territorial Army before the Second World War, during which he was a staff sergeant in the Royal Army Ordnance Corps in Scotland. He was discharged medically unfit in 1941.

Walter was a Freemason – Govanhill Lodge No.1222 and Holyrood House Lodge No.44. He died at West Saville Terrace, Mayfield, Edinburgh on 17th March 1965 and was cremated at Warriston Crematorium, Edinburgh. His ashes were placed in Niche C-20, but it no longer exists.

In addition to the VC and French Croix de Guerre, he was awarded the 1914 Star with Mons clasp, British War Medal 1914–20, Victory Medal 1914–19, 1939–45 Star, War Medal 1939–45, George V Silver Jubilee Medal 1935, George VI Coronation Medal 1937 and Elizabeth II Coronation Medal 1953. Although not mentioned in the London Gazette entry, his Croix de Guerre carries the Palme emblem.

The VC was first sold at Sotheby's for £1,700 on 30th September 1970. It has been sold, or at least listed, a number of times since. It was listed by John Burridge for $A22,000 on 1st November 1981 and sold to a private collector. Its current whereabouts are unknown. The bugle carried by Walter throughout the war is held by the Highlanders Museum, Fort George, Inverness.

G/3281 PRIVATE ROBERT EDWARD RYDER
12th Battalion, The Duke of Cambridge's Own (Middlesex Regiment)

Robert Ryder was born in Harefield Workhouse, Breakspear Road North, Middlesex on 17th December 1895. His father, Charles Ryder (born 1856), was variously a labourer, cowman and night watchman at Harefield Hospital. His mother was Jane née Howard (1861–1952). She married Charles at St Mary the

Virgin, Harefield on 21st December 1878. The family was living at Fishery Cottages, Rickmansworth, Hertfordshire in 1881 and the Old Workhouse, Harefield, Middlesex in 1891. By 1911 they were at Breakspear Road, Harefield and in 1915 Jane was living at 8 Park Terrace. Robert had twelve siblings including:

- Charles James Ryder (1880–1952) owned a property in Kensington, London and became a lodging house keeper at 21 Upper Phillimore Place, Kensington. One of his clients was Clementine Ogilvy Hozier, who in 1908 married Winston Churchill. He married Alice Maria Greenaway (1866–1852) at Deptford in 1898 and they had two daughters: Audrey Alice Lawlison Ryder (1901–60) married William Herbert Lugg in 1922, and Doris May Ryder, born and died 1902.
- Emily Martha Ryder (1883–1980) married George Henry Breen (1871–1960) in 1906. George was from Ireland and was a coachman in 1911 living with his family at Hill End, Uxbridge. They had three children: Maisie Dorothy Breen (1911–99), George C Breen born and died 1921 and Joan P Breen 1922, who married as Cook and served in the WAAF during the Second World War.
- William Robert Ryder (1886–1927) was a carter on a farm. He married Johanna O'Neill (1897–1958) in 1921 and they had two children: Stephen WC Ryder born 1922, served in the REME 1943–47; and Marie JA Ryder (1925–2009), who married Leslie Clarence Simser (1922–2001) in 1945 and had four children. Both children emigrated to Canada. Johanna married Henry William Hiley in1930.
- Harry Reginald Ryder (1888–1971) was a carter on a farm and later a labourer. He married Matilda Louisa Hawkins (1888–1949) at Poplar in 1908 and they lived at Shrubs Cottages, Harefield. They had at least three children: Hilda May Ryder 1909, Dorothy L Ryder 1913 and Gladys Emily Ryder 1914–89. Harry enlisted in the Middlesex Regiment (3273) on 3rd September 1914 and was allocated to 12th Battalion on the 5th. He was described as 5′ 5½″ tall, weighing 123 lbs, with grey eyes, light brown hair and his religious denomination was Church of England. He was discharged from Colchester on 19th September as unlikely to become an efficient soldier due to flat feet.
- Dorothy Louisa Ryder (1890–1967) was a domestic servant in 1911 at Walwyns, Peterborough Road, Harrow-on-the-Hill, Middlesex. She married Walter George Drury (1889–1955), a jobbing gardener, in 1914. They had a son, Kenneth Walter Drury 1916–2005.
- Alfred Joseph Ryder (1892–1939) was a carter. He enlisted in the Royal Garrison Artillery (85788) at Mill Hill on 1st December 1915. His next of kin was his mother, living at 8 Park Terrace, Harefield. He trained at No.1 Depot RGA at Fort Burgoyne, Dover and went to France on 17th September 1916, where he served in 39th Siege Battery from 19th October. He was granted leave in Britain 13th-27th November 1917 and qualified for Class 1 Proficiency Pay as a gun layer

on 4th December. Alfred was in hospital sick 4th-15th July 1918 and was granted leave in Britain 6th-20th December. Posted to Shorncliffe, Kent 26th January 1919 and was discharged on 1st March. He married Alice Gathercole in 1919.

- Adelaide Mary Ryder (1894–1939) was a twin with Lucy. She married Alfred S George (1892–1962) in 1914 and they had a son, Sydney Charles George 1916–92.
- Lucy Lilian Ryder (1894–1964) was a twin with Adelaide. She was a domestic servant in 1911 at 4 Western Gardens, Brentford, Middlesex. She married Richard Jesse Scott (1892–1953) in 1915.
- Eva Elizabeth Ryder (1897–1982) was a joint-maker. She emigrated to Australia, arriving on 24th March 1920 and settled at Campsie, Parkes, New South Wales. She married an Australian soldier, William Thomas Blake (1892–1973), at St Philip's Church, Sydney. They had two children: Pearl Blake and Keith Frederick Blake (1923–84), who married Dorothy May Hodge in 1945 and they had seven children.
- Edna Constance Ryder (1901–90) moved to Australia, arriving at Sydney on 15th February 1921. She married Edwin George Stray in 1921 and had a daughter, Irene Constance Stray, at the end of that year.
  Edna returned to Britain and her death was registered at Watford in the 4th quarter of 1990.

Jimmy Wilde (1892–1969) was a South Wales miner before turning to boxing. In February 1916 the 'Mighty Atom' won the British Flyweight title and two months later was the International Boxing Union World Flyweight champion. Later that year he joined the army and went to France to the Physical Training and Bayonet School at St Pol. He continued to box and on 18th December 1916 became the first official World Flyweight Champion, as the IBU title was only recognised in Europe. He retired in 1923 after losing his world title to Filipino Pancho Villa, only his fourth defeat in 147 professional fights, a record that makes Wilde one of the greatest boxers of all time.

Robert was educated at Harefield Council School and also attended the local Sunday School. He was a Boy Scout. As a youth he was a skilled amateur boxer and once went fifteen rounds with the British and World Flyweight champion, Jimmy Wilde, but lost on points. From 1910 he was employed driving a hay cart to London overnight. In 1913 he became a bricklayer and later worked as a labourer at the United Asbestos Works, Harefield, but described himself as a farm labourer on enlistment, working for United Asbestos.

During the 4th quarter of 1913, Robert Ryder married Bessie Gabrielle Carty (16th August 1896–1936). They lived at Shah Cottages, High Street, Harefield and had three or four children:

- Robert William Ryder (23rd January 1914 – 31st August 1998) served in 2nd Middlesex and was captured by the Germans in 1940, but escaped and walked to St Nazaire, where he caught a boat to England. An injury to his arm rendered him unfit for service and he was discharged in 1943. He married Kathleen 'Kitty' George in 1941 at Portsmouth and they had four children: Ellen H Ryder 1942, Larry AT Ryder 1944–2007, Colleen M Ryder 1946 and Dixie A Ryder 1948.

- Edna M Ryder (born 1921) emigrated to Australia and married as Coulson. They had at least one son, Robert Coulson, who was commissioned in the Royal Australian Army Service Corps and served in Vietnam 1969–70.
- Frank Ryder (1923–2011) was educated at the Duke of York's Royal Military School, Dover 1935–38. He served in 2nd Middlesex in Northwest Europe until 1944 and Palestine and Egypt until 1948. Frank then served with the Surrey Police 1949–76. He married Joan M Wearing in 1949 and they had two children: Andrew K Ryder 1953 and Paul R Ryder 1964.
- Betty Ryder, born about December 1931, was adopted on 24th May 1934 by a family named Dean. She may have been the fourth child, but there are no records that match such a birth.

Colchester Military Hospital.

Robert enlisted on 3rd September 1914 and joined 12th Battalion on 25th September. He was described as 5′ 5″ tall, weighing 133½ lbs, with blue eyes, brown hair and his religious denomination was Church of England. He had tattoos on both arms. Robert was admitted to Colchester Military Hospital 9–17th February 1915 with catarrh and went to France on 25th July, where he was sentenced to twenty-one days Field Punishment No.1 on 1st September.

Awarded the VC for his actions at Thiepval, France on 26th September 1916, LG 25th November 1916. He received a gun shot wound to the left hand, fracturing the proximal phalanx, on the same day and was evacuated to Britain via No.3 Canadian General Hospital on 28th September on HMHS *St Denis*, where he was treated at Norfolk War Hospital until 14th October, when he transferred to the Auxiliary Hospital, Union House, Swainsthorpe, Norwich. He returned to duty on 18th November and served in 6th (Reserve) Battalion from 27th November. The VC was presented by the King at Buckingham Palace on 29th November.

Robert was appointed unpaid lance corporal on 6th January 1917 and was promoted lance corporal on 27th February. **Awarded the Italian Bronze Medal for Military Valour, LG 26th May 1917 (18th Division Routine Order 854 dated 13th March 1917).** On 4th June he was admitted to Barnwell Military Hospital, Cambridge from hospital in Chatham to be treated for gonorrhoea and was discharged to duty on 3rd September. He returned to France on 12th September, was posted to the Base Depot BEF next day and to 11th Battalion on 14th September. Robert returned to 12th Middlesex from 41st Infantry Base Depot on 23rd September and rejoined next day.

He was almost taken prisoner as a result of a ruse. A German in British uniform led him and other volunteer reinforcements into the German lines, but Robert and another man made a dash for nearby woods and escaped. He was promoted corporal on 19th February 1918 and slipped on a duckboard on 1st March while carrying ammunition and injured his knee. Appointed acting sergeant on 10th March.

The Italian Bronze Medal for Military Valour.

Robert received a gun shot wound to the left buttock on 7th April 1918 and was admitted to 2/3rd Home Counties Field Ambulance on 10th April and 5th General Hospital at Rouen on 12th April. He was evacuated to England on HMHS *Grantully Castle* next day. He was treated at Bagthorpe Military Hospital, Trent Bridge, Nottingham 16th April – 9th May, having reverted to corporal. From 19th April he was on the strength of the Infantry Command Depot. He sprained his left knee while recovering at the Command Depot in Tipperary, Ireland and was admitted to the Special Military Orthopaedic Hospital, Blackrock, Dublin on 23rd July. He had treatment for his left knee there until discharged 'no longer fit for war service' on 14th February 1919.

Robert was wounded again in September and was evacuated to Britain on the 14th via the Infantry Base Depot BEF on 13th September. He was on the held strength of 11th Battalion until returning to 12th Battalion on 23rd September. Promoted corporal 19th February 1918 and acting sergeant 10th March. He slipped on a duckboard on 1st March while carrying ammunition and injured his knee. He was wounded (gun shot or shell fragment) in the left buttock on 7th April 1918 and admitted to 5th General Hospital in Rouen on the 12th, prior to being evacuated to Britain on HMHS *Grantully Castle* on 13th April. He was treated at Bagthorpe Military Hospital, Trent Bridge, Nottingham 16th April – 9th May. While recovering

HMHS *Grantully Castle* (7,612 tons) was built in 1910 on the Clyde. In January 1915 she became a troopship and was involved in transporting troops during the Gallipoli campaign. On 1st May 1915 she was commissioned as a hospital ship with 552 beds. She returned to the Union-Castle Line in March 1919 and was scrapped in 1939.

Staff of the Military Hospital housed in the pavilion of Nottinghamshire County Cricket Club at Trent Bridge, Nottingham.

at the Command Depot in Tipperary he sprained his left knee. He was treated at the Special Military Orthopaedic Hospital, Blackrock from 23rd July for his left buttock until discharged from the Army on 14th February 1919. He was awarded Silver War Badge B159852 on 9th May. One of his cousin's, G/14679 Private Herbert Winwright (1879–1917) 11th Queen's, was killed in action on 1st August 1917 (Ypres (Menin Gate) Memorial),

Shortly afterwards he stopped a pair of runaway horses in Uxbridge High Street as they headed towards children coming out of school. Robert struggled to find work after the war but was eventually taken on as a builder's labourer for five years. Bessie became ill as a result of inhaling asbestos dust at work, so the family moved to New Milton, Hampshire on 16th August 1931 and took lodgings at Wooton. Robert found temporary employment with Milton Urban District Council on new sewerage schemes. He had great difficulty finding work to support his ailing wife and children. Bessie was admitted to Boscombe Hospital, Bournemouth, Dorset in September 1931 for an operation. Her health continued to decline and her death was registered in the 1st quarter of 1936 at Wandsworth, London.

Station Road North in New Milton, Hampshire, around the time Robert Ryder moved his family there.

Robert's second marriage to Rose Frearson (née Fairbrother) (6th October

RMS *Queen Elizabeth* was launched in September 1938 as a passenger liner, but she was almost immediately pressed into service as a troopship, making her maiden voyage to New York. During the war she carried over 750,000 troops and afterwards was engaged in repatriating them. In 1946 she underwent a major refurbishment on the Clyde and at Southampton, prior to commencing transatlantic services. Her belated maiden passenger voyage to New York commenced on 16th October 1946. She was withdrawn from service in 1968. A venture to turn her into a floating hotel in Florida failed and she went to Hong Kong to be converted into a university, but before completion was the victim of arson and sank in the harbour. The picture shows the ship in the King George V dry dock at Southampton. The dry dock was used to train the commandos on the St Nazaire raid in March 1942, which resulted in five VCs being awarded.

Robert Ryder while serving in the Royal Engineers during the Second World War.

1890–1977) was registered at Uxbridge, Middlesex in the 4th quarter of 1936. Rose had been married previously to Archibald Frearson (1887–1926) in 1909 and they lived at 76 Gibb Street, Long Eaton, Derbyshire, where he was a lace maker. Rose and Archibald had three children: Harold Frearson 1910, Norman D Frearson 1915 and Marion R Frearson 1921. In the 4th quarter of 1932, the birth of Brenda R Freason (sic) was registered at Uxbridge; the mother's maiden name was Fairbrother. As Archibald Frearson died in 1926, it is almost certain Brenda was Robert Ryder's child. Brenda Ryder, born on 21st November 1932, later emigrated to Canada with her parents and married there.

On 10th September 1939, Robert re-enlisted as a sergeant instructor in the Royal Sussex Regiment and transferred to the Royal Engineers in Derbyshire in May 1940. He was discharged on 21st August 1944.

Robert and Rose emigrated to Hartland, Canada with their daughter Brenda aboard RMS *Queen Elizabeth* on 26th December 1946, arriving in January 1947. He

During the First World War the Ordnance Factory at Chilwell was a National Filling Factory and the scene of a horrific explosion on 1st July 1918, in which 134 people were killed and 250 were injured.

worked in a lumber mill and then purchased a 100–acre mixed farm at Avondale, near Woodstock, New Brunswick. He farmed there until 1953, when he was forced to sell it following an accident in which a tree fell on him. It was then discovered that a piece of shrapnel remained in his leg and was causing partial disability. They returned to England on RMS *Ascania*, arriving at Southampton on 10th March 1953 and settled at 189 Station Road, Long Eaton, Nottinghamshire, but the marriage ended in divorce. Rose returned to Canada, arriving at Montreal on SS *Empress of Scotland* on 18th October 1955, where she lived with her daughter Marion from her first marriage, who had emigrated there having married a Canadian soldier. Robert worked at the Ordnance Factory, Chilwell, Nottinghamshire.

Robert's third marriage to Alice Edna Thornley (née Houldsworth) (31st August 1895 – 5th August 1988) was registered in the 1st quarter of 1960 at Basford, Nottinghamshire. She had previously married John W Thornley in 1917. In 1964 she embroidered a tablecloth with the names of all 1,346 VC recipients with the Victoria Cross and badge of the Middlesex Regiment in the centre. They lived at 'Jacwyn', Main Road, East Keal, Spilsby, Lincolnshire and moved to 58 Co-operative Avenue, Hucknall, Nottinghamshire in 1977–78. Later they moved to 62 Annesley Road, Nottingham.

He was one of twelve VC holders invited by the Ministry of Defence to attend the 50th anniversary of the Battle of the Somme at Thiepval, France 1st – 3rd July 1966. Robert needed his wife to accompany him, as his leg required frequent dressing. The British Legion and the Middlesex Regiment offered to cover the cost, but the Government agreed to his request and both went. During the VC/GC Reunion in 1966, he and his wife had their suitcase stolen. The thief may have assumed the VC and other medals were in it, but Edna had them in her handbag.

St Mary the Virgin Churchyard, Harefield, where Robert Ryder is buried.

Robert Ryder suffered for most of his life from the shrapnel wound in his hip and developed emphysema and thrombosis later. He died at home at 62 Annesley Road, Hucknall, Nottinghamshire on 1st

December 1978 after a long illness and a spell in Nottingham General Hospital. He is buried in St Mary the Virgin Churchyard, Harefield, Middlesex. His funeral, with full military honours, took place on 11th December, with buglers and seven men from the Queen's Division Depot as pall bearers. He is buried close to his boyhood hero, Lieutenant General GL Goodlake VC, whose grave he visited as a child.

Edna fell on hard times after Robert's death, but refused to sell his medals, which at the time were valued at £12,000. News of her hardship leaked out and £600 was donated by various anonymous benefactors, but she appealed for them to stop.

In addition to the VC, he was also awarded the 1914–15 Star, British War Medal 1914–20, Victory Medal 1914–19, War Medal 1939–45, George VI Coronation Medal 1937, Elizabeth II Coronation Medal 1953, Elizabeth II Silver Jubilee Medal 1977 and the Italian Bronze Medal for Military Valour. Edna donated the medals to the Imperial War Museum in February 1979 in accordance with her husband's wishes. During the presentation ceremony she met HRH Prince Charles. The medals are held in the Lord Ashcroft Gallery at the Imperial War Museum.

Robert is also commemorated at Middlesex Guildhall, Westminster and a Heritage Blue Plaque was unveiled at The Old Workhouse, Harefield, Hillingdon, Middlesex on 1st June 2010 by the Mayor of Hillingdon, Councillor David Yarrow. Robert was the model for the life-size soldier on the 12th Battalion War Memorial in Middlesex Guildhall. The Secretary of State for Communities and Local Government, Eric Pickles MP, announced that Great War VCs would have commemorative paving stones laid in their birth places on or close to the 100th anniversary of their VC actions. Robert Ryder's stone was dedicated at Harefield War Memorial, Village Green, Breakspear Road North, Middlesex on 4th November 2014.

3203 CORPORAL GEORGE SANDERS
1/7th Battalion, The Prince of Wales's Own (West Yorkshire Regiment) (Leeds Rifles)

(Leeds Museum)

George Sanders was born at 7 Thornton Place, New Wortley, Leeds, Yorkshire on 8th July 1894. His father was Thomas Sanders (1859–1936), an iron tool maker in 1901. His mother was Amy née Hargreaves (1863–1904), a wool filler in 1881. Thomas and Amy married in 1882. The family lived at 7 Weston Grove, Holbeck in 1901 and 3 Shand Grove, Holbeck, Leeds in 1911. Thomas married Amy's sister, Martha Elizabeth Bland (née Hargreaves), (1873–1939) in 1908. In 1891 Martha was a servant at 49 Cromwell Street, Leeds, the home of William H Bland (1873–1906), a mineral water manufacturer, and his wife Sarah, née Williamson. Sarah died in 1899 without issue. William and Martha married immediately thereafter. They had two daughters

Thornton Place, where George Sanders was born on 8th July 1894 (Leodis photographic archive).

Shand Grove, Leeds (Leodis photographic archive).

previously: Florence Hargreaves 1890 and Emily Bland Hargreaves 1892. George had six siblings:

- Emily Sanders (1883–1962) was a tailoress machine presser in 1901. She married Richard Brooke (1883–1971), a tailor, in 1910. They had twins, Edith and George Brooke in 1913.
- Edith Sanders (born 1884) was a tailoress finisher in 1901. She married George Sharp, a locomotive engine fitter in 1907 and they had a son, Ernest Sharp (1909–11). They were living at 10 Moorview Place, Leeds in 1911.
- John Sanders (born 1886) was a steel moulder in 1911.
- Ethel Sanders (born 1888) was a tailoress finisher in 1901 and was living with her sister Edith in 1911.
- Thomas Sanders (born 1890) was a tailor's cutter, living with his sister Edith in 1911.
- Mary Louisa Sanders (born 1892) was a tailoress in 1911. She married Edward Bland McCurrie (1887–1958) in 1917. He was a soldier at the time.

St John's Church, where George sang in the choir.

George was educated at Little Holbeck School and afterwards was an apprentice fitter at Airedale Foundry, Hunslet. He was a member of the choir of St John's

Church, Holbeck. He enlisted on 9th November 1914 (later number 265913) and went to France on 16th April 1915. Appointed unpaid lance corporal 4th October and promoted lance corporal 11th November. He was in hospital with conjunctivitis 1–6th April 1916. Appointed acting corporal 15th April.

Awarded the VC for his actions near Thiepval, France on 1st July 1916, LG 9th September 1916. He was recommended for the Victoria Cross by the CO of the Royal Irish Rifles. Promoted corporal 15th July. On 10th August he was wounded in the face by shrapnel and temporarily deafened, but returned to duty on 15th August. Promoted lance sergeant 30th August. He returned to Britain on leave on 14th November and the VC was presented by the King at Buckingham Palace on 18th November.

George applied for a commission on 22nd December. He left France on 12th January 1917, joined the Depot on 14th January and was posted to No.8 Officer Cadet Battalion at Lichfield on 8th March. He was commissioned in 2nd West Yorkshire on 27th July (June in his service record) and was attached to 1/6th Battalion. Appointed acting captain 20th December while commanding a company.

Rügen island in the Baltic, where George was held prisoner. It is a popular holiday destination.

Awarded the MC for his actions at Kemmel Hill on 25th April 1918 whilst commanding C Company 1/6th West Yorkshire. After the enemy had penetrated the front line he organised his men in support and held them up for some time inflicting, heavy casualties. Although wounded in the leg and right arm he continued to fight with his revolver in his left hand and at one time was seen on top of a pillbox rallying his men and firing his revolver point-blank, LG 16th September 1918. He was taken prisoner in the same action and held on Rügen island in the Baltic until released on 16th December and repatriated on 26th December. Promoted lieutenant 27th December. He was demobilised on 20th March 1919, but appears in the Army List until February 1920. He relinquished his commission and retained the rank of lieutenant on 1st September 1921.

Meadow Lane Gas Works, Leeds (Leeds Engine).

George Sanders married Nellie Newby (1896–1968) at Leeds on 5th April 1920.

By June 1920 they were living at 12 Lumley Walk, Burley, Leeds. They had two children:

- Kenneth George, born on 3rd April 1921. He enlisted in the Yorkshire Hussars in 1937, which during the Second World War served in 6th Cavalry Brigade, 1st Cavalry Division in Palestine from January 1940. In August 1941, 1st Cavalry Division reorganised into 10th Armoured Division and went to Egypt, but the Yorkshire Hussars went to Cyprus in March 1942 as the Armoured Striking Force. In January 1943 it went to Egypt to rejoin the division, which took part in the Battles of Alam el Halfa and Second El Alamein. Kenneth came back to Britain with the Yorkshire Hussars late in 1943. The Regiment converted to reconnaissance, ran D-Day embarkation camps April-August 1944 and was later a holding unit for reconnaissance personnel. He was married and living at 6 Iveson Rise, Leeds in 1950.
- Margaret Sanders, born on 6th December 1927.

St James's Hospital, Leeds.

George was employed as a foreman at Meadow Lane Gas Works under Leeds Corporation (later North-East Gas Board) after the war, as was William Butler VC. George attended the funeral of John Crawshaw Raynes VC on 16th November 1929, together with ten fellow VCs (W Edwards, F McNess, C Hull, A Mountain, F Dobson, A Poulter, W Butler, S Meekosha, AE Shepherd and JW Ormsby).

During the Second World War, George was a major in 8th West Riding (Leeds) Battalion Home Guard from 1st February 1941. He transferred to 18th West Riding (Leeds) Battalion from 1st February 1944.

Carlton Barracks in Leeds, HQ of the Leeds Rifles, during a parade in 1914.

George Sanders died at St James's Hospital, Leeds on 4th April 1950. The cause of death was collapse of lung and pleural endothelioma. He was living at 3 Stratford Street at the time. He was given a full military funeral on 6th April, followed by cremation at Cottingley Crematorium, Leeds, where his ashes were scattered. In addition to his family, the funeral was attended by four VCs (WB Butler, A Mountain, W Edwards and C Hull). Also in attendance were members of the Leeds Rifles Old Comrades Association, Home Guard, British Legion and the Leeds Group of the North-East Gas Board. Harry Daniels VC sent a wreath, as he was too ill to attend. Sanders' medals were carried by his old sergeant major, Frank Stembridge. Three volleys were fired by a party from 45th Battalion, Royal Tank Regiment (TA) (successors to 7th West Yorkshire) as the coffin left the chapel, and two buglers sounded Last Post and Reveille.

In addition to the VC and MC, he was awarded the 1914–15 Star, British War Medal 1914–20, Victory Medal 1914–19, Defence Medal and George VI Coronation Medal 1937. A plaque at the Garden of Rest, Victoria Gardens, The Headrow, Leeds commemorates all Leeds VC winners: AL Aaron, A Atkinson, WB Butler, L Calvert, H Daniels, W Edwards, DP Hirsch, C Hull, E McKenna, F McNess, A Mountain, J Pearson, A Poulter, JC Raynes, G Sanders, C Ward and J White. The VC is held privately.

12067 PRIVATE WILLIAM HENRY SHORT
8th Battalion, Alexandra, Princess of Wales's Own (Yorkshire Regiment)

William Short was born at 11 William Street, Eston, near Middlesbrough, Yorkshire on 4th February 1885. His birth was registered as William Henry Sivill. William was known as Twig or Twiggie, as he always had one in his mouth. His father is not known. His mother was Anne Stephenson Sivil (born 1867), whose birth was registered at Stockton as Annie Stephenson. She married James Short (c.1868–1939) in Middlesbrough in 1888 and he may have been the father. James was a blast furnace man in 1891, living with his family at his mother-in-law's at 11 William Street, Eston. By 1901 he was a cupola charger at a steel works at the same address. By 1911 the family was living at 38 Lee Road, Grangetown, Yorkshire. They moved to 35 Vaughan Street by 1914 and later to 18 Leighton Road. William had eight siblings:

- Mary Sivil, born as Sivill in 1888, married John C Crossman in 1911. They had four children: Phyllis Crossman 1915, Doris Crossman 1916, Leslie Crossman 1918 and John G Crossman 1932.

- Annie Eliza Short (1890–1970), married Francis Dunn (1893–1945) in 1923 and they had three daughters: Edith A Dunn 1924, Florence Dunn 1925 and Ann D Dunn 1928.
- Florie Short born 1893.
- Alfred James Short (1894–1977) was a sample catcher in 1911 and a steelworks labourer in 1914. He enlisted in the Yorkshire Regiment (11009) on 25th August 1914 at Middlesbrough. He was described as 5′ 6⅛″ tall, weighing 149 lbs, with fresh complexion, brown eyes, brown hair and his religious denomination was Church of England. He joined 6th Battalion at Richmond, Yorkshire the following day, but was discharged on 13th November 1914 at Grantham, Lincolnshire, 'Not being likely to become an efficient soldier'. He had a mal-united fracture of the tibia and was unable to march. He married Eva Gofton (born 1894) in 1918 and they had nine children: Alfred J Short 1919, Edna Short 1921, Louisa Short 1923, John Short 1925, May Short 1927, Olive & Ronald Short 1929, Herbert Short 1930 and Donald Short 1933.
- Mary Ann S Short (1897–1921) married Alfred E Leek (c.1896–1955) in 1919. He married Winifred Smith in 1933.
- Enoch Short (1899–1952), served in 3rd Durham Light Infantry (80755) 26th-29th March 1918 and 14th London Regiment (London Scottish) (S/41853 and later 516168) until the end of the war, by when he had been promoted to lance corporal. He married Esther Lavinia Clark (1898–1967) in 1917 and they had two sons: Eric Short 1920 and Philip Short 1922.
- Harry Short, born 1901.
- Arthur John Short, born 1905.

Grangetown Council School, founded in 1884, one of five schools opened to cater for the town's growing population.

Bolckow, Vaughan & Co steelworks at Eston in 1907.

William was educated at Grangetown Board School (later Grangetown Council School). He was employed as a general labourer at Eston, Middlesbrough in 1901 and later worked as a craneman at Bolckow, Vaughan & Company steelworks at Eston. He enlisted on 2nd September 1914 and went to France on 26th August 1915.

Awarded the VC for his actions at Munster Alley, near Pozières, France on 6th August 1916, LG 9th September 1916. He died at Contalmaison, France on 7th August 1916 of wounds received during his VC action. He is buried in Contalmaison Chateau Cemetery (II B 16). The first his parents knew about William's death was a note from an old friend, Jack Dixon, who was serving with him in C Company:

William Short's grave in Contalmaison Chateau Cemetery.

> *It is with deepest regret that I should have to write these few lines & break the sad news to you about poor Will. He died of wounds received on 7.18.16* (sic). *I thought it was my duty to let you know & believe me Jim, your son proved himself a Good*

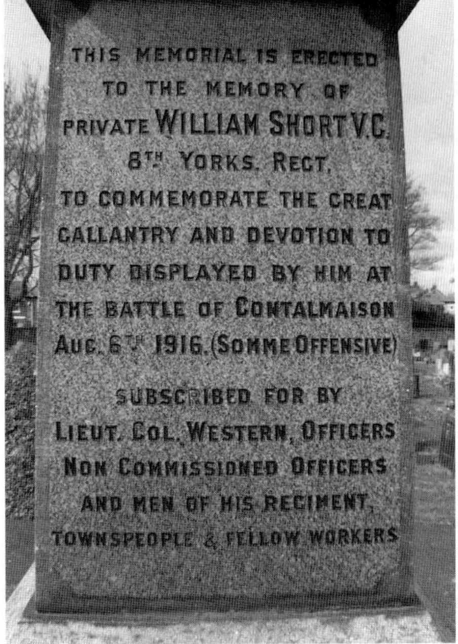

The memorial obelisk to William Short originally stood in Grangetown, but was later moved to Eston Cemetery (Ray Wilkins).

Soldier & died a Hero. He is sadly missed by his officers who always found a good name for him & also all his Comrades.

Well, Jim, you can rest assured he was laid to rest in a very nice place & was followed by his Comrades who saw the last of him.

Write and let me know when you receive this letter.
Remember me to all the Boys &
I remain your Friend,
Jack

As William never married, his VC was presented to his father by the King at Buckingham Palace on 29th November 1916. In addition to the VC, he was awarded the 1914–15 Star, British War Medal 1914–20 and Victory Medal 1914–19. The medals were sold to the Regiment by William's youngest and only surviving brother in April 1979 and are held by the Green Howards Museum, Trinity Church Square, Richmond, Yorkshire. William is commemorated on an obelisk of Cleveland ironstone at Grangetown, unveiled by Councillor WG Grace on 26th July 1919 and paid for by subscriptions from the officers, NCOs and men of his Regiment, the townspeople and fellow workers. It stood in the town square until moved to Eston Cemetery. Short's Commanding Officer, Lieutenant Colonel BCM Western, who lost an arm during the war, was present at the unveiling.

15888 SERGEANT JAMES YUILL TURNBULL
17th Battalion, The Highland Light Infantry

James Turnbull was born at 49 Park Road, Glasgow on 24th December 1883. His second name has also been seen as Youll and Young. His father was James Turnbull (1841–1922). He was a master joiner, employing two apprentices in 1881. His mother was Elizabeth née Dunlop (1842–1904) a dairymaid in 1861. James and Elizabeth were married on 29th December 1870 at Glencorrum, Kirn, Argyll. The family lived at various times at 82 and 90 Houston Street, Govan, 103 Renfrew Street, Glasgow, 7 Kenmure Street, Glasgow and Hardington Mains, Bargeddie, Coatbridge. James had four siblings:

- John Turnbull (born 1871) enlisted on 1st December 1915 in 79th Overseas Battalion CEF (150651) at Brandon, Manitoba. He gave his year of birth as 1872 and was living at Cromer, Manitoba at the time. He was described as 6′ 1/2″ tall, with dark complexion, blue eyes, iron grey hair and his denomination was Presbyterian. The tip of his left ear was missing. His sister, Mrs McLeod of 427 Paisley Road West, Glasgow, was his nominated next of kin. John claimed thirteen years previous service with 1st Lanark Rifles. He was later attached to the Canadian Pay Department in London.

- Thomas Dunlop Turnbull (born 1873) was an apprentice joiner in 1891.
- Gavin Yuill Turnbull (1875–1917) was an assistant warehouseman in 1901. He served as 147979 Sapper G Turnbull, 38th Divisional Signal Company RE and died on 17th October 1917. He is buried at Estaires Communal Cemetery Extension, Nord, France (V B 16).
- Elizabeth Bruce Turnbull (1879–1946) was living at 102 Ledaid Road, Glasgow at the time of her marriage to John McLeod (born c.1874), a marine engineer in 1912. They were living at 36 Duke's Avenue, Chiswick, London in 1922 and had at least a son, N McLeod.

Third Lanark FC, winners of the Scottish Cup in 1889. James Turnbull played for the team some years later.

James was educated at Albert Road Academy Glasgow. He was employed by Messrs Wallace, Scott & Co, wholesale speciality tailors of Cathcart; and later by William Chalmers of Oban. He was a keen footballer, playing for Third Lanark Volunteers FC, which formed in 1872 and was one of the founder members of the Scottish League, winning the Scottish Cup in 1889 and the First Division Championship twice in the 1930s. James was also a member of Cartha Athletic Club, Glasgow and Lorn Corinthian Yacht Club, Oban.

James Turnbull's grave in Lonsdale Cemetery. In the background on the right is the top of the Thiepval Memorial and on the left the trees that now cover the Granatloch in the Leipzig Salient, where he won his VC.

James served in 3rd Lanark Volunteer Battalion of the Cameronians. He enlisted on 13th September 1914 and went to France on 22nd November 1915. **Awarded the VC for his actions at the Leipzig Redoubt, near Authuille, France on 1st July 1916, LG 25th November 1916.** He was killed during his VC action and is buried in Lonsdale Cemetery, Authuille (IV G 9).

As he never married, the VC was presented by the King to his father and sister at Buckingham Palace on 2nd May 1917. In addition to the VC, he was awarded the 1914–15 Star, British War Medal 1914–20 and Victory Medal 1914–19. The VC is held privately. A memorial tablet was unveiled in the reading room of Lorn Corinthian Yacht Club, Oban on 11th September 1925 by Sir Thomas Dunlop GBE.

20572 PRIVATE THOMAS GEORGE TURRALL
10th Battalion, The Worcestershire Regiment

(Worcestershire Regiment)

Thomas Turrall was born at Speedwell Road, Hay Mills, Yardley, Birmingham on 5th July 1886. His surname has also been seen as Turrell. His father was William Turrall (1856–1932), a coal carifer in 1891, a labourer in a brickworks in 1901, a carter in 1911 and a labourer at Birmingham Small Arms Co Ltd in 1920. His mother was Ellen née Adams (c.1861–1895). William and Ellen married in 1882. William married Louisa late Adkins née Slaytor (c.1862–1941), a tailoress, in 1896. She had married John Robinson Adkins (1859–94) in 1885 and they had three children: William Henry Adkins (1886–1947), John Edward Adkins (1888–1954) and Charles Frederick Adkins (1890–1962).

In 1891, Thomas Turrall's family was living at 1 Back 63, Aston, Warwickshire. By 1901 they had moved to 2 Back 44 Baker Street, Aston and by 1911 to 23 Ronald Road, Saltley, Birmingham. William Turrall was living at 23 Oakley Road, Small Heath, Birmingham in 1920. Thomas had six siblings:

- Frederick William Turrall (1884–1939).
- James Alfred Turrall (1898–1952) married Leah Hill in 1918 and had four children: James A Turrall 1918, Betty L Turrall 1920, Doreen A Turrall 1928 and June Turrall 1931.
- May Turrall (born c.1893) was a general domestic servant in 1911.
- Rose Turrall (born c.1897).
- Lily 'Lillie' Turrall (born 1900).
- Violet Pearl Turrall (born 1903).

The houses beyond the brickworks quarry are on Speedwell Road (Ruston - Bucyrus Ltd, Lincoln).

Thomas was educated at Dixon Road School, Small Heath, Birmingham, before being employed as a decorator. He was a

Birmingham Small Arms factory at Small Heath, where William Turrall worked (BSA).

member of Smethwick Crescent Wheelers cycling club, as was Harold Colley, who won the VC on 25th August 1918. Thomas Turrall married Mary Lilian née Mansell (1889–1915) in the 2nd quarter of 1913 at Aston. They had a daughter, Lilian M Turrall, born in the 3rd quarter 1914; she died unmarried in 1942.

Thomas enlisted on 29th December 1914 and went to France on 2nd September 1915. **Awarded the VC for his actions at La Boisselle, France on 3rd July 1916, LG 9th September 1916.** The VC was presented by the King at Buckingham Palace on 30th December 1916. He was given a hero's welcome by Small Heath on his return and was presented with £250 and a gold watch. The Lord Mayor of Birmingham, the future Prime Minister Neville Chamberlain, also offered his congratulations.

Thomas transferred to the Reserve on 9th April 1919 and was employed as a barman and later was a partner in a painting and decorating business. On 17th July 1920 he married Daisy May late Dennis née Phillips (1894–1961). Her first marriage was to Thomas E Dennis in 1917. Thomas and Daisy lived at Hall Green, Birmingham and did not have any children.

Dixon Road School, Small Heath (Oosoom).

Thomas Turrall died at Selly Oak Hospital, Birmingham on 21st February 1964 and is buried in Robin Hood Cemetery, Solihull (A-4 North, Grave 193). The Secretary of State for Communities and Local Government, Eric Pickles MP,

Thomas Turrall outside Buckingham Palace prior to his investiture on 30th December 1917. He is holding his daughter, Lilian, with his father, William Turrall, and his second wife, Louisa, behind (Worcestershire Regiment).

Neville Chamberlain was Lord Mayor of Birmingham 1915–17 before he entered Parliament as MP for Birmingham Ladywood and went on to become Prime Minister 1937–40 (Associated Press).

announced that Great War VCs would have commemorative paving stones laid in their birth places on or close to the 100th anniversary of their VC actions. Thomas Turrall's stone was dedicated at the Walk of Heroes, Hall of Memory, Centenary Square, Birmingham on 7th December 2015. In addition to the VC, he was awarded the 1914–15 Star, British War Medal 1914–20, Victory Medal 1914–19, George VI Coronation Medal 1937 and Elizabeth II Coronation Medal 1953. The VC is held by the Museum of the Worcestershire Soldier, Foregate Street, Worcester.

One of Thomas' cousins served as 242493 Corporal Leonard Ward (1890–1917) in 2/6th Royal Warwickshire. He went to France after 31st December 1915, probably on 21st May 1916, and was killed in action on 8th December 1917. He is buried in Metz-en-Couture Communal Cemetery British Extension, France (II F 15). His wife, Edith, lived at 7 Rue Armand Carrel, Paris, France.

10799 PRIVATE THEODORE WILLIAMS HENRY VEALE
8th Battalion, The Devonshire Regiment

Theodore Veale was born at 30 or 34 Clarence Street, Dartmouth, Devon on 11th November 1892. His date of birth has been recorded as 11th November 1893,

including on a Blue Plaque at Dartmouth, and 11th November 1890. However, the birth was registered at Totnes on 22nd December 1892 and he was baptised at St Saviour's, Dartmouth on 9th February 1893. His father was Henry Peake (or Peek) Veale (1865–1932), a builder, mason and plasterer. His mother was Ada King née Williams (c.1871–1959), a professional concert pianist. Henry and Ada were married at Plymouth, Devon, registered in the 4th quarter of 1890. The family was living at Horn Lane, St Saviour, Dartmouth, Devon in 1891. They moved to 12 Mansard Terrace, Dartmouth and later to Lower Street, Dartmouth. By 1911 they were living at 3 St Clair Terrace, Dartmouth. Theodore's uncle, Percy Veale (born 1880), enlisted as an electrician in the Royal Navy on 26th April 1902 and served until 25th April 1923. During this time he served on many ships and shore establishments, including HMS *Defiance, Vivid, Exmouth, Aboukir, Britannia, Espiegle, Bulwark, Pomone, Hibernia, Centurion, Emperor of India* and *Ajax*. Theodore had two siblings:

- Lawrence John Veale (1894–1958) was a carpenter and served as a sergeant in 1/7th (Cyclist) Battalion, The Devonshire Regiment (290046). During the war he served in 2nd Devonshire and was disembodied on 19th April 1919. He married Elsie M Parker in 1925 at Totnes and they lived at Maidenway Road, Paignton. He went into partnership with Daniel Joseph Woodhouse, trading as Veale and Woodhouse, builders and contractors, at Kingskerswell and Newton Abbot, Devon until 6th April 1938.
- Thora Florence Ada Veale (1911–61) never married.

Theodore was educated at Dartmouth Council Schools. He was a member of Dartmouth United Football Association and Dartmouth Athletic Reserves, winning numerous trophies for his sporting achievements. After school he was employed in his father's building business in Dartmouth.

Mr Welch, a Licensed Victualler of South Town, Dartmouth, noticed personal items were disappearing from his house. While PC Barnacott was concealed in the house on 24th October 1912, Theodore entered using a key and stole a number of items, including a sweater, clippers, razor, cigarette case, pocket knife, slippers, necktie, compass and strands of a child's hair. Theodore was arrested for housebreaking and theft, appeared before Dartmouth Magistrates' Court the following day and pleaded

Lower Street, Dartmouth. These buildings have since been demolished.

Theodore rowing before the war (Tim Saunders).

guilty at Devon County Assizes at Exeter Castle on 1st November. Fortunately Mr Justice Bucknill regarded the offence more as a boyish prank and bound him over in his own recognisance of £5 to be of good behaviour for a year.

Theodore enlisted on 4th September 1914. He was 5′ 9¼″ tall and weighed 134 lbs. The Battalion trained at Aldershot and Farnham. He went absent without leave at Rowledge, Hampshire 24th-26th January 1915 and was fined seven days' pay. For taking an overcoat on leave belonging to Private Conibear on 23rd January and for having a dirty rifle on parade on 27th January, he was confined to barracks for twenty-one days. He was absent from parade twice on 15th February and forfeited seven days' pay. On 20th-22nd April he was again absent without leave and was confined to barracks for seven days and forfeited two days' pay.

Although his disciplinary record was poor, Theodore partly redeemed himself as an athlete. His trainer and chief opponent was Lieutenant Eric Savill, the man whose life he later saved. During a battalion sports day Theodore won the mile and two miles races and came second to Savill in the half mile. He also won the three and seven miles races at the Southern Command Championships.

Theodore went to France with the Battalion on 27th July. He was fined fourteen days' pay on 10th August and on the 17th was admitted to 6th Casualty Clearing Station with influenza. He was moved to 16th General Hospital at Le Tréport with enteritis on 22nd August, until transferred to 3rd Infantry Base Depot at Le Tréport on 29th August. He was absent from tattoo on 8th December and underwent seven days' Field Punishment No.2 and forfeited two days' pay.

Ill-health continued to dog him. He was admitted to 22nd Field Ambulance with laryngitis on 16th March 1916, returning to duty on 21st March. He was next admitted to 23rd Field Ambulance with debility on 28th April and moved to 22nd Field Ambulance with myalgia next day. On 6th May he was admitted to 21st Casualty Clearing Station with trench fever and transferred to 11th Stationary Hospital at Rouen on the 8th with influenza. He was discharged to Harfleur on 19th June, arrived at 6th Infantry Base Depot at Le Havre next day and rejoined the Battalion on 8th July.

Awarded the VC for his actions east of High Wood, France on 20th July 1916, LG 9th September 1916. During a soccer match the game was halted and a bugler sounded 'Fall In'. Captain James informed Theodore he had been awarded the VC and a general pinned the VC ribbon to his football jersey. The battalion was given a

Hospital Ship *Dunluce Castle*, 8,114 tons, launched in 1904, was requisitioned from the Union-Castle Line in August 1914 as a troopship. She became a hospital ship for 755 patients on 6th July 1915 and was used at Gallipoli and Mudros to transfer patients to the White Star liner *Britannic*. On 23rd February 1917 she was stopped by a U-boat but allowed to proceed when it was clear that she was complying with the Hague Convention. *Dunluce Castle* returned to commercial service on 2nd April 1919. She was to be scrapped in 1939, but was used for accommodation in the Humber during the Second World War and not broken up until 1945.

Raglan Barracks, Devonport.

day's leave to celebrate. Theodore received a letter from Edwin Savill, thanking him for saving his son's life. Eric Savill gave him a gold watch and chain.

He was appointed acting corporal on 27th July and was subsequently promoted corporal backdated to 25th July. On 29th September he went on leave until 9th October, but this was extended to 15th December. On 30th September the Mayor of Dartmouth, T Wilton JP, on behalf of the inhabitants, presented him with an illuminated address and an inscribed silver coffee service and salver plus £60. When he visited Raglan Barracks, Devonport on

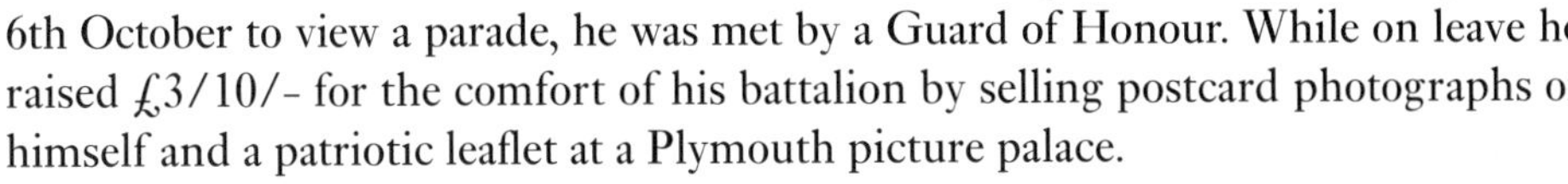

6th October to view a parade, he was met by a Guard of Honour. While on leave he raised £3/10/- for the comfort of his battalion by selling postcard photographs of himself and a patriotic leaflet at a Plymouth picture palace.

The day after he returned to France he was admitted to 23rd Field Ambulance with bronchitis, transferred to 22nd Field Ambulance next day and 44th Casualty Clearing Station on 17th December. On 24th December he was moved to 16th General Hospital at Le Tréport and evacuated to England aboard Hospital Ship *Dunluce Castle* on the 28th. He was admitted to 5th Northern General Hospital, Leicester

5th Northern General Hospital, Leicester.

Ealing Studios.

Dartmouth Volunteer Fire Brigade in Market Square in 1925. Theodore Veale is second from the right front row (Torquay Herald Express).

St Saviour's Church, Dartmouth, where Theodore Veale was baptised on 9th February 1893 and where he married Amy Rose Pinsent on 13th April 1920.

on 30th December and on 2nd February 1917 transferred to Hambleton Hall VAD Hospital, Oakham, Rutland, suffering from gas poisoning and rheumatism. While at these hospitals he was a member of the Hambleton Hall Hospital Pierrot Troupe, singing in a series of concerts in aid of the Red Cross. He also sang during the National School Boys' entertainment at Oakham in aid of the same charity.

On 5th February, he was presented with the VC by the King at Buckingham Palace. Having recovered, he was posted to the Depot at Exeter and was employed with the 3rd Battalion at Devonport on 29th March. On 12th June he returned to France to the Infantry Base Depot at Rouen and joined the 2nd Battalion. However, his stay was short and on 29th June he was posted to 31st Prisoner of War Company.

Theodore transferred to the Labour Corps (564359) on 15th July. He was posted to the Garrison Battalion Base Depot at Étaples on 31st August. On 17th September he was posted to 254th Prisoner of War Company at Villers-Bretonneux. He proceeded on leave on 18th November, returning on 17th December. Theodore forfeited a day's pay on 20th January 1919. He was medically examined on 6th February at Villers-Bretonneux, complaining of shortness of wind and swelling of the trapezoid after carrying weights. Theodore was sent to Fovant, Wiltshire on 13th February and was discharged to the Class 'Z' Reserve on 15th March.

Theodore returned to his father's building business and also played small parts in a number of films, including *The Battle of the Somme*, *The Call of the Sea* and *Q Ships*. He also worked at Ealing Studios with his brother-in-law as a studio electrician. Talking films impacted on the studio he worked for and he was laid off. He found work difficult to come by and even placed an advertisement in a London newspaper. He ended up working for his brother, Lawrence, in Devon and was a member of the Dartmouth Volunteer Fire Brigade until moving to London in 1927.

Theodore Veale married Amy Rose née Pinsent (born 1900) at St Saviour's Church, Dartmouth, Devon on 13th April 1920. The family moved to London before returning to Devon during the Second World War. However, after the war they split up. Theodore and Amy had three children:

- Graham Saville Peek Veale, born on 10th July 1920, registered at Totnes, Devon, played soccer for Kingston Hill Football Club, Surrey. He served as a pilot in the Royal Air Force Volunteer Reserve during the Second World War and married Phyllis E Reed (born 1919) in the 4th quarter of 1941, registered at Surrey North Eastern. She was given away by her brother, Edward, who was serving in the Royal Tank Regiment.
- Doris BR Veale, whose birth was registered in the 3rd quarter of 1921 at Lambeth, London. She married Arthur G Tucker, registered in the 3rd quarter of 1940 at Plymouth, Devon. They had three children: Michael A Tucker 1941, Maria A Tucker 1943 and Andrea P Tucker 1955. Doris and Arthur divorced and both married again in 1958; Doris to Charles E Doel and Arthur to Edith PE Bone.
- Theodora Amy Veale, born on 20th August 1928, registered at Brentford, Middlesex. She married John S Grindell (born 1925), registered in the 2nd quarter of 1948 at Totnes. They had two children, Jennifer Grindell 1949 and Graham Grindell 1956–67. Theodora died in 2006.

Theodore was one of the Devonshire trio of VCs, 'Veale, Sage and Onions'. They met for the first time at the VC Dinner at the House of Lords on 9th November 1929. On 20th July 1931, while working at Paignton Pier, Devon, he was struck on the head by a falling packing case and had to give up work. He suffered from fits and following one attack found himself crying on a rifle range. He also had numbness in his left leg and buzzing in his head. X-rays in December 1932 and January 1933 revealed thinning of part of the skull bone and thickening of the membrane pressing on the brain. These conditions were not present on X-rays taken after the accident. Subsequent tests revealed lack of sensitivity in the left thigh, reduced grip in his left hand and some loss of taste and smell; all symptoms indicative of pressure on

Paignton Pier.

the brain. He successfully sought damages against Montague Williams of Paignton, lessee of the Pier, for an undisclosed amount, in February 1933. Theodore was later employed as a chauffeur by the Bentall family, owners of the Bentall Department Store in Kingston on Thames.

During the Second World War Theodore tried unsuccessfully to return to his old Regiment, even writing to Lord Gort VC, commanding the BEF in France. Instead he served as aircraftman 2 (842858) at Crewe with 949 Balloon Squadron Auxiliary Air Force and then at Clapham, London, with 904 (County of Surrey) Balloon Squadron Auxiliary Air Force on barrage balloons.

After the war Theodore was a porter at Earlsfield and was in the Corps of Commissionaires for a time, working at the Daily Mail Ideal Home Exhibition in 1968. He also continued to work as a chauffeur for Procea products.

Theodore Veale died at his daughter's home, 11 Ware Road, Hoddesdon, Hertfordshire on 6th November 1980. Following a full military funeral on 12th November, he was cremated at Enfield Crematorium, where his ashes were scattered in Area M3 – D8.

In addition to the VC, he was awarded the 1914–15 Star, British War Medal 1914–20, Victory Medal 1914–19, 1939–45 Star, Defence Medal 1939–45, War Medal 1939–45, George VI Coronation Medal 1937, Elizabeth II Coronation Medal 1953 and Elizabeth II Silver Jubilee Medal 1977. The VC is held by the Devonshire and Dorset Regiment Museum, Bridport Road, Dorchester, Dorset. The Mentioned in Despatches oakleaf is on the Victory Medal ribbon, but no entry can be found in the London Gazette.

Earlsfield Station.

Theodore is commemorated on a plaque in the Veale/Savill Garden, close to the war memorial in Royal Avenue Gardens, Dartmouth. The garden marks the connection between Dartmouth and Windsor Great Park through Theodore Veale and Eric Savill. The plaque was unveiled on 10th November 2002 by his daughter, Mrs Theodora Grindell, and her daughter, Jennifer, laid a wreath. The ceremony was attended by General Sir John Wilsey GCB CBE, Colonel of the Devonshire and Dorset Regiment and Commodore Charles Anthony Johnstone Burt of Britannia Royal Naval College, together with the Chief Executive of South Hams District Council, the Mayor of Dartmouth and the Chairman of Kingswear Parish Council. The following day a similar ceremony took place at Kingswear to unveil a memorial plaque to Lieutenant Colonel Herbert 'H' Jones VC OBE. Veale Drive in Exeter, Devon is one of two VC-named roads (with Masterson Street) in the Wyvern Park housing development built in 2006–07 on the site of the former Wyvern Barracks.

Eric Savill (1895–1980) later became Sir Eric Savill KCVO CBE MC. He worked for the Royal Family at Windsor Great Park, becoming Deputy Surveyor in 1930, Deputy Ranger in 1937 and Director of Forestry to the Crown Estate in 1958. The Savill Gardens at Windsor were named after him by George VI in 1951. Sir Eric laid the foundations for the National Collection of Magnolias there.

CAPTAIN ARCHIE CECIL THOMAS WHITE
6th Battalion, Alexandra, Princess of Wales's Own (Yorkshire Regiment)

Archie White was born at Boroughbridge, Yorkshire on 5th October 1891. His father was Thomas White (1838–1911), born at Youlgreave, Derbyshire as Thomas Wright. By 1861 he was an assistant draper and grocer at Brigg, Lincolnshire with the surname White. In 1871 he was Thomas Wright again, living with his wife Mary (born c.1841 at Birchover, Derbyshire), a milliner, at Boroughbridge, Yorkshire. He was still Thomas Wright in 1881, a draper and outfitter, living at Fishergate, Boroughbridge with his wife Kate (born c.1843 at Derby) and children. By 1891 his surname was White and he was living with his family at Norwood House, Langthorpe near Boroughbridge, before moving to Horsefair, Boroughbridge by 1901, where he ran an outfitters shop. Archie's mother was Jean 'Jeannie' nee Finlayson (c.1852–1924), born in Aberdeenshire. She was living with her son Archie at Horsefair, Boroughbridge, Yorkshire in 1911. Archie had four siblings from his father's three marriages:

- Godfrey William Wright (1877–1962), a half-brother from the second marriage, changed his surname to White prior to his marriage to Gladys Elding (1887–1967) in 1909. They had at least seven children: Godfrey P White 1912, Archie White 1914, Thomas G White 1916, Gladys HC White 1917, Marion White 1919, Marjorie White 1922 and John S White 1929.

- John Finlayson White (1894–1915), a full brother, was commissioned in 6th Yorkshire and killed in action during a night assault on Lala Baba at Suvla, Gallipoli, on 7th August 1915 (Helles Memorial, Turkey).
- Mary Ellen Wright, (1871–1941) a half-sister from the first marriage.
- Kate Blanche Wright (1876–1930), a half-sister from the second marriage, married William Arthur Elliott (1875–1917), a railway clerk, in 1907 at Great Ouseburn. They were living at 7 Belvoir Street, Hull in 1911 and at 31 Manor Road, Scarborough, Yorkshire in 1915. William attested in the Canadian Overseas Expeditionary Force at Montreal, Quebec on 18th January 1915. He was described as 5′ 4½″ tall, of ruddy complexion, with blue eyes, fair hair and his religious denomination was Wesleyan. He transferred to 1/7th King's (267248) and died on 13th November 1917 (St Sever Cemetery Extension, Rouen, France – P III R 1A). Kate had moved to 35 Manor Road by 1917. Kate and William had a daughter, Catherine Foster Elliott 1908.

Archie was educated at Harrogate Municipal Technical School (later Harrogate Grammar School), where he was friendly with Donald Bell VC. He gained a scholarship to King's College London (BA English Literature 1913) and was a member of the OTC. He became a teacher at Westminster School.

Harrogate Grammar School.

Archie was commissioned in 6th Yorkshire on 12th September 1914 and appointed temporary lieutenant on 10th December. He was appointed temporary captain on 15th May 1915 and sailed with the Battalion from Liverpool on 3rd July. The Battalion arrived at Lemnos on 10th July and disembarked on the 11th, although Archie's Medal Index Card gives his qualification date for the 1914–15 Star as 1st July. The Battalion landed at Suvla Bay (B Beach), Gallipoli on 6th August, but Archie almost certainly missed the landings due to dysentery and joined the Battalion ashore a few days later, by when his brother, John, had died on 7th August. Archie was wounded in an attack on 21st August and was evacuated to Egypt. He went with the Battalion to France in July 1916.

Awarded the VC for his actions at Stuff Redoubt, near Thiepval, France on 27th September and 1st October 1916, LG 26th October 1916. The VC was presented by the King in Hyde Park on 2nd June 1917. Archie returned to France as a GSO3 from 30th June. As a result of the award of the VC, he was made a Fellow of King's College London in 1917. He was appointed brigade major to Brigadier General J V Campbell VC commander of 137th Brigade 28th March – 20th October

1918. **Awarded a periodic MC for distinguished service in connection with military operations in France and Flanders, LG 3rd June 1918.**

Archie was appointed temporary captain and GSO3 of 238th Brigade 25th April – 28th May 1919. Promoted captain 12th May 1919, with seniority from 15th May 1915. He went to Russia on 13th May 1919 and was appointed brigade major in the Archangel Relief Force on 29th May. He departed Russia on 29th September, but remained brigade major until 5th October, when he returned to Britain. Appointed brevet major 11th November for distinguished service in connection with military operations in Archangel, North Russia and was demobilised the same day. He relinquished his commission on 13th November 1920.

Archie White married Jeanie Georgina nee Will MA (23rd May 1892 – 1960) on 14th June 1920. Jeanie was born at Schoolhouse, New Pitsligo, Tyrie, Aberdeenshire, daughter of James Will (1856–1933), headmaster of Pitsligo Public School 1883–1920. Jeanie was also a teacher and governess. Archie was living at 20 Manor Road, Scarborough at the time. Jeanie and Archie had three daughters:

- Alison Jean Sutherland White (twin with Cecilia), born on 19th April 1921 at New Pitsligo, Tyrie, Aberdeenshire. She married Robert D Baird in 1944 and had three children: Andrew N Baird 1948, Christopher R Baird 1950 and Joanna C Baird 1955.
- Cecilia Mary Sutherland White (twin with Alison) was commissioned assistant section officer in the Administrative and Special Duties Branch WAAF (8431) on 11th July 1945. She married Terence GF Hudson in 1950.
- Jean Lesley Sutherland White, born on 5th December 1922 at Reading, Berkshire. She married Randolph GH Ricketts in 1947 and they are understood to have had three children: Alistair I Ricketts 1949, Anthony G Ricketts 1952 and Diana L Ricketts 1956.

Queen Victoria's School, Dunblane, was the idea of Queen Victoria as a memorial to the Scottish dead of the Boer Wars. The School was opened in 1908 by Edward VII for the education of the sons of Scottish soldiers. Over the years it became coeducational and admitted members of all three services regardless of where they came from. It has two sister schools – the Duke of York's Royal Military School in Dover and the Royal Hibernian School in Dublin, which merged with the Duke of York's in 1924.

Archie was appointed Organiser to the Federation of British Industry (later Confederation of British Industry) in 1920, but was soon back in uniform. He was appointed major in the Army Educational Corps on 25th November 1920. Appointed GSO2 Instructor at Sandhurst 2nd February 1921 – 7th January 1925, following which he was Commandant of Queen Victoria's School, Dunblane until 28th August 1929. He returned to Sandhurst as Senior AEC Instructor 29th August 1929 -1st February

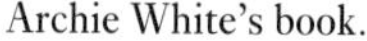
Archie White's book.

Archie White later in life.

1933, followed by tours of duty in India and Burma (Naini Tal). Appointed brevet lieutenant colonel 1st January 1933. From 1st September – 14th October 1939 he was a Cipher Officer and then became a Senior Umpire Home Forces until 11th November 1940. Appointed acting lieutenant colonel 6th November 1939. Appointed Command Education Officer Home Forces (Northern, Southern and AA Commands) 12th November 1940 – 15th August 1943. Appointed temporary lieutenant colonel 6th February 1941 and acting colonel 20th November. Promoted lieutenant colonel 11th March 1942 and temporary colonel 20th May. Appointed Chief Education Officer 21st Army Group 16th August 1943 – 13th June 1945. **MID, LG 9th August 1945.** Archie served in South-East Asia before retiring as honorary colonel 17th November 1947.

'Three Greyhounds Inn' on Horsefair, Boroughbridge.

He became Principal of the City Literary Institute 1948–56 and returned to give classes after his retirement. He was also a member of the Civil Service Council for Further Education 1950–

55 and London University Senate 1953–56. Appointed Deputy Colonel Commandant Royal Army Educational Corps 1960–69. Archie wrote *The Story of Army Education 1643–1963* and was one of twelve VCs who took part in the official 50th anniversary commemorations of the Battle of the Somme 1st – 3rd July 1966.

Archie White died at his home 'Brucklay', Upper Park Road, Camberley, Surrey on 20th May 1971 and was cremated at St John's Crematorium, Woking. His ashes were scattered in Tennyson Lake Garden and his name is listed in Bay 19/173. He is also commemorated:

A total of 85,235 George V Silver Jubilee Medals were awarded to members of the Royal Family, servants of the Royal Household, ministers, government officials, mayors, public servants, local government officials, members of the armed forces and police in Britain, the colonies and Dominions.

- On a blue plaque on the former 'Three Greyhounds Inn', the site of his father's outfitters shop at Horsefair, Boroughbridge.
- Victoria Block, Army Recruiting and Training Development Staff Leadership School, Army Training Centre, Alexander Barracks, Pirbright, Woking, Surrey, completed in April 2007, is divided into four VC – named wings – Egerton, Nelson, Speakman and White, the latter after A.C.T. White.

In addition to the VC and MC, he was awarded the 1914–15 Star, British War Medal 1914–20, Victory Medal 1914–19 with Mentioned-in-Despatches Oakleaf, 1939–45 Star, France & Germany Star, Defence Medal, War Medal 1939–45 with Mentioned-in-Despatches Oakleaf, George V Silver Jubilee Medal 1935, George VI Coronation Medal 1937 and Elizabeth II Coronation Medal 1953. The VC is owned privately but held by the Green Howards Museum, Richmond, North Yorkshire.

LIEUTENANT THOMAS ORDE LAUDER WILKINSON
7th Battalion, The Loyal North Lancashire Regiment

Thomas Wilkinson was born at the Lodge Farm on the Dudmaston estate at Quatt, Bridgnorth, Shropshire on 29th June 1894. His father was Charles Ernest Orde Wilkinson (1862–1934). He was educated at the Royal Agricultural College, Cirencester, Gloucestershire and became a farmer and land agent. His mother was Edith Mary née Lawder (1860–1938), a high school teacher born in Madras, India. Charles and Edith married on 17th December 1889 at St

St Thomas' Cathedral, Bombay, India where Thomas Wilkinson's parents married.

Thomas' Cathedral, Bombay, India. Amongst the widespread places where the family lived were:

- Hyderabad, India.
- Lazo, Comox, British Columbia, Canada.
- Ardanoir, Foynes, Co Limerick, Ireland.

Charles died on 12th March 1934 at Villa La Pagoda, Alassio in Italy and Edith died on 7th January 1938 at 9 Pine Close, Pinelands in South Africa. Charles left £6,044/3/- in his will. Thomas had five siblings:

Hyderabad in the 1890s.

- Wilfred Wilkinson born and died the following day in October 1890 at Hyderabad, India.
- Alan Frederick Lawder Wilkinson (1892–1948) was born at Secunderabad. He served as a lieutenant in the Royal Canadian Navy aboard HMCS *Hochelaga* (as the *Israel* she made an attempt to transport 550 Jewish settlers

HMCS *Niobe*. Thomas' brother, Alan Frederick Lawder Wilkinson, served on her as a lieutenant in the Royal Canadian Navy. *Niobe* started life as a Diadem class cruiser of the Royal Navy. Built by Vickers at Barrow-in-Furness, she entered service in 1898. During the Boer War, she escorted troop transports from Gibraltar to South Africa and in 1901 was one of two escorting cruisers for the world tour of the future King George V. She was transferred to the RCN on its formation in 1910. In October 1914 she joined the 4th Cruiser Squadron on the North America and West Indies Station, intercepting German ships. Her final patrol was in July 1915 when she returned to Halifax worn out and became a depot ship. She was damaged in the Halifax Explosion in 1917, but remained in use until 1920 and was broken up in 1922 (Admiral Digby Collection).

to Palestine in 1946) and *Niobe* (the first ship of the newly formed RCN) before working in Intelligence in Ottawa and later transferring to the Royal Naval Volunteer Reserve. He was promoted sub lieutenant on 1st January 1916 and lieutenant 25th August 1917. Alan was attached to HMS *Hermione* while on a course at Greenwich from 14th September 1916 and served on ML *225* from 25th August 1917. He was demobilised on 7th June 1919 and was later appointed district commissioner in the Gold Coast, Africa. Alan married Dorothy Leonard née Pike (1894–1926) in 1917 and they had two sons, Frederick W Wilkinson 1921 and George A Wilkinson 1923. Dorothy was the daughter of Vice Admiral Frederick Owen Pike DSO CMG (1851–1921), who served in the Royal Navy 1865–1906 and was recalled 1915–18 to serve as a temporary captain on HM Yachts. He was awarded the DSO for engaging an enemy submarine from HM Yacht *Valiant*, LG 4th June 1917. He was also awarded the Italian War Cross, LG 22nd January 1920. Dorothy died of blackwater fever in 1926. Alan married Evelyn Dorothea Birch née Reynardson (1900–c.1986) in 1930. Evelyn's uncle, William John Birch-Reynardson, married Violet Maxwell in 1859, sister of Francis Aylmer Maxwell VC. Alan was living at Ashley House, Box, Somerset at the time of his death on 24th October 1948. He left £5,719/5/1 in his will. Thomas's VC was left to his brother Henry.

- Henry Michael Lawder Wilkinson (1901–74), born at Corgigg Lodge, Shanagolden, Rathkeale, Co Limerick, Ireland was appointed assistant superintendent, Northern Rhodesia Police. He married Beryl Gordon née Bayly (1912–2005) in 1937 at Cathedral Church, Ndola, Zambia. She was born at Innisfail, Alberta. They had four children, including: Alan Michael Gordon Wilkinson, born in 1938 at Livingstone, Northern Rhodesia and Brian Peter Wilkinson born in 1943 at Kitwe, Northern Rhodesia. Henry died on 15th February 1974 at Vancouver Island, British Columbia. Beryl died on 19th August 2005 at St Albans, Hertfordshire.
- Dora Beatrice Wilkinson (1897–98), born at Dudmaston, Bridgnorth, Shropshire.
- Margaret Lawder Wilkinson (1899–1981) was born at Hillside, Yatton, Somerset. She married Eric Stephen Dumsday (1892–1963) in 1926 at Cape Town, South Africa. They had three children, including Stephen Michael Dumsday (1939–42), and divorced in 1952.

Thomas' paternal grandfather was Reverend Frederick Paget Wilkinson (1825–92), Vicar of St John, Ruyton-of-the-Eleven-Towns, Shropshire, for thirty-three years. He married Jane Ellen née Orde (1828–93), daughter of Sir John Powlett Orde, in 1857 at St George's, Hanover Square, London. In addition to Charles they had nine other children:

St John, Ruyton-of-the-Eleven-Towns, Shropshire, where Thomas' paternal grandfather was vicar for thirty three years.

- Frederick Lionel Paget Wilkinson (1858–64).
- Beatrice Emma Paget Wilkinson (1859–1949) married Reverend Algernon Barrington Simeon (1947–1928) in 1883 and they had five children: Violet Barrington Simeon 1883, Lionel Barrington Simeon 1885, Charles Barrington Simeon 1886, Rosalind Barrington Simeon 1887 and Mary Felicia Barrington Simeon 1891.
- Lancelot Campbell Wilkinson (1863–1933) was Vicar of Berwick, Shrewsbury, Shropshire.
- Cecil Parker Wilkinson (1864–87) joined HMS *Britannia* as a cadet on 15th January 1878. He was a midshipman on HMS *Temeraire* from 19th March 1880. Promoted sub lieutenant 19th March 1884. Served on HMS *Duke of Wellington* from 12th May 1884, HMS *Excellent* 15th April 1884, HMS *Helicon* 10th July 1885, HMS *Leander* and *Gannet* January 1886 and HMS *Dolphin* 27th January 1886. He died on 25th July 1887 at Gibraltar. The Lych Gate at the Church of St John the Baptist, Ruyton-of-the-Eleven-Towns, was erected in 1887 in memory of the two brothers, Cecil and Wilfred.

- Wilfred Paget Wilkinson (1866–86).
- John Edward Francis Wilkinson (1867–97).
- Arthur Godfrey Wilkinson (1868–1948), a twin with Henry, was a farmer living at Wicksted Hall, Wirswall, Cheshire in 1901. He married Evelyn Frances née Rimington (c.1884–1967) in 1907 at Penrith, Cumberland. They were living at Walton House, Brigstock, Northamptonshire in 1911. They had two children: Henry Frederick Lawrie Wilkinson 1908 and Mary 'Molly' Rimington Wilkinson 1920.
- Henry Fenwick Williams Wilkinson (1868–99) died on 26th March 1899 after falling from a horse at Baschurch, Shropshire.
- Helena Mary Wilkinson born and died on 25th July 1870.

Thomas' uncle, Cecil Parker Wilkinson, was a midshipman aboard HMS *Temeraire* in the 1880s. *Temeraire* was a unique ironclad battleship, with her armament partly in traditional broadside batteries and partly in disappearing barbettes on the upper deck. She was built at Chatham and commissioned in 1877 for service in the Mediterranean. On 3rd October 1890, she became the last ship of the Royal Navy to enter harbour under sail alone, at Suda Bay, Crete; it took five hours.

Thomas' maternal grandfather was Major General Edward James Lawder, Madras Staff Corps (1821–1900). He was commissioned in the Indian Army 18th June 1839 and served with 41st Madras Native Infantry from 5th December and 44th Native Infantry from 11th June 1844. Promoted lieutenant 17th August 1844. Appointed DAQMG Madras 20th October 1849 – 6th December 1851 and AQMG Madras next day until 27th September 1861. Transferred to the Madras Staff Corps before 1858. Appointed DQMG Madras 28th September 1861 – 27th September 1866. Promoted captain 1st May 1854. Appointed brevet major 20th July 1858. Promoted major 18th February 1861 and lieutenant colonel 18th June 1865. Appointed brevet colonel 18th June 1870 and paid colonel's allowance from 18th June 1877. Promoted major general 1st July 1881. He served during the Indian Mutiny 1858–59 and was Mentioned in Despatches 18th April 1859. He married Dora Jane née Moore-Lane (1828–77) in 1845 in Madras, India. In addition to Edith they had ten other children:

Sir George Clement Bertram, Bailiff of Jersey 1884–98, married Thomas' aunt, Anna Maria Lawder (theislandwiki).

- Anna Maria Lawder (born 1845) married George Clement Bertram (1841–1915) in 1866. There were no children. George was educated at Victoria College in Jersey and Sherborne College before studying law at Cambridge University. Called to the Bar in Jersey 1865. Solicitor General 1877. Attorney General 1880. Bailiff of Jersey 1884–98. Knighted by Queen Victoria at Osborne House, Isle of Wight on 1st August 1885. He was succeeded as Bailiff by Charles Malet de Carteret, who was distantly related to Harold Ackroyd VC MC.
- James Ormsby Lawder JP DL (1847–1928) was born at Trinchinopoly, India. He was a civil engineer of Lawderdale, Co Leitrim and High Sheriff of Co Leitrim in 1901. He married Jane Eliza née Thomas (c.1846–1933) in 1872. They had three children: Violet Eliza Dora Lawder 1873, Cecil Edward Lawder 1877 and Pearl E Lawder 1882.
- Edward John Grant Lawder (1849–1922) was a doctor. He married Margaret née Ellis (c.1860–1933) in 1885. They were living at 7 Blakesley Avenue, Ealing, London in 1918. They had four children: Noel Wilfred Lawder 1886–1916, Mildred M Lawder 1890, Iris Mary Lawder 1899 and Beryl MM Lawder 1900. Noel Wilfred Lawder was commissioned in 1st Bedfordshire on 29th August 1906. Promoted lieutenant 30th September 1907. Employed with the West African Frontier Force 1st June 1910 – 31 August 1915. Promoted captain 22nd January 1913. Appointed temporary major from 16th February 1916. He was killed in action on 4th September 1916 (Thiepval Memorial).
- Thomas Moore Lane Lawder (1851–88) was commissioned as an Ensign in 96th Regiment on 14th September 1870. Promoted lieutenant 1st November 1871 and was appointed adjutant, serving at Perak, Straits Settlements. He died on 23rd January 1888 and is buried at San Remo, Italy.
- Charles Alfred Browne Lawder (1853–1925) worked for the Indian Postal Department. He married Mary Sophia Clare née Arkwright (1861–1945) in 1901 at Ootacamund, Madras. They had three children: Dorothy EC Lawder 1902, Clare Valerie M Lawder 1904 and Robert Julius FA Lawder 1906.
- Dora Ellen Lawder (1855–1943) married Francis Godfrey Bertram (c.1847–1913) in 1874. He was born at Bahia, Brazil. They had two children: Emily Dora Bertram 1867 and Francis George Lawder Bertram 1875.
- Eliza Kate Lawder (1856–1951) was born at St Helier, Jersey. She died unmarried at Barham, Kent.
- Francis Ernest Lawder (1862–1943) was born in Madras. He worked for the Hyderabad Civil Service and was a District Officer for the Malay States. He married Elizabeth née Macleod (1862–1917) in 1888 in Chelsea, London. They had four children: an unknown Lawder 1889, Patrick Bruce Lawder 1891, Keith Macleod Lawder 1893 and Edward Francis Lawder 1895. Francis married Helen Dorothea Biggs (1868–1942) in 1921 at Long Ashton, Somerset.
- Elizabeth Lawder (1864–1962) was born in the state of Tamil Nadu, India. She died unmarried at Bridge, Kent.

- Arthur Henry Lawder (1866–1949) was born in India. He married Blanche Adeline Luff (1863–1919) in 1892. They were living at Greenwood City, British Columbia in 1901, where he was a member of the police force. They had two children born at Oak Lake, Manitoba: Dora Blanche L Lawder 1893 and Rynd Augustus L Lawder 1895. Arthur returned to Britain at the outbreak of the Great War. Arthur married Mabel F Dixon (c.1876–1948) in 1922 at Atcham, Shropshire.

Wellington College.

Thomas was educated at Mr Potts' Preparatory School, Parkside, Ewell and Wellington College, where he was a member of the OTC and represented the school in the Public Schools Boxing Competition for three years. He emigrated to Canada in 1912, where he was employed as a student surveyor in the Comox and North Burnaby areas of British Columbia. In 1913 he passed the preliminary surveyors examinations in Victoria, British Columbia.

SS *Andania*.

Thomas enlisted in 16th Battalion Canadian Expeditionary Force on 23rd September 1914 (28804). He departed Quebec for Britain on SS *Andania* on 7th October, five days after the first Canadian contingent. He was commissioned in 7th Loyal North Lancashire on 23rd December. There was confusion in the Canadian Forces administration about what became of him. A note in his records dated 4th November 1915 states that his whereabouts were not known and it was not until 1936 that his record was completed with his commissioning details from December 1914. He went to France in July 1915 and was promoted lieutenant 1st February 1916. **Awarded the VC for his actions at La Boisselle, France on 5th July 1916, LG 26th September 1916.** He was killed during the VC action and is commemorated on the Thiepval Memorial.

SS *Andania* at Quebec, with members of 14th and 16th Battalions CEF aboard prior to sailing for Britain.

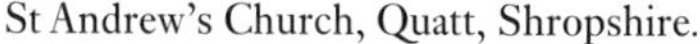

St Andrew's Church, Quatt, Shropshire.

The 49¢ postage stamps issued by Canada Post on 21st October 2004.

As he never married, the VC was presented to his father by the King at Buckingham Palace on 29th November 1916. In addition to the VC, he was awarded the 1914–15 Star, British War Medal 1914–20 and Victory Medal 1914–19. The VC was in the safe custody of the National Bank, Notting Hill Gate, London in April 1965. The owner at that time was Thomas' brother Henry, who was living in Rhodesia. The medals were listed by JB Hayward for £22,000 on 10th January 1975. They were sold to a private buyer at a Glendining's auction in London for £21,232.50 on 1st June 1991. The purchaser, Richard Nichols at Kensington, had been saving to buy a Porsche until he visited the battlefields in France. He was so taken with the story of Wilkinson's gallantry that he decided to spend the money on the VC group instead. The medals are on loan from Richard Nichols and are displayed in the Lord Ashcroft Gallery at the Imperial War Museum, Lambeth, London.

Thomas is commemorated:

- On a path-side plaque in St Andrew's churchyard, Quatt, Shropshire, unveiled by Lieutenant Colonel MJ Glover, Queen's Lancashire Regiment, on 17th October 2004.
- On a memorial obelisk to all Canadian VCs at Military Heritage Park, Barrie, Ontario dedicated by The Princess Royal on 22nd October 2013.
- Two 49 Cent postage stamps were issued by Canada Post on 21st October 2004 in honour of all Canadian VCs on the 150th Anniversary of the first Canadian VC's action, Alexander Roberts Dunn VC.

Sources

The following institutions, individuals and publications were consulted:

Regimental Museums

Royal Army Medical Corps Historical Museum, Aldershot; Royal Ulster Rifles Museum, Belfast; King's Own Royal Lancaster Regiment Museum, Lancaster; RHQ Devonshire and Dorset Regiment, Exeter; The Royal Gloucestershire, Berkshire and Wiltshire Regiment Museum, Salisbury; Lancashire County and Regimental Museum, Preston; Museum of the Manchesters, Ashton-under-Lyne; RHQ Worcestershire and Sherwood Foresters, Beeston; Royal Green Jackets Museum, Winchester; The Worcestershire Regiment Museum Trust, Worcester; The Royal Irish Fusiliers Regimental Museum, Armagh; Regimental Headquarters Coldstream Guards, London; HQ Scots Guards, London; Green Howards Museum, Richmond, Yorkshire; RHQ Queen's Lancashire Regiment, Preston; RHQ Prince of Wales's Own Regiment of Yorkshire, York; Canadian War Museum, Ottawa.

Individuals

Clive Adlam, Doug & Richard Arman, Gaye Ashford, L Bennett, Glen Bird, Peter & Shirley Birkett, Rev'd John & Mrs Waveney Brooks, P A Buddle, Margaret Carey, Mike Chapman, Ann Clayton, Maj John Cotterill, Jonathan Cremer, Mark Davies, David Downie, Margaret VB Doyle, Percy Dunbavand, Estelle Emms, John Ervey, Jean Foster, Lord Valerian Freyberg, John & Theodora Grindell, Bernard Holland, Niall Holland, Dr Norman Holland, Cecilia Hudson, Tom Hughes, Tom Johnson, Ian Jones, Alan Jordan, Henry Keown-Boyd, Stephen G Lane, Sid Lindsay, Geraldine Longstaff, Alasdair Macintyre, Robert Mansell, Margaret Marsh, Nick Metcalf, Col Gerald Napier, James Peck, Bryan Perrett, Lt Col Fred Phillips, Ian Riley, Bill Ritchie, Walter Ritchie, Paul Ryder, Francis Rynn, Kenneth Sanders, Derek Seaton, Tom Sharratt, Ruby Short, Alison Skene, Brandon Smith, Margaret Smith, Frank Snape, John Starling, Iain Stewart, Vic Tambling, Robert Taylor, Dave Thompson, Liz Turner, Heather Ward, Ray Wilkins.

Record Offices, Libraries and Local Museums

Birmingham Central Library, Cheshire Record Office, Nuneaton Library.

Schools and Universities

Clongowes Wood College, Clane, Co Kildare; Eton College; Liverpool College; University of Liverpool; Stonyhurst College; Worksop College.

Divisional Histories

The Guards Division in the Great War. C Headlam. Murray 1929. Two volumes.
The History of the Second Division 1914–18. E Wyrell. Nelson 1921. Two volumes.
Iron Division, The History of the 3rd Division. R McNish. Allen 1976.
The Fifth Division in the Great War. Brig Gen A H Hussey and Maj D S Inman. Nisbet 1920.
The Seventh Division 1914–18. C T Atkinson. Murray 1927.
Ireland's Unknown Soldiers – The 16th (Irish) Division in the Great War. Terence Denman. Irish Academic Press 1992.
The 18th Division in the Great War. Capt G H F Nichols. Blackwood 1922.
The History of the 19th Division 1914–18. E Wyrell. Arnold 1932.
The History of the 20th (Light) Division. Capt V E Inglefield. Nisbet 1921.
The 23rd Division 1914–19. Lt Col H R Sandilands. Blackwood 1925.
The History of the 36th (Ulster) Division. C Falls. Linenhall Press 1922.
A Short History of the 49th West Riding and Midlands Infantry Division (TA). Lt Col F K Hughes. Stellar 1958.
The Story of the 55th (West Lancashire) Division. Rev'd J O Coop. Liverpool Daily Post 1919.
The Royal Naval Division. D Jerrold. Hutchinson 1923. (63rd Division).

Brigade Histories

The 54th Infantry Brigade 1914–18 – Some Records of Battle and Laughter in France. E R. Gale & Polden 1919.

Regimental/Unit Histories In seniority order:

The Hood Battalion, Royal Naval Division: Antwerp, Gallipoli, France 1914–18. L Sellars. Leo Cooper 1995.
Gallant Deeds. Compiler Vice Admiral W H D Boyle. Gieves, Portsmouth 1919.
Records of the 4th (Royal Irish) Dragoon Guards in the Great War 1914–18. Rev'd H Gibb. Canterbury 1925.
History of the Royal Regiment of Artillery, Western Front, 1914–18. Gen Sir M Farndale. Dorset Press 1986.
The Coldstream Guards 1914–18. Lt Col Sir J Ross of Blankenburg. Oxford University Press 1928. Two volumes with a separate volume of maps.

A History of the Coldstream Guards Victoria and George Cross Holders. Sergeant L Pearce. RHQ Coldstream Guards 1995.
The Scots Guards in the Great War 1914–18. F Loraine Petre, W Ewart and Maj Gen Sir C Lowther. Murray 1925.
A Guide to the Queen's Regiment. G Blaxland. Elvy & Gibbs.
History of the Queen's Royal Regiment Volume VII. Col H C Wylly. Gale & Polden 1925.
The King's Own, The Story of a Royal Regiment, Volume III 1914–50. Compiler Col J M Cowper. Gale & Polden 1957.
The History of the King's Regiment (Liverpool) 1914–19. E Wyrell. Arnold 1928–35. Three volumes.
The Liverpool Scottish 1900–19. A M Gilchrist. Young 1930.
The Devonshire Regiment 1914–18. Compiler C T Atkinson. Eland Bros 1926.
The Bloody Eleventh: History of the Devonshire Regiment Volume III: 1914–1969. WJP Aggett. Devon and Dorset Regiment 1995.
The West Yorkshire Regiment in the Great War 1914–18. E Wyrell. The Bodley Head 1924–27. Two volumes.
History of the Sixth Battalion West Yorkshire Regiment, Volume I 1/6th Battalion. Capt E V Tempest. Country Press 1921.
The East Yorkshire Regiment in the Great War 1914–19. E Wyrell. Harrison 1928.
This Righteous War. B S Barnes. Richard Netherwood 1990.
The 16th Foot, A History of the Bedforshire and Hertfordshire Regiment. Maj Gen Sir F Maurice. Constable 1931.
The Story of the Bedfordshire and Hertfordshire Regiment Volume II – 1914–58. Compiled by Lt Col T J Barrow DSO, Maj V A French and J Seabrook Esq. Published privately 1986.
The Green Howards in the Great War 1914–19. Col H C Wylly. Butler & Tanner 1926.
The Green Howards – For Valour 1914–18. Anon. Published 1964.
The History of the Green Howards – 300 Years of Service. G Powell. Arms and Armour 1992.
The History of the Cheshire Regiment in the Great War. A Crookenden. W H Evans 1938.
Ever Glorious, The Story of the 22nd (Cheshire) Regiment Volume I. B Rigby. Evans & Sons 1982.
That Astonishing Infantry, The History of the Royal Welsh Fusiliers 1689–1989. M Glover.
Regimental Records of the Royal Welsh Fusiliers (23rd Foot), Volume III 1914–18 France & Flanders. Compiler Maj C H Dudley Ward. Forster Groon 1928.
The War Diary of 10th (Service) Battalion Royal Welch Fusiliers 1914 -18. Editor Lt Col F N Burton. William Brendon 1920.
The Royal Inniskilling Fusiliers in the World War. Sir F Fox. Constable 1928.
The Gloucestershire Regiment in the Great War 1914–18. E Wyrell. Methuen 1931.
The Slasher, A New Short History of the Gloucestershire Regiment 1694–1965. Anon.

The Worcestershire Regiment in the Great War. Capt H FitzM Stacke. G T Cheshire 1929.

History of the Duke of Wellington's Regiment (West Riding) 1702–1992. J M Brereton and A C S Savoury. Amadeus 1993.

The South Lancashire Regiment. Col B R Mullaly. White Swan Press.

Ich Dien, The Prince of Wales's Volunteers (South Lancashire) 1914–34. Capt H Whalley-Kelly. Gale & Polden 1935.

The Loyal North Lancashire Regiment, Volume II 1914–19. Col H C Wylly. Royal United Services Institute 1933.

A Year on the Western Front. E S Underhill, editor A Milledge. London Stamp Exchange 1988 (previously published privately 1924).

The Northamptonshire Regiment 1914–18. Regimental Historical Committee. Gale & Polden.

Four VCs in Forty Months, The Proud Record in World War One of the 6th (Service) Battalion The Northamptonshire Regiment. G Moore. G Moore 1979.

The Die Hards in the Great War, A History of the Duke of Cambridge's Own (Middlesex Regiment). E Wyrall. Harrison 1926–30. Two volumes (1914–16 and 1916–19).

The Annals of the King's Royal Rifle Corps, Volume V The Great War. Maj Gen Sir S Hare. John Murray 1932.

Somme Harvest. Giles E M Eyre. London Stamp Exchange 1991.

The King's Royal Rifle Corps Chronicles 1914, 1915, 1916 and 1917.

History of the Manchester Regiment, Volume II 1883–1922. Col H C Wylly. Forster Groom 1925.

16th, 17th, 18th and 19th Battalions The Manchester Regiment (1st City Brigade), A Record 1914–18. Anon. Sherratt & Hughes 1923.

Manchester Pals, 16th-23rd Battalions The Manchester Regiment. M Stedman. Leo Cooper 1994.

Proud Heritage, The Story of the Highland Light Infantry, Volume III 1882–1918. Lt Col L B Oates. House of Grant 1961.

The 17th Highland Light Infantry (Glasgow Chamber of Commerce Battalion) Record of War Service 1914–18. Editors J W Arthur and I S Munro. David J Clark 1920.

Seaforth Highlanders. Editor Col J Sym. Gale & Polden 1962.

The History of the First 7 Battalions The Royal Irish Rifles in the Great War, Volume II. C Falls. Gale & Polden 1925.

The Royal Irish Fusiliers 1793–1950. M Cunliffe. Oxford University Press 1952.

Blacker's Boys – 9th (Service) Battalion, Princess Victoria's (Royal Irish Fusiliers) (County Armagh) & 9th (North Irish Horse) Battalion, Princess Victoria's (Royal Irish Fusiliers). Nick Metcalfe. Writersworld 2012.

The Connaught Rangers, Volume III. Lt Col H F N Jourdain and E Fraser. Royal United Services Institute 1928.

The History of the Prince of Wales's Leinster Regiment (Royal Canadians), Part II The Great War and the Disbandment of the Regiment. Editor Lt Col F E Whitton. Gale & Polden 1924.

Stand To – A Diary of the Trenches 1915–18. Capt F C Hitchcock. Hurst & Blackett 1937.

Crown and Company, The Historical Records of the 2nd Battalion Royal Dublin Fusiliers, Volume II 1911–22. Col H C Wylly. Gale & Polden 1923.

Neill's Blue Caps, Volume III 1914–22. Col H C Wylly. Gale & Polden 1923.

The History of the Rifle Brigade in the War 1914–18. Volume I August 1914 – December 1916. R Berkley. Rifle Brigade Club 1927.

As above. Appendix – List of Officers and Other Ranks of the Rifle Brigade awarded Decorations or MID for services during the Great War. Compiled by Lt Col T R Eastwood and Maj H G Parkyn. Rifle Brigade Club 1936.

Rifle Brigade Chronicles 1915 – 1920. Editor Col W Verner. John Bale 1916 – 1921.

A Rifle Brigade Register 1905–63, Part 1 – A Roll of Officers who have served in the Regiment. Compiled by Col W P S Curtis. Culverlands Press 1964.

Not Least in the Crusade, A Short History of the Royal Army Medical Corps. P Lovegrove. Gale & Polden 1951.

History of the Great War, Medical Services, Volume IV General History. Maj Gen Sir W G MacPherson. HMSO 1924.

Medical Officers in the British Army, Volume II 1898–1960. Lt Gen Sir R Drew. Wellcome Historical Medical Library 1968.

The Royal Army Medical Corps. R Mclaughlin. Leo Cooper 1972.

The Medical Victoria Crosses. Col WEI Forsyth-Jauch. Arrow Press 1984.

The Army Medical Services Magazine.

Official History of Australia in the War of 1914–1918, Volume III – The Australian Imperial Force in France, 1916. 12th edition 1941.

They Dared Mightily. Lionel Wigmore, Jeff Williams & Anthony Staunton 1986.

Tales of Valour from The Royal New South Wales Regiment. Maj Gen GL Maitland 1992.

The Fighting 10th: A South Australian Centenary Souvenir of the 10th Battalion, A.I.F. 1914–1919. Cecil Bert Lovell Lock. Webb & Son, Adelaide 1936.

Official History of the Canadian Army in the First World War – Canadian Expeditionary Force 1914–19. Col GWL Nicholson 1962.

The History of the 16th Battalion (The Canadian Scottish) Canadian Expeditionary Force in the Great War, 1914–1919. HM Urquhart 1932.

The New Zealand Division 1916 – 1919, A Popular History Based on Official Records. Col H Stewart CMG DSO MC. Whitcombe & Tombs Ltd 1921.

Official History of the Otago Regiment in the Great War, 1914–1918. AE Byrne. J Wilkie 1921.

The History of the South African Forces in France. John Buchan 1920.

General Works

A Bibliography of Regimental Histories of the British Army. Compiler AS White. Society for Army Historical Research 1965.

A Military Atlas of the First World War. A Banks & A Palmer. Purnell 1975.
The Times History of the Great War.
Topography of Armageddon, A British Trench Map Atlas of the Western Front 1914–18. P Chasseaud. Mapbooks 1991.
Before Endeavours Fade. R E B Coombs. Battle of Britain Prints 1976.
British Regiments 1914–18. Brig E A James. Samson 1978.
Orange, Green and Khaki, The Story of the Irish Regiments in the Great War 1914 – 18. T Johnstone. 1992.
Leeds in the Great War 1914–1918. Leeds Libraries and Arts Committee 1923.
The First Day on the Somme. Martin Middlebrook. Allen Lane 1971.
Delville Wood. Ian Uys. Uys Publishers 1983.

Biographical

The Dictionary of National Biography 1901–85. Various volumes. Oxford University Press.
The Cross of Sacrifice, Officers Who Died in the Service of the British, Indian and East African Regiments and Corps 1914–19. S D and D B Jarvis. Roberts Medals 1993.
Australian Dictionary of Biography.
Whitaker's Peerage, Baronetage, Knightage & Companionage 1915.
Our Heroes – Containing Photographs with Biographical Notes of Officers of Irish Regiments and of Irish Officers of British Regiments who have fallen or who have been mentioned for distinguished conduct from August 1914 to July 1916. Printed as supplements to Irish Life from 1914 to 1916.
The Roll of Honour Parts 1–5, A Biographical Record of Members of His Majesty's Naval and Military Forces who fell in the Great War 1914–18. Marquis de Ruvigny. Standard Art Book Co 1917–19.
Birmingham Heroes. J P Lethbridge. Newgate Press 1993.
Bloody Red Tabs: General Officer Casualties of the Great War 1914–1918. Frank Davies and Graham Maddocks. Leo Cooper 1995.
The Dictionary of Edwardian Biography – various volumes. Printed 1904–08, reprinted 1985–87 Peter Bell Edinburgh.
This Gallant Steelback. William Ewart Boulter VC. Derek Seaton. Abbotts Creative Print 2010.
Armageddon Road – A VCs Diary 1914–1916. Billy Congreve. Edited by Terry Norman. William Kimber 1982.
Arthur Blackburn, VC. An Australian hero, his men, and their two world wars. Andrew Faulkner. Wakefield Press 2008.
I Laughed Like Blazes: The Life of Private Thomas 'Todger' Jones VC DCM. Dave Thompson 2002.

Specific Works on the Victoria Cross

The Register of the Victoria Cross. This England 1981 and 1988.

The Story of the Victoria Cross 1856 – 1963. Brig Sir J Smyth. Frederick Muller 1963.

The Evolution of the Victoria Cross, A Study in Administrative History. M J Crook. Midas 1975.

The Victoria Cross and the George Cross. IWM 1970.

The Victoria Cross, The Empire's Roll of Valour. Lt Col R Stewart. Hutchinson 1928.

The Victoria Cross 1856 – 1920. Sir O'Moore Creagh and E M Humphris. Standard Art Book Company, London 1920.

Victoria Cross – Awards to Irish Servicemen. B Clark. Published in The Irish Sword summer 1986.

Heart of a Dragon, VC's of Wales and the Welsh Regiments. W Alister Williams. Bridge Books 2006.

The Seven VC's of Stonyhurst College. H L Kirby and R R Walsh. THCL Books 1987.

Devotion to Duty, Tributes to a Region's VCs. J W Bancroft. Aim High 1990.

For Conspicuous Gallantry, A Brief History of the recipients of the VC from Nottinghamshire and Derbyshire. N McCrery. J H Hall 1990.

For Valour, The Victoria Cross, Courage in Action. J Percival. Thames Methuen 1985.

VC Locator. D Pillinger and A Staunton. Highland Press, Queanbeyan, New South Wales, Australia 1991.

Black Country VCs. B Harry. Black Country Society 1985.

The VC Roll of Honour. J W Bancroft. Aim High 1989.

A Bibliography of the Victoria Cross. W James McDonald. W J Mcdonald, Nova Scotia 1994.

Canon Lummis VC Files held in the National Army Museum, Chelsea.

Recipients of the Victoria Cross in the Care of the Commonwealth War Graves Commission. CWGC 1997.

Victoria Cross Heroes. Michael Ashcroft. Headline Review 2006

Monuments to Courage. David Harvey. 1999.

The Sapper VCs. Gerald Napier. The Stationery Office, London 1998.

Liverpool Heroes – Book 1 & Book 2. Ann Clayton. Noel Chavasse VC Memorial Association.

Beyond the Five Points – Masonic Winners of The Victoria Cross and The George Cross. Phillip May GC, edited by Richard Cowley. Twin Pillars Books, Northamptonshire 2001.

Irish Winners of the Victoria Cross. Richard Doherty & David Truesdale. Four Courts Press, Dublin, Ireland 2000.

The Victoria Crosses and George Crosses of the Honourable East India Company & Indian Army 1856 – 1945. National Army Museum 1962.

Our Bravest and Our Best: The Stories of Canada's Victoria Cross Winners. Arthur Bishop 1995.

VCs of the First World War: The Somme. Gerald Gliddon. Sutton Publishing 1994.

A Breed Apart. Richard Leake. Great Northern Publishing 2008.

Beyond Their Duty – Heroes of the Green Howards. Roger Chapman. Green Howards Museum 2001.

Other Honours and Awards

Recipients of Bars to the Military Cross 1916–20. J V Webb 1988.
Distinguished Conduct Medal 1914–18, Citations of Recipients. London Stamp Exchange 1983.
Recipients of the Distinguished Conduct Medal 1914–1920. RW Walker.
The Distinguished Service Order 1886–1923 (in 2 volumes). Sir O'Moore Creagh and E M Humphris. J B Hayward 1978 (originally published 1924).
Orders and Medals Society Journal (various articles).
The Old Contemptibles Honours and Awards. First published 1915. Reprinted by J B Hayward & Son 1971.
Burke's Handbook to the Most Excellent Order of the British Empire. A Winton Thorpe (Editor). Burke Publishing Co Ltd, London 1921.
South African War – Honours and Awards 1899–1902.

Official Publications and Sources

History of the Great War, Order of Battle of Divisions. Compiler Maj AF Becke. HMSO.
History of the Great War, Military Operations, France and Belgium. Compiler Brig Gen Sir J E Edmonds. HMSO. Published in 14 volumes, with 7 map volumes and 2 separate Appendices between 1923 and 1948.
Location of Hospitals and Casualty Clearing Stations, BEF 1914–19. Ministry of Pensions 1923.
List of British Officers taken Prisoner in the Various Theatres of War between August 1914 and November 1918. Compiled from Official Records by Messrs Cox & Co, Charing Cross, London 1919.
London Gazettes
Census returns, particularly for 1881, 1891 and 1901.
Officers and Soldiers Died in the Great War.
Service records from the Australian War Memorial.
Service records from the Canadian Archives.
Service record in New Zealand Government Archives.

National Archives

Unit War Diaries under WO 95.
Imperial Yeomanry Attestation Papers under WO 128/13.
Military maps under WO 297.
Medal Cards and Medal Rolls under WO 329 and ADM 171.
Soldier's Service Records under WO 97, 363 and 364.
Army Officer's Records under WO 25, 76, 339 and 374.
RAF Officer's Records under Air 76.
Chinese awards 29 December 1942 – 27 May 1949 in WO373/145/2.
Colonial medals for the Boer War 1899–1902 – WO 127.

Births, Marriages and Deaths records formerly in the Family Records Centre, Islington, London.

Official Lists

Navy Lists.
Army Lists – including Graduation Lists and Record of War Service.
Air Force Lists.
Home Guard Lists 1942–44.
Indian Army Lists 1897–1940.
India List 1923–40.

Reference Publications

Who's Who and Who Was Who.
The Times 1914 onwards.
The Daily Telegraph 1914 onwards.
Kelly's Handbook to the Titled, Landed and Official Classes.

Internet Websites

I hesitate to include websites because they change frequently, but the following were particularly useful and deserve a mention:
History of the Victoria Cross – www2.prestel.co.uk/stewart – Iain Stewart.
Commonwealth War Graves Commission – www.yard.ccta.gov.uk/cwgc.
Roland Bradford VC – www.geocities.com/bradcrem/bradford_rbb_biog.html.
Scottish General Registry Office – www.origins.net/GRO.
Noel Chavasse VC – www.chavasse.u-net/chavasse.html
Free Births, Marriages and Deaths – www.freebmd.com
Memorials to Valour – www.memorialstovalour.co.uk

Periodicals

Various editions of:
This England
Coin and Medal News – various editions.
Journal of The Victoria Cross Society
Gun Fire – A Journal of First World War History. Edited by AJ Peacock, but no longer published.
Yachting Monthly dated August 1917.

Useful Information

Accommodation – there is a wide variety of accommodation available in France. Search on-line for your requirements. There are also numerous campsites, but many close for the winter from late September.

Clothing and Kit – consider taking:

Waterproofs.
Headwear and gloves.
Walking shoes/boots.
Shades and sunscreen.
Binoculars and camera.
Snacks and drinks.

Customs/Behaviour – local people are generally tolerant of battlefield visitors but please respect their property and address them respectfully. The French are less inclined to switch to English than other Europeans. If you try some basic French it will be appreciated.

Driving – rules of the road are similar to UK, apart from having to drive on the right. If in doubt about priorities, give way to the right, particularly in France. Obey laws and road signs – police impose harsh on-the-spot fines. Penalties for drinking and driving are heavy and the legal limit is lower than UK (50mg rather than 80mg). Most autoroutes in France are toll roads.

Fuel – petrol stations are only open 24 hours on major routes. Some accept credit cards in automatic tellers. The cheapest fuel is at hypermarkets.

Mandatory Requirements – if taking your own car you need:
Full driving licence.
Vehicle registration document.
Comprehensive motor insurance valid in Europe (Green Card).
European breakdown and recovery cover.
Letter of authorisation from the owner if the vehicle is not yours.
Spare set of bulbs, headlight beam adjusters, warning triangle, GB sticker, high visibility vest and breathalyzer.

Emergency – keep details required in an emergency separate from wallet or handbag:
Photocopy passport, insurance documents and EHIC (see Health below).
Mobile phone details.
Credit/debit card numbers and cancellation telephone contacts.
Travel insurance company contact number.

Ferries – the closest ports are Boulogne, Calais and Dunkirk. The Shuttle is quicker, but usually more expensive.

Health

European Health Insurance Card – entitles the holder to medical treatment at local rates. Apply online at www.ehic.org.uk/Internet/startApplication.do. Issued free and valid for five years. You are only covered if you have the EHIC with you when you go for treatment.

Travel Insurance – you are also strongly advised to have travel insurance. If you receive treatment get a statement by the doctor (*feuille de soins*) and a receipt to make a claim on return.

Personal Medical Kit – treating minor ailments saves time and money. Pack sufficient prescription medicine for the trip.

Chemist (*Pharmacie*) – look for the green cross. They provide some treatment and if unable to help will direct you to a doctor. Most open 0900–1900 except Sunday. Out of hours services (*pharmacie de garde*) are advertised in Pharmacie windows.

Doctor and Dentist – hotel receptions have details of local practices. Beware private doctors/hospitals, as extra charges cannot be reclaimed – the French national health service is known as *conventionné*.

Rabies – contact with infected animals is very rare, but if bitten by any animal, get the wound examined professionally immediately.

Money

ATMs – at most banks and post offices with instructions in English. Check your card can be used in France and what charges apply. Some banks limit how much can be withdrawn. Let your bank know you will be away, as some block cards if transactions take place unexpectedly.

Credit/Debit Cards – major cards are usually accepted, but some have different names – Visa is Carte Bleue and Mastercard is Eurocard.

Exchange – beware 0% commission, as the rate may be poor. The Post Office takes back unused currency at the same rate, which may or may not be advantageous. Since the Euro, currency exchange facilities are scarce.

Local Taxes – if you buy high value items you can reclaim tax. Get the forms completed by the shop, have them stamped by Customs, post them to the shop and they will refund about 12%.

Passport – a valid passport is required.

Post – postcard stamps are available from vendors, newsagents and tabacs.

Public Holidays – just about everything closes and banks can close early the day before. Transport may be affected, but tourist attractions in high season are unlikely to be. The following dates/days are public holidays:

1 January
Easter Monday
1 May
8 May
Ascension Day
Whit Monday
14 July
15 August
1 & 11 November
25 December

In France many businesses and restaurants close for the majority of August.

Radio – if you want to pick up the news from home try BBC Radio 4 on 198 kHz long wave. BBC Five Live on 909 kHz medium wave can sometimes be received. There are numerous internet options for keeping up with the news.

Shops – in large towns and tourist areas they tend to open all day. In more remote places they may close for lunch. Some bakers open Sunday a.m. and during the week take later lunch breaks. In general shops do not open on Sundays.

Telephone

To UK – 0044, delete initial 0 then dial the rest of the number.

Local Calls – dial the full number even if within the same zone.

Mobiles – check yours will work in France and the charges. Beware roamer charges and/or disable them before getting on the ferry.

Emergencies – dial 112 for medical, fire and police anywhere in Europe from any landline, pay phone or mobile. Calls are free

British Embassy (Paris) – 01 44 51 31 00.

Time Zone – one hour ahead of UK.

Tipping – a small tip is expected by cloakroom and lavatory attendants and porters. Not required in restaurants, when a service charge is included.

Toilets – the best are in museums and the main tourist attractions. Towns usually have public toilets where markets are held; some are coin operated.

Index

Notes:
1. Not every person or location is included. Most family members named in the Biographies are not listed in the Index.
2. Armed forces units, establishments, etc are grouped under the respective country, except for Britain's, which appear under the three services. Royal Naval Division units appear under British Army for completeness.
3. Cemeteries/crematoria, Churches, Hospitals, Schools, Universities and Commonwealth War Graves Commission cemeteries/memorials appear under those group headings.
4. All orders, medals and decorations appear under Orders.